To Graham, with love, on your birthday,
from Pat.   29th January 1981.

A DICTIONARY OF
BRITISH SHIPS AND SEAMEN

Grant Uden and Richard Cooper

A Dictionary of British Ships and Seamen

Illustrated by Lionel Willis
and with prints

That art untouched by softness, all that line
Drawn ringing hard to stand the test of brine;
That nobleness and grandeur, all that beauty
Born of a manly life and bitter duty . . .
They mark our passage as a race of men,
Earth will not see such ships as those agen.

John Masefield, 'Ships'

Allen Lane/Kestrel Books

TO OUR WIVES,
JO AND DOROTHY

ALLEN LANE/KESTREL BOOKS
Published by Penguin Books Ltd, Harmondsworth,
Middlesex, England

Text copyright © 1980 by Grant Uden and Richard Cooper
Illustrations copyright © 1980 by Lionel Willis

First published 1980

ISBN 0 7226 5242 9

Printed in
Great Britain by
Fakenham Press Limited
Fakenham, Norfolk

Contents

Acknowledgements

Thanks are due to Olive Cooper for her patient secretarial assistance, and the authors are indebted to Judith Wardman for her scrupulous and exacting editorial work.

Acknowledgements for the illustrations are given on p. 589.

Foreword

We hope this book will be of value and interest to all who love Great Britain's naval heritage and especially to those who, enjoying tales of the sea or maritime history, meet with unfamiliar nautical references.

To the best of our knowledge, no encyclopedist has ever ventured to compute the number of vessels that, since the dawn of history, have been launched down the beaches and slipways of the British Isles. Still less has any statistician computed the number of men (and women) who have gone down to the sea in ships by choice, chance or compulsion: from family tradition, pushed in by patronage, flying from justice, gathered by the press and the pimps, scraped up from the jails and workhouses: born to it, thrown into it, exulting in it, hating it. No book can hope to cover more than a fraction of the ships and men born of a great seafaring nation like Britain.

So there is unlikely to be anyone, however generously disposed, who will not find some memorable or favourite name missing, or some familiar word or phrase. Some seafarers we have selected are famous – or infamous – some virtually unknown. Some, in Admiral Hopwood's words, voyaged 'small and lonely', some 'with fame, the happy fortune of the few'. But we trust they will be accepted as at least representative of all those, good, bad and indifferent, who have served, defended, sustained and, if only occasionally, disgraced their country; and the book as a small testimony to those who, if they often knew hardship and cruelty, met, too, humanity and comradeship, whether in peaceful pursuits or in the smoke of battle; found, enduringly or fleetingly, some honour and, for Britain through the centuries, ensured our prosperity and, in times of danger, deliverance.

R.C., G.U.,
L.W.

Abbreviations

A.D.	*anno Domini*	H.M.	Her (or 'His') Majesty's
b.	born	in.	inch, inches
B.C.	before Christ	lb.	pound, pounds
c.	about	mm	millimetre, millimetres
cf.	compare	N.	north
Co.	County	NATO	North Atlantic Treaty
d.	died		Organization
E.	east	R.N.	Royal Navy
ed.	edited by	S.	south
e.g.	for example	trans.	translated by
fl.	flourished	vol.	volume
ft	foot, feet	W.	west

Cross-references

Cross-references are printed in SMALL CAPITALS (*ITALIC* for the names of ships or books etc.). We have treated cross-references selectively, and have normally inserted them only when the entry referred to adds new information on the subject in hand.

A

A1 at Lloyd's: first-class, the very best (often contracted to simply 'A1'). LLOYD'S Register classifies the character of a ship's hull by a letter and the condition of anchors, cables, stores etc. by a number. Thus 'A1' means a first-class vessel in all respects; 'A2' means a first-class hull with equipment somewhat less good. 'A1' has passed into common speech and is often applied to non-maritime things.

'A' arc: the arc over which most of the ship's guns could bear.

A.B.: *see* ABLE SEAMAN.

Aback: a ship is taken aback when the wind brings her sails back against the mast; hence the figurative meaning, 'unpleasantly surprised' or 'astonished'.

Abaft: on or towards the aft, hinder or stern part of a ship.

Abeam: at right angles to the middle of the ship's side. *See p. 577.*

Aquatint by Thomas Rowlandson, 1799.

Able Seaman: originally 'able-bodied seaman'; usually abbreviated A.B. In both the Royal and Merchant Navies an A.B. must have reached certain standards of proficiency in a seaman's duties to achieve this rating.

'Aboukir': name of several ships of the Royal Navy. The first of the name was the French ship *Aquilon* (third rate), captured at the Battle of the Nile (1798). The last was a cruiser torpedoed in 1914.

Aboukir Bay, Battle of: *see* NILE, BATTLE OF THE.

A-box: the yards on a sailing ship are a-box when, on different masts, they are braced in different directions.

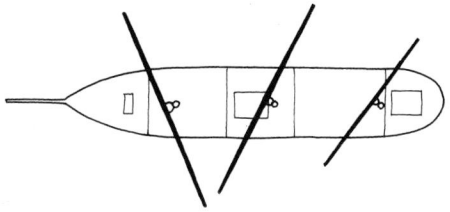

Acapulco galleons: another name for MANILA GALLEONS, Acapulco being the Mexican depot port for the Spanish fleets. As well as the ship captured by Anson in 1743, another Acapulco galleon, valued at £3,000,000, was taken in 1762, during the Seven Years' War.

Accommodation ladder: a ladder lowered flush with the ship's side to allow easy transfer to and from smaller boats.

'Achilles': name of several British warships, one of the best-known being the 74-gun ship launched in 1794, which fought at Trafalgar (1805) under Captain Richard King, forcing the surrender of the Spanish *Argonauta* and the French *Berwick* and sustaining 72 killed and wounded, including nine officers.

The other immortal *Achilles* was the cruiser which took part in the Battle of the RIVER PLATE (1939). She was transferred to the Indian Navy in 1948 and renamed *Delhi*. At present (1978), still carrying some of the scars of the River Plate encounter, she is destined for the scrapyard unless sufficient funds can be found to preserve her as a museum.

Achines: apparently the nearest the Spaniards could get to managing the surname of Sir John HAWKINS.

'A' class submarines: British submarines, built 1945–8, of 1120 tons, 281 ft over-all, with 18 knots surface speed and 8 knots submerged.

A-cockbill: an anchor is a-cockbill when hanging from the hawse-pipe and waiting to be let go.

Acre: ancient port on the coast of modern Israel. It had a long history even before being attacked by the Crusaders in the 12th century and has subsequently changed hands many times. It was besieged by Napoleon in 1799, captured by Mehemet Ali in 1832, taken by the British in 1840, restored to the Ottoman Empire, and again taken by the British in 1918.

'Active': Royal Navy frigate commissioned at Southampton in July 1977. Of 2500 tons, she carries a 4·5-in. automatic gun, two 20-mm cannon and Seacat missiles. She also mounts a Lynx anti-submarine helicopter.

Adams, John (?1760–1829), *alias* Alexander Smith: seaman on H.M.S. *Bounty* who took part in the mutiny (1789) and sailed to PITCAIRN ISLAND, where he founded and governed an English-speaking settlement. *See also* BLIGH, WILLIAM.

Adams, William (*d.*1620): English navigator and adventurer, the first Englishman in Japan. Entering a merchant ship at the age of twelve, he became a pilot and in 1598 sailed as master-pilot with a fleet of five Dutch merchant ships bound for the East from Texel. After a disastrous voyage, in which the fleet was scattered and many lives lost, Adams, in the *Charity*, with the crew in desperate state, reached the island of Kiushiu, Japan, where he was first imprisoned. Later, because of his knowledge of ships and shipbuilding, he found favour with the shogun, or ruler, Iyeyasu, and was presented with an estate, where he settled, married a Japanese wife and raised a family. He obtained trading privileges for Dutch merchants, helped found an English factory and took part in several voyages to Siam and Cochin-China in its service. He was buried on a hill overlooking Yokosuka harbour, had his name (in Japanese, Anjin Sama) preserved in a street name in Yedo, and was honoured annually on 15 June.

Admiral (from Arabic *amir*, *emir*, a prince): commander of a fleet or one of its chief divisions. The post of Lord Admiral or High Admiral (later Lord High Admiral) became established in Tudor times, but the title as commander-in-chief at sea was not carried till Blake's time, *c*.1650. Thereafter developed an elaborate hierarchy, based on the three main squadrons – the red, the white, and the blue – in which fleets were long organized. The highest rank was Admiral of the Fleet. Each squadron was big enough to be divided into the front (or van), the middle and the rear divisions, with an admiral in command of each. The senior admiral was the Admiral of the Red Squadron. By the 18th century there was a well-established ladder of promotion which ran thus:

> Rear-Admiral of the Blue
> Rear-Admiral of the White
> Rear-Admiral of the Red
>
> Vice-Admiral of the Blue
> Vice-Admiral of the White
> Vice-Admiral of the Red
>
> Admiral of the Blue
> Admiral of the White
> Admiral of the Red
> Admiral of the Fleet

This system of squadronal colours was not finally abolished till 1864. It survives in the allocation of different ensigns to the three main branches of the sea service. To the Royal Navy went the St George's Cross on the white field, with the Union flag in one corner – the White Ensign. The Royal Navy Reserves use the Blue Ensign; and the Merchant Service appropriated the Red Ensign – the famous 'Red Duster'.

The ranks of Admiral and Vice-Admiral and Rear-Admiral as second and third in command still survive, along with the special flags they wear in the ships carrying them. An admiral flies the St George's Cross, and the vice- and rear-admirals indicate their lower rank by one or two red balls in the quarters.

'Admiral Graf Spee': *see GRAF SPEE.*

'Admirals, Lives of the': *see* CAMPBELL, DR JOHN.

'Admiral Scheer': sister POCKET BATTLESHIP to the *Admiral GRAF SPEE*. She was sunk at Kielin (1945) in the course of the Allies' 'saturation' bombing.

Admiral's eighth: under the old system, the flag-officer's share of PRIZE MONEY earned by ships under his command, whether he was present at the action or not.

Admiralty: (1) the government department (the Board of Admiralty) which controls naval affairs in Britain; (2) the former headquarters of this department (in Whitehall); (3) sovereignty at sea, as in Kipling's lines:

> If blood be the price of admiralty,
> Lord God, we ha' paid in full!
>
> 'The Song of the Dead'

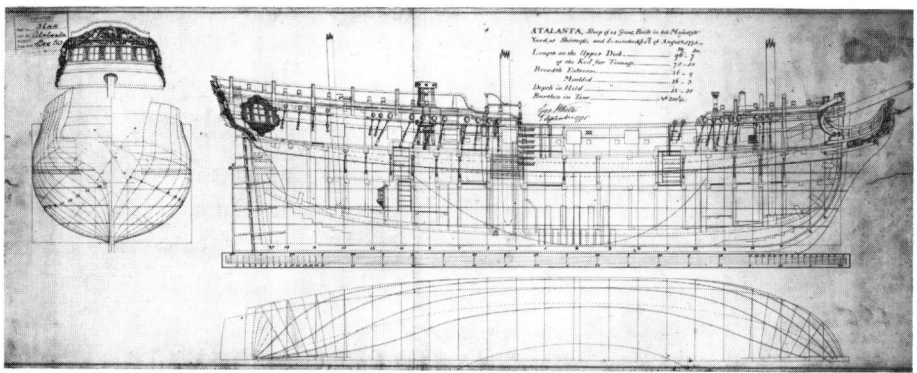

The draught of H.M. sloop *Atalanta*, 1775.

Admiralty draughts: original plans of Royal Navy ships, showing in great detail dimensions, methods of construction etc. at various periods, making an invaluable source of information to the student of maritime history. Many thousands, from 1700 onwards, are preserved at the National Maritime Museum, Greenwich, as well as a large collection relating to merchant and private ships.

Admiralty Instructions: *see* REGULATIONS.

Admiralty Islands: group of coral islands N.E. of New Guinea. Discovered by the Dutch in 1616, they were annexed by Germany in 1885 and mandated to Australia after the First World War. Taken by the Japanese in the Second World War; recaptured by the Allies in 1944.

Adriatic: sea lying between Italy and Yugoslavia, an arm of the Mediterranean. At its head lies Venice. It is 500 miles long, varying in width from 110 miles to 45 at its southern limit.

Adriatic, Marriage of the: ceremony conducted on Ascension Day every year from 1177 to 1789 under the Doges of Venice. The Venetians, in a procession of boats led by the Doge in the state galley, 'married' the sea by casting into it a sacred ring symbolizing their mastery of it. *See also* BARGE.

'Adventure': one of the ships in Captain Cook's second voyage (1772–5). Originally a Whitby collier, she was purchased by the Admiralty and was considerably altered to fit her for the expedition. Of 336 tons burden, she entered the Navy as the *Rayleigh* and carried ten carriage guns and ten swivels.

For another *Adventure, see* MEDALS.

Adventurer (or **Venturer**): often, in its old sense, a member of, or participator in, a sea-going commercial enterprise, e.g. one of the Adventurers to the New Found Lands (1501–2), a syndicate formed under a patent granted by Henry VII to trade with any new lands they might discover, as yet unknown to Christians. *See also* MERCHANT ADVENTURERS.

Adze: tool with a curved cutting blade set at right angles to the handle, much used by early shipwrights for shaping beams.

Aegean Sea: an arm of the eastern Mediterranean bounded by Greece to the

Adze.

west and north, by Turkey to the east, and by the islands of Crete and Rhodes to the south. The Aegean contains many islands and island groups, the southernmost of which is called the Dodecanese, with Rhodes as the chief island. Further north lie the Cyclades and Sporades and many scattered islets. The Aegean was at the heart of the ancient Greek civilization, and its islands have again mostly reverted to Greek sovereignty after many years of contention with the Turks and also the Italians, who occupied the Dodecanese

from 1911 until late in the Second World War.

Affleck, Sir Edmund (?1723–1788): admiral who distinguished himself under Rodney at the Battle of the Saints (1782) and elsewhere. His brother Philip (1726–99), who also became an admiral, served at the same period with equal distinction, especially under Boscawen at LOUISBOURG (1758).

Africa: the second largest continent, extending both sides of the Equator, with the greater area in the northern hemisphere. It was the rounding of the southern limits of Africa that opened up the sea route to India and the East, and this was mainly due to the Portuguese with the support of Prince Henry the Navigator. Bartholomew Diaz in 1487–8 rounded the Cape of Good Hope and reached Mossel Bay before returning. It was left to Vasco da Gama to complete the discovery of the route to India (1497–9) in one of the greatest sea voyages of exploration.

'Africa': 64-gun Royal Navy ship, built on the Thames in 1781. She played a

Marriage of the Adriatic: the Doge's state galley leading the grand procession. Detail from a drawing by Canaletto.

conspicuous part in the attack on San Domingo (21 March 1796), and at the Battle of Trafalgar (21 October 1805), when, having lost sight of the fleet during the night before the battle, she made all sail and joined in the main action, sustaining severe structural damage and over 60 casualties. She was broken up in 1813, after 33 years' hard service.

Aft: towards the stern or hinder part of a ship. *See also p.577 and* FORE.

Aftercastle: *see* CASTLES.

After-jigger: *see* MAST.

After-spanker: *see* MAST.

Agadir: Moroccan seaport which figured in a serious incident (1911) in the events leading up to the First World War. In the struggle for the control of N.W. Africa, the German government, annoyed at the dispatch of a French military expedition to Fez, retaliated by sending the gunboat *Panther* to Agadir. Amidst widespread reaction throughout Europe, Lloyd George, the British Chancellor of the Exchequer, warned the German government that if war were forced on France

Britain would inevitably become involved. In subsequent negotiations between France and Germany, the French Protectorate over Morocco was confirmed, Germany being compensated by the acquisition of a large part of the French Congo.

'Agamemnon': 64-gun ship imperishably associated with the name of Nelson and considered by him 'without exception the finest 64 in the service'. Built at BUCKLERS HARD and launched in 1781, she came under Nelson's personal command in 1793 and was engaged in many exploits, including the battering into submission of the French 100-gun *Ça Ira*, which Nelson said was 'absolutely large enough to take the *Agamemnon* in her hold'. At Trafalgar she fought in the weather line, sustaining ten killed and wounded. After an outstanding career, she went aground in Maldonado Bay (1809) and had to be abandoned; a gunner recorded that some of her men cried like children when ordered to leave her.

Agulhas, Cape: *see* CAPE AGULHAS.

Agulhas Current: strong south-westerly current off the S.E. shores of South Africa.

Agamemnon getting in her lower masts at Portsmouth, 1781.

It has a return north-easterly current running closer to the shore, which was used by sailing ships on passage from Cape Town to Natal.

Ahoy: call used by sailors for hailing or attracting attention.

Aircraft-carrier: a ship carrying and operating aeroplanes from her deck. The first successful flights from and onto warships were made as early as 1911. During the First World War flying from warships fitted with specially constructed platforms became frequent, but flying onto a warship was less common until the first true aircraft-carrier, with a flight deck over her whole length, H.M.S. *Argus*, was completed in 1918. In the inter-war years many aircraft-carriers were built by the great naval powers, and the changes they brought to naval warfare were fully seen in the Second World War, when carriers played a vital part, especially in the vast expanses of the Pacific Ocean. The Battle of the CORAL SEA (1942) was the first ever fought between fleets which never came in sight of each other, being decided by aircraft operating from carriers a hundred miles or more apart.

The United States has the greatest carrier force in the world with thirteen in commission, six in reserve, and two building. The powerful fleet which Russia has built over recent years has hitherto favoured helicopter-carrying cruisers rather than aircraft-carriers, but in 1976 she brought into commission the *Kiev*, the first of a new class of carriers of which she is building two, and probably three, others. For the Royal Navy's present-day aircraft-carrier, *see* ARK ROYAL.

'Ajax': an illustrious name in the Royal Navy, dating from 1767 and borne by several famous ships. The 74-gun ship launched at Rotherhithe in 1798 was at the Egyptian expedition of 1801 and Trafalgar in 1805. During the Dardanelles expedition of 1807, she caught fire (14 February), burned throughout the night and eventually blew up on the island of Tenedos, where she had drifted. Some 250 people were lost. In the Second World War, another *Ajax* was one of the cruisers at the Battle of the RIVER PLATE.

The owner of a commercial firm in the U.S.A. is said to have built a LIGHTER named *Ajax*. He was so impressed with the name that he built three others called *Bjax*, *Cjax* and *Djax*.

'Akbar': reformatory training ship, opened for delinquent boys in 1855. The Royal Navy refused to take boys direct from reformatory ships, so that most entered the merchant service. The first *Akbar* was originally H.M.S. *Cornwallis*. In 1862 she was replaced by H.M.S. *Wellington*, which also took the name *Akbar*.

'Alabama': *see* NEUTRALITY.

'Alarm': Royal Navy frigate which was the first ship to have its hull copper-sheathed as a protection against the teredo worm (1761).

Albatross: sea-bird with large wing-span and great powers of flight, inhabiting the oceans of the southern hemisphere. There was an old superstition that trouble would assail a ship if an albatross were killed, and such a deed forms the theme for Coleridge's haunting poem *The Rime of the Ancient Mariner*:

> And I had done a hellish thing,
> And it would work 'em woe:
> For all averred, I had killed the bird

15

That made the breeze to blow.
'Ah, wretch!' said they, 'the bird to slay
That made the breeze to blow!'

Albemarle, Duke of: *see* MONCK, GEORGE.

Albemarle, George Keppel, third Earl of: *see* HAVANA, CAPTURE OF.

Albion: an ancient name for Britain, dating from the 2nd century A.D. The name was used by the Romans and perhaps had association with the white cliffs of the Channel coast: from Latin *albus*, meaning white.

'Albion': Royal Navy 90-gun sailing line-of-battle ship, launched at Devonport in 1842. She suffered severe damage during the bombardment of Sevastopol (1854) and was converted into a screw ship in 1861.

Aldis lamp: a flashing electric lamp for signalling by Morse code. It is designed with an angled movable mirror which reflects the flash, whose light cannot easily be seen except by those in whose direction it is pointed.

'Alecto': paddle-driven sloop which in 1845 took part in a famous trial of strength in the search for a strong mover whose

Aldis lamp.

method of propulsion did not interfere with fire-power (as the great paddle-boxes did, restricting the broadside, which was the Navy's chief battle-winner). H.M.S. *Alecto* was lashed stern-to-stern with the screw-driven H.M.S. *Rattler*, of identical tonnage and horsepower, and the order 'Full steam ahead' was given to both. After a short struggle the *Rattler* took over and went ahead at about $2\frac{1}{2}$ knots, towing the *Alecto*; and in a race over 100 miles *Rattler* also won. *See also* PROPELLER.

A-lee: on the side away from the wind, on the leeward side.

Aleutian Islands: a chain of volcanic

The contest with the *Rattler*, 3 April 1845.

islands separating the North Pacific Ocean from the Bering Sea and forming a bridge between Asia and North America. The islands were bought from Russia by the U.S.A. in 1867 as part of the Alaska purchase. An attack on the Aleutian Islands by the Japanese in the Second World War in 1942 was part of their tactical plan for the capture of Midway Island. They occupied Kiska and Attu, but came under heavy attack from the Americans, who in the following year drove them out.

Alfred (or **Aelfred**; 849–901): king of the West Saxons, often called 'the Father of the English Navy' because of his shipbuilding activities. In reality, his chief contribution lay in the then very new idea that the best way to deal with a sea-borne invader was not to let him land but meet him in equal strength at sea. In Geoffrey Callender's paraphrase of his policy: 'there is no advantage of living on an island unless your navy rides in undisputed sway over the waters that surround it' (*The Naval Side of British History*, 1924). The idea was powerfully restated in the 15th century in a book called *The LIBELLE OF ENGLISH POLICIE.*

Algerine pirates: *see* ALGIERS.

Algiers: ancient port on the Mediterranean coast from which modern Algeria takes its name. From the 14th century, and perhaps even before that, Algiers was notorious as the chief centre of pirates or corsairs known as the Algerine or BARBARY pirates. In spite of many expeditions from England, Holland, France and America from the 17th to the early 19th centuries, the Algerine pirates continued their depredations on shipping and harbours and capture of thousands of Christians to be sold as slaves in the market of Algiers. At last in 1816, when the Dey, or Governor, refused to end these practices in spite of continued demands, an Anglo-Dutch fleet under Sir Edward PELLEW bombarded Algiers harbour and destroyed its shipping and forts, thus breaking the pirates' power. In 1830 the French took Algiers and brought Algeria under their rule, which continued until 1962, when, after a long and fierce war of revolt against France beginning in 1954, the country gained its independence.

Alkin, Elizabeth: *see* PARLIAMENT JOAN.

Allin, Sir Thomas (1612–85): one of a notable group of merchants (BLAKE being the supreme example) who took to the sea during the Civil War period and achieved a new, and greater, reputation as naval commanders. Allin was in trade in Lowestoft and supported the royalists. He held several posts as commander-in-chief at sea, fought successfully against the French, the Dutch and the Barbary pirates, and became an admiral and a comptroller of the Navy.

From a drawing by Godfrey Kneller, 1685.

Almanac: *see* NAUTICAL ALMANAC.

Aloft: above the decks of a ship, on or up the masts or rigging.

> While the raging seas did roar,
> And the stormy winds did blow,
> And we jolly sailor-boys were all up aloft,
> And the land-lubbers lying down below.
>
> anon., 'The Mermaid'

Amazon River: the largest river in the world in size, though exceeded in length by the Nile. The volume of fresh water flowing from the river is noticeable many miles out to sea. First reports of it were brought to Europe by the Spaniard Pinzon (1500), and Orellana descended the Amazon from the Andes in 1541, but it was little known until the middle of the 19th century, when exploration and trade, with the help of steam navigation, brought more detailed knowledge. The period 1910–27 saw a number of expeditions, some simply exploratory, some for industrial and scientific purposes. In 1913–14 a notable journey was made by Theodore Roosevelt, former President of the U.S.A., at the age of 65: with Colonel Candido Rondon, a Brazilian, he covered 900 miles down the so-called 'River of Doubt', an area of primeval wilderness beset with perils of all kinds. The party eventually struggled back to civilization at the confluence of the Amazon and the Madeira. More tragic was the expedition of the British explorer Colonel P. W. Fawcett, who in 1925 set out to explore the Xingu-Tapajos region of Brazil and disappeared. Although there was evidence that the party had been murdered, rumours long persisted that Fawcett had survived and was living with Indians.

Ambergris: from the French *ambre gris* ('grey amber'); a waxy substance formed in, and cast up by, the sperm whale. It is often found floating at sea or on the shore, and is much prized for making perfumes.

Amboyna (or **Ambon, Amboina**): a seaport in the Moluccas islands in Indonesia, discovered and settled by the Portuguese, who were expelled by the Dutch in 1605. English traders began to settle there in 1615, but in 1623 occurred the 'Massacre of Amboyna' when the English were killed by the Dutch. The port became an object of fierce dispute between the two nations and was captured by the British in 1796 and again in 1810. In 1817 it was restored to the Dutch. After Japanese occupation (1942–5) the town and island became part of Indonesia, but the Moluccas islanders seek their independence.

American Independence, War of (1775–83): the struggle for freedom from British rule by the thirteen American colonies. On the naval side of the war, Professor Michael Lewis gave a terse summary (not necessarily accepted by all historians), referring to the four main theatres of the war at sea – home waters, North America, the West Indies, and the Indian Ocean:

> The fighting in the first should have been fatal to us but was not. In the second it should not have been disastrous but was. In the third we lost heavily on points in the earlier rounds but, evading a knock-out, won the last round handsomely. In the fourth we held our own till the last round when, possibly, the bell saved us from taking the count.
>
> *The History of the British Navy* (1957)

In North American waters, for some six years the British fleet managed to keep communications open with our armies in America. Then, with those forces divided for strategic reasons, the whole complexion of affairs was changed in 1781 by the arrival of the French admiral Comte de Grasse with his entire fleet. Cornwallis's army, marching northwards, had reached the sea-inlet of the River Chesapeake and, to support it, the British admiral Thomas Graves sailed to Chesapeake Bay with 19 ships, expecting to meet only the small Rhode Island French squadron. Instead he encountered de Grasse's whole fleet of 24 ships. Even so, with enterprise and a disregard for conventions, Graves could have pulled off a spectacular victory. However, he played safe and half the British fleet was never brought into action. De Grasse out-manoeuvred him and Graves withdrew to New York. To quote Lewis again, 'he had lost no engagement, no ships – none was lost on either side. He had merely lost America.' General Cornwallis, with no support at sea, was forced to surrender and the war was, in effect, lost. *See also* JONES, JOHN PAUL; NEW ENGLAND; VERSAILLES, PEACE OF.

Amidships: either midway between stem and stern, or the position of the rudder when it is in line fore and aft with the ship. The word is shortened to 'midships' when the order is given to the helmsman. *See p.577.*

Amiens, Peace of (25 March 1802): treaty between Britain and France, after the war that had lasted since 1793. The peace was of very short duration; war was again declared, on Napoleon, the next year.

Anchor: device laid on the sea-bed and held by rope, cable or chain, for holding a craft in position in the water.

The parts of an anchor are the ring for securing to the cable or chain, the stock, the shank, which has a gravity band at the point of balance, the arm, crown, fluke and pea or bill.

Primitive anchors consisted of stones or other weights. The Admiralty pattern anchor, introduced at the beginning of the 19th century, has curved arms and flukes to give a better hold on the bottom, and has a detachable stock for convenience in stowing. In commonest use today is the patent or stockless anchor, on which the

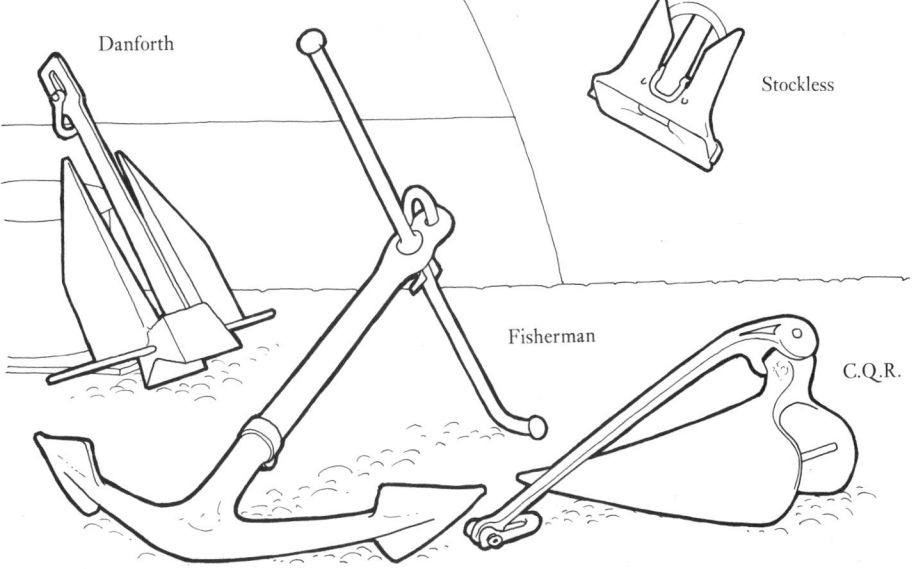

Danforth

Stockless

Fisherman

C.Q.R.

arms tip to give a better bite into the sea-bed; it can also be easily stowed. There are several other types of anchors.

A ship's main and largest anchors are its bower anchors, which stow in the hawse-pipes (the openings in the bows of a ship through which the cable passes from the chain-locker). A SHEET ANCHOR is an additional bower anchor; a STREAM anchor is a stern anchor.

A KEDGE anchor is one taken out in a boat and laid away from a ship; the ship is then hauled onto it. A SEA ANCHOR (or 'drag anchor') is a floating contrivance to assist a ship in keeping head to wind.

Ring and shank, stock and fluke,
  She's coming into ken,
Give a long and heavy heave, she's coming
  into ken.
Chorus: Bring home! Heave and rally!

Old anchor chanty

'Andromache': known to seamen as 'Andy (or "Andrew") Mack'. One *Andromache*, a 32-gun frigate, was in Rodney's Battle of the Saints (1782). Another, of 28 guns, helped force the passage of the Bocca Tigris (7–9 September 1834), when British ships were fired upon by Chinese forts.

Angel-shot: a particularly damaging form of shot in which a cannon-ball was cut in two and linked by a length of chain. The name is an example of the grim humour of men at war, comparable with the name 'holy water sprinkler' for the medieval military flail or 'morning star' for the mace.

Anglo-American War (1812–15): war was declared on Britain by the United States, whose trade was seriously affected by our BLOCKADE and who strongly objected to British enforcement of 'right of search' and to the impressment of American seamen into British ships. Though the States had no line-of-battle ships, they converted a number of cut-down two-deckers into highly effective frigates, more heavily gunned than the British equivalents. Some 16 vessels flew the new Stars and Stripes, and at the outset they scored some notable successes against their mighty opponent, who began by regarding them contemptuously. In 1813, Captain (later Admiral Sir Philip) Broke somewhat redeemed the British Navy's reputation when, commanding the frigate *Shannon*, he captured the U.S. frigate *Chesapeake* outside BOSTON. On Napoleon's final defeat in 1815, the war ended by mutual consent.

Resolved, That this Meeting view with sincere regret the recent declaration of War against Great Britain, by the United States of America; but being satisfied that Hostilities have been *unprovoked* on the part of our Government, we are determined to give our most zealous and active support, for the vigorous prosecution of a just and necessary War, as the best means, under Divine Providence, for attaining a secure and honourable Peace.

Resolution at a meeting of the merchants
and housekeepers of St John's,
Newfoundland (8 July 1812)

Anglo-Dutch Wars (or **Dutch Wars**): series of naval wars with Holland in the 17th century, brought about by trade rivalry and the NAVIGATION ACTS, which badly hit the Dutch carrying trade.

The *First Dutch War* (1652–4) saw half-a-dozen major actions, mainly between England's Robert BLAKE and the equally redoubtable Dutch admiral TROMP. It was after the Battle of Dungeness (or the Ness) that the latter is said to have hoisted a broom to his mast-head to signify that he had swept the Channel clear. But the chief honours were with England, and the Dutch were glad to sign the Treaty of Westminster in 1654.

For the *Second War* (1665–7) the Dutch found a worthy successor to Tromp in DE RUYTER, under whose leadership Holland had, on the whole, the best of the struggle, with de Ruyter actually sailing up the MEDWAY in defiance of the English fleet. The war concluded with the Treaty of Breda.

In the *Third War* (1672–4), after setbacks at Solebay and the Texel – which were due, not to any lack of courage or seamanship on the part of the English (under Prince RUPERT), but rather to the inefficiency of their French allies – England withdrew from the war. Thereafter a bond of union developed between England and Holland which has endured through the fluctuating fortunes of Europe.

Anglo-Spanish Wars: principally, the 1585–1603 maritime struggle between England and Spain, occasioned by religious and – much more important – commercial differences. After years of scarcely concealed hostility, the struggle flared into open war, culminating in the defeat of the Spanish ARMADA (1588). Other Anglo-Spanish conflicts include that waged by Cromwell; the so-called War of JENKINS' EAR (1739–41); and the undeclared struggles of the 1710s and 20s.

'Anne Ager': the custom of naming ships after wives and girl-friends is of very long standing. Sir Humphrey Gilbert named this 250-ton ship after his wife when he set sail (1578) in an expedition to plant an English colony overseas – an effort which failed completely, though it is worthy of record as the first attempt.

'Anne Gallant': one of Henry VIII's ships that took part in actions against the French fleet – chiefly ram-fitted galleys – in 1545. The *Anne Gallant* and her sister ship the *Mistress* were a new and significant departure from the old 'round ship', being relatively longer and narrower and of the type that was to culminate in the great line-of-battle ships with their fearful 'broadside' power.

> The *Mistress* and the *Anne Gallant* did so handle the galleys, as well with their sides as with their prows, that your great ships in a manner had little to do.
>
> John Dudley, Viscount Lisle, Great Admiral, in a dispatch to Henry VIII

'Ann McKimm': see BALTIMORE CLIPPER.

Annus Mirabilis (Latin for 'the wonderful year'): (1) the year 1666, which saw the Great Fire of London and, at sea, the war against the Dutch which included the crushing defeat inflicted on de Ruyter in the St James's Day Fight (25 July). John Dryden wrote a long poem with the title *Annus Mirabilis*, describing both the Fire and the victory at sea:

> Our Fleet divides, and straight the Dutch appear,
>   In Number, and a fam'd Commander, bold:
> The Narrow Seas can scarce their Navy bear,
>   Or crowded Vessels can their Soldiers hold.

> The Duke, less numerous, but in courage more,
>   On wings of all the winds to Combat flies:
> His murdering Guns a loud Defiance roar,
>   And bloody Crosses on his Flag-staff rise.

(2) The year 1759, also known as the WONDERFUL YEAR.

Anson, George, first Baron Anson (1697–1762): admiral who has been described as 'the last of the great corsairs'.

21

Almost as a by-product of his attacks on Spanish shipping and treasure (*see* MANILA GALLEONS), he circumnavigated the globe, reaching Spithead in June 1744 after an absence of three years and nine months. He subsequently defeated the French off Cape Finisterre (1747) and carried out dockyard and administrative reforms. *See also* WALTER, REV. RICHARD.

In private life the Admiral's most marked characteristic was his invincible habit of silence.

C. R. L. Fletcher

Antarctic: the Antarctic Ocean consists of the southern parts of the Atlantic, Pacific and Indian Oceans, and surrounds the continent of Antarctica. Its strong north-westerly winds and tremendous seas are notorious among sailors. James Cook was the first to cross the Antarctic Circle (1774); for the history of the exploration of the Antarctic, *see* POLAR EXPLORATION. The International Geophysical Year (1957–8) saw many nations acting together in scientific study of the region. By an international agreement signed in 1959 it was decreed that Antarctica should be freely open to all nations who wished peacefully to pursue scientific study of the continent, and this is being undertaken by Americans, British, Russians and others in various research bases.

Anthony, Anthony (*fl.*1540–50): compiler of an important Roll of the Navy (1546), containing coloured drawings of each of the royal ships, and particulars of tonnage, guns, powder, shot and other stores. Samuel Pepys obtained a great part of the Roll from Charles II, and it is preserved in the Pepysian Library at Magdalene College, Cambridge.

Antilles: the great arc of islands in the Caribbean Sea known as the West Indies and stretching from the southern point of Florida to the northern coast of South America. They are divided into two

A section of Anthony's Roll depicting the *Mary Rose*.

groups: the Greater Antilles, consisting of the larger islands Cuba, Jamaica, Hispaniola and Puerto Rico, and the Lesser Antilles, many smaller islands grouped as the Leeward and the Windward Islands. The islands were the first part of the New World to be discovered during the voyages of Columbus, who believed he had reached the Indies of Eastern Asia. The Antilles (or West Indies) were the scene of much colonial rivalry between Spain, England, France and the Dutch, being considered of strategic and great economic importance in many wars, particularly the Napoleonic. Wholly within the Tropics the islands have an equable warm climate with a rainy summer season, at the end of which the area is often the gathering ground of violent hurricanes which sweep up towards the southern United States.

Antipodes: from Latin and Greek meaning 'having the feet opposite'; those parts of the world lying diametrically opposite to any given point. In Britain we think of New Zealand as the antipodes.

Apron: (1) a timber at the stern of a boat; (2) any protecting flap or piece of canvas, e.g. the canvas apron which, secured to the shrouds, held and protected the leadsman as he took soundings.

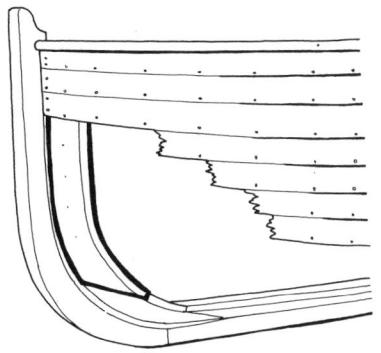

Archangel: principal port on the White Sea at the mouth of the River Dvina on the northern coast of Russia. Though frozen up during the winter, Archangel and ice-free Murmansk were terminal ports for the Allied Arctic convoys taking supplies to Russia from 1941 during the Second World War. In 40 convoys, 98 merchant ships and 18 warships were lost, but some four million tons of war supplies were delivered.

Archipelago: originally the Greek name given to the Aegean Sea with all its islands; now used to describe any chain or cluster of islands extending from the mainland.

Arctic: the Arctic Ocean, largely land-locked, is the most northerly of the great seas, and its most northerly part around the Pole is permanently covered by ice. Through the Arctic Ocean the NORTH-WEST and NORTH-EAST PASSAGES were sought by the early navigators, and their names (Hudson, Frobisher, Davis, Baffin and many others) are found upon the map. The American submarines *Nautilus* and *Skate* were the first to traverse the Arctic by passing under the Polar ice-cap (1958–9; *see* POLAR EXPLORATION). *See also* POLES.

'Arethusa': the last ship to go into battle entirely under sail. Launched in 1849, she took a leading part in the bombardment of Sevastopol (October 1854–September 1855), when her main and lower decks were set on fire by red-hot shot and shell from the Russian shore guns. Several other vessels were ignited in the same way, serving as a hard lesson that the old 'wooden walls' were no match for the modern shell.

This *Arethusa* later achieved fame as a training ship, berthed at Greenhithe, Kent, from 1874 until 1933, when, condemned as unfit for further service after 80 years, she went to the breaker's yard in Woolwich. A replacement *Arethusa*, a new four-masted steel barque of 3000 tons, was commissioned in 1933 and berthed on the Medway. In the 1930s, about 25 per cent of *Arethusa* boys went into the merchant service and the rest into the Royal Navy.

An earlier *Arethusa* (38 guns) was commanded by the famous frigate captain Sir Edward Pellew (later Lord Exmouth). She gained the sobriquet 'Saucy', first given in a somewhat doggerel poem, 'The *Arethusa*', by Prince Hoare (1755–1834). The poem referred to an action against the French *Belle Poule* (in which, as a matter of fact, the *Arethusa* got the worst of it!).

> Come, all ye jolly sailors bold,
> Whose hearts are cast in honour's mould,
> While English glory I unfold,
>   Huzza for the *Arethusa*!
> She is a frigate tight and brave,
> As ever stemmed the dashing wave,
>   Her men are staunch
>   To their fav'rite launch,
> And when the foe shall meet our fire,
> Sooner than strike, we'll all expire,
>   On board of the *Arethusa*.

Argosy: large old-time merchant ship, especially from the Dalmatian port of Ragusa, from which the name is derived. The word is now used only poetically.

> There where your argosies with portly sail,
> Like signors and rich burghers on the flood,
> Or as it were the pageants of the sea,
> Do overpeer the petty traffickers.

Shakespeare, *The Merchant of Venice*, I.1

'Argus': *see* AIRCRAFT-CARRIER.

'Ariel': famous clipper ship, built in 1865 by R. Steele & Co. at Greenock; tons register, 853; length between perpendiculars, 197·4 ft; breadth, 33·9 ft; depth in hold, 19·6 ft. A composite ship, she took part in the most celebrated of clipper races to get first home with the China tea crop (1866). Three of the clippers, *Ariel*, *Serica* and *Taeping*, having left Foo-chow-foo almost together and lost sight of each other during the whole voyage, docked in the Thames on the same tide, each having taken a record 99 days. *See also* TENDER.

'Ark Royal': a famous name in the Royal Navy, though, strangely enough, it was not revived for centuries after Tudor times. The first *Ark Royal*, originally *Ark Ralegh*,

Ariel.

was purchased by the Crown and renamed just in time to help defeat the Spanish Armada (1588), when she carried the flag of the Commander-in-Chief, Lord Howard of Effingham. By the 1588 method of rating she was a ship of 800 tons. Then the name disappeared till the 20th century, when *Ark Royal* took the seas again as an aircraft-carrier. One was sunk in 1941 in the Western Mediterranean while serving under Admiral Somerville's 'Force H', but not before her Swordfish aircraft had so slowed down the German cruiser *BISMARCK* that a combined attack by destroyer, cruiser and battleship turned the enemy ship into a blazing wreck.

The third 20th-century *Ark Royal*, an aircraft-carrier of 36,800 tons, went to the scrapyard in 1978 after 23 years' service. For many years she had been the largest warship in the Royal Navy; she was built in the 1950s at a cost of £21·5 million and modernized in 1967–70 at a further cost of £32·5 million. Happily the name *Ark Royal* is to be perpetuated in the 1980s in a new through-deck Royal Navy cruiser.

Armada: an armed fleet, especially the Spanish Armada (*see below*).

> Drake, he's in his hammock till the great
>   Armadas come,
> (Capten, art tha sleepin' there below?)

> Sir Henry Newbolt, 'Drake's Drum' (1896)

Armada, the Spanish (1588): often called simply 'the Armada', and, along with Trafalgar (1805), the most famous sea-fight in English history. Philip II of Spain, delayed for a year by Drake's raid on CADIZ (1587), sent an invading fleet of 132 vessels, manned by 8066 sailors and 2088 galley slaves, and carrying over 21,600 troops and 2680 pieces of artillery. ELIZABETH I mustered 197 ships of all sorts and sizes, made up of 34 royal ships and 163

belonging to her subjects. In fire-power, however, the royal ships contributed over 80 per cent. The command was given to Charles Howard of Effingham, Lord High Admiral; Drake, Hawkins and Frobisher were chief subordinate commanders. The Spanish commander-in-chief, reluctant and no skilled seaman, was the Duke of Medina Sidonia. In the Netherlands, the Duke of Parma waited with another army to be ferried to England.

The Spanish fleet was first sighted off the Lizard on 19 July, swung in a great seven-mile crescent. In the subsequent engagements (21 July–3 August) the so-called 'Invincible Armada' was out-manoeuvred, out-gunned and demoralized by its own inefficiencies, the last blow being gales that scattered their wrecks along the inhospitable west coasts of Connaught and the Western Isles (*see* GRAVELINES, BATTLE OF). Of the great fleet that had left the Tagus, only 53 battered vessels struggled home.

Too much has often been made of the supposed vastly superior Spanish fleet daringly opposed by a puny English fleet. Daring there was in plenty; but the truth is that the Armada was doomed when it set sail; the famous Protestant gale ('God blew with his winds and they were scattered') was only the final misfortune.

> From Eddystone to Berwick bounds, from
>   Lynn to Milford Bay,
> That time of slumber was as bright and busy
>   as the day;
> For swift to east and swift to west the ghastly
>   war-flame spread,
> High on St Michael's Mount it shone: it
>   shone on Beachy Head.
> Far on the deep the Spaniard saw, along each
>   southern shire,
> Cape beyond cape, in endless range, those
>   twinkling points of fire.

> Lord Macaulay, *The Armada*

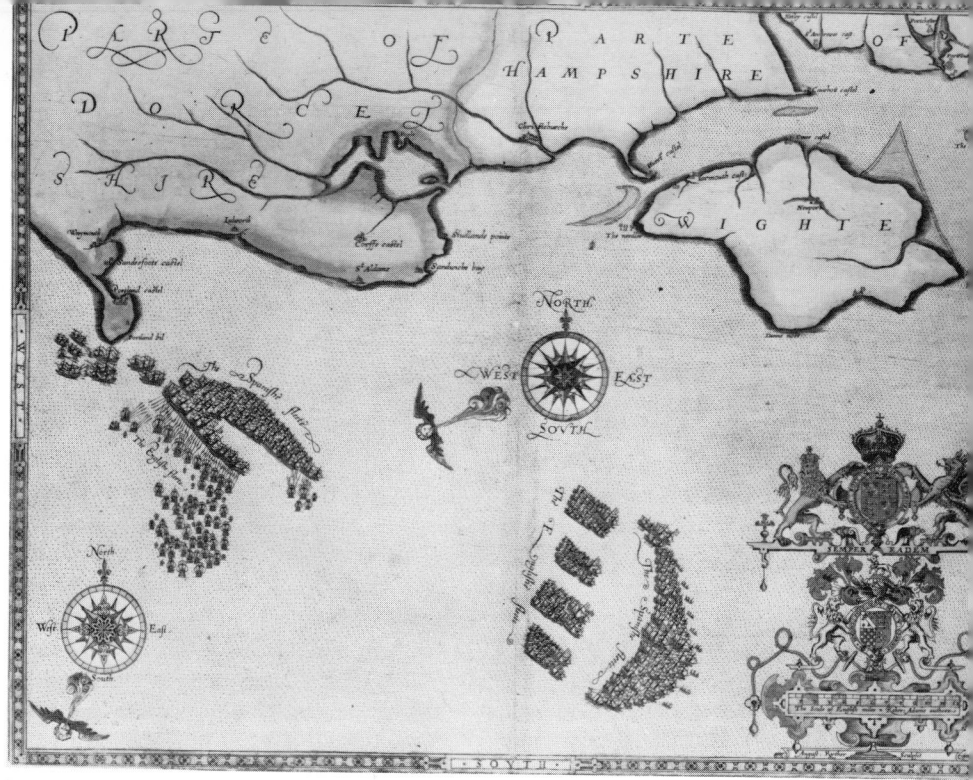

Coloured wash chart showing the Armada engagement, by Robert Adams, 1590.

Hugh de Moncada died,
Shot in his burning ship by Calais side,
Cheering his men to save her. Pimentel
Sank in a galleon shambled like a hell
Rather than yield, and in a whirl of flames
Pedro Mendoza, Captain of St James,
Stood with Don Philip thrusting boarders back
Till their Toledan armour was burnt
    black . . .
And there they fell,
Shot down to bleed to death. They perished
    well,
Happy to die in battle for their king
Before defeat had fallen on their friends;
Happier than most, for where the merrows
    sing
Paredes and his brother met their ends,
And Don Alarcon, cast alive ashore,
Was killed and stripped and hanged upon a
    tree.
And young Mendoza, whom the flagship bore,
Died of starvation and of misery.
But hundreds perished, King; why mention
    these?

Battle and hunger, heart-break, and the seas
Have overwhelmed the chivalry of Spain.

John Masefield, *Philip the King*

Armament: the offensive guns and other weapons carried by a warship. The history of armament starts with the first crude placement of firearms and small guns in the castles of early 15th-century ships. Then came the invention and development of the BROADSIDE from heavier guns firing through portholes, probably used first in Henry VIII's Navy. The 16th-century guns were smooth-bore and MUZZLE-LOADING, and fired round SHOT.

This form of armament continued on similar lines until the middle of the 19th century. There were improvements in the powder used in the charge, the gun carriage, and control of the recoil, with a consequent increase in the rate of firing, but no great increase in RANGE.

In the mid-19th century came a great revolution in armament, with the development of the elongated exploding shell, the rifling of guns and breech-loading, giving far greater range and accuracy. There was then a change from the broadside firing through portholes to the placing of turreted guns in both the forward and after parts of the ship. H.M.S. *DREADNOUGHT* (launched 1906) was armed with ten 12-in. guns; technical improvements continued towards the huge 15- and 16-in. guns carried by the great battleships which were constructed up to the close of the Second World War. The last great British battleship was H.M.S. *VANGUARD*, completed in 1942 with eight 15-in. guns, but scrapped in 1960 when the long history of the gun-carrying battleships had closed and the line of battle was no more. Up to the end of the First World War the gun had remained supreme, but the coming of the aeroplane, the development of the aircraft-carrier, the growth in the power of bombs and torpedoes, altered the nature of sea battles. Today the armament of ships depends chiefly on a whole range of new weapons and missiles, including nuclear, which are controlled by electronics and can seek their enemy under, on or over the sea; but guns of smaller size, many of them automatically controlled and fired, are still in use.

Armed neutrality: coalitions entered into by the Northern powers (*c.*1780–1800), resisting British claims to right of search of all neutral vessels in order to prevent war supplies reaching the enemy. The neutrals claimed that 'the flag covers the goods', i.e. that in their own ships, beneath their own colours, they could do as they pleased.

Armour: plating of iron or steel attached to the sides and deck of warships as protection against shells, torpedoes, bombs and other missiles. Primitive forms of extra protection using wood, hides and felt, and even iron, had been attempted in early times, but it was not until the development of the shell in the mid-19th century that the necessity of armour was forced upon the builders of warships. Armoured floating batteries, i.e. wooden barges protected by iron plates, were first used by the French in 1855 at the close of the Crimean War. The first ironclad warship was the French *La Gloire* (launched 1859); the first British ironclad was the *WARRIOR* (launched 1860). In these the armour or iron-plating, $4\frac{1}{2}$ in. thick, was fixed directly on the hull of timber ships. In the following years even thicker iron armour was used in an endeavour to keep pace with improved gunnery, and H.M.S. *INFLEXIBLE* in 1881 had a belt of armour 24 in. thick in two layers of 12 in. Steady improvements, however, in making steel gave a lighter,

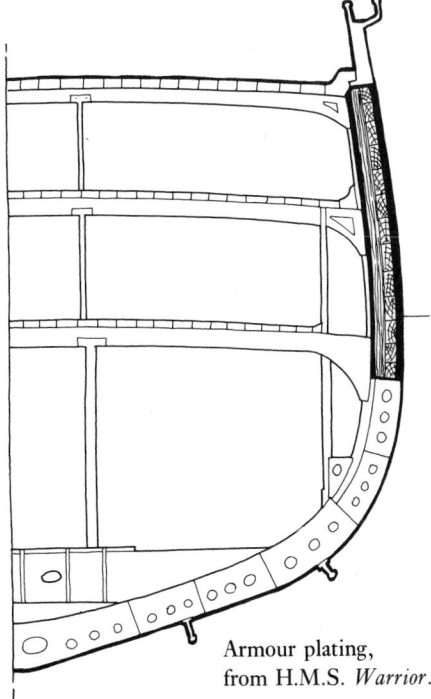

Armour plating, from H.M.S. *Warrior.*

thinner and tougher form of armour. Even so, as the ironclad evolved into the battleship of the first half of the 20th century, armour using nickel-steel or nickel-chrome alloys was employed up to a thickness of 14 in., as, for example, on the main belt of the ill-fated H.M.S. *HOOD*, sunk in 1941. The last great class of British battleships, the King George V class, broken up in the years after the Second World War, had armour up to 15 in. thick on the main belt, and up to 16 in. on the main turrets. With the changed nature of naval warfare today, and the decrease in the size of most naval ships, there is no longer need for such large thicknesses of armour.

Armstrong, Sir William (1810–1900): designer of a gun which revolutionized the art of gunnery. The Armstrong gun introduced polygroove rifling in the barrel (previously used only on hand guns), elongated cylindrical explosive shells, and a breech-loading mechanism. Although tested and approved by the Navy in 1858, the gun as finally fitted to H.M. ships reverted to the old tried and tested MUZZLE-LOADING system, which was not replaced by the modern breech-loading principle until 1880.

Articles of War: the regulations, embodied in various official ordinances and Acts, by which the Royal Navy is governed. Based on medieval sea laws and instructions to captains on individual voyages, the first official Articles of War appeared in 1652. The most famous part of the Articles is the Preamble: 'It is upon the Navy, under the good Providence of God, that the safety, honour and welfare of this realm do chiefly depend.' Modern regulations are embodied in the NAVAL DISCIPLINE ACT.

Artificer: *see* TIFFY.

Ascension Island: discovered by the Portuguese on Ascension Day 1501, this small volcanic island lies in the South Atlantic halfway between Africa and South America. It was occupied as a British naval station when Napoleon was exiled to ST HELENA, and in his *Voyage of the Beagle* Darwin gives a description of the island as it was when he visited it in 1836. The island became an important international cable station, and today has a satellite tracking station and a landing strip for aircraft.

Asdic: an underwater device using ultrasonic waves for detecting submarines etc. It takes its name from the initials of the *A*llied *S*ubmarine *D*etection *I*nvestigation *C*ommittee set up in the First World War, and came into effective operational use in the Second World War. *See also* SONAR.

Asia: the largest of the continents, 17,600,000 square miles in area. European exploration and conquest began with the voyage of Vasco da Gama round the Cape to India (1498). The Portuguese established an early monopoly of trade, but strong competition soon came from England, Holland and France. In particular, the English East India Company (founded 1600) and the Dutch East India Company (1602) developed a thriving trade and settlements on the coasts and in the islands. The continuing commerce saw the building of great lines of ships especially designed to cope with the voyages, notably the East Indiamen and the racing clippers.

Asiento, the: the contract to supply negro slaves to the Spanish colonies in the New World, a right that was disputed between Dutch, French and English traders, but was transferred to Britain by the Treaty of UTRECHT (1713). The Asiento was ended in 1752. *See also* SLAVE TRADE.

Engraving of the wreck of the *Association*, by an unknown artist.

'Association': the ship in which Admiral
Sir Cloudisley SHOVELL and all hands were
lost on 22 October 1707. A second-rate of
90 guns, she and three other ships
returning from the Mediterranean were
wrecked, with great loss of life, on the
Bishop and Clerk rocks off the Scilly Isles
because of an error in navigation. In 1968
divers discovered the remains of the
Association and brought to the surface
many coins, guns, silver plate and other
relics.

Astern: at, in or towards the stern or
hinder part of a ship. To 'go astern' is to
move the ship stern first. *See p.577.*

Astrolabe: an early astronomical instrument, probably of Greek origin, used for
measuring the altitude or position of any
celestial body. *See also* INSTRUMENTS.

Thyn Astrolabie hath a ring to putten on the
thoumbe of thy right hand in taking the height
of things.

Geoffrey Chaucer,
A Treatise on the Astrolabe (*c.*1391)

Love alone, with yearning
Heart for astrolabe,
Takes the star's height burning
O'er the babe.

Swinburne, 'A Rhyme'

A gilt copper astrolabe by Erasmus Habermel,
1585.

'**Athenia**': Donaldson liner torpedoed without warning on the first day of the Second World War by the German U-boat *U30*; she sank with loss of 112 lives.

Athwart: across, from one side to the other.

Atlantic: the world's second largest ocean, separating Europe and Africa from the Americas and at its northern and southern extremities linking with the Arctic and Southern Oceans. The North Atlantic Drift, or Gulf Stream, moved by the prevailing westerly winds, has a great moderating influence on the climate of N.W. Europe.

Speculation about the unknown Atlantic, so far as England was concerned, began to take active form in the 15th century, but did not become a national concern till the late Tudor period, when adventurers and traders crossed in ever-increasing numbers. By the end of the 17th century, in the words of the historian James A. Williamson,

The ocean was a great lake fringed by European settlements carrying on a variety of enterprises all complementary to one another; and the English share of these holdings, and still more of their trade, had grown preponderant . . . All this enterprise, in its thousands of little sailing ships, began and ended in a few home ports. Bristol and Boston were opposite numbers, New York and others were on a lower scale, but London by far transcended them all.

The Ocean in English History (1941)

Atlantic, Battle of the: the long struggle (1939–43), in the Second World War, between German U-boats and Allied shipping carrying supplies to sustain the war effort. At first, the menace was mainly confined to enemy submarines operating alone; then the German commander-in-chief, Admiral Karl Dönitz, who had been a U-boat commander in the First World War, developed the idea of the WOLF-PACK, several U-boats hunting together and often used as surface raiders rather than underwater craft. Allied losses at times assumed terrifying proportions; e.g. in 1942 U-boats sank 239 ships in convoy and 840 sailing unprotected. Intense bombing raids on the U-boat bases on the French Biscay ports proved largely ineffective, but at last the tide was turned: radar, long-range aircraft flying from shore bases, new weapons, heavier depth charges, and above all the development of a more powerful and efficient counter-attack on the U-boats by special support groups of destroyers and frigates enabled the Allies gradually to obtain the upper hand. The period March–May 1943 saw a dramatic change. In the first three weeks of March the Allies lost half a million tons of shipping for the destruction of a single U-boat. But in one phase in May, enemy submarines attacked 24 times without sinking a single ship and losing seven themselves. At the end of May, 41 U-boats had been destroyed, and Dönitz withdrew the rest from the North Atlantic. Sporadic attacks continued, but the Battle of the Atlantic had been won.

There was, of course, a vital struggle on the Atlantic in the First World War, but this is not usually separately christened.

Atlantic Cable: telegraph cable linking the United Kingdom and North America. After several failures, this momentous development in the history of communication was finally achieved in 1865–6, using Brunel's *GREAT EASTERN*. The cable was laid from Valentia, Ireland, to Heart's Content, Newfoundland, a distance of 2174 nautical miles, under the

Coiling the cable on board the *Great Eastern*.

auspices of the Anglo-American Telegraph Company, a prominent member of which was the American Cyrus K. Field. The most important figure on the British side was Sir Richard Glass (1820–73), manufacturer of the cable.

Her Majesty the Queen of the United Kingdom of Great Britain and Ireland.

The President of the United States acknowledges with profound gratification the receipt of Her Majesty's dispatch and cordially reciprocates the hope that the Cable that now unites the Eastern and Western Hemisphere may serve to strengthen and perpetuate peace and amity between the Government of England and the Republic of the United States.

Andrew Johnson
The Executive Mansion,
Washington
11.30 a.m. 30 July

(Message via the Atlantic Telegraph from the President of the U.S. to Queen Victoria, 1866. The transmission took 11 minutes, at 7·36 words per minute, including one stoppage for acknowledgement)

Atlantic greyhound: a term first applied to the Guion Line's *Arizona*, which in 1879 won the Atlantic Blue Riband. Afterwards it became a general term for any fast transatlantic liner. The fastest crossing by a British ship (3 days, 15 hours, 48 minutes) was made in September 1946 by the Cunard Line's *Queen Mary* at an average speed of 30·86 knots (35·54 m.p.h.). The record is held by the United States Line Company's *United States*, which on her maiden voyage (July 1952) crossed in 3 days, 10 hours, 40 minutes, at an average speed of 35·59 knots (40·98 m.p.h.). *See also* SPEED.

Atlantis: a legendary land described by

31

Plato and believed to have been rich and powerful until submerged beneath the Atlantic Ocean. Francis Bacon, between 1614 and 1618, wrote of the *New Atlantis*, another imaginary land, but this time discovered in the northern Pacific. One of the inhabitants had this to say about shipping in remote times:

You shall understand, that which you will scarce think credible, that about three thousand years ago, or somewhat more, the navigation of the world, especially for remote voyages, was greater than at this day . . . The Phoenicians, and especially the Tyrians, had great fleets. So had the Carthaginians their colony, which is yet further west. Toward the east, the shipping of Egypt, and of Palestine, was likewise great. China also, and the great Atlantis, that you call America, which have now but junks and canoes, abounded then in tall ships.

Atoll: a ring of coral reef surrounding a lagoon. Part of the reef may be above water and form low-lying islands.

Aurora australis: *see* AURORA BOREALIS.

Aurora borealis (Latin for 'northern dawn'; also called **Northern lights**): a varying display of light seen at night in northern latitudes. A similar phenomenon, electrical in origin, occurs towards the South Pole and is known as aurora australis, or 'southern dawn'.

Austen, Charles John (1779–1852), Rear-Admiral, and **Austen, Sir Francis William** (1774–1865), Admiral of the Fleet: sailor brothers of the novelist Jane Austen. They entered the Navy through the Naval Academy at Portsmouth, and though, after the custom of the time, they were helped by some patronage, they rose steadily to various commands by their own efficiency and bravery. Francis ('Frank' to his sister) became a lieutenant in 1792 after

six years' sea service in the frigate *Perseverance* in the East Indies. Seven years later he was made Commander, and was in 1801 Flag-Captain to Rear-Admiral Louis on *Canopus*. After being at the Battle of San Domingo (1806) he commanded the *St Albans* (64 guns), and in 1810 was Flag-Captain to Admiral Lord Gambier in command of the Home Fleet. From 1811 to 1814 he saw further sea service in the Baltic. Achieving Rear-Admiral's rank in 1830, he eventually rose to Admiral of the Fleet two years before his death. His brother Charles had a less distinguished but no less steady progression towards his final rank of Rear-Admiral.

It was through these two brothers that Jane Austen was able to show in her novels considerable knowledge of, and sympathy for, the Navy. Amongst the several naval officers characterized by her are William Price in *Mansfield Park*, who may have his prototype in her brother Charles, and the kindly Admiral Croft and other naval figures in *Persuasion*.

The navy, I think, who have done so much for us, have at least an equal claim with any other set of men for all the comforts and all the privileges which any home can give. Sailors work hard enough for their comforts, we must all allow.

Persuasion

Australia: the smallest of the continents and the last to be discovered by Europeans, though the existence of TERRA AUSTRALIS INCOGNITA had been a belief of geographers from earliest times. Australia lies to the south-east of Asia between the Indian and Pacific Oceans. The north and west coasts were first explored by the Dutch in the 17th century, and the land was named New Holland. In 1642 Tasman sailed south about the continent and discovered Tasmania, which he named Van Diemen's

Land. The English voyager William Dampier navigated along the west coast in 1688, but it was not until after the first of Captain Cook's great voyages (1768–71) that Australia began to be more thoroughly known and settlement began. Cook landed at Botany Bay and named New South Wales.

Austrian Succession, War of the (1741–8): war brought about by the death of Charles VI, Emperor of Germany, who left no male heir, so that the question of the succession to the Austrian dominions and the empire lay open to a protracted dispute between Bavaria, Spain, France and Britain. The war, which was ended by the Peace of Aix-la-Chapelle in October 1748, eventually resolved itself into the question of the naval supremacy of Britain or France, heading leagues of various countries and states, and did much to establish the former's control of the sea.

Auxiliary: a Fleet Auxiliary is a ship servicing or supplying others. *See also* RESERVES; ROYAL FLEET AUXILIARY SERVICE.

Avast: from the Dutch *houdvast* ('hold-fast'); a nautical order meaning stop or cease.

A-weather: on the weather or windward side, in contrast to the lee side.

A-weigh: when the anchor is raised off the sea-bed it is said to be a-weigh.

Ay-ay (or **aye-aye**): seaman's customary acknowledgement of an order.

'Sink me the ship, Master Gunner – sink her,
    split her in twain!
Fall into the hands of God, not into the hands
    of Spain!'
And the gunner said 'Ay, ay', but the seamen
    made reply,
'We have children, we have wives,
And the Lord hath spared our lives'.

Tennyson, 'The *Revenge*'

Ayscue, Sir George (*fl.*1646–71): admiral; he was knighted by Charles I but served under Cromwell during the Commonwealth, the later years of which he spent in Sweden as naval adviser and at one time commanding the Swedish fleet. At the Restoration he managed to secure appointment as a Commissioner of the Navy, but returned to sea and was taken prisoner by the Dutch in the Four Days' Battle (1666).

Azores: group of widely separated islands, of volcanic origin, in mid-Atlantic, settled by the Portuguese from the 15th century. For the Battle of Flores (1591), *see* GRENVILLE, SIR RICHARD.

Azov, Sea of: a shallow sea on the north of the Black Sea, to which it is connected by the Strait of Kerch. Rich in fish, and providing the exit and entry to the great Don-Volga waterway, it has the disadvantage of being frozen for some six months in the year.

B

Backing (of the wind): *see* SHIFT.

Backing and filling: so handling the sails of a ship that the wind catches them alternately before and behind, especially when the tide is with the vessel and the wind against it – a manoeuvre frequently used when navigating in narrow waters. The phrase is also used figuratively to describe irresolution or vacillation.

Back-staff (also known as **Davis's quadrant**): an instrument of navigation invented by Captain John DAVIS (*c*.1594) for observing the altitude of the sun. It consisted of a large and a small arc, with a horizon-vane at the common centre, an eye-vane on the large arc and a shadow-vane on the smaller. It was an improvement on the CROSS-STAFF, which it gradually replaced.
See also INSTRUMENTS.

Baffin, William (*d*.1622): discoverer and navigator whose voyages included expeditions to Greenland to search for the North-West Passage. He made many valuable charts and wrote accounts of his voyages. He was killed while serving in an expedition for the East India Company, attempting to expel the Portuguese from Ormuz in the Persian Gulf.
Baffin (or Baffin's) Bay, west of Greenland, is named after him.

Nowhere will such a mad sea be raised in such an incredibly short time as when the autumn boreal winds, marshalling in Baffin's Bay,

charge southward, and, crowding through the narrows of Davis Strait, hurl every intruder out . . .

Robert Peary, *Northward over the Great Ice* (1898)

Baker, James (*fl. c*.1530): shipwright to Henry VIII. His chief contribution was the revolutionary step of piercing the sides of warships to permit the mounting of guns on the lower deck. He was given a pension of 4d. a day in 1537.

Baker, Matthew (*b*.1530): son of James BAKER and the first to be called (in 1572) Master Shipwright. Some of his actual draughts of ships – the only 16th-century plans known to survive in England – are preserved in the library of Samuel Pepys at Magdalene College, Cambridge. Pepys entitled them 'Fragments of Ancient English Shipwrighty'.

Balchen (or **Balchin**), **Sir John** (1670–1744): admiral; a distinguished officer who saw service in the West Indies, on the Spanish coasts, in the Mediterranean etc. In October 1707, commanding the *Chester* and sailing with a convoy of 130 merchantmen, he was captured by the French admiral René Duguay Trouin after a spirited engagement and was honourably acquitted at the subsequent court-martial. Soon after being knighted (1744) he was caught in a violent storm and lost on the voyage home after seeing a convoy of food and store ships safely into Gibraltar.

Balinger: a small, sloop-like, sea-going vessel in use during the 15th and 16th centuries. The exact nature of a balinger is somewhat obscure, as the word has not been applied to any particular kind of ship for several centuries. The *Oxford English Dictionary* traces the origin of the name to old French *baleinier*, meaning a whale-

Matthew Baker: a ship draft illustrating the 'cod's head, mackerel tail' principle of hull design.

ship, but it was evidently applied in a general sense to early light sailing vessels, perhaps with oars also, apparently used for transporting goods and sometimes fighting men.

Ballast: shingle, iron, or any other heavy substance loaded into the hold of a ship to settle her in the water and give her greater stability. A vessel is 'in ballast' when she is carrying no cargo, only ballast.

But Sir Richard bore in hand all his sick men
    from the land
Very carefully and slow,
Men of Bideford in Devon,
And we laid them on the ballast down
    below . . .
           Tennyson, 'A Ballad of the Fleet'

Baltic: inland sea of N. Europe, connected with the Atlantic by a series of channels and bordered by Denmark, Germany, Poland, Russia, Finland and Sweden. For the British Navy the pine forests around the Baltic were a vital source of supply for masts and tar (*see* STOCKHOLM TAR), especially in the 18th century and in the Napoleonic Wars; hence the constant British endeavours to prevent the Baltic from falling under the domination of any one power.

For the 'Battle of the Baltic', *see* COPENHAGEN, BATTLE OF.

Baltimore clipper: fast type of American sailing ship, popular with pirates, smugglers and slave traders, as well as with the U.S. Navy, for its turn of speed. One of its distinguishing features was its sharp bows. It is usually shown as schooner-rigged, though in its earlier stages of development it was probably rigged like a cutter. There has been much discussion as to which was the first true clipper; some have settled for the Baltimore-built *Ann McKimm*, a 500-ton schooner of 1832. Baltimore is the chief city and seaport of Maryland.

See also colour section and CLIPPER.

Band of Brothers (or **The Chosen Band**): the distinguished group of captains who fought with Nelson at the Battle of the Nile (1798), selected and trained in the tough school of Admiral John Jervis (Earl St Vincent). The term was used by Nelson to describe this fellowship of some of the finest seamen of the day, many of them his life-long friends. Among them were:

    Alexander Ball (later Admiral Sir
        Alexander), 1757–1809
    Edward Berry (later Admiral Sir
        Edward), 1768–1831
    Thomas Foley (later Admiral Sir
        Thomas), 1757–1833
    Benjamin Hallowell (later Admiral
        Sir Benjamin), 1760–1834

Samuel Hood (later Admiral Sir
Samuel), 1762–1814
Ralph Miller (killed during the
defence of Acre), 1762–99
James Saumarez (later Admiral
Baron de Saumarez), 1757–1836
Thomas Thompson (later Admiral
Sir Thomas), 1766?–1828

It will be noticed how much of an age-group they all were, three being born in the same year – Nelson himself was born in 1758 – and how distinguished a band they were, all except the prematurely (and accidentally) killed Miller attaining flag rank and at least a knighthood.

Banks, Joseph: *see* BOTANY BAY.

Banner: the rectangular flag, originally of greater depth than length, carried on a ship to indicate the presence of a king or some other person of high degree. Accounts for the tenth year of the reign of Henry V mention a banner for the ship *Trinity Royal*, 'of the royal arms and St George'. Henry VIII's *Henri Grâce à Dieu* was provided with the 'banners of England, England and Spain, Castille, Guienne, Wales, Cornwall, the pomegranate and rose, the rose of white and green . . .' Early merchant ships also flew the royal banner, as is shown by the medieval seals of such ports as Lyme Regis, Hastings, Bristol and Yarmouth.

And when the ships were fulfilled with arms and provisions, and knights and sergeants, the shields were ranged round the bulwarks and castles of the ships, and the banners displayed, many and fair.

Geoffrey de Villehardouin, *Chronicle of
the Fourth Crusade* (1204)

See colour section.

Bantry Bay: bay in Co. Cork, Southern Ireland. Among the events in its history was the arrival of a French fleet (May 1689) bringing to Ireland the exiled James II of England and an array of soldiers to support his cause. With the disembarkation completed, the French withdrew after a short engagement with a British squadron under Admiral Herbert. A landing in Bantry Bay was also the unfulfilled objective of the French in 1796. A squadron with 20,000 troops on board had sailed from Brest in the hope of raising an insurrection in Ireland. Adverse winds and navigational errors prevented the landing, and after a fortnight, the expedition straggled back to France.

Bantry Bay was also the scene, in December 1801, of the last serious mutiny in the fleet till the next century. Two months earlier, an armistice had been agreed with France and the preliminaries of peace signed. The Bantry Bay squadron, eagerly anticipating getting home, was instead ordered to sail to the West Indies, and mutinied. There was no violence, the men exercising a marked degree of self-discipline, only resolving 'not to start an anchor except for England'. After a week the mutiny was broken by the courage of Captain Eyles of the flag-ship *Temeraire* and by the failure of the marines to support the mutineers. Eleven men were hanged at the yardarm and others were flogged through the fleet or imprisoned. Ironically, in the end the squadron was not sent on foreign service.

Banyan days: in old sailing times, days on which no meat was served to the ship's crew; from the banyan tree, or Indian fig.

Barbary: literally, 'the land of the Berbers'; region of North Africa consisting of the area covered by Morocco, Algeria,

Tunis, Tripoli and Barca. It was colonized very early and came to great power under the Carthaginians. Its greatest reputation, however, for several centuries was as a centre of pirate hordes (see below). Shakespeare mentions them in *Hamlet* and *Othello*.

Barbary corsairs (or **pirates**): the redoubtable group of pirate states on the North African coast was founded by the brothers Uruj and Khizr Barbarossa *c*.1512. By their ruthlessness and courage they soon made themselves supreme on the coast and built up a pirate empire which, though its power fluctuated, did not end till the 19th century, when Sir Edward PELLEW bombarded Algiers into submission (1816); the final extinction came with the French conquest of Algiers in 1830.

The North African pirates did not by any means confine their activities to the Mediterranean. They made their raids as far afield as Iceland and even North America; they cruised in the English Channel and between 1609 and 1616 captured 466 ships, taking the surviving crews into slavery. At times they even landed on the coast of Britain and took away men, women and children. John Masefield's poem 'Enslaved' gives a vivid picture of this sort of happening. *See also* PIRATES.

> However great may be the dangers . . . they cease not their irritating performances, kindling warfare in all the coasts of the Christian nations. It is there that they exercise their infamous piracies, and there also that they glory in the most shameful of all commerce . . . Indeed, experience has taught all Christian merchants that the infidels of the coast of Barbary are all brigands. Among these, those of Algiers carry off the prize for riches, for ships, for strength, and for villainy.
>
> Frère Pierre d'An, *Histoire de Barbarie et ses Corsaires* (1637)

Barber, Francis (*fl*.1752–89): Dr Johnson's Negro servant, who, despite his master's pronouncement that 'No man will be a sailor who has contrivance enough to get himself into a jail', at one time joined the Navy. Johnson was in such distress about this that he sought the good offices of friends who might exercise some influence at the Admiralty on the grounds that 'the boy is a sickly lad, of a delicate frame, and particularly subject to a malady in his throat, which renders him very unfit for his Majesty's service.' Johnson's efforts were successful and Barber served the lexicographer for the rest of the writer's life.

Barbette: a circular armoured platform with a hood to protect the guns on a warship.

Barents Sea: an arm of the Arctic Ocean lying off the north of Norway and N.W. of Russia. It feels the last effects of the North Atlantic Drift and so is generally ice-free, allowing access to the port of Murmansk. The sea was named after the Dutch explorer and navigator Willem Barents, who sailed these waters in his voyages between 1594 and 1596 during his search for the NORTH-EAST PASSAGE.

Bare poles: *see* UNDER BARE POLES.

Barfleur and La Hogue, Battles of (19 and 23–4 May 1692): two battles on the northern coast of France between the forces of Louis XIV, supporting the cause of the exiled James II of England, and the Anglo-Dutch fleet. Off Cape Barfleur on 19 May, Admiral Tourville's fleet was scattered by the much superior force under Admiral RUSSELL. A few days later three French ships that had reached Cherbourg (including Tourville's flag-ship, the *Soleil Royal*) were destroyed by a cutting-out

Prince Frederick Louis's state barge, 1737.

expedition sent in by Admiral Delavall; and at La Hogue Sir George Rooke, in sight of James II, destroyed twelve French battleships that had sought shelter in the fortified harbour. The luckless (and scarcely tactful) James II is said to have exclaimed to his French allies: 'None but my British tars could have done so gallant a deed!'

Barge: (1) flat-bottomed freight-boat used on inland rivers and canals; (2) large, richly ornamented state or pleasure boat used by high dignitaries; (3) the second largest of a man-o'-war's boats, the largest being the launch; (4) boat used to carry flag-officers, e.g. 'admiral's barge'.

From the purely decorative point of view, state barges are some of the most magnificent boats ever built. Ceremonial barges were used by the Doges of Venice for the annual Marriage of the ADRIATIC. A fine model of the last of these Venetian state barges, the *Bucentaur* of 1729, is in the possession of the Elder Brethren of Trinity House, London. The National Maritime Museum, Greenwich, has the original splendidly gilded state barge of Frederick Louis, Prince of Wales, father of George III, used by him on the River Thames; and

a model of the Barge of the Worshipful Company of Shipwrights, used *c.*1750 in the Lord Mayor's procession on the Thames.

The barge she sat in, like a burnished throne,
Burned on the water. The poop was beaten gold;
Purple the sails, and so perfumèd that
The winds were lovesick with them. The oars were silver . . .

Shakespeare, *Antony and Cleopatra*, II.2

Barham, Lord: *see* MIDDLETON, CHARLES.

'Barham': *see WARSPITE.*

Bark: *see* BARQUE.

Barkers: the old-time seamen's name for the lower deck guns.

Barnacle: type of crustacean or shell-fish which, in the adult stage, attaches itself permanently to a rock or a ship's bottom. The word has a curious and confused history, apparently originating from the same source that gives us a type of goose: the barnacle, bernacle, or Arctic goose. One 17th-century writer actually speaks of 'broken pieces of old ships on which is found certain spume or froth, which in time breedeth into shells, and the fish which is hatched therefrom is in shape and habit like a bird.'

Heavily encrusted ships could be badly slowed up, and barnacles and other marine life have to be removed by scraping or careening.

Barometer (or **weather-glass**): instrument for recording the pressure of the atmosphere. The commonest type is the mercurial barometer, in which a column of air is balanced by a column of mercury set against a graduated scale marked in millibars or inches. Three other different types of barometer, however, are commonly carried in ships: the aneroid barometer, the precision aneroid barometer and the barograph. The aneroid barometer consists of a thin metal chamber, partly exhausted of air and sealed, and thus sensitive to the smallest changes of external pressure. A pointer from the chamber is contrived to show the changes of pressure on a dial. The precision aneroid barometer is more complicated and also more accurate. The barograph records variations in atmospheric pressure by means of a sensitive lever and pen registering on paper on a slowly revolving drum. The drum, driven by clockwork, makes one revolution in seven days, and so the barograph has the advantage of giving a continuous record in addition to its ability to register minor fluctuations less easily seen in other types of barometer. To obtain accurate readings of a barometer certain corrections have to be made. A marked lowering of barometric pressure may foretell an approaching storm.

Barque (or **bark**): small three-masted sailing vessel, having fore and main masts square-rigged and mizzen mast fore-and-

aft rigged. The name is also used poetically, but incorrectly, for almost any sailing vessel.

Barquentine: small three-masted sailing vessel with the fore mast square-rigged and the other two masts fore-and-aft rigged.

Bar-shot: *see* SHOT.

'Bartimeus': pen-name of Captain Sir Lewis Anselmo Ritchie (1886–1967). Born da Costa Ricci, he changed his name by deed poll in 1941. Having entered the Royal Navy in 1901, he retired as Captain in 1944. Over most of that period he produced a series of fine tales of the sea, beginning with *Naval Occasions* (1914).

Bass, George (*fl.*1790–1812): naval surgeon who explored the coast of New South Wales and circumnavigated Tasmania. Bass Strait, 80–150 miles wide, separating Tasmania from Australia, is named after him.

Bathyscaphe: *see* BATHYSPHERE.

Bathysphere: a specially strengthened spherical chamber used for deep oceanic descent and exploration, but lowered from a surface ship by a cable. An American, William Beebe, was the first to make deep descents in a bathysphere; on 15 August 1934, off Bermuda, he descended to a depth of 3028 ft. In 1949 one of his colleagues, Otis Barton, descended in a steel sphere known as the benthoscope to a depth of 4500 ft off California.

The bathysphere suspended by cable gave way to specially designed free-moving submersibles known as bathyscaphes. Very strongly built to resist the great pressure of water at extreme depths, the bathyscaphe was designed and first used in 1948 by Auguste Piccard. Ballast tanks using petrol for buoyancy and iron shot held in place by electro-magnets gave control of descent and ascent, and electrically driven pro-pellers gave the bathyscaphe a limited horizontal movement. After experimental developments by the French and Italians, the American Navy acquired Piccard's bathyscaphe named the *Trieste*. In January 1960, in the deep sea trench off the Marianas Islands in the Pacific, Jacques Piccard, son of the designer, and an American, Donald Walsh, descended in the *Trieste* to a depth of over six miles (to be precise, 35,820 ft or 6000 fathoms).

Batten the hatches: secure all the hatches (deck openings) firmly, usually against bad weather.

Battle cruiser: large warship of a kind which evolved early in this century: armament was nearly as heavy as that of a battleship, but speed was greater. Battle cruisers formed an important section of the Royal Navy during the two World Wars; *Repulse* and *Renown*, launched in 1916 and each of 32,000 tons, were of this class. So too was the ill-fated *HOOD*, sunk by the *Bismarck* in May 1941. In the same year the *Repulse* and the *Prince of Wales* were sunk by Japanese aircraft off the coast of Malaya, sealing the fate of Singapore and revealing the vulnerability of the big ship against superior air power.

Battle-lanterns: lanterns of thick horn used on ships of the line to lessen the risk of fire and explosion. If an action was fought at night, the gunners fought by the light of these lanterns, one to a gun.

Bayeux Tapestry: the 11th-century tapestry, preserved in the Cathedral of Bayeux in Normandy (a full-size reproduc-tion is in the Victoria and Albert Museum, London), showing the history of King Harold II of England and the invasion of William the Conqueror, and giving vivid glimpses of contemporary ships, both

The battle cruiser H.M.S. *Renown* at sea, 1943.

Saxon and Norman. They are, in fact, little different from earlier Viking ships, the vessels being clinker-built, with tall figureheads and stern carvings rearing vertically. There is a square sail on a single mast, and a steering paddle is carried on the starboard quarter. Harold's own ship, the *Mora*, has sixteen oar-ports a side. The knights and soldiers shipped their shields along the gunwales.

See colour section.

Bayonne ship: a large ship, 186 ft long and 46 ft in breadth, that a contemporary record shows was being constructed at Bayonne for Henry V of England in the year 1419. This was unusually large for a ship of the period and it is probable that the shipwrights could not overcome the technical problems involved, since it was apparently never completed. The largest known ship of Henry V, the *JESUS OF THE TOWER*, was of 1000 tons – about 200 tons less than the Bayonne ship would have been.

Beach, on the: either temporarily ashore or having left the sea for good.

Beach-comber: a long rolling wave that rakes over the beach; hence, a dock loafer or any white man on a foreign shore living an idle existence.

Beachy Head: a well-known Sussex landmark, the tallest headland on the south coast of England, 575 ft above sea level. At the foot of the chalk cliffs lies the Beachy Head lighthouse, built in 1902 to replace the one still to be seen on the cliff top. The granite tower of the lighthouse shows from its lantern a double-flashing white light every 20 seconds.

Beachy Head, Battle of (30 June 1690): action in which a combined English and Dutch fleet suffered a defeat at the hands of the French admiral Tourville. The fault lay not so much with the English admiral, the Earl of Torrington, as with the government, who ordered him to attack against his advice that his squadron was wholly insufficient to take on the entire French fleet, and with the Dutch, who either misunderstood or deliberately disobeyed his orders. Torrington, before retreating into the Thames, had to destroy one English and several Dutch ships to prevent their capture. He was thrown into the Tower, and, although he was later acquitted by his fellow-officers at a court-martial, he never held command again.

'Beagle': Royal Navy 10-gun brig of 235 tons, commanded by Captain Robert FITZROY, on which Charles Darwin sailed as naturalist on a scientific expedition that lasted five years. It began on 27 December 1831, when Darwin was an untried young scientist not yet 23 years of age. He returned an accomplished zoologist and geologist, having had a variety of experiences that determined the whole of his future career and thought. But despite the importance of the voyage, Darwin had no love of the sea. Looking back, he wrote:

If a person suffer much from sea-sickness, let him weigh it heavily in the balance. I speak from experience: it is no trifling evil, cured in a week . . . And what are the boasted glories of the illimitable ocean? A tedious waste, a desert of water, as the Arabians call it.

Beak (and **beak-head**): the long projecting structure at the head or bows of a ship, very much like the beak of a bird (or, in some cases, the snout of a crocodile) and typical of Elizabethan ships. This long beak continues till well on into the 17th century, when it becomes wider and

41

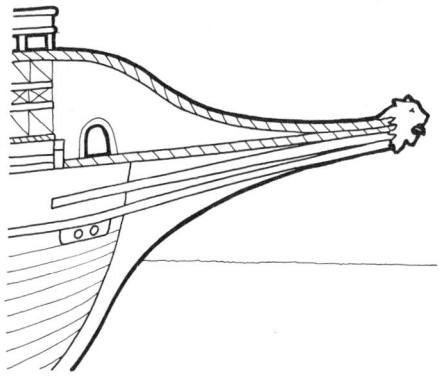

the wind; to 'bear off' is to move to a distance or keep clear of something.

> Bore up for the French fleet lying off Aboukir Roads.
>
> Log of H.M.S. *Vanguard* (1 August 1798)

> Saw the enemy's fleet bearing S.S.W., distance 7 or 8 miles.
>
> Log of H.M.S. *Culloden*, Battle of Cape St Vincent (1798)

> The winter star doth now appear,
> So, boys, the anchor weigh,
> 'Tis time to leave this cold country,
> And for England bear away, brave boys!
> And for England bear away!
>
> Sea song, 'The Greenland Fishery'

shorter and is set higher than in Tudor ships. The bird-like appearance is sometimes curiously reinforced by the hawsehole (the hole in the bows for a cable to pass through), which looks very much like an eye.

Beam: (1) the width of a ship or boat (e.g. 'The beam of Nelson's *Victory* was just over 51 ft'); (2) a transverse piece of timber supporting the deck.

Various expressions derive from this: a 'beamy' ship was a broad one; 'abaft the beam' means astern of an imaginary line drawn across the vessel amidships; 'on the starboard beam' is away on the right side of the ship, and 'on the larboard (or "port") beam' is on the left side of the ship facing the bows; a ship is 'on her beam-ends' when she is so far heeled over (e.g. by a great wind) that she is almost on her side; and a man 'on his beam-ends' is in a similar position of acute difficulty, without money or means of support.

Bear: in nautical language, a word always connected with direction and ship manoeuvre: e.g. to 'bear away' is to change the course of a ship when close-hauled and put her before the wind; to 'bear down (on)' is to sail in the direction of; to 'bear up' is to put the helm up so as to put the ship before

The complexities of nautical terms and their definition, not only for the layman but even at times for the seaman, are well illustrated in the appendix to the 1817 edition of Dr John Campbell's *Lives of the British Admirals*, where the bewildered editor writes:

Bearing-up, or *bearing away*, in navigation, the act of changing the course of a ship, in order to make her run before the wind, after she had sailed some time with a side wind, or close hauled; it is generally performed to arrive at some port under the lee, or to avoid some imminent danger occasioned by a violent storm, leak, or enemy in sight.

This phrase, which is absurd enough, seems to have been derived from the motion of the helm, by which this effect is partly produced; as the helm is then bore up to the windward, or weather side of the ship. Otherwise, it is a direct contradiction in terms, to say that a ship bears up, when she goes before the wind; since the current of the wind, as well as that of a river, always understood to determine the situation of objects or places within its limits. In the first sense we say, up to windward and down to leeward; as in the latter we say, up or down the river. This expression, however, although extremely improper, is commonly adopted in the general instructions of our navy, printed by authority, instead of bearing-down or bearing-away.

'Bear': *see WHITE BEAR.*

Beat: (1) make way against the wind; to 'beat to windward' is to sail on a series of tacks into the wind. (2) For 'beat to quarters' etc., *see* QUARTERS.

Beatson, William: a well-known ship-breaker of the early 19th century, who bought many ships 'sold out of the service', often at public auction, and demolished them in his yard at Rotherhithe on the River Thames. The most famous ship brought to his yard was the *TEMERAIRE.*

Beatty, David, first Earl Beatty (1871–1936): Admiral of the Fleet. In 1896 he won the D.S.O. for his leadership of a gunboat force on the Nile, and so continued his dashing and courageous career that in 1910 he became the youngest flag-officer for over 100 years. He was naval secretary to Winston Churchill (1912–13), commanded a battle-cruiser squadron (1913–16), and became Commander-in-Chief, Grand Fleet (1916–19), accepting the surrender of the German High Sea Fleet (November 1918). He was described as 'of dauntless moral and physical courage', with a wonderful clarity of judgement in times of crisis. His character, and even the unmistakably jaunty set of his cap, made him a national figure.

Beatty, Sir William (*d.*1842): surgeon in H.M.S. *Victory* who attended Nelson when he was shot at Trafalgar. He afterwards published *An Authentic Narrative of the Death of Lord Nelson . . . and Several Interesting Anecdotes* (1807); for a quotation from this, *see* HARDY, SIR THOMAS MASTERMAN.

Beaufort, Sir Francis (1774–1857): admiral and hydrographer. After much notable survey work he was appointed Hydrographer to the Navy (1829), a post he held for more than a quarter of a century. He is most remembered for the famous BEAUFORT WIND SCALE.

Beaufort (Wind) Scale: a numerical scale for assessing and recording the force of the wind. It was devised by Admiral Sir Francis Beaufort in 1808 and has since been revised from time to time. The scale numbers attributed according to the observed force of the wind are given in the table on pp. 44–5.

The case of surgeon's instruments belonging to Sir William Beatty and used by him on board H.M.S. *Victory* at Trafalgar.

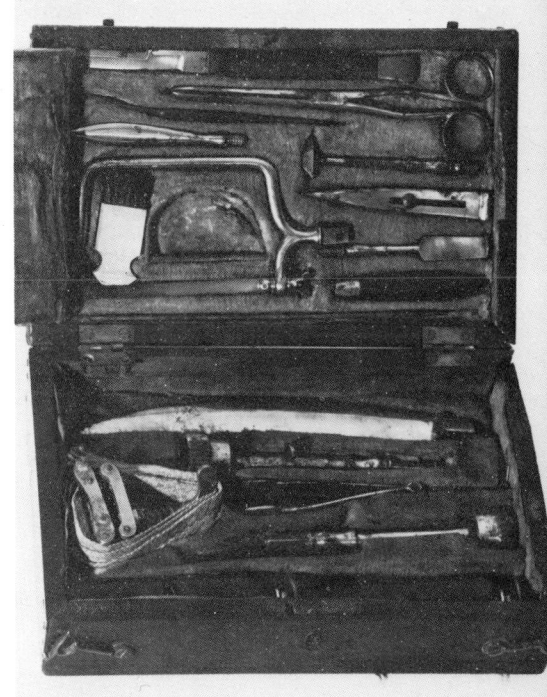

Beaufort number	Velocity (nautical miles per hour)	Descriptive terms	Sea criterion
0	Less than 1	Calm	Sea like a mirror
1	1–3	Light airs	Ripples with appearance of scales are formed, but without foam crests
2	4–6	Light breeze	Small wavelets, still short but more pronounced; crests have a glassy appearance and do not break
3	7–10	Gentle breeze	Large wavelets. Crests begin to break. Foam of glassy appearance. Perhaps scattered white horses
4	11–16	Moderate breeze	Small waves, becoming larger; fairly frequent white horses
5	17–21	Fresh breeze	Moderate waves, taking a more pronounced long form; many white horses are formed
6	22–27	Strong breeze	Large waves begin to form; the white foam crests are more extensive everywhere
7	28–33	Near gale	Sea heaps up, and white foam from breaking waves begins to be blown in streaks along the direction of the wind
8	34–40	Gale	Moderately high waves of greater length; edges of crests break into spindrift. The foam is blown in well-marked streaks along the direction of the wind
9	41–47	Strong gale	High waves. Dense streaks of foam along the direction of the wind. Crests of waves begin to topple, tumble and roll over. Spray may affect visibility
10	48–55	Storm	Very high waves with long overhanging crests. Foam in great patches is blown in dense white streaks along the direction of the wind. On the whole, the surface of the sea takes on a white appearance. The tumbling of the sea becomes heavy and shock-like. Visibility affected

Beaufort number	Velocity (nautical miles per hour)	Descriptive terms	Sea criterion
11	56–63	Violent storm	Exceptionally high waves. The sea is completely covered with long white patches of foam lying along the direction of the wind. Everywhere the edges of the wave crests are blown into froth. Visibility affected
12	64 and over	Hurricane	The air is filled with foam and spray. Sea completely white with driving spray; visibility very seriously affected

Becket: a ring or loop of rope, or a hook, used to hold ropes, spars etc. in position. *See* KNOTS.

Beckets, hands out of: old-time order to a youngster on board ship to get his hands out of his pockets.

Bedlam: a corruption of 'Bethlehem', from the Priory of St Mary of Bethlehem, London, founded in 1247 and three hundred years later given to the Mayor and Corporation of London and incorporated as a royal foundation for the care of lunatics. The Navy had its own wards at the Bethlehem or Bethlem Hospital and in the early years of the 19th century was discharging as many as 40 or 50 men a year to its care. The surgeon Sir Gilbert Blane revealed that, at that period, there was more than seven times the amount of insanity among sailors than among landsmen. He suggested, as one reason, that this was due to head injuries received by men constantly bumping their heads in the narrow space between decks, something they were particularly liable to do when intoxicated.

Beechey, Frederick William (1796–1856): admiral and geographer. He accompanied Sir John Franklin on his 1818 Arctic expedition and published an account of it. He surveyed the coasts of North Africa, South America and Ireland and was a President of the Royal Geographical Society.

Belay: (1) to fasten a running rope by making it fast round a strip of wood or belaying-pin; **(2)** word of command meaning 'Stop!' or 'Cancel', e.g. 'Belay there!', 'Belay that order!'

Belaying-pin: strong pin in the side of a ship, or elsewhere, round which a rope can

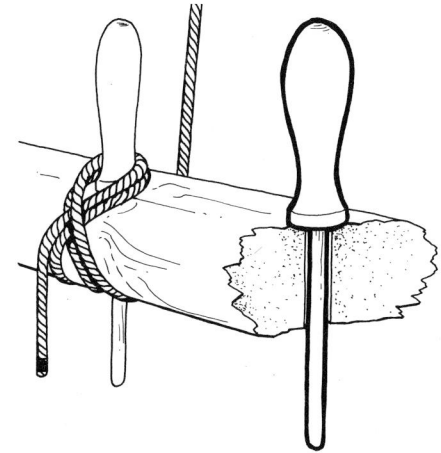

be fastened or 'belayed'. Made of wood or iron, it could be used as a formidable weapon.

> The winds is never nothin' more than just
>   light airs,
> 'N' no one gets belayin'-pinned, 'n' no one
>   ever swears . . .
>
> John Masefield, 'Port of Many Ships'

'Belfast': light cruiser, displacing 11,500 tons, completed by Harland and Wolff in Belfast in 1939. In November of that year, shortly after the outbreak of the Second World War, *Belfast* broke her back when she exploded a German magnetic mine in the Firth of Forth. After repair she played an important part in the Battle of the North Cape (December 1943), when the German battleship *Scharnhorst* was destroyed, and in 1944 she took part in the bombardment of the coast during the landing of the Allied forces in Normandy. Her armament consisted of twelve 6-in. guns in triple turrets and a number of 40-mm anti-aircraft guns. Her torpedo tubes were removed and her tripod masts replaced with lattice masts when she was refitted in 1959. Paid off in 1971, H.M.S. *Belfast* now has a permanent berth on the Thames near Tower Bridge, London, where she can be visited by the public.

Belfry: the frame from which a ship's bell is hung.

'Bellerophon': the famous 'Billy Ruffian' of Nelson's seamen (and their descendants), who refused to get their tongues round many of the difficult ships' names selected by the Admiralty. The Trafalgar *Bellerophon* was a 74-gun ship, launched on the Medway in 1786 and first commissioned in 1790. She served for more than a quarter of a century, constantly in action under a number of distinguished commanders. Her most famous day was 21 October 1805, when she was in the lee line (led by Admiral Collingwood) and was commanded by Captain John Cooke, who was killed almost at the same time and in the same way as Nelson. When the ship received Nelson's signal 'England expects . . .', Cooke made the rounds, giving the gun crews the Admiral's message. In reply, they chalked 'Death or glory' on their guns. Her casualties were 132 dead and wounded. Her last passenger of note was Napoleon, when he was brought to the coasts of England in 1815 after his defeat at Waterloo. Sadly enough, after such a career, *Bellerophon* finished up as a convict ship, renamed the *Captivity*. Her figurehead is preserved in Portsmouth Dockyard.

Bells: *see* SAND-GLASS; WATCHES.

Benbow, John (1653–1702): admiral; one of the rare examples in the 17th century of a 'tarpaulin' (a seaman who came from the lower deck into the officer class). Benbow was a fine seaman and had seen hard service as a mate and master's mate, but he was a tough, awkward character who, when he reached high command, could not always secure the loyalty of the captains under him. In 1702 he was sent with a squadron of ships to prevent a threatened French occupation of some Spanish West Indian territories. He came up with the French fleet off Santa Marta and gave chase for several days, fighting an almost single-handed action while most of his captains failed to support him. Two were subsequently tried and shot. Benbow, having behaved with great heroism, died of his wounds at Fort Royal. The French admiral involved, du Casse, was so angry at the contemptible behaviour of the British captains that he wrote to Benbow:

The wounded Benbow extolling his men during the chase, 1702.

I had little hope on Monday last but to have supped in your cabin [i.e. to have been taken prisoner]; but it pleased God to order it otherwise, and I am thankful for it. As for those cowardly captains who deserted you, hang them up; for, by God, they deserve it.

English public opinion agreed with du Casse, and Benbow became a popular hero, celebrated in many stories and ballads.

Bend: (**1**) a knot by which one rope is fastened to another, to a spar etc.; *see* KNOTS. (**2**) To bend a rope, cable etc. is to make it fast; to bend a sail is to attach it to yard or boom.

Bering Sea and **Strait:** in the northernmost Pacific; named after Vitus Bering (1681–1741), Danish sailor and explorer. He served in the Russian Navy and was appointed by Peter the Great to discover whether Asia and North America were connected by land. In 1728 he passed through the Bering Strait into the Arctic Ocean, proving the separation of the two continents. At its narrowest the Strait is 53 miles wide. *See also* SEALING.

Bermuda rig: almost standard on modern racing yachts: mainsail, headsail and no bowsprit. The Bermudan sail, introduced from across the Atlantic, is tall, narrow and triangular, enabling the vessel to sail very close to the wind. There is no space between mast and sail, which is sewn on to slides running in a metal track. *See also* SAIL.

Bermudian: old term for a 'wet' ship, one that took on a great deal of water; from a type of three-masted schooner of Napoleonic times, built in Bermuda, that did not rise to the waves but went through them.

Berry, Sir Edward (1768–1831): admiral; one of the 'Band of Brothers', and Nelson's flag-captain at the Battle of the Nile (1798).

The support and assistance I have received from Captain Berry cannot be sufficiently expressed. I was wounded in the head, and obliged to be carried off the deck; but the service suffered no loss by that count: Captain Berry was fully equal to the important service then going on, and to him I must beg leave to refer you for any information relative to this victory.

Nelson to Admiral John Jervis,
Commander-in-Chief off Cadiz, after the
Battle of the Nile

In fact Berry was not able to deliver the promised information. Sent off in the *LEANDER* with dispatches, he was captured by the French and severely wounded. He was later released on parole and, after reaching London, was knighted. He was also with Nelson at Trafalgar, commanding one of the latter's favourite ships, the *Agamemnon*. When Nelson heard that the 64-gun ship was approaching, he is reported to have exclaimed: 'Here comes Berry! Now we shall have a battle!' In all, Berry was in eight major fleet actions (more than any other captain in the Navy) as well as many minor engagements, and received three gold medals – a record apparently equalled only by Collingwood.

Berth: (1) place for mooring a ship at a quay, wharf or dock; (2) a room in a ship where the officers or some other section of the ship's company feed and spend their off-duty time (e.g. 'the midshipmen's berth', which, in Nelson's time, was often a dingy, very restricted space below the water-line); (3) a post or situation on a ship; and, hence, a situation of any kind.

A good berth I wish you, in a ship that's well
    found,
With a decent crowd forrard, an' her gear all
    sound.

Cecily Fox-Smith, 'So Long!'

To 'give a wide berth to' means to keep clear of or deliberately avoid (from the need to give a berthed ship room to swing at anchor).

Bethlehem Hospital: *see* BEDLAM.

Between wind and water: that part of a ship's hull that is just below the water-line except when the ship heels over under the pressure of wind. The phrase was used with special reference to the danger of being holed by cannon shot along this line. It is now used metaphorically: a hit between wind and water is a damaging blow to someone's plans.

Bibles: one of the seamen's names for the HOLYSTONES.

Bight: (1) a large bay or indentation in the coastline, e.g. the Bight of Benin, the Great Bight of Australia; (2) a loop of rope; *see* KNOTS.

Big Triangle: a familiar route sailed by cargo ships – from Britain to Australia, thence to the west coast of South America and home again.

Big-wigs: now a slang term for any important official or dignitary; but it seems to have originated at sea, applied to senior officers wearing the full wigs typical of the 17th and early 18th centuries.

Bilboes: *see* IN IRONS.

Bilge (or **bilges**): the broadest part of a ship's bottom, on which she would rest if aground; hence, 'bilge-water' (the water allowed to collect in the bottom of a ship, often becoming contaminated and smelly), and 'bilge-pump' etc. To 'taste like bilge-water' is a common expression for unsavoury food or drink, as is 'Don't talk bilge!' to someone talking rubbish. *See also p.577 and* PUMPS.

Bill-board: reinforcement fitted over the bow planking to prevent damage to the hull when the anchor is hoisted aboard.

Bill of lading: a statement or description of a ship's freight or cargo.

'Billy Blue': *see* CORNWALLIS, SIR WILLIAM.

'Billy Ruffian': *see BELLEROPHON.*

Binnacle: the case or box containing the ship's compass. It was usually provided with a light so that it could be read at night. H.M.S. *Victory*'s binnacle, which can still be seen at Portsmouth, has a copper flue to let the lamp-smoke escape. Some early

Bill-board.

binnacles were very beautiful and ornate structures. The word originally meant 'a dwelling place'.

Birkenhead: large town and port in Cheshire, at the mouth of the River Mersey. The 19th century saw rapid development, particularly in shipbuilding; many famous ships were built in the universally known yards of Cammell Laird. In April 1962 a dock capable of taking ships of 100,000 tons was opened.

'Birkenhead': Royal Navy frigate of 1845 which became a troop transport and was wrecked off the coast of South Africa in February 1852, with a loss of 436 men.

Biscay, Bay of: that part of the Atlantic which lies immediately to the west of France. Its reputation for storms and huge seas made it a fearsome area in the days of sail. Here some of the finest feats of British seamanship were performed during the wars with France, from the Seven Years' War and Hawke's victory at Quiberon Bay (1759) to the long, exhausting blockades of the Napoleonic Wars.

Bishop Rock: the highest point of the south-westernmost island of the Scillies. It carries a granite-built lighthouse 167 ft high, which shows a double-flashing white light every 15 seconds. The light was first established in 1858 after an attempt at building an earlier structure had been destroyed in a gale. The present tower was enlarged and strengthened in 1887. Bishop Rock marks a most dangerous approach from the Atlantic, and it was not far from Bishop Rock that H.M.S. *ASSOCIATION* and three other ships were wrecked in 1707.

'Bismarck': German battleship of 45,000

tons, launched in 1939. On 24 May 1941 the *Bismarck* sank the British battle cruiser *Hood* while attempting to reach the open spaces of the Atlantic. In a running battle which involved such ships as *PRINCE OF WALES*, *Norfolk*, *Suffolk*, and the aircraft-carriers *Victorious* and *Ark Royal*, the *Bismarck* was finally crippled by torpedo hits from Swordfish aircraft. Unable to steer, and leaking fuel oil, she was battered into a wreck by a sustained heavy barrage from the British battleships *Rodney* and *King George V*, and was finally sunk by torpedoes launched from the cruiser *Dorsetshire*.

Bitts: strong upright timbers to which ropes, cables etc. can be fastened. The word can be traced in such expressions as 'to the bitter end'. The 'bitter end' was the end of the rope fastened to the bitts; when the bitt or 'bitter end' was reached, there was no more rope to run out.

All Thy waves and storms have gone over me, but I have borne up under them to the bitter end.

Psalm 42.9

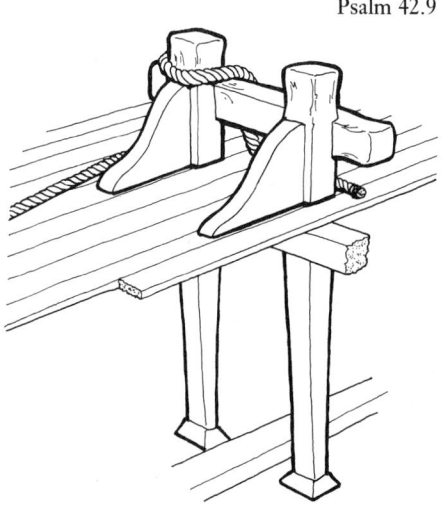

'Blackbeard': *see* TEACH, EDWARD.

Blackbirder: ship engaged in the slave trade.

'Black Charlie': *see* NAPIER, SIR CHARLES.

'Black Dick': *see* HOWE, RICHARD.

'Black Joke': an unusually named Royal Naval vessel, carrying one long 18-pounder gun and 34 men, commanded by Lieutenant Henry Downes. In 1829, while serving as a tender to the *Sybille*, engaged in the suppression of the slave trade on the west coast of Africa, she encountered the Spanish slaver *Almirante* in the Bight of Benin and carried on a running fight alone against an armament of ten 18-pounders and four long 9-pounders for eleven hours. For this exploit Downes was promoted to commander and presented by his commanding officer with 'a splendid vase of polished Heart of Oak, with appropriate ornaments in silver gilt'.

Black Sea: large enclosed sea bounded on the south by Turkey, on the north and east by Russia, and by Bulgaria and Rumania on the west. It is linked to the Mediterranean by a narrow south-western outlet through the Bosporus, Sea of Marmara and Dardanelles, and is therefore of vital importance to Russia for reasons of trade and naval power. The Black Sea stretches over 700 miles from east to west and nearly 400 miles from north to south. It is tideless, but subject to sudden storms. The many large rivers such as the Danube, Dnieper and Don discharging great quantities of fresh water into the Black Sea reduce its salinity, but also cause strong surface currents flowing out through the Bosporus.

Black ships: sailing ships built of teak in Indian yards. Numbers of these were built for the Royal Navy and the East India Company, partly to overcome the increasing shortage of oak (*see* TIMBER) and partly to avoid the mounting costs and corruption in the home dockyards.

Blackwall: Thames-side district of S.E. London, well-known for its docks and warehouses and formerly a considerable shipbuilding centre.

Blackwall frigate: famous type of ship built at Blackwall in the 19th century. Many were engaged in the East Indies trade. In design they were much like the Royal Navy frigates of the day, with the old square stern, though they later developed finer lines. Probably the earliest Blackwall frigate was the *Seringapatam* of 818 tons, built in 1837. The largest was about 1400 tons. Not all so-called Blackwall frigates were built at Blackwall; later vessels were commissioned by various Blackwall firms to be constructed in other yards, e.g. at Sunderland.

Blackwall ships were among the best and speediest of their day, strongly manned and attracting an excellent type of seaman. Many were ex-Royal Navy men. An eye-witness in the 1860s described how there could be seen at Calcutta, when the Blackwallers were at the height of their prosperity,

stretched along from bow to next ship's stern, from twenty to thirty of the handsomest ships in the world, flying the famous house-flags of Green, Money Wigram, Joseph Somes, Marshall, Smith, Willis and Dunbar. Man of war style and discipline were always maintained . . . Each ship was provided with a fiddler, who played at least four hours daily.

Cecily Fox-Smith, *A Book of Famous Ships* (1924)

As a good example of a Blackwaller, the *Newcastle*'s career may be outlined. Built by Messrs Green, she was 198 ft 8 in. long and 36 ft 6 in. in breadth, with a registered tonnage of 1137. Her maiden voyage began

The *Seringapatam* hove to, from an oil painting by J. Lynn, 1837.

in April 1859 and she continued, in the hands of various owners, for 28 years. She was employed in a number of different trades, including the Indian passenger service, conveying coolie labour to the West Indies, and on the Australian emigrant run. She often made more than 250 miles a day, her fastest trip being 77 days between Melbourne and London. In 1876 she is recorded as having run 302 miles in a day, scurrying before a gale with all sails set. In the eight days before that she had made 258, 251, 246, 260, 249, 238, 258, and 201 miles.

Blackwood, Sir Henry (1770–1832): admiral; a distinguished officer who entered the Navy as a volunteer in 1781 and saw service all over the world. He is best remembered for his share in the Battle of Trafalgar, when, on the *EURYALUS*, he commanded the inshore squadron outside Cadiz and kept watch over the French and Spanish shipping. *See also* HARVEY, SIR ELIAB.

Blake, Robert (1599–1657): admiral and General at Sea; one of England's greatest naval commanders, the strange thing being that, although he knew a good deal about ships, he did not enter the Navy till he was 50, and his career lasted only eight years. He came of a merchant shipping family in Bridgwater, Somerset, and became prominent as a commander of Parliamentary forces on land during the Civil War. In 1649 he was appointed General at Sea and won great victories against Prince Rupert, the Dutch and the Spaniards. *See also* ANGLO-DUTCH WARS; DUNGENESS, BATTLE OF; SANTA CRUZ.

Admiral Blake, as to his person, was of middle stature, about five feet and a half, a little inclining to corpulence; he was of a fresh, sanguine complexion, his hair was of the frizzled

kind, and, as was then the mode, he wore whiskers, which he curled up when he was in any ways provoked.

John Oldmixon, *The History and Life of Admiral Blake* (1746)

Blane, Sir Gilbert (1749–1834): physician; honoured in connection with the improvement of the health and sanitary conditions of the Navy, on which he published important statistics and recommendations. *See also* SCURVY.

Bligh, William (1754–1817): admiral. He accompanied Captain Cook as sailing master on his second voyage round the world, but is best remembered as the central figure of the famous mutiny of the *Bounty*. In response to representations by a number of merchants and planters, an expedition was sent to introduce breadfruit trees from the Southern Pacific islands into the West Indies. A small vessel, the 250-ton *Bounty*, was bought and fitted out for the purpose, and put under the command of Lieutenant William Bligh, with a ship's company of just over 40. They sailed from Spithead just before Christmas 1787 and reached Tahiti in October 1788, after a voyage of over 26,000 miles. By the time the *Bounty* left again, with a cargo of over a thousand bread-fruit trees and other plants, they had lingered more than five months, with many opportunities for the crew to get slack. Moreover, though Bligh was a seaman of great courage and strength, he had a foul tongue and an unfortunate gift for irritating and provoking the men under him. Three weeks after leaving Tahiti, the crew mutinied, led by the second-in-command, Fletcher Christian. With 18 other members of the ship's company, Bligh was forced into an open boat and set adrift, with a small quantity of food and drink, a quadrant and compass, but no sextant, maps or time-keeper. By a superb feat of seamanship, after 41 days in their 23-ft long boat and a voyage of 3618

From a sketch portrait by George Dance, 1794.

nautical miles, Bligh and his company landed at Timor with the loss of only one man. (For the fate of the mutineers, *see* PITCAIRN ISLAND.)

Bligh later made another expedition to transport bread-fruit, this time without incident; but he incited another mutiny after he had been made Captain-General and Governor of New Zealand, 16 years after the *Bounty* affair. This time the soldiers deposed him and put him in prison. He returned to England in 1811 and finished up as Vice-Admiral of the Blue.

The bread-fruit, as we call it, grows as large as a tree, as big and as high as our largest apple trees; it hath a spreading head, full of branches and dark leaves. The fruit grows on the boughs like apples; it is as big as a penny loaf . . . and hath a thick, tough rind; when the fruit is ripe, it is yellow and soft, and the taste is sweet and pleasant. The natives of Guam use it for bread. They gather it when full-grown, while it is green and hard; then they bake it in an oven, which scorcheth the rind and makes it black, but they scrape off the outside black crust and there remains a tender thin crust; and the inside is soft, tender, and white.

William Dampier, *Voyage Round the World* (1697)

Block: a contrivance for leading a rope in a desired direction and for increasing pulling power. Many kinds are used on board ship – single, double, treble, and so on. *See also* SNATCH BLOCK.

Blockade: the investment of a place, especially by sea, to prevent supplies or reinforcements reaching it, or to confine ships inside it. One of the most famous and effective blockades in history was the ceaseless surveillance of the French ports by British ships during the Napoleonic Wars. The best testimony to its results comes from the pen of an American naval historian:

They were dull, weary, eventless months, those months of watching and waiting of the big ships before the French arsenals. Purposeless they surely seemed to many, but they saved England. The world has never seen a more impressive demonstration of the influence of sea-power upon its history. Those far-distant, storm-beaten ships, upon which the Grand Army never looked, stood between it and the dominion of the world.

Admiral A. T. Mahan, *The Influence of Sea Power upon History* (1890)

Blockade runner: a ship, captain or owner attempting to run into, or out of, a blockaded port.

Block-and-block: *see* CHOCK-A-BLOCK.

Blockhouse Fort: original name of the headquarters of Flag-Officer, Submarines, at Gosport on the western entrance to Portsmouth harbour; now known as H.M.S. *Dolphin*.

Blue: *see* ADMIRAL; NAVY BLUE.

Blue Ensign: the flag of the Royal Naval Reserve, blue with the Union Flag in the top left-hand corner. *See also* ENSIGN.

Bluenose: name given to (**1**) inhabitants of Nova Scotia, perhaps because of the tinge produced by the prevailing easterly winds; (**2**) ships built between 1840 and 1870 in the maritime provinces of Canada, which at the height of their sea-going prosperity could boast well over 7000 vessels, aggregating 1,333,015 tons.

There she goes – a ramping, stamping, hard-driving Bluenose – wooden ships with iron men commanding them.

Contemporary comment on the Nova Scotiaman *W. D. Lawrence* of Maitland

Blue Peter: a blue flag with a white square in the centre (flag P in the International Code), hoisted as a signal that the ship is ready to sail.
See colour section.

Blue Riband: the 'trophy' or symbol held for the fastest crossing of the Atlantic. The 'blue ribbon' of any sport or profession is 'the highest point of honour attainable therein'; the title probably derives from the blue ribbon of the Order of the Garter, the premier order of chivalry. *See also* ATLANTIC GREYHOUND; SPEED.

Board, to: to go on a ship, to attack and enter it by force. Two distinct words, one meaning board or plank, and the other border or rim, seem to have become associated very early; hence the many ship words and expressions in which 'board' appears, e.g. 'on board', 'aboard', 'ship-board', 'by the board'. 'Gone by the board' originally meant lost overboard, but is now in common use to describe anything lost or dropped, e.g. a plan or arrangement.

Boarding axe: small heavy weapon with steel axe-head and spike, useful for slicing through the enemy rigging, stays etc. and so affecting the manoeuvrability of the ship.

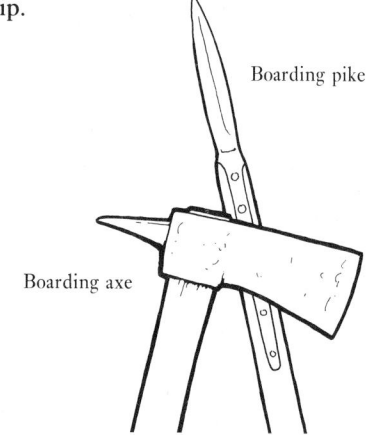

Boarding pike

Boarding axe

Boarding nets: strong nets erected at the side of a ship to hamper an enemy trying to board.

Boarding pike (or **half-pike**): steel spike on a wooden shaft, useful for repelling boarders.

Boat: small vessel, usually without a deck and propelled by oars or sails; but the name is also applied to engined craft such as fishing vessels and passenger steamers. To 'be in the same boat' means to share an unpleasant condition or predicament, like survivors from a shipwreck in an open boat.

Boats, ships': boats carried on ships for shore expeditions and as a safety precaution, so that passengers and crew can get away in case of accident. On modern passenger liners, merchant ships etc., the number is prescribed by regulations and must be sufficient for everyone on board. Many ships carry out regular 'boat drill', so that passengers and crew, equipped with life-jackets, know exactly how to get to boat-stations without fuss or panic.

In the old sailing Navy, certain boats were standard equipment: e.g. Nelson's *Victory* carried a 34-ft launch, a 32-ft barge, a 28-ft pinnace and an 18-ft cutter.

Boatswain (pronounced and often spelt **bos'n**): petty officer in charge of boats, sails, rigging etc.

When one of His Majesty's Ships is commissioned, the Boatswain is to exert himself to get on board all the Stores committed to his charge as expeditiously as possible; he is to examine them very carefully, and to inspect very minutely all rigging fitted in the Dock Yard.

Regulations and Instructions Relating to His Majesty's Service at Sea (1808)

The keys of the boatswain's store-room will be always hung on the outside of the first lieutenant's cabin; and the boatswain, for whatever he may want, is to apply to the officer of the watch . . . The boatswain is to pay the greatest attention to the conduct of his mates, and to prevent them from inflicting any punishment with their sticks or canes, unless ordered by their superior officers.

Observations and Instructions for the Use of the Commissioned, the Junior and other Officers of the Royal Navy (1804)

Boatswain is the oldest title in the British Navy. Along with the gunner and the carpenter, he formed the 'age-old triumvirate of "standing officers" to be found in every ship of war'. His reputation among the crew did not stand high, for he was always associated with the need to jump to duty, and (despite the regulation quoted above) he and his mates carried the means of enforcing it, not always with higher authority, with their rope 'starters' and their canes. It was often the boatswain's mates who inflicted the floggings with the cat-o'-nine-tails when men were sent to the gratings for punishment. Honesty was also traditionally rare in a boatswain; Admiral Lord Duncan is reputed to have said to one 'Whatever you do, Mr Bone, I hope and trust you will not take the anchors from the bows.' Though there were many thoroughly worthy and honest boatswains, their poor reputation in this respect finds some confirmation in the court-martial records; e.g.

Robert Hook, of H.M.S. *Lyme* (1750), dismissed the service for embezzlement of stores.

John Campbell, of H.M.S. *Terror* (1761), forfeited 12 months' pay and dismissed for embezzlement of stores.

Benjamin Lavery, of H.M.S. *Swift* (1769), dismissed the service for 'frequently sending on shore some stores committed to his charge.'

J. Chapman, of H.M.S. *Deal Castle* (1777), sentenced to be 'rendered incapable of ever serving in the navy and drummed through the fleet with a halter round his neck', for embezzling stores.

Boatswain's call (or **pipe** or **whistle**): a curiously curved small whistle, of ancient origin, with which the boatswain's mate used to pipe different orders by varying cadences. Today in the Royal Navy the boatswain's pipe survives for the ceremony of 'piping the side', that is, the formal reception of important naval officers or civilian dignitaries when they step on board a ship. But although in modern ships orders are given by a loudspeaker system they are still said to be piped. 'Pipe down' was the order for hands to turn in and for quiet on the messdecks, hence its continued use to tell someone to be quiet. Many of the old boatswain's calls were made of silver and are now highly prized as collector's items.

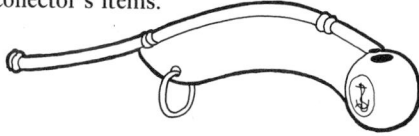

Boatswain's chair: a small seat hoisted aloft for attending to masts or rigging, or lowered over the side for painting and repairing.

Bobstay: the standing rigging which secures the bowsprit downwards and is made fast to the stem at a point above the water-line. *See also* RIGGING.

Bollard: large post of wood, stone or metal, usually on quay, wharf or dockside, for making ships fast.

Boltrope: rope sewed round the edge of sails or awnings.

Bomb: *see* BOMB-KETCH.

Bombay: territory in western India acquired by Charles II through his marriage to Catherine of Braganza (1661) as part of her dowry. It had belonged to Portugal since 1530. This gave Britain a useful base in East Indian waters, an area which the Dutch regarded very much as their own. In 1668 it was granted to the East India Company and became a great commercial centre.

Bombay oyster: name given in training ships to a repulsive drink issued in the sick-bay, a glass of milk with a double dose of castor oil mixed in.

Bomb-ketch (or **bomb**): type of vessel introduced by the French towards the end of the 17th century to carry mortars — short, wide-barrelled guns for firing 'bombs' at a high angle. Bomb-ketches were similar to ketches and were very strongly built to withstand the recoil. The shot weighed some 200 lb, compared with that from the ordinary 'great guns', which fired 48 lb shot. The first mortar bombardment from the sea was that of Algiers, centre of the Barbary pirates, by the French admiral du Quesne (1682). These ketches, usually referred to just as 'bombs', were quickly built by other navies. At the end of William III's reign (1702) the British Navy had twelve, each carrying from four to ten guns and from 30 to 65 men.

See also MORTAR BOATS.

'Bonaventure': a famous name in Tudor times, meaning 'good adventure'. The *Elizabeth Bonaventure* was Drake's flagship in the raid on CADIZ (1587). She was a ship of 600 tons, her keel rather less than 100 ft and her breadth about 30 ft.

The wind commands me away. Our ships are under sail. God grant we may so live in His fear as the enemy may have cause to say that God doth fight for Her Majesty as well abroad as at home. Haste! From aboard Her Majesty's good ship the *Elizabeth Bonaventure*, this 2nd April 1587.

> Drake to Sir Francis Walsingham, from
> Plymouth, just before he sailed for Cadiz

In all this time there never came a spoonful of water into her well . . . except a ship had been made of iron, it were to be thought impossible to do as she had done; and it may be well and truly said that there never was nor is in the world a stronger ship than she is.

> Lord Howard of Effingham, describing
> the *Elizabeth Bonaventure* when he went
> aboard after she had run aground at
> Flushing and was held fast for two tides
> before she could be got off

For the *Edward Bonaventure*, *see* CHANCELLOR, RICHARD; LANCASTER, SIR JAMES.

Bonaventure mast (or **bonaventure mizen**): an extra, or fourth, mast, carried on many Tudor and early Stuart ships, set right at the stern and carrying its own rigging and sail. Henry VIII's *Henri Grâce à Dieu* (launched 1514) had one, as did ten of the largest English ships that defeated the Spanish Armada. In James I's reign the proportion of four-masters was about half the royal fleet. By 1640, however, the bonaventure mast had virtually disappeared, since it was found to be more effective to carry extra sail on the ordinary mizen mast.

'Bonhomme Richard': the 40-gun American warship, commanded by John Paul Jones, which was blown in two off FLAMBOROUGH HEAD (1779). To mark the bicentennial of the Declaration of American Independence (4 July 1776) the

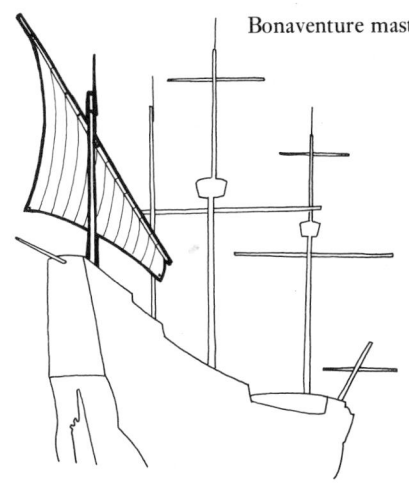

Bonaventure mast.

Americans launched a multi-thousand-dollar scheme to locate the sunken *Bonhomme Richard* and recover anything possible from her remains.

Bonnet: long strip latched to the foot of a sail to help catch the wind when it was very light.

I let them set all sails, the main course with two bonnets, the fore course, the spritsail, the mizen, the topsail and the boat's sail on the half deck.

> Christopher Columbus, Log-book
> (24 October 1492)

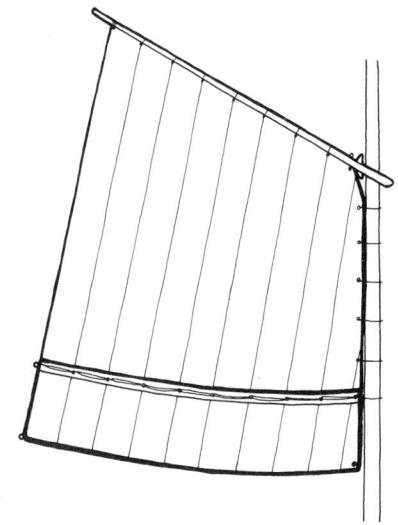

Boom: (1) a long spar used to extend the foot of a sail or the bowsprit; hence 'jib-boom', 'stunsail boom' etc.; (2) a floating barrier to protect the entrance to a harbour.

Boot-topping: from the keel to a short distance above the water-line a ship's hull is often painted a different colour from the upper part. This is known as 'boot-topping' because the most frequent colour is black.

Bora: strong northerly or north-easterly wind experienced in the Adriatic.

Bore: (1) the inside of a gun's barrel; (2) a steep wave which passes rapidly up a narrow inlet or river mouth, especially where the range of tides is big. In England the Severn Bore is a well-known example.

'Boreas': one of Nelson's early commands, a 28-gun frigate for which he was commissioned in March 1784 to sail to the West Indies.

On last Friday I was commissioned for the *Boreas* . . . I understand she is going to the Leeward Islands, and I am asked to carry out Lady Hughes and her family . . . so I must put up with the inconvenience and expense, two things not exactly to my wish.

> Nelson to Captain William Locker
> (23 March 1784)

Lady Hughes was the wife of Admiral Sir Richard Hughes, commanding on the Leeward Islands station. Despite Nelson's reluctance to take her, she proved to be a good friend and, according to Nelson, 'a fine talkative lady'.

H.M.S. *Boreas* was paid off at Sheerness at the end of November 1787, and Nelson was then unemployed for five years.

Borough (or **Burrough**), **Stephen**

(1525–84): navigator; master on CHANCELLOR's ship, the first to reach Russia (1553). According to his epitaph, he 'discovered Moscovia by the Northern Sea', and he named North Cape. On a second voyage (1556) he discovered the entrance to the Kara Sea, and in 1560–61 he made another voyage to Russia. He wrote records of his voyages, published by Richard Hakluyt. The name is found spelt in many other ways, including Burrowe and Borrows.

Borough (or **Burrough**), **William** (1536–99): brother of the above and his companion, as a common seaman, on several of his Russian voyages. By then a thoroughly experienced seaman, he was appointed Vice-Admiral in Drake's expedition to CADIZ (1587), but fell out badly with him because he disapproved of Drake's dashing methods and his failure to take proper counsel with his captains before going into action, as was the traditional method. Drake put him under arrest and would have liked to execute him for what he considered cowardice, mutiny and desertion – charges which he could not properly justify. After a long wrangle, the charges were dropped. Borough became Comptroller of the Navy and commanded a ship against the Armada. *See also GOLDEN LION.*

Boscawen, Edward (1711–61): admiral. He was Commander-in-Chief at the siege of LOUISBURG (1758), when the fortress and harbour were seized. His greatest triumph was at LAGOS (1759) when he learned that the Toulon fleet of French ships had broken the British blockade and slipped out into the Atlantic to join the Brest squadron.

Boscawen was dining ashore when he heard the news [at Gibraltar]. With one bound he was out of the house, and a few minutes later was on board his ship, galvanizing his whole fleet into activity. In three hours the first vessels were ready and, weighing anchor, dashed off in order to set the pace. The rest struggled out as best they could and, like a huntsman, the Admiral rounded them up and whipped them on to the trail. Before breakfast the next day the French were sighted, and ere the sun set Boscawen had overwhelmed them or scattered them to the four winds. Never before was battle like the battle of Lagos . . .

> Sir Geoffrey Callender, *The Naval Side of British History* (1924)

Bos'n: *see* BOATSWAIN.

Boston: capital of Massachusetts, U.S.A., first settled in 1630. It was one of the chief centres of resistance to British rule in the War of AMERICAN INDEPENDENCE; it witnessed the celebrated BOSTON TEA PARTY, and later, during the ANGLO-AMERICAN WAR, the equally famous encounter between the British frigate *Shannon* of 38 guns and the similarly armed American frigate *Chesapeake*, which had been fitting out at Boston.

Captain Philip Broke of the *Shannon* wrote to Captain James Lawrence of the *Chesapeake*, rather in the manner of the old-time tournament, inviting him to come out and do battle:

> I request you will do me the favour to meet the *Shannon* ship to ship, to try the fortune of our respective flags . . . I entreat you, sir, not to imagine I am urged by personal vanity . . . We have both noble motives . . . Favour me with a speedy reply. We are short of provisions and water, so we cannot stay long here.

Lawrence does not, in fact, appear to have received the message, but he obligingly sailed out on 1 June 1813 to do battle. In the subsequent hard-fought action, Lawrence was killed in a desperate hand-to-hand fight on board his frigate and, despite his plea 'Don't give up the ship', the *Chesapeake* was taken as a prize.

Boston Tea Party (16 December 1773): occasion when three ship-loads of tea were thrown overboard into Boston harbour as a demonstration against the British taxation on tea.

Bosun: *see* BOATSWAIN.

Botany Bay: inlet to the south of modern Sydney in New South Wales. It was here that, in 1770, Captain James Cook in the *Endeavour* landed and proclaimed British sovereignty over the east coast of Australia. The name given to the Bay arose from the number of new plants observed there by the famous botanist Joseph Banks, who accompanied Cook. It was originally called Sting-Ray Harbour (or Stingrays Bay) but was renamed on the homeward voyage, apparently by Cook himself, in tribute to his enthusiastic colleague, who had fitted out his quarters at his own expense.

Boteler, Nathaniel (*fl.*1625–35): naval captain and writer. His *Six Dialogues about Sea Services between an High Admiral and a Captain at Sea* (written *c.*1634 but not published until 1685) contains much valuable information about the conduct of the fleets of his day, their signalling systems etc.:

Admiral. Colours and Ensignes I take to be all one, but wher are they to be placed and wherefore serve they?
Captain. They are placed in the Sternes or Poops of Ships; and very few Ships there are, whether Men of Warre or Merchantmen, that are without them. And there special service is, that when any strange Shypps meet one with another at Sea, or fynde one another in any Harbour or Rode, by the shewinge abroade thes Ensigns or Colours, it is knowne one to another of what country they are and to what place they belong . . .

Admiral. What are the Pendants you mentioned even now, and wherefore serve they?

Captain. A Pendant is a long Piece of silk or other stuff, cut out pointed wise towards the end in the form of a streamer, wher they are slit into two partes, and the use of them, to distinguish the Squadrons of great fleetes by hanging them out in the topps of such Shypps as carry noe flaggs. As, for example, all suche Shypps as are of the Admiralls Squadron are to hang them out in their maine topps, thoes of the Vice Admiralls Squadron in their Fore-tops and those of the Reare Admiralls in their Missen-tops.

Boulogne-sur-Mer: famous French port about 17 miles from Calais and a town of note from Roman times. It enters many times into English history, but came into greatest prominence during the Napoleonic Wars, when Napoleon assembled there his fleet for the invasion of England, consisting of 160,000 men, 10,000 horses, 17,000 seamen and 1300 boats to convey them all across the Channel.

'Bounty': *see* BLIGH, WILLIAM.

Bow (or **bows**; pronounced to rhyme with 'now'): the pointed or rounded forward part of a ship. The name comes from an Icelandic word meaning 'shoulder', and should be distinguished from the entirely different word of the same spelling pronounced to rhyme with 'flow'. *See also p.577.*

From the part of the ship come many other words and expressions, e.g. 'bow chaser', a gun carried in the bow for firing when in pursuit of another vessel; 'bower', one of the ship's main anchors, carried in the bow; 'bow oar', a seaman rowing in the forward part of a boat; 'on the bow', that part of the horizon within 45° each side of the straight line ahead: hence 'on the port bow' (left side) and 'on the starboard bow' (right); *see also* SHOT ACROSS THE BOWS.

Bowen, James (1751–1835): admiral. After commanding a ship in the Africa and West India trades, he served as a master in the Royal Navy from 1781 to 1789, and again in the 1790s, when he was master on Howe's flag-ship, the *Queen Charlotte.* He reached the rank of rear-admiral by a mixture of skill, intrepidity and, sometimes, scant respect for his superiors. He made a celebrated laconic rejoinder to Sir Roger Curtis, who, when Bowen was guiding a British squadron into Torbay in very thick weather, remonstrated: 'If you do make a mistake, recollect you will be responsible for the loss of the whole fleet.' 'The fleet won't be lost', Bowen replied; and, despite the hazards, he brought the ships to a safe anchorage.

On another famous occasion Bowen bandied words with the redoubtable 'Black Dick' Howe. As master of the *Queen Charlotte* on the 'Glorious First of June' (1794) he warned the Admiral that he was in danger of running foul of the enemy flag-ship.

'What's that to you, sir?'

'Damn'd if I care, if you don't. I'll take you near enough to singe your black whiskers.'

> Christopher Lloyd, *The British Seaman* (1968)

Howe rewarded his nerve with a lieutenancy.

Bower: *see* BOW.

Bowline: (1) rope used to keep the weather edge of a sail tight forward when the ship is sailing close-hauled; (2) the name of various ways of bending a rope to give a loop which does not jam; *see also* KNOTS.

Bows: *see* BOW.

Bowsprit: the spar running out from the bows of a vessel. It is virtually a subsidiary mast carrying its own sail, which is a great help in making progress against contrary winds. It was in use in the Mediterranean in the early centuries A.D. and then, for some mysterious reason, almost disappeared from about the 8th to the 15th century. The bowsprit reappeared in the 13th century but not for another 200 years did the square spritsail come into general use again. As some indication of its size and importance, the length of the bowsprit on Nelson's *Victory* was 7/11th of the main mast, and its diameter was only 2 in. less. *See also* RIGGING.

Box battery ship: *see* CENTRAL BATTERY BATTLESHIP.

Box the compass: *see* POINT, COMPASS.

Boy: a grade of seaman, in Nelson's day numbering about 8 per cent of the total ship's company, i.e. about 40 on a first-rate ship. They were volunteers, whose ages ranged from about 12 to 18 and who were divided into three main classes, First, Second and Third. Formerly they were carried on the books as 'Servants', each officer being allowed a certain quota. In the 1790s the three classes were defined as:

1. 'Young Gentlemen intended for the Sea Service . . . to be styled Volunteers and allowed wages at the rate of £6 per annum.'

2. 'Boys between 15 and 17 years of age to be divided into watches with the seamen in order to make them such, at £5 per annum.'

3. 'Boys between 13 and 15 years of age of whom Lieutenants and other officers who are now allowed servants might be permitted to recommend to the Captains, each of them one, to be attendant upon such officers, at £4 per annum.'

The First Class were reckoned boys of the future officer class; the Second and Third Classes were normally regarded as part of the ordinary ship's company and rarely rose above the rank of warrant officer.

Braces: ropes running from the ends of all yards in a square-rigged ship by which the yards are slewed and braced so that the sails make the best use of the wind. *See also* RIGGING.

Break: a change in the level of the deck; e.g. 'the break of the forecastle'.

Breakwater: (1) solid pier or mole to break the force of the sea and give calmer water; (2) a V-shaped screen across the forecastle to deflect seas breaking over the bows.

'Brecon': new 725-ton mine countermeasures vessel launched at Southampton in June 1978, the world's largest glass-reinforced plastic ship. It is estimated that by the time she joins the fleet in 1979 she will have cost £25,000,000, i.e., ton for ton, four times more than the largest warship in the world's navies, the 91,000-ton American nuclear-powered aircraft-carrier *Nimitz*. Some £10,000, however, was spent on initial research and development for the

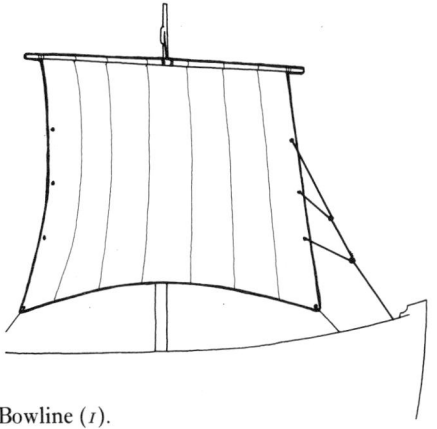

Bowline (*1*).

Brecon, which will later be joined, according to present plans, by eleven sister ships.

The launching produced a *bon mot* from the chairman of the firm of Vosper Thornycroft, which built the ship: 'the unrottable in close pursuit of the unchartable.'

Breeches buoy: life-saving device which runs on a rope from a wrecked ship to shore. The name arises from the canvas 'breeches' which support the person being brought to safety.

Breechings: *see* RECOIL.

Breech-loading: *see* MUZZLE-LOADING.

'Brendan': leather square-rigged vessel, 36 ft long, designed to prove that the Irish monk St Brendan (*c*.484–578) could have made the transatlantic voyage attributed to him in many medieval sagas. Made of 40 ox-hides over an oak and ash frame, the *Brendan*, manned by a crew of four, set out from the west coast of Ireland in May 1976 and, after wintering in Iceland, successfully completed the expedition in June 1977, for the last few miles accepting a tow from a Canadian coastguard cutter and anchoring in Musgrave Harbour, Newfoundland. The leather hull, greased with an ancient tallow and cod-oil recipe, contradicted all the gloomy predictions by remaining in remarkably seaworthy condition. One of the few concessions made by the leader, Timothy Severin, and his crew of mixed nationalities was the use of modern navigational and communications equipment.

See colour section.

Brest: one of the greatest French naval bases, in N.W. France. It played a conspicuous part in the Hundred Years'

War and, four and a half centuries later, in the Napoleonic Wars, when Britain maintained a strong blockading squadron off the port. It was Napoleon's plan that Admiral Ganteaume's fleet, in Brest, should link up with Villeneuve's for the invasion of Britain in 1805. Ganteaume did his best, but Villeneuve failed to keep the rendezvous and entered Cadiz instead, a decision that has been assessed as 'the bitterest incident in Napoleon's career'. *See also* FINISTÈRE.

Bridge: a raised superstructure on a ship from which the ship, or, in the case of an admiral's bridge, a squadron or group of ships, is directed. *See p.577.*

Brig: (1) a two-masted vessel, square-rigged; (2) in the U.S. Navy, punishment quarters.

Brigantine: a two-masted vessel, square-rigged on the fore mast and schooner-rigged on the main mast.

Brightwork: unpainted metalwork, generally of brass, which required much cleaning to maintain a smart appearance. It is less evident in modern ships.

Bristol: seaport in S.W. England, from the 12th to the 18th century the most flourishing in the kingdom after London. It was from Bristol that John Cabot sailed in 1496 and 1497. *See also* SHIPSHAPE AND BRISTOL-FASHION; SLAVE TRADE.

The merchants of this city have not only the greatest trade (for before the American war, the annual amount of the customs was more than £200,000) but they trade with more independence of London than any other town in Britain. Whatever exports they make, they are able to bring the full returns back, and dispose of them at their own port; and, as they have a great trade abroad, so they have always sufficient buyers at home for their returns . . . Their trade to the West Indies, of which they were some of the first discoverers and adventurers, is very considerable; as is also their Guinea trade. Their West India ships sail and arrive in fleets. They carry on the Dutch, Hamburgh, Norway, Eastland and Russian commerce. They send ships to Newfoundland and the Mediterranean, and import great quantities of fruit, wine and oil.

Daniel Defoe, *A Tour through the Island of Great Britain* (1778)

Bristol-fashion: *see* SHIPSHAPE AND BRISTOL-FASHION.

Britannia: a famous personification, destined to become symbolic of British naval power. The first known appearance of the figure, in typical pose, is on a Roman coin of Antoninus Pius (A.D. 138–161). She turned up again, with a less respectable prototype, on the copper coinage of Charles II, the model having been Frances Stuart (afterwards Duchess of Richmond), mistress of the King. A new design was made in 1825.

'Britannia': as might be expected, a name borne by many British ships, including a number of ROYAL YACHTS and the famous training ship that was the forerunner of the ROYAL NAVAL COLLEGE, DARTMOUTH. At the Battle of Trafalgar the 100-gun *Britannia*, built at Portsmouth in 1762, carried the flag of the Earl of Northesk, third in command. In the Merchant Navy, the name was carried by the first Cunarder, which crossed the Atlantic from Liverpool to Boston in 14 days, 8 hours (1840); *see* CUNARD STEAMSHIP COMPANY.

Britannia Royal Naval College: *see* ROYAL NAVAL COLLEGE, DARTMOUTH.

Brixham: *see* TORBAY.

Broach: (1) to come broadside on to the sea; (2) to 'broach a cask or barrel': to open it for use.

Broad pennant: flag of command flown by a commodore, i.e. an officer holding temporary rank and in charge of a number of ships, but with no authority over captains senior to him. Originally fourteen times as long as it was wide at the head, the pennant (or pendant) gradually became shorter till it was only twice as long as its breadth. It could be red, white or blue according to the class of commodore.

Broadside: simultaneous volley from all the guns on one side of a ship of war. It was the greatest weapon of the English sailing Navy and was used with terrible effect on countless occasions (*see also* ARMAMENT; RANGE). Probably the earliest description of it is in a dispatch from John Dudley, Lord Lisle, Great Admiral of England, to his master Henry VIII after an encounter with a French squadron in August 1545:

The *Mistress* and the *Anne Gallant* did so

63

handle the galleys, as well with their sides as with their prows, that your great ships in a manner had little to do.

The effect of the fully developed broadside can be judged from another dispatch, 260 years later:

... the three-decker *Temeraire*, which had doubtless seen that the English flag-ship was no longer fighting and would inevitably be taken, fell on us to starboard and at point-blank range, riddled us with her whole broadside. Nothing can describe the resulting slaughter; more than 200 men were put out of action.

Captain Jean Lucas of the French ship *Redoutable*, writing to the Minister of Marine after Trafalgar

From the gunnery term comes the colloquial use of 'broadside' for a devastating verbal attack on an opponent.

Broke, Sir Philip Bowes Vere (1776–1841): admiral who, though he served on other ships and in other theatres of war, will always be chiefly associated with his command of the *Shannon* and the capture of the American frigate *Chesapeake* (*see* BOSTON).

Bronze John: a colloquial name for yellow fever (*see* HEALTH AND HYGIENE).

Brown George: an old term for bread supplied to the Navy by contractors, or for a coarse ship's biscuit.

Brown paper warrant: warrant issued not by the Admiralty (as in the case of commissioned officers) but by the captain of a vessel to warrant officers (e.g. the boatswain, gunner and carpenter). The captain could demote these officers if they failed to give satisfaction and, in effect, tear up the flimsy warrant.

Brunel, Isambard Kingdom (1806–59):

famous engineer son of a famous engineer father, Sir Marc Isambard Brunel (1769–1849). For thirteen years I. K. Brunel was chief engineer of the Great Western Railway and many fine constructions remain to his credit. But he is also remembered as a great ship constructor and innovator, building the *GREAT WESTERN* (the first steam boat to make regular passages across the Atlantic), the *GREAT BRITAIN*, and the huge *GREAT EASTERN*, whose launching Brunel survived by only a week. His versatility manifested itself in other fields; he contributed to the improvement of great guns and designed a floating gun-carriage.

Brygandyne (or **Brigandin**), **Robert** (*fl.*1490–1520): one of the earliest naval officials known in English history, Clerk of the Ships to Henry VII. The first permanent dry dock in England, at Portsmouth, was built under his superintendence (1495–6). *See also* SHIPWRIGHT.

Buccaneers: a swashbuckling word with unromantic origins, the original *boucaniers* in the Caribbean being those who lived on and traded in *boucan*, or smoke-dried meat and hides. Later these settlers, chiefly of French origin, took to the sea and made an easier living by plundering Spanish ships. Adventurers from other nations joined the sea-borne *boucaniers*, so that a 'buccaneer' became any member of the body of lawless seafarers who banded together under various leaders in the fellowship of the so-called 'Brethren of the Coast'. The buccaneer, rogue though he was, did not usually prey on ships of his own country and may therefore perhaps be regarded as one step better than a pirate.

'Bucentaur': *see* BARGE.

Bucklers Hard: 18th- and 19th-century shipbuilding port in Hampshire on the Beaulieu River, which flows into the Solent. The earliest record of a warship being built there is of the 48-gun *Salisbury*, launched in 1698. The *Elephant*, to which Nelson transferred at Copenhagen because of her lighter draught for shallow waters, was partly built at Bucklers Hard. Others were the 74-gun *Victorious* and 36-gun *Hussar*. But perhaps most famous of all was the *AGAMEMNON*. Not only Royal Navy ships were built there. Many fine East and West India merchantmen came off the slipways before the decline set in and the Master Shipbuilder's house became a hotel, popular with the yachting fraternity which frequents the single street once piled so high with stacks of timber that they over-topped the houses.

Bucko: tough and fond of physical violence; often applied to a mate on a sailing ship, of the type described by Cecily Fox Smith in 'Words of Wisdom':

And if you go further and pause to admire
A ship that's as neat as your heart could
    desire,
As smart as a frigate aloft and alow,
Her brasswork like gold and her planking like
    snow . . .
Look round for a mate by whose twang it is
    plain
That his home port is somewhere round
    Boston or Maine,
With a jaw that's the cut of a square block of
    wood,
And . . . beat it, my son, while the going is
    good!

A Sea Chest (1927)

Bulkhead: movable partitions on board ship, making separate cabins, store-rooms etc. When the ship was in action they could quickly be moved to give long clear decks. Later, bulkheads became permanent, giving additional strength and providing water-tight compartments.

Bulwarks: the sides of a ship above the upper deck; often used figuratively of some strong defence or protection.

The royal navy of England hath ever been its greatest defence . . . the floating bulwark of the island.

Sir William Blackstone (1723–80)

Bum boat: a small boat which came out to ships at anchor or at moorings to sell provisions and other goods.

Buntlines: ropes leading through tackles to the footropes of square sails to prevent bellying of the sail and to assist in furling. *See also* RIGGING.

Buoy: a moored mark to assist safe navigation. Navigational buoys are of many kinds, shapes and colours, and there is now an internationally agreed system to give a measure of uniformity. Starboard and port-hand buoys are placed so that they should be passed on the ship's starboard and port sides respectively when the ship is going in the direction of the main flood stream. Other buoys may mark shoals, wrecks or other hazards. They may be lighted and give different-coloured flashes at stated intervals; or sound a bell swinging with the swell of the sea; or be named or numbered. A mooring-buoy is a floating buoy for securing a ship.

See also colour section and MIDDLE GROUND.

Burden (or **burthen**): *see* TONNAGE.

Burgee: small swallow-tailed or triangular flag flown at mast-head, especially by yachts. Apart from identification purposes, it serves also as a wind-vane.

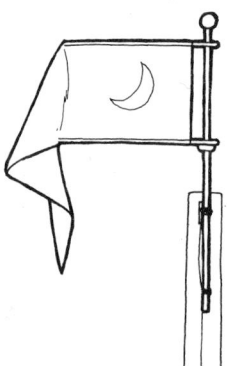

Burgoo: slang naval word for porridge.

Burlesdown Wreck: wreck found at Burlesdown, on the River Hamble, Hampshire; thought to be Henry V's ship *Grâce de Dieu*, built at Southampton in 1418 and destroyed by fire in 1439. She was a two-masted ship, with a keel of 112 ft, a remarkably large vessel for her time.

Burnham Thorpe: Norfolk village where Lord Nelson, son of the Rev. Edmund Nelson, was born in the Parsonage House (29 September 1758). After the *Boreas* frigate was paid off (1787), Nelson was unemployed for five years and kicked his heels back at Burnham Thorpe, doing everything he could to get another ship. To help pass the time, he constructed a pool in the rectory garden the shape of a man-o'-war, to float a model ship in.

Burrough: *see* BOROUGH, STEPHEN and WILLIAM.

Burthen (or **burden**): *see* TONNAGE.

Buss: small, strongly built vessel, much used in the fishing industry. A print of *c*.1480 shows a Dutch ship of this type, much the same in general structure as those of several centuries later.

Buys Ballot's Law: named after a Dutch scientist (C. H. D. Buys Ballot, chief of the Dutch Meteorological Services from 1854 to 1889), the law states that, if you face the true wind, the centre of low pressure (cyclonic depression) will be on your right hand in the northern hemisphere and on your left hand in the southern hemisphere. This is because air in movement, i.e. wind, is drawn towards a centre of low pressure and, by the Earth's rotation, is deflected to the right in the northern hemisphere and so creates an anti-clockwise circulation. When there is a high pressure centre from which the air moves outward, the circulation is in a clockwise direction. In the southern hemisphere these directions are reversed.

By and large: sailing fairly close to the wind, i.e. keeping the head of the vessel fairly near the quarter from which the wind is blowing. The phrase is often used by landsmen to mean 'in general' or 'on the whole'.

A buss: detail from *The Dutch herring fishery* by Abraham Van Salm, 1733.

Byng, John (1704–57): admiral, fourth son of Viscount Torrington. After his failure to relieve MINORCA from the French (1756), he was court-martialled and shot on the quarter-deck for lack of resolution. This face-saving act by the government brought strong condemnation from many quarters.

Dans ce pays-ci il est bon de tuer de temps en temps un amiral pour encourager les autres. ('In this country [England] it is thought well to kill an admiral from time to time, to encourage the others.')

Voltaire, *Candide* (1759)

The man I never saw but in the street, or in the House of Commons, and there I thought his carriage haughty and disgusting. From report, I had formed a mean opinion of his understanding; and from the clamours of the world, I was carried away with the multitude in believing he had not done his duty . . . When his pamphlet appeared, I read it and found he had been cruelly and scandalously treated . . .

The fatal morning arrived, but was by no means met by the Admiral with reluctance . . . He took an easy leave of his friends, detained the officers not a moment, went directly to the deck, and placed himself in a chair with neither ceremony nor tightness.

Some of the more humane officers represented to him that his face being uncovered might throw reluctance into the executioners, and besought him to suffer a handkerchief. He replied with the same unconcern: 'If it will frighten *them*, let it be done: they would not frighten me.'

Horace Walpole, *Memoirs of the Reign of King George II* (1822)

To the perpetual Disgrace
of publick Justice,
The Honourable John Byng, Esq.
Admiral of the Blue,
Fell a Martyr to political
Persecution
March 14th, in the year 1757;
when Bravery and Loyalty
were insufficient Securities
for the Life and Honour of
A Naval Officer.

Transcribed by James Boswell (1781) in
Southill Church, Bedfordshire

Byron, the Hon. John (1723–86): admiral. A midshipman under ANSON in his voyage round the world, he saw so much hard weather and misfortune that the sailors nicknamed him 'Foul Weather Jack'. He was appointed Governor of Newfoundland in 1769. In 1779 he fought a curious action with the French while trying to save the island of Grenada. He arrived to find the enemy squadron sailing out of the harbour to meet him. Despite their superior strength, he ordered 'General chase!' as if the French ships were on the run. The result could have been disastrous. As it was, the English ships fought furiously to extricate themselves and limped home badly damaged; and the French admiral d'Estaing, almost contemptuously, let them go, having attained his main objective in capturing Grenada. Both admirals escaped censure, but Byron was not employed again.

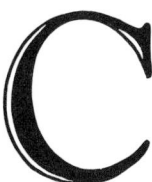

Cable: (1) a strong rope or chain for pulling or securing anything, particularly a ship's anchor; (2) a measurement of distance, a tenth of a nautical mile or approximately 200 yards. *See also* TIER.

'Cable Venture': chief ship of the Royal Navy Cable and Wireless fleet, a 10,000-ton cableship launched at Immingham in 1977 after a £3-million modernization and refit, and capable of laying every type of modern submarine telecommunication.

Caboose: derived from the Dutch for 'cabin-house'; originally a small space on deck for cooking, and later applied to any little enclosure or store.

Cabot, John (*fl.*1476–98): explorer, father of Sebastian CABOT. John, probably a Genoese by birth, became a naturalized Venetian and arrived in Bristol between 1490 and 1495, to seek backing for a voyage westwards across the Atlantic to the east coast of Asia, in search of spices and other merchandise. It seems certain, in the light of modern research, that Bristol seamen had already discovered Newfoundland and its valuable fishing grounds before John Cabot made his first voyage.

Backed by letters patent from Henry VII, Cabot set sail from Bristol in 1496 on his first voyage, but apparently turned back because of bad weather, shortage of food and difficulties with his crew. The famous expedition in the *Matthew* was his second, and began on 20 May 1497. The ship, of only 50 tons and with a crew of 18 or 20, made landfall in either Maine or Nova Scotia on 24 June. Cabot was back in Bristol in early August, had an audience of Henry VII on 10 August, and, as 'the great Admiral', became a popular figure at Court and in the streets of London.

He sailed again with a larger and better-equipped fleet early in May 1498. No definite news of this voyage has ever come to light, and it seems probable that all the ships, five in number, were lost. A pension was still being paid in 1499, but, it may well have been to Cabot's wife Mattea.

Cabot, Sebastian (*c.*1484–1557): map-maker and geographer, son of the above. Modern research has upset many of the previous accounts of his life; e.g. there is no evidence that he ever accompanied his father on his voyages, and he was never really a great seaman or a discoverer, though he led one expedition in 1508 or 1509 to search for the North-West Passage. Most of his life was spent in the service of Spain, but he was eventually given a pension in England. He was the first governor of the Merchant Adventurers of

England (1551) and, as 'chiefest setter forth of this journey or voyage', sent out Willoughby's 1553 expedition. He also drew what was undoubtedly one of the greatest maps of the time, finely illuminated in gold and colours, a copy of which is in the Bibliothèque Nationale, Paris.

In a sense, he was his own worst enemy, since he laid claim, if only by implication, to exploits that were not his own and, perhaps through vanity, was a considerable liar; thus he cast suspicion on his true accomplishments as a geographer, cartographer and contributor to the science of navigation. Stephen BOROUGH, who sailed on the third voyage sent out by the Merchant Adventurers (1556), wrote:

The 27th, being Monday, the right worshipful Sebastian Cabota came aboard our pinnace at Gravesend, accompanied by divers gentlemen and gentlewomen . . . and the good old Master Cabota gave to the poor most liberal alms, wishing them to pray for the good fortune and prosperous success of the *Serchthrift*, our pinnace. And then at the sign of the Christopher, he and his friends banqueted and made . . . great cheer; and for very joy that he had to see the towardness of our intended discovery, he entered into the dance himself amongst the rest of the young and lusty company.

Cachalot: another name for the sperm whale.

Cadiz: a seaport on the Atlantic coast of southern Spain which has played a prominent part in Anglo-Spanish naval history. Its ancient prosperity was renewed after the discovery of America and the growth of Spain's empire in the New World, and it became the headquarters of the Spanish treasure fleets.

In 1587 Sir Francis Drake carried out his famous exploit of 'singeing the King of Spain's beard' when his fleet sailed into Cadiz harbour and sank, burned or captured over 30 Spanish ships preparing for the invasion of England. This delayed the sailing of the ARMADA for a year. Drake on his way home also captured the *San Felipe*, a great Spanish treasure ship. *See also* BOROUGH, WILLIAM.

Nine years later the Earl of Essex and Lord Charles Howard of Effingham made a further attack, sacked the city and destroyed 40 merchant ships and 13 warships; in the words of Medina-Sidonia, 'Neither ship, nor fleet, nor galleons, nor Cadiz was left'.

The port was further fortified and was able to repel later English fleets under the Duke of Buckingham (1626), Admiral Robert Blake (1656), and Sir George Rooke and the Duke of Ormonde (1702). During the war with France it was blockaded by the British fleet (1797–8) and bombarded by Nelson (1800).

Caique: light sailing or rowing boat of Turkish origin.

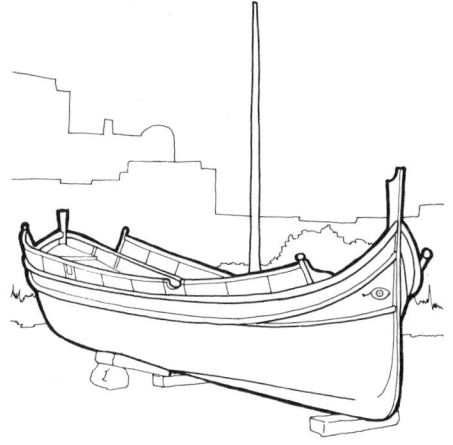

Calais: on the coast of N.E. France, the nearest continental port to England, from which it is separated by just 20 miles of the

Straits of Dover. It was besieged by the English under Edward III and finally reduced in 1347 by famine. From that time it remained in English hands until 1558, when it was recaptured by the French in the reign of Mary Tudor, who said 'When I am dead and opened, you shall find "Calais" lying in my heart'. When the Armada anchored in Calais Roads (1588), fire-ships sent in by Howard and Drake drove out the Spanish fleet. In 1940, when the German armies overwhelmed the British and French, Calais was the scene of a brave defensive delaying action by some 6000 men, who thus assisted the escape of their comrades at DUNKIRK.

Calcutta: large Indian city standing on a distributary of the River Ganges at the head of the Bay of Bengal. Calcutta was an important early centre for the East India Company and later became a great trading city. From 1833 to 1912, when it was superseded by Delhi, Calcutta was the capital of India.

In 1756 Calcutta's small British garrison was attacked by the troops of Surajah Dowlah, the Nawab of Bengal, and was forced to surrender. 146 prisoners including one woman were forced into a cell no more than 18 feet square, as a result of which 123 of them died, an outrage which became known as the Black Hole of Calcutta. In the following year Admiral Charles Watson and Colonel Robert Clive retook Calcutta, Clive defeated Surajah Dowlah at the Battle of Plassey, and Bengal, with Calcutta as its chief city, became the first extensive area of British rule in India.

Calder, Sir Robert (1745–1818): admiral. He entered the Navy in 1759 and got off to a good start by sharing, three years later, in the prize money for the Spanish

Hermione, the richest prize on record. He was at the Battle of CAPE ST VINCENT and was knighted after he brought home the dispatches. On 22 July 1805, with fourteen ships, he fought an indecisive action off Ferrol against the French admiral Villeneuve, who had twenty ships. Calder captured two ships and inflicted heavy damage; but on the following days he failed to renew the battle. He was court-martialled (at his own request) and censured for not pressing home his advantage, though he was acquitted of any suspicion of cowardice. He was promoted to flag rank in 1810 but was never again sent on active service.

Calibre: the internal bore or diameter of a tube, particularly of a gun, measured in inches. A 4"/50 gun is 4 in. in bore diameter and 50 calibres (200 in.) long.

Calicut (modern name **Kozhikode**): port on the Malabar coast in S.W. India. In 1664 it became an important trading post of the East India Company, and from its name was derived our word 'calico', cloth of that kind being one of its chief exports.

Callender, Sir Geoffrey: *see* GREENWICH; *VICTORY*.

Camel: a device for lifting ships, consisting of a water-filled tank which is secured alongside or under the ship; the tank is then pumped out and the resultant buoyancy lifts the ship.

Camouflage: a broken pattern of colours painted on a ship etc. to make identification difficult and to confuse the enemy as to the vessel's size or course. The practice of camouflaging ships was much used and highly developed during World War I.

See colour section.

Campbell, Gordon: *see* MYSTERY SHIPS.

Campbell, Dr John (1708–75): writer. Intended for the law, he early turned to writing and produced a considerable number of works, of which one of the most successful was *The Lives of the Admirals and other Eminent British Seamen.* It was first published between 1742 and 1744 and reappeared in many later editions, some of them revised and expanded by other authors long after Campbell's death. Campbell was a member of Samuel Johnson's circle and is mentioned several times by Boswell. Dr Johnson said of him 'I am afraid he has not been in the inside of a church for many years; but he never passes a church without pulling off his hat. This shows he has good principles.' But Campbell once told Boswell that he had drunk thirteen bottles of port at one sitting!

Campbell, Thomas (1777–1844): a poet whose longer works are not much read now, though he is remembered for at least two of his shorter pieces of sea verse: 'The Battle of the Baltic' (*see* COPENHAGEN) and

Ye Mariners of England
That guard our native seas!
Whose flag has braved, a thousand years,
The battle and the breeze!

'Camperdown': *see* VICTORIA.

Camperdown, Battle of (11 October 1797): sea-fight between a British fleet, under Admiral Duncan, and the Dutch under Admiral de Winter. Camperdown is a village on the dunes of North Holland. Duncan, with a force reduced by the 1797 mutinies to only two ships, had been blockading the Texel, where were lying 16 Dutch line-of-battle ships, 20 frigates, and a French army of about 30,000 waiting for an invasion of Ireland. For a time Duncan carried out a gigantic bluff by signalling from his flag-ship to his only supporting vessel, a frigate on the horizon, which made a great show of passing on the messages to an imaginary fleet lurking somewhere in the background. When the Dutch eventually came out, under cover of bad weather, Duncan, with his fleet by this time returned to duty, inflicted a crushing defeat, capturing the commander-in-chief, nine ships of the line and two frigates. He was immediately raised to the peerage as Viscount Duncan of Camperdown. *See also* ETCHES, RICHARD CADMAN.

Can, carry the: a slang naval phrase meaning to take the blame for anything. Its origin may lie in the unwelcome duty of taking the can back after an issue of rum or food from the galley.

Canals: *see* INLAND WATERWAYS.

Canary Islands: a group of islands of volcanic origin off the N.W. coast of Africa. Gran Canaria and Tenerife are the two largest, and the peak of the latter rises to over 12,000 ft. They have belonged to Spain since 1483; it was from Gran Canaria that Columbus set out on his discovery of the New World in 1492. In British naval history the islands are associated with Blake and Nelson: *see* SANTA CRUZ.

'Canberra': Pacific and Orient Line passenger ship of 45,000 tons, built in 1960 and capable of carrying 2250 passengers in comfort. Like others of her class, she is virtually a floating luxury hotel, with shops, swimming baths, dance-floors etc., and is now almost exclusively engaged in holiday cruises.

Cancer, Tropic of: a line of latitude ($23\frac{1}{2}°$ N.) which marks the most northerly point at which the sun is directly overhead at mid-day during the northern hemisphere's summer.

Canister shot (or **case shot**): a development of the solid round shot or cannon ball, consisting of a metal container, filled with small projectiles, which burst after firing. It was a precursor of the explosive shell.

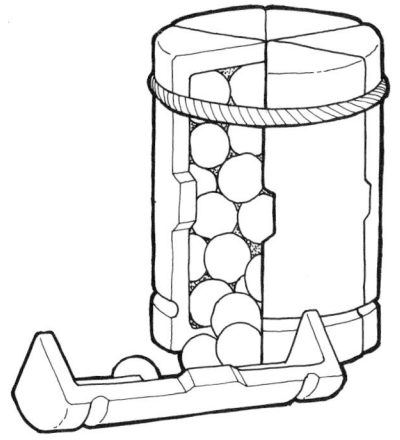

Cannon: used as a general term to describe the large pieces of muzzle-loading ordnance used on land and in ships before the coming of the shell-firing rifled gun. Cannon were of many types and sizes (e.g.

the CULVERIN) and were divided into cannon royal or double cannon, whole cannon, demi-cannon, the perier etc. They were strong battering guns throwing round-shot of different weights. The demi-cannon with a 32-lb. shot was favoured by the British Navy and probably had a range of about a mile, though this is open to debate. The principle of the cannon was the same from the Armada to Trafalgar, and it is interesting to note that no ship at Trafalgar was sunk by gunfire alone. The term cannon has in modern times been applied to new types of gun used also on land and in aircraft.

Cannon-perier: *see* PERIER.

Canton (modern name **Kwangchow**): great city and port in S. China, the first Chinese port with which Europeans established trade. As early as 1699 the East India Company began bringing back tea, spices, silk and Chinese manufactures. French, Dutch and other traders soon followed. Difficulties and restrictions led to a war with Britain (1839–42; *see* CHINESE WARS).

Canvas: a strong coarse cloth made of

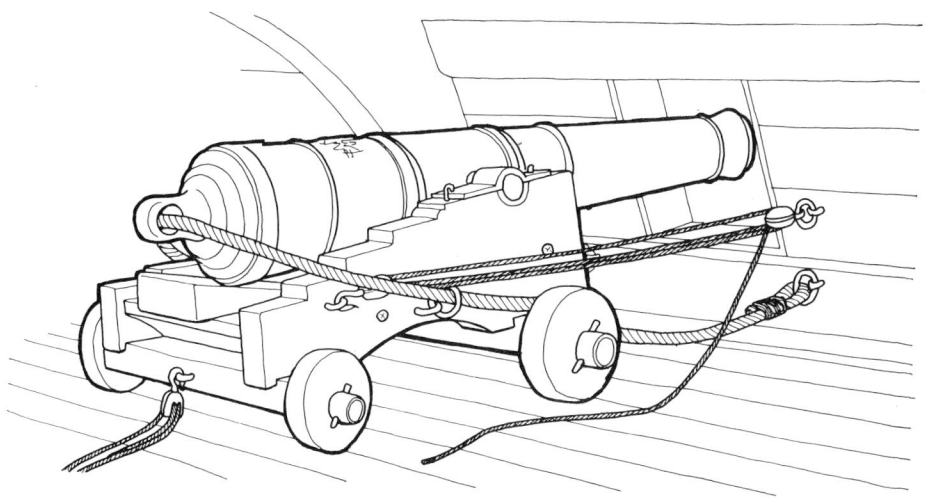

hemp or flax and used for sails, awnings etc. The word is also used as a general term for the sails carried by a ship, thus 'under storm canvas', 'a full spread of canvas' etc.

> As ships becalmed at eve, that lay
> With canvas drooping, side by side,
> Two towers of sail at dawn of day
> Are scarce long leagues apart descried.
>
> Arthur Hugh Clough,
> '*Qua Cursum Ventus*'

Cape Agulhas: the most southerly point of the African continent. The name is the Portuguese for 'needles', and the rocky promontory can be treacherous for navigation.

Cape Bar (or **Cap-a-Bar**): a curious phrase in use in the early 19th century in reference to the misappropriation of government stores. Earl St Vincent (John Jervis) wrote to Admiral Markham in 1806 giving a warning against one Tom Wolley: 'He is the meanest thief in the whole profession, abounding as it still does with Cape Bar men' (quoted by G. J. Marcus, *A Naval History of England*, Vol. II, 1971).

Cape Cod: a long low-lying peninsula at the eastern extremity of Massachusetts, U.S.A., so named because of the wealth of fish off the coast. It was here that the Pilgrim Fathers landed (1620); the development of settlements with fishing and whaling industries made the area the breeding ground of fine sailors.

Cape Finisterre: a promontory on the N.W. Atlantic coast of Spain; the most westerly point of Spain. *See also* FINISTERRE, BATTLES OF.

Cape Gris Nez: a promontory on the N.E. coast of France between Calais and Boulogne and overlooking the Straits of Dover. Cape Gris Nez was watched with anxiety from the English coast during the Napoleonic wars, and again during the Second World War, when the whole area was massed with German gun batteries, which from August 1940 fired on Allied convoys and shelled the town of Dover.

Cape Horn: the most southerly point of South America, notorious for its stormy weather. Possibly first seen by Drake in 1577, it was named by the Dutch (after the town of Hoorn in Holland) some forty years later. ANSON, in his great voyage round the world, suffered terrible storms here in 1741, and the rounding of Cape Horn, achieved by many famous later sailors, became a real test of endurance and fine seamanship. 'Cape Horners' is the name given to those mariners who have rounded Cape Horn under sail.

Capel, Sir Thomas Bladen (1776–1853): admiral. He entered the Navy in 1792, though he had been entered as a 'Captain's Servant' ten years earlier. In the *Vanguard*, he was Nelson's signal officer at the Battle of the Nile (1798), was given command of the brig *Mutine* and brought the first news of the victory to England. In 1802 he was appointed to the famous frigate *Phoebe* and was one of the 'eyes of the fleet' at Trafalgar, stationed to windward of the weather column and receiving warm praise from Collingwood. He completed a distinguished career as Commander-in-Chief, Portsmouth.

Cape Matapan, Battle of (28 March 1941): action in the Second World War fought to the south-west of Cape Matapan, which lies at the southern extremity of Greece, between British and Italian battle fleets and resulting in a victory for the British, who suffered no loss. The engagement arose from the knowledge that an Italian fleet was likely to move into the eastern Mediterranean to attack British troop convoys on their way to Greece. Accordingly Admiral Sir Andrew Cunningham gave orders for a British light force of cruisers and destroyers to rendezvous south of Crete, while he himself sailed from Alexandria with a fleet consisting of the battleships *Warspite*, *Barham*, and *Valiant*, the aircraft-carrier *Formidable* and nine destroyers. Early in the morning the British light force made contact with the Italians, whose battleship the *Vittorio Veneto* opened fire. The British ships turned to lure the Italians towards Cunningham's fleet, but it turned westward. Aircraft from the *Formidable* located the enemy fleet and during three strikes the *Vittorio Veneto* was damaged and her speed somewhat reduced, and the Italian cruiser *Pola* was brought to a stop, all by air-borne torpedoes. Two other Italian cruisers, the *Zara* and *Fiume*, and a number of destroyers were ordered to stand by the damaged *Pola*, while the *Vittorio Veneto* headed towards Italy. About an hour before midnight the British cruisers located the *Pola*, and Cunningham led his battleships towards her. As he did so the other Italian cruisers were revealed and were almost immediately destroyed at very close range. The *Pola* was later finished off by destroyers. Cunningham was unable to find the rest of the Italian fleet before they reached the cover of their own shore-based aircraft, and accordingly returned with his undamaged fleet to Alexandria.

Cape of Good Hope: a jutting peninsula at the southern, but not most southerly, point of Africa. It lies between Table Bay and False Bay. Bartholomew Diaz reached this point, which he named Cape of Storms, in 1487. It is not known whether it

was Diaz or the King of Portugal who afterwards changed the name to its present optimistic description. The Portuguese were followed by the Dutch, and the Cape was in turn taken by the British in 1795. In the days of sail, rounding the Cape was always a hazard, for gales are frequent; but before the SUEZ CANAL lessened its importance, the Cape was a vital point on the sea route to Asia, the East Indies and Australia (*see also* SIMONSTOWN).

Cape Passaro, Battle of (31 July 1718): action off Cape Passaro on the coast of Sicily, in which George Byng (later Viscount TORRINGTON) defeated a large Spanish fleet that was attempting to take Sicily from the French.

Cape St Vincent, Battle of (14 February 1797): victory won by Admiral John JERVIS (later created Earl St Vincent) with a fleet of 15 sail over a Spanish fleet of 27. Falling on them off Cape St Vincent (a headland at the S.W. extremity of Portugal) as they were running for Cadiz, Jervis smashed through their faulty line, dividing them into two parts. Jervis ordered his ships, when they were through the Spanish line, to tack one by one after the leader and prevent the gap from being closed. Nelson, last but two in the line, seeing that this manoeuvre would not be completed in time and making an on-the-spot decision, sailed the *CAPTAIN* into the gap and took on seven Spanish ships, including the *Santissima Trinidad*, the largest ship in the world, and two other three-deckers. Reinforcements arrived, and by nightfall four ships had been captured and ten others crippled. Jervis was generous in his praise of Nelson.

Employed cutting the remains of the foresail away and clearing ourselves from the wreck of the fore topmast. At 7 the *Minerve* took us in tow, our standing rigging and running rigging with all the bending sails being cut to pieces. Our wheel and fore topmast shot away and the other masts severely wounded, the main mast having three shots through the heart.

> Log of Philip Thomas, Master, H.M.S. *Captain* (14 February 1797)

No language I am possessed of can convey the high sense I entertain of the exemplary conduct of the flag-officers, captains, officers, seamen, marines and soldiers, embarked on board every ship of the squadron I have the honour to command, present at the vigorous and successful attack made upon the fleet of Spain on the 14th instant.

> John Jervis to his ships (morning of 16 February)

For the 1780 battle off Cape St Vincent, *see* MOONLIT BATTLE.

Capital ship: a warship of the most powerful type, e.g. a battleship, battle cruiser or aircraft-carrier.

Capricorn, Tropic of: a line of latitude ($23\frac{1}{2}°$ S.) which marks the most southerly point at which the sun is directly overhead at mid-day during the southern hemisphere's summer.

Capstan: a cylindrical revolving device used for hauling a cable, especially the anchor cable. It was originally worked by the deck hands pushing on capstan-bars inserted in sockets at the top of the capstan; but modern capstans are power driven.

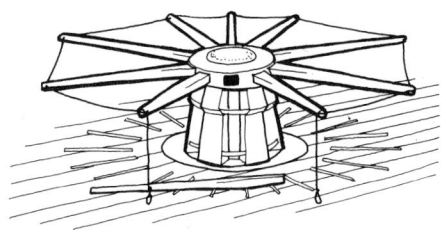

Captain: leader or commander of a Royal Navy or merchant ship. The term is often confusing since, in earlier times, it was not a fixed *rank*. The man concerned held not a personal commission, but a 'post-commission'; i.e. he was appointed to a particular ship for a particular occasion. When the job finished he reverted to being a private individual again, waiting for his next appointment. Not till 1860 was the full 'general commission' established, although the change-over was begun by Samuel Pepys, giving the holder the *rank* rather than the temporary *post*. Lieutenants and Commanders in charge of a ship would be given the courtesy title of 'Captain' on board their ships, even though they did not hold the rank.

> Drake he's in his hammock an' a thousand mile away
> (Capten, art tha' sleepin' there below?)
>
> Sir Henry Newbolt, 'Drake's Drum' (1896)

> Oh, I am a cook and a captain bold,
> And the mate of the Nancy brig,
> And a bo'sun tight, and a midshipmite,
> And the crew of the captain's gig.
>
> Sir W. S. Gilbert, 'The Yarn of the *Nancy Bell*'

No person shall be appointed to command a Ship of War of Twenty Guns or upwards, nor shall have the Rank of Captain, until he shall have been one complete year a Commander.

> *Regulations and Instructions relating to His Majesty's Service at Sea* (1808)

See colour section.

'Captain': name of several well-known ships in the Royal Navy. The *Captain* of 1708, a third-rate of 70 guns, was at Sir George Byng's defeat of the Spaniards off Cape Passaro (1718). A fine contemporary model of her, built by a young shipwright of Portsmouth, is in the London Science

Museum. At the Battle of CAPE ST VINCENT (1797) Nelson, in the *Captain* (74 guns), boarded and captured the *San Josef* (112) and the *San Nicolas* (80). The mid-19th-century *Captain* was a curious and ill-fated attempt to combine the old and the new. Built in a private yard by Captain Cowper Phipps Coles (1870), she was a rotating-gun-turret ironclad still fully rigged as a sailing ship. Seriously unstable, she capsized in a moderate gale and was lost, with nearly all hands, in three minutes.

'Captain Scott': *see* TRAINING SHIP.

Captain's servant: in former times, a back-door and privileged entry into the officer class on H.M. ships. Young men of good social standing were taken into the service under this heading by friendly captains without reference to the Admiralty. Later (1796) the title became First Class Volunteer (*see* VOLUNTEERS).

Caravel: name applied at various times to different types of ships. In a 13th-century manuscript the Portuguese word *caravela* is used to describe a fishing vessel. A 16th-century Portuguese *caravela* was present at the capture of Tunis (1535), but this was

more like an Elizabethan galleon, with a projecting ram instead of a figurehead. The *Nina* and the *Pinta*, the two ships that sailed with Columbus's *Santa Maria*, are reckoned to have been caravels, as were the long-ranging ships of Henry the Navigator down the west coast of Africa. Though we have little precise information, the typical caravel was probably long, fairly light and of shallow draught, with a sharp bow and concave waterlines. A distinction can be made between the *caravela latina* (i.e. with a lateen sail on all three masts) and the *caravela redonda* (a square-sailed caravel).

Carcass: an iron shell filled with inflammable materials. Its effective use at

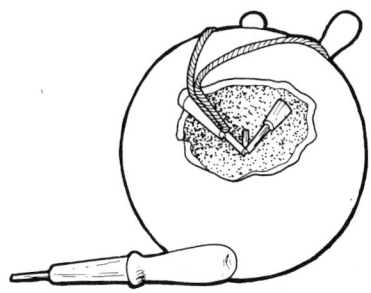

sea was first shown by an Englishman in the naval service of the Tsar of Russia, Sir Samuel Bentham, who in 1788 destroyed a Turkish fleet with the help of carcasses.

Cardinal points: the four main points of the compass, North, South, East and West.

Careen: to careen a ship is to heel her over on her side so that the bottom can be cleaned. In the past ships were often careened on the sand between high- and low-water marks, or they could be careened by tackle pulling them over whilst in harbour. *See p.78.*

Cargoes: *see* STOWAGE.

Cargo liner: *see* TRAMP.

The *Lucille* careened at Union Street wharf, San Francisco, 1901.

Caribbean Sea: a tropical sea bounded by the Antilles and the northern coast of South America. Following Columbus's voyages it was the first part of the New World to be explored, and was for long the scene of intense rivalry between the Spanish, British, French and Dutch, in a long series of wars during which countless naval engagements were fought.

Carpenter, ship's: an essential member of the crew in the days of wooden ships. By constant attention to hull and deck, masts and yards, the carpenter made and mended, and his duty was to keep the ship in going condition. As ships changed to metal his importance and standing diminished, but it was not until 1918 that the name was changed to 'Shipwright'. His former responsibilities were taken over by the engineers and artificers. Many merchant ships still carry a ship's carpenter, 'Chips' or 'Chippy' as he is familiarly called.

Carrack: large merchant ship much in use

in the Mediterranean and Adriatic in the 15th century. They were normally of 600–800 tons burden, three-masted, carvel-built, with an overhanging forecastle. Columbus's *Santa Maria* was probably a carrack, as distinct from his two other vessels, which were CARAVELS.

A ship's carpenter: from an aquatint by Thomas Rowlandson, 1799.

Carronade: a short-barrelled, light gun, firing a heavy (68-lb.) shot over a short distance. First used in British ships in 1779, it takes its name from the Carron Iron Works in Falkirk, Scotland, where it was made. Colloquially known as the 'smasher', it was a formidable weapon for fighting at close quarters, and was much relied upon in the French and Napoleonic Wars in the late 18th and early 19th centuries. It was its lack of RANGE that eventually caused its disappearance.

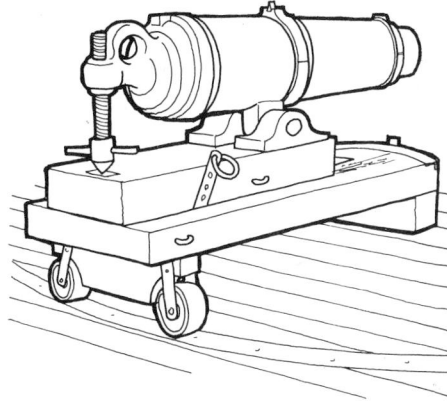

Cartagena (or **Carthagena**): ancient city and port on the Mediterranean coast of S.E. Spain; named after Carthage, the native city of Hasdrubal, its founder in the 3rd century B.C. It has a splendid harbour, much strengthened in the 16th century by Philip II. During the War of the Spanish Succession, the port was occupied by Sir John Leake in 1706 and by the Duke of Berwick in 1707.

Carter, John: *see* KING OF PRUSSIA.

Carteret, Sir George (*d.*1680): sailor and governor of Jersey. He saw service against the Sallee pirates, was Comptroller of the Navy in 1639 and was offered a command by Parliament in the Civil War. His sympathies, however, lay with the royalists, to whom, from Brittany, he sent arms and supplies. As governor of Jersey he gave refuge to other royalists there, eventually surrendering to the Commonwealth forces in 1651. After a period of exile, he returned to important administrative posts at the Restoration, holding office as Treasurer of the Navy and Naval Commissioner.

Cartography: *see* SURVEYING.

Carvel-built: with the outer boards or planks of the hull lying flush with each other. Compare CLINKER-BUILT.

Casemate: an armoured enclosure for guns.

Castaway: someone cast upon an uninhabited island either by shipwreck or, in former times, as a punishment (*see* MAROONING). Alexander SELKIRK was abandoned at his own request on Juan Fernandez Island (1704–9); his story was the basis for Defoe's *Robinson Crusoe*, whose hero is the best-known castaway in literature. In Robert Louis STEVENSON's *Treasure Island* poor Ben Gunn is the castaway or marooned pirate found on the island.

Castles: when medieval merchant ships were used by the king for war, they were adapted by erecting fighting platforms at each end to give the advantage of height in attacking the enemy. These structures looked like towers and came to be known as castles. With the coming of the gun the castles seemed the natural place for positioning the new weapons, so they were strengthened and raised, becoming a permanent feature of the ship of war until this form of attack from the castles was replaced by the invention of the broadside in Tudor times; but the names FORE-CASTLE and 'aftercastle' continued, and the former remains very much in use.

Cat: the CAT-O'-NINE-TAILS. Space was needed to wield it effectively, so the phrase 'no room to swing a cat' has come to describe any cramped, narrow quarters.

Catamaran: (1) a craft with twin hulls, which give greater stability. The word is Indian in origin, and craft of this kind are used in southern India and Sri Lanka (Ceylon). The name is also given to boats with an outrigger such as the Polynesians use, and with a sail has today developed into a sporting craft. **(2)** A raft of floating timber or metal used in harbours and dockyards.

Cathead: a construction at the bows of a ship for securing the anchor when hoisted.

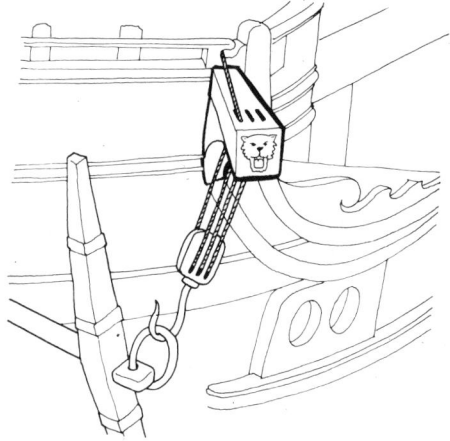

Cat-o'-nine-tails: a whip with nine lashes at the end of its handle, formerly used for punishment by FLOGGING. *See also* CAT; TAKE TOKO.

Cat's paw: (1) a light breeze; **(2)** a hitch in a rope to give loops for hoisting.

Caulk: in order to make a ship water-tight, OAKUM was forced between the planks, and the seam was then covered with pitch; this was known as caulking.

Cavendish, Thomas (1560–92): circum-navigator; a gentleman of Suffolk who in 1586 fitted out three ships for privateering and discovery purposes, his own being the *Desire*. He made an unsuccessful attack on Sierra Leone, but scored a major triumph by capturing the great Spanish treasure ship *Santa Anna* from Manila. He reached home in September 1588, the second Englishman to sail round the globe. On the way, he had discovered Port Desire, Patagonia. He died at sea on his way home from another voyage of discovery, this time in the *Leicester*, from Brazil.

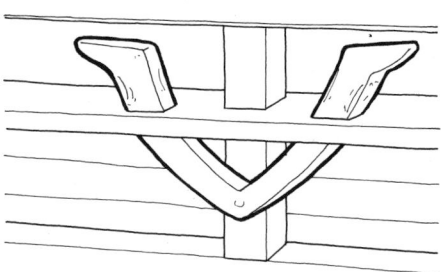

Cavils: heavy V-shaped wooden cleats on early ships, fixed at various places on the planked inside of the bulwarks for securing the ropes fastened to the lower corners of sails.

Cay: *see* KEY.

Central battery battleship: ship with the heaviest guns placed mid-ships and protected by extra-strong plating. A good example was the French *L'Océan* of 1868, which had a central battery of four $10\frac{1}{2}$-in. guns protected by $6\frac{1}{2}$-in. armour plating ($8\frac{1}{2}$ in. thick at the water-line).

Some ships had walls of plating set up fore and aft to further safeguard the central guns. These were known as 'box battery ships'.

'Centurion': H.M. ship of 50 guns

imperishably associated with the name of ANSON. In her he made his circumnavigation and captured the *Nuestra Señora de Covadonga* (*see* MANILA GALLEONS).

'Cerberus': *see* RHODE ISLAND.

Chain-locker: a compartment below decks in which the anchor chain or cable is stowed.

Chains: a fitting for securing rigging on the outside of a vessel. It was used as a place from which to heave the lead, and the name came to be given to any small platform in the bows on which the LEADSMAN stood to take the depth when the ship was sailing in uncharted or shallow waters.

Chain-shot: *see* SHOT.

'Challenger': one of the best-known Royal Navy research and survey ships, which, on a famous voyage (1872–6) instigated by the Royal Society, covered 79,000 miles of the world's oceans and added greatly to knowledge of the sea. Of 2300 tons, she had begun life as a corvette, launched at Woolwich in 1858. Her civilian scientific staff was headed by Professor Wyville Thompson, and for her scientific work she was fitted with a fully equipped laboratory, a detailed model of which

can be seen in the geophysics and oceanographic gallery in the Science Museum, London. The *Challenger* (the fifth of her name in the Royal Navy) finished her service on harbour duty at Chatham.

For the present-day *Challenger*, *see* OCEANOGRAPHY.

Chancellor, Richard (*d*.1556): navigator and explorer. He commanded the *Edward Bonaventure* in Sir Hugh Willoughby's expedition to discover the NORTH-EAST PASSAGE (1553). Sailing as pilot-general of the expedition (and with Stephen Borough as master of his ship), he became separated from Willoughby in a gale (August 1553) and pushed on without him, entering the White Sea and subsequently journeying overland to Moscow, where he was hospitably received by Ivan IV, who promised 'free mart with all free liberties through my whole dominions'. Chancellor sailed home in 1554 and wrote the first account of the Russian court and people for English readers. Following up his success, he returned to Moscow with several merchants who were to stay in Russia to organize regular trade. Chancellor drowned when his ship, returning from Russia in November 1556, was wrecked off the Aberdeenshire coast.

Channel: *see* ENGLISH CHANNEL.

Chanty (or **shanty**): a song sung by sailors, usually to lighten the labour when working the ship. Some chanties are very old, and most have a soloist, or chantyman, whose words are followed by the refrain or chorus. Chanties are of different kinds and rhythms according to the job to be done: there are halyard chanties for heavy work such as hoisting a mainsail; capstan or windlass chanties for long steady work; short-drag chanties where a few sharp strong pulls would be required; and there are chanties in the forecastle or on deck during off-duty times. A typical capstan chanty runs:

> Yeo, heave ho! Round the capstan go,
> Heave, men, with a will,
> Tramp, and tramp it still!
> The anchor must be weighed,
> The anchor must be weighed.
>
> *Chorus*
> Yeo ho! heave ho!
> Yeo ho! heave ho!

Haul away, Joe is a short-drag chanty; all hands give a mighty pull on the word 'Joe'.

> Way, haul away, we'll haul away
>   the bowlin'.
> Way, haul away, we'll haul away, Joe.

Charleston: a historic city with a fine harbour in South Carolina on the eastern seaboard of the U.S.A. It was established by English colonists in 1670 and named after Charles II. During the American War of Independence it was held as a key port by the British from 1780 to 1782. It was the capture of Fort Sumter in Charleston Harbour by the Confederates (1860) that sparked off the American Civil War, and the town was blockaded by Union land and sea forces.

'Charlotte Dundas': reckoned to be the first steamship of practical use; built by William Symington for Lord Dundas, who wished to replace the horses used for pulling barges along the Forth and Clyde Canal. In March 1802 the *Charlotte Dundas* towed two 70-ton barges along the canal for nearly 20 miles against a head wind, taking about six hours. She was a paddle steamer driven by a 10 h.p. engine. Despite her good performance, there were fears that the canal banks might be eroded by eddies from the whirling paddle-blades and she was laid up. She was 56 ft long, 18 ft wide and 8 ft deep.

See also INLAND WATERWAYS.

Charlotte Dundas steaming on the Forth and Clyde Canal.

Chart: the seaman's map of the sea, showing details of depths, lights, coasts, buoys, landmarks etc., to assist accurate and safe navigation. *See also* SURVEYING.

Charter: an agreement in writing setting out the terms for the hire and cargo of a vessel.

Charybdis: *see* SCYLLA AND CHARYBDIS.

'Charybdis': Royal Navy ship which on one occasion left Australian waters in company with the immortal clipper *THERMOPYLAE*. Under press of sail, the clipper quickly forged ahead and *Charybdis*'s commander signalled: 'Goodbye! You are too much for us. You are the finest model of a ship I ever saw. It does my heart good to look at you.'

Chase: *see* GENERAL CHASE.

Chatham: town and port on the River Medway in Kent, one of the great home bases and dockyards of the Royal Navy. Those navy-conscious monarchs Henry VIII and Elizabeth I established the dockyard, and under the later Stuarts Chatham became the chief naval port. To the east of the town there may still be seen defences erected at the time of the threat of invasion by Napoleon in 1803–5.

Chatham Chest: a fund for disabled seamen which was founded in 1590 by Drake, Sir John Hawkins and Lord Howard of Effingham. Seamen paid 6d. a month from their pay into the fund; the chest in which the money was kept is now in the National Maritime Museum, Greenwich. In 1814 the fund was amalgamated with the GREENWICH CHEST.

Chaucer, Geoffrey: *see* DARTMOUTH; *MAGDELAYNE.*

Chebeck: *see* XEBEC.

Cherbourg: an important French Channel port, on the N. coast of the Cotentin peninsula. During the many and long wars between France and England, from the Hundred Years' War onward, Cherbourg's strategic position opposite the S. coast of England made it a key port. During the Second World War it was fiercely and bravely defended by the German occupying forces after the Normandy landings of the Allied armies (1944). It is the main French terminal of the Atlantic liner traffic.

'Chesapeake': U.S. frigate captured in 1813 by Captain Broke of H.M.S. *Shannon* outside BOSTON.

Chesapeake Bay: a huge inlet on the coasts of Maryland and Virginia, which is really the drowned lower valley of the Susquehanna River. On it are many famous towns and ports, e.g. Baltimore, Annapolis, Newport News and Norfolk. At its entrance was fought the important naval engagement in 1781 during the War of AMERICAN INDEPENDENCE.

Chief Petty Officer: *see* PETTY OFFICER.

China Seas: the South China Sea and the East China Sea, arms of the Pacific Ocean lying off South-East Asia. The former lies between the Philippines, Borneo and the mainland coast of China; the latter lies to the north, between Taiwan, Japan and the mainland. The whole area, particularly the South China Sea, is subject to violent tropical storms, known as TYPHOONS.

For many years pirates were active in the South China Sea, often boarding ships as passengers or members of the crew, and then seizing control and sailing the vessel to be pillaged in a secret rendezvous. Piracy still occurs, largely because of the unsettled political conditions of the area. In his book *The China Clippers* (1914) Basil Lubbock told how in the South China Sea it was considered risky to employ a Chinese pilot, for some of them were in the pay of the pirates and would purposely steer the ship into their clutches:

There were other dangers in the China Seas to be reckoned with besides indifferent pilots, rocks, shoals and treacherous currents. Pirates swarmed along the coast. For protection against these, every tea clipper was provided with an armoury of muskets, pistols and cutlasses, besides two cannons, which were capable of more than ornamental or sailing duties. And they had special magazines for powder, ball and grape shot, small arms, ammunition etc.

Chinese Wars: the war of 1839–42 was chiefly concerned with the discreditable opium trade. The Chinese authorities protested against the importation of opium by British traders and, in 1839, seized and burnt large quantities of the drug. After the capture of Chusan, Hong Kong and Amoy, peace was concluded, and Hong Kong, together with a number of other ports, was opened to European traders. China agreed to pay 21,000,000 dollars in indemnity and as compensation for the confiscated opium.

The immediate cause of the second war (1855–8) was the capture by the Chinese of the cutter *Arrow* on a charge of piracy. The charge was probably justified, but the *Arrow* was British-registered and her surrender was demanded. Her crew was set at liberty, but war broke out with the bombardment of Canton by the British. After the fall of the Taku forts the Treaty of Tientsin was concluded, the Chinese paying an indemnity of £4,000,000.

Chin-stay: the ribbon strap used for securing a seaman's cap in windy weather.

'Chips': originally the pieces cut away in the process of shaping ships' timbers, which were regarded as the lawful perquisites of the workmen and dockyard officials. Later, the term degenerated to cover any articles removed by fraud and embezzlement. That 'chips' were a useful supplement to wages is shown by the fact that in 1803 the spare bits of timber from Plymouth Dockyard were sold for £3204 2s. 9d., which should be multiplied many times to get a modern equivalent. In 1801 the Navy Board ordered that, in return for an increase in daily wages, 'chips' were to be collected up and sold to the public.

There were some monstrous examples of fraud and over-charging. Soon after 1800, two contractors, Michael and John Hedges, supplied goods to the Navy worth £264 7s. and put in bills for £3671 9s. 2d. In Jamaica a case came to light of a naval storekeeper buying slaves, hiring them from himself to work in the dockyard, and paying himself at a high rate out of public money. The office of Treasurer of the Navy was for long, in the words of David Hannay, 'one great impudent Chip. The Treasurer did nothing, and was known to do nothing except pocket his emoluments.' There were, of course, distinguished exceptions, but, since all money from the Exchequer for naval purposes was for long

banked in the Treasurer's name, it is not surprising that the 'chips' system operated even at this high level. When the Commissioners of Public Accounts were investigating this anomaly, they found that the executors of the estates of Viscount Falkland, who left the Treasurership in 1689, still owed the Navy over £27,000 nearly a hundred years later.

See also CARPENTER, SHIP'S.

Chock-a-block (or **block-and-block** or **two blocks**): when two blocks are as close together as they can go. 'Chock-a-block' is now used as a slang term for 'full' and for 'fed-up', and is often abbreviated to 'chocker'.

Chops of the Channel: the entrance to the English Channel from the Atlantic.

Chosen Band, the: *see* BAND OF BROTHERS.

Christian, Fletcher: *see* BLIGH, WILLIAM.

Christ's Hospital: school founded by Edward VI (1553) on the site of a Grey Friars' monastery. In the history of the sea it played an important part in providing the first centre of organized instruction in navigation. Letters Patent were issued on 19 August 1673, with an endowment of £7000, authorizing an establishment

. . . for the mayntenance of forty poore Boyes in the said Hospitall whoe having attained to competence in the Grammer and Comon Arithmatique to the Rule of Three in other Schooles of the said Hospitall may be fitt to bee further educated in a Mathematical Schoole and there taught and instructed in the Art of Navigacon and the whole Science of Arithmatique until their age and competent proficiency in these parts of the Mathematiques shall have fitted and qualified them in the judgment of the Master of Trinity House for the tyme being to bee initiated into the practices of Navigacon and to bee bound out as Apprentices for seaven yeares to some Captaines or Comanders of Sipps.

See also EDUCATION.

Chronometer: a very accurate watch or clock used in ships for reckoning longitude. *See also* INSTRUMENTS; HARRISON, JOHN.

Church: in past times churches often had close associations with ships. Ship models were sometimes used as votive offerings ·(*see* MODEL SHIPS). *See also* NAVE.

Churchill, Sir Winston (1874–1965): statesman, soldier and author, imperishably associated with the leadership and inspiration of the British people during the Second World War. Although his own military service was as a soldier, he had close connections with, and a great affection for, the naval forces; and he was First Lord of the Admiralty 1911–15 and 1939–40.

We are waiting for the long-promised invasion. So are the fishes.

> Broadcast to the French people
> (21 October 1940)

. . . the whole fortunes of our race and Empire, the whole treasure accumulated during so many centuries of sacrifice and achievement, would perish and be swept utterly away if our naval supremacy were to be impaired.

> Speech in Glasgow (9 February 1912)

'Cimba': *see* MILTIADES.

Cinque Ports (pronounced 'sink . . .'): originally the five ports of Hastings, Romney, Hythe, Dover and Sandwich on the English Channel, which, in return for certain privileges, undertook in medieval times to supply ships and seamen for guarding the Channel and carrying the king's army. Later Rye and Winchelsea were associated with the five, and so were a number of lesser places. Up to the 14th century the Cinque Ports were certainly the main providers of ships for royal needs, but they fell into decline, largely because their rivers and harbours became silted up and other ports had developed, so that at the time of the Spanish Armada (1588) they could supply no more than five ships. The Lord Warden of the Cinque Ports, also Constable of Dover Castle, was the Admiral of the Ports with maritime jurisdiction, and this title, today a courtesy one, is still conferred upon distinguished men, e.g. Sir Winston Churchill.

Circumnavigation: sailing completely round, usually the world. The first circumnavigation of the world was achieved in the years 1519–22 by the Spanish expedition which set out under the leadership of the Portuguese Ferdinand Magellan. He discovered the Strait of MAGELLAN into the Pacific; a member of the crew called Pigafetta wrote 'Wednesday the twenty-eighth of November we came forth out of the said strait and entered into the Pacific Sea, where we remained three months and twenty days without taking in provisions or other refreshments, and we only ate old biscuit reduced to powder, and full of grubs, and stinking . . . and we drank water that was yellow and stinking. We also ate the ox-hides that were under the main-yard.' Terrible hardships, including scurvy, were endured before land was eventually reached. Magellan was killed in a quarrel with the natives in the PHILIPPINE ISLANDS, and it was left to one of his captains, del Cano, to complete the voyage in the *Vittoria*, the only ship to return out of the five which set out. The next great circumnavigation was by Sir Francis DRAKE (1577–80), who avoided the Magellan Strait and sailed round Cape Horn. The second English circumnavigator was Thomas CAVENDISH. Where the pioneers sailed, others (e.g. George ANSON) followed; the first scientific circumnavigation was by Captain James Cook in 1768–71. The venturing spirit of these great sailors endured in those who have sailed single-handed round the world, of whom the American Joshua Slocum (1844–1910) is generally acknowledged as the first. Setting out from Boston in 1895 he completed his circumnavigation in the sloop *Spray* in 1898, and recorded his experiences in *Sailing Alone around the World* (1900). Famous British names amongst the growing list of recent single-handed circumnavigators are Sir Francis Chichester, Sir Alec Rose, Robin Knox-Johnson and Naomi James.

Civil War (1642–9): at the outbreak of the English Civil War, the majority of the fleet immediately joined the Parliamentary side, a matter hardly to be wondered at since, in the words of Professor Michael Lewis, 'Many ships were years behind in wages, and the best captains were selling their ships' masts and sails to feed and clothe their starving, naked men' (*The History of the British Navy*, 1957). Parliament promised to look after them, and, by and large, kept its word. Although the war is generally thought of as an almost exclusively land affair, in reality the Navy's role was decisive. The major ports resisted the King, the fleet prevented the military aid of Louis XIII of France, and the City of London dipped into its coffers and helped the Parliament forces as a safer investment than a king bereft of his navy. *See also* SHIP-MONEY.

Claw off: when in danger of being driven

on to a lee shore, a sailing ship had to 'claw off' by beating to windward.

Clear: the word is used in many nautical senses, but in general means free of any obstruction, unencumbered or empty, e.g. a clear anchor as opposed to a foul anchor; 'the gun is clear', i.e. is not loaded. A ship can clear the harbour or a navigational danger. To 'clear for action' means to prepare at once to engage the enemy. 'Clear lower deck' is the order for all the crew to muster.

Cleat: a kind of double-ended peg or similar device for securing or hitching a rope.

Clerk: title formerly carried by various officials in the naval administration. The Clerk of the Ships (or Clerk of the Acts) was the head of the secretariat, corresponding rather to a Permanent Under Secretary in modern government. Samuel Pepys was at one time 'Clerk of the King's Ships'. The Clerk of the Cheque supervised the number of men employed in the dockyards, the hours they worked (or failed to work). The Clerk of the Ropeyard had, as his title implies, special responsibility for the ropewalks which turned out the vast quantities needed for the Navy. Other offices included the Clerk of the Survey.

Clew (or **clue**): (1) the two lower corners of a square sail, but only the aftermost lower corner of a fore-and-aft sail. To 'clew up' a sail is to haul it up to the yard ready for furling. This is done by means of clew lines and by tackle called clew garnets on lower square sails. 'Clewed up' in nautical talk has come to mean that a job of work is completed. *See also* SAIL. (**2**) 'Clews' is the name given to the cords and lanyards of a hammock by which it is slung.

Clinker-built (or **clincher-built**): with the outer boards of the hull overlapping each other. Compare CARVEL-BUILT.

Clipper: type of large, fast, fine-lined sailing vessel that developed and flourished 1830–70; probably the most praised, most written about and most romanticized ships of all time. Their chief characteristics were their slim lines, their sharp bows (the 'fine, clean bows' of Masefield's poem, 'D'Avalos' Prayer') and their towering cloud of sail – on the famous *Lightning*, for example, 13,000 square yards of spread canvas. Most clippers were between five and six times as long as they were broad, a big difference from, e.g., the old ships of the line, which were about three-and-a-half times as long as their breadth. The streamlined construction can be judged from the fact that, in the *Thermopylae*, anyone standing as much as 15 ft from either stem or stern could touch both sides of the ship with outstretched arms and 'if anyone pressed a Malacca cane along her side at any point the cane would have to bend, as there was not a straight line in her'.

Many of the finest early clippers were built at Baltimore, Maryland; and some experts have decided that the 500-ton Baltimore-built *Ann McKimm* (1832) was, in fact, the first true clipper. These fast American ships were able to cope with the demands for speedy passages brought about by the Gold Rush to California (1847 onwards) and the discovery of gold in Australia (1851). English owners, before the home product began to come off the slipways, ordered new ships from the American yards, which had begun to build vessels of up to 1800 tons register.

From about 1850, composite construction became common; i.e. all the interior framework was of iron, and the keel, stem and stern-posts were of wood, as was the external planking, which, below the water-line, was copper-sheathed.

Clippers were much used for the China tea trade and for Australian wool, where speed was of great importance; hence the famous races and the many records set up. Some of these are noted in separate entries for such famous clippers as the *CUTTY SARK, LIGHTNING, ARIEL, THERMO-PYLAE, TAEPING, FLYING CLOUD* etc. *See also* TEA CLIPPER; WOOL CLIPPER; FRUIT CLIPPER; OPIUM CLIPPER.

The opening of the Suez Canal (1869) spelt the end for this great line of ships. Some of them served on, cut about, mishandled, down-graded, for many years; but their great days were over. They would never again, as Masefield wrote movingly of the clipper *Wanderer* in his poem of the same name,

Come as of old a queen, untouched by Time,
Resting the beauty that no seas could tire.

See also colour section.

Closed galleries: the old two- and three-deckers usually had open stern galleries, decorative and popular among senior naval officers for limited promenading and taking the air. Towards the end of the 18th century a great many of these were closed in, giving the double advantage of greater strength and added protection from the weather, especially during the bleak months of the winter blockades. Sometimes the galleries were cut completely away and the ship given a so-called circular stern, which could be equipped with further gunports. Some ugly-looking ships resulted, and the reactionary British seamen were apt to point out that their ships were not accustomed to running away and, until they developed the habit, they needed no stern guns.

Close-hauled: with sails trimmed so that the ship sails as nearly as possible towards the direction from which the wind is blowing.

Close quarters: formerly strong bulwarks or barriers erected as a defence against boarders; hence 'at close quarters', meaning in close contact, hand-to-hand.

Close-reefed: a sailing ship is close-reefed when it has taken in or reefed its sails to the full extent.

Cloth of Gold, Field of the: meeting in June 1520 between Henry VIII of England and Francis I of France at Guines, south of Calais; so-called from the lavishness and splendour of the preparations. It was not a maritime event, but is of considerable interest to naval historians because of the large contemporary painting (ascribed to Vincent Volpe, who worked at the English court from 1514 to 1530) showing Henry VIII's departure from Dover for the famous meeting. It was long thought that the largest ship portrayed is the *Henri Grâce à Dieu*, but in fact that ship was not present and it is more likely to be the GREAT BARKE.

The picture (now at Hampton Court Palace, London) shows clearly how the fleet, to take the greater weight of armament carried in Henry VIII's reign,

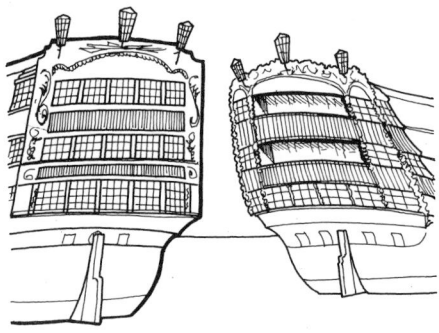

had gunports cut in the hull rather than just in the superstructure. Other new features are the top-gallant sails carried by the larger vessels and the greater strength given to the warships by being carvel-built instead of clinker-built (i.e. with the planks strongly butted edge to edge instead of overlapping).

See colour section.

Cloud cleaner: *see* MOONRAKER.

Clove hitch: *see* KNOTS.

Club-haul: means of moving or tacking a ship by letting go an anchor and slipping the cable.

In Marryat's *Peter Simple* (1834) Captain Savage saves the *Diomede* by club-hauling, and this classic description of how it was done was for many years learnt by heart by naval cadets for their examination.

'Luff now, all you can, quartermaster,' cried the captain. 'Send the men aft directly. My lads, there is no time for words – I am going to *club-haul* the ship, for there is no room to wear. The only chance you have of safety is to be cool, watch my eye, and execute my orders with precision. Away to your stations for tacking ship. Hands by the best bower anchor. Mr Wilson, attend below with the carpenter and his mates, ready to cut away the cable at the moment I give the order. Silence, there, fore and aft. Quartermaster, keep her full again for stays. Mind you ease the helm down when I tell you.'

Clue: *see* CLEW.

Coach: in the 17th century this referred to the ante-room of the large cabin at upper-deck level; later it became an alternative name for the roundhouse or cabins at the after end of the quarter-deck.

Coachwhipping: ornamental work, usu-ally of cordage, plaited on to boathooks or stanchions to give a smart appearance.

Coamings: the raised borders round hatches etc. to prevent water pouring below deck.

Coaster: vessel which sails from port to port in the same country, keeping close to land.

Dirty British coaster with a salt-caked smoke
    stack
Butting through the Channel in the mad
    March days,
With a cargo of Tyne coal,
Road-rail, pig-lead,
Firewood, iron-ware, and cheap tin trays.

John Masefield, 'Cargoes'

Coastguards: body of men whose functions have varied through the centuries, their chief work having been devoted to the prevention of smuggling, signalling, the sighting of vessels in distress and assistance with shipwrecks. They maintain close liaison with such bodies as the Royal National Lifeboat Institution in the saving of human life. During, and after, the Napoleonic Wars, the service was normally staffed by half-pay naval officers, working alongside the revenue and preventive men. Until 1831 the control of the coastguard service resided with the Customs, but in that year, after a process of reorganization, the force came under the aegis of the Admiralty and formally took the name of Coastguards. In 1856 was passed the Coastguard Act, one provision of which was that in time of war the coastguard service was to be used in coastal defence and as a naval reserve force. Its numbers are now reduced and its chief functions have reverted to life-saving, though a recent development has been maintaining a sharp look-out for landings of illegal immigrants. Staffed by retired naval officers and pensioners it is now supervised by H.M. Inspectors of Coastguards.

Coble: type of fishing boat, usually flat-bottomed and square-sterned, with a lug sail and propelled by several pairs of oars.

Cochrane, Sir Alexander Forrester Inglis (1758–1832): admiral; served with credit on various stations, including the West Indies and America, finishing his career as Commander-in-Chief, Portsmouth.

Cochrane, Thomas, tenth Earl of Dundonald (1775–1860): admiral, nephew of the above and at one time his flag-captain. A conspicuously successful officer, with many captures and successful cruises to his credit, he sometimes earned the jealousy of his contemporaries and made himself unpopular with the government by attacking naval abuses and corruption. In 1814 he was falsely accused of complicity in a stock-exchange fraud, dismissed from the Navy and deprived of the Order of the Bath and his seat in Parliament. He was at once re-elected by his Westminster constituents, but was continually victimized by the government with imprisonment and with fines that were paid by popular penny subscriptions.

Indefatigable and irrepressible, he accepted command of the Chilean Navy and by a series of brilliant successes against Spain secured the independence of Chile and Peru. As admiral of the Brazilian fleet, he also liberated Brazil, and he went on to serve the Greek Navy. Perhaps in bewildered self-defence, the British government reinstated him and promoted him to rear-admiral in 1832. One of the most original minds of his day, he was the first to employ steam power in ships of war, urged the introduction of screw propellers and constantly showed an independence and fertility of ideas that were too often frustrated by short-sighted and envious opponents. His autobiography reveals both his strengths and his weaknesses. *See also RISING STAR.*

On the occasion of William the Fourth's accession to the throne he was at length reinstated in his place in the British Navy; and on 22 May 1847, although it had until then been most inconsistently withholden, the Order of the Bath was restored to him, an act which of course re-establishes his Lordship's character, but not more fully proves his innocence than it clearly indicates the debt of reparation due to him for having been so long suffered to bear the stigma of unmerited disgrace.

> William O'Byrne, *Naval Biographical Dictionary* (1849)

The moral of my chequered career is this: That they who, in political matters, propose to themselves a strict and rigid adherence to the truth of their convictions, irrespective of personal consequences, must expect obloquy rather than reward; and that they who obstinately pursue their professional duty in the face of routine and official prejudice, may think themselves lucky if they escape persecution.

> Thomas, tenth Earl of Dundonald, *Autobiography of a Seaman* (1861)

Cocked hat: (1) a type of hat formerly used for full dress by naval officers of appropriate rank (*see* ROTHERHAM, EDWARD). (2) A triangle formed by lines of bearing on a chart, and caused by some error in observing or plotting the bearings.

Cockpit: in the old sailing warships there were two cockpits, fore and aft. The after cockpit was on the lowest deck and was dark and stuffy. Here lived the 'young gentlemen', or midshipmen, and they shared their unattractive quarters with the Master's Mates and other lesser folk. In battle the after cockpit was used as an emergency sick-bay for the wounded, and was the scene of many an amputation by the surgeon. The fore cockpit was in the bows and was the quarters of the boatswain and the carpenter.

Codrington, Sir Edward (1770–1851): admiral. He commanded the *Orion* (74 guns) at Trafalgar, taking the French *Intrepide* and assisting in the capture of the *Swiftsure*, for which services he received the gold medal, a sword of honour from the Patriotic Fund, and the thanks of Parliament. Among his other distinguished services was his part in the Anglo-American War of 1812–15, including the capture of Washington. He was commander-in-chief in the Mediterranean 1826–8 and led the British, Russian and French squadrons engaged in the pacification of Greece, shattering the Turkish-Egyptian fleet at the Battle of NAVARINO (1827).

Cod Wars: the name informally given to a series of disagreements between Iceland and Britain over fishing rights in Icelandic waters. In 1952 Iceland began extending her fishing limits, at first to four miles and then in 1958 to twelve miles, because she was gravely concerned at the over-fishing of the seas around her coasts and felt that fish stocks must be conserved, since they were her main source of income. But Icelandic waters for a very long time had been traditional fishing grounds for British and other fishing fleets. The British reacted by banning Icelandic boats from landing their fish in United Kingdom ports. This first Cod War was ended by agreement in 1961. The second Cod War began in February 1973, when Iceland extended her exclusive fishing zone to fifty miles. This dispute was ended in November of the same year by a temporary agreement, though in July 1974 the International Court of Justice ruled that Iceland was not entitled to exclude British and other fishing vessels between the twelve- and fifty-mile limits.

In 1975 Iceland declared that from 15 October her fishing limits would extend to 200 miles, so concerned was she for the conservation of fish stocks. All foreign vessels were forbidden within the fifty-mile zone and only limited permits were to be given for the 200-mile zone. British trawlers ignored these restrictions, and the third Cod War began. Icelandic gunboats started harassing British trawlers and cutting their warps so that they lost their nets. Britain offered concessions, but could not accept the limitation of her catch to the very small tonnage demanded by Iceland. Talks broke down, and many more incidents occurred on the fishing grounds. At first four civilian vessels were sent to assist the British trawlers, but the fishermen demanded Royal Naval protection, and three frigates were sent. Relations between the two countries continued to deteriorate and on the fishing grounds dangerous encounters became more frequent. The warships were withdrawn as a precondition to negotiations in January 1976, but when these failed they returned, with a continuation of incidents damaging ships and gear. In February Iceland broke off diplomatic relations with Britain, and the stability of NATO was threatened in spite of attempts at mediation.

Eventually the third Cod War was ended in June 1976 by an agreement which severely limited the British catch in Icelandic waters, and with which the fishing industry felt very dissatisfied. Opinion had turned against the British case as more and more countries were coming to accept the 200-mile limit for TERRITORIAL WATERS. (*See also* TUG.)

91

Coffer dam: *see* OIL-CARRIER.

Cog: type of early merchant vessel closely associated with the 12th- and 13th-century group of European trading towns known as the HANSEATIC LEAGUE. Many are shown on the seals of these towns. They were roomy, deep-draught vessels, sharp-ended and with a high freeboard.

Collier: ship employed in the coal-carrying trade. The colliers formed a very important class of merchantmen, trading from the Tyne to London, and further afield to Northern Europe and the Mediterranean. They were strong, bluff-bowed and broad-sterned, the larger ones of 300–400 tons burden. The Admiralty purchased numbers of them for general service; for all three of his voyages of discovery (1768–80) Captain Cook used Whitby colliers, the most famous of them the *ENDEAVOUR*.

Collingwood, Cuthbert, first Baron Collingwood (1750–1810): vice-admiral and second-in-command at Trafalgar. It was Collingwood in *ROYAL SOVEREIGN*, leading the lee column, who first broke the enemy line, earning the exclamation from

Nelson: 'See how that noble fellow Collingwood carries his ship into action!' In a period of harsh punishments, he ran some of the best-disciplined and most efficient ships in the fleet without excessive flogging. When tough and dangerous sailors were brought before Nelson, he was known to say: 'Send them to Collingwood. He will tame them, if no one else can.' *See also* SICILY; TIMBER.

What a beautiful day! Will you be tempted out of your ship? If you will, hoist the Assent and *Victory*'s Pendants.

Lord Nelson to Collingwood
(19 October 1805)

Collision: *see* RAM; RULE OF THE ROAD.

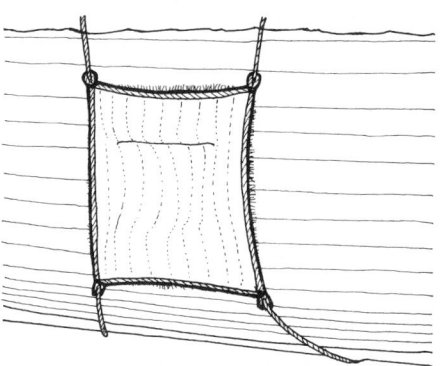

Collision mat: a large square stuffed canvas mat secured by ropes and lowered over the side to cover a hole in the hull caused by collision or other mishap. The pressure of the seawater holds the mat firmly against the hole and prevents excessive intake of water. Using a collision mat is known as fothering; *see also* THRUM.

Colomb, Philip Howard (1831–99): admiral who entered the Navy in 1846 and later in his career made important reports to the Admiralty on day and night signalling, himself devising (1858) the 'Colomb's Flashing Signals' system. He was in the forefront in perceiving what revolutionary changes in the Navy were demanded by steam power, and he made important contributions to new conceptions of tactics and the conduct of war, many of them embodied in his *Naval Warfare* (1891). His conclusions on the main causes of collisions at sea led to new international regulations, adopted following the Washington conference of 1889.

'Colossus': 74-gun ship, built at Deptford (1803). At Trafalgar she suffered very heavy casualties, with 40 killed and 160 wounded. Her main mast was so badly damaged that it had to be cut away, her fore mast was shot through and she lost several anchors and ship's boats. She was so closely in action that she knocked off several of her lower-deck gunports by running on the Spanish *Argonauta*. Her crew were cheered on by a cockerel which escaped from the hen-coop, perched on the shoulder of the captain (James Nicoll Morris) and crowed loudly.

An earlier H.M.S. *Colossus* went down in a storm off the Scillies on 10 December 1798. Apart from her human cargo, she was carrying a magnificent collection of Greek and Roman antiquities built up by Sir William Hamilton (1730–1803), the diplomatist and archaeologist who is usually chiefly remembered for his wife Emma's association with Nelson. Sir William had already been the means of the British Museum acquiring one great collection in 1772 after he had served as British plenipotentiary at the Court of Naples from 1764. He then proceeded to build up another, which he considered even finer. In 1798, when Italy was threatened with imminent invasion by Napoleon's armies, this collection was hastily packed and shipped for home on board the *Colossus*. Among it were some 200 Greek vases dated between 700 and 400 B.C. Thousands of shards have recently been recovered from the wreck by divers.

Some wit once commented that Sir William Hamilton would be remembered as 'the man who shared his wife with the admiral and his treasure with the sea.'

Colours: the general name given to the flag or ensign flown by a ship to indicate her nationality. Sailing under false colours has been an accepted ruse in time of war, but true colours must be hoisted before an attack is made. For 'hauling down the colours' *see* STRIKE, TO; *see also* NAIL ONE'S COLOURS TO THE MAST. 'Colours' is also the name for the naval ceremony of hoisting the ensign in the morning and hauling down at sunset. *See also* ENSIGN; FLAGS.

'Columbus': curious vessel built (1823–4) at Quebec by Charles Wood of Port Glasgow, Scotland, with the idea of evading the British tax on oak and squared pine imported from Canada. The scheme was to build a solid ship of such timber, sail her to Britain and break her up there. A 3690-ton vessel, 301 ft in length, she was packed with timber and rigged as a four-masted barque. While being towed down the St Lawrence she ran aground and had to jettison some of her timber; but she arrived safely at Blackwall, London. Her cargo of timber was discharged, but the owners then refused to allow her to be broken up as originally planned and sent her back to St John, New Brunswick, for another cargo – an ill-advised decision since she foundered on the voyage. Another vessel of similar type was the *Baron of Renfrew* of 5294 tons, launched in 1825, and having five decks with a height of about seven feet between each, packed close with squared timber. She ran

93

aground after she had reached the English Channel and then broke up on the French coast, scattering her timbers over the beaches.

At a broadside view from a distance, the *Columbus* looks a tremendous length and, though seemingly hogged or broken-backed and very much under-rigged, there is something sneaking and dangerous in her show. As you approach her, however, she looks as she is – an immense mass of timber knocked together for the purposes of commerce, without any regard to beauty and little attention to the principles of naval architecture.

The Times (November 1824)

Commander: in the Royal Navy, the rank below Captain and above Lieutenant-Commander.

See colour section.

Commerce-raider: as the name implies, a ship used for attacking the merchant shipping of an enemy. Any swift well-armed ship would serve the purpose and, through the centuries, it has been realized that merchant ships, carrying vital supplies, are a legitimate and very vulnerable

target. According to Geoffrey Callender, 'it is only by the destruction of sea-borne commerce that naval forces can exercise the pressure employed by an army on land.'

At the outset of the First World War Germany had a number of ships well positioned to carry out such raids – the *Königsberg* in the East Indies, the *Karlsruhe* and the *Dresden* in West Indian waters, and the famous *Emden*, the most formidable raider of them all. In the Second World War the role was largely taken over by U-boats, hunting singly or in WOLF PACKS.

Commission: (1) a ship is 'commissioned' when it is brought into service; it is then said to be 'in commission' (compare 'in ORDINARY'); (2) a commission is also the authority given to officers of sub-lieutenant's rank and above; they are 'commissioned officers' (*see* OFFICER).

Commissioner: official formerly in charge of each royal dockyard.

Commissioners of the Navy: officials appointed to inquire into the state of, or to

The German commerce-raider *Karlsruhe*.

manage the affairs of, the Navy. A Commission of 1617–18 made an outspoken report on the sad condition into which the Navy had fallen in the 15 years since the accession of James I. Another was established in 1686–8, which did much to bring the Navy back into good shape and remove at least some of the effects of many years of maladministration and corruption. The most effective work ever achieved by the Commissioners of the Navy was probably the great series of thirteen reports compiled 1805–7, entitled 'Reports of the Commissioners for Revising and Digesting the Civil Affairs of His Majesty's Navy'. They were to:

revise the System and Mode of accounting for the Receipt and Expenditure of Money and Stores; and likewise the Instructions and Standing Orders for the Government of the Civil Department of His Majesty's Naval Service . . . having it carefully in view to adapt the Mode of accounting for Monies and Stores, and likewise the whole body of such Orders and Instructions, to the present extensive Scale of the Naval Service; and to take Measures for keeping up the said System and Digest in all time to come.

Commodore: (1) the senior captain of a line or fleet of merchant ships; (2) in the Royal Navy, an officer holding temporary rank above a captain and below a rear-admiral for the performance of a particular duty or assignment; (3) the president of a yacht club.

See colour section.

Companion way (or **companion ladder**): the steps leading below to cabins or saloons in a merchant ship.

Company, ship's: everyone serving in a particular ship.

Company Ship: a ship of the Honourable East India Company (often abbreviated H.E.I.C.), or a government vessel on the Indian coast even after the Company was dissolved (1874).

Compass: an instrument to help guide a ship on a certain course or to observe the direction and bearing of landmarks or other objects. For its history, *see* INSTRUMENTS. For its functioning the compass depends on the earth's magnetic field, and the needle of the compass points to magnetic north, which is not the same as true north, the difference between the two being known as the magnetic variation (*see* MAGNETIC POLES). The compass needle is also affected by local magnetism, especially that of the ship itself if she is built of iron or steel; this is known as the deviation of the compass. Both these phenomena were gradually understood and mastered; every chart now shows the magnetic variation for its area, and the deviation of the modern liquid magnetic compass, most widely used in ships, is reduced and recorded in a procedure known as swinging ship.

Today many ships rely on the electrically driven GYRO-COMPASS, which depends on the rotation of the earth for the principles of its directive force. The gyro-compass consists of a heavy wheel, very rapidly rotating with the minimum of frictional resistance. The axis on which it spins when set in a north–south line holds that position and, being free from magnetic interference, provides the direction of true north. The master gyro-compass is usually set low down in a ship, and from it gyro-headings giving true direction and bearing can be repeated electrically wherever needed in the ship.

See also POINT, COMPASS.

Compass timber: *see* TIMBER.

Composite ship: one built of both wood

Composite ship: a line-and-wash shipyard drawing indicating the diagonal iron frames beneath the wooden planking.

and iron. Such ships were constructed during the 19th-century transition from wood to iron. *See also* CLIPPER.

Comptroller: official first appointed by Henry VIII to manage and supervise the whole machine of naval administration. His duties included the surveying of all stores and the superintendence of all payments made by the NAVY BOARD. He was a watch-dog over the Treasurer and Surveyor and had the job of balancing the accounts for annual presentation. The spelling, though it persists in some quarters, is simply the archaic form of 'controller'.

Con: to con a ship is to direct her course and to give orders for this purpose.

Congreve, Sir William: *see* ROCKET.

Conning tower: originally that part of a warship from which the ship was directed or conned, but now used to describe the upper part of a submarine below her bridge.

'Conqueror': 74-gun ship built at Graham's Yard, Harwich, in 1800 and broken up at Chatham in 1821. Her most distinguished service was at Trafalgar, where she was commanded by Israel Pellew (later Admiral Sir Israel Pellew), brother of the celebrated Sir Edward. *Conqueror* was much damaged and sus-

tained twelve casualties. Captain Atcherley of the ship's company of marines was sent on board the French flag-ship *Bucentaure* to receive the sword of Admiral Villeneuve.

'To whom,' asked Admiral Villeneuve, in good English, 'have I the honour of surrendering?'

'To Captain Pellew of the *Conqueror*.'

'I am glad to have struck to the fortunate Sir Edward Pellew.'

'It is his brother, sir,' said Captain Atcherley.

'His brother! What! are there two of them? Hélas!'

> Edward Fraser, *The Enemy at Trafalgar* (1906)

Conrad, Joseph (1857–1924): author. Born Jozef Teodor Konrad Korzeniowski, he came from Russian Poland, and changed his name on becoming a British subject in 1886. At the age of 14 he went to sea, working in French ships and voyaging to the West Indies. He joined his first British ship at Marseilles and in her came to England in 1878. In the following years he qualified by examination as Second and First Mate, and then obtained his Master's Certificate. During this time he made voyages to the Far East and Australia, and was also in charge of a river steamer on the Congo. All this experience gave him the material for his novels and short stories, to which he devoted himself after abandoning the sea when his first novel, *Almayer's Folly*, was published in 1895. The sea provides the setting or background to most of his novels and short stories, and his love and awe of it are shown in a book of reminiscences, *The Mirror of the Sea* (1906). Among his many great sea stories are *The Nigger of the Narcissus* (1898), *Lord Jim* (1900) and *Typhoon* (1902).

'Constitution': most famous of early U.S. ships, nicknamed 'Old Ironsides' because of her heavy timbers. She was a 55-gun (officially 44) frigate, launched at Boston (1797), and was more powerfully armed than most other frigates of her day, as well as being more heavily built. On one occasion an American privateer, the *Decatur*, mistook her for a British warship and, in her haste to get away, toppled twelve of her fourteen guns overboard. In the 1812 war the *Constitution* met a powerful British squadron soon after the outbreak of hostilities and had to make a run for it. Not long after, profiting by her escape, she captured the British frigate *Guerrière* after an action fought gallantly on both sides. The English captain, Dacres, won the admiration of the Americans by sending ten American subjects among his crew below rather than make them fight against their own countrymen, despite the odds against him. The *Constitution* has been preserved and restored and, fittingly, may still be seen in the shipyards at Boston which gave her birth.

Container ships: ships specially designed to carry cargo in large crates or box units ('containers') of standardized size for ease, safety and economy in stowage and handling. The containers are not only stowed in the holds, but are also carried neatly stacked and secured on the upper deck, which for this purpose is designed free of any obstruction. The containers are quickly loaded and discharged by dockside

equipment also specially designed, as are the lorries and wagons on which the containers are transported by road and rail. The container shipping trade has seen a major development over the last twenty years.

Continental System: Napoleon's attempt to create a 'fortress of Europe' and virtually blockade Britain, not with warships but by cutting off the main markets for her exports; *see also* PAPER BLOCKADE.

Contraband: goods which, by law, cannot be imported or exported; smuggled goods.

Convoy: a fleet of merchant and non-combatant ships sailing under the protection of warships. Possibly convoys were first introduced as a protection against pirates, but their origin in British naval history certainly goes back to medieval times, and from the 13th century onwards convoys were organized in time of war both to protect trade and to secure the safe passage of fighting forces. Other nations, particularly the French and Spanish, also used the convoy system, and the Spanish Armada (1588) was one example of a highly organized convoy with 93 transports and 37 fighting ships. The Spanish treasure ships from the New World were also protected by convoy.

In the 17th and 18th centuries convoys were the normal practice in time of war, and in 1731 convoy instructions were embodied in the first issue of what is known as 'Queen's Regulations and Admiralty Instructions'. Those who undertook marine insurance were energetic in pressing forward the Admiralty's organization of convoys by showing how much safer they were than 'runners' or ships sailing independently, and consequently lower premiums were charged on convoyed ships. During the American War of Independence, and in the wars against Revolutionary and Napoleonic France, convoy organization became more and more highly developed, being very extensive up to 1815; but, even so, losses from privateers and other enemy ships were severe for the ten years after Trafalgar.

During the later 19th century all the experience and belief of the past were cast aside, so that in the First World War the absence of a convoy system led to severe losses, mainly from enemy submarines, culminating in a loss of 350 ships in the one month of April 1917, when at last the organization of convoys began again in earnest, and with beneficial results.

In the Second World War the convoy system was once again highly developed to counteract the submarine and surface raider, though aircraft added a new threat to the protection of ships, especially on some of the most dangerous convoys such as those to Malta or through Arctic waters

to Northern Russia. Though again grievous losses occurred, the number of sinkings gradually decreased, and, as one important factor in this, the convoy system justified itself.

'Conway': famous training ship, moored for many years in the Mersey and, in the 1870s and 80s, one of a group of five in the river – the guard-ship *Defence*, *Conway*, and three other training ships, *Akbar*, *Indefatigable* and *Clarence*. The first H.M.S. *Conway* had taken part in the capture of the island of Chusan (1849) and made the first survey of the entrance to the River Yangtze. She was fitted up for her new purpose at Devonport (1858–9) and sent to Liverpool, primarily, in the words of one supporter, 'to train boys and bring them up as gunners as well as seamen, selecting them from the sons of seafaring people'. In 1861 H.M.S. *Winchester* was substituted and renamed *Conway*, and in 1875 H.M.S. *Nile* took over, again being renamed.

Cook, James (1728–79): circumnavigator; one of the greatest of English seamen. He began life as an ordinary sailor, first in the Baltic trade, then in the Royal Navy, and 'came up through the hawsehole' to captain's rank and unequalled navigational achievements.

While a Master (the equivalent of navigator) in the *Mercury* he played a great part in the capture of QUEBEC (1759) by discovering and buoying the deep-water channel of the St Lawrence. On his first great voyage of discovery (1768–71), in the *ENDEAVOUR*, he charted the coasts of New Zealand, the east coast of Australia and part of New Guinea, establishing the fact that Australia is an island continent (*see also* BOTANY BAY). This voyage was remarkable not only for its geographical significance but for Cook's successful experiments with antidotes to the curse of SCURVY.

From 1772 to 1775, with the *RESOLUTION* and the *ADVENTURE*, Cook made his second voyage, circumnavigating the Antarctic continent and discovering incidentally the important islands of New Caledonia and South Georgia (*see also* TERRA AUSTRALIS INCOGNITA).

After only a short interval, Cook, now promoted post-captain, offered to take command of a new expedition to explore the North Pacific. He set out in 1776 with the *Resolution* and the *Discovery*. On the voyage home in 1779, having returned to Hawaii to refit after a gale, he was murdered by the natives. In the words of C. R. L. Fletcher, 'In eleven years, this simple, modest sailor had added a quarter of the globe to the map, and had made long sea-keeping voyages without that loss of life which, before his time, had invariably attended them.' He was described as

above six feet high . . . plain both in address and appearance. His head was small; his hair, which was dark brown, he wore tied behind. His face was full of expression . . . his eyes . . . quick and piercing; his eyebrows prominent, which gave his countenance altogether a look of austerity.

See colour section.

Cook, Thomas (1808–92): the best-known of British tourist agents who, if he had few pretensions to being a seaman, was responsible for hundreds of thousands of men and women going to sea. Beginning his business life as a printer, a missionary and a wood-turner, he found his true *métier* when he organized the first publicly advertised train excursion in England in 1841. Thereafter the organization of tours at home and abroad, with attendant handbooks of information, became his life's work. In 1855 there was a 'Cook's Tour' from Leicester to Calais and back for £1 10s. in connection with the Paris Exhibition. Switzerland and the whole of Europe were subsequently embraced in his schemes. In 1882, when war broke out with Arabi Pasha, Thomas Cook & Son conveyed General Sir Garnet Wolseley and his staff to Egypt and transported the sick and wounded up the Nile. In 1884 the firm was employed to convey, first, General Gordon to the Sudan and, later, the men and stores sent belatedly to relieve him at Khartoum. In 1889 Thomas Cook was given the exclusive right to carry, on behalf of the Egyptian Government, all mail, soldiers, officials and supplies of coin along the Nile.

Copenhagen: capital and chief port of Denmark. For the battle of 1801 see below. In September 1807 Copenhagen again came under attack when, after heavy bombardment, the British took possession of the citadel and captured the whole of the Danish fleet, including 18 sail of the line.

Copenhagen, Battle of (or **Battle of the Baltic**; 2 April 1801): battle in which Sir Hyde Parker and Nelson, having taken the British fleet through the narrow King's Channel under the guns of the Danish fleet and batteries, inflicted a heavy defeat and effectively broke up the NORTHERN CONFEDERACY against Britain. It was in this engagement that there occurred the celebrated incident of Nelson putting his telescope to his blind eye when, with the issue still undecided, Hyde Parker made the recall signal.

'Leave off action? Now, damn me if I do! You know, Foley, I have only one eye – I have a right to be blind sometimes': and then, putting the glass to his blind eye, in that mood of mind

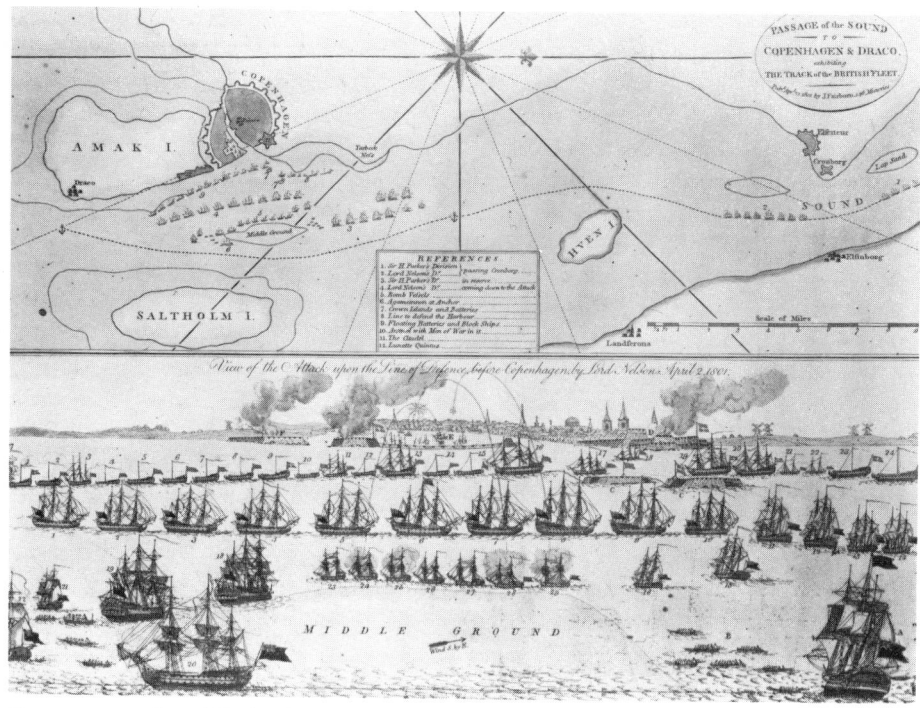

Contemporary plan of the battle lines by J. Fairburn.

which sports with bitterness, he exclaimed, 'I really do not see the signal!'

Robert Southey, *The Life of Nelson*
(1813)

There are two schools of thought about the reason for Parker's decision. The more generous is that, after three hours' action, he wished to save Nelson, even at the risk of his own reputation. Others have ascribed it to Parker's irresolution. Southey unflinchingly credits him with the more worthy motive:

The fire, [Parker] said, was too hot for Nelson to oppose; a retreat, he thought, must be made; he was aware of the consequences to his own reputation, but it would be cowardly in him to leave Nelson to bear the whole shame of the failure, if shame it should be deemed. Under a mistaken judgment, therefore, but with this disinterested and generous feeling, he made the

signal for retreat . . . I have great pleasure in rendering this justice to Sir Hyde Parker's reasoning. The fact is here stated upon the highest and most unquestionable authority.

Under the less familiar name for this encounter, 'the Battle of the Baltic', Thomas CAMPBELL wrote a well-known poem, beginning:

Of Nelson and the North
Sing the glorious day's renown,
When to battle fierce came forth
All the might of Denmark's crown,
And her arms along the deep proudly shone;
By each gun the lighted brand
In a bold determined hand,
And the Prince of all the land
Led them on.

Copper sheathing: device to protect wooden ships against the ravages of the *teredo navalis*, long known as the ship-worm, but towards the end of the 18th century established as a mollusc (i.e. a creature belonging to the same order as snails and mussels). It attacks wood under water, and makes long cavities, each separate from the other, so that a ship can become riddled, usually along the grain. It is probably true to say that the teredo was responsible for the destruction of more fine ships from classical times to the 18th century than gales or enemy action. While it normally flourishes in water approximating in salinity to that of the open sea, it has been known to invade much fresher water, especially when there has been a temporary increase in salt content. In the four years 1917–21, for instance, San Francisco suffered teredo damage to wharves and other woodwork estimated at 25 million dollars.

Many methods were tried to protect the timbers – lead, pitch, tar, tallow, lime, deal planking over oak, even layers of brown paper; but it was not till October 1761 that the Navy Board in England announced that it proposed to experiment with thin plates of copper. The 32-gun frigate *Alarm*, bound for service on the West India Station, was sheathed with copper at Woolwich Dockyard, and in a few years nearly all H.M. ships were being similarly protected. At first iron bolts were used to fasten the plates, but these oxidized so quickly that they were soon useless. Eventually copper bolts were substituted, and the battle was won. One drawback was the considerable cost. In 1798 the estimates for a new 90-gun ship of the line included £1870 for copper bolting and £2000 for coppering. In fact, the copper was so valuable that, when old ships were sold to breakers at the end of their service, the Admiralty stipulated that all the copper should be returned.

Coracle: primitive small boat with wickerwork or wooden ribs covered with hide or oiled cloth. Used primarily for fishing etc. on inland water in Wales and Ireland, it is similar to the Greenland oomiak (*see* KAYAK).

Coral Sea, Battle of the (May 1942): decisive battle of the Second World War, in which American sea and air forces defeated the Japanese. Eleven Japanese warships were sunk off the Solomon Islands. The encounter was remarkable in that no surface ships came within gun-range; instead of the great guns of the old Navy, the whole assault, with only occasional submarine help, was carried out by aircraft, almost all of which flew from carriers.

'Cornwall': reformatory training ship (instituted 1859), an old two-decker moored for many years off Gravesend. Convicted boys were sentenced for terms of not less than three years, but they were often allowed to leave after two years if they had qualified and had a good record while on board. About 80 per cent went into the Merchant Navy.

Cornwallis, Sir William (1744–1819): admiral, nicknamed 'Billy Blue', from his habit of flying the Blue Peter, even when driven into shelter by a gale, as a sign that he was about to sail again. He was commander-in-chief in the East Indies (1789–93) and of the Channel Fleet (1801 and 1803–6).

Coromandel Coast: a name given in the days of the East India Company to the eastern seaboard of India. *See also* MADRAS.

Coronel, Battle of (1 November 1914): a gallant action fought off Coronel, Chile, in the First World War between a crack

German squadron under Admiral von Spee and a weaker British force under Admiral Sir Christopher Cradock. Von Spee declined action till dusk, when, in the words of Geoffrey Callender, 'the setting sun behind the English ships silhouetted them like targets against the western sky. Then, satisfied that he could give, without receiving punishment, he opened fire with his unanswerable weapons, and the *Good Hope* and *Monmouth*, fighting till the waves closed over them, went down with their colours flying' (*The Naval Side of British History*, 1924).

The fight was a preliminary to the Battle of the Falkland Islands a month later, when the tables were turned.

Corposant: *see* ST ELMO'S FIRE.

Corsica: a large island in the Western Mediterranean lying south of the Gulf of Genoa. Famous as the birthplace of Napoleon Bonaparte, the island has had a long and chequered history, being considered a strategic prize by all the powers who have fought in the Mediterranean.

Corvette: originally a ship of war with a flush deck and single tier of guns; later, a small, fast escort vessel, lightly armoured, with anti-submarine and anti-aircraft weapons.

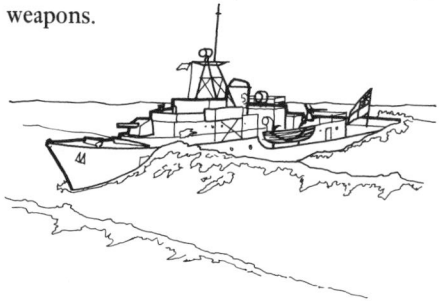

Costin gun: a gun used for throwing a line, generally between ships at sea, so that a stronger line may be passed for any purpose such as towing or transfer of stores or mail.

Country ship: an East India Company ship built in one of the Indian yards; or, later, a ship owned by natives or engaged in the Indian coastal trade.

Course: (1) the line or direction taken by a ship and usually expressed today in angular degrees, though in the past the points of the compass, e.g. 'North-East by East', were also used when orders were given to the helmsman; (2) the lowest sail on a square-rigged mast; hence 'main course', 'fore course' etc. *See also* SAIL.

Court-martial (plural **'courts-martial'**): court for naval (or military) offenders, composed of officers, none of whom, normally, are of lower rank than the accused. An Act of 1661 (*see* DUNGENESS, BATTLE OF) conferred the right to hold courts-martial, but there were so many limitations and inconsistencies about the setting up and composition of the courts that serious injustices could easily occur. Most of these were removed by an Act of 1749, in George II's reign. This limited the number of officers sitting in court to not less than five and not more than thirteen. The court's power to imprison was restricted to two years, and to a month for contempt. The best-known alterations made by the 1749 Act were incorporated in the 12th and 13th Articles of War. The 12th Article now covered the punishments to be handed out to 'Every Person in the Fleet who through Cowardice, Negligence, or Disaffection, shall in Time of Action withdraw or hold back, or not come into the fight or Engagement, or shall not do his utmost to take or destroy every ship which it shall be his Duty to engage, and to assist and relieve all and every one of his

Year	Name	Rank	Charge	Sentence
1750	Thomas Griffin	Vice-Admiral	Misconduct and negligence	Suspended from his rank. (Reinstated later, but not employed again)
1751	Peter Slater	Surgeon	Writing malicious letters	Dismissed from his employment
1755	Thomas Golden	Seaman	Theft, and desertion	350 lashes
1757	Robert Roddam	Captain	Loss of his ship, in striking to a French 64 after an engagement	Honourably acquitted
1759	Richard Steel	Lieutenant of Marines	Selling his clothes, sash and sword and keeping low company	Dismissed the service
1759	William Cleaver	Master-at-Arms	Purloining candles, being a seditious fellow and ignorant of discipline	Broken from his employment and put on board a King's ship to serve as a landsman
1777	Francis Reynolds	Captain	Loss of ship by fire	Acquitted, as ship caught fire in action
1779	Hon. Augustus KEPPEL	Admiral	Misconduct and neglect of duty on various occasions	Fully and honourably acquitted; declared to have behaved as a judicious and brave officer
1779	Thomas Wood	Impressed seaman	Attempting to blow up part of the deck and to poison the ship's company	300 lashes
1780	Philip Boteler	Captain	Loss of his ship, it being captured by the French	Dismissed the service, as it appeared he did not do his utmost to prevent her capture
1781	John Swaddle	Pilot	Refusing to take charge of the ship and absenting himself from duty	Six months' imprisonment in the Marshalsea
1791	John Gold	Lieutenant	Neglect of duty, disobedience	Adjudged insane and to be kept in safe custody
1805	Sir Robert CALDER	Admiral	Not having done his utmost to renew an engagement with the French	Severely reprimanded, but acquitted of cowardice and disaffection

103

Majesty's Ships or those of his Allies which it shall be his duty to assist and relieve.' The 13th Article paid particular attention to anyone who was backward in the 'Chase' or did not help 'a known Friend in View to the utmost of his Power'. At some periods the only sentence allowed for offences of this nature was death, but this severity was later modified. The selection of cases from 1750 onwards listed on p.103 shows the range of ranks dealt with, offences and punishments.

It should be noted that there is automatically a court-martial if one of H.M. ships is lost. Sometimes, as in the case of Calder, an officer can be court-martialled at his own request in the hope (not always realized) of clearing his name from rumours and imputations.

Cowper, William (1731–1800): poet. He pronounced his name 'Cooper', and, though he was no sailor, he is recorded here for his stirring poem 'On the Loss of the *Royal George*', beginning

> Toll for the Brave!
>   The brave that are no more!
> All sunk beneath the wave,
>   Fast by their native shore!

The *ROYAL GEORGE* had gone down at Spithead (1782). Admiral Kempenfelt and many men were lost, but the cause of the disaster was not, alas, as Cowper wrote, that 'A land-breeze shook the shrouds', but the rotten state of the hull and errors of seamanship in the degree to which the ship was heeled.

Coxswain (pronounced 'cox'un'): **(1)** seaman in charge of a boat, who generally steers; **(2)** a senior rating in smaller warships.

Crank ship: a ship that lists or tilts easily.

Crete: a mountainous, and the largest, island in the Greek Archipelago in the E. Mediterranean. 1941 saw yet another remarkable episode in Crete's long and often turbulent history, for in that year the island was captured by German air-borne forces in what was in effect the first oversea invasion to by-pass naval power. After being driven out of Greece, British and Allied troops had withdrawn to Crete, but they were consequently not fully organized and equipped. 22,000 German troops were landed by air in a few days and captured the island. Some 16,500 British troops were evacuated by the British Navy, but at the cost of great losses: over 2,000 dead, the sinking of three cruisers and six destroyers, and damage to other ships, including two battleships and an aircraft-carrier.

Crew: in naval usage, those men manning a boat, gun turret, operations room etc; in a merchant ship, all on board except the ship's officers and passengers.

Crimean War (1853–6): war against Russia by Turkey, Britain, France and Sardinia, though the declarations were not all made at the same time. So far as the Navy was concerned, the war caught Britain in a transitional stage, with a few minor steamships and her main battle-fleet still consisting of the old wooden walls under sail. At the bombardment of SEVASTOPOL (1854), the sailing ships of the line were hauled into position by steam tugs and were almost helpless against the Russian shore guns, which wreaked havoc. It was the clearest indication possible that the old Navy must turn to steam. Another pointer to the future came near the end of the war, when the French brought into action several 'armour-plated' ships, in this case small wooden steamships covered with $4\frac{1}{2}$-in.-thick iron plating, against which the

Russian shot was ineffective. *See also*
LUCAS, CHARLES DAVIS.

Cro'jack (or **crossjack**): a sail bent to the
lower yards of the mizen mast; a mizen
course. *See also* SAIL.

Crossing the Equator (or **crossing the
line**): a mock ceremony is often held to
initiate those who are crossing the Equator
for the first time. The occasion is one for
dressing up amid much high spirits and
fooling as King Neptune and his attendants
come aboard to receive the initiates into his
court. The ceremony is probably of pagan
origin and dates from ancient times when
rites were performed before a voyage to
propitiate the sea-gods.

Crossing the T: the naval tactic of sailing
across a line of enemy ships at approximately right angles to their line of
advance. This manoeuvre has an interesting history, for from being almost
disastrous it became an advantage to the
crosser. In the era of fighting galleys the
really vulnerable points were the oars and
oarsmen along each side, so the galleys held
to close line abreast and attacked from their
bows. If their line was crossed then the
crossing ships were exposed on their beam
where the rowers were. When the era of the
broadside arrived we find the position
reversed; the advantage was now with the
ships crossing the T, for they could bring
all their port or starboard guns to bear on
the enemy, whereas he was limited to his
few bow guns if in line abreast, and if in line
ahead to the bow guns of his leading ships
only. Crossing the T continued as a naval
tactic into the days of the battleship with
turreted guns. Two classic occasions on
which it was performed were the Battle of
Tsushima (1905), when the superior speed
of the Japanese ships enabled them to cross

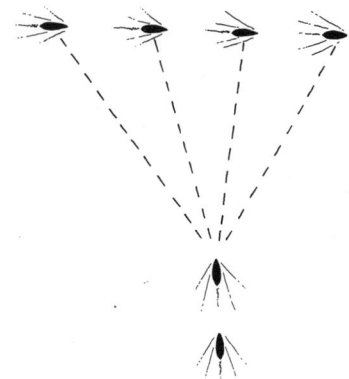

the T of the Russians with some success,
and the Battle of Jutland (1916), when
Jellicoe crossed the German line of battle,
but was prevented from reaping full
advantage of this manoeuvre because of
mist and darkness. But the advantages of
the T-crossing ships could be quickly
reduced, as they were at Jutland, if the
enemy turned away as a countering move.

Crossjack: *see* CRO'JACK.

Cross-staff (or **fore-staff**): an early
navigating device for measuring the
elevation of the sun or a star. It was simply
a staff about 3 ft long with a sliding crosspiece. Introduced as a successor to the
mariner's astrolabe in the 16th century, it
continued long in use, being improved and
developed, but John Davis's BACK-STAFF
eventually took its place. *See p. 106.*

Crosstrees: strong horizontal timbers at

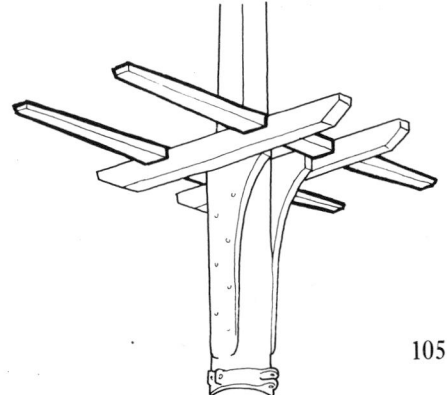

105

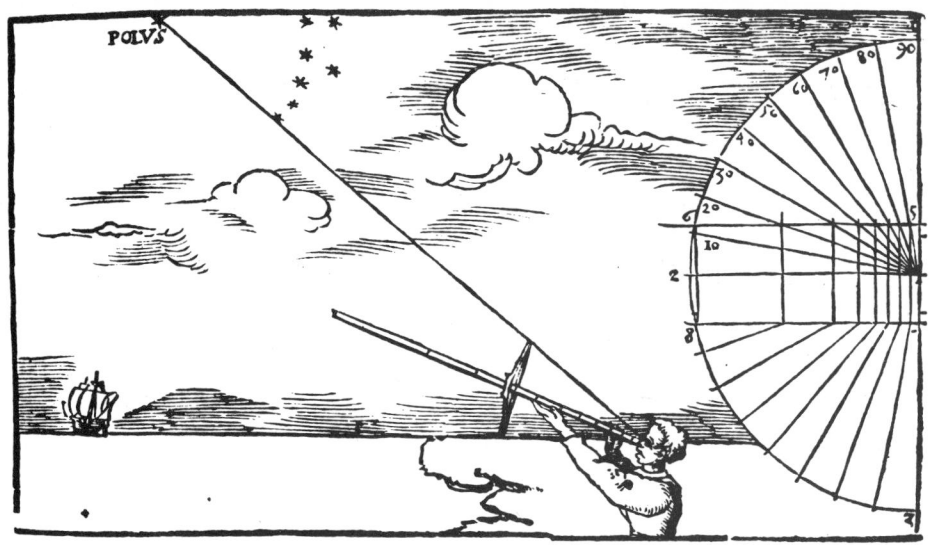

An early woodcut showing a navigator using a cross-staff.

the top of the main and top masts, supporting rigging etc.

Crow's nest: a small area high on a ship's fore mast where the look-out was posted.

Cruiser: usually considered a fairly modern word, but it was certainly in use in the 18th century to denote a fast, well-armed warship. Cruisers came to be divided into four classes: BATTLE CRUISER; armoured cruiser; protected cruiser; and light cruiser.

Crusades, the: series of military expeditions by the nations of Western Europe to rescue Jerusalem and the Holy Land from the Saracens (Moslems). Eight in number, they stretched in time from 1096 to 1270. Little is known about English ships of the period, most of the available evidence coming from such sources as the official seals of the Cinque Ports, which are inevitably distorted, frescoes etc. Most would have been two-masters, though there is an account of a large three-masted Saracen ship having been sunk by Richard I in the Mediterranean (1191). During the 13th century fore and after castles began to be used for fighting purposes, first as only temporary structures. Also in the early part of the century, the bowsprit seems to have come into use and the old steering paddle gave way to the rudder.

One chronicler gives a dramatic picture of Richard I on board ship, leaving the Holy Land, to which he had given the best of his years and energies:

And all night long the vessel sped on by starlight, till, as the morning broke, the King, after long reflection, broke out into prayer: 'O Holy Land, to God do I entrust thee. May He, of His mercy, only grant me such span of life that, by His good will, I may bring thee aid . . .' And with this prayer, he pressed his sailors to set all sail.

When the Count of Brienne first landed in Palestine he arrived with

his galley all painted, within and without, with escutcheons of his arms . . . He had at least three hundred rowers in his galley, and for each rower there was a targe with the count's arms thereon, and to each targe was a pennon attached with his arms wrought in gold.

'Culloden': *see* MUTINY.

Culverin: a long-barrelled cannon of about 5-in. calibre, much favoured by the Elizabethans, and probably the main armament of the English ships in the fight against the Armada. It fired a ball weighing about 18 lb., whereas a cannon fired shot up to 50 lb. Its range is open to debate, but its longest possible carry was about $1\frac{1}{4}$ miles, whilst its effective range was about 350 yards. There were many types of culverin, which remained in favour for many years.

Cunard Steamship Company: famous steamship company, taking its name from its founder, Sir Samuel Cunard (1787–1865), who secured from the British Admiralty the contract to carry the American mail. The original fleet (1840) consisted of four wooden paddle-wheel steamers, the *Britannia, Acadia, Columbia* and *Caledonia,* each 207 ft long, built on the Clyde and with an average horsepower of 440. The maiden voyage, made by the *Britannia,* took 14 days 8 hours from Liverpool to Boston. After a series of 13 wooden steamers, the company went over to iron, and the iron paddle steamer *Persia* (1856) was for a time the fastest powered ship afloat, capable of 14 knots. In the Crimean War the company loaned 14 Cunarders to the British government. Cunard ships broke many records, the *Scotia* (launched 1862) having an average speed of 14·4 knots and reducing the New York–Liverpool time to 8 days 22 hours. *Servia* (1881), the largest ship of her day, with a speed of nearly 17 knots, was the first of the company's vessels to be constructed of steel and to have electric light. The *Carmania* (1905) was the first Atlantic liner to be equipped with turbine engines. Other famous Cunarders were the *Lusitania,* sunk

A cruiser.

by a German torpedo (7 May 1915) with the loss of 1198 lives, and the immortal *Mauretania* which, in 1924, did the 3198 miles from Ambrose Channel Light Vessel to Cherbourg Breakwater in 5 days 1 hour 49 minutes, at an average speed of 26·25 knots. *See also QUEEN ELIZABETH; QUEEN MARY.*

Cunningham (of Hyndhope), **Andrew,** first Viscount (1883–1963): admiral and First Sea Lord (1943–6). One of the most distinguished modern naval commanders, he won the D.S.O. and two bars in the First World War, and in the Second World War he was Commander-in-Chief Mediterranean and Allied Commander-in-Chief in the North African campaign. Apart from his British decorations he was honoured by France, Greece, Holland and the U.S.A.

From a portrait by R. Langmand, 1942.

Currach: primitive small boat used in Ireland, especially on the west coast and in the Aran Islands. In construction it is very similar to the CORACLE.

Curtis, Sir Roger (1746–1816): admiral. In the course of more than 40 years' service he saw action in many parts of the world. At one time he commanded Lord Howe's flag-ship, and he destroyed the floating batteries at Gibraltar (1782).

Cutlass: a fairly broad, often curved, sword; in the Navy used by the ship's company as distinct from the officers' swords. In the 1790s some seamen were using a cutlass about 28 in. long and $1\frac{1}{2}$ in. wide, with an ivory grip, heavy brass pommel and brass knuckle bow. By 1800 the weapon was rather cheaper, with a straight blade, iron grip and guard. There were several changes of pattern in the 19th century, the weapon at times being little different from that used by a heavy cavalry trooper. In fact, in 1903 the Army sold to the Admiralty a quantity of old so-called 'pioneer' saw-backed swords for use as naval cutlasses, though the Navy apparently never issued them.

Cutter: type of vessel much used for scouting and similar purposes in the 18th and 19th centuries. The first cutters to enter the Royal Navy were purchased in 1763. Though built for speed, they were strong and seaworthy. Single-masted, they carried a large mainsail with several subsidiary sails, and anything up to twelve guns, with additional carronades and swivels.

A cutter is also one of the standard ship's boats, smaller than a barge.

Cutting-out: the act of entering a port or harbour and seizing a ship or ships by sudden surprise attack. The expedition was usually carried out by ship's boats. The following is typical:

Proceeding next to the Mediterranean, he [Lieutenant George Mitford Monk] participated there in much boat-service on the coasts of Spain, France, and Italy. On 16 May 1813, we find him aiding, in the boats of his own ship and the *Euryalus* 36 . . . at the capture and destruction of *La Fortune* xebec of 10 guns, 4 swivels, and 95 men, and of 22 vessels collected under the enemy's batteries (which were likewise taken) in the harbour of Cavalarie.

William O'Byrne, *Naval Biographical Dictionary* (1849)

'Cutty Sark': the best-known of British clipper ships, though not, as is often thought, the fastest. She was built in 1869 by Scott and Linton, Dumbarton, for the China trade, though it was after she moved over to the Australian wool run that she achieved her greatest reputation. The *Cutty Sark* is a composite ship, with wooden planks over iron frames, and wooden keel, stem and stern. Her length is 212·5 ft; breadth, 36 ft; depth, 21 ft; tons register, 963. She could carry a cargo of something over 5000 bales of wool; her record was 5304 bales, which lowered her two inches below her Plimsoll marks. 'Cutty sark' means 'short shirt', though the famous figurehead is clothed in adequately long garments.

With the decline of the clipper trade, the ship fell on hard times and lost much of her original beauty. She was rescued (1922) by Captain DOWMAN; and now, magnificently restored, she is in permanent dry dock at Greenwich.

See also MOODIE, CAPTAIN GEORGE; OLD WHITE HAT; TIPTAFT, CAPTAIN W. E.; WOODGET, CAPTAIN RICHARD.

> Ay, many a time he's seen her,
>   All splendid from the sea,
> Come swaying up from south'ard
>   With chests of China tea,
> Or, loaded to her hatches
>   With Riverina bales,
> Lead home the racing wool fleet
>   Rip-roaring for the sales!

Cecily Fox Smith, 'The *Cutty Comes Back*'

Cutwater: the fore-part of a ship's prow or bow, which cuts through the water. *See p.577.*

Part of a seaman's neckerchief illustrating cutlass exercise.

D., D.D. and **R.**: familiar abbreviations found in old ships' logs, standing for 'Discharged' (i.e. to another ship), 'Discharged Dead' (from shipboard accident, sickness or in battle) and 'Run' (deserted).

Dakar: an important port in Senegal on the coast of W. Africa. In September 1940 Dakar was the scene of an abortive British expedition in which General de Gaulle was a key figure. It was hoped that the port, at that time part of the French colonial empire, would, under a show of force and the persuasion of General de Gaulle, turn from the Vichy government of France and side with the Allies. A French squadron had, however, passed the Straits of Gibraltar, eluded the British ships and arrived at Dakar to strengthen resistance. All overtures by de Gaulle and his Free French were spurned, and fighting began between the British and French ships and shore batteries. The French battleship *Richelieu* lay in the harbour as well as other ships, and though she was damaged, so were the British battleship *Resolution* and the cruiser *Cumberland*. The engagement was a failure due to a combination of mischances, and the only beneficial outcome was that it put a limit to the spread of Vichy influence in W. Africa, for within a fortnight the Free French cause was established at Duala in the French Cameroons.

Damant, Guybon Chesney Castell: *see LAURENTIC.*

Dampier, William (1652–1715): Royal Navy captain, hydrographer and pirate. In an extraordinary career which began with a spell as a merchant seaman and work on a Jamaica plantation, he joined a company of buccaneers and shared in the raids of 1679–81 on Porto Bello, the Isthmus, Peru and Chile. Further piratical and privateering voyages over a period of eight years took him round the world, till in 1691 he arrived back in England with a journal which he had carefully written over a long period and carried round with him concealed in hollow bamboos. His *New Voyage Round the World* (1697) and *Discourse of Winds* (1699) brought him fame and influential friends and proved him to be much more than a pirate: in fact, a gifted narrator and an acute observer of natural and scientific phenomena. He was commissioned captain in the Navy in 1698 and commanded a voyage of exploration in

William Dampier: from a portrait by T. Murray.

the *ROEBUCK*. His career as a more respectable member of society was, however, much less successful than his former life, since, though he was a tough and hardy seaman, he showed few talents as a commander and leader.

It is at least to Dampier's credit that, on his . . . last voyage, as pilot in Woodes Rogers's privateering cruise (1708–11) round the world, he picked up Selkirk and brought him home in time for him to become, under the name of 'Robinson Crusoe', the hero of an Odyssey hardly inferior to Homer's.

C. R. L. Fletcher, *Historical Portraits* (1919)

(Dampier had also been commander of the privateering expedition in which Alexander SELKIRK had set out.)

See colour section.

Dana, Richard Henry (1815–82): American writer, remembered for his book *Two Years before the Mast* (1840), in which he gave his experiences as a common sailor. He became an authority on maritime law, and also wrote *The Seaman's Friend* (1841).

Dan buoy: a buoy consisting of a spar surrounded by a metal float chamber, put down to mark a particular position.

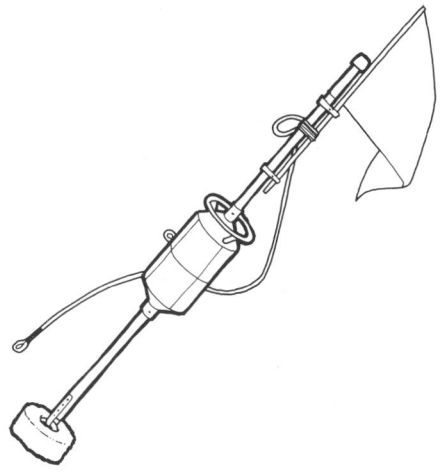

Dance, Sir Nathaniel (1748–1827): commander under the East India Company. At the end of January 1804 he sailed from Canton in the *Earl Camden* with a convoy of about 40 ships without the protection of any of H.M. ships. Encountering a French battle-squadron under Admiral Linois, Dance put on such a show of expert manoeuvring and potential force that Linois was bluffed into flight. For this exploit Dance was knighted.

Dandy: (1) sloop or cutter with a jigger mast on which a lug-sail is set; (2) a small sail carried at or near the stern of small craft.

Dandyfunk: in the old days, a ship's biscuit, pounded up with water, marmalade and fat, then baked.

Danes: the Danish invasion of Anglo-Saxon England began with raids early in the 9th century A.D., and these were soon followed by conquest and settlement. The Saxons, particularly under Alfred, fought bravely, but Mercia and Northumbria were overrun and became the Danelaw, whose southern extension was limited from Saxon Wessex by Alfred's treaty with the invaders. These northmen, vikings or warriors, came from Denmark, southern Sweden and Norway, and crossed the

North Sea in long clinker-built open ships propelled by oars with the addition of a square sail on a single mast. 'Over the low waist of the brightly painted ship hung the line of round shields, yellow and black alternately, while the high dragon-prow broke the billows in front, a terror to Christian men who saw it coming' (G. M. Trevelyan, *History of England*, 1926).

For the year 851 the *Anglo-Saxon Chronicle* gives the first record of a sea-battle in English history, when Athelstan, the under-king of Kent, defeated a Danish force off Sandwich. Gradually, after years of terrible fighting, the Saxons and the Danes, of kindred stock, came together; but, following a period of comparative freedom from invasion, a second wave of viking descents on Britain began towards the end of the 10th century. *See also* VIKINGS.

Dardanelles: a narrow strait connecting the Aegean with the Sea of Marmara, which in turn leads into the Black Sea through the Bosporus. The channel has always been of great strategic and commercial importance. Across it Xerxes in 480 B.C. built a bridge of boats for the invasion of Greece, and in 334 B.C. Alexander the Great passed over the Dardanelles to begin his invasion of Asia.

In the struggle against Napoleon a British squadron under Sir John Duckworth was sent to force the Dardanelles with a view to assisting the Russians (1806). The passage was made and the British ships anchored within eight miles of Constantinople, but had to withdraw because they had insufficient military force in support.

In 1915 the Dardanelles was the scene of an unsuccessful attempt by the Allies to take the GALLIPOLI peninsula, with Constantinople as its objective.

Darien: a name given to the eastern part of the Isthmus of Panama. It was the scene in 1510 of the first attempted European settlement in South America. Three years later Balboa crossed the Isthmus to reach the Pacific Ocean.

Darien Company: company formed in 1695 with the object of colonizing the Atlantic side of the Isthmus of Panama, thus providing a commercial entrepôt between the east and the west. Formed under an Act passed by the Scottish Parliament, with support from the English representative, it caused such an outcry at Westminster, on the grounds that special privileges were being given to the northern Parliament, that William III disowned his commissioner's act and all English capital was withdrawn. Led by the banker William Paterson, however, the scheme went ahead, indifferently planned, ill-equipped and under-financed. When the small fleet sailed in 1698, not even the exact destination was known, and, for the purposes of trading with Spaniards and Indians in tropical conditions, the colonists took with them such incongruous goods as cumbersome periwigs, heavy woollen materials and hundreds of English Bibles. The first settlement, named New Caledonia, failed miserably and, with their numbers badly depleted, the intended colonists would not even await the arrival of reinforcements from home. Four more ships, with 1300 men, were sent in 1699, but their attempts to do better were thwarted by sickness, internal squabbles, and the threat of armed intervention by Spain, who claimed the territory and sent a squadron of ships.

Darling, Grace Horsley (1815–42): name imperishable in the annals of the sea for her heroism in rescuing a number of survivors from the *Forfarshire*, a steamer bound from

From a portrait by H. Perlee Parker.

Hull to Dundee with 63 passengers on board, which was wrecked on the Farne Islands (7 September 1838). Her father, William Darling, was keeper of the Longstone (Farne) lighthouse. In the teeth of the gale, father and daughter reached the wreck in their coble and brought back four men and a woman. Two of the rescued men and William Darling then returned and brought off the four other survivors. Grace and her father were much fêted, received a public subscription and the Gold Medal of the Humane Society. Doubtless her exposure on this and other occasions contributed to her death from consumption at the early age of 27.

A museum at Bamburgh, Northumberland, still houses the coble used in the rescue – a frail open rowing boat, 21 ft long and 6 ft wide. It was built c.1830 and continued in use at the Longstone till 1873. Among the other relics in the museum is a page from Grace Darling's school copybook, with the sentence 'Friends in adversity are not often found.'

Darning the water: in the old days, plying backwards and forwards before a blockaded port or harbour.

Dartmouth: town and seaport on the Dart estuary on the Devon coast east of Plymouth. It is the home of the Britannia ROYAL NAVAL COLLEGE, where so many thousands of R.N. officers have received their early training. But its history goes back to at least the Middle Ages, when there was a wine trade with Bordeaux:

> A Shipman was ther, wonynge fer by weste.
> For aught I woot, he was of Dertemouthe...
> Ful many a draughte of wyn had he ydrawe
> Fro Burdeux-ward, whil that the chapman
>   sleep.
>
> Chaucer, *The Canterbury Tales* (c.1387)

In 1190 Richard Coeur de Lion's Crusaders set out from Dartmouth, and in 1620 the *Mayflower* on her way to America anchored off the town. In the Second World War it was one of the ports of embarkation of American troops for the invasion of Normandy.

See also MAGDELAYNE.

Darwin, Charles: *see BEAGLE.*

Date Line (or **International Date Line**): an imaginary line running from north to south through the Pacific Ocean, corresponding to the 180th meridian, but with some variations to avoid land. On crossing this line, which is of equal longitude east and west of Greenwich, it is internationally accepted that the date changes, forward by one day if travelling west, and similarly backward by one day if travelling east. The reason for this is that for every 15° of longitude the time by the sun varies by one hour. Thus when it is noon at Greenwich it is by the sun one hour past noon at 15° east of Greenwich, and one

113

hour before noon at 15° west; and when 180° have been travelled either east or west there is respectively a difference of plus or minus twelve hours. This would give travellers different days and dates as they went round the world. So to meet the problem it is agreed that a day is subtracted when crossing the International Date Line from the east and added when crossing it from the west. In other words, the same day and date are used on two successive days on the eastward crossing, and one calendar day is lost or omitted on the westward crossing.

Dauber: the name given to the ship's painter and lamp-man; and the title of a long poem by John Masefield, full of seafaring interest and information.

Davis (or **Davys**), **Captain John** (*c.*1550–1605): explorer and navigator who gave his name to the Davis Strait separating Greenland from North America and connecting Baffin Bay with the open Atlantic. In 1585 he commanded an expedition, financed mainly by London and West Country merchants, to discover a NORTH-WEST PASSAGE to China and named a number of places after friends and supporters at home – Mount Ralegh, Cape Walsingham, Gilbert Sound etc. After several other important voyages he was killed in an encounter with Japanese pirates off Singapore.

A staunch Puritan, he was one of the greatest Tudor seamen, with an indomitable faith in the maritime destinies of England. He invented the BACK-STAFF, and his published works include *The Worldes Hydrographical Description, whereby it appears that there is a short and speedie Passage into the South Seas to China* (1595) and *The Seamens Secrets* (1594).

There is no doubt but that we of England are

this saved people, by the eternal and infallible presence of the Lord predestinated to be sent unto these Gentiles in the sea, to those Isles and famous Kingdoms, there to preach the peace of the Lord.

Davis, in Richard Hakluyt's Principall Navigations (1589–1600)

See MOONSHINE.

Davis, John (*d.*1622): navigator who made a voyage to the East Indies and wrote *A Ruter … for Readie Sailings into the East India* (1618).

Davis's quadrant: *see* BACK-STAFF.

Davit (pronounced 'dayvit'): the davit is an upright construction for lowering and hoisting a ship's boats and is generally used in pairs, with falls or tackle secured to the bows and stern of the boat. There are many different patterns of davit, the simplest being manually operated, and others in bigger ships either by a hand winch or by power.

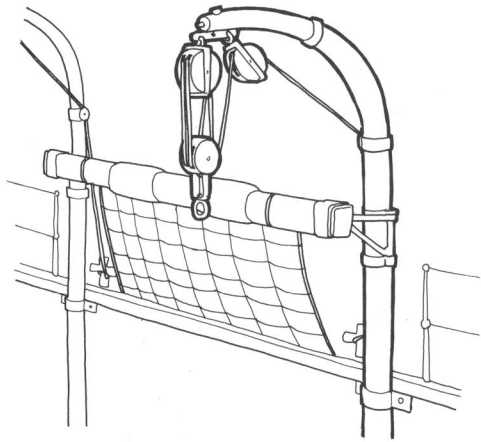

Davy Jones's locker: in old-time sailors' language Davy Jones was a popular name for the evil spirit of the sea, and his locker was at the bottom of the sea where drowned men go.

Davys: *see* DAVIS, CAPTAIN JOHN.

D-Day (6 June 1944): the day during the Second World War when the Allies landed in northern France, with an invasion fleet of over 4000 vessels.

Dead-eye: a block with three holes for tightening a rope.

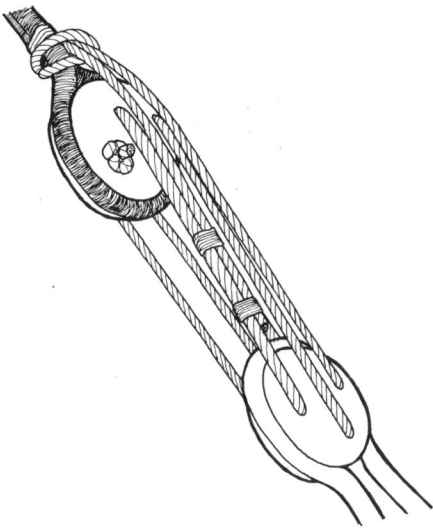

Deadlight: a strong metal hinged plate secured over a scuttle (or porthole in landlubbers' parlance). Its purpose is to exclude (or conceal) light and to give extra strength to the opening.

Dead reckoning: the calculation of a ship's position since it was last fixed by observation of the heavenly bodies or of the land. From the last known position, the course steered and the distance run, with allowance for the effect of any tide, current and wind, or leeway, are laid on the chart to give the dead reckoning position.

Dead reckoning inevitably was formerly the principal method of navigation, especially when celestial observation might be impossible for days on end, before the use of the chronometer for calculating longitude, and before the invention of the many modern navigational aids. Nevertheless, dead reckoning is still much used for a quick check between fixes.

Deal: one of the original Cinque Ports on the coast of East Kent. It remained of considerable importance until the mid-18th century, for the town supplied and serviced ships anchored in the DOWNS.

Deane, Sir Anthony (1638?–1721): shipbuilder and inventor. A friend of Samuel Pepys, he became master shipwright at Harwich (1664) and a Commissioner of the Navy (1675). He wrote the *Doctrine of Naval Architecture* (1670), the manuscript of which belonged to Pepys and is preserved at Cambridge. He also invented a new type of cannon, the 'Punchinello'.

Mr Deane and I did discourse about his ship *Rupert*, built by him, which succeeds so well as he hath got great honour by it, and I some, by recommending him.

Samuel Pepys, *Diary* (19 May 1666)

Deane, Richard (1610–53): admiral and 'General at Sea'; an artillery expert who had probably made sea voyages in his youth and who, having commanded the Parliamentary guns in Cornwall and at Naseby (1644–5), was put in charge of the coast from Portsmouth to Milford Haven (1649) and was with Blake in the battle off Portland Bill (1653). He was killed in the Battle of the GABBARD in the same year.

De Burgh, Hubert (*d.*1243): chief justiciar of England who, in a varied career, showed some talent for naval command. In August 1217 he completely defeated a French invasion fleet, one of his devices apparently being to blind the enemy by throwing quick-lime into their eyes. A vivid illustration of the battle occurs in Matthew Paris's *Chronica Majora* (1245–59).

Decatur, Captain Stephen (1779–1820): distinguished U.S. naval officer, several times wounded in action. In the 1812 Anglo-American War he captured H.M.S. *Macedonian*; but in 1815 his frigate the *President* was captured by the British, chiefly as the result of the sustained pursuit and attack by the frigate *ENDYMION*. William James gives an instructive account of the methods adopted by ships to gain speed when pursued:

> Towards noon the wind decreased; and the *Endymion*, in consequence, began to leave the *Majestic* and gain upon the *President*. At 1h.15m. P.M., the American frigate commenced lightening herself, by starting her water, cutting away her anchors, throwing overboard provisions, spare spars, boats, and every article of the sort that could be got at: she also kept her sails constantly wet from the royals down.
>
> *Naval History of Great Britain* (1822)

Decatur eventually became a Navy Commissioner and held office till he was killed in a duel. One phrase of his has passed into the standard books of quotations – 'our country, right or wrong':

Our country! In her intercourse with foreign nations may she always be in the right; but our country, right or wrong.

'Decatur': *see CONSTITUTION.*

Deckers: in the old navy, ships were described according to the number of their gundecks: thus, 'three-decker' (ships of the first and second rates), 'two-decker' etc.

Deckhead: the underside of the deck or what a landlubber would call the 'ceiling'.

Deck-house: any small enclosure or shelter on the upper deck.

Decks: the various horizontal levels in a ship used for a variety of purposes – movement, accommodation, stowage etc. In the old sailing ships of the line the lowest deck was the orlop, in which there were no ports. Above this came the lower deck, where the heaviest guns were found and where most of the seamen lived (hence today the words 'lower deck' refer to the men not of officer rank). Above the lower deck came the middle deck, where the medium-sized guns were found, and then

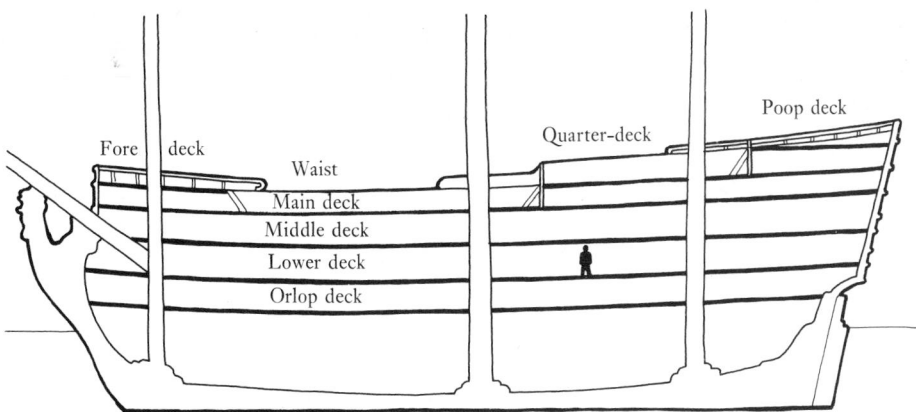

Fore deck
Waist
Quarter-deck
Poop deck
Main deck
Middle deck
Lower deck
Orlop deck

above this the main deck, with the 18-pounder guns. Partial decks above the main deck gave the quarter-deck, the preserve of the officers, and the poop, which was right aft and from which the ship was steered and commanded. Right forward was the forecastle, another partial deck with the capstan or windlass; and in between was the waist. With the development of the ship, both war and merchant, many different decks with different names were developed; thus we have decks designated weather deck, flight deck, cargo deck, promenade deck etc.

'Defence': a celebrated name in the Royal Navy. The most famous of the line is the 74-gun ship launched from Plymouth Dockyard in 1763. She was with Rodney when he sailed to the relief of Gibraltar (1779), shared in the capture of the important Spanish Caracas convoy (January 1780) and, a week later, in an action against a fleet of 14 Spanish ships of the line, when seven ships were captured or destroyed, the *Defence* suffering 31 killed or wounded. But her most glorious days were yet to come, when she fought at the Glorious First of June, under Howe, and at the Nile and Trafalgar with Nelson. Despite some disparaging references to her as a 'praying ship' under the deeply religious Gambier, she showed no meek piety when she was the first to break the enemy line at the FIRST OF JUNE, losing 54 killed and wounded and having all her masts shot away. At Trafalgar she captured the Spanish *Ildefonso*. After surviving battle and tempest for nearly 50 years, she was lost on the coasts of Jutland on Christmas Eve 1811, with the loss of most of her crew of 530.

Defoe, Daniel: *see ROBINSON CRUSOE.*

Delavall, Sir Ralph (*d.*1707): admiral. He held various commands, including that of the rear squadron at Beachy Head (1690) and Barfleur (1692). He was removed because of his sympathies with the exiled Stuarts.

Demi-cannon: a smaller piece of ordnance than the whole cannon. It threw a 32-lb. shot, had a range of about a mile, and was the largest gun in the Elizabethan navy.

Demi-culverin: a long and effective gun somewhat smaller than the full CULVERIN, and throwing a shot of about 9 lb.

Denmark: Denmark consists of the peninsula of Jutland and groups of islands, of which Funen and Zealand are the chief, commanding the entrance to the Baltic. In addition to the early invasions of England by the DANES, Denmark's long history touches upon British naval history principally through the Armed Neutralities of 1780 and 1800. These were combinations of the Baltic powers (of which Denmark was one) to resist the British claim that enemy goods were prizes of war no matter in what ships they were carried, whether in neutral convoy or not. It was in opposing the Second Armed Neutrality that Nelson destroyed the Danish fleet in COPENHAGEN harbour (1801). In 1807, to forestall Napoleon's threat to Denmark, which would give France the command of the entrance to the Baltic, a British fleet was sent to lay off Elsinore, and troops were landed to bombard Copenhagen and force the surrender of the Danes, so that most of their fleet passed into British keeping for the duration of the war.

Departure: the last fixing of a ship's position by a sight of the land.

The Departure is not the ship's going away from her port any more than the Landfall can be looked upon as a synonym of arrival ... the seaman takes his Departure by means of cross-bearings which fix the place of the first tiny pencil-cross on the white expanse of the track-chart ...

Joseph Conrad, *The Mirror of the Sea* (1906)

Depression: a circulating mass of air having the lowest pressure at its centre. The air circulates in a counter-clockwise direction in the northern hemisphere, and clockwise in the southern hemisphere. In the latitudes of the British Isles much of the weather is produced by depressions, and will vary according to the intensity of the depression in the strength of the wind and amounts of cloud and rain.

Deptford: an area of S.E. London on a reach of the River Thames. The first royal dockyard was founded here, by Henry VIII in 1509, when, of course, Deptford lay outside London, but it is further up river than Greenwich. It continued as a naval shipyard until as late as 1870.

Depth charge: an explosive weapon, dropped or projected, and set to explode at a given depth to destroy submarines.

H.M.S. *Holmes* depth-charging a suspected submarine, 1944.

Derelict: a vessel abandoned at sea, usually in the expectation of disaster, but sometimes in more mysterious circumstances. One of the most famous derelicts in history was the *MARY CELESTE*. Particularly in the days of wooden ships, derelicts could sometimes wander the seas for years, following unpredictable courses and covering thousands of miles with no one on board. Under the laws of salvage, an abandoned ship, especially with her cargo intact, can mean rich rewards for those who bring her into port.

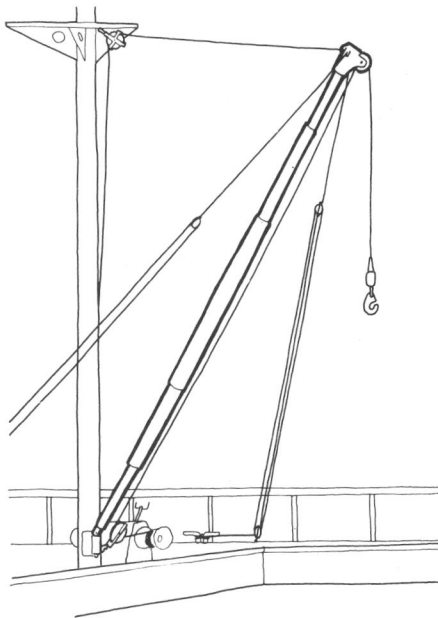

Derrick: a strong spar or boom, pivoted at the base and rigged so that it can be used for hoisting in a variety of positions.

De Ruyter, Michael Adrianzoon (1607–76): Dutch admiral, one of the most redoubtable opponents of England in the ANGLO-DUTCH WARS, his most celebrated exploit being to bring his fleet up the

Thames itself (1667). One of his friends described him as

well-made in figure, agile, robust, and as if born for work. He had a wide forehead, a ruddy complexion, somewhat high in colour ... He had a bushy, curled-up moustache, in the fashion of sailors of former times ... He was naturally healthy, but in his youth he had once been accidentally poisoned through eating bad fish; this had resulted in a slight trembling in all his limbs, which lasted to the end of his life.

Desertion: the abandonment of a ship without leave. In the hard days of the sailing Navy, desertion was a constant problem: ships' log-books often show 'R.' or 'Run' in their muster-rolls, meaning 'deserted'. The East Indiaman *Sulivan*, which left for a voyage to India and China in 1792, had 52 out of a crew of 110 'run' at Plymouth – the last chance before the round trip of nearly two years (though, in other cases, hard-used seamen would sometimes desert in a foreign port and forfeit all their wages). Desertion in the Royal Navy was a very serious offence and was invariably heavily punished if the offender was caught. Cases of 500 lashes with the cat-o'-nine tails, and many

Part of a contemporary account depicting de Ruyter's attack on the British fleet in the Medway.

A destroyer.

sentences of death, can be found in 18th-century records. Nevertheless, thousands of seamen annually were prepared to take the risk. One record shows that in the short period May 1803–June 1805 over 12,000 deserted.

Destroyer: the development of the torpedo and of torpedo boats during the 1880s led to the building of torpedo boat destroyers. The first of these, *Havoc* and *Hornet*, completed in 1893, were the forerunners of the modern destroyer; they were very fast (27 knots), only 180 ft long, with $5\frac{1}{2}$ ft draft, and a displacement of 320 tons. Their armament consisted of torpedo tubes, a 12-pounder and three 6-pounder guns. The size of destroyers and their capacity for different duties increased, and in both the First and Second World Wars the part they played in anti-submarine and convoy escort duties was enormous, whilst in a multitude of actions as supporting forces their prestige and value were continually enhanced. For general anti-submarine and escort duties the frigate has replaced the destroyer, but a new class of modern destroyers is now building, of which the *Sheffield* was commissioned in 1975. This ship displaces over 3000 tons, has a speed of 30 knots and a crew of 300 officers and men. She carries an anti-submarine helicopter and is armed with missile launchers as well as guns.

'Deutschland': *see* POCKET BATTLE-SHIPS.

'Devastation': one of the first modern battleships, in that she marked the end of the sailing warship. Designed by Sir Edward Reed (1830–1906), she was 285 ft long, 62·3 ft wide, armour-plated to a thickness of 10–14 in. on the gun turrets ($8\frac{1}{2}$–12 in. on the hull) and equipped with four 12-in. muzzle-loaders. Launched in 1873, she was with the fleet at Con-stantinople (1878), became a guardship at Plymouth (1900), and was broken up in 1908.

Devereux, Robert, second Earl of Essex (1567–1601): a favourite of Queen Eliz-abeth I, a cousin of hers on her mother's side. Throughout his life he showed himself a strong-willed, hot-tempered, generous, impulsive and courageous man, as when he slipped away secretly in 1589 and joined an expedition with Drake, an action which he knew the Queen would veto. Nevertheless, this 'rash and temera-rious youth' was put in command of one of the squadrons which attacked CADIZ under Lord Howard of Effingham in 1596. Essex captured Cadiz with his forces and returned home virtually the hero of the expedition. A year later he was given command of the Islands' Voyage to capture the Spanish treasure ships and the Azores. Here he showed incapacity as a leader, and his reputation steadily declined until, after an ill-advised rising in the City of London itself, he was executed on 25 February 1601.

Deviation: the iron in a ship, or any other local source of magnetism, will deflect the needle of the compass from the magnetic meridian. The extent of this deflection will depend on the relative strength of the earth's and of the local magnetic fields and on their relative directions. When this is determined, it is known as the deviation of the compass.

Devitt & Moore: shipping firm that played a great part in nautical education. In 1890, with Earl Brassey, they inaugurated a scheme for training officers in ocean-going sailing ships, such as the *Harbinger* and *Hesperus*. This scheme was maintained till 1909 when a new company, Messrs Devitt & Moore's Ocean Training Ships Ltd, was formed, the shareholders being a number of the chief shipping companies. This in turn ceased in 1917 when the Devitt family established the Nautical College at PANG-BOURNE. *See also MACQUARIE.*

Devonport: lying on the estuary of the River Tamar, Devonport was begun as an extension of PLYMOUTH at the end of the 17th century (*see* DOCKYARD), and was given its modern name in 1824. It is an important base and dockyard for the Royal Navy, and the estuary, known as the Hamoaze, provides an extensive anchorage. Devonport was the birthplace of Captain Robert Falcon Scott of Antarctic fame.

Devonshire: perhaps no county in England has a greater association with the sea than Devon. Lying on the south-western peninsula at the mouth of the English Channel, its harbours, ships and seamen have been famous down the ages, particularly in Tudor times: Drake, Ralegh, Humphrey Gilbert, Richard Grenville and Hawkins were all men of Devon. Plymouth, Dartmouth, Bideford and the many small harbours and the rocky coasts were the breeding ground for a proud maritime history.

Dhow: an Arab trading vessel, rigged with a lateen sail, and usually with one mast. Some dhows are now power-driven. They are commonly to be seen in the north-western coastal areas of the Indian Ocean.

Diagonally doubled: system of planking a wooden ship in which a second layer of planks was laid over the first. This 'doubling' was arranged vertically amidships, but diagonally fore and aft, an arrangement thought to give greater strength and resistance to stress.

Dibdin, Charles (1745–1814): actor, dramatist and song-writer, chiefly remembered for his sea songs, of which the earliest success was 'Blow high, blow low', written in a gale during a thirteen hours' passage from Calais (1776). But his best-known nautical song is 'Tom Bowling', said to have been in memory of his sailor brother Tom. He wrote some 90 sea songs, all of which have appealing gusto, but these were but a part of an enormous output of other songs, plays and sketches.

> Here, a sheer hulk, lies poor Tom Bowling,
> The darling of our crew;
> No more he'll hear the tempest howling
> For death has broach'd him to.

Dinghy: a very small rowing boat with or without a sail; a name also given to small collapsible boats for emergency use by airmen.

Dipsey (dipsie or **dipsy):** a corruption of 'deep sea', used in sailing days for the 'deep-sea' lead for sounding depths. The word has also been applied to both the float and the sinker of a fishing line.

Dirk: naval weapon, usually associated with midshipmen, though in fact it was sometimes worn by commissioned officers and even admirals. No precise specification for the dirk was issued till 1856, so that up to that time there was considerable variety. Before 1825 it was usually a light weapon with a tapered blade, double-edged and anything from 8 to 18 in. long. The 1856 dirk had a lion's-head pommel and white fish-skin grip, with a blade $1\frac{1}{8}$ in. wide and only about a foot long – a cause for complaint among midshipmen when they found themselves involved in hand-to-hand fighting ashore. The length was later increased to about 18 in.

'Discovery': as is fitting, a famous ship name in the annals of exploration. One *Discovery* sailed with Captain Cook on his third voyage (1776–9). Another conveyed Robert Falcon Scott in the National Antarctic Expedition (1901–4). This *Discovery* is now permanently moored at the Victoria Embankment, London, and public access is given to the wardroom, upper deck, bridge and Scott's cabin. Fears have recently been expressed for her future, since it was estimated that £100,000 (more than twice the cost of her original building) was needed to cure the extensive rot revealed by surveys.

Discovery, Age of: term frequently applied to the period *c*.1420–1600, which saw a great series of voyages and expeditions by various countries and nationalities. Especially notable were the voyages down the west coast of Africa by Prince Henry the Navigator's captains, following the establishment of his geographical seminary at Cape Sagres (1419); the rounding of the Cape of Good Hope by Bartholomew Diaz (1487); Vasco da Gama's voyage to India via the Cape (1497); John Cabot's second voyage (1497); Columbus's voyages (1492–1504); Amerigo Vespucci's two expeditions to the New World (1499–1502); Ferdinand Magellan's circumnavigation of the globe

Discovery forcing the pack ice during the Antarctic expedition.

(1519–22), and Drake's circumnavigation (1577–80). *See also* CIRCUMNAVIGATION.

Displacement: *see* TONNAGE.

Distress signals: *see* ROCKET; SIGNALS; SOS.

Ditty bag (or **box**): a small container for holding a sailor's personal possessions. The origin of the word 'ditty' in this sense is not known.

Diving: a general term covering underwater action by man or the submerging of a submarine. There is a great variety of apparatus to allow man to dive and work underwater, either with air supplied from above or freely, as with the modern aqualung, the development of which owes much to the work of the Frenchman Captain Jacques Yves Cousteau. *See also* DIVING BELL; HALDANE, JOHN SCOTT; SALVAGE.

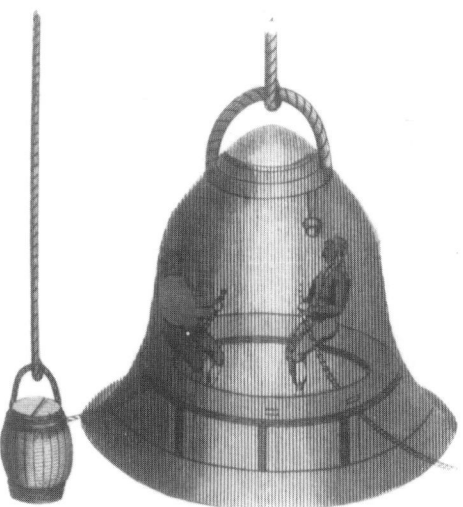

Diving bell: a metal chamber in which persons can be lowered into the water, kept dry and supplied with air, for the purpose of underwater work and inspection. History records that as early as the 4th century B.C. Alexander the Great descended into the ocean in a machine called a *colimpha*, which admitted light and kept the occupant dry; and Francis Bacon (1561–1626) described 'a hollow vessel, made of metal' which was 'let down equally to the surface of the water, and thus carried with it to the bottom of the sea the whole of the air which it contained'. In 1683 Archibald Miller examined through a window in a diving bell the wreck of a Spanish galleon which had gone down a hundred years before in TOBERMORY BAY. *See also* BATHYSPHERE.

Divisions: a ship's company in the Royal Navy is divided into divisions, each under a Divisional Officer, who has a general responsibility for the work and well-being of his men. The word is also the name for the muster or assembly for inspection and other purposes.

Docks: sheltered spaces for the loading,

123

discharge, and storing and repairing of ships. They are of many kinds, and can be open to the rise and fall of the tide or enclosed with a water level regulated by gates. A dry dock or graving dock can be pumped or drained dry to allow attention to a ship's hull, which can also be done in a floating dock.

Dockyard: a general term given to all the area of docks and buildings concerned with the building and working of ships. The term 'dockyard port' generally refers to one under the jurisdiction of the Royal Navy, for example Devonport. *See also* ROYAL DOCKYARDS; NAVAL BASES.

Dog-days: a name popularly given to the hottest part of the year in July and August, formerly so named because it is the time of the year when Sirius, the dog-star, rises and sets with the sun.

Dogger Bank: an extensive shallow part of the North Sea between England and Denmark. For centuries it was famous as a fishing ground, but in recent years catches have diminished. The area is part of the North Sea oilfield, and oil-rigs now stand gaunt above the waves.

Dogger Bank, Battles of the: (1) inconclusive action fought on 5 August 1781 between the English and Dutch; although vigorous, it was fought in the old line-ahead style and no ship was lost on either side; (2) battle of the First World War fought on 24 January 1915 between a British naval squadron under Admiral Beatty and a German reconnoitring force under Admiral Hipper. When the attack began, the Germans made for their home base of Heligoland, losing the cruiser *Blücher* in the process. On the British side, the *Lion* was disabled.

Dog-star: a popular name for Sirius, the principal star in the constellation Canis Major.

Dog watches: the two-hour WATCHES between 1600 and 1800 hours and 1800 and 2000 hours.

Doldrums: those areas on and either side of the Equator where calm or very light inconstant winds prevail and where consequently sailing ships often made little progress. Hence to be 'in the doldrums' means to be downcast.

Dolphin: (1) a sea mammal similar to the porpoise and a member of the whale family, but only about 5 to 10 ft long; (2) a strong structure of wood or stone standing in the water and to which ships can be secured.

Dolphin-striker: an old name for a stay on the bows used in rigging the jib.

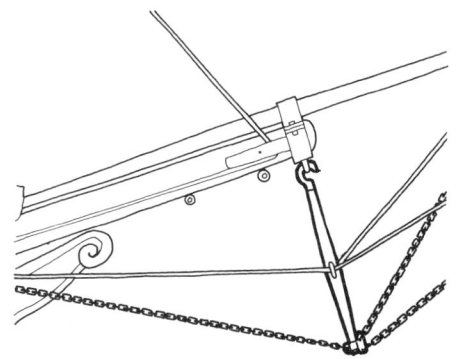

Domett, Sir William (1754–1828): admiral who rose from humble West Country farming stock to flag rank and a Commissionership of the Navy. He commanded Howe's flag-ship, the *Royal George*, at the 'Glorious FIRST OF JUNE' (1794) and was Fleet Captain in the Baltic expedition and the Battle of Copenhagen (1801).

Dominica: an island of the Lesser Antilles in the Caribbean Sea. It was named (from the Spanish for 'Sunday') by Columbus, who discovered it on a Sunday (3 November 1493) during his second voyage. It was settled by the French in 1635, but during the wars with France in the 18th century it changed hands several times, as did other West Indian islands. In the Seven Years' War it was taken by Britain, to whom it was assigned at the peace in 1763. After France's entry on the side of the Americans during the War of Independence Dominica was recaptured by the French (1778) but it was retaken after Rodney's victory at the Battle of the Saints (1782). It continued to be contested during the Napoleonic Wars, but finally after 1805 it became British. In 1978 the island became an independent republic.

Donkey engine: any small auxiliary engine used for various purposes such as turning the capstan or pumping.

Dorling, Captain H. T.: *see* TAFFRAIL.

Dory: a small open boat used by cod-fishers off the North American coast; *see also* FISHING CRAFT.

Double-hulled: having an inner and outer hull with a water-tight space between to give extra strength and buoyancy.

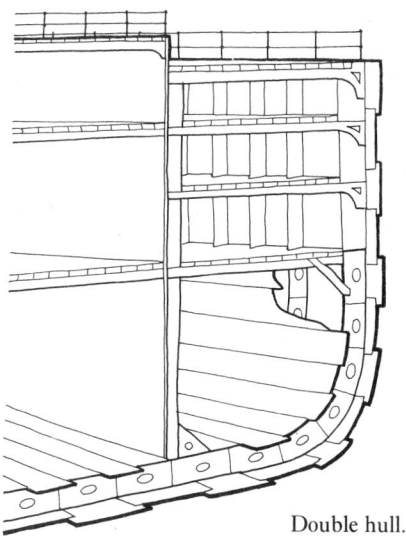

Double hull.

Double-shotted: a cannon is double-shotted when it is loaded with two shots. Ships might fire a double-shotted broadside.

Double voyage: in the days of the East Indiamen, the extended voyage on to China after the Indian ports. The owner or ship-broker usually received an extra payment per ton.

Doughty, Thomas (*fl. c.* 1577): a gentleman-adventurer companion of Francis Drake when he set sail from Plymouth (1577); accused of mutiny, he was court-martialled on charges of conspiracy and mutiny and was executed, after kneeling side by side with Drake and receiving Holy Communion. Thomas's brother John was also on board, but was acquitted of involvement. Unrest on board continuing, Drake later made a famous speech to the assembled companies of his ships:

For by the life of God it doth even take my wits from me to think on it. Here is such controversy between the sailors and the gentlemen, and such stomaching between the gentlemen and the sailors that it doth even make me mad to hear it . . . I must have the gentleman to hale and draw with the mariner, and the mariner with the gentleman.

Douglas, Sir Charles (1725–89): admiral. His most distinguished services were the relief of Quebec (1776) and his flag-captaincy of Rodney's fleet at the Battle of the Saints (1782), when five French ships were captured. He was also an inventor in naval gunnery: *see* RECOIL.

Dover: a cross-channel port with an unbroken history of maritime importance. It commands the narrow Straits of Dover, and from Roman times has played a proud part in naval history. In 1217 the ships of the CINQUE PORTS secured a victory against the French off Dover. During the First World War it was the base for the DOVER PATROL, and in the Second World War, though shelled from Cape Gris Nez on the French coast, Dover played an invaluable part in the evacuation at Dunkirk (1940) and throughout the rest of the war.

Dover, Straits of: the narrowest part of the sea between England and France, no more than 20 miles wide at its narrowest. Today the Straits are more crowded with shipping than any other part of the ocean, and special procedures for the passage of ships have been introduced.

Dover Patrol: during the First World War Dover was the headquarters of a naval force known as the Dover Patrol, whose duties were to guard the narrows of the English Channel and hunt submarines.

Dowman, Captain Wilfred (*c*.1878–1936): the sailing-ship skipper who, in retirement, saw the famous clipper *CUTTY SARK*, after she had fallen on evil times,

bought her back from her Portuguese owners (1922) and moored her in Falmouth, thus beginning the great story of her preservation and restoration to her former glory. In 1938 Mrs Dowman presented the ship to the Thames Nautical College and *Cutty Sark* was towed round to the Thames, where she served as part of the cadet training establishment.

Down Easter: originally a seaman from the extreme north-eastern state of Maine, U.S.A., which bred many fine, tough seamen; or a ship from one of its yards. Later the term came to mean any 'bucko' or hard-case officer or mate.

Downhaul: any rope for hauling down, but more specifically a rope for hauling down the jib in sailing ships.

Downs, the: a roadstead and former anchorage in part of the Straits of Dover inside the Goodwin Sands.

Now the signal was made for the grand fleet to
    anchor,
All in the Downs that night for to meet . . .

anon., 'Spanish Ladies'

Armed trawlers of the Dover Patrol in the outside harbour.

Downs, Battle of the (21 October 1639): an abject experience for the English fleet, when they signally failed to protect a Spanish fleet anchored in the Downs with Charles I's consent. Shamelessly violating British neutrality, the Dutch under Martin Tromp smashed the Spanish ships without a gun being fired in their defence.

Downton, Nicholas (*d*.1615): East India Company commander who, in company with Sir Henry Middleton, established trade connections among the Red Sea ports, and eventually became 'general' of the Company's ships in the East Indies.

Draft: a variant spelling of DRAUGHT, but in this form its naval meaning is a selected number of men to be sent to or from a ship, or to a particular duty. To draft is to select men for this purpose.

Drake, Sir Francis (1543?–1596): with Nelson, the most famous English naval commander. Brought up among ships and sailors, he made a series of voyages from 1566 onwards, several of them in association with his cousin Sir John HAWKINS. His fame and reputation, both in England and in Spain, began with his dedicated missions to defend Protestantism against Philip II of Spain and to destroy the Spanish monopoly in the New World – objectives covertly encouraged by Elizabeth I, especially as she was a substantial gainer financially. Of all Drake's exploits, probably those best remembered are his capture of the Spanish treasure train en route from Panama to NOMBRE DE DIOS (1573) and his sighting of the Pacific; his CIRCUMNAVIGATION of 1577–80 (*see also* DOUGHTY, THOMAS), after which he was knighted by the Queen at Deptford; his raid on CADIZ (1587), which set back the Armada preparations for a year; and his

Engraved portrait from the frontispiece of Drake's book *The World Encompassed*.

share in the subsequent destruction of Philip II's attempted invasion the next year. He died of yellow fever at Porto Bello in January 1596 and was buried at sea in Nombre de Dios bay.

Drake was the greatest seaman of his age, a fanatical Protestant and patriot, quick-thinking, often intolerant of less agile minds, invincibly courageous, at once kindly and ruthless, courteous and over-bearing. He was a supreme naval tactician, in many ways a pioneer and innovator in his appreciation of gun-power, his insistence on attack rather than supine defence, and his use of combined sea and land forces. *See also* EL DRAQUE; *JUDITH*.

> Round-headed, brown hair, full-bearded, his eyes round, large and clear, well-favoured, fair and of a cheerful countenance.
>
> John Stow, *Annales* (1580)

> He is called Francisco Drac, and is a man of about 35 years of age, low of stature, with a fair beard, and is one of the greatest mariners that sail the seas, both as a navigator and as a commander... He is served on silver dishes with gold borders and gilded garlands, in which are his arms. He said that many of these had been given to him by the Queen.
>
> Don Francisco da Zarate, in Richard Hakluyt's *Principall Navigations* (1589–1600)

Drake, John (*fl.*1575–95): cousin of Sir Francis Drake. He accompanied him on his circumnavigation, and on a Muscovy Company expedition which left Southampton in 1582, Francis contributed a frigate of 40 tons (named *Francis* after him) with John as its captain. The leader, Edward Fenton, lost heart at Sierra Leone; but John Drake carried on, crossed the Atlantic to the River Plate and there ran his vessel on a rock. He and his companions were held captive by the natives for some 15 months, after which he escaped in a canoe and eventually surrendered to the Spaniards. At first he was hospitably entertained by the Governor of Buenos Aires, but when his hosts learnt of his relationship to Sir Francis, the atmosphere changed and he was taken to Lima to be closely examined by the Inquisition, though he had by that time learnt Spanish and professed to be a Catholic. He was eventually granted his life but after 1595 was not heard of again.

Drake's Drum: the famous drum, by tradition once belonging to Sir Francis Drake, brought home by his brother Thomas from Nombre de Dios Bay and guarded through the centuries by his descendants at Buckland Abbey, Devon, now a museum. According to legend, if the drum was ever beaten in time of national emergency, Drake would return to deal with England's enemies.

Take my drum to England, hang it by the shore,
Strike it when your powder's running low;
If the Dons sight Devon, I'll quit the port o' Heaven,
An' drum them up the Channel as we drummed them long ago.

Sir Henry Newbolt, 'Drake's Drum' (1896)

Draught: the depth at which a vessel floats in the water; e.g. a ship may be said to 'draw twenty feet', and this is her draught. Draught varies, however, with the amount of loading and again with the nature of the water on which the ship is afloat. The draught permitted on British merchant ships is known by the Plimsoll marks or LOADLINES.

Draughts: *see* ADMIRALTY DRAUGHTS.

Draw, to: (1) to require an amount of water in order to float; e.g. a ship 'draws twenty feet' (*see also* DRAUGHT).

(2) To collect stores, cordage, victuals, ammunition etc. from store aboard or ashore.

(3) To gain or lose position in relation to another ship; e.g. to 'draw clear', 'draw ahead' or 'draw away'.

(4) To fill with wind; a sail draws when it takes the wind. To 'let draw' in a sailing boat is to haul taut the lee sheets after going about.

Dreadnought: a generic name given to a class of all-big-gun battleships of which the 1906 *Dreadnought* (*see below*) was the prototype. Admiral Sir John Fisher, as First Sea Lord, was largely instrumental in introducing these powerful, speedy, well armed and well armoured warships.

'Dreadnought': one of the ships in Drake's famous raid on Cadiz (1587), commanded by his trusted friend Thomas Fenner; and the name of other great ships, including Admiral Fisher's *Dreadnought* (1906), 'the first all-big-gun ship'. She carried ten 12-in. guns mounted in five turrets, so disposed that six could be fired forward, six aft and eight broadside. She did, in fact, have smaller guns too, for repelling torpedo boat attacks – 27 of them – as well as five torpedo tubes. She was the fastest battleship at that time (21 knots),

and the first large warship to be equipped with turbine engines. (*See also* SKEERED O' NOTHING.) *Dreadnought* was also the name chosen for Britain's first nuclear-powered submarine.

Dredger: a vessel designed to dredge and deepen channels, fairways and harbours. A dredger works by means of a revolving chain of buckets passing through her hull to take mud and other material from the sea bottom.

Dressed overall: *see* DRESS SHIP.

Dress ship: on special occasions and for celebrations such as a visit by royalty, a ship is 'dressed overall' by running a line of flags from the jack-staff up to the fore mast, then to the after mast or masts, and then down to the ensign staff on the stern.

Drifter: a fishing vessel using drift nets for catching fish, e.g. herring and mackerel, which are found in the upper layers of the sea.

Driver: (1) some sailing ships had as many as five masts, and the fifth one nearest the stern was called the driver; **(2)** another name for the SPANKER.

Drogher: a slow heavy coaster, carrying timber, cotton, lumber etc.

Drogue: the word has several applications to constructions of wood or canvas which serve as a drag at the end of a harpoon line, or as a sea anchor, or as a truncated canvas cone towed by an aircraft as a target for firing practice from a ship's anti-aircraft guns.

'Droits de l'Homme': French 74-gun ship of the line discovered off Ushant in January 1797 by Captain Sir Edward Pellew in his 44-gun frigate *Indefatigable* and the accompanying smaller frigate, *Amazon*. The action continued all through the night of 13 January, and at daybreak the *Droits de l'Homme* went ashore with terrible loss of life. The *Amazon* was also wrecked, but most of her crew landed safely and were made prisoner.

Dromon (or dromond): a large medieval

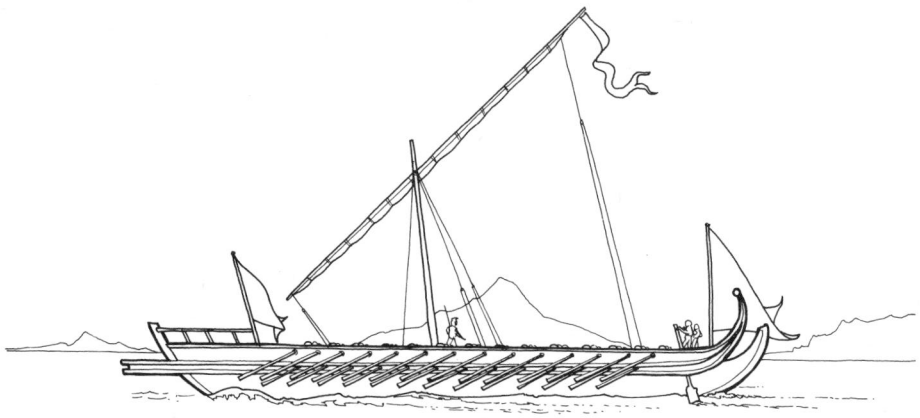

vessel propelled by many oars, and with or without a single sail.

Drowning the miller: putting too much water into the grog.

Dry dock: *see* DOCKS.

Duckworth, Sir John Thomas (1748–1817): admiral. He entered the Navy at the age of 11, and saw a great deal of action for half a century. He received a gold medal and the thanks of Parliament for his share in the three-day battle off Ushant (1794; *see ORION*) and, in 1801, the Order of the Bath and a pension of £1000 a year for taking St Bartholomew, St Thomas, and other Swedish and Danish possessions in the West Indies. He was Governor and Commander-in-Chief of Newfoundland 1810–13. *See also* DARDANELLES.

Duff (or **plum-duff**): a sailor's name for steamed suet pudding with currants.

Duff, George (1764–1805): commander of H.M.S. *Mars* at Trafalgar, killed early in the action. His young son Norwich was also on board, serving as a midshipman; he survived the battle and rose to flag rank.

Duncan, Adam, Viscount Duncan of Camperdown (1731–1804): admiral, chiefly remembered for his victory over the Dutch admiral de Winter off CAMPERDOWN (1797). Duncan had the reputation of being one of the handsomest men in the Royal Navy: 'upwards of six feet four inches in height, with limbs of proportionate frame and strength, his forehead high and fair, and his hair as white as snow'. Robert Louis Stevenson put it otherwise: 'And you will observe this is no naked Viking in a prehistoric period, but a Scotch member of Parliament with a smattering of the classics, a telescope, a cocked hat of great size and flannel underclothing.' *See also* LUTINE BELL; MUTINY.

Dundas, George (*fl.*1780–1820): admiral. He commanded some famous ships in the course of his career, including the frigate *Juno* and the 74-gun *Elephant*, but the most unusual exploit in which he was involved occurred at the Cape of Good Hope when some of his friends wagered that Dundas 'and one other' would consume sixteen pounds of tripe at a single sitting. With all the bets taken, a time and place were appointed and the officers gathered round to watch the Homeric feat. Despite his fondness for tripe, Dundas laid down his knife and fork after the first two or three pounds; whereupon his friends led in a large bear, who quickly polished off the remainder. There were loud protests and a committee of officers met to decide whether or not the wager had been won. They solemnly decided that 'and one other' satisfactorily covered the bear and that the terms had been fulfilled.

Dundas, Sir Richard Saunders (1802–61): admiral. He received the C.B. for his services in the Chinese War of 1841, became a junior lord of the Admiralty, and was Commander-in-Chief of the Baltic Fleet 1855–61.

Dundee: an ancient city and port on the north of the Firth of Tay in Scotland. The jute and associated industries developed very rapidly in the late 19th century, the raw material coming mainly from the Ganges Delta. Many ships were employed; and the convenience of picking up a deck cargo of oranges in Spain on the homeward voyage is said to have led to the making of Dundee marmalade.

Dundonald, Earl of: *see* COCHRANE, THOMAS.

Dunes, Battle of the (1657–8): actions against the pirates based on Dunkirk and Mardyke who raided English commerce in the 17th century. When Cromwell allied himself with Louis XIV against Spain, it was part of the agreement that a combined French and English army should besiege the pirate strongholds and that the towns should thereafter belong to Britain. Mardyke was captured in September 1657 and Dunkirk surrendered in June of the next year, despite a great effort by the Spaniards to raise the siege. Dunkirk remained in British hands till 1662, when,

with its dependencies, it was redeemed by Louis XIV for five million livres.

Dungeness: a shingly promontory, the most southerly point of Kent. Dungeness's lighthouse lamp, 140 ft high, and its famous lifeboat station have played an important role in the story of the sea. *See also* DUNGENESS, BATTLE OF.

Dungeness (or **the Ness**), **Battle of** (30 November 1652): encounter between the Dutch under Tromp and de Ruyter, and the English under Robert Blake, who were hopelessly outnumbered but fought a gallant action. It was after this fight that de Ruyter is alleged to have hoisted a broom to his mast-head as a sign that he had swept the sea, though there is probably little substance to the story. Much more important, the battle was to have revolutionary effects on the conduct of maritime war and the whole of naval history. The merchantmen in Blake's fleet had not properly supported him, and from then on there grew a clear differentiation between the specialized fighting ship and the merchant vessel. Moreover, Blake complained to the Admiralty that he had no legal power to punish the captains who had had no stomach for the battle. As a result, the right to hold courts-martial was granted to the commander-in-chief, and this became a potent disciplinary weapon in building the Navy into a supreme fighting force.

Dunkirk: an ancient seaport in N.E. France, lying on the Straits of Dover. It has been besieged and destroyed many times in its long history. After the Battle of the DUNES it was in English hands for four years (1658–62). In 1713 by the Treaty of Utrecht the port was destroyed and it was not allowed to be rebuilt until 1783.

Dunkirk was badly damaged during the First World War, and was almost completely destroyed in the Second World War, when the beaches of Dunkirk saw the evacuation of over 330,000 British and Allied troops before the town was taken by the Germans (1940).

Dunkirk privateers: fast-sailing pirate ships operating out of Dunkirk in the 17th century, especially on the east coast of England. At one time they established an effectual blockade of the Thames, levying a toll on London's merchants. In 1636 two famous Dunkirkers, the *Swan* and the *Nicodemus*, were captured and yielded up the secrets of their design, so that the way was open for building similar fast frigate-type ships for the British Navy.

Dunnage: (1) planks or baulks of timber used in protecting and stowing cargo securely; (2) a sailor's personal gear.

'Dunraven': *see* MYSTERY SHIPS.

Durham, Sir Philip Charles Henderson Calderwood (1763–1845): admiral. Entering the Navy in 1777, he had a long and distinguished career, including actions at Gibraltar, Cape Finisterre, Trafalgar (where he was wounded), Martinique and Guadeloupe. The most remarkable episode was his survival from the sinking of the *Royal George* off Portsmouth (1782), when he was pulled under twice by a struggling marine who had hold of his waistcoat; Durham freed himself only by tearing off the garment. Half a century later, when divers were working in the wreck of the ship, they came across the stamp, made of hard wood capped with brass, used by Durham to mark his personal possessions. It was packed up and forwarded to him on his Scottish estate in 1841.

Duster, Red: *see* RED ENSIGN.

Dutch courage: a temporary burst of courage induced by liquor. The cluster of expressions libelling the Dutch can be traced back to the 17th century and the Dutch Wars, though in this case there may be some foundation for the story, according to a report in *Notes and Queries*, October 1892:

> In the Dutch wars... the captain of the Hollander man-of-war, when about to engage with our ships, usually set... a hogshead of brandy abroach before the mast, and bid the men drink... and our men felt the force of the brandy to their cost.

It should be said, however, that the British were not above distributing an extra ration of grog for the same reason.

Dutch East India Company *see* EAST INDIA COMPANY, DUTCH.

Dutch hoy: *see* HOY.

Dutchman's anchor: anything accidentally left behind, from the doubtless apocryphal story of the Dutch skipper who, after he had wrecked his ship, said he had had a very good anchor but had left it at home.

Dutchman's breeches: a small patch of blue sky, just about enough to make a pair of breeches.

Dutchman's log: a primitive method of reckoning a ship's speed by timing the passage of a floating object from bow to stern.

Dutch reckoning: a mistaken calculation of a ship's position or distance run.

Dutch Wars: *see* ANGLO-DUTCH WARS.

E

E.28: the former 'E' flotilla British submarines were numbered from 1 to 56, but, for some unaccountable reason in the Admiralty, No. 28 'went missing'. An amateur researcher eventually discovered that No. 28 had in fact been ordered and placed on the official list, but the order was cancelled before the ship was built.

'Eagle': a name which appears in many ship actions through the centuries. H.M.S. *Eagle* took part in Hawke's victory off Finisterre (14 October 1747) and in Sir Edward Hughes's encounter with the French squadron under Suffren in the East Indies (12 April 1782). At the beginning of the War of American Independence, the *Eagle*, Howe's flag-ship in the Hudson River, was the subject of an early submarine attack (1776), when the American Sergeant Ezra Lee tried to blow her up with the first working SUBMARINE, the *Turtle*, built in 1775 by David Bushnell. There was room for only one on board, and Lee had to manage screws, valves, pumps and changes in ballast single-handed. A mine was hung over the *Turtle*'s rudder, but when Lee tried to attach it to the underside of the *Eagle* he was foiled by the copper sheathing, and the mine drifted away.

Another *Eagle* was built at Northfleet in 1804 as a 74-gun ship and was later (1831) converted to a 50-gun frigate. She was the last ship to be fitted with a circular stern, with a lantern-like projection aft.

The long line was continued with the launch in 1946 of the aircraft-carrier *Eagle* of 36,800 tons. She had a sea speed of 31 knots and flew up to 110 aircraft.

Eagled: spread or tied up for punishment; a colloquial shortening of 'spread-eagled'.

> I saw a poor fellow spread-eagled up to the grating.
>
> Captain Marryat, *Frank Mildmay* (1829)

'Earl Balcarras': a well-known East Indiaman, one of the largest built for the Honourable East India Company. Constructed entirely of teak at Bombay in 1815, she continued in service till 1833. She was of 1488 tons burden, carried a crew of 130 and two tiers of guns, on the upper and middle decks, with the typical additional row of painted dummy ports below, to make her appear more heavily armed than she actually was.

'Earl Camden': famous East Indiaman and flag-ship of Commodore Nathaniel DANCE. In the 1804 encounter the *Earl Camden* was a new ship, 'built on the bottom' (in the old phrase) of the former ship of the same name. This was familiar practice, since the Indiamen rarely lasted more than six voyages.

Earthquakes, marine: movements of the earth's crust, sometimes originating in the deep trenches of the ocean floor, may be followed first by a withdrawal of the coastal waters and then by an advancing and fast-moving destructive wave popularly and wrongly called a 'tidal wave'. Numerous instances have been recorded throughout history. For example, in 1755 the Lisbon earthquake was followed an hour afterwards by a huge wave on the coast at Cadiz, and the waters are said to have risen 50 ft above normal level. Earthquakes off the western coast of South America in 1868 set up a withdrawal and advance of the waters which carried boats a quarter of a mile inland. In 1883 the volcanic explosion of Krakatoa in the Sunda Strait between Java and Sumatra caused a 100-ft wave which inundated villages and drowned thousands of people. The shock wave travelled round the world, though with diminishing effect. In 1946 a movement of the earth's crust in the deep of the Aleutian Islands set up waves which travelled at great speed to the islands of the mid-Pacific. Seismological stations can now provide predictions of the likelihood and time of arrival of these so-called 'tidal waves' once the position and strength of the centre of the earthquake has been recorded.

East country ships: old name for Baltic trading ships.

East End: a general name for that part of London lying to the east of Tower Bridge. At the end of the 18th century the congestion of shipping in the Thames was so serious that there began a gradual shift of the PORT OF LONDON down stream. In the first half of the 19th century the increasing size of ships and the tidal nature of the river led to the building of enclosed basins and the opening of the great docks – the West India, London, St Katharine, East India. Later, and further east, were built the Royal Victoria and Albert Docks, and in this century the great King George V Dock. All this dockland led to the growth of the East End. Much of it was destroyed by air-raids in the Second World War; much was rebuilt, but much still awaits redevelopment.

Easterling: old name for a Baltic trader or a native of a country east of Britain.

Eastern hemisphere: that half of the world which includes the great land mass of Europe and Asia, Africa and Australasia. In atlases it is generally shown opposed to the western hemisphere, consisting of the Americas and the vast tracts of the Pacific Ocean.

East India Company, British: company granted a charter in 1600 to trade with the eastern hemisphere. From 1623 onwards (*see* EAST INDIES) it concentrated its activities in India. In the 18th century, as a result of Clive's victories over the French, culminating at Plassey (1757), the company developed vast power both politically and economically over enormous territories, so much so that the British government gradually assumed first indirect, then more direct, control. The monopoly on the India trade was abolished in 1813 and that with China twenty years later. Trading activities finished in 1833, and the complete transference of administrative power took place in 1858, after the Indian Mutiny. From the full title 'Honourable East India Company' came the abbreviations H.E.I.C. and 'The Honourable Company'. It was also familiarly known as 'John Company' ('John' may be a perversion of 'Hon.').

As early as 1609, the company constructed its own shipbuilding yard at Deptford; but the vast increase in trade led to extensive chartering and purchase of ships from other yards, both British and foreign, though these were usually built to an approved design. *See also* EAST INDIAMAN; LANCASTER, SIR JAMES.

In old times John Company employed four thousand men in its warehouses.

Edward Walford, *Old and New London* (1897)

East India Company, Dutch: company granted a charter in 1602 by the

The *Hindostan* and the fleet of the East India Company manoeuvring at sea, by Nicholas Pocock.

government of the Netherlands to trade with the EAST INDIES. Despite considerable successes, such as the capture of Ceylon and the Malabar Coast from the Portuguese (1658–63), its influence gradually weakened in the face of mounting British competition and it was finally wound up in 1798.

East Indiaman: generally, any ship, including the Dutch, trading from Europe to the East Indies; but specifically the ships owned by, or chartered by, the British EAST INDIA COMPANY. The larger East Indiaman did not differ very much from the Royal Navy man-o'-war, was admirably maintained and disciplined, and indeed frequently included ex-R.N. officers and men in her complement. This fine line of ships died out after 1833, when the East India Company ceased trading activities. Examples of the East Indiaman were the *EARL BALCARRAS* and the *EARL CAMDEN*. Although the East Indiamen were well-armed and able to cope with

privateer attacks, it was common practice to make them look more formidable than they actually were, e.g. by painting a row of dummy gunports so that the ship had all the appearance of a two–decker warship (*see also* LETTERS OF MARQUE).

East Indies: a great archipelago of islands off South-East Asia, of which Sumatra, Java, Borneo and Celebes are the largest. Formerly India and the Malay Peninsula were also looked upon as part of the East Indies, and it was in the latter, where Malacca fell to the Portuguese in 1511, that the incursion of the West may be said to begin. It was the spices and many varied products of the East Indies which drew the Portuguese to establish trading posts on the islands in the first half of the 16th century, but their power fell away and in the next century they were succeeded by the Dutch, with the English following in contention for a share in the valuable trade. The rivalry between the Dutch and the English East India Companies culminated in 1623 in the massacre of the English traders at Amboyna in the Moluccas, after which for a time the English withdrew to the mainland of India. The Dutch extended their hold on the islands, but British pressure continued, and by the Treaty of Paris in 1784 the right to trade in East Indian waters was conceded. During the Napoleonic Wars Java fell in 1811 to a British East India Company's force under Lord Minto, who appointed Thomas Stamford Raffles, the founder of Singapore, as Lieutenant-Governor; but the island was returned to the Dutch after the defeat of Napoleon. By the beginning of the 20th century the Dutch had established their control of the islands, but the British had suzerainty over a large part of northern Borneo and over the Malay States of the peninsula. The whole area was occupied by the Japanese in 1942 during the Second World War, after which the Dutch hopes of re-establishing their power were frustrated by the rising tide of nationalism, which culminated in the establishment of the United States of Indonesia in 1949. British North Borneo (now Sabah) and Sarawak have since 1963 been independent states within the Federation of Malaysia, whilst Brunei, a small area in Borneo, is an independent Malay Sultanate, but remains a British Protected State.

Easting: the distance covered by sailing to the eastward.

Easy!: an order to go gently or to rowers to stop rowing.

Ebbsfleet: part of the Isle of Thanet, in the parish of Minster, where, according to the *Anglo-Saxon Chronicle*, the invaders Hengest and Horsa landed in A.D. 449 or 450. It is also thought to have been the landing-place of St Augustine in 597.

Ebb tide: the falling or going down of the tide or tidal stream; the opposite of flood tide.

E-boat: a general name given to German light coastal craft used during the Second World War. E-boats operated against British shipping and forces in the English Channel and North Sea.

Echo-sounder: an electromagnetic device that indicates the depth of water by producing a sound-wave beneath a ship and recording its return or echo from the sea-bed. The known basic speed of sound in water enables the depth to be calculated and automatically recorded on a calibrated dial. The echo-sounder is found today on almost every type of ship, including quite small craft. It not only ensures that the ship is in sufficient and safe water, but can be used also for navigation by comparing soundings against those on charts. Fishermen can also use the echo-sounder for locating large shoals of fish.

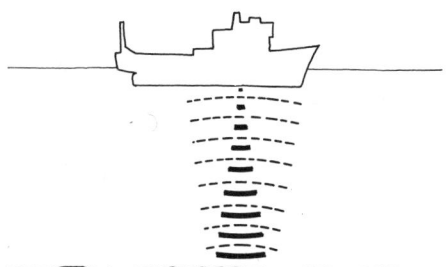

Eddy: a small whirlpool or swirling of the waters, which can be variously caused by the current of rivers flowing against the tide, by wrecks or other obstructions, by rocks or sandbanks, etc.

Eddystone: the dangerous rocks or reef on which the present lighthouse and its four predecessors were built lie some 14 miles S.S.W. of Plymouth. The first lighthouse

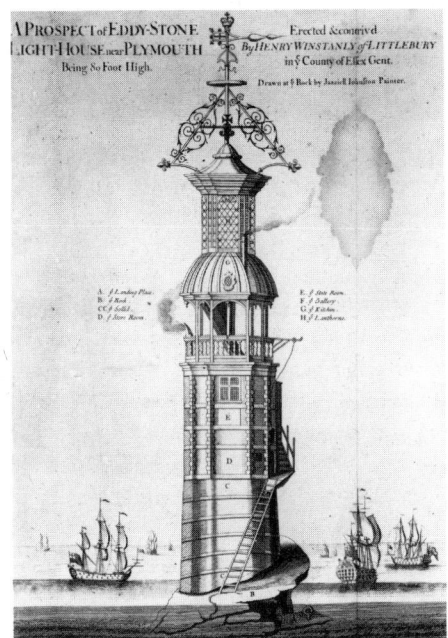

An engraving of Winstanley's first lighthouse on the Eddystone Rock, 1696.

was begun by Henry Winstanley in 1696; three years later it was rebuilt and raised to 100 ft in height. In 1703, however, the lighthouse was completely demolished in a very severe gale, and Winstanley himself and the men with him perished. The third lighthouse was erected by John Rudyerd in 1709 and lasted till 1755, when it was destroyed by fire from its own lanterns. The fourth, which was the first stone lighthouse, was completed to John Smeaton's design in 1797 and stood for 120 years. It became unsafe, so in 1878 James Douglass began a new lighthouse on a different part of the rock. The stump of Smeaton's tower still stands, and some of the upper part was removed and re-erected on Plymouth Hoe as a memorial to him. Douglass's improved design was based on a massive foundation of sufficient strength and size to break the first force of the waves and so protect the upper tower and light. It

began operating in 1882 with a light 135 ft above mean high water and visible to a range of nearly 18 miles. *See also* LIGHTHOUSE.

Eden, Richard (?1521–1576): not a sailor, but a civil servant whose writings and translations exerted a considerable influence on exploration and the science of navigation. Among his books were *A Treatise of New India* (1553), *The Decades of the New World, or West India* (1555) and *De Natura Magnetis* (1574).

Education, naval: Samuel PEPYS once wrote: 'No kind or degree of the land-education in use among us in England, whether of the liberal or servile sorts, qualifies a man at all for sea-employment ... or gives him any considerable help towards it'. There had been a few attempts to provide some sort of sea-education for a very limited number of people: Sir Humphrey Gilbert, in about 1572, put up a proposal for a 'Queen Elizabeth's Academy' where a few selected boys would be taught the applications of science to everyday life; and some 25 years later, Gresham College opened its doors to do more or less what Gilbert had visualized but never brought into effect. As a result of private enterprise there had been public lectures in navigation, astronomy and hydrography, but ordinary schools would have none of that sort of teaching. It was left to Pepys to help in bringing about a change, and as a result of his persuasion, mathematical teaching was developed at Christ's Hospital, which regularly provided navigators for the Navy thereafter. Other schools soon followed; Dartmouth Grammar School began to teach navigation in 1679, and Pepys, in a letter of 1685, refers to Sir William Boreham's 'new Mathematical School at Greenwich, in imitation of the King's at Christ's Hospital'. This therefore preceded the Royal Hospital School at Greenwich, which was begun in 1717. There were also Williamson's Mathematical School at Rochester (1704), the Naval Academy at Portsmouth (1733) and the Hull Trinity House Nautical School of about the same date. Jonas HANWAY, who with others had founded the MARINE SOCIETY, was influential in starting a 'Maritime School on the banks of the Thames near London', though it is thought not to have opened until the year of his death, 1786.

But the very great majority of those who became naval officers did not have the advantage of preliminary theoretical training in such schools; they learnt their navigation and other professional skills at sea. Such were the 'young gentlemen' who, as KING'S LETTER BOYS (until 1729) or as captain's protégés (CAPTAIN'S SERVANTS, as they were known), went directly to sea at the early age of 11 or 12, learnt from experience, and after three years' service were rated as midshipmen. But even so there was a recognition that further, more formal teaching was needed. An Order in Council of 1702 recognised the SCHOOL-MASTER, albeit in a very lowly status, for the purpose of teaching navigation to the 'young gentlemen and other youths'. Herein lies the origin of the modern highly qualified INSTRUCTOR BRANCH of the Royal Navy, but in fact few ships in the 18th century carried schoolmasters, and when the position was filled it was sometimes by most unsuitable men. Conscientious captains saw to it that their midshipmen were disciplined and trained. For long one of the midshipmen's regular exercises was the completion of the 'day's work', that is calculating 24 hours of celestial navigation, and satisfying their supervising officer with the accuracy of their workings. From this comes the phrase 'all in a day's work'.

In 1854 H.M.S. *Illustrious*, moored in Portsmouth harbour, began to be used as a training ship for young seamen, but three years later it was turned over to the training of naval cadets, as young future officers had now become called. A larger ship was soon needed, and in 1859 H.M.S. *Britannia*, a 120-gun three-decker, was chosen for the purpose. In 1861 she was moved to Portland, and then eighteen months later to Dartmouth, where she remained the training ship for cadets until 1905.

By this time the Selborne Scheme of 1902 had introduced new regulations to provide a common entry for all future officers so as to ensure a full general education as well as training in specialized professional subjects. To meet the demands of the new system ROYAL NAVAL COLLEGES were established at Osborne in 1903, and at Dartmouth where new buildings were opened in 1905 to become what is now known as the Britannia Royal Naval College. Osborne was closed in 1923, but Dartmouth remains as the future officers' great starting point for naval training and education. The Royal Naval College at Greenwich, set up to provide for 'the education of naval officers ... in all branches of theoretical and scientific study bearing upon their profession', now serves as a staff college and has been described as the Navy's university.

In the 19th century the merchant service, like the Royal Navy, made improvements in regulating entry and training. The Mercantile Marine Service Association did much to provide pre-sea training courses for potential officers. Ships such as *Conway*, *Worcester*, *Arethusa* and *Mercury*, permanently moored as school training ships, were to send many boys into the mercantile marine. Today training for the Merchant Navy is largely sea-based, via cadet-training schemes, many of them run by the bigger shipping companies. Sailing training ships are greatly favoured by some maritime nations. Nevertheless longer periods have to be spent ashore at technical colleges, for modern merchant navy officers have to be more than navigators, such is the pace of technological development. All merchant seamen, however, officers and ratings, must still take Department of Trade examinations to acquire statutory certificates of competency to serve on board ships in particular grades.

Edward III (1312–77): king of England. Although not renowned for having much influence on maritime history, he issued a well-known gold coin (noble) in 1344 that provides a valuable representation of a ship of the time; and the chronicler Jean Froissart has given us a delightful picture of the King in a naval action, that of Les ESPAGNOLS SUR MER (29 August 1350):

He was in high good humour, as joyous as ever he was in his life, I was told by those who saw him. He stationed himself right up in the fore of his ship and, dressed in a black velvet jacket with a small beaver hat on his head, summoned his musicians and ordered them to strike up a dance ... There he sat, the English King, hands and feet keeping time with the gay rhythm, as excited as a schoolboy at the prospect of a battle upon the summer sea ... The King could hardly wait to get into action. He pointed out the nearest Spanish vessel, bearing down at a great rate, and shouted to the master of his ship: 'Get me alongside that Spaniard! I must joust with him!'

Effective occupation, doctrine of: doctrine that exclusive trading rights in a territory can be claimed by a power only when it is in actual occupation and control,

such things as papal dispensations and paper claims being valueless. Thus Henry VII, in his patronage of Cabot and his patent to the men of Bristol, made it clear that he would respect only effective occupation; and Queen Elizabeth would not admit Portuguese claims to the African trade, maintaining that in most parts of the coast the negroes were independent people, not under Portuguese rule.

Effingham: *see* HOWARD OF EFFINGHAM, LORD CHARLES.

Elba: a small and rocky island off the west coast of Italy in the Tyrrhenian Sea. Well-known from earliest times for its iron ore (now almost exhausted), Elba has over the centuries come under Italian, Spanish and French rule. In 1802 it was assigned to France and was recognized as an independent principality with Napoleon Bonaparte as ruler when he was exiled there in 1814. He remained until 26 February 1815, when he returned to France for the famous Hundred Days, culminating in his defeat by Wellington and Blücher at Waterloo. Today Elba belongs to Italy.

Elder, John (1824–69): shipbuilder and marine engineer who successfully developed compound engines. In 1868 he read a paper to the United Service Institute entitled 'Circular Ships of War with increased motive power'.

Elder Brethren: Masters of TRINITY HOUSE.

Eldest: an old-time word, now obsolete, for the senior in rank or standing.

El Dorado: literally, the gilded or golden one, a name originally applied to a South American tribal king or priest who was reputed to have covered himself with gold or gold dust at an annual religious festival; then to a legendary city or country where gold could be found in superabundance. Many explorers searched for it, chiefly Spanish; but, fired by their accounts, Sir Walter Ralegh headed an English expedition in 1595 to search for Manoa, the empire ruled by the gilded king.

His ascent of the River Orinoco in rowing boats, until the rainy season compelled his return, and his talks with Indians, left him convinced that El Dorado existed. On his return to England he wrote (1596) his *Discovery of the Large, Rich and Beautiful Empire of Guiana*, in the mountains of which he located the fabulous golden state. His theme was political – that it was Spain's Indian gold which 'endangereth and disturbeth all the nations of Europe' and that, by seizing El Dorado, England would hold the mastery and Europe would be safe.

Ralegh made another expedition in 1616–18 (*see* GUIANA), and other English seamen also engaged in the fruitless search – 'ship after ship in nameless expeditions.'

Yet something remained... Rapids barred access by the rivers, but in their estuaries a trade developed. Then, with the Spanish peace, colonies began, a score of plantations that failed and are forgotten. But they played their part in history, for they trained the men who colonized the West Indies.

James A. Williamson, *The Ocean in English History* (1941)

'El Draque': 'the Dragon', the name given by the Spaniards to their hard-hitting enemy, Sir Francis Drake. Even in modern times Spanish mothers dealing with difficult children have been known to threaten: '*El Draque* will get you!'

'Elephant': chiefly remembered as the 74-gun ship of the line carrying the flag of Vice-Admiral Lord Nelson at the Battle of COPENHAGEN (1801) when the famous 'blind eye' incident took place.

Elevation: the elevation of a gun is the vertical angle to which it is raised from the horizontal.

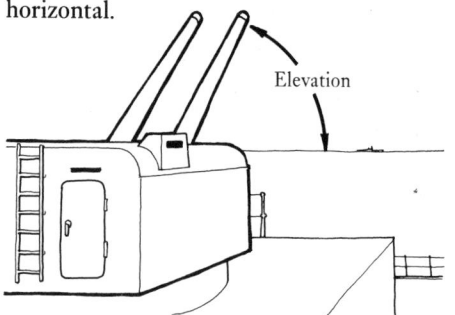

Elevation

Elizabeth I (1533–1603): queen of England, not herself a seafarer, but her reign was the inspiration and breeding time of a great number of seamen and maritime exploits. She was an adroit manipulator of men, and she had a happy command of the English language, as in her famous speech at Tilbury when the Spanish Armada was approaching:

I know I have the body of a weak and feeble woman, but I have the heart and stomach of a king, and of a king of England too; and think foul scorn that Parma or Spain, or any other prince of Europe, should dare to invade the borders of my realm.

The development of the Navy under Elizabeth may best be estimated from the words of William Harrison (1534–93), a canon of Windsor who in 1577 published a *Description of England*. An estimate of 1552 puts the fleet at '24 ships and pinnaces in good state to serve'. Harrison wrote:

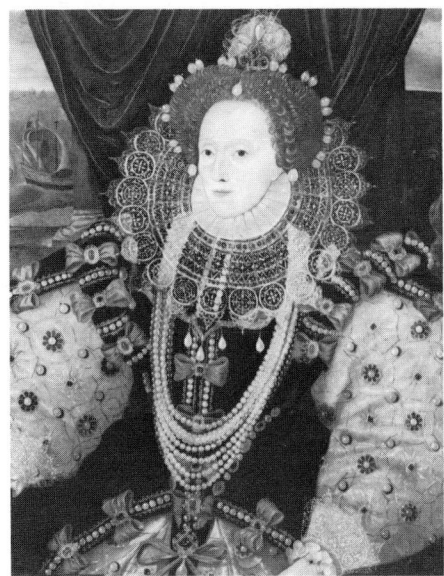

fire-power in that part. The elliptical form gave the same advantages but allowed a better appearance and a return to the old stern windows and quarter-galleries.

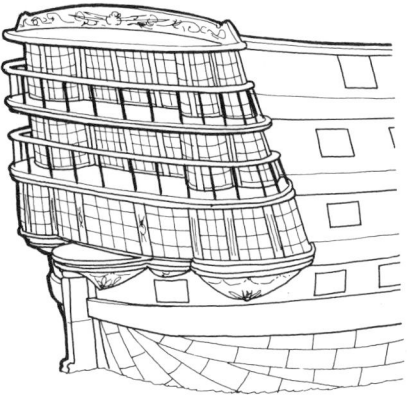

The Queen's Highness hath at this present already made and furnished, to the number of One Hundred and Twenty Great Ships, which lie for the most part in Gillingham Road. Beside these, her Grace hath other in hand also; she hath likewise three notable Galleys, the *Speedwell*, the *Tryright*, and the *Black Galley*, with the sight whereof, and the rest of the Navy-Royal, it is incredible to say how marvellously her Grace is delighted.

But to get the picture right (and to put Harrison's lyrical description in true perspective), it must be added that to meet the ARMADA eleven years later the Queen mustered 197 ships – 34 of them true Navy-Royal ships and 163 belonging to her subjects, begged, borrowed and hired. Her father HENRY VIII could boast just over 100.

'Elizabeth Bonaventure': *see BONA-VENTURE*.

Elliptical stern: modified form (introduced by Sir William Symonds in 1827) of the round sterns which had been provided to give men-o'-war greater strength and

Elphinstone, George Keith, Viscount Keith (1746–1823): admiral who held a series of important commands, including those of the India squadron (1795), ships in Spanish waters (1799) and the North Sea (1803). He was mainly responsible for the suppression of the Sheerness mutiny (1797), and in his later years he acted as intermediary between the British government and Napoleon regarding the Emperor's exile to St Helena.

Elphinstone, John (1722–85): Royal Navy captain who also became a rear-admiral in the service of Russia and defeated a Turkish fleet. At one time, in his curious dual capacity, he was ordered to discontinue setting the watch in Portsmouth harbour because he was a foreign admiral. After abandoning the Russian service he commanded the *Magnificent* in the battle off Grenada (1779) and was with Rodney in 1780 in his encounters with Admiral de Guichen.

Embargo: the detention of merchant

vessels or other property in ports to prevent their departure and to deny their goods to a hostile state. There are many instances of the use of embargo. In 1807 the United States passed an Embargo Act when Napoleon's Continental System and the British Orders-in-Council were felt to be violating American international rights. There were many embargoes in the First and Second World Wars, and since then there have been international cases: for example, in 1951 the United Nations placed an embargo on the shipment of arms and materials to China and the North Korean Communists; a more recent instance is the embargo relating to Rhodesia.

Embark: go or take on board ship either men or supplies and stores.

'Emden': famous German cruiser of the First World War which, commanded by Captain von Müller, 'gave the world a classic example of how a lone raider should operate' (Michael Lewis, *The History of the British Navy*, 1957). After a brilliant run of success, especially in the Indian Ocean, she was destroyed by the Australian cruiser *Sydney* on 9 November 1914.

Emigrant ships: the movement of people from one country to another has gone on throughout history, but 'emigrant ships' is generally taken to refer to those ships carrying the vast numbers of men, women and children who left the Old World to settle in the New World, Australia and New Zealand between about 1820 and 1914. The ships were often overcrowded and conditions appalling.

'Empress of India': a well-known name in both the Royal Navy and the merchant fleet. The 1891 *Empress* was a first-class battleship of 14,150 tons displacement. Better known to a generation of passengers was the Canadian-Pacific *Empress of India* on the Vancouver–Yokohama run, with her yellow funnels and house-flag of chequered red and white. Cecily Fox-Smith mentions her 'pretty clipper bow with its bust of Queen Victoria... so familiar a sight in Victoria Harbour'.

'Endeavour': the most famous ship of the name was Captain Cook's barque, the first discovery vessel of which we have precise details. Built as a COLLIER by Messrs Fishburn of Whitby in 1764 and named *Earl of Pembroke*, she was purchased by the

Emden.

Emigrant ships: *The Departure*, an engraving by J. J. Tissot, 1902.

Admiralty in 1768 and renamed *Endeavour Bark*, 'Bark' being added because there was already an *Endeavour* in the Navy List.

She was described as 'cat-built', i.e., with a stern very full on the water-line and with comparatively narrow upper-works – a design characteristic of much merchant shipping of the time. For the special purposes of Cook's first great voyage (1768–71) the cabin accommodation was improved by raising and lengthening the poop deck slightly. She was of 366 tons burden, 97·7 ft long (lower deck), 29·2 ft broad and 11·3 ft deep in the hold. As armament she carried ten 4-pounder guns on carriages and 12 swivels. She was equipped with five anchors and three ship's boats. The small vessel carried a total of 94 officers, crew, scientists and servants.

See colour section.

'Endymion': one of the most interesting ships of the name was the frigate built in 1797 for the Royal Navy. She was prepared in draught as an exact replica of *La Pomone*, a captured French ship which it was thought could provide lessons for English ship-builders. Though in the outcome there were slight modifications, the *Endymion* was in fact considered one of the speediest ships in the Navy. Of 1277 tons burden, she was 159·3 ft along the gun-deck and 42·6 ft in breadth. She carried twenty-six 24-pounder guns on the gun-deck, fourteen 32-pounder carronades on the quarter-deck, four other carronades on the forecastle, and two long 9-pounders. She lasted over 60 years in the service. *See also* DECATUR, CAPTAIN STEPHEN.

Engineer Officer: a rank that developed after the arrival of power-driven ships. The Engineer Officers' first permanent recognition in the Royal Navy was in 1837, when they were made warrant officers. Ten years later Senior Engineers became commissioned officers, and from that time the Engineer's status and importance have risen. The Royal Naval Engineering College was founded at Keyham in 1880. For the first quarter of the present century an attempt was made to coalesce the Seaman and Engineer functions, but in 1925 they were separated because of the increasing need for specialization. Today, after initial training ashore and afloat, those who are selected to become Engineer Officers begin a three-year course at the Royal Engineering College, Manadon, Plymouth, where they study for degrees in electrical or mechanical engineering. In practice the work of Engineer Officers is separated into six sub-specializations, viz. Weapon and Electrical (Surface ships or Submarines), Marine (Surface ships or Submarines), Air (Mechanical or Electrical). In the Merchant Navy the Engineer Officer is qualified by holding a Certificate of Competency, second class or first class, or Extra Chief Engineer for steam or diesel engines.

English Channel (or **Channel**): the long arm of the Atlantic Ocean dividing England from France. Its French name, La Manche, meaning 'The Sleeve', is apt. The Channel narrows from its wide western entrance of over 100 miles between Land's End and Ushant to a mere 20 miles between Dover and the French coast.

Over the centuries the English Channel has seen countless naval actions and countless wrecks; it has seen great fleets such as the Spanish Armada in 1588, and in the Second World War it saw the huge Allied fleet sail from English ports for the invasion of Normandy in June 1944.

The English Channel is the main outlet to the Atlantic for the industrialized nations of N.W. Europe and it has become the busiest, often most congested, of the world's great seaways.

Enright, Captain Anthony: *see LIGHTNING.*

Ensign (pronounced 'ensin'): name given in the 16th century to the striped flag flown on the poop of ships. The term 'colours' was also used for the ensign but was later extended to cover other flags. The story of the ensign's development is long and complex: one of the most important steps was the limiting in the 17th century of the Union Flag (or Union Jack) to Royal Navy ships, merchant vessels being obliged to fly a different ensign. Thus eventually came about the WHITE ENSIGN of the Royal

Navy and the RED ENSIGN (the famous 'Red Duster') of the merchant service. The BLUE ENSIGN is the flag of the Royal Navy Reserve. A curious variation of the spelling and pronunciation of 'ensign' in earlier centuries was 'ancient'.

'Enterprise': obviously a fine ship name, used through the centuries for many types of craft, ranging from the tiny 4-gun Royal Navy armoured sloop of 1864 to the giant $1101\frac{1}{2}$-ft-long U.S. aircraft carrier, with a displacement of 85,350 tons. One well-known *Enterprise* took part in the 1848 and 1850 expeditions sent out to search for Sir John Franklin.

Entrepôt: a 'put-between' place: i.e. a port or other centre where foreign merchandise is held in bond before being re-exported; or a commercial centre where goods are sent for distribution.

Entry port: an opening in a ship's side for the loading of cargo or embarkation of passengers. The idea of cutting a hole in the ship's side for such a purpose is attributed to a French shipwright in Brest in 1501, and from this there developed the cutting of smaller ports for guns when the broadside was introduced.

Epaulette (or **epaulet**): an ornamental piece on the shoulder worn by officers of the Royal Navy in full dress. An important

innovation in the development of British naval dress came in 1795, when epaulettes were allocated to distinguish rank, as follows:

Admiral: gold epaulettes, each with three silver stars.

Vice-Admiral: gold epaulettes, each with two silver stars.

Rear-Admiral: gold epaulettes, each with one silver star.

Captain of three or more years' standing: plain gold epaulettes.

Captain of less than three years' standing: a single plain gold epaulette worn on the right shoulder.

Commander: a single plain gold epaulette worn on the left shoulder.

See colour section

Equator: the great circle running round the earth halfway between the North and South Poles. *See also* CROSSING THE EQUATOR.

Equinoctial gales: storms which tend to occur at about the time of the equinoxes, especially the autumnal equinox.

Equinox: the times at which the sun is directly overhead at the Equator at mid-day, namely on 20 March and 22 or 23 September. At these times day and night are of equal length.

'Erebus': a great and sad name in the annals of discovery: one of the two ships on Sir John FRANKLIN's last voyage, from which neither vessels nor explorers returned. *Erebus* had previously been to the Antarctic with Ross and Crozier, but had been refitted for Franklin, using steam and a screw propeller.

Espagnols sur Mer, Les (29 August 1350): battle of 'the Spaniards on the Sea', fought off Winchelsea. The King of Castile, the ally of France, had sent a large fleet through the Channel to the Flemish ports. As it sailed back, EDWARD III, the Black Prince and their chivalry bundled themselves on board a scratch fleet and came charging down as if they were fighting a tournament or land battle, watched admiringly by Queen Philippa and her ladies on the cliff-tops. The royal line of England narrowly escaped some drastic losses that day, and it is difficult to avoid the picture of a rather hilarious and hearty schoolboy affair. But there was much true valour and as night fell the Castilian fleet made off as best it could, leaving some 24 captured and destroyed ships behind. The day finished appropriately with a notable feast.

Essex, Earl of: *see* DEVEREUX, ROBERT.

Establishment: (1) ('the Establishment') the officially recognized or authorized strength of the Royal Navy in ships and men at any period, specifying the standard dimensions of every class of vessel, their style of decoration, etc.

(2) All the shore-based activities which serve the Royal Navy and provide the backing for ships afloat. It includes establishments concerned with the building and repair of ships, with training, research, health and education etc. Permanent naval shore establishments are commissioned and named as H.M. ships (e.g. H.M.S. *Excellent* at Portsmouth); *see also* STONE FRIGATE.

Estuary: the broad mouth of a river into which the tide flows. Some estuaries are sunken or 'drowned' river valleys and are known as 'rias': e.g. Dingle and Bantry Bays in S.W. Ireland or the estuaries at Falmouth and Plymouth.

Etches, Richard Cadman (*fl.c.*1797): smuggler and spy who, before the Battle of Camperdown, gave early warning that some Dutch move was preparing against the coasts of Essex and Suffolk. These daring operators outside the law were often of service in this way, as a result of their frequent sea crossings in fast-sailing craft; *see* SMUGGLING.

'Euryalus': famous 36-gun frigate built (1803) at Adam's Yard, Bucklers Hard, to the design of Sir William Rule, Surveyor of the Navy. She was nicknamed 'Nelson's Watch Dog', and it was from her deck that the first signs of positive activity by French and Spanish ships were spotted, three days before Trafalgar. With her consorts she kept unremitting vigilance, firing a signal gun at every movement of the enemy, and burning a blue light to show she was still on watch, the messages being relayed by a chain of ships to the Admiral. Before battle was joined, Nelson summoned *Euryalus*'s commander, Captain Henry Blackwood, on board *Victory* and thanked him personally for his services. After the battle Collingwood, the acting Commander-in-Chief, shifted his flag to her, and she took the *Royal Sovereign* in tow.

After other distinguished service *Euryalus*, sadly enough, finished her career as a convict ship and was eventually sold out of the service in 1859 at Gibraltar for £337 6s. 8d.

At daylight observed the enemy's ships in Cadiz with topgallant yards across, and eight ships having their topsails hoisted to the mast heads. At 7. saw the northernmost ships under way. At 7.20 dispatched the *Phoebe* to repeat signals between us and the English fleet. At 8, saw 19 of the enemy under way. All the rest, except the Spanish Rear-Admiral and another line-of-battle ship, with their topsails to the masthead. The *Defence* in sight from the mast head west. *Phoebe* WNW, firing three minute guns. At 8.10, came within hail the *Naiad*, and ordered her to repeat as many signals as possible between us and the *Phoebe*. Made a telegraph message to the *Weazle*, intelligence to Gibralter and Tetuan. At 9, ordered the *Pickle* to proceed with all possible dispatch off Cape Spartel, and inform all ships that the enemy is out.

Log of H.M.S. *Euryalus* (19 October 1805)

Eustace the Monk (*fl.*1200–1217): a mercenary fighter, at one time in the employ of King John, who brought over a fleet of some 80 ships from Calais to reinforce Prince Louis of France, who had carried out a successful minor invasion of England in 1216–17. The French fleet was heavily defeated by Hubert DE BURGH, and Eustace, despite the offer of a great price for his life, was summarily beheaded.

'Evangelicals': body of officers of strong Low Church and Methodist persuasions who considerably influenced the conduct of ships in the late 18th and early 19th centuries. Two such were Admiral Lord Barham (1726–1813) and Admiral Lord GAMBIER. Though some were scoffed at, their attitude and example brought about a considerable decrease in barbaric punishments and general improvement in shipboard conduct and conditions.

Captain Marryat, writing in the 1820s, observed:

Whoever has been fifteen years in the Navy, and will compare what took place at the period of his entrance with the present usages in the service, must acknowledge that swearing and abusive language, the oppression of the midshipmen's berth, the custom of starting [*see* STARTER] and severe punishments at the gangway, have been discountenanced and checked.

Quoted in Christopher Lloyd, *Captain Marryat* (1939)

Evans, Edward Radcliffe Garth

Russell ('Evans of the *Broke*'; 1880–1957): admiral. He entered the Navy in 1897 and soon saw service in the Antarctic, 1902–4 and 1909–13, commanding the latter expedition after the death of Captain Scott. He came to national fame in 1917 when, commanding the *Broke* and in company with H.M.S. *Swift*, he defeated six German destroyers and was especially promoted Captain for services in action. Many subsequent honours and decorations came his way from France, Norway, Belgium, Italy, Portugal, Hungary and the United States, not the least being gold and silver medals for saving life at sea.

Evans, Sir Frederick John Owen (1815–85): hydrographer. He surveyed the Coral Sea, Great Barrier Reef and Torres Straits (1841–6) and served as Hydrographer to the Admiralty (1874–84). As Superintendent of the Compass Department he published *A Report on Compass Deviations in the Royal Navy*.

Evelyn, John (1620–1706): diarist, remembered chiefly for his valuable chronicle of the period 1640–1706. He was also of service to the Navy. In 1664 he was given the responsibility for the sick and wounded of the Dutch War (*see* SICK AND WOUNDED BOARD) and also for the prisoners, an unenviable task for which inadequate funds were provided and whose accounts he was still trying to get settled more than twenty years later. In 1695 he accepted the treasurership of Greenwich Hospital for old sailors and laid the first stone of the new building in 1696. But perhaps his greatest contribution was the publication (1664) of *Sylva, or a Discourse of Forest Trees, and the Propagation of Timber in His Majesty's Dominions*, a work which created a tremendous interest in the planting and propagation of TIMBER, soon to be needed for the rebuilding of the Royal Navy and the wars of the 18th and early 19th century.

I need not Acquaint Your Majesty how many Millions of Timber-Trees (beside infinite others) have been Propagated and Planted throughout Your vast Dominions, at the Instigation, and by the sole Directions of this Work; because Your Gracious Majesty, has been pleas'd to own it Publickly for my Encouragement... And, indeed, what more August, what more Worthy Your Majesty, or more becoming our Imitation? than whilst You are thus solicitous for the Publick Good, we pursue Your Majesty's Great Example; and by Cultivating our decaying Woods, contribute to Your Power, as to our greatest Wealth and Safety.

Preface to *Sylva* (1678 edition)

Evolution: the name given to any drill or practice in seamanship or readiness for action.

'Excellent': the Royal Navy's gunnery training school at Portsmouth (*see* WHALE ISLAND). *Excellent* was the name of the ship on board which the school for naval gunners was first established at Portsmouth in 1830.

The Admiralty have recently considered it expedient to establish a permanent corps of seamen to act as captains of guns; and they have also fitted out a ship in Portsmouth harbour for the express purpose of affording instruction to the officers and men of His Majesty's Navy in the theory and practice of naval gunnery... His Majesty's ship *Excellent*, an old line-of-battle ship, of which Lord Collingwood was captain on 1st June [1794] has been appropriately selected for this purpose...

Captain Basil Hall, R.N., *Fragments of Voyages & Travels* (3rd series, 1833)

Executive Branch: before 1956, the name given to those officers of the Royal Navy responsible for the command and military aspects of ships at sea, as opposed to the Engineer and other branches of the Service. The Executive Branch corresponded to the modern Seaman specialization, officers from which are the only ones eligible to command ships at sea. Today all branches are amalgamated within the General List, but with specializations and sub-specializations.

'Exeter': cruiser in the Second World War, forming part of 'Force G', which defeated the *Graf Spee* at the Battle of the RIVER PLATE. In the early stages of the action *Exeter* received the full weight of the German ship's 11-in. broadside, sustaining heavy damage and many casualties. After several more direct hits, she listed heavily to starboard and, with only one turret left in action, had to discontinue.

Exmouth: town on the east side of the estuary of the River Exe in Devon. In the days of sail it was of maritime importance for fishing and shipbuilding, but today it is a seaside resort and yachting-centre.

Exmouth, first Viscount: *see* PELLEW.

Experimental Squadron: squadron formed (1844–5) to carry out a series of tests in various types of seas and winds: smooth water, head seas, in strong breezes, with the wind abeam etc. The experiment was part of the important programme of ship design carried out by Sir William SYMONDS. Five of the ships were actually built in 1844 and were almost identical in dimensions and tonnage, though by different designers. These, the *Mutine*, *Flying Fish*, *Espiegle*, *Daring* and *Osprey*, were from 101·5 to 112 ft in length, 31·4–32·4 ft in breadth, 13·6–15·5 ft in depth, and from 425 to 445 tons. In addition, there were the 1831 *Pantaloon* (323 tons) and the 1828 brig *Cruizer* (384 tons).

Exploration: the exploration of the world by sea and the slow discovery of the extent and nature of the oceans and land masses began at the dawn of history. Minoans, Phoenicians, Greeks, Romans and Arabs all extended geographical knowledge beyond the confines of their own lands. But the great age of European discovery by sea, which led to the final shaping of the map of the world and has been called the Age of DISCOVERY, was in the 15th and 16th centuries. Many motives impelled the voyagers: plunder and profit, adventure and trade, political rivalry and missionary zeal, and thirst for knowledge and fame. In the 18th century Captain Cook's voyages in the Pacific between 1768 and 1780 are said to mark the beginning of the Age of Scientific Discovery because of his careful observations and records. Much inland and pioneer exploration of the Americas, Africa and Australasia was left for the 19th century, whilst for the 20th there remained the penetration of the uttermost parts of the earth including the North and South Poles (*see* POLAR EXPLORATION).

Eye: (1) a loop of rope or wire cable; (2) the eye of a storm is the centre of an intense cyclonic depression where pressure is lowest and into which wind moves with great force, especially in tropical depressions: *see* HURRICANE; TYPHOON.

'Eye of the Wind': barquentine in 'Operation Drake', a project for young people launched by the Prince of Wales in 1977 to attempt a new circumnavigation in honour of the 400th anniversary of Drake's exploit.

Faeroe (or **Faroe**) **Islands**: a group of islands in the North Atlantic between Shetland and Iceland. The Faroese rely greatly on fishing as their main trade, and they are skilful and hardy sailors. When Germany occupied Denmark in 1940 the British took control of the islands, and their fish became a valuable food supply. In 1947 the islanders became a self-governing community associated with the kingdom of Denmark, under whose control they had previously been.

Fag: the unravelled ends or strands of a rope.

Fairborne, Sir Stafford (*d*.1742): admiral. He commanded the *Warspite* at the Battle of Beachy Head (1690) and distinguished himself in a number of other actions, including an onslaught on a gang of Newfoundland pirates in 1700.

Fairfax, Robert (1666–1725): admiral. He was at Bantry Bay and the relief of Londonderry (1689). Five years later he was court-martialled for failing to overtake a French squadron off Cape Palos, but was acquitted. In 1708 he retired in a huff, having been appointed Vice-Admiral of the Blue and then had the commission withdrawn. His pride was perhaps restored as M.P. for the city of York and Lord Mayor.

Fairlead: an opening in the gunwale to allow the easy passage of a rope.

Fairway: the cleared navigable channel leading into an estuary or harbour and generally marked with buoys.

Falcon and **falconet**: light cannon of the 15th and 16th centuries, throwing shot of $2\frac{1}{2}$ to 3 and $1\frac{1}{4}$ to 2 lb. respectively.

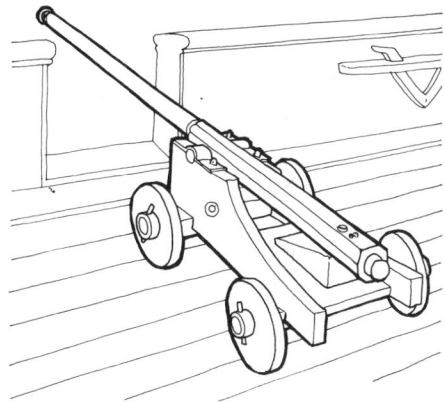

Falconer, William (1732–69): the Scottish author of a long poem, *The Shipwreck*, which from its appearance in 1762 enjoyed great popularity. The poem is full of the language of the days of sail, and the rules, maxims and orders given during the great storm described were thought to be very valuable to the seaman. Falconer was himself a sailor, first in the merchant service and then, after the appearance of his poem, in the Royal Navy, being rated a midshipman in the *Royal George*. In 1769 he obtained the appointment of purser in the *Aurora* frigate, which was not heard of

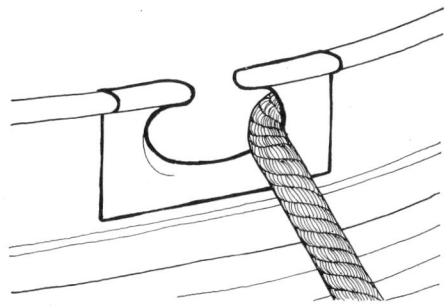

again after leaving the Cape in late December. In the year of his death Falconer had produced his *Universal Dictionary of the Marine*.

The following lines, describing the operation of reefing and balancing the mizen, are typical of Falconer's skilful use of nautical terms in verse:

Now down the mast the yard they lower away,
Then jears and topping-lift secure belay;
The head, with doubling canvass fenced
    around,
In balance near the lofty peak they bound:
The reef enwrapped, th'inserting knittles tied,
The halyards throt and peak are next applied –
The order given, the yard aloft they swayed,
The brails relax'd, th'extended sheet belayed;
The helm its post forsook, and, lashed a-lee,
Inclined the wayward prow to front the sea.

(The knittle is a short line used to reef the sails by the bottom; the throt is the part of the mizen yard close to the mast.)

Falconet: *see* FALCON.

Falkland Islands, Battle of the (8 December 1914): action between two British battle cruisers under Admiral Sturdee and the crack German cruiser squadron of Admiral von Spee, which had been inflicting considerable damage on merchant shipping at the outset of the First World War. The German squadron was destroyed, except for one light cruiser.

Falls: the ropes used in the tackle for lowering a boat from the davits.

Falmouth: because of its situation on a deep estuary Falmouth has had a prominent place in the maritime history of Cornwall from early times. The town stands on the western shore of Carrick Roads, which provided safe haven for sailing ships; its position less than 40 miles

from Land's End made it an important port of arrival and departure.

...Whose entrance is from sea so intricately
    wound,
Her haven angled so about her barbarous sound,
That in her quiet bay a hundred ships may ride,
Yet not the tallest mast be of the tall'st descried.

Michael Drayton, 'Falmouth Haven' (1612)

Faroe Islands: *see* FAEROE ISLANDS.

Fast, make: secure a rope or line so that it will not shift.

Fastnet: an area of sea south of the south coast of Ireland, so named for purposes of weather forecasts broadcast regularly to shipping, and taking its name from the Fastnet Rock off the coast of S.W. Ireland, on which stands a powerful lighthouse.

'Father': *see* OLD MAN.

'Father of the Navy': a title often awarded to King Alfred (849–901), who tried to teach that the best way to deal with an invader was not to fight him on the beach but to build ships and meet him at sea. Later, Edward III liked to think of himself as 'King of the Sea'. But perhaps the strongest case can be made out for Henry VII, the first Tudor, who greatly increased the tonnage of merchant ships, encouraged deep-water seamen and hired out his own ships for trading. Other kings have built more ships of war, but it has ever been the case that the Royal Navy moves in to protect and hold what the merchant ship has pioneered.

Fathom: originally the width of the outstretched arms, it became standardized at six feet and was used as a measure of the depth of water. Admiralty Charts showed the depth of the water in fathoms until the recent change to metric measurement.

Faulknor, Robert (1763–95): Royal Navy captain whose most remarkable exploit was his share in the capture of Fort Royal, Martinique (1794). The line-of-battle ship *Asia* having failed to get into the attack, he ran his little sloop *Zebra* right up to the walls of the fort and, in spite of the hail of grape-shot poured on her, 'leaped overboard at the head of his ship's company, and assailed and took this important post' (Sir John Jervis). After a number of other gallant actions he was killed while commanding the frigate *Blanche* and endeavouring to lash to her capstan the bowsprit of the French frigate *Pique*, which was subsequently added to the British Navy.

Fearnought: a stout woollen cloth of great thickness, formerly much used by seamen for cold-weather wear. A thick felt of the name was also used in such places as the powder magazine to avoid sparks flying.

Fegen, Captain: *see JERVIS BAY.*

Fellowship of Seamen: one of the 18th-century attempts to introduce a register of seamen which, by a type of limited conscription, would provide an alternative to the press-gang. In 1780 a parliamentary committee was set up to examine methods of encouraging the recruitment of seamen. In the suggested fellowship, members were to be conscripted by age-groups and do their service by rotation. Although a Bill reached its second reading in the House, the scheme was finally defeated by the chief shipping interests, who would have had to face a levy on a tonnage basis to finance the plan.

Felucca: a small Mediterranean boat with lateen sails.

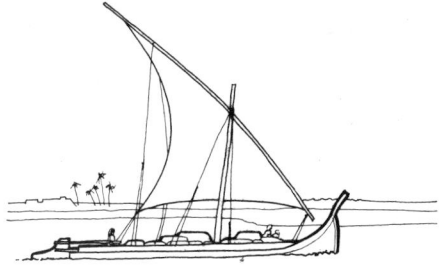

Fender: a device used to reduce impact and prevent damage when a boat is berthing or coming alongside another. Various sizes and shapes of fender are used, and they may be constructed of various materials: wood, cane, cork, rubber, old rope etc.

Ferriby Boats: two early wooden boats, dating from the first centuries A.D., found at North Ferriby, on the Humber, in 1937. Though far from complete, they afford valuable evidence of one method of early shipbuilding. The more complete of the two was a flat-bottomed boat about 45 ft long and 7½ ft across. The sides were three planks high and the bottom was also made of three oak planks set edge to edge. The planks were fastened tight together with yew withies and the seams caulked with moss.

151

Ferrol, Battle of (or **Battle of Vigo**; 22 July 1805): pre-Trafalgar encounter off Ferrol, on the N.W. Coast of Spain, between Sir Robert CALDER and the French admiral Villeneuve.

Ferry: the name for a vessel or any pontoon-like construction used for crossing the waters of a river, estuary or narrow sea. Many ferries are specially constructed ships to allow cars to drive on and off, and others can take railway trains (*see* TRAIN FERRY).

Fid: a tapered wooden hand-tool used to open out a rope's strands when splicing.

Fiddle bow: a stern or bow curving inwards such as many clippers had.

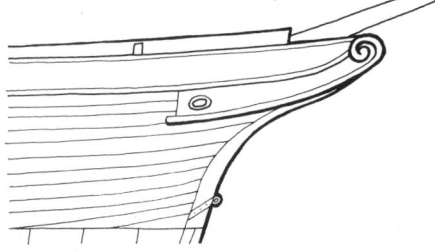

Fiddle-head: *see* FIGUREHEAD.

Fiddler's Green: a fanciful name for a happy place to which sailors go after death. Dancing and singing chanties to the fiddle may have been in mind, along with unlimited grog and tobacco.

'Fiery Cross': famous clipper built (1860) at Liverpool for the China tea trade. She was of wood, sheathed in yellow metal. For some years she was the finest and fastest clipper afloat, winning four of the tea races from China in the years 1861–6. Her two fastest passages were 101 days out from China. She was bought by Norwegian owners in about 1880 and continued in service till the end of the century.

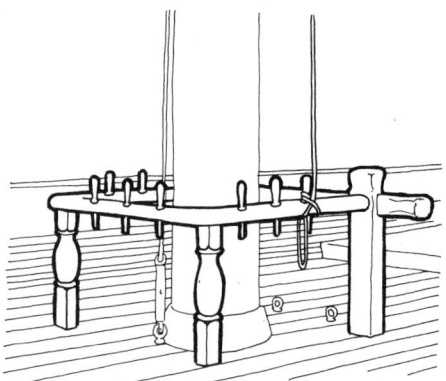

Fife rail: a rail ringing the mast of a sailing ship in which belaying pins were stowed, handy for use on the upper deck.

Fighting Instructions: the first Fighting Instructions were introduced in 1653 with orders for line ahead in battle. They were made by the 'Generals at Sea' Blake, Deane and Monck. These orders and advice to officers for the tactics to be employed in naval engagements were added to later in the 17th century during the wars with the Dutch, from the experience of which emerged the Fighting Instructions of 1691, effectively putting the control of an action into the hands of one man. After Admiral Rooke's further revisions (1703) they became the Permanent Fighting Instructions, which were the 'Law of the Line' for 18th-century naval warfare. In fact, they had a cramping effect on initiative: *see* LINE AHEAD.

Fighting sails: when a ship was going into action sails were reduced to the essential, often courses and topsails only.

Fighting Temeraire: *TEMERAIRE.*

Fighting top: a small platform on the mast occupied by sharpshooters in engagements between sailing ships; *see also* TOP.

Figurehead: ornamental carving on the prow of a ship, above the cutwater and below the bowsprit. The use of figureheads goes back to remote antiquity, first as a superstitious means of giving the ship 'eyes' amidst the mysteries of the waters and, later, to lend the vessel additional grimness or majesty, calculated to inspire fear or respect. Hence creatures such as dragons and lions were popular. In England, figureheads attained a rich degree of beauty and gilded ornamentation, especially on the first-rates. In the reign of Charles I, all men-of-war below first-rates used the crowned lion, but the custom of allowing individual figureheads to smaller ships gradually spread till they were generally accepted in the middle of the 18th century. Imagination – often, of course, related to the ship's name – was allowed full play. Merchant ships of all shapes and sizes were also fond of their figureheads. They tended to be cruder and less sophisticated, but had their own primitive sturdiness and charm. Standing detached from their proper place in some junk-yard, antique shop or museum they often appear lifeless and ugly, but in their right element they had their true beauty.

The full majesty of the figurehead can be seen on many contemporary models of 17th- and 18th-century ships; and visitors to *Victory* at Portsmouth can see the new figurehead designed for her in 1802 when she was under repair at Chatham, the shield carrying the royal arms with the arms of Hanover superimposed, the whole with attendant cherubs and intricately enriched with fruit and flowers. In the 1790s the Admiralty, in an economical fit, tried to forbid the use of elaborate figureheads and confine H.M. ships to a simple carved scroll or 'fiddle-head'; but the move was never fully successful and individual ships' captains were often prepared to spend their own money to retain the proper thing, which was so much beloved of them and their seamen (*see also* LEDDY).

> At the bows an image stood,
> By a cunning artist carved in wood,
> With robes of white that far behind
> Seemed to be fluttering in the wind.
> It was not shaped in a classic mould,
> Not like a Nymph or Goddess of old,
> Or Naiad rising from the water,
> But modelled from the Master's daughter!
>
> H. W. Longfellow, 'The Building of the Ship' (1850)

See colour section.

Finistère: the French 'land's end': a rocky and often stormy and dangerous peninsula jutting into the Atlantic off N.W. Brittany. The great harbour and naval base of Brest lies to the south, and it was in watching the French fleet there that British ships during the Napoleonic Wars kept their long and arduous vigil on the seas off Finistère.

Finisterre, Battles of (3 May and 14 October 1747): two actions in the War of the Austrian Succession. Although given the same name, they were fought hundreds of miles apart. In the first, Admiral Anson captured nine French warships and other vessels from two convoys near Cape Finisterre (Spain). It was for this victory that Anson was given his peerage.

In the second engagement, far out in the Atlantic, Admiral Hawke captured six French battleships protecting a large convoy. The victories had considerable effect on the war and were great morale-boosters. The second action is sometimes known as the 'Battle of Ushant'.

Finisterre, Cape: *see* CAPE FINISTERRE.

Fire precautions: fire, always one of the greatest hazards at sea, was guarded against with particular care in the days of wooden ships. In the POWDER MAGAZINE, men wore slippers to reduce the risk of a flying spark, and floor and walls were covered with felt. In action, decks were wetted and strewn with sand. Buckets of water were plentifully disposed and at all vulnerable points were wet screens and blankets, aimed at stopping sparks and flying embers.

He [the Captain] is to be extremely attentive in taking every possible precaution to prevent accidents by fire. He is not to suffer any, except the most careful Officers or Men, to have berths, or to sleep in the Orlop or Cable Tiers, where lights are never to be used without his express permission, but in good lanthorns. He is not to allow any person to smoke Tobacco in any other place than the Galley. He is strictly to forbid the sticking of candles against the beams, the sides or other part of the Ship. He is strictly to enjoin the Officers not to read in bed by the light of either lamps or candles: nor to leave any light in their Cabins without having some person to attend it. He is to direct the Carpenter to see that the holes in the decks through which the funnels of the stoves are passed are well leaded. The funnels are to be cleaned every morning before the fires are lighted. At the setting of the watch all fires and lights are to be extinguished by the Master at Arms and Ship's Corporals, except those which the Captain shall expressly permit to be kept burning...

Regulations and Instructions Relating to
His Majesty's Service at Sea (1808)

Fire-ships: vessels loaded with inflammable materials, such as pitch and tallow and also with gunpowder, which were taken near to the enemy ships in harbour or at anchor and set alight, whilst their crews escaped and returned to their own ships in small boats. Wind or tide would then drift the burning fire-ships amongst the enemy. They were used in ancient times, but the best-known instance in British naval history was when fire-ships were used to drive the Spanish Armada from its anchorage off Calais (1588). They were also employed against the French by Lord Cochrane in 1809, and, unsuccessfully, by the Confederates against the Union fleet in 1862 during the American Civil War.

Set 'un blazin', good your Lordships, for the
    tide be makin' strong,
Proper breeze to fan a fire-ship, set 'un driving
    out along!
'Tis the 'Torch', wi' humble duty, from Lord
    Howard 'board the 'Ark',
We'm a laughin'-stock to Brixham, but a terror
    after dark,

154

Hold an' bilge anigh to burstin', pitch and
sulphur, tar an' all,
Was it so, my dear, they'm fashioned for my
Lord High Admiral?

R. A. Hopwood, *The Old Way*

See colour section.

First Lieutenant: normally the second in
command and executive officer of one of
H.M. ships. He may be of lieutenant-
commander's rank or below, but if the ship
has a commander as executive officer, then
the senior officer of the seaman branch,
either a lieutenant-commander or lieutenant, would be the First Lieutenant.

See colour section.

First Mate: the chief officer after the
Master in a merchant ship; the second in
command.

First of June, Battle of the (or **The
Glorious First of June**; 1794): action in
the French Revolutionary Wars, fought in
the Atlantic, about 400 miles west of
Ushant, between Lord HOWE, commanding the Channel fleet, and the French
admiral Villaret-Joyeuse trying to bring
home a large convoy of over 100 vessels
with grain from America to relieve near-
famine conditions as the result of the poor
harvest of 1793 in France. 1 June was, in
fact, only the culmination of a series of
manoeuvres and minor actions, and it was
not in the full sense a victory, since the
grain consignment was brought safely into
port; but six French ships were captured
and a seventh sunk. Tactically it marked a
new principle, with Howe 'breaking the
enemy's line at all points to windward' and
so taking the leeward station and cutting off
the enemy line of retreat: and the battle was
a great and much-needed morale-booster.

After a smart and most decisive action, we
have, thank God, gained one of the most
splendid victories ever fought at sea. The
French fought with desperate bravery . . . It was
a desperate business, and the victory was gained
by our breaking the line.

Lieutenant J. Smith of the Queen's
Regiment, on board the *Royal George*, in
a letter to his mother (2 June 1794)

See colour section.

First-rate: a sailing warship of the first
'rate'; *see* RATING OF SHIPS.

Fish, to: apart from its primary meaning
this verb has two other nautical uses. A
yard or spar is 'fished' when another timber
is lashed to it like a splint; and to 'fish the
anchor' was formerly used to describe the
action of securing an anchor over the
gunwale by its flukes.

Fisher, John Arbuthnot, first Baron
Fisher of Kilverstone (1841–1920), known
as 'Jackie' or 'Jacky': admiral and First Sea
Lord (1904–10 and 1914–15). One of the
greatest administrators in the history of the
Navy, he held important commands at sea
and shore appointments over a long period,
from about 1875 onwards. Whatever he
touched he increased in efficiency, and his
many innovations and reforms did much to
shape the modern service. Above all,
perhaps, he prepared Britain for the

growing menace of Germany and for the First World War, reorganizing the distribution of the fleet and introducing the Dreadnought type of battleship and battle cruiser.

Fisheries: a thriving fishing industry is considered important not only for food but also as a valuable national reserve of ships and seamen. British fisheries are fortunate in geographical position and in long experience. The cod of the Grand Banks off Newfoundland were discovered and taken in Tudor times, and so too were the fish of the Arctic waters off Iceland and Norway, while at the same time a rich haul came from the waters of the Continental Shelf surrounding the British Isles. Today British fishing grounds have somewhat changed with the changed habits of certain fish such as cod and herring, but they may be divided into (i) the distant-water fishing grounds of the Arctic Circle in the Barents and White Seas, and off Iceland and Norway; the distant-water trawlers may be away for weeks at a time, cleaning, preparing and freezing their catch on board; (ii) the middle-water grounds off the Faeroes, the Norwegian coast and in the Irish Sea; and (iii) the inshore grounds off the British coasts.

The main trawler ports for landing fish are Hull and Grimsby, but Fleetwood, Aberdeen and other ports all play their part. The inshore fishing boats are centred on local ports all round the coast, but their numbers have declined in recent years. The development by other nations of modern fishing fleets has led to a large increase in the total catch and the series of international agreements which have been made to control and define fishing rights are more than ever necessary today.

See also COD WARS; FISHING CRAFT; SEALING; WHALING.

Fisherman's bend: *see* KNOTS.

Fishguard: a Welsh port on the N. coast of Dyfed, formerly Pembrokeshire; a packet

The herring fleet at Scarborough, September 1897.

station for the passage across St George's Channel to Rosslare and Waterford in Ireland.

Fishing craft: vessels specially designed or adapted for fishing, of which there are many kinds with a variety of local names. Many of the older types of inshore fishing boats have disappeared as the fishing industry has become more centralized and dependent upon expensive and highly equipped boats to handle larger catches. Today fishing boats are generally named by the type of gear they use. Of those that use nets, TRAWLERS are the best-known, catching fish for the most part in the lower layers of the sea. Also using nets, of a different kind and in a different way, are drifters and seiners, taking fish in the upper sea layers. Other boats use lines and hooks, often of great length, a method still found in various parts of the world and once much used by the cod-fishers on the Grand Banks off Newfoundland. Small boats called dories would set out from a mother ship, often a schooner, set their lines and return with their catch. *See also* FISHERIES; IDENTIFICATION MARKS.

Fitch, Ralph (?1550–1611): traveller and merchant adventurer. Originally a member of the Leathersellers' Company, he sailed with John NEWBERY's 1583 expedition and over the next 28 years was an indefatigable traveller and trader, often involved in hair-raising adventures and escapes. He was one of the first Englishmen to accomplish the overland route to India and the first to visit Burma and Siam. When he returned home in 1591 from a journey begun in 1586, he found his family had given him up for lost and had divided his estate.

Fitzroy, Robert (1805–65): admiral and distinguished hydrographer and meteorol-

ogist. From 1829 to 1836 he commanded the *BEAGLE* and so took part in the survey of Patagonia and the Straits of Magellan in which Darwin participated. He became head of the meteorological department in 1854. The Fitzroy barometer was named after him; he was responsible for a system of storm warnings; and he originated the first systematic weather forecasts.

Five-masted vessels: not a frequent type in sailing-ship history and not very successful when constructed, either on grounds of beauty or safe handling. For two examples *see FRANCE* and for a seven-masted vessel *see THOMAS W. LAWSON*.

Fix: a position calculated from bearings.

Flag: *see* FLAGS; HONOUR OF THE FLAG.

Flag-captain: the officer commanding the flag-ship in which the flag-officer sails.

Flag deck: *see* FLAG-LIEUTENANT.

Flag-lieutenant: an officer acting as a personal assistant to an officer of flag rank, i.e. rear-admirals and above.

Closely associated with the flag-lieutenant and his attendant yeomen in the sailing Navy was the flag deck, that part of the upper deck used in the old days for hand-signalling by flag and semaphore. In 1978 a new Defence Council decree obliterated this venerable reminder of the past by ordering that it be known henceforth as the 'signal deck', on the grounds that, in spoken communications, confusion was sometimes arising with 'flight deck'.

Flag-officer: an officer with the rank of rear-admiral or above. An officer promoted to admiral's rank was said to 'receive his flag'. From early times admirals flew special flags, their rank being indicated by colour, design and the positions in which they were hoisted. The story is a complicated one, since many sets of instructions were issued to keep pace with the development of squadronal colours and methods of warfare.

> I am sensible of the honour their Lordships have done me by permitting me to hoist my flag on so desirable a ship.
>
> Admiral William Cornwallis to the Admiralty on being given the *Royal Sovereign*, a new ship of 100 guns (1794)

> *Victory* is ordered to sea; whether my Flag goes out in her I have not heard. I am satisfied you may hoist your Flag whenever you please; and I do assure you that it will always give me pleasure to see your Flag fly in any Fleet under my command.
>
> Nelson to Rear-Admiral Murray (31 August 1805)

> And so the Admiral of a Fleet or Squadron hath his flag in the Main-top; the Vice-Admiral in the Fore-top and the Rear Admiral in the Missen-top.
>
> Nathaniel Boteler (*c*.1634)

Flags, naval: flags, under a wide variety of names and of many shapes, have been in use at sea from earliest times, their uses ranging from the purely decorative to elaborate and detailed communication between ships. To quote some interesting early English examples, the accounts for 1574 show the Queen's Serjeant Painter having prepared for her 'newe shippes' 24 ensigns of 'bolonia sarcenett of diverse coulors'. Some of the streamers were 84 ft long and 9 ft broad at the head. Drake and Hawkins, when they set out on their 1594 voyage, were provided with:

4 flags gilt with Her Majesty's arms
30 flags of St George

3 streamers with the Queen's badges in silver and gold
80 other streamers
26 ensigns

The total cost was £221 (or some thousands of pounds in modern value).

Apart from the purely decorative functions, the following chief types may be distinguished:

1. *Flags of command*, e.g. the Royal Standard, the Admiralty Flag, the flags of individual admirals, and pendants of command flown by commodores and senior officers. The Admiralty flag, a red flag displaying a gold FOUL ANCHOR and originally the flag of the Lord High Admiral, is flown continuously over the Admiralty building and is not lowered to half-mast even on the death of a sovereign.

2. *Flags* (or Colours) *of distinction*, i.e. those flown by ships of war (public and private), public ships used for other purposes than war, merchant shipping, and pleasure craft.

3. *Signal flags* for communication between ships of the same squadron or fleet, and between ships of different nations.

4. *Ceremonial flags* to mark particular circumstances and events.

Certain flags and signals have become particularly well known and some have passed into everyday speech. To 'show the white flag' is to surrender, the black flag was the emblem of piracy, the yellow flag indicated contagious disease on board, half-masting a flag is a sign of mourning, and so on.

See also BANNER; COLOURS; ENSIGN; HOUSE FLAGS; PENDANT; SIGNALS; STANDARD.

Flag-ship: ship carrying the admiral or

commander-in-chief, and flying his flag of command.

Flags of convenience: dodge adopted by a number of shipping companies to reduce their taxes and wage-bills, by registering with one of a number of foreign ports whose fees and safety standards, including manning levels, are less strict than those of the front-line maritime nations, such as Britain, Norway and the U.S. The main flags of convenience today are those of Liberia, Panama, Singapore and Cyprus. Technically speaking, Liberia at present has the world's largest fleet – according to Lloyd's Register of Shipping in mid-1976 2600 ships, of which 953 were tankers. Panama had 2680 ships, 260 of them tankers. Some of the flag-of-convenience nations, including the two just named, are setting up a much more stringent ship inspectorate to enforce maritime law.

One highly important aspect of the 'flag-of-convenience' device is the way it can affect safety at sea. It has been said that in some parts of the world a master's certificate can be purchased for £50 – which, in turn, could give the owner control of a supertanker several times the size of a football stadium. It may not be without significance that some of the most spectacular losses of recent years have been among ships sailing under such flags, with a low standard of proven navigational competence.

Flak: anti-aircraft fire, from the German word for anti-aircraft cannon, *Fliegerabwehrkanone* (or *Flugabwehrkanone*).

Flamborough Head: chalk headland, with a lighthouse, on the Yorkshire coast. On 23 September 1779 an action was fought off Flamborough between John Paul JONES, commanding a squadron consisting of the 40-gun *Bonhomme Richard*, the American frigate *Alliance* and two French frigates, and two British ships, the 44-gun *Serapis* (Captain Richard PEARSON) and the 22-gun *Countess of Scarborough* (Captain Thomas Piercy), convoying the Baltic fleet. With most of his crew disabled or killed, Pearson struck his colours, but the convoy was saved and the *Bonhomme Richard* later sank.

Flannel: a seaman's vest, originally made of flannel but now of cotton. The word is also used as service slang to describe unconvincing or pompous talk.

Flare: (1) a pyrotechnic signal, either held in the hand or fired from a special pistol, giving off a coloured smoke for day signals or a bright coloured light for night signals. Flares are generally used to attract attention or indicate distress.

(2) The widening out of the curve of a vessel's bows and sides.

Flatboat: a general name given to a flat-bottomed boat for transporting heavy objects or for landing men and materials on shallow shores.

Fleet: a number of ships in company; a

A flatboat armed with a small carronade.

division of a Navy under a single command; all the warships of a nation (e.g. 'the British fleet') or all the ships owned by a company (e.g. 'the P. & O. fleet'). The term is also used to describe all the ships of a particular kind (e.g. 'the tanker fleet', 'the fishing fleet').

Fleet Air Arm: all those officers, men and establishments concerned with flying, maintaining and controlling aircraft of the Royal Navy, whether afloat or ashore. *See also* ROYAL NAVAL AIR SERVICE.

'Fleet in being': technique of holding ships in a dilatory or evasive role, either to await reinforcements or to avoid head-on battle. It is essentially the strategy of a weaker force. The phrase originated with the Earl of Torrington in 1690 when he preferred to keep his 'fleet in being' while awaiting further ships, rather than risking immediate action with the French (*see* BEACHY HEAD, BATTLE OF).

Fleming, Captain Thomas (*fl.*1580–90): Elizabethan sailor whose chief claim to fame is that, while cruising in the *Golden Hind* pinnace, he sighted off the Lizard the Andalusian squadron of fifteen galleons commanded by Pedro de Valdes and sped to Plymouth with the news of the approach of the Spanish Armada. Whether or not he interrupted Drake's famous game of bowls is another (and not very important) matter.

Fletcher, Francis (*fl.*1570–80): chaplain to Sir Francis Drake on the famous voyage of 1577–81. He was a supporter of Thomas DOUGHTY, executed by Drake for treason, and, though Fletcher found it expedient to conceal his feelings and hold his tongue on the voyage, he later gave vent to strong criticism of his commander.

Flinders, Matthew (1774–1814): naval captain, surveyor and discoverer. He assisted George Bass in a survey of the coasts of New South Wales and Van Diemen's Land and, in command, first, of the *INVESTIGATOR*, then of the *Cumberland*, made the first survey of a large part of the coast of Australia (1801–3). In December 1803 he put in at Mauritius without knowing that England and France were at war, and he was detained there by the French for over six years. His published works include valuable data on magnetism, hydrography and meteorology; and he seems to have been the first navigator to discover the errors in the compass caused by the presence of iron in ships.

Flinders' bar: a small piece of iron used on the binnacle to correct compass error caused by a ship's magnetism.

Floating dock: a dock so built that it floats but can be flooded to allow ships to enter; it is then pumped dry to allow attention to the ship's hull or propellers.

Floating Republic, the: name given in parts of the press to the ships that mutinied at Spithead and the Nore (1797); *see* MUTINY.

Flogging: one of the most barbaric and longest-lived methods of punishment on board ship, usually inflicted on the bare back with the 'cat-o'-nine-tails' – a short wooden stick with two-foot-long knotted cords. Offenders were brought up on deck and lashed, sometimes across a cannon, but more often to one of the gratings borrowed from the hatches. Sentence was carried out before the captain, lieutenants, and a full muster of the hands. Theoretically, at least for a period, a court-martial was necessary for a sentence of more than twelve lashes; but it was always possible to circumvent this by awarding twelve lashes for each of several regulations breached by the same offence: e.g. a drunken seaman, as well as being drunk, could easily start a fight,

swear, be incapable of carrying out an order etc.

Heavier punishments could bring unconsciousness, permanent disfigurement or, in extreme cases, death. Often they ruined a good seaman by breaking his health, his pride and his spirit, so that, in the words of one observer, 'he rarely held up his head or did his best again'. It took a great deal to convince the Navy that indiscriminate punishment of this sort was not only ineffective but unnecessary. Yet such commanders as COLLINGWOOD, one of the finest of Nelson's officers, rarely had recourse to it.

An alternative to punishment at the gratings was flogging round the fleet, in which the sufferer was brought alongside every ship in the anchorage and lashed by a boatswain's mate to the accompaniment of the 'Rogue's March' thudded out by the drums.

From about 1830 returns of punishment

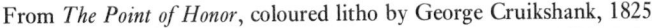

From *The Point of Honor*, coloured litho by George Cruikshank, 1825.

were submitted quarterly; and (making the rash assumption that all captains were scrupulously honest in their records) we know that in 1839 2007 men were flogged in the Royal Navy. Six years later the number was only 860, a sign that flogging was, at long last, on its way out. The Naval Discipline Act of 1866 limited the punishment to 48 lashes. It was subsequently 'suspended', first in peace-time, then in war-time; but, oddly enough, it was never formally abolished, as it was (1881) in the Army.

The grim humour of the seaman was not suppressed even by such barbarous punishments. Being flogged over a cannon was called 'kissing (or "marrying") the gunner's daughter'; another description of flogging was 'putting on a red check shirt'.

Flood tide: the inflow or rise of the tide in a channel or river estuary; the opposite of ebb tide.

Flores, Battle of: *see* GRENVILLE, SIR RICHARD.

Flory boats: old name for the watermen's boats, especially on the River Thames, which used to ferry steamship passengers to and from the landing stages.

Flotilla: a word of Spanish derivation meaning a little fleet or a number of small ships. The name is now used for a group of ships of a particular kind or for particular duties within a fleet.

> Come you back to Mandalay,
> Where the old Flotilla lay,
> Can't you 'ear their paddles chunkin' from
> Rangoon to Mandalay?
>
> Rudyard Kipling, 'Mandalay'

Flotsam: any material or goods lost at sea

and floating on the water. Compare JETSAM.

Fluke: the broad, flat and pointed end of the arm of an anchor.

Flush deck: with the weather deck forming one continuous surface, with no raised or lower part.

'Flying Cloud': reputed to have been the fastest of all American clippers. Built by Donald McKay and launched in 1851, she was 209·5 ft long and 40·7 ft wide. Her greatest achievements were two passages from New York to San Francisco via Cape Horn in 89 days.

'Flying Dutchman': phantom ship reputed to appear in stormy weather off the Cape of Good Hope. According to one story, the original vessel, carrying precious metal, was the scene of murder and plague and, unable to find home in any port, is condemned to wander the seas for all time.

Flying jib: a small triangular sail, uppermost of the sails on the jib-boom of a ship. *See also* SAIL.

Fo'c'sle: *see* FORECASTLE.

Fog: one of the great hazards of the sea, often causing collisions and faulty navigation. Sound signals have to be made by ships in fog, either by foghorn or whistle; and fog signals are also provided, by a variety of devices, from the shore, from light-ships or buoys.

Foley, Sir Thomas (1757–1833): admiral; one of Nelson's 'Band of Brothers' and with him at the Nile (1798), where, commanding the *GOLIATH*, he led the English line into action, and at Copen-

Flying Cloud.

hagen (1801), where he was flag-captain on the *Elephant*.

Foot rope: a rope under the yards and on which men stood to furl the sails.

Forbes, Captain James Nicol (1821–74): popularly known as 'Bully' Forbes and one of the most colourful seamen of the clipper era, he is credited with the saying 'Hell or Melbourne!' He commanded the *MARCO POLO* and brought over the famous *Lightning* on her maiden voyage from Donald McKay's Boston yard to Liverpool (1854). He seems to have been a showy, daring character who appealed to the popular imagination. He also had, according to one writer, 'that peculiar sort of sixth sense which has belonged to most of the noted ship-captains of the past and which in these days of wireless and other scientific aids to navigation is perhaps hardly needed.' However, his sixth sense seems to have deserted him when he lost the new clipper *Schomberg* (1855), stranded on a sand-bank where she finally went to pieces. Though he was exonerated by a court of inquiry, he never came back to top command. His

163

memorial bears the simple inscription 'Master of the famous *Marco Polo*'.

Forbes, John (1714–96): admiral. One of his distinctions is that, as a Lord of the Admiralty, he refused to sign the warrant for the execution of BYNG. Another is his connection with the evolution of the uniform of the Royal Navy: *see* NAVY BLUE.

Fore: the nautical word for 'front' and used as a prefix in many words connected with ships; for example, the sails on the fore mast were termed fore top gallant, fore royal etc. See the entries below.

Fore and aft: lengthwise, from bows to stern.

Fore-and-aft rigged: with sails that lie in the direction of the ship's length and are set abaft the mast. *See also* RIG (*1 and 2*).

Forecastle (or **fo'c'sle**; pronounced 'foksl'): the foremost part of the weather deck. (*See* CASTLES for the origin of the name.) In merchant ships the crew's quarters were originally below the forecastle, and so the word was sometimes used for the crew itself, e.g. 'a forecastle hand'. *See p.577.*

Fore course: a square sail set on a ship's foreyard. *See* SAIL.

Forefoot: the foremost part of the keel where it curves upward to meet the stern. *See p.577.*

Fore mast: the foremost mast in a vessel. In a sailing ship of only two masts the fore mast is only so called if the after mast is the main mast.

Forenoon: the later part of the morning before 12 noon. The forenoon watch is from 0800 to 1200; the morning watch is from 0400 to 0800.

Forepeak: a compartment, generally small, in the bows of a ship.

Fore River Shipbuilding Company: shipbuilding company of Quincy, Massachusetts, who built the only seven-masted schooner, the *THOMAS W. LAWSON*.

Foresail: the lowest sail on the fore mast, above which on a three-masted square-rigged ship were the fore lower topsail, the fore upper topsail, the fore top-gallant, the fore royal and the fore skysail. In smaller craft the name can apply to a sail set forward of the mast. *See also* SAIL.

Fore-staff: *see* CROSS-STAFF.

Forester, Cecil Scott (1899–1966): novelist. Turning from medicine to writing, Forester established himself as a story-writer whose tales won many readers. After earlier successes with novels of the Peninsular War he wrote in 1937 *The Happy Return*, the first of the Hornblower stories for which he is chiefly known. Horatio Hornblower appears to be a fictional reflection of Nelson, and the many novels about Hornblower's exploits at various stages of his career not only grip the reader but also present an excellent picture of the Navy and sailing ships at the time of the French and Napoleonic Wars.

Foretop: originally a small platform at the top of the fore mast; used also as a name for one of the divisions into which a ship's company was grouped.

Foreyard: the lowest yard on the fore mast of square-rigged vessels.

'**Forfarshire**': *see* DARLING, GRACE.

Forties: an area of sea between Scotland and Norway, one of the divisions of the seas round the British Isles variously named to localize meteorological forecasts. *See also* ROARING FORTIES.

Forward (pronounced 'forr-ard'): a position near or towards the bow of a vessel.

Fother: a hole or leak is said to be 'fothered' when it is stopped by covering it with a COLLISION MAT, a sail or other material.

'**Foudroyant**': an honoured name which first came on to the English Navy List in 1758, when the French 84-gun ship was captured off Cape de Gapa by vessels from the Mediterranean fleet under Admiral Henry Osborne, eventually surrendering to the *Monmouth*. As was customary, the ship retained her foreign name; she was broken up in 1787. The next *Foudroyant*, a second-rate built in 1798, had an exceptionally long life, becoming a training ship in 1862 and being eventually wrecked off Blackpool in 1897. The third started as the *Trincomalee*, a fifth-rate of 46 guns built at Bombay (1817), later reduced to a sixth-

rate. Renamed *Foudroyant*, she served as a famous training ship and was actually requisitioned for naval service in 1941–7, when she was the oldest shp afloat. In the last stage of her fine career she provided short courses of instruction for thousands of boys and girls from schools all over Britain.

Foul anchor: an anchor is 'foul' when it is aweigh and the cable or chain is entangled round its shank, arms or flukes. The device used on the Admiralty flag (and on the buttons of naval uniform) is a foul anchor. The anchor in association with the English Lord High Admiral's arms occurs in 1558

Foudroyant in dry dock during a recent survey.

(in Scotland on seals of 1515), but it can be assumed that it was in use earlier. The foul anchor is first found on a seal of Howard of Effingham after he became Earl of Nottingham in 1596.

'Foul Weather Jack': *see* BYRON, JOHN.

Four Days' Battle (1–4 June 1666): battle off North Foreland in the Second Dutch War, one of the hardest ever fought by the Royal Navy, with 60 English ships commanded by George Monck, Duke of Albemarle (then nearly 60 years old), against 90 Dutchmen under de Ruyter. Monck fought stubbornly for two days, then retreated towards the Thames; but, sighting Prince Rupert's squadron coming to his aid, he went back on the offensive and broke through the enemy line from leeward. On the fourth day, de Ruyter had had enough and withdrew; but, numerically, he had by far the best of the encounter, with only seven or eight ships lost but twenty English ships captured or destroyed. The remarkable thing is that Albemarle, 'hitching up his breeches, as was his wont', was at sea again seven weeks later with 90 sail (*see* ST JAMES'S DAY FIGHT).

Four-masted barques: a number of fine four-masted barques were built in the late 19th century, particularly in Scottish yards. Among them were the 'Counties' East India Line ships; the *Loch Torridon* and *Loch Moidart*, considered the finest four-masters ever built and used on the Australian wool-run; and the 'Falls' group (Falls of *Earn*, *Gary*, and *Halladale*). All these were iron ships, varying in tonnage from 1865 to 2386 (gross register).

Four-masters: the earliest known four-masted vessel in England was the *Regent*, built in 1487. *See also* JAMES I.

'Fox': *see* MCCLINTOCK, SIR FRANCIS LEOPOLD.

Fox (or Foxe), Luke (1586–1635): navigator. In 1631 he sailed from London in the *Charles* pinnace in search of a NORTH-WEST PASSAGE, returning after a six-month voyage. He published a book with the curious title *The North-west Fox, or, Fox from the north-west Passage*, containing valuable information on the ice, tides, compass etc. A channel on the west shore of Baffin Land is named after him.

Frame: the main outline of the ship – keel, ribs, beams etc. – before any planking was laid on. In the old days ships often stood 'in frame' for a year or more, on the mistaken theory that exposure to the elements

The *Loch Torridon* moored off Gravesend, 1881.

seasoned the timber. In practice, this often meant that deterioration and decay had already set in when the ship was launched.

'France': five-masted barque built of steel at Glasgow (1890) for the French Navy and designed for handling nitrate cargoes. Her sail area was 49,000 square ft, and for a short time she was the largest sailing vessel ever built in a British yard (gross register 3784), but she was soon eclipsed by the five-master *Maria Rickmers* (3822 tons), built at Glasgow the following year for the Germans and the rice trade with the East. Both ships were lost at sea, the *France* in 1901 after having been abandoned by her crew, and the *Maria Rickmers* in 1892 on the return trip from her maiden voyage. Neither was easy to handle, the safety margin was small and, at least with the latter ship, it was thought her crew of 40 was insufficient in bad weather.

Frankland, Sir Thomas (?1717–1784): admiral. He was especially well-known as a frigate captain on the Bahama station

(1740–45), capturing many ships, including a number of privateers.

Franklin, Sir John (1786–1847): Arctic explorer. After an early career which included service as a midshipman at Copenhagen and Trafalgar, his energies were almost entirely given over to exploration and discovery, and his name is imperishably associated with the Arctic. He commanded the *Trent* in an expedition of 1818 and then headed the 1819–22 expedition which traversed North America from Fort York to the mouth of the Coppermine, where the party embarked on the Arctic Sea and eventually, after great privations, reached Fort Providence and York via the 'Barren Grounds'. Another major expedition followed in 1825–7, after which he was knighted for his services.

After a period as Lieutenant-Governor of Van Diemen's Land (1837–43), where he did much to improve conditions for the convicts, he was appointed – at the age of nearly 60 – to command an expedition in search of the NORTH-WEST PASSAGE. He

167

From a photograph taken before the sailing of the *Erebus*, May 1845.

left England in May 1845 with a party of 129 officers and men in the *EREBUS* and *Terror*. The ships were sighted in Baffin Bay in July 1845 but were not heard of again. No fewer than thirty-nine expeditions were sent out to discover their fate. At last in 1859 Captain MCCLINTOCK discovered a cairn containing a log of the expedition up to April 1848, which indicated that Franklin's ships had been held fast in the ice near King William Island. He himself had died on 11 June 1847. In 1848 his men had abandoned the ships and set out overland, but all had evidently perished on their journey.

One of the most courageous and indomitable organizers of the search expeditions was Franklin's wife, who shares his memorial in Westminster Abbey. The point reached by his last expedition fully entitles him to the honour of being the discoverer of the North-West Passage, the prize sought by so many seamen through the centuries.

An old man, with broad shoulders... grey hair, full face and bald head. He wore spectacles, was quite lame, and appeared sick... But despite his ill health he was always laughing.

> A description given to Captain Charles Hall by two Eskimoes

The value of such expeditions as his... is not to be measured in terms of use or profit, but in terms of immortal honour and example. It is on record that Franklin took the command in the teeth of remonstrance, on the score of his age, at head-quarters; 'But you are fifty-nine, Sir John,' said Lord Haddington to him; '*Not quite*,' answered the fine old seaman.

> C. R. L. Fletcher, *Historical Portraits*

Fraser of North Cape, first Baron, Admiral of the Fleet Bruce Austin Fraser (1888–   ): successively Commander-in-Chief Home Fleet (1943–4), Eastern Fleet (1944), Pacific Fleet (1945–6), and Portsmouth (1947–8); First Sea Lord and Chief of Naval Staff (1948–51). The exploit most associated with his name is the destruction of the German battle cruiser *SCHARNHORST*.

Fred Wunpound: a Royal Navy cat; before he 'swallowed the anchor', the longest serving member of the survey ship *Hecate*, with the title Leading Seacat. He was pressed into service in 1966 in return for a payment to the Plymouth R.S.P.C.A. of a bounty of £1, from which he took his name. He acquired a proper dossier of service documents, showing his promotion from Junior Hecat to Ordinary Hecat and Able Hecat, and qualified for a kit allowance. He travelled over a quarter of a million miles before new anti-rabies regulations brought about his discharge. He had earned two good conduct medals and one disgraceful conduct badge following an incident in Brixham fish-market.

Freeboard: the vertical clearance between the water-line and the gunwale of any craft. *See* LOADLINES.

Freedom of the seas: in general, the right to sail on, and trade in, the oceans of the world without special restrictions, rights of boarding, insistence on salutes etc., that have characterized certain periods of maritime history. In practice, many countries still impose certain territorial limits for economic reasons and considerations of national safety.

Freedoms of motion: the types of movement a ship can make, basically reduced to six, though there can be combinations of them.

Rolling: a rotation about the ship's horizontal fore-and-aft axis.

Pitching: a rotation about the ship's transverse horizontal axis.

Heaving: a vertical lifting and falling.

Yawing: a swing off-course by the bow or stern.

Swaying: a horizontal sideways movement of the ship.

Surging: a strong forward movement with some recoil.

The movements are due partly to tricks of wind, weather and water, but, equally important, to the design of the ship.

Freighter: a cargo vessel generally, but the name also applies to an agent arranging the shipment of goods.

Fremantle, Sir Thomas Francis (1765–1819): admiral; a distinguished officer who entered the Navy in 1778 and saw service in many engagements, including Santa Cruz under Nelson (where he was wounded), Copenhagen, and Trafalgar, where he commanded *Neptune* and afterwards received the gold medal and a sword of honour from the Patriotic Fund. He was also decorated by a number of other countries.

His wife Betsy is well-known in her own right as an amusing and vivid diarist. She had been evacuated from Italy in 1796 when Napoleon's troops were arriving, fell in love with Fremantle, then commanding the *Inconstant* which brought her away, and married him. In the early days of her marriage she was on board Fremantle's *Seahorse* at Santa Cruz when Nelson's right arm was shattered. Nelson was rowed to the *Seahorse*, the nearest ship, but, though nearly unconscious and in great pain, he refused to go on board because he did not wish to alarm Betsy, anxiously awaiting her husband's return from the beaches. 'I will die', he said, 'rather than alarm Mrs Fremantle by her seeing me in this state when I can give her no tidings of her husband.' Her diaries were published in 1940.

French prizes: ships captured from the French were an important source not only of increased naval strength but, at times, also of improved design. The French treated naval architecture as a science long before their English counterparts, and kept precise records from about 1660. Many of the improvements in English ship design can be traced to some French prize.

French Wars: it is strange to reflect that, up to the beginning of the 20th century, 'the Great War' meant the war against

France at the end of the 18th and beginning of the 19th century. The French Wars fall into two periods:

1. *The French Revolutionary Wars* (1792–1802). Despite Napoleon's brilliant campaigns on land, Britain maintained her maritime supremacy in the Atlantic and Mediterranean, and the victory at the Nile (1798) temporarily isolated the Emperor and ensured the failure of his Egyptian expedition.

2. *The* NAPOLEONIC WARS (1803–15).

The final punishment was inflicted by avenging armies on the battlefields of Leipsic and Waterloo. But the decisiveness of these encounters should not obscure the fact that it was England's maritime shield which saved the world... The truth did not escape the mind of the Emperor... 'In all my plans,' he said with something of the petulance of a child, 'I have always been thwarted by the British fleet.'

Geoffrey Callender, *The Naval Side of British History* (1924)

Frigate: from Tudor times the name has been given to many different types of ship, but the two types which are most memorable are the frigates of Nelson's times and the modern frigate. In the latter half of the 18th century the frigate was next in importance to ships of the line and was used for many purposes in addition to cruising and scouting, for it was a fast vessel, three-masted and fully-rigged, and on a single deck carried a formidable power of up to 50 guns. Nelson's remark in 1798,

'Was I to die at this moment want of frigates would be found stamped on my heart', shows how valuable frigates had become.

During the transition from sail to steam several curious types of ship were called frigates, but the evolution of the cruiser replaced the name until it was revived in the Second World War when the Admiralty built a class of ship, larger and more powerful than the sloop and corvette, and designed especially for convoy work. These new frigates appeared in 1943, and the type has developed until today the Navy has a large number with an average displacement of over 2000 tons and 360 ft in length. The most recently completed frigates carry an anti-submarine helicopter, have a speed of 34 knots, and are armed with missile launchers, guns and torpedoes.

See also BLACKWALL FRIGATE; STONE FRIGATE.

Frobisher, Sir Martin (1539–94): navigator who, while still a boy, was noted by his grandfather, Sir John York, as being 'of great spirit and bold courage and natural hardiness of body'. When only about 14 he joined an expedition to the Guinea coast. In the course of the next 20 years he led an adventurous life, at one time being captured and imprisoned by the Portuguese. He was an active pirate/privateer, often holding commissions from Protestant foreigners such as William of Orange, and

was arrested by the English government five or six times, though he seems to have escaped punishment, probably because the Queen and her ministers found his unorthodox services useful. In 1576 began the most important part of his career, when he set out on the first of three voyages to the Arctic, one object being the search for the NORTH-WEST PASSAGE, in which he had long been interested. Of his three ships, one deserted him and another was lost, so that he was left with the *Gabriel* and 18 men. Despite appalling weather and 'monstrous great ilands of ise' he continued northwards, entered and named Frobisher's Strait, exchanged gifts with the Eskimoes and brought one native home, complete with kayak. He also brought back a specimen of the sulphide of iron known as iron pyrites (later called 'fools' gold'), which, despite the denial of English goldsmiths that it had an auriferous content, became the chief object of a second expedition, which returned with 200 tons of it. A third expedition set out in 1578 with the intention of bringing back 2000 tons, but the only important result was Frobisher's entry into what is now known as Hudson's Strait. (Frobisher called it 'Mistaken Strait' because it was not where he intended to be.) Other piratical ventures followed. He was with Drake's West Indian expedition of 1586 and he commanded the *Triumph* against the Armada (*see* PORTLAND BILL). After this he was knighted for his services. Between 1589 and 1592 he made three voyages to the Azores and captured, among other prizes, the *Madre de Dios*, worth some £150,000. The end of his turbulent career, marked by physical endurance, invincible courage and great seamanship, came when he was killed while in command of a squadron sent by Queen Elizabeth to help the French Huguenots.

Frock: naval officers used to wear a coat cut long and similar in style to the civilian frock-coat. Its use was for semi-formal occasions when full dress was not required, such as on Sundays and when officer of the watch in harbour. The name is also given to thick white woollen sweaters issued to submarine crews.

Fruit clipper: type of ship designed especially for such traffic as the West Indian fruit trade, built primarily for speed because of the perishable nature of the cargo. A characteristic was the deep heel (after-end of the keel). SALCOMBE fruit clippers were one well-known type.

'Frying pans': name given to the old Whitby collier brigs from the wind-vane they carried at the top of the main mast, a large disc with pointer attached.

Full and by: sailing close-hauled to the wind.

Full-rigged ship: a vessel with three or more masts, carrying square sails on all of them. *See also* RIG.

Fulton, Robert (1765–1815): American engineer and inventor. Among his successes was the *Clermont*, the first commercially profitable steam boat, built in 1807 and put into service on the River Hudson between New York and Albany. His *Fulton*, a 38-ton vessel with central paddle-wheels, was the first steam warship. He also experimented with submarine explosives; *see NAUTILUS. See also PHOENIX.*

Funnel: a ship's chimney providing passage to the atmosphere for the smoke, fumes or gases from the furnace or engines. Most merchant shipping lines decorate their ships' funnels with their own distinctive colours, badges or symbols.

Furl: to furl sails is to fold or bundle them up, making them secure on yard or mast so that they no longer take the wind.

Futtock: (1) a crooked lower timber below the deck of a sailing vessel. (2) 'Futtock plates' are iron plates in a ship's top to which rigging is secured; (3) 'futtock shrouds' are short shrouds from the futtock plates to a lower mast. The word probably derives from 'foot-hook'.

Gabbard, Battle of the (2–4 June 1653): an encounter in the First Anglo-Dutch War, fought between the English commanders-in-chief Monck and Deane and a Dutch fleet under Tromp on the *Brederode*. Deane was killed in the first broadside, but Monck went on to win a decisive victory, nearly capturing Tromp himself. To save his flag-ship, when the English had boarded her, Tromp, with what remained of his powder, blew the boarders and his upper deck into the sea, escaping badly burnt.

The Gabbard is a sand-bank off the coast of Suffolk.

Gaff: the spar which extends and secures the upper edge of a four-sided fore-and-aft sail ('gaff topsail'). To 'blow the gaff' was to show the ship's colours suddenly at this point, and has now the colloquial meaning of divulging a secret.

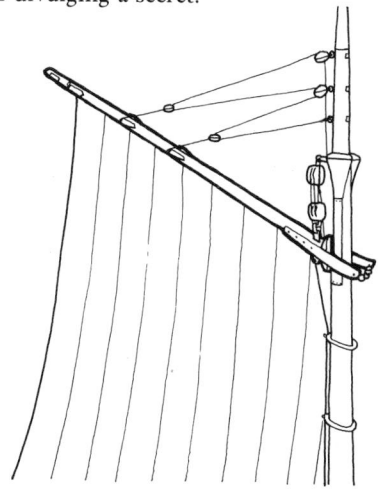

Gage (or **gauge**): to have the 'weather gage' is to be in a position of advantage by being to windward of another vessel or vessels. The 'lee gage' is the position of a ship to leeward of others.

Gage, Thomas (*d.*1656): author of *The English-American his Travail by Sea and Land* (1648), a work translated into French, Dutch and German. A complex and hardy spirit, he began his career as a friar of a Spanish Dominican order, living for some time among the Indian tribes of South America. He developed an itch for travel, crossed Nicaragua and the Isthmus of Panama, and reached England in 1641, in time to join the Parliamentarian forces in the Civil War. He renounced his Roman Catholicism and held two Church of England livings in Kent.

Gagging: a minor punishment in the old Navy, sometimes inflicted for bad language, impertinence etc. The offender's hands were tied behind his back and an iron marline spike, of the sort used for forcing apart the strands of a rope, was lashed between his teeth for several hours.

Gale: a wind classed on the BEAUFORT SCALE as Force 8, fresh or near gale, blowing at 34–40 nautical miles per hour, or Force 9, strong gale, blowing at 41–47 nautical miles per hour. More loosely used, 'gale' describes any strong wind of Force 8 or more.

Galiot (or **galliot, galyot**): sometimes a small galley with, for example, a single mast and 15 to 20 seats for rowers; more often, a one- or two-masted Dutch or Flemish merchantman with a large gaff mainsail. But it is difficult to be dogmatic with many early names and types of vessel. Some early Navy Lists, for example, make

little or no distinction between galiots and hoys.

Galleass (or **galliass** etc.): a combination of galley and galleon, a war vessel usually three- or four-masted but carrying a large number of oars as well as sails. Extensively used by Mediterranean peoples, especially the Venetians, the galleass disappeared from northern European waters after about 1600.

See colour section.

Galleon: a term used indiscriminately, and often inaccurately, for 16th-century ships and especially those built by Spain. The galleon was built to some extent on galley lines but higher out of the water, usually four-masted, and with a long beakhead. It was also a true ship of war, carrying cannon on decks within the ship, though the Spaniards also used large galleons for trading with their American possessions. The Elizabethan galleon in England developed comparatively fine lines, with a forecastle set well back from the stem. As an example of dimensions, the *Elizabeth Jonas*, rebuilt in 1597–8, was 100 ft along the keel, with a rake forward of 36 ft and aft of 6 ft, a breadth of 38 ft and a depth in the hold of 18 ft. The precise armament is uncertain, but was in the neighbourhood of nearly 50 guns (demi-cannon, cannon perier, culverins, demi-culverins and sakers), along with smaller guns.

Gallery: a narrow platform running round the stern of a ship; e.g. QUARTER-GALLERY. *See also* CLOSED GALLERIES.

Galley: (1) ship's kitchen; (2) originally a sea-going vessel, long, narrow and of shallow draught, propelled by banks of oars and particularly suited to inland seas. The descendants of the war galleys of Greece and Rome continued in the Mediterranean till the end of the 18th century. By the 15th century a single-decked vessel had evolved using sails in addition to oars. The term is usually associated with Mediterranean countries; but Henry VII had a *Galley Subtile* in 1546, and as late as 1704 Captain Thomas Bowrey caused Richard Wells of Rotherhithe to build for the India trade the *Mary Galley*, a small merchantman which, as well as having the usual complement of masts and sails, could also be driven by eight oars. She made one voyage to Batavia, but on the return trip was captured off the coast of Jutland by privateers.

Behold this galley, my friends: fancy you hear her tell how once she was the fastest among ships, able to show her heels to any keel afloat, whether driven by oars or sails! . . . And you, O Pontic Amastris, and Cytorus green with box . . . well you also know it: for on your top she stood a tiny tree, in your waters first dipped her oars, and thence through stormy seas she brought her master, now close-hauled on the port tack, now on the starboard, now running free with a following wind . . .

Catullus, 'To a Galley' (*c.*50 B.C.)

Galliot: *see* GALIOT.

Gallipoli: town and peninsula in Turkey on the Dardanelles, the scene of an

A contemporary model of a galley of the Knights of Malta.

unsuccessful attempt by the Allies in 1915 to take the peninsula and then Constantinople in an effort to eliminate Turkey from the First World War and link up with Russia. The preliminary naval attack failed: two British battleships and a French ship sank, and others were damaged by Turkish mines. A month later British and Anzac Troops (*A*ustralian and *N*ew Zealand *A*rmy *C*orps) made landings with great bravery and heavy losses. The attempt had to be abandoned, the failure being largely due to poor planning, since the advantage of surprise had been lost after the earlier naval attack. (*See p. 176.*)

In the Dardanelles five great battleships have gone down. In the southern lands such losses would cause countless comments; but they cause Englishmen to become only more silent, thoughtful and busy.

M. Lazare Kossovac in *Samouprava*
(*The Times*, 26 June 1915)

Ship after ship, crammed with soldiers, moved slowly out of harbour, in the lovely day, and felt again the heave of the sea. No such gathering of fine ships has ever been seen upon this earth, and the beauty and the exaltation of the youth upon them made them like sacred things as they moved away. All the thousands of men aboard them gathered on deck to see, till each rail was thronged... they cheered and cheered till the harbour rang with cheering. As each ship crammed with soldiers drew near the battleships, the men swung their caps and cheered again, and the sailors answered, and the noise of cheering swelled, and the men in the ships not yet moving joined in, and the men ashore... They left the harbour very, very slowly; this tumult of cheering lasted a long time; no one who heard it will ever forget it, or think of it unshaken.

John Masefield, *Gallipoli* (1916)

Gambier, James, first Baron Gambier (1756–1833): admiral. He took part in the

175

British troops going ashore at Gallipoli, passing H.M.S. *Implacable*.

capture of Charlestown (1780), was the first to break the enemy line on the 'Glorious FIRST OF JUNE' (1794) and led the fleet at the bombardment of Copenhagen when the Danish fleet surrendered (1807). Despite all this he was in many ways an incompetent commander and administrator: on one occasion, while commanding the Channel fleet, he failed to destroy the French ships in the Basque Roads on the grounds that the use of fire-ships was a 'horrible anti-Christian mode of warfare' (1809). One of his captains (Admiral Eliab Harvey) in a fit of temper described him as a canting methodist, psalm-singer and hypocrite; but he was an upright, if stupid, man. *See also* EVANGELICALS.

Gammon (or **gammoning**): to lash or secure the bowsprit to the stem of a vessel, or the lashing or chain so used.

Ganger: old term for a member of the press-gang.

'Ganges': the last British sailing line-of-battle ship, of 84 guns, launched at Bombay in 1821. When she was paid off in 1861, no other sailing ship of the line remained in the Navy. In 1866 she became a training ship, moored in Falmouth Bay. The establishment became shore-based in 1905, at Shotley Gate, near Ipswich, Suffolk. Some 100,000 men trained in *Ganges*, some of them rising to flag rank and many rendering distinguished service. It closed down in June 1976, with an impressive ceremony attended by many of its old

Gammon.

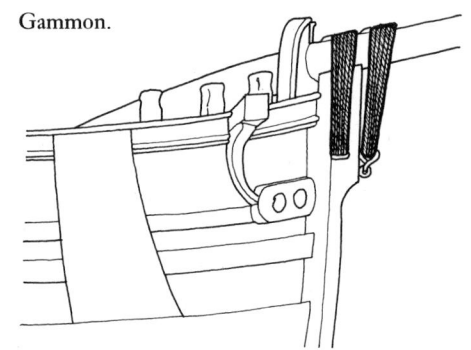

company. The tall mast, raised ashore by traditionalists so that the shore establishment still looked something like a ship, is retained as a memorial.

Gangway: any free passage way, but more particularly the point of access to a ship from the wharf or jetty; the construction used to provide it; in its simplest form, a gang plank.

Gantline: *see* GIRT-LINE.

Gap, Battle of the: name sometimes given to that part of the struggle in the Second World War when British shipping, because of the range involved, could not be protected by air-cover. The gap was gradually closed by longer-ranging aircraft, merchantmen so converted that they could fly their own air-cover, and the use of bases nearer the critical areas.

Garboard strake: a row of planks or plates running along and outside a ship's bottom next to the keel.

Gardner, Alan, first Baron Gardner (1742–1809): a distinguished sailor who was created a baronet for his services in Howe's battle off Ushant, 1 June 1794 ('The Glorious FIRST OF JUNE') and was later raised to the peerage. He had previously fought in a number of other actions, including Quiberon Bay (1759) and Rodney's victory over de Grasse in the West Indies (1782). In 1797 he had the responsibility of interviewing the mutineers at Spithead (*see* MUTINY). He became Rear-Admiral of the Blue in 1799 and full Admiral in 1808. He is not to be confused with his less well-known son, Alan Hyde Gardner, second Baron, who was appointed Rear-Admiral of the Blue in the same year as his father became Admiral of the Red. (In the years 1760–1815 there were at least ten Gardners commissioned in the Navy and almost as many Gardiners, the spellings sometimes being interchanged.)

Gash: naval slang for any waste, particularly from mess-deck or galley.

Gasket: a small piece of rope or canvas used to secure a furled sail to the yard.

Gauge: *see* GAGE.

General chase (or **chase**): the general pursuit of the enemy on the run. In the days of the sailing line-of-battle ships in the 18th century, British naval commanders were bound by the Permanent Fighting

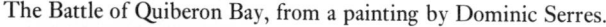

The Battle of Quiberon Bay, from a painting by Dominic Serres.

Instructions, which laid down formal battle procedures and insisted on the preservation of the line of battle (*see* LINE AHEAD). The exception occurred in Article 25:

> If the enemy be put to the run, and the Admiral thinks it convenient the whole fleet shall follow them, he will make all the sail he can himself after the enemy, and fire two guns out of his fore-chase; then every ship in the fleet is to use his best endeavour to come up with the enemy and lay them on board.

This was known as the general chase, and developed from a disorganized free-for-all into a fairly precise and well-ordered manoeuvre. One of the most famous successes illustrating the organized general chase was Hawke's victory over the French at the Battle of Quiberon Bay (1759; *see p. 177*).

Generals at Sea: senior commanders at sea before the title of Admiral came generally into use for the sea service. 'General' did not at one time have an exclusively military connotation, so that Drake, for example, was on occasion named 'General'. The group to whom the name is specifically applied are the three army officers sent afloat in one ship during the Commonwealth – Edward POPHAM (?1610–1651), Richard DEANE (1610–53) and Robert BLAKE (1599–1657).

Gibraltar: Gibraltar lies at the western end of the Mediterranean where its peninsular rock fortress commands the Straits of the same name. In antiquity it was known as one of the Pillars of Hercules, and throughout the ages it has had an eventful history. Gibraltar came into British possession in 1704 during the War of the Spanish Succession, being taken by Dutch as well as British forces under Sir George Rooke. In 1713 by the Treaty of Utrecht the cession of the Rock to Britain was accepted by Spain, but that country has ever sought its return to her sovereignty. After the failure of an assault in 1726 Spain once more laid siege to Gibraltar for over three years (1780–83) during the War of American Independence. The siege nearly succeeded at times, but the Rock was three times relieved by British naval forces, the first under Admiral Sir George Rodney, the next under Admiral George Darby, and the third in 1782 under Admiral Lord Howe. With the opening of the Suez Canal (1869) Gibraltar became of increasing importance as a port and naval base. Extensive harbour improvements were made, and the strengthening of its defences was continued during the Second World War to counter the threat of a possible German-Spanish attack, which never materialized. In recent years the Spanish have continued to press their claim to Gibraltar, but in 1967 the Gibraltarians overwhelmingly voted to continue their link with Britain, and Gibraltar still has the only remaining royal dockyard outside the British Isles.

Gig: a ship's boat, light and fast, with oars and sail, generally used by the commanding officer.

> Oh, I am a cook and a captain bold,
> And the mate of the Nancy brig,
> And a bo'sun tight and a midshipmite,
> And the crew of the captain's gig.
>
> Sir W. S. Gilbert, 'The Yarn of
> the *Nancy Bell*'

Gilbert: *see* HARD A-GILBERT.

Gilbert, Sir Humphrey (?1539–1583): explorer and colonizer. His first expedition (1578) was a failure (*see ANNE AGER*). In 1583 he left Plymouth with five ships in an effort to colonize Newfoundland. He landed on 5 August at the site of St John's and there founded the first English colony in North America. For several weeks he explored the south coast of Newfoundland, then sailed for home on 1 September, but was lost in a storm off the Azores. The historian of the voyage attributes to him the famous remark 'We are as near to heaven by sea as by land':

Monday, the ninth of September, in the afternoon, the frigate was near cast away, oppressed by waves, yet at that time recovered; and giving forth signs of joy, the General, sitting abaft with a book in his hand, cried out unto us in the *Hind*, so oft as we did approach within hearing: 'We are as near to heaven by sea as by land!'; reiterating the same speech, well beseeming a soldier, resolute in Jesus Christ, as I can testify he was.

> Edward Hayes, 'A report of the voyage, and success thereof, attempted in the year of our Lord 1583 by Sir Humphrey Gilbert, Knight...', in Richard Hakluyt's *Principall Navigations* (1589–1600)

See also EDUCATION.

Gimbals: rings devised for suspending the mariner's compass, chronometers or other instruments, so that they remain horizontal when the ship rolls or pitches.

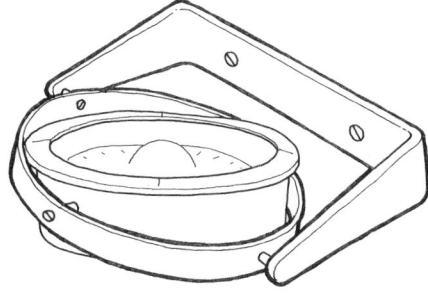

Gingerbread rigging: the old sailor's name for wire rigging when it was introduced (*c.*1850) in place of hemp.

The highly decorated stern of the *Naseby*, 1656. She was captured by the Dutch, and the central portion of the carving is preserved at the Rijksmuseum, Amsterdam.

Gingerbread work: elaborate gilded and painted carvings, coats of arms and figureheads, were much favoured by the builders of ships in earlier times, and the fanciful scroll work was known as gingerbread work. It can still be seen in state barges. From it comes our phrase 'to take the gilt off the gingerbread', meaning to reduce the appeal of anything.

'Gin Palace': the sailors' irreverent name for every H.M.S. *Agincourt*.

Girt-line (or **gantline**): the first rope used in rigging a ship, passing through a block, on the head of the masts, to hoist up the rigging.

Give way: (**1**) an order to start rowing; (**2**) to give way to another craft: to keep out of its course.

Glasgow: the largest city of Scotland, situated on the Clyde, and centre of a great commercial, shipbuilding and industrial area. After the Union with England (1707)

Glasgow developed rapidly, the tobacco trade with America being specially important. With the Industrial Revolution and the coming of steam power, the city was ideally situated to become the centre of the great Clyde shipyards, in which so many famous ships were built during the 19th and early 20th centuries. Marine engineering and shipbuilding are still important, but Glasgow has today many different industries.

Glass: *see* SPY-GLASS.

Glorious First of June: *see* FIRST OF JUNE.

Glory hole: originally a steward's store room in a passenger ship; now used to describe any small space, with implications of untidiness.

'Glory of the Seas': the last clipper built by Donald McKay (1869). With the glory of the days of sail over she became a hulk, a cold-storage vessel used by a fish company. One American wished to tow her round to the east coast and restore her, as the *Cutty Sark* was saved and restored; but she was by then in no condition to stand the strain of the voyage. In the end, some 50 years after her launch, she was hauled up on the beach at Seattle and burnt – not, viking-like, as a last triumphant gesture, but for the commercial value of her copper fastenings.

G.M.T.: abbreviation for GREENWICH MEAN TIME.

'Gneisenau': a new 11-in.-gun German battle cruiser in the Second World War, successfully employed as an ocean raider. In 1942 she was ordered north from Brest to attack Russian convoys and, having passed unchecked through the Straits of Dover, was mined off the Frisian Islands. She remained in the Baltic and was later taken by the Russians when they entered Gdynia.

An earlier *Gneisenau* figured in the First World War at the Battle of Coronel (*see MONMOUTH*) and was sunk by Admiral Sturdee's battle cruisers at the Battle of the Falkland Islands (1914).

Go about: change course in sailing, from one tack to another.

Gokstad Ship: 9th-century viking ship excavated on a farm near Oslo in 1880 and now preserved in the Viking Ship Hall at

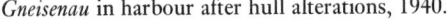

Gneisenau in harbour after hull alterations, 1940.

Bygdoy. She is a superb example of the type that used to raid the shores of Britain, sea-going and powered by oar and sail (*see also* LONG SHIP). She had a single mast carrying a large square sail and was driven by, probably, sixteen oars on each side. Steering was by an oar on the 'steerboard' side. Her overall length was 79 ft, and her breadth 16 ft 8 in.; she carried about 70 men, with their shields stowed along the gunwales.

See colour section.

Golden Gate: the name given to the narrow entrance, about a mile wide, to the superb huge harbour of San Francisco Bay in California. The Golden Gate may have been seen by Sir Francis Drake in 1579, but it was the Spanish who first penetrated the area in the 18th century. The name Golden Gate seems to have arisen during the time of the California gold rush. In 1937 the Golden Gate was spanned by a magnificent suspension bridge.

'Golden Hind': one of the most famous ships in history. Often called just the *Hind* and originally christened the *Pelican*, she is celebrated for carrying Francis Drake round the world (1577–80). He renamed her during the circumnavigation, in honour of Sir Christopher HATTON, a shareholder in the voyage, whose badge was a golden hind.

Strangely enough, though the ship is a favourite for the art (and imagination) of the model-maker, we have very little precise information about her. But fortunately she was preserved in dry dock at Deptford for nearly a century. The dock was specially built (at a cost of £370) and the remains of the brickwork suggest that the *Golden Hind*, including beak and figurehead, must have been only about 75 ft long. Other approximate figures are:

The *Golden Hind*, from the bottom portion of a map by Hondius.

breadth, 19 ft; depth in hold, 9–10 ft; tonnage, about 100. There seems little doubt that she eventually dropped to pieces at Deptford, modern methods of preservation being unknown.

The Queen 'consecrated the ship with great ceremony, pomp and magnificence, eternally to be remembered.' She decreed that the ship should be placed in a dock and a house built over it so that more than the memory of it should live to hearten and inspire other daring men.

A. E. W. Mason, *The Life of Sir Francis Drake* (1941)

Golden Hind was also the name of the pinnace commanded by Captain Thomas FLEMING (1588).

Golden Horn: the name given to the deep arm of the sea joining the Bosporus with the Sea of Marmara, and separating the city of Istanbul into two parts. The name is a translation of the Greek and perhaps originally referred to the wealth of fish found there.

'Golden Lion': ship of 500 tons which, commanded by William BOROUGH, took part in Drake's expedition to Cadiz (1587). In 1588 she was one of Lord Howard of Effingham's squadron against the Armada.

'**Goliath**': 74-gun ship, commanded by Captain Thomas Foley, that led the attack at the Battle of the NILE (1 August 1798). Although the French admiral had so anchored his fleet that he considered nothing could pass between it and shore, Foley brought the *Goliath* through the rocks and shoals, and was followed by four other ships.

The log of the *Goliath* is a simple record of occurrences, and contains nothing to indicate that her captain considered the fact of his having led inside the French line was worthy of special remark.

> Navy Records Society, *Logs of the Great Sea Fights*

The Enemy were moored in a strong Line of Battle for defending the entrance of the Bay, (of Shoals,) flanked by numerous Gun-boats, four Frigates, and a Battery of Guns and Mortars on an Island in their Van; but nothing could withstand the Squadron your Lordship did me the honour to place under my command.

> Nelson to Earl St Vincent (3 August 1798)

Goodwin Sands: an area of shifting sand-banks off the E. coast of Kent. They lie at the entrance to the Straits of Dover from the North Sea and are separated from the coast by The DOWNS. Traditionally the sands were once part of an island owned by Earl Godwin or Godwine (*d.*1053), Earl of the West Saxons. According to William Camden (1551–1623) the sands were formed in 1097 as a result of tempestuous seas and violent wind and rain. Despite safeguards such as buoys, flashing lights and LIGHT-SHIPS, the sands have brought disaster to many ships through the centuries.

Goose-neck: a hinged metal connection between gaff, boom or swinging spar and a mast, allowing the former to move freely both horizontally and vertically.

Gould, Rupert T. (1891–1948): retired naval officer and mechanical genius who restored to perfect working condition John HARRISON's chronometers (now at the National Maritime Museum, Greenwich) after a century and a half of neglect and destruction. When Gould saw them in 1920 many parts were missing, and previous clumsy attempts at repair had left the delicate and intricate mechanisms wrongly assembled. Gould described No.1 as looking 'as though it had gone down with the *Royal George* and had been on the bottom ever since', and of one task he said that it was 'like trying to thread a needle stuck into the tailboard of a motor-lorry which you are chasing on a bicycle'.

In all, Gould spent twelve years on the work, No.3 alone taking the best part of seven years. This contained 753 separate parts, which all had to be cleaned, polished and lacquered to prevent future corrosion. New parts had to be made, without any reliable drawings to go by; and in some cases the function of parts had to be determined by patient experiment.

> I finished ... with a gale lashing the rain on to the windows of my garret, about 4 p.m. on February 1st, 1933 – and five minutes later No.1 had begun to go again for the first time since June 17th, 1767: an interval of 165 years.

'**Grâce à Dieu**': *see* HENRI GRÂCE À DIEU.

'**Grâce Dieu**': one of Henry V's ships, built in 1418. She was equipped, according to the records, with one 'great mast', one 'mesan' (mizen), two bowsprits, six sails and eleven 'bonnets' (some of the sails and bonnets would have been spares). *See also* BURLESDOWN WRECK.

This pious (and perhaps placatory) name was also given to a number of 15th- and 16th-century ships, culminating in the

Graf Spee at the fleet review, 1937.

HENRI GRÂCE À DIEU. On one occasion a captured Portuguese caravel was immediately rechristened *Grâce Dieu* by Hawkins.

'Graf Spee' (or **'Admiral Graf Spee'**): famous German 11-in. gun POCKET BATTLESHIP, the focus of the Battle of the River Plate. Nominally the same size as a cruiser, she was much more heavily armed and proved a highly successful surface raider at the beginning of the Second World War. After the RIVER PLATE battle (13 December 1939) she made for the neutral port of Montevideo, on the River Plate, to refuel and repair her comparatively minor damage. She stayed in the harbour for the maximum time allowed (*see* NEUTRALITY), but on 17 December she had to sail. Convinced, as a result of a British bluff, that a superior force awaited her and she could not escape, her commander, Langsdorff, scuttled her outside the three-mile limit and committed suicide.

Grand Fleet: the name given to the main British fleet during the First World War.

'Grand Guy': not a modern yacht or dinghy but, improbable though it sounds, a French-built Spanish galleon of 600 tons captured by Drake at San Domingo (1586), the flag-ship of the station. Drake brought her away laden with treasure and, since he had attacked on 2 January and was not without the grace of humour, he renamed her *New Year's Gift*.

Grape-shot: a cluster of iron balls clamped together in a frame and formerly fired from cannons so that the balls (or shot) were released and scattered.

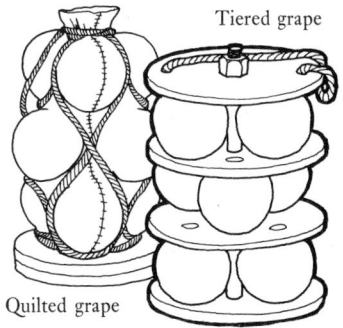

Tiered grape

Quilted grape

Grapnel: a device like a small anchor but with several sharply upturned flukes, once

used for grappling another ship and securing it alongside for boarding. The device is still used for retrieving sunken or elusive objects.

Gratings: latticed or open-work movable boards forming part of the deck or flooring in a small boat. A sailor was sometimes lashed to an up-ended grating when he was to be punished by flogging.

Gravelines, Battle of (29 July 1588): that part of the Spanish Armada expedition following the attack of the English fire-ships, when the Spaniards, with their formation broken, made for the open sea from the Calais Roads, cables cut and anchors lost. At close range, with superior mobility, the English ships, led by Drake, poured in murderous broadsides till the evening, when the powder gave out, and they left the staggering fleet to founder on the coasts of Connaught and the Western Isles.

> Weary and overwrought
> We strove to make all taut;
> But when the morning brought
> The dawn to light us,
> Drake, with the weather gage,
> Made signal to engage,
> And, like a pard in rage,
> Bore down to fight us.
>
> From their van squadron broke
> A withering battle-stroke,

> Tearing our planked oak
> By straiks asunder,
> Blasting the wood like rot
> With such a hail of shot,
> So constant and so hot,
> It beat us under.

> The Messenger to Philip II in John Masefield's 'Philip the King'

Graves, Admiral Thomas: *see* AMERICAN INDEPENDENCE, WAR OF.

Gravesend: an out-port and ferry point in the Thames estuary on the N. coast of Kent. Gravesend became increasingly important with the development of British maritime trade; it is a centre for customs duties, for the Port of London Health Authority and for Trinity House Pilots.

Graving: the cleaning and repair of a ship's outside hull below the water-line. *See also* DOCKS.

Gray, Thomas (1832–90): *see* THOMAS GRAY MEMORIAL TRUST.

Greaser: any member of a merchant ship's engine-room crew responsible for greasing the machinery.

'Great Barke': one of Henry VIII's ships, probably depicted in Vincent Volpe's painting of the King's departure for the meeting at the Field of the CLOTH OF GOLD. She was a vessel of 500 tons, and is shown in the picture as having ten guns. By 1546 she was mounting twelve.

Great and **Little Belts:** the narrow entries to the Baltic on the eastern side of Denmark.

'Great Britain': steamship launched (1843) in a bid by a British company to

In heavy seas during the trial voyage, 1845.

smash the monopoly of the North Atlantic passenger trade held for so long by America. Designed by Isambard Kingdom Brunel for the Great Western Steamship Company of Bristol, she was in many ways of revolutionary design, using iron frames for strength, a screw propeller weighing four tons, and with six masts (nicknamed by the days of the week, Monday to Saturday). The hull was constructed of overlapping iron plates approximately 6 ft by 2 ft 6 in. On her first voyage to New York she covered the 3300 miles in 14 days 21 hours, the only problems being considerable rolling and vibration. On her fifth voyage she ran aground on the coast of County Down owing to a navigational error in thick weather, attributed to the ship's speed. She had left Liverpool on 22 September 1846 and was not salvaged and brought back till the end of August 1847. Facing a bill of nearly £22,000 for a ship insured for only £17,000 (she had cost nearly £140,000), the company sold her for £18,000 to Gibbs, Bright & Co. of Liverpool, in whose hands she underwent extensive alterations. Over the next 36 years she carried a wide variety of cargoes and passengers, including the first English cricket side to Australia, gold from the newly discovered fields there, and troops to the Crimean War. For another half century

the *Great Britain* was used at the Falkland Islands as a storage hulk for coal and wool. Finally she had holes punched in her bottom and was allowed to settle in shallow water several miles out from Port Stanley. Thirty-three years later she was refloated and began a 7500-mile tow back to Britain and her home-port of Bristol to be restored as an enduring monument to a great engineer. *See also* IRON SHIPBUILDING.

Great circle: any imaginary circle on the surface of the Earth and of which the plane passes through the centre of the Earth. Great-circle sailing is a route on an arc of a great circle and provides the shortest distance between two points.

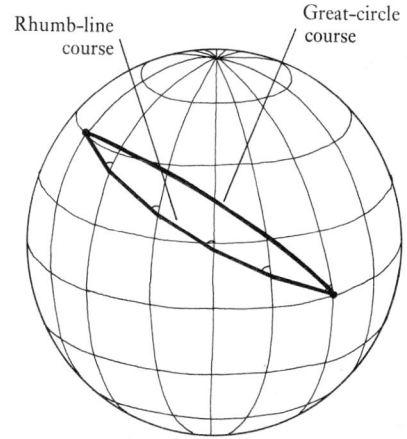

Beached at New Ferry, Cheshire, prior to breaking up, 1888.

'Great Eastern': iron transatlantic steamer designed by Isambard Kingdom Brunel and built by Scott, Russell & Co. at Millwall on the Thames. Of 18,914 tons, she was too large for normal launching and had to be launched sideways – a manoeuvre during which she several times stuck on the ways (1857). 692 ft long and 82·7 ft wide over the paddle-boxes, she was the only vessel in the world with both paddle-wheels and propeller. She had five funnels; her six masts carried a sail spread of 58,000 square ft, and her maximum speed was about 15 knots. Cargo capacity was approximately 6000 tons and there was passenger accommodation for 4000 in three classes in addition to a crew of 400. The hull was divided into ten water-tight compartments and her iron plating was double from keel to water-line, with a space of 2 ft 9 in. between inner and outer plates. Destined for the India and Australia trade, she proved an economic failure for a combination of reasons, among them the fact that she was underpowered for her bulk, it was difficult to

find ports to accommodate her, and she was an uncomfortable ship for passengers because of her roll. She was sold for scrap in 1888; but she had had one outstanding success, when she laid the ATLANTIC CABLE (1865–6).

I think you're on the right tack, and you'll succeed in laying the Atlantic cable; but you'll have two failures to one success, and you'll have to ask us for the *Great Eastern* at last.

Brunel to Sir Richard Glass (manufacturer of the cable)

...one of the greatest, & it is certainly without any degree of comparison the boldest and most successful conquest of mind over weather ever achieved by men.

Letter from W. H. Russell (the famous newspaper correspondent)

'Great Harry': *see HENRI GRÂCE À DIEU.*

'Great James': large ship burnt by the Dutch under Admiral de Ruyter in the MEDWAY (13 June 1667).

'**Great Republic**': American clipper, built by Donald McKay and launched in 1853, probably the largest wooden ship ever built: four-masted, 325 ft long and 53 ft wide. Unfortunately she caught fire when setting out on her maiden voyage and was so mauled during the extensive repairs that followed that she never had a fair chance to show her paces.

'**Great Western**': transatlantic paddle steamer, designed by Isambard Kingdom Brunel for the Great Western Steamship Company, built by Patterson at Bristol in 1837. Of 1340 tons, she left Bristol on 7 April 1838 on her first voyage to New York and was the first steamship to cross the Atlantic without rebunkering. She was sold to the Royal Mail Steam Packet Company in 1847 and broken up in 1856. *See also* HOSKEN, JAMES.

Greek fire: an inflammable mixture used for setting fire to enemy ships; first used by the Greeks of Constantinople against the Saracens in A.D. 673. They in turn later employed Greek fire against the Crusaders. It is not known for certain what substance was used, but it appears to have been projected at the enemy from tubes, and in that sense was a forerunner of the modern flame-thrower.

Green: the colour of the navigation side light shown on the starboard side; hence 'green' is used to give a quick bearing on the starboard side, e.g. 'green zero four five', meaning 45° on the starboard bow.

Greenland: the world's largest island, lying mostly within the Arctic Circle between the North American and European land masses. The whole of the interior is covered by a vast ice-cap and only the coastal areas are ice-free. The southern coasts were discovered and settled by Norsemen in the 10th century. Eric the Red, having spent three years there (982–5), urged further settlement and is said to have named it Greenland to make it sound more attractive. In the 15th century the settlements became extinct and there was no contact from Europe until Martin Frobisher landed on the west coast in 1578. Other Englishmen to visit Greenland were John Davis (1585–7), Henry Hudson (1607) and William Baffin (1616). Greenland was recolonized by the Danes in the 18th century, and when in 1814 the combined kingdoms of Norway and Denmark separated, it remained part of the Danish Kingdom. In 1979, after a referendum, it achieved home rule, although retaining certain links with Denmark. During the last century-and-a-half many expeditions have mapped Greenland's coasts and explored the ice-cap.

In earlier years Greenland was largely dependent on whaling and sealing, but today fishing, especially for cod, is more important, and the island economy has shown considerable development. Greenland's strategic importance for the Arctic air routes and for the defence of America has led to the establishment of an important NATO base at Thule in the north of the island. The Denmark Strait between Greenland and Iceland was the scene of the sinking of H.M.S. *Hood* by the German battleship *Bismarck* (1941).

Greenlander: apart from its obvious meaning, a whaling ship in northern waters, or a seaman serving on her.

Greenock: a port famous for shipbuilding and marine engineering on the Firth of Clyde, lying some 20 miles N.W. of Glasgow. The Greenock yards have produced many fine clippers, warships and passenger liners. During the Second World

War Greenock was a base for the Free French naval forces.

Greenwich: the group of buildings housing the Royal Navy College and the National Maritime Museum, on the banks of the lower Thames at Greenwich Reach, between Deptford and Woolwich, is one of the noblest in Europe and holds much of the story of England for 500 years.

Its history begins in 1427, when Duke Humphrey of Gloucester built himself a house, 'Bella Court', in the midst of a peaceful estate near the river, a house that later developed into a sprawling palace. From about 1450 (and particularly from 1485), the buildings became a royal palace, in Tudor times known as Placentia. Henry VII's sons, Prince Arthur and Henry (afterwards Henry VIII), were born there, as was the future Queen Elizabeth I. In 1553 the Court and Privy Council at Greenwich watched Willoughby and Chancellor setting off on their voyage in search of the North-East Passage. The knighting of Drake after his circumnavigation and the signing of the orders to resist the Armada are only two of many other events connected with Greenwich. In 1617 James I commissioned Inigo Jones to build the beautiful Queen's House (now part of the Museum) for Anne of Denmark (*see also* KIDD, WILLIAM). In 1675 the Royal Observatory was established by royal warrant, the first Astronomer Royal being the Rev. John Flamsteed.

By charter dated 25 October 1694 the Royal Hospital at Greenwich was founded by William III and Mary for 'the relief and support of seamen . . . who by reason of age, wounds, or other disabilities shall be incapable of further service at sea, and unable to maintain themselves', provision also being made for widows and orphans (*see also* PENSIONS). A magnificent new range of buildings was designed and built by a number of great architects, including Wren, Hawksmoor and Vanbrugh. The first 42 pensioners arrived in January 1705. By 1814 there were 2710 in residence. Thereafter numbers steadily declined as fewer wars were engaged in and more out-pensions were granted. The Hospital was finally closed in 1869, and in 1873 the ROYAL NAVAL COLLEGE was transferred to its buildings.

Along with the Hospital a School was run which began in 1717 and which paid particular attention to the teaching of navigational subjects. After a time, with the numbers at 600, it was transferred to the Queen's House, which was afterwards increased by two wings to house 950 boys, the headmaster occupying Anne of Denmark's Palace. In 1933 the School was moved to Holbrook, near Ipswich, and its buildings were made over to the NATIONAL MARITIME MUSEUM.

Several notable naval historians (quoted in a number of entries in this book) have been associated with the Royal Naval College and the National Maritime Museum, chief among them Sir Geoffrey Callender (1875–1946), Professor of History at the College and first Director of the Museum, Professor Michael Lewis and Professor Christopher Lloyd.

Greenwich Chest: one of the early pension funds instituted for the relief of wounded and disabled seamen (*see* PENSIONS). It was amalgamated with the Chatham Chest in 1814, though for some time documents continued to be addressed separately to 'the Directors of the Chest at Greenwich' and 'the Governors of the Chest at Chatham'. At the time of the amalgamation the value was one and a quarter million pounds. *See also* SIXPENNY OFFICE.

Greenwich Mean Time (or **G.M.T.**): the mean time by the sun at the PRIME MERIDIAN (0° longitude) on which Greenwich stands. By agreement, G.M.T. is the basis for standard time, that is, the time kept in any of the zones east or west of Greenwich, which in general are in bands of 15° of longitude and which will accordingly be either in advance of or behind G.M.T.

Grenada: the southernmost of the Windward Islands in the West Indies, discovered in 1498 by Columbus and named Concepcion. It became a British possession in 1627, but in 1650 was sold to the French, from whom it was captured during the war against France in 1762. After being retaken by the French it was restored to Britain by the treaty of 1783. For the encounter between British and French ships off Grenada in 1779, *see* BYRON, JOHN.

Grenville, Sir Richard (?1541–1591): naval commander and hero of the immortal last fight of the *Revenge*. Previously, in 1585, he had led Ralegh's first expedition to plant a colony in North America and, on the voyage home, had captured the Spanish *Santa Maria*, whose rich cargo more than paid for the whole expedition. He was appointed second-in-command to Lord Thomas Howard of the Azores fleet (1591) and, with 95 men sick ashore and Lord Thomas having beaten a strategic retreat, was left to fight his single ship, the *Revenge*, against 53 Spanish ships off Flores, one of the Azores islands. He withstood their attacks for fifteen hours, so damaging fifteen of the enemy that they were 'far more willing to hearken to a composition [i.e. truce] than hastily to make any more assaults'. Mortally wounded, Grenville was at last carried aboard the Spanish flagship and received with great honour.

All the powder of the *Revenge* to the last barrel was now spent, all her pikes broken, forty of her best men slain, and the most part of the rest hurt. In the beginning of the fight she had but one hundred free from sickness... a small troop to man such a ship, and a weak garrison to resist so mighty an army... Unto ours there remained no comfort at all, no hope, no supply either of ships, men or weapons; the masts all beaten overboard, all her tackle cut asunder, her upper work altogether razed... Sir Richard, finding himself in this distress and unable any longer to make resistance... commanded the master gunner, whom he knew to be a most resolute man, to split and sink the ship; that thereby nothing might remain of glory or victory to the Spaniards... The master gunner readily condescended and divers others; but the Captain and Master were of another opinion...

> Sir Walter Ralegh, 'Report on the truth of the fight about the Iles of the Azores, this last sommer...'

The remark most often quoted – 'Sink me the ship, Master Gunner' – is from Tennyson's 'The *Revenge*'.

Greville, Sir Fulke, first Baron Brooke (1554–1628): courtier and Treasurer of the Navy. His chief claim to fame (one that he included in the epitaph he wrote for himself) is that he was the friend of Sir Philip Sidney. In 1598 he became 'Treasurer of the Wars' and of the Navy. Some interesting figures have survived from his period of office. In 1600, for example, he received £4988 for press and conduct money (i.e. for impressing men into the Navy and conveying them to their assigned ports) and for sea stores to victual and furnish ten ships for three weeks; and £3290 for the payment of wages on board.

Gridiron: slang term for the old flag of the Honourable East India Company, consisting of horizontal red and white stripes, the number varying from nine to thirteen.

Grimsby: fishing port on the S. bank of the Humber estuary. The original settlement was Danish; the town's importance increased with the development of the North Sea fisheries and with the rise of British maritime power. Its position as a foremost fishing port was helped by the coming of the railways, the building of fine docks and the introduction of modern methods of freezing, curing and handling fish, so that it became the home port for a large trawler fleet making their catch in the Greenland, Iceland and White Sea areas. Recently, however, there has been a decline in the number of fishing vessels fully employed; *see* FISHERIES.

Gripe: rope, canvas or matting band used in pairs diagonally on the outboard side of a ship's boat to prevent it swinging and chafing when secured to the davits.

Grog: any spirit, generally RUM, mixed with water. The word is said to be derived from 'Old Grog', the nickname of Admiral VERNON, who introduced it (1740). Our modern expression 'feeling groggy' for feeling unwell derives from this source, though it is now not necessarily associated with liquor.

Guardship: a warship with special duties such as providing a formal guard for a royal person, for defence against surprise attack, or for regulating naval affairs.

'Guerrière': *CONSTITUTION.*

Guiana (modern **Guyana**): formerly known as British Guiana until it became independent in 1966, Guyana lies on the N.E. coast of South America. The territory was taken by the British from the Dutch West Indian Company in 1796 during the Napoleonic Wars, and was ceded to Britain in 1814. Columbus had sailed along Guiana's tropical coast in 1498, and it was in these parts that the myth of EL DORADO arose. Ralegh's vain expedition up the River Orinoco (1595) hoped to break into the gold-bearing centre of the Spanish Empire in the New World. In 1616 Ralegh was released from prison to make his final expedition to Guiana. He himself was delayed in Trinidad by fever, but his

Gripe.

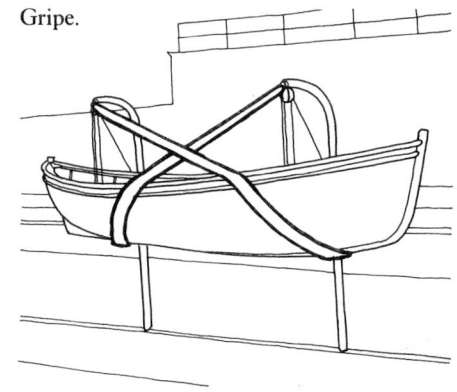

Guided missiles: H.M.S. *Hampshire* firing a Sea Slug missile.

lieutenant became embroiled in an attack on a Spanish garrison against the English king's orders. Ralegh returned home after the failure of the expedition and was executed in disgrace in 1618.

Guided missile: a general term for a whole variety of modern weapons which rely on controlling the direction of their missiles by internal or external devices, so that they seek and strike their target. Guided missiles may be air-to-air, surface-to-surface, surface-to-air, air-to-surface, air-to-underwater, surface-to-underwater, underwater-to-air, underwater-to-surface and underwater-to-underwater.

Guinea boat: type of fast open pulling boat used, especially on the Kent coast, for smuggling gold and contraband goods to and from France during the early-19th-century French Wars.

Gulf Stream: the great drift of warmed water which moves from the Gulf of

Mexico and Florida out into the North Atlantic. There it continues to flow under the influence of the prevailing winds and spreads out in a clockwise direction to become the North Atlantic Drift. The relative warmth of this current raises the temperature of the air of the westerly winds, which thereby have a considerable effect in moderating the climate of N.W. Europe.

Gulf Stream Drift: *see* NORTH ATLANTIC DRIFT.

Gunboat: general name given to a small naval vessel, well-armed and often of shallow draught for use in rivers and close inshore. 'Gunboat diplomacy' came to mean the presence of a gunboat in an area of dispute to enforce diplomatic pressure.

Gun captain: a seaman in charge of a gun crew. In Nelson's Navy the gun crew looked after two guns, one on each side of

A gunboat.

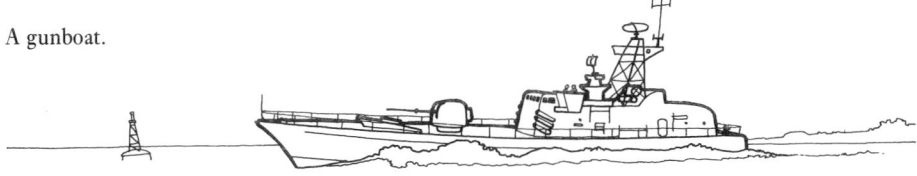

the ship. The gun captain put the cartridge through the touch hole and filled the hole with powder, he armed the cannon and he released the flintlock trigger when the order to fire was given. His crew hauled out the guns, sponged them out before reloading, fetched and carried, and were detailed and trained for any emergency.

Gunlayer: *see* LAY.

Gunner's daughter: *see* FLOGGING.

Gunport: the hole in the side of a ship through which the cannon fired a broadside. When guns were not run out it was closed by a covering hinged at the upper side and secured on the inside.

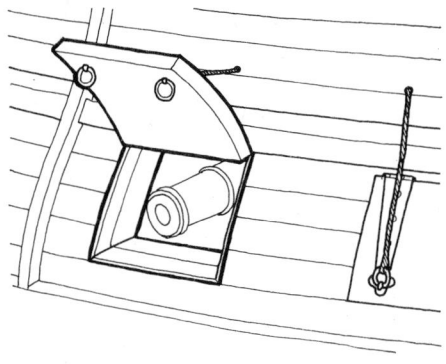

Gunroom: originally a room for the use of the gunner, and then the mess used by the most junior naval officers when afloat.

Guns: *see* ARMAMENT; RANGE; SHOT.

Guns, blowing great: a phrase describing a very strong and tempestuous wind.

Gun turret: armoured, revolving structure for housing a ship's guns. The advantage of the gun turret over the broadside method of firing began to appear with the building of the *MONITOR* during

the American Civil War. The lessons of her encounter with the Confederate *Merrimac* (1862) were closely considered by other maritime powers, and the advantage of being able to aim the guns without putting the ship into a broadside position became apparent. After much debate, gun turrets placed about the ship, instead of in a central battery, won the day. The first all-big-gun ship in the British Navy was H.M.S. *Dreadnought* (1906), with five gun turrets, each containing two 12-in. guns. The gun turrets of the great battleships of the first half of the 20th century increased in size and strength, commonly housing guns of 15- and 16-in. calibre. Though such battleships are now obsolete, the principle of the gun turret is still widely used in housing the armament of modern warships, both guns and guided missiles.

Gunwale (pronounced and sometimes spelt **gunnel**): the upper edge of a ship's or boat's side. Planks known as wales strengthened this upper edge, and the gunwale was probably so called because the upper guns were aimed from it.

Guy: any rope, chain or wire used as a stay for a spar, derrick or boom, etc.

Gybe (a variant of 'jib'): to allow a fore-and-aft sail to swing so that the wind is brought on to its opposite side.

Gyro-compass: a navigational instrument based on the principle of the gyroscope, namely that a freely rotating body will maintain a fixed direction in space. A gyro-compass, being free from magnetic interferences, can provide the direction of true north, and is therefore of great value in ships and submarines. *See also* COMPASS.

Gyro-pilot: *see* GYROSCOPE.

Gyroscope: a rapidly rotating wheel, so mounted that it is free to turn about any axis. It has certain characteristics of behaviour which have been adapted to many uses, particularly nautical (e.g. the GYRO-COMPASS); other applications are in gyroscopic gun sights, in the stabilization of fire-control systems, in the mechanisms of guided missiles, and in the gyro-stabilizer, a device located below decks to counteract the rolling of a ship. Yet other uses of gyroscopic principles are found in the gyro-pilot, a form of automatic steering for ships, and in the roll-and-pitch recorder and the track recorder.

H

Hadley, John (1682–1744): mathematician and scientific inventor. Hadley became a Fellow of the Royal Society in 1717, and two years later demonstrated his great improvement of the reflecting telescope. His second success was the invention in 1731 of the reflecting quadrant, a considerable advance on the previously used octant. Hadley's quadrant became indispensable at sea: 'By means of two small mirrors on a portable instrument it was now for the first time possible to note easily the angle subtended by two distant objects independently of small changes of place in the centre of observation' (*Dictionary of National Biography*). Hadley's quadrant was the immediate forerunner of the sextant, which appeared in 1757.

Hadley's quadrant: *see* HADLEY, JOHN.

Hakluyt, Richard (?1553–1616): an English divine who never went to sea but devoted his life to collecting and publishing accounts of maritime enterprises. His best-known work was *The Principall Navigations, Voiages, and Discoveries of the English Nation*, published in 1589 and enlarged in 1598–1600. These first-hand narratives told the world of the achievements, hitherto little known, of navigators such as the Cabots, Willoughby, John Hawkins, Drake, Gilbert, Frobisher and other less famous voyagers.

The Westminster boy found lying open upon a board in his cousin's room certain books of cosmography and a universal map. In these, he displayed some curiosity, whereupon his kinsman began to instruct his ignorance by explaining to him the divisions of the earth according to the old account and the new learning. With a wand Richard Hakluyt [the boy's relative of the same name] pointed out to the youth all the known seas, gulfs, bays, straits, capes, rivers, empires, kingdoms, dukedoms and territories . . . Then he touched the boy's imagination by taking down the Bible, and, turning to the 107th Psalm, directed him to read in the 23rd and 24th verses that 'they which go down to the sea in ships and occupy the great waters, they see the works of the Lord, and his wonders in the deep.'

> C. N. Robinson and John Leyland in *The Cambridge History of English Literature* (1932)

Halcyon: the Greek myth of Halcyon and Ceyx, which were changed into birds, gave rise to a belief in a fabulous bird who built a floating nest on the sea, the eggs being hatched during a period of calm around the time of the winter solstice. Hence 'halcyon days' refers to such weather, and so, figuratively, to any period of tranquillity and happiness.

Haldane, John Scott (1860–1936): physiologist invited by the Admiralty to investigate the respiratory difficulties attending deep diving. In 1907 he drew up detailed compression tables which were for many years regarded as the diver's bible, enabling him and those controlling the dives to calculate the extent of nitrogen saturation and the timing of the slow decompression process. In recent years, especially for emergency deep dives, further experiments have been necessary and modifications made.

When I was about twelve my father was very interested in diving. There was some talk at the time of the dangers of going down to any considerable depth, dangers which my father

194

pooh-poohed. He said that any healthy boy could go down to forty feet, and he proceeded to try the experiment with me. My own training for this experience was a short sojourn in a compressed-air chamber, which taught me the necessity of swallowing when pressure increased . . . Next day I was put into a diving suit and sent down to a depth of forty feet, where I stayed for half an hour. It was not altogether a pleasant experience, for the dress was too small and leaked horribly, and by the time I was pulled up I was wet to the neck and most horribly cold.

J. B. S. Haldane, biochemist, son of John Scott Haldane

Half deck: a deck extending over half or a smaller part of a vessel. In the past it was generally in the after part of the ship and gave access to officers' cabins.

Half-pay: introduced by Charles II in 1667, half-pay was a form of retaining fee for certain selected captains of first and second rates. In 1693 half-pay was extended to all unemployed officers, but in 1700 the numbers who could receive it were limited to 50 captains, 100 lieutenants, and 30 masters. However, this limitation was soon rescinded, and half-pay became the rule for those officers whose services were not being used. Out of these practices came the idea of established rank as opposed to rank according to the post held, and also the idea of seniority within that rank. Half-pay for unemployed naval officers continued to be the rule until as late as 1938.

Half-pike: *see* BOARDING PIKE.

Half seas over: literally, half across the sea, but used colloquially to mean half-drunk.

Half tide: *see* TIDES.

Half topsails under: having only half topsails showing above the horizon (a position sometimes arising when enemy ships were being chased).

Halifax: capital and largest city of Nova Scotia, Canada; founded (1749) by Edward Cornwallis to counter the French settlement at Louisburg on Cape Breton Island. Its magnificent harbour soon made it into an important naval base and strong-point for the British attack on French Canada during the Seven Years' War. Ice-free during the winter when the St Lawrence waterway is frozen, the port and town continued to grow and became the eastern terminal of the Canadian National Railway. During the First and Second World Wars, Halifax was an important naval base and assembly point for Atlantic convoys. In 1917 the harbour was the scene of a terrible marine disaster when a French ship carrying high explosives collided with a Norwegian vessel. The resulting explosion killed close on 2000 people, injured as many others, and caused vast damage to property.

Halifax Steam Squadron: the original Cunard Line fleet.

Halliard: *see* HALYARD.

Hallowell, Sir Benjamin (1760–1834): admiral; one of the 'Band of Brothers', a Canadian-born seaman 'of gigantic frame and vast personal strength', variously described as looking like a bear and a prize-fighter. His main service was in the Mediterranean (1781–1814), and he commanded the *Swiftsure* at the Battle of the Nile (1798). In 1828, after succeeding to some property, he took the surname of Carew.

Halyard (or halliard; derived from 'haul

yard'): any rope or tackle for hoisting a sail, a flag or other signal.

Hamilton, Sir Edward: *see HERMIONE.*

Hamilton, Sir William and **Lady (Emma):** *see COLOSSUS.*

Hammock: a hanging bed made of canvas, with clews and lanyards at each end for slinging and securing to hooks or rails. Formerly, all ratings and midshipmen slept in hammocks, which, when not in use, were neatly lashed up and stowed. In the days of the fighting sailing ship, hammocks were stowed in the NETTINGS. Hammocks were normally slung to a standard distance of only 14 in. to a man, though when a larboard-starboard watch system ·was operated, only half the hammocks were occupied at a time, so that the seaman had a little more space to swing. They were introduced in Tudor times, and till the late 18th century were usually called 'hammacoes', indicating a Caribbean origin.

Hampden, John: *see SHIP-MONEY.*

Hance: the curve or rise of rails or bulwarks from the waist of a ship to the quarter-deck.

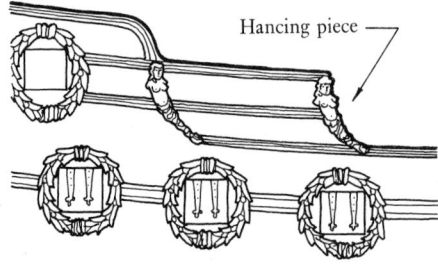

Hancing piece ⌐

Hand: a member of the ship's crew. 'All hands on deck' and 'all hands to muster' are common usages. 'Leading hand' is the colloquial name for the sailor holding the leading rate in any branch. The word is also used to indicate direction, as in 'on the starboard hand' or 'a port-hand buoy'.

Hand flag: flag used in hand-signalling, e.g. by semaphore code.

Hand-organs: one of the seamen's names for the HOLYSTONES.

Hand, reef and steer, to: the traditional capabilities demanded of an able seaman; in other words, to take in and furl a sail, and handle the wheel.

Handsomely: in a nautical sense, carefully and gradually.

Handspike: a strong lever for moving heavy objects such as guns; also a spoke for the capstan or windlass.

Handy billy: a luff tackle, consisting of a double and single block purchase; one end made fast to the stem of a boat and the other to a stake on the beach, or behind it, enabled one man to pull up a fair-sized boat, preferably with the aid of greased sleepers for the keel to run on.

Hangfire: delay in the explosion of the charge of a gun.

'Hanging Jervis': nickname for John JERVIS, Earl St Vincent, renowned for his strict discipline, but one of the greatest leaders and administrators the Navy produced.

Hanseatic League: a commercial association of mainly German towns formed in the 13th century for the protection and furtherance of their trade in the Baltic, N.W. Europe and the Low Countries. The name derived from the German *Hanse*, meaning 'company'. The League grew in power and influence during the 14th and 15th centuries until at its height about 100 cities were members. Lübeck, Rostock, Stralsund, Wismar, Hamburg and Danzig were prominent in the League's activities, which became monopolistic and commanded at one time much of the trade from the eastern Baltic to the North Sea. There were establishments of Hanseatic merchants overseas, including London, where the Steelyard at Blackfriars was their base. Inevitably the endeavour by so many different trading towns to produce a common policy was fraught with difficulties, and after successes (political and military as well as commercial) the League began to decline during the late 15th century. The Scandinavian powers became more independent, and the British and Dutch more thrustful in their own trade, whilst the discovery and opening up of the New World turned Western Europe's attention away from the Baltic. *See also* MERCHANT ADVENTURERS.

Hanse towns: *see* HANSEATIC LEAGUE.

Hanway, Jonas (1712–86): philanthropist, writer and traveller, with a special interest in marine education. He himself made a notable journey down the Volga and by the Caspian Sea to Persia with a caravan of woollen goods. He included an account of his travels in *A Historical Account of British Trade over the Caspian Sea* (1753), and wrote over 70 other printed works, mostly pamphlets connected with his philanthropic activities, e.g. *The Sea Lad's Trusty Companion*, *A Proposal for County Naval Free Schools to be Built on Waste Land*, and *The Seaman's Christian Friend*. Largely owing to his influence a marine school was opened in 1786. This was rebuilt in 1841 and reorganized as a 'Navigation School' in 1854. The school was under the direction of Trinity House. He also founded the MARINE SOCIETY. Hanway was an eccentric: he is reputed to have been the principal pioneer of the umbrella in England and was the first Londoner habitually to employ one, much to the indignation of the hackney coachmen. *See also* EDUCATION.

Harbour: any area of water in ocean, sea or river that is sufficiently sheltered from the elements and deep enough to provide ships with a safe haven or anchorage. Most of the world's great harbours started as natural features, but have been improved by building moles, breakwaters, wharves and docks. An instance of a purely artificial harbour was the MULBERRY HARBOUR.

Hard: a firm landing-place, wharf or jetty, as in 'Portsmouth Hard'.

Hard a-Gilbert: old version of the order 'Hard a-port', Gilbert having been a wine-merchant who supplied the wardroom port.

Hard a-lee, hard a-port etc.: order to helmsman of sailing ship to put the wheel fully over; also indicates closeness to the leeside, portside etc. *See also* WHEEL.

Hard and fast: fixed and firm; generally of ships run aground with small hope of getting off.

Hard tack: ship's biscuits, very dry and hard, and in the old days often weevil-ridden. 'Tack' means food or provisions: compare 'soft tack', meaning bread and other good and more palatable food.

Hardy, Sir Thomas Masterman (1769–1839): admiral, imperishably associated with Nelson and his last moments at Trafalgar. One of the great 'Band of Brothers', he commanded the *MUTINE* at the Battle of the Nile (1798) and was Nelson's flag-captain for almost the whole of the period 1798–1805, on the *San Josef*, *St George*, *Vanguard*, *Foudroyant*, *Amphion* and *Victory*. He was knighted after Trafalgar, was commander-in-chief on the South American station, and became First Sea Lord (1830) and governor of Greenwich Hospital (1834).

Nelson's devotion to this fine seaman is exemplified in an incident in 1796 when their ship was being pursued by a Spanish squadron which was coming up fast. An English sailor fell overboard and Hardy lowered a boat and went to the rescue. Despite the risk of capture, Nelson shouted: 'I'll not lose Hardy! Back the mizen topsail!' Boat, Hardy and the seaman were retrieved.

In April 1977 Hardy's presentation sword, given him by the City of London in recognition of his gallantry at Trafalgar, was auctioned at Christie's. Valued at the time of presentation at 100 guineas, it sold for near a hundred times that sum.

Captain Hardy now came to the cockpit to see his Lordship a second time, which was after an interval of about fifty minutes from the conclusion of his first visit . . . Lord Nelson and Captain Hardy shook hands again, and while the Captain retained his Lordship's hand, he congratulated him, even in the arms of death, on his brilliant victory: which, said he, was complete; though he did not know how many of the enemy were captured, as it was impossible to perceive every ship distinctly. He was certain however of fourteen or fifteen having surrendered. His Lordship answered, 'That is well, but I bargained for twenty': and then emphatically exclaimed, '*Anchor*, Hardy, *anchor*!' . . . Captain Hardy then said, 'Shall *we* make the signal, sir?' – 'Yes,' answered his Lordship, 'for if I live, I'll anchor' . . . He then told Hardy he felt that in a few minutes he should be no more. 'Then . . . you know what to do . . . Kiss me, Hardy.' The Captain now knelt down, and kissed his cheek; when his Lordship said, 'Now I am satisfied. Thank God I have done my duty.' Captain Hardy stood for a minute or two in silent contemplation: he knelt down again, and kissed his Lordship's forehead. His Lordship said 'Who is that?' The Captain answered: 'It is Hardy'; to which his Lordship replied, 'God bless you, Hardy!'

Surgeon William Beatty's *Narrative* (1807)

Harmattan: a dry, parching wind blowing from the Sahara to the Gulf of Guinea off West Africa during December–February. It is called 'The Doctor' locally.

Harness-cask: formerly, a cask in which salt meat was kept for immediate use.

Harpoon: a barbed iron spear with rope attached used for catching whales. In the early days of whaling it was hurled by hand from a boat, but in modern whalers it is fired from a gun specially designed for the purpose.

Harrison, John (1693–1776): horologist; a carpenter's son who never served a single day's apprenticeship in the highly skilled

Harrison's first time-keeper, 'No. 1', 1735.

and delicate art of clockmaking but who, where scientists, mathematicians, astronomers and other inventors had failed, succeeded in solving the problems Sir Isaac Newton had summarized as 'the Motion of a Ship, the Variation of Heat and Cold, Wet and Dry, and the Difference of Gravity in different Latitudes', so that accurate time could be kept at sea.

In 1714 the British government offered a scale of rewards for 'a generally practicable and useful' method of accurately finding longitude at sea and thereby avoiding tragic

blunders in navigation that had cost thousands of lives. For a time-keeper that, at the end of a six-week voyage, resulted in an error of not more than 60 nautical miles, the reward would be £10,000; if the error was less than 40 miles, the prize would be £15,000; and if it was only 30 miles or less, the sum would rise to £20,000. Though many inventors and cranks offered solutions, it was more than twenty years before the answer was brought to the special body of commissioners known as the Board of Longitude.

Harrison submitted his ideas in 1728 and then took six years (1729–35), with the aid of a London clockmaker, George Graham, to make his first marine clock. It was tried out first on a barge on the Humber and then on a voyage to Lisbon and back, when it behaved with an accuracy that amazed the shipmaster when he compared it with the traditional methods of calculation. It was not taken to sea again, but kept going continuously for thirty years without ever being stopped for cleaning and oiling. During 1737–9 Harrison made a second time-keeper to the same design, but more strongly built. This was never taken to sea, probably because the country was at war and the Admiralty did not wish it to fall into enemy hands.

Harpoon.

199

The third time-keeper took 17 years (1740–57) to complete and contained 753 parts. Harrison also constructed a large watch (now known as Harrison's No. 4) which would be easier to handle and to carry on deck, and which has been called 'the most famous time-keeper which ever has been or ever will be made'.

No. 4 was taken by Harrison on board H.M.S. *Deptford* in 1761 for a voyage to Jamaica via Madeira. Nine days out of sight of land, Harrison calculated that they would sight Madeira the next day. The captain, an experienced sailor, did his own sums and bet five to one they would not. On the morrow the look-out sighted Madeira; and on arriving at Jamaica, they found Harrison's time-keeper was only five seconds slow – equivalent to an error of less than one geographical mile.

There could not have been a clearer case for payment of the full £20,000 award. But, governments being what they are, Harrison was given only £2500 till further tests were made. The results were equally impressive. The Board of Longitude then altered the conditions, insisting that Harrison should reveal all the secrets of his invention to a special committee, which would include three watchmakers. They would then give him a further £7500, making a total of £10,000. It was not till the personal intervention of George III ('By God, Harrison, I'll see you righted!') that the inventor, now an old man with failing sight, received the full amount – well, almost. Shifty to the end, the Board so juggled the figures that he finished up £1250 short.

For the sequel to this remarkable story, *see* GOULD, RUPERT T.

'Harry Grâce à Dieu': *see HENRI GRÂCE À DIEU.*

Harry Tate's Navy: jocular term applied

before the First World War to the Royal Naval Volunteer Reserve but, all honour to it, dropped completely after its distinguished services. Harry Tate was a popular music-hall comedian.

Hartland: N. Devonshire village, in Tudor times an important town, with a long sea history. In 1566 an Act of Parliament authorized the building of a quay, among the sponsors being Sir Walter Ralegh, Sir Francis Drake and Sir John Hawkins. It is a jagged, ruthless coast, with a lighthouse at Hartland Point. In the days of sail it was an accepted fact that any ship inside Hartland Point with an onshore wind was as good as lost. One local historian compiled a list of 35 wrecks between 1862 and 1904. Regrettably, not all those who rushed down to the shore to a stricken vessel were intent on providing help. The owner of Hartland Abbey, a friend of HAWKER, often helped him by rounding up volunteers and equipping them with pistols to protect the lives and goods of lost ships from plunderers.

Harvey: *see* TORPEDO.

Harvey, Sir Eliab (1758–1830): admiral; a courageous and ebullient seaman whose most famous exploit was at Trafalgar, where, commanding the *TEMERAIRE*, he battered *Fougueux* and *Redoutable* into submission and rescued *Victory*. In 1809 he was court-martialled and dismissed the service for insubordination under Gambier's command in the Channel, but he was reinstated a year later. He owned considerable estates in Essex, was M.P. for Maldon and was, according to Walpole, a considerable gambler, losing £10,000 in one night's gambling.

Captain Blackwood . . . had used every argument to get his beloved commander-in-chief [Nelson] away from the point of extreme danger at the head of the weather line. He reasoned, quite properly, that the fight could be directed in greater safety from one of the frigates . . . Now Blackwood tried another line. Could not Nelson at least let another ship lead the weather line? The obvious choice was the *Temeraire* . . . riding light, since she had been at sea for many weeks and had used up much of her heavy stores. Nelson, reluctantly, yielded to this importunity, and . . . Harvey received the message to take the lead and endeavour to break the enemy's line about the 14th ship from the van. Eagerly, the *Temeraire* crept ahead, her head level with *Victory*'s stern windows, with the mizzen mast, with the quarter deck . . . There was a sudden commotion on *Victory*, and Nelson was at the ship's side, his slightly nasal Norfolk voice bellowing sharply across the narrow space of water:

'Captain Harvey, I'll thank you to keep your station, which is astern of *Victory*!'

> Grant Uden, *The Fighting*
> *Temeraire* (1961)

(This incident is well authenticated. *Temeraire*'s log shows that she was only a ship's length behind *Victory* and at one time cut away the studding sails and hauled to the wind to avoid overtaking her.)

Harwich: port on the E. coast of Essex, serving the sea routes to Holland and Scandinavia. From Harwich, Martin Frobisher set out on his Arctic expedition in 1578. During the First World War Harwich was an important naval base for a Destroyer Force, and in the Second World War for Coastal Forces.

Harwood, Sir Henry (1888–1950): admiral. A torpedo specialist by training, he is chiefly remembered for the Battle of the RIVER PLATE (1939); then a Commodore, he was in command of the *Ajax*, *Achilles* and *Exeter*.

Haslar: naval hospital in Gosport at the western entrance to Portsmouth harbour. Opened in 1754, it marked the beginning of a proper medical and hospital service for the Royal Navy, primitive and harsh though the provision must have been during the early years of its existence. Many improvements were made later in the eighteenth century by Dr Thomas TROTTER.

Hatch: deck opening for loading cargo or for entry to another deck. Raised walls or coamings generally surround hatches, which are covered and made water-tight by various methods. 'Confined below hatches' was used of slaves or prisoners kept below.

Hatton, Sir Christopher (1540–91): Elizabethan statesman; not a seaman, but he had a financial interest in several voyages, and he merits a niche in maritime history because one of the most famous ships of all time, originally the *Pelican*, was renamed by Drake the GOLDEN HIND in his honour.

Haul: a word with many applications, but basically meaning 'pull'. Thus to 'haul away' is to start pulling; 'haul down' is to lower the flag (see also STRIKE, TO); 'haul out of line' is to move out of the line of ships; 'haul one's wind' is to change direction of sailing, to bring closer to the wind. 'Haul the anchor' means, colloquially, to retire from seafaring.

> Way, haul away, we'll haul away the bowlin'.
> Way, haul away, we'll haul away, Joe.

> Chorus of old chanty (on the word 'Joe' all hands gave a mighty pull)

Havana, Capture of (1762): the culmination of a two-month siege by the British fleet under Admiral George Pocock and George Keppel, Earl of Albemarle, with heavy losses on both sides. France lost twelve sail of the line and money and property worth about £3,000,000.

Haven: an inlet of the sea giving shelter for ships; a harbour.

Hawke, Edward, first Baron Hawke (1705–81): Admiral of the Fleet. A brilliant and daring seaman, he was for much of his life dogged by jealousy and professional neglect of his talents. Early in his career he showed a disregard for conventional regulation tactics, and it was this spirit which characterized the finest exploit of his career when, at QUIBERON BAY (1759), he engaged in a running fight with the French amidst rocks and shoals on a lee shore. The French Atlantic Fleet was virtually wiped off the ocean and all plans for an invasion of England were at an end. It was the culmination of Hawke's long blockade of the port of Brest, maintained ceaselessly throughout the summer and autumn.

Hawke had reached flag rank through the personal intervention of George II. After Quiberon Bay he received the thanks of Parliament and at long last became First Lord of the Admiralty. But his pension of £1500 was a mean one in view of his services, and he had to wait for his peerage till he was over seventy. Lord Anson seems to have nourished a grudge against him, and he was never trusted by Pitt, who resented some of Hawke's outspoken criticism of the government and his objections to ministerial interference.

Hawker, Robert Stephen (1803–75): eccentric, poet and for 40 years vicar of Morwenstow on the N. Cornish coast, where he always wore sea-boots beneath his cassock and continually laboured for the shipwrecked sailors who all too frequently came to grief on the treacherous coast. The Morwenstow churchyard contains plentiful reminders of these tragedies, among them the figurehead of the *Caledonia* of Arbroath, dashed on the rocks in a gale in 1843. Hawker had many good sea stories to tell, for instance one about a stranger watching a smuggler's cargo being brought ashore on the Cornish coast without any interference. He demanded whether there was not a magistrate or J.P. near at hand and was told there was none for eight miles.

'Well, then, is there no clergyman hereabout? Does no minister of the parish live among you on this coast?'

'Aye! to be sure there is.'

'Well, how far off does he live?'

'That's he, sir, yonder with the lantern.'

Looking in the direction indicated, the scandalized stranger saw the vicar obligingly holding the lantern while his congregation brought the contraband ashore. *See also* HARTLAND.

Hawkins, Sir John (1532–95): naval commander and administrator, merchant and ship-owner, son of William HAWKINS and a cousin of Francis Drake. Before he was 30 John had already amassed a fortune of £10,000 (a considerable sum in the 16th century) as a result of trading ventures in partnership with his brother William, principally to the Canaries. Then he turned his attention to the SLAVE TRADE and made three voyages (1562, 1564–5 and 1567–8) partly engaged in this sorry traffic, though it should be remembered that public opinion of the day saw no reason to disapprove of it. The Queen herself was a shareholder in the last two expeditions; she lent Hawkins the royal ship *JESUS OF LUBECK* and ordered that the royal standard should be flown as well as the banner of St George. The third voyage had particularly important political con-

From a portrait by Hieronymous Custodis, 1591.

sequences: it brought Hawkins (and Drake, who accompanied him) into head-on conflict with Spain when a treacherous attack at San Juan de Ulloa in Mexico cost the expedition several ships (including the *Jesus*), much treasure and many lives. Drake's ship, the *JUDITH*, and Hawkins's were the only ones to return.

This left Hawkins with a passionate hatred for the Spaniards. His opportunity for revenge came when he was appointed Treasurer (1577) – and later also Comptroller (1589 – of the Navy. He proved himself a great administrator and successful innovator, building faster ships with finer lines, improving their armament and taking revolutionary steps towards greater hygiene by reducing overcrowding and supplying better victuals, including fresh meat and fruit on some vessels. He remained a first-rate commander at sea, taking the *Victory* against the Armada and receiving his knighthood during the battle (1588). He was one of the founders of the CHATHAM CHEST, and he built an almshouse at Chatham known as Sir John Hawkins's Hospital. In 1595 he set out with Drake on an expedition to raid the West Indies, but he died at sea off Porto Rico.

This many-talented man was one of the greatest of his age: seaman, navigator, strategist, administrator, businessman, Member of Parliament, innovator and patriot. Nineteenth-century historians tended to see him through spectacles gloomed over by their detestation of all things connected with slavery. But, though Hawkins was no saint, modern research has accorded him his rightful place as one who contributed as much to the salvation of England and the humiliation of Spain as Sir Francis Drake. *See also* ACHINES; HAWKINS, SIR RICHARD.

Serve God daily, love one another, preserve your victuals, beware of fire and keep good company.

Hawkins's order to his ships, quoted in
C. R. N. Routh, *Who's Who in History* (1964)

Hawkins, Sir Richard (?1562–1622): naval commander, the only son of Sir John Hawkins. In 1582 he sailed with his uncle William Hawkins to Brazil. He commanded the *Duck* galiot in Drake's West Indies expedition (1585) and the *Swallow* against the Armada. Two of his own merchant vessels were used as FIRE-SHIPS at Calais. Having built his own galleon, the *Dainty*, 'pleasing to the eye, profitable for stowage, good of sail and well-conditioned', he sailed in her to the Azores with his father (1590) and set out in 1593 to make a voyage round the world. Starting from Plymouth, he passed through the Strait of Magellan, plundered Valparaiso and in June 1594 was defeated in San Mateo Bay, Peru. He was held prisoner for three years in Peru and was then taken to

Madrid; he was eventually released in 1602 for a ransom of £3000. On his return he was knighted; later he was a Member of Parliament and a mayor of Plymouth. The valuable *Observations of Sir Richard Hawkins, Knight, in his Voiage into the South Sea, A.D. 1593* were written in 1603–4 but not published until 1622. *See also* SCURVY.

Hawkins, William (*c.*1495–*c.*1553) and his son, also **William** (*c.*1519–1589): merchants and sailors, respectively father and brother of Sir John HAWKINS. Both were prominent citizens of Plymouth, both held the mayoralty several times, and both were much involved in trading ventures. The elder William sent trading expeditions as far as Guinea and Brazil; the younger became more involved in political affairs: his ships went privateering against France and Spain, he cooperated with the Huguenots in the Protestant struggle, and he helped fit out seven ships for the fight against the Armada.

Hawse: that part of a ship's bows which contains the hawse-pipes through which the anchor cable runs, and the hawse-pipes in which the anchor is stowed. 'Clear hawse' and 'foul hawse' when a ship is anchored or moored indicate respectively whether the cables are clear or twisted across each other. To 'come up through the hawse-hole' is naval slang for PROMOTION from the lower deck to officer rank.

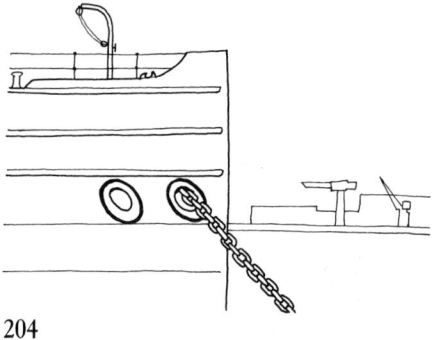

Hawser: a long rope or wire cable used for securing a ship alongside, or for towing, mooring etc.

Hawser-laid: made of three small ropes twined together, the usual form of cordage.

Hay-making: a yachtsman who neglected to clean the weed and seagrass from his vessel was apt to be asked by a smarter rival when he meant to begin hay-making.

Heads: the seamen's lavatories or latrines, so named because they were generally in the head or fore part of a ship.

Headsail: any sail set forward of the fore mast.

Health and hygiene: in the nature of his work the old seaman lived in very unhealthy conditions, so crowded that any contagion was sure to spread. He was subjected to foul air and damp, often indifferently fed and deprived of essential chemical substances. Hammocks were usually slung at 14 in. to the man, and such inconveniences as thousands of RATS and weevil-infested biscuits were commonplace.

Many captains and even ships' SURGEONS (who were frequently ill-qualified and the lowest representatives of their profession) did not realize that a clean orderly ship was a happier and more efficient fighting and trading unit. It is an odd fact that the Admiralty did not issue soap to seamen till 1810, and even then the price of a piece was knocked off a man's wages. Some of the effective steps progressively, if spasmodically and slowly, put into effect were:

1. Dirty and verminous recruits from the slums, portside hovels and prisons were put into 'receiving ships', where they were scrubbed down, had their rags burnt and

were kitted out with 'slops' – clean clothes from the store.

2. Better supplies of fresh air were ensured below decks through wind-sails diverting air below and air funnels.

3. Hammocks were scrubbed and aired.

4. Various efforts were made to fumigate the crew's quarters and produce a drier atmosphere: smouldering pans of gunpowder previously soaked in vinegar, acid on hot sand, burning tobacco, red-hot irons in tar, the fumes of sulphur, brimstone and charcoal.

Strained muscles, broken limbs and lacerated hands were all part of the day's work. Rupture, brought about by handling heavy casks, constant heaving on ropes and capstans, and lying out on the yards, was so common that, for example, over the years 1808–15 the Admiralty issued an average of 3714 trusses a year.

Another almost inevitable evil was drunkenness, largely brought about by the official daily issue of RUM, offered as some compensation for, and as an anaesthetic against, the terrible conditions in which seamen lived and worked. Writing in 1812, Admiral Lord Keith declared:

It is observable and deeply to be lamented that almost every crime except theft originates in drunkenness, and that a large proportion of the men who are maimed and disabled are reduced to that situation by accidents that happen from the same abominable vice . . . for although their spirits are mixed with four times the quantity of water, and issued at two separate periods of the day sufficiently distant from each other, yet not only young and raw lads from the country, but the more crafty and experienced who contrive to purchase or cheat their messmates are often so drunk as to be insensible of the most severe fractures by falls, or even of having fallen overboard when under the influence of drink.

It has been noted elsewhere in this book (see BEDLAM) that drunkenness may have led directly to another distressingly common disorder, lunacy.

In earlier days the most serious scourge of all was SCURVY. Typhus fever (called ship, gaol or camp fever), another killer, was virtually obliterated by the improved standards of hygiene described above. It was not till about 1900 that another menace was defeated – yellow fever (the dreaded 'Yellow Jack' or 'Bronze John'), a hot-climate fever picked up in such areas as the East and West Indies. Its virulence can be judged from the fact that in the attack on Martinique in 1794, 1100 men and 46 masters were reported to have been lost from it in the transport vessels alone. Doses of quinine helped, but many captains were lax about issuing them. Yellow fever was finally conquered by the same remedies as had been applied to malaria.

Perhaps the most damning evidence of conditions in the old Navy comes from the lists of fatal casualties issued from time to time. The year 1810 can serve as an example:

Men killed in action	281
Men died of wounds	150
Men lost through wreck, foundering, fire etc.	530
Men lost by accidents	1630
Men lost by disease	2592
	5183

That is, more than three-quarters (over 80 per cent) of the *fatal* casualties came, not from battle or tempest, but from accident and disease.

'Heart of Oak': frequently and wrongly referred to as 'Hearts of Oak', this stirring sound is the Royal Navy's official march. The words were written for a pantomime by David Garrick in 1759; the music is by William Boyce. It echoes the spirit of the

WONDERFUL YEAR of victories in 1759. *See also* QUARTERS.

> Heart of oak are our ships,
> Heart of oak are our men,
> We always are ready,
> Steady, boys, steady!
> We'll fight and we'll conquer
> Again and again.

One of the verses refers to the threat of invasion by the French.

> They swear they'll invade us, these
>   terrible foes,
> They frighten our women, our children,
>   and beaus;
> But should their flat-bottoms in darkness
>   get o'er,
> Still Britons they'll find, to receive them
>   on shore.
> Heart of oak are our ships, *etc.*

Heath, Edward Richard George (1916–): probably the only British Prime Minister with any claim to be regarded as a seaman. A keen yachtsman, he won the Sydney to Hobart Ocean Race (1969), and captained Britain's victorious Admiral's Cup Team (1971).

Heave to: allow a ship to lie to the wind in bad weather, or slow or stop a ship for a particular purpose. When this is accomplished, a ship is said to be 'hove to'.

Heaving line: a light line thrown from or to a ship, to which a heavier hawser can be attached and taken inboard or ashore; used when coming alongside.

Heavy weather: general term for rough, unpleasant weather at sea; see also WEATHER.

Hebber man: early name for a Thames fisherman down river, probably because he usually fished on the ebb tide.

He-cat: quite properly, and inevitably, the sailor's preferred name for every H.M.S. *Hecate* that has appeared in the Navy.

Heel: (1) the lean of a vessel to one side, caused by the wind or by centrifugal force when an engined craft turns at speed. It is neither a list, which is continuous, nor a roll, which is intermittent. (**2**) The lower end of a mast or upright spar; the inboard end of a boom. (**3**) The point where the aftermost part of the keel joins the base of the stern-post.

Heeling error: inaccuracy of the compass caused by the heeling of the ship.

Height of breadth: curious old shipbuilding term, meaning the distance of the ship's greatest breadth above the keel. It was one of the most important things to be decided in designing a ship and was usually a few feet above the water-line when the vessel was loaded.

Helideck: platform for the landing of helicopters.

Heligoland, Battle of (28 August 1914): encounter during the First World War when Admiral (then Commodore) Keyes with a force of submarines and of destroyers led by Commodore Tyrwhitt, broke through the defences under the guns of the German stronghold and, backed up by the light and battle cruisers of Jellicoe and Beatty, destroyed three enemy cruisers and a destroyer and crippled three other ships.

Helm: the handle of the rudder: the TILLER in small boats and the steering WHEEL of a vessel. A ship is said to 'answer the helm' when it responds to the helmsman's movement of the tiller or wheel to port or starboard.

Henri Grâce à Dieu, from a painting by Cruikshank after Holbein.

Hemp: fibre obtained from hemp plants and made into ROPE. It produces a soft, fairly heavy but flexible rope.

'Henri Grâce à Dieu' (known also as the **'Harry Grâce à Dieu'** and **'Great Harry'**): Henry VIII's famous warship, built in 1514, a four-master of 1000 tons, three decks high in the poop and four in the forecastle from the evidence available. Her lofty spread of sail marked a great advance over her predecessors and she carried a formidable armament of no less than 186 guns, including 122 iron serpentines (breech-loading) and four of brass (muzzle-loading). When the ship was rebuilt in 1540, the number of guns was reduced to 122. *See also* BONAVENTURE MAST; HERALDRY; POPPENRUYTER, HANS.

Henry V (1387–1422): king of England. Interesting details have survived of his fleet, which numbered some 35 vessels, described as 'of the Tower' (i.e. the Tower of London), the medieval equivalent of 'H.M.S.'. They included several ships of exceptional size for the period, e.g. the *Jesus of the Tower* of 1000 tons, some carracks of 500–600 tons and five of 400 tons upwards. Fighting ships were usually of 400–600 tons and merchantmen were somewhat smaller. *See also* BAYONNE SHIP.

Henry VII (1457–1509): king of England. In the first years of his reign, beginning in 1485, the first Tudor hired merchantmen for most royal purposes, but soon began a special shipbuilding programme. The *Regent* of 1000 tons and the *Sovereign* of 800 were on the stocks in 1487, the former being the first four-master known in English shipbuilding. Henry VII's ships were typical carracks, with the forecastle projecting considerably over the stem and, at least with the large vessels, both poop and poop-royal aft. *See also* FATHER OF THE NAVY.

Henry VIII (1491–1547): king of England. His reign gives us many more documentary records than those of his predecessors, since the Navy-Royal was not only greatly enlarged but put on a more or less permanent footing. To this period belongs the great Roll of Anthony ANTHONY, giving details of the Navy in 1546, still preserved in the Pepysian Library at Magdalene College, Cambridge. Henry built his fleet 'with the deliberate intention of using it to destroy an invading army on the sea . . . Henry's fleet was different in design from all its predecessors . . . It was designed, and created, for one purpose only – to fight' (Professor Michael Lewis). He came to possess over 100 ships, from the great *Henri Grâce à Dieu* of 1000 tons to a number of row-barges (small swift vessels of about 20 tons). Of these ships he actually built 46, the rest having been acquired by purchase and capture, with just a few inherited from his father. His greatest innovation, one that was to revolutionize naval warfare, was to locate the ships' guns, not in the 'fighting castles', but the length of the cargo deck, with ports cut in the sides.

Heraldry: with a multitude of standards, banners, ensigns, pendants and streamers, often bearing heraldic devices, medieval and Tudor ships must have made a brave sight on great occasions, especially when the king and important nobles were aboard. A roll of 1350, describing the flags made for the royal ships, mentions streamers charged with dragons, leopards' heads, lozenges, green and red roses, chequered flags, the royal arms surrounded by a blue

garter, and the figure of St Mary. Another roll, of Henry V's time, lists guidons of the Holy Trinity, St Mary, St Edward and St George, and devices of the swan, ostrich feather and antelope. Henry VIII's *HENRI GRÂCE À DIEU* flaunted the banners of England, England and Spain, Castile, Guienne, Wales and Cornwall, with other flags showing the pomegranate, rose, dragon, greyhound, lion etc.

Most of this splendour has departed, though a few essential FLAGS have survived. Otherwise we must look to such things as the crests and badges of H.M. ships as the sometimes humdrum survivors of early pageantry. In former times, their heraldry was erratic and often inaccurate; but the design of these badges is now the responsibility of the College of Heralds, and is subject to Admiralty approval.

Herbert, Arthur: *see* TORRINGTON, EARL OF.

Her Majesty's Ship: *see* H.M.S.

Hermaphrodite brig: a two-masted sailing vessel with square sails on the fore mast, and a fore-and-aft sail with a square topsail above on the main mast. It was therefore neither strictly a brig nor a brigantine, but had characteristics of both – in fact a hermaphrodite.

Hermaphrodite rig: combining in one ship features of sails and rigging of different types.

'Hermes': Royal Navy aircraft-carrier of 28,700 tons, launched in 1953 and first commissioned in 1959. By means of regular refits, it is hoped to keep her in service till at least 1984–5. For ten years she carried fixed-wing aircraft and was then adapted to operate helicopters and convey some 750 Royal Marine commando troops with their vehicles and equipment. Late in 1979 it is planned to equip her with the first operational squadron of Royal Navy Sea Harrier fighters, in addition to nine Sea King anti-submarine helicopters.

'Hermione': 32-gun frigate which featured in a famous cutting-out exploit (1799). In September 1797, as a result of the brutality of her captain, Hugh Pigot, the crew had mutinied, killed Pigot and most of the other officers, then carried the ship into La Guayre, where they handed it over to the Spaniards. The ship was reconditioned by them, her guns and crew number were increased and she was put into the service of Spain.

In October 1799 Captain Edward Hamilton of the 28-gun frigate *Surprise* found her in the harbour of Puerto Cabello, moored between two strong batteries of guns and manned by 320 men. Hamilton left the *Surprise* with six boats at 8 a.m. and, despite fire from the batteries, boarded the *Hermione* just after noon, overcame the resistance and cut the cables. By 2 p.m. the ship had been towed out of gun-shot, with a British casualty list of ten wounded against a Spanish loss of over 200 killed and wounded. Hamilton received a knighthood and the *Hermione* was restored to the British Navy but, fittingly enough (and doubtless to erase as far as possible the associations with the mutiny), she was renamed *Retribution*.

Herring buss: type of vessel used for net-

A modern model of a herring buss, made from drawings by Henrik af Chapman, the 18th-century Swedish naval architect.

fishing in the North Sea in the 16th–18th centuries. They were normally of 45–80 tons burden, round-bowed, narrow-pooped and fitted with three masts, each of which carried a square sail, with a topsail on the main mast. A 17th-century writer recorded that in 1601 the Dutch had the substantial fishing fleet of 1200 busses. This type of vessel developed into the fishing lugger of 1790–1830.

Herring pond: a humorous name given particularly to the North Atlantic, but also at times to other dividing seas, e.g. the North Sea.

'Herzogin Cecile': one of the last of the great sailing ships, wrecked on the coast of Devonshire in 1936. Built as late as 1920, she was used on the Australian wool run and during the years 1925–9 won the race home three times, averaging 100 days for the passage.

Ashore at Bolt Head, Salcombe, 1936.

Hide boats: primitive sea-going craft in general use in Northern Europe during the Stone and Bronze Ages. The more recent Eskimo umiak and Irish currach clearly demonstrate the toughness of these craft in heavy seas. *See also BRENDAN.*

High seas: all that area of sea not within territorial waters; that is, not within the sovereignty of any state. With the proposed international 200-mile limit for territorial waters, the high seas would be restricted to the larger oceans. *See also* NARROW SEAS.

Hillary, Sir William: *see* LIFEBOAT.

Hilo: the principal town and port of Hawaii; Johnny's destination in the windlass and capstan chanty:

Oh – wake her!
Oh – shake her!
Oh – wake that girl with the blue dress on
When Johnny comes down to Hilo,
Poor old man.

Hitch: a knot for securing a rope temporarily to a rail, bolt, or any structure, rather than to another rope; *see* KNOTS.

H.M.S. (Her (or 'His') Majesty's Ship): the prefix for ships of the Royal Navy, for certain shore establishments commissioned as ships, and also for some training ships not strictly part of the fleet.

Hobbler: *see* HOVELLER.

Hogging: constructional fault or weakness in a ship when the centre part of the keel and bottom arch upwards. All wooden ships were liable to it. In *Victory*'s present keel there is about 18 in. of 'hogging'. But even a steel ship can 'hog' under stress, as the commanding officer of H.M.S. *Exe* found in a China Seas typhoon:

When she hit the succeeding sea, the ridge-rope suddenly slacked to such an extent that my feet felt the deck and, for a moment, I thought the ridge-rope had carried away, but, to my astonishment, as I hung on, I felt it tauten again like a bar. Thus it dawned on me how a destroyer could, thanks to modern steel, bend without breaking.

> Quoted by Admiral Sir Christopher Cradock, *Whispers from the Fleet* (1907)

Hoggy: craft used in the south coast of England in the 19th century, very round in shape (its length less than two widths) and eminently suitable for dragging up on the beach.

Hoist: (1) an apparatus for lifting or hoisting; (2) the vertical height of a sail, flag or yard; (3) an assembly or combination of flags when signalling, etc.; (4) to lift or raise, e.g. a sail or flag.

Hold: the space below decks in a merchant ship within which cargo is carried; also the lowest deck in a warship. *See also page 577.*

Holiday: a gap or a part missed out when painting ship.

Holk: *see* HULK.

Holmes, J. W.: *see LEUCADIA.*

'Holmes's Bonfire': raid following the St James's Day Fight (25 July 1666), when the Dutch retreated and were followed up by George Monck, Duke of Albemarle, to the Texel, where he sent in Sir Robert Holmes to destroy the shipping in the Vlie. The town of Brandaris, a long range of storehouses and at least 150 Dutch ships were destroyed.

Holystones: stones used for scrubbing the deck. One theory on the origin of the name is that a quantity of broken monuments from St Nicholas Church, Great Yarmouth, was once used for this purpose. 'Bibles', 'hand-organs' and 'prayer books' were alternative names. *See also* PHILADELPHIA CATECHISM.

Home port: (**1**) formerly, the port from which a ship was manned; (**2**) a port on which a ship is based; (**3**) a port where a merchant ship is registered or its owners have their headquarters.

Hondius, Jodocus (real name Joos or Josse de Hondt; 1563–1611): famous Flemish engraver who came to England from Ghent and who, among his other work, constructed globes and illustrated the voyages of Drake and Cavendish.

A celestial globe by Hondius, dated 1603.

Hong Kong: British colony off the coast of southern China. The territory consists of Hong Kong Island, ceded in 1842 at the end of the Opium War, and the New Territories on the mainland and other islands, of which the British obtained a 99 years' lease in 1898. It was a powerful naval base in the early years of the century, but in 1922 Britain agreed not to fortify Hong Kong further. When the Japanese entered the Second World War they had little difficulty in capturing the colony (Christmas Day 1941), and they held it until August 1945. Since that time the population of Hong Kong has grown enormously with the entry of Chinese from the mainland, and now numbers over four million. At the same time Hong Kong has become one of the great industrial centres of Asia, exporting a wide range of manufactured goods and providing an important financial centre.

Honourable East India Company: *see* EAST INDIA COMPANY, BRITISH.

Honour of the flag: recognition of another nation's flag by dipping colours, firing gun salutes, etc.; in extreme cases, insistence on the acknowledgement of maritime supremacy.

A celebrated case occurred in the year 1554, when Lord William Howard was sent with a fleet of 28 sail to bring Philip II of Spain up the English Channel, *en route* to his marriage with Mary I in Winchester Cathedral.

Prince Philip was accompanied by 160 of his own ships: and the Spanish Admiral came along proudly with the Spanish flag flying at the main topmast-head. He was probably surprised to find himself greeted with a good round shot by Lord William Howard, who flatly refused to give the Prince any other welcome till the Spanish colours were hauled down.

Sir Arthur Quiller-Couch (ed.), *The Story of the Sea* (1898)

See also MONSON, SIR WILLIAM; SALUTES.

Hood: a family which has been the despair (and occasionally the downfall) of naval historians, since there were two Alexanders and two Samuels all serving at roughly the same time; three of them became admirals and two contrived to die in the same year.

1. *Alexander Hood*, first Viscount Bridport (1726–1814), was the brother of Samuel Hood, first Viscount Hood (1724–1816). He saw much action, with Hawke and Howe among others, entered Parliament in 1784, first received his flag in 1794 and was created Viscount Bridport in the same year, after the Glorious FIRST OF JUNE.

2. *Alexander Hood* (1758–98), brother of Sir Samuel Hood (1762–1814), was a naval captain who accompanied Captain Cook on his second voyage and fought at St Kitts (1782) and Dominica (1782).

3. *Samuel Hood*, first Viscount Hood (1724–1816), saw much service with Rodney, commanded on the North America station (1767–70), was a Lord of the Admiralty and governor of Greenwich Hospital. He became a vice-admiral in 1787 and full admiral seven years later. *See also* ST KITTS.

4. *Sir Samuel Hood* (1762–1814), who also became an admiral, was one of the 'Band of Brothers'. Among his other actions he was with Nelson at Santa Cruz (1797) and the Nile (1798), Gambier at Copenhagen (1807) and Saumarez in the Baltic (1808). *See also* JUNO.

The two sets of brothers were cousins.

Hood, Sir Horace (1870–1916): admiral, a descendant of Viscount HOOD. He died in the Battle of Jutland (*see* INVINCIBLE).

Hood, Samuel: *see* HOOD.

Hood, William John Thomson (1794–1857): naval captain and inventor.

He entered the Navy at the age of 10 and was present at Trafalgar in H.M.S. *Achilles* as a Volunteer First Class. As well as seeing much action he was an officer of great ingenuity, receiving a number of awards. In 1824 he was given the Gold Medal of the Society for the Encouragement of Arts for his invention of improved screen glasses for quadrants and sextants, and he gained a Silver Medal for his special saw to help the progress and escape of ships surrounded by ice. Floating bridges and rocket shafts were among his other successful inventions.

'Hood': it is fitting that a great seafaring family should be commemorated in the naming of a great ship, or a line of them. The 1849 *Hood*, a two-decker of 80 guns, was designed as a sailing ship but she was replanned before she was completed, and was launched as a screw battleship ten years later. As originally designed, she was of 2600 tons burden. The 1891 *Hood* displaced over 14,000 tons, was heavily armed and carried seven torpedo tubes. Her eight boilers and 32 furnaces drove her at 17 knots. Twenty-seven years later her successor, of 41,000 tons displacement and equipped with geared turbines, could steam at 32 knots. One of the worst moments of the Second World War came on 24 May 1941 when this old battle cruiser, along with the new battleship *Prince of Wales*, was brought out to tackle the German *Bismarck* and *Prinz Eugen* in the Denmark Strait. A pre-war plan to reinforce her outdated thin armour had been dropped and she was no match for the modern 15-in. shells of the powerful *Bismarck*. All her turrets opened fire on *Hood*, followed by all the 8-in. guns of the *Prinz Eugen*.

. . . a 15-in. shell from the *Bismarck* hit the *Hood* just forward of her funnel. Her inadequate armour plate did nothing to prevent the shell

Undergoing sea trials, 1920.

from penetrating deep inside her and by a terrible stroke of fate it ploughed its way into the main magazine and 300 tons of high explosives. For a brief second the pressure of the resultant explosion was confined inside the hull of the ship; then the plates burst outwards and the *Hood* disintegrated. When the smoke from the explosion cleared she had disappeared below the icy water and 1416 men out of the crew of 1419 were dead.

John Welch, *Famous Sea Battles* (1964)

Hopper: a barge with discharge openings at the bottom for disposing of mud etc. from a dredger.

Hopping, Ann: *see* TOWNSHEND, JANE.

Hopwood, Ronald Arthur (1868–1949): admiral. It is not always realized that the modest R. A. Hopwood who appears in a number of poetical anthologies was, in fact, a naval flag officer. Some of his verse is cherished in naval circles and deserves to be better known than it is. His publications include *The Old Way*, *The Secret of the Ships* and *The New Navy*.

Horizon: the line at which sky appears to meet sea or land. Its distance is determined by the observer's height of eye, and is affected by the refraction of light. An artificial horizon is a device used to give a fixed point for observations of altitude.

Hornblower, Horatio: the fictional hero of many of the stories of C. S. FORESTER.

Hornpipe: an old wooden instrument fitted with horn at each end, which gave its name to the sailors' dance and to the tune itself. The dance was originally a solo jig, and so was adopted by sailors because it could be danced by men alone. During the 18th and 19th centuries the hornpipe was danced on board ship by the sailors on festive occasions and in their leisure hours.

Horse latitudes: areas of the ocean about 30° N. and S. subject to calms, especially in the North Atlantic. The origin of the name is uncertain.

Horse marines: 'tell that to the horse marines' is a facetious reply to an incredible story. The origin of the phrase may lie in

213

an incident in 1796 when cavalry being transported in a ship acted as marines; thus a 'horse marine' is an awkward or foolish person, quite out of his element.

Hosier, Francis (1673–1727): admiral. From 1714 to 1717 he was suspended as a suspected Jacobite, but he came back to command a squadron in the West Indies, where he died of fever. Richard Glover (1712–85) wrote a popular but inaccurate ballad called 'Admiral Hosier's Ghost' suggesting that the Admiral died of a broken heart when Admiralty orders prevented him from fighting the Spaniards.

Hosken, James (1798–1885): pioneer of transatlantic steam navigation, taking the *Great Western* from Bristol to New York in 15 days (1838) and in 13 days the following year. He commanded the *Great Britain* (1844–6) and a hospital ship in the Baltic (1854–5). He was commissioned Captain in 1857 and Vice-Admiral twenty years later.

Hospital ship: a ship equipped as a hospital with medical services, and attached in time of war to a fighting fleet. Hospital ships are non-combatant, carry no arms of any kind, and display the red cross on funnels and sides, these being illuminated at night when at sea in war-time.

Hoste, Sir William (1780–1828): naval officer who may well have set up some sort of record for capturing ships. In 1808–9, with the *Amphion* and other ships, he took or destroyed some 200 French and Venetian vessels in the Adriatic, and in the next year he added another 46 sail. In 1811 he defeated a greatly superior force off Lissa, being severely wounded in the process but refusing to leave the deck:

The number of men in the British squadron appears to have been about 880, and the number in the Franco-Venetian squadron, at the lowest estimate, 2500. Hence the British had opposed to them a force in guns full one-third, and in men nearly two-thirds, greater than their own . . . But the foe was met, the action fought, and the victory won; and fresh and unfaded will be the laurels which Captain Hoste and his gallant companions gained at Lissa.

William James, *The Naval History of Great Britain* (1822)

Undeterred by his damaged right arm, Hoste went on capturing ships, including a large number of gunboats, and by way of variety he helped the Austrians take Cattara and Ragusa (1813–14), after which he was made a baronet and a Knight of the Bath.

Hotham, William, first Baron Hotham (1736–1813): admiral, whose career ended rather tamely after a lively beginning. In 1757 he was promoted captain for his capture of a French privateer. He was in action with Rodney, Howe and Hood, but in 1795 he twice let an inferior French fleet off when a more resolute commander might have annihilated it. His nephew, another *William Hotham* (1772–1848), also made flag rank and was knighted in 1815.

Hot press: an urgent and determined raid by the press-gang.

Hour-glass: *see* SAND-GLASS.

House-boat: boat equipped for living in as a home, usually moored with direct access to land but occasionally drawn up on the shore.

. . . we the Inhabitantes of the towne of Wivenhoe doe informe your worshippes of one Edward Mayer the elder of our towne, an obstenate and refracterie fellowe who will not live in Ranke and order amongst his neyghbours in a house, But will live in a boate drawn up on dry land in which he hath built a chimney . . .

Essex County Record Office, record of a
court action (Michaelmas 1641)

If it had been Aladdin's palace, roc's egg and all, I suppose I could not have been more charmed with the romantic idea of living in it. There was a delightful door cut in the side, and it was roofed in, and there were little windows in it; but the wonderful charm of it was, that it was a real boat which had no doubt been upon the water hundreds of times, and which had never been intended to be lived in, on dry land . . . Peggotty opened a little door and showed me my bedroom. It was the completest and most desirable bedroom ever seen – in the stern of the vessel; with a little window, where the rudder used to go through . . .

Charles Dickens, *David Copperfield*
(1850)

House flags: distinctive flags flown by individual merchant shipping lines and companies, cargo and passenger. Thus ships of the Lamport and Holt Line, Liverpool, have a flag with two red stripes and a white band between carrying the letters L.H.; Clan Line steamers fly a red flag with a white central diamond and red lion; and the Athel Line a blue flag with a white diamond and the word 'Athel'. Some lines and companies who belong to special shipping groups (e.g. The British and Commonwealth) fly a group burgee above their own house flag.

Hoveller (or **hobbler**): an unlicensed boatman; one who helps save life and property from a wreck (or, in more barbarous days, plundered it). Other meanings of the word included a small coasting vessel and, for some unexplained reason, the watcher of a beacon or lighthouse.

Hovercraft (also known as **air cushion vehicle** or **A.C.V.**): a craft designed to travel close to but above water or ground by forcing air beneath it to create a lift. A surrounding skirt around the hull helps to retain the lifting air, while forward motion is provided by air (or water) propellers driven by the same engines as produce the lifting thrust.

The idea of the hovercraft was patented in December 1955 by Christopher Cockerell, who was knighted in 1969 for his contribution to the development of this new form of transport. After the difficulties of the early experimental stage, the first full-size $3\frac{1}{2}$-ton 30-ft-long craft (SR.N1) was launched in May 1959 and made its first Channel crossing in July of that year. Since then the hovercraft has developed rapidly and become a fast and economical form of transport, especially on short sea ferry routes for passengers and motor vehicles. A regular hoverferry service was opened across the Channel between Dover and Boulogne in August 1968 and soon after between Ramsgate and Calais. These routes were operated by large hovercraft, known as the SR.N4, of 168 tons and capable of carrying some 250 passengers and 30 cars. In reasonably calm weather these craft can cruise at 65 to 70 knots, and in rough seas averages of 35 to 40 knots are maintained, the hovercraft being able to continue in winds up to Force 8. In 1978 an enlarged version of the SR.N4 was completed, giving it a carrying capacity of over 400 passengers and 30–60 cars.

Many other nations are developing hovercraft, large and small, not only for ferry services but also for military use. Several of the larger navies already maintain hovercraft and continue with experiments in their employment as amphibious assault and landing ships, for mine counter-measure operations, and as fast attack craft. The ability of hovercraft to operate at speed in shallow water and on land, to transfer from one to the other without special port facilities, and to overcome conditions too difficult for normal ships and vehicles makes it likely that it will be developed for many different uses. Already in Canada hovercraft have been adapted for ice-breaking and for working in swamp land.

See colour section.

Hove to: *see* HEAVE TO.

Howard, Lord Thomas, first Earl of Suffolk and first Baron Howard de Walden (1561–1626): statesman who also fought against the Armada (1588) and was vice-admiral of the fleet sent to Cadiz (1596) under the Earl of Essex and Lord Charles Howard of Effingham. *See also MERE HONOUR.*

Howard of Effingham, Lord Charles, second Baron Howard of Effingham and first Earl of Nottingham (1536–1624): Lord High Admiral of England (1585–1618). He was the chief commander against the Spanish Armada (1588), and his service (military as well as naval) also included the expedition to CADIZ (1596). He was a courageous and wise commander, if slow to grasp that the whole concept of war at sea was changing under a race of captains such as Drake. But Ralegh wrote that he was 'better advised than a great many malignant fools were that found fault with his demeanour'. One of his finest points was his concern for the well-being of his seamen and his stout opposition to the meanness of the government's treatment of them. He was Lord High Admiral for 34 years and retained the trust and affection of the throne to the end of his long life.

Howe, Richard, Earl Howe (1726–99): admiral, nicknamed 'Black Dick', either because of his dark complexion or, it has been suggested, because of his reputation of only smiling when there was the prospect of a fight. A strict disciplinarian, he had a distinguished record of service and, as captain of the *Dunkirk* in the 1755 expedition to North America, he fired the first shot in the Seven Years' War – which had not at that stage been declared. He held the North American command during the American War of Independence (*see* NEW YORK; RHODE ISLAND), but he disliked the whole operation and, at odds with the government, laid down his command (1778) and went into retirement for four years. He came back to hold the Channel command, to effect the relief of Gibraltar against great odds and to serve as First Lord of the Admiralty. But, whatever the tale of success (and occasional failure), his place in English history is most firmly assured by his victory of the Glorious FIRST OF JUNE (1794), when he sank one French ship and captured six others. Even so, there were critics, Nelson among them, who thought he let the French off too lightly by not pushing home his advantage more vigorously. Nelson, in fact, sometimes ungenerously referred to any success not sufficiently followed up as 'a Lord Howe victory'.

Among the sailors he was known, for his dark complexion, by the epithet of 'Black Dick'. If no genius could be discovered in the lines of his face, there was in them an expression of serene and placid fortitude, which could not be mistaken.

Sir William Wraxall, *Historical Memoirs of My Own Life* (1815)

Howling Fifties: a name given to the very stormy latitudes between 50° and 60° S. in the Southern Ocean. Compare 'Roaring Forties'.

Hoy: coasting vessel, often sloop-rigged, useful for conveying goods or as a ship–shore tender. Since voyages were usually short, and quick loading and unloading an important factor, the main hatch was often very large. They are often called Dutch hoys, but numbers were built in British yards.

'Huascar': *see SHAH.*

Hudson, Henry (*d.*1611): navigator and explorer. His name is commemorated in Hudson Strait, Bay and River, though he did not actually discover any of them. Nevertheless, he explored farther than his predecessors, and on his final voyage, in search of the North-West Passage, he reached Hudson Strait and the bay beyond. The tragic end to a courageous life came when mutineers abandoned him in Hudson Bay. *See also* NORTH-EAST PASSAGE.

Hudson Bay: inland sea in E. central Canada, 850 miles long, 650 miles wide. It is linked with both the Arctic and the Atlantic and, except for the July–October period, is largely icebound.

Hudson's Bay Company: English trading company founded by royal charter (1670) to search for the NORTH-WEST PASSAGE and to exercise a fur-trade monopoly in the region of Hudson Bay. The original charter was granted to Prince Rupert and seventeen other noblemen and gentlemen, forming the 'Governor and Company and Adventurers of England trading into Hudson's Bay'. The first settlements, known as Rupert's Land, were on James Bay and the Churchill and Hayes Rivers. The enterprise continued as a great commercial success, despite considerable inroads by the French, till the 19th century, the chief sufferers being the Indians, who were demoralized by the plentiful supply of spirits offered as a bribe by rival companies, and the fur-bearing animals, which were slaughtered in and out of season. In November 1869 the Company ceded its territories and rights of government to the Dominion of Canada, but it continues as a private trading company.

Huggins, William John (1781–1845): marine painter. He served with the East India Company and later, when he had settled ashore in London, specialized in depicting East and West Indiamen. In 1834 he was appointed marine painter to William IV, for whom he painted three large canvases of Trafalgar.

Hughes, Sir Edward (?1720–1794): admiral; described as a fine seaman, an inspiring leader and a determined fighter, whose greatest limitation was his insistence on sticking to the book and to restrictive Admiralty conventions of battle. During the struggle for control of India (1782–3), he fought five full-scale actions in the space of just over a year with the great French admiral Suffren – all of them indecisive. Sir Joshua Reynolds painted a fine portrait of him in full dress as a Vice-Admiral and looking remarkably well-fed. *See also* MADRAS.

Hughes, Sir Richard (?1729–1812): admiral. Unusually for a sailor who attained flag rank, little is known about his origins. His first command was the *Lark* (1748); ten years later he served under Admiral Saunders in the Louisburg and Quebec campaigns. At various periods he commanded at Halifax, Nova Scotia, and in the West Indies. He was a fine seaman and tough fighter who early in his career learned 'how not to do it' when his squadronal commander, Admiral Lestock, failed to support his superior in an action. Nelson, when commanding the *Boreas*, took Lady Hughes out to the West Indies and considered her 'a fine talkative Lady'.

'Hugin': a replica of a Viking long-ship of *c.* A.D. 700 rowed from Denmark to England in 1949. She cost some £5000 to build, and was 71 ft long and 18 ft wide, with a mast nearly 40 ft high. In true style, she carried a striped sail, a dragon figure-head and rows of shields along the bul-warks. Her volunteer crew manned 32 oars.

Hulk (or holk): (1) late medieval heavy cargo vessel, clinker-built, with fore and aft castles, simple square sails and triangular lateen mizen; a Scandinavian example shows the sails with 'bonnets'; **(2)** an old vessel cut down to serve as a convict ship (*see* PRISON HULKS), store, etc.

Hull: the body of a ship excluding its superstructure, masts and rigging, and funnels. A ship is 'hull down' when only its superstructure is showing above the horizon.

Humber: an estuary on the E. coast of England carrying the Rivers Ouse and Trent into the North Sea. A dredged channel runs upstream as far as Goole, but Hull and Immingham on the north side, and Grimsby on the south, are the chief ports.

Humber keel: type of cargo-carrying vessel in general use on Yorkshire waterways in the Middle Ages, double-ended, decked fore and aft, with hatch-covers amidships, carrying a square sail on a single mast. Other types of 'keel' were the Tyne and the Norfolk. Capacity varied from 20 to 50 tons, the larger craft being able to make longer voyages, e.g. to the Low Countries. *See also* NORTHIAM SHIP.

Humboldt Current (or **Peruvian Current**): one of the world's most important and valuable currents, flowing northward along the W. coast of South America, and so more often known as the Peruvian Current. It was named after Alexander von Humboldt (1769–1859), the famous German traveller and geographer. The Humboldt Current carries the cold Antarctic waters northward, and is con-tinuously reinforced by upwelling of the lower oceanic layers. Its waters are remarkable for their richness in minerals and the variety and abundance of fish life. The latter feeds vast colonies of sea-birds, whose droppings of guano provide the world with a very rich fertilizer, dug and exported from the islands and shores where it has accumulated over the centuries.

Hundred-and-seventy-gun ship: a draught of such a ship exists, dated 1809 and 'proposed' by Joseph TUCKER. Perhaps fortunately, she was never built, and in fact no ship with anything like this armament, or with four complete gun-decks, was ever seen in the British Navy. About 120 guns was the normal limit; e.g. *NELSON* (1814).

Hundred Years' War, the: the long period (approximately 1338–1453) of almost uninterrupted dispute and warfare between England and France. Though

A 20th-century square-rigged keel.

perhaps chiefly remembered for its land battles at Crécy, Poitiers and Agincourt, the sea also played its part: *see* ESPAGNOLS SUR MER; LA ROCHELLE and SLUYS, BATTLES OF.

Hurricane: a violent tropical storm in the West Indies and the Pacific. The hurricane revolves round an area of deep low pressure and blows anti-clockwise in the northern hemisphere and clockwise in the southern. Low cloud, poor visibility, torrential rain, violent squalls and fierce winds accompany the storm, which may have a diameter of over 100 miles. The hurricane moves on a course known as the track, and its centre is called the eye or vortex. In the West Indies hurricanes occur from June to November and are most frequent in September. On the Beaufort Scale a hurricane rates as Force 12 with winds of 65 nautical miles per hour and above.

Hurricane deck: a light upper deck on a steamship.

Husband: *see* SHIP'S HUSBAND.

Hydrofoil: a device on a fast motor-boat so designed that it will raise the hull and thus reduce the resistance of the water; and also the name given to a vessel so equipped.

Hydrographer: a person who studies and is versed in HYDROGRAPHY.

Hydrography: the scientific study of the waters on the earth's surface, including the art of SURVEYING and charting them. The Admiralty's Hydrographic Department is responsible for the production of charts, tide-tables and all navigational data and is headed by the Hydrographer of the Navy. Admiralty charts and Notices to Mariners are relied on throughout the world.

Hydrophone: an underwater device with microphone for detecting a submarine by the noise it makes.

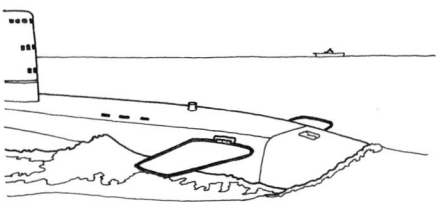

Hydroplane: a plane or fin projecting from a submarine enabling it to be steered upwards or downwards; also a plane fitted to a motor-boat assisting it to skim along the surface; or the boat itself. The name was also used for aeroplanes which could alight and float on water.

Hythe: one of the CINQUE PORTS on the S. coast of Kent which supplied ships for the royal service in medieval times. Originally a broad haven protected by a shingle bank, the harbour became silted up and Hythe lost its value as a port.

I

Iberian Peninsula: that part of S.W. Europe consisting of the countries of Spain and Portugal. The W. coast facing the Atlantic was the starting-point for many of the famous voyages of the Spanish and Portuguese navigators, who opened up the sea routes to the New World and round Africa to India and the East. From the struggle with Spain in Tudor times through the era of Britain's naval supremacy, the Iberian Peninsula was always an area of concern in relation to both the Atlantic and Mediterranean. Gibraltar, at the peninsula's southern extremity and commanding the entrance to the Mediterranean, has been British since 1704. *See also* PENINSULAR WAR.

Iceberg: a great mass of ice which has broken away from a glacier or ice-sheet and floated out to sea; only about a ninth of the iceberg appears above water. A most dangerous area for icebergs is the North Atlantic, where they are 'calved' from the great glaciers of Greenland and float southwards on the Labrador Current. One of the greatest sea disasters, the sinking of the *Titanic* (1912), was caused by an iceberg. In 1929 an international agreement established an ice-patrol service to report on and give warning of icebergs in the North Atlantic. This patrol work is undertaken by ships of the United States Coast Guard assisted by long-range aircraft operating from Newfoundland.

Ice blink: (1) the name given by the Danes to the ice cliffs of Greenland; (2) a curious luminous appearance of the sky caused by reflection of light from a mass of ice.

Ice-breaker: a powerful vessel specially designed, heavily plated and strengthened to break sheet ice and force a navigable passage for other ships. Ice-breakers are used in the St Lawrence and Great Lakes waterways, in the Baltic, the Arctic etc. For the nuclear-powered ice-breaker *Lenin*, *see* NUCLEAR-POWERED SHIPS.

See also colour section.

Iceland: a volcanic and mountainous island in the North Atlantic just south of the Arctic Circle and about 180 miles S.E. of Greenland. First settled by the Norsemen in the 9th century, Iceland in early times was linked with Norway, and then for five centuries came under the rule of Denmark, but since 1946 it has been an independent republic. Relatively barren and with a harsh climate, Iceland depends on the wealth of fish in the seas off the coasts. Here the mingling of cold and warm currents provides rich feeding and spawning grounds for many fish, especially cod, haddock and herring. Since medieval times Icelandic waters have attracted the fishermen of the maritime countries of N.W. Europe, and English ships were amongst the earliest to exploit them. Over-fishing and the consequent depletion of stocks have recently led to conflict between Iceland and other fishing nations (*see* COD WAR).

Identification marks: every ship must be able to be identified. Her nationality, under which she is registered, will be indicated by the flag or ensign flying at her stern on the ensign staff. This may be the national flag or a special ensign such as the Red Ensign, flown by British merchant ships, or the

White Ensign, flown by the Royal Navy. Many merchant ships are now registered under the flags of Liberia, Panama and other small countries though their ownership is elsewhere; these are known as FLAGS OF CONVENIENCE. A merchant ship will generally have her name on either side of her bows and also, with the port of registration added, on the counter of her stern; but this is by no means universal. All ships, however, including many small yachts, have an International Call Sign for radio which can also be indicated visually by a flag hoist, especially when entering or leaving harbour. These are known as her signal letters; the first one or two letters indicate the country, and the others the ship. For example, British ships have G or M as the first of their signal letters, whilst for the U.S.A. it is K, N or W.

Most of the major shipping lines maintain a distinctive pattern of painting their ships' hulls; the funnel may bear a painted emblem; and the company's house flag will be flown. Often two colours to give contrast are used for the hulls, one for the topsides and one for the boot-topping; e.g. ships of the Cunard Company may be grey with orange or white with red, and the Union Castle use lilac grey with brown and have a red and black funnel. Thus the painting of merchant ships can be a helpful part of their identification.

More strictly defined identification marks are to be found on naval and on fishing vessels. Ships of the Royal Navy are given 'pennant numbers' consisting of a letter and a number painted on their sides. Different letters are used for each general type of ship according to the following key: R for aircraft-carriers or commando ships; S, submarines; C, cruisers; D, destroyers; F, frigates; L, assault landing ships; N, minelayers; A, support ships and auxiliaries; M, minesweepers; P, boom defence

vessels and light forces. Similar systems are used in other navies.

British fishing vessels are identified by letters indicating their port, followed by a number. The letter prefix may consist of one, two or three letters; the following are a few examples: A for Aberdeen; BM, Brixham; DE, Dundee; FD, Fleetwood; FR, Fraserburgh; GE, Goole; GY, Grimsby; H, Hull; HH, Harwich; HL, Hartlepool; INS, Inverness; LT, Lowestoft; M, Milford Haven; NN, Newhaven; PD, Peterhead; PZ, Penzance; SH, Scarborough; SN, North Shields; SSS, South Shields; WA, Whitehaven; WY, Whitby; YH, Yarmouth.

Flaunt out O sea your separate flags of
    nations!
Flaunt out visible as ever the various ship-
    signals!
But do you reserve especially for yourself and
    for the soul of man one flag above the
    rest . . .
Token of all brave captains and all intrepid
    sailors and mates,
And all that went down doing their duty . . .
A pennant universal, subtly waving all time,
    o'er all brave sailors,
All seas, all ships.

    Walt Whitman, 'Song for all Seas, all Ships'

Idlers: a name, not to be taken literally, from sailing-ship days for men or boys of lowly status who did not keep a watch but were employed in a variety of duties, e.g. servants, cooks, butchers, barbers, tailors. The term was used also to include some non-watch-keeping officers such as the surgeon, purser and marine officer. In merchant sailing ships, where the name may have originated, idlers were men such as carpenters and sailmakers, who similarly did not keep a watch at sea. For ships of each rate the number of idlers was specified. Thus, at the beginning of the

19th century, a first-rate carried as many as 60 idlers, and a sixth-rate, 20.

'Illustrious': perhaps best-known in the 19th century as the stationary training ship for naval cadets, commissioned at Portsmouth in 1854 and converted from the old ship of the line. The 1896 *Illustrious* was a battleship of the Majestic class. In more recent times the aircraft-carrier *Illustrious* played an important part in the Second World War, when her aircraft sank the new Italian battleship *Littorio* and two older warships in the harbour at Taranto (11 November 1940; *see also* TORPEDO). *Illustrious* was severely damaged by German dive-bombers in 1941, but reached Malta under her own power and fought till the end of the war. *See also* INVINCIBLE.

'Implacable': the best-known H.M.S. *Implacable* began life as the French ship of the line *Duguay Trouin*. She escaped at Trafalgar only to be captured three weeks later by Captain Sir Richard Strachan, who fell in with six French ships off Ferrol and, after a costly action, brought in four of them to Plymouth as prizes. The renamed *Implacable* took part in several subsequent actions, commanded by Thomas Byam Martin. The 1898 *Implacable* was a London class battleship. The aircraft-carrier of the name was part of the British Pacific Fleet in the Second World War.

Impressment: the recruiting of seamen by means of the PRESS-GANG.

Inchcape Rock (or **Bell Rock**): a dangerous reef some 15 miles off the entrance to the Firth of Tay on the E. coast of Scotland. The abbot of Arbroath fixed a floating bell near the reef to warn sailors of the danger; Southey's ballad, 'The Inch-cape Rock', tells how Ralph the Rover, to spite the abbot, cut away the bell but was himself wrecked on the rock on his homeward voyage.

'Indefatigable': the 44-gun *Indefatigable*, commanded by one of the greatest frigate captains, Sir Edward Pellew, shared in the famous action of 13–14 January 1797, when the great French ship of the line, the *DROITS DE L'HOMME*, was driven ashore after an all-night fight. The *Indefatigable* also led the capture of four Spanish treasure ships in October 1804 and was in Gambier's action at the Basque Roads (1809).

The 1848 frigate of the same name was built at Devonport; there is a fine half-model of her in the National Maritime Museum, Greenwich. True to the name, another *Indefatigable*, this time a battle cruiser, was at the Battle of Jutland (1916), when shells from the German *Von der Tann* reached the magazine and 'turned the huge vessel over like a toy', with the loss of over 1000 men. The name lived on in the aircraft-carrier, which suffered a Japanese kamikaze raid on 1 April 1945, fortunately with only minor damage.

Indenture: a contract binding an apprentice to an employer. The document was written in duplicate and divided along a serrated or indented line so that the two halves would tally when brought together. In the past many boys took up indentures so that they could learn a trade or profession, and were bound to their master for a number of years, generally seven. The practice was common in the merchant service of the last century.

India husband: the owner of an East Indiaman, as compared with the Company, to which she had been chartered.

Indiaman: *see* EAST INDIAMAN; WEST INDIAMAN.

Indian Ocean: the world's third largest ocean after the Pacific and the Atlantic. Its northern extensions, the Arabian Sea and the Bay of Bengal, surround the Indian sub-continent; on the west it is bounded by Africa, on the east by South-East Asia and Australia, while to the south it merges with the Southern Ocean extending to the coasts of Antarctica. Groups of islands, both coral and mountainous, such as the Cocos, Seychelles and Mauritius, rise from the ocean floor, which in places is very deep, reaching over 3000 fathoms to the south of Java. The Indian Ocean is usually associated with the monsoons which, often accompanied by violent tropical storms, blow from the S.W. from June to September, and from the N.E. from December to March. But every kind of weather may be experienced according to latitude, ranging from the stormy westerlies of the Roaring Forties in the south to the steady S.E. Trades and equatorial calms and monsoon areas as one sails north.

Indies: *see* EAST INDIES; WEST INDIES.

'Indomitable': sister ship of the 1907 *INVINCIBLE*. She was at the bombardment of the outer Turkish forts protecting the Dardanelles, an enterprise later described as 'an act of sheer lunacy', since it prompted Turkey to strengthen the defences before the combined attack on GALLIPOLI (1915). She also took part in the sinking of the *Blücher* (1915).

The aircraft-carrier *Indomitable* was Admiral Sir Philip Vian's flag-ship in the Pacific Fleet when, in 1945, the mass of kamikaze attacks was launched by the Japanese, mainly from airfields in northern Formosa. In an extraordinary incident, the

Indomitable was hit but escaped damage, the kamikaze bouncing over the side with its bomb explosion delayed.

For the newest H.M.S. *Indomitable, see INVINCIBLE.*

'Inflexible': the name of several well-known ships in the Royal Navy, the most impressive of which was probably the one launched in 1876, and completed in 1881, described by her designer as having 'reached the extreme limit in thickness of armour for sea-going vessels'. Her ARMOUR was, in fact, 2 ft thick, and she was the only one of her class built for this country, though Italy tried to copy and outdo her. Her displacement was 11,800 tons; her engines of 6500 h.p. gave a maximum speed of nearly 15 knots. Length was 320 ft, beam 75 ft and draught 26 ft 4 in. She carried four 16-in. muzzle-loading rifled guns in her turrets, eight 4-in. breech-loaders, 21 anti-torpedo boat guns and four torpedo tubes. The weight of a single discharge was 6800 lb., which was not exceeded for another 25 years.

Imagine a floating castle . . . rising 10 feet out of the water, and having above that again two round turrets, planted diagonally at its opposite corners. Imagine this castle and its turrets to be heavily plated with armour, and that each turret has two guns of about 80 tons each. Conceive these guns to be capable of firing, all four together, at an enemy ahead, astern, or on either beam, and in pairs towards every point of the compass . . .

Part of the designer's description to the Institution of Naval Architecture (1874)

In irons: (1) secured to the deck by iron bars and shackles on the ankles as a punishment. The device was known as the bilboes, a word which probably derives from the town of Bilbao in Spain, famous for its iron foundries.

(2) When some sails are full of wind and others are aback, a ship is unmanageable and is said to be in irons.

Inland waterways: any rivers or canals that can be used for navigation. The rivers of England provided entries for the early Saxon and Norse invaders, and for centuries afterwards, as trade developed, rivers were of great importance for the transport of goods. As ships became larger, and some rivers silted up, the use of the smaller rivers fell away, and the larger harbours developed only on the deeper estuaries. The 18th century saw the great era of canal-building, and this was carried on into the 19th century. The Bridgewater Canal from Worsley to Manchester was opened in 1761. This was followed by the Trent and Mersey Canal and many others, until there were over 4000 miles of navigable waterways. After 1830 the building of railways slowed the development of canals, and much of the network of inland navigation which had been built up fell into disuse. *See also* NARROW BOAT.

Inshore: close to the shore. An inshore squadron was a number of ships lying closer to the coast than the main body of the fleet. During the wars with France in the 18th century, and against Napoleon in the early 19th, inshore squadrons were employed for long periods keeping a watch on the French ports, so that any movements of the enemy could be reported.

Instructor Branch: the corps of commissioned naval officers responsible for professional and general education in the Royal Navy. They are concerned chiefly

A photograph of the 'navigators' working on the construction of the Manchester Ship Canal, 1890.

with instruction in navigation, meteorology, electronics and many other branches of learning which are an essential part of a modern officer's training. From the early 18th century some ships carried a SCHOOLMASTER, and his standing rose during the 19th century. In 1862 there was a division of rank between the Naval Schoolmaster, a warrant officer looking after the boy ratings' training, and the Naval Instructor, a commissioned officer looking after officers' training. In 1919 the Naval Instructor became an Instructor Officer, and the rank of Warrant Officer Schoolmaster is now obsolete.

Instruments, navigation: perhaps the oldest and simplest of devices used for navigation was the LEAD, a weighted rope thrown by the leadsman and marked off in fathoms with different colours and materials by which he could judge the depth of water beneath the ship. The lead was much used when approaching the coast or when in unknown waters. But it was the COMPASS that was to be the most important and lasting instrument to help men find their way at sea. It is believed to have originated in China and to have come to the West via the Arab world. The first known written reference to it was made by an Englishman writing in 1180. The compass-rose dividing the horizon into points was probably added in the 13th century, though it was a long time before the variations of the compass, and difference between magnetic and true north, were properly understood.

The compass gave direction, but the distance travelled had to be estimated by the LOG-LINE, a log tied to a line with knots at intervals. According to the number of knots paid out over the stern in a given time, measured by a sand-glass, the speed of the ship was calculated at so many knots or nautical miles per hour. The course and distance might then be plotted with pegs on a TRAVERSE BOARD. Even when the effects of wind and tide were also allowed for, this method of sailing, known as DEAD RECKONING, could only give an approximate position. The navigator required to know how far north or south he was, that is, his latitude. This was done by observation of the heavenly bodies, whose angles above the horizon were measured by a succession of instruments, the mariner's ASTROLABE, the QUADRANT and CROSS-STAFF. The BACK-STAFF, which was an improvement on the cross-staff, was invented c.1594, and became the forerunner of HADLEY's quadrant (really an octant) of 1731. In 1757 came the SEXTANT, a refinement of which is in regular use today. The observations of sun, moon and stars made with these instruments were used in conjunction with manuals of navigation and books of tables giving astronomical data to assist the calculations. Over the centuries these were steadily improved in usefulness and accuracy to the level of the Nautical Almanac of today.

But the problem of the accurate reckoning of longitude was not solved satisfactorily until the coming of John HARRISON's chronometer, the first of which he made in 1735. The marvellous time-keeping of the improved chronometer enabled the navigator to calculate his longitude based upon Greenwich Time, and by the close of the 18th century the chronometer superseded other methods of working out east or west position.

In more recent times the art of navigation, as it was first called, has become more of a science. Old instruments have been improved, and new ones developed. The trailing, propeller-driven mechanical log and new optical instruments such as the range-finder appeared, but more important

225

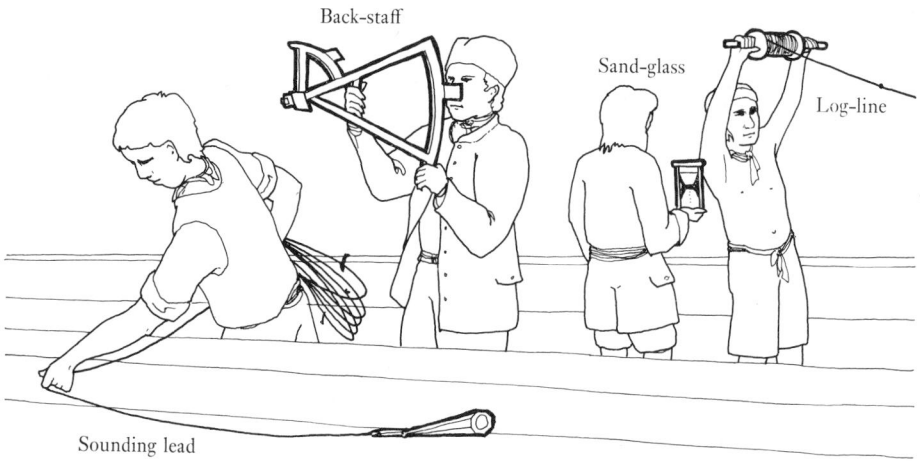

Back-staff

Sand-glass

Log-line

Sounding lead

was the introduction of the GYRO-COMPASS, now universally in use in larger naval and merchant ships.

But it was the advent of radio and electronics which, especially during and since the Second World War, contributed most to modern navigation. The master gyro-compass repeats its readings electrically wherever needed in the ship; there is the ECHO-SOUNDER giving continuous readings of sea depth; and RADAR gives the bearing and distance of ships, shore and other objects, whatever the visibility. RADIO provides not only contact with shore and accurate time-signals, but also a variety of navigational systems, some long-range depending on the timing of the arrival of pulses transmitted from synchronized shore stations, others, like the Decca system, based on beacon stations in Great Britain and on the Continent sending a continuous medium radio wave received by special equipment in the ship, whose position can then be immediately pin-pointed on special charts. Further developments in navigation have taken place with the use of computers, with a system known as inertial navigation, and with the use of satellites. *See also* NAVIGATION.

Insurance, marine: a system of contract whereby one party agrees to pay compensation for any loss or damage of the other party's ships or goods at sea, in return for the payment of a fee or premium. Marine insurance is ancient in origin, but its development owed much to the practice of the Hanseatic cities and the merchants of Elizabethan times. The rise of London as the great centre for marine insurance coincided with the growth of British sea-power, and the modern system largely originated in the late 17th century, when Edward Lloyd's coffee-house became a centre for shipping intelligence and a favourite resort for marine insurers. From these beginnings grew the great institution of LLOYD's, a name now known all over the world. Today the main insuring clause of marine policies is almost unchanged from the original wording used at Lloyd's, but many additional clauses cover different eventualities. The huge sums involved require the risks to be shared by a number of individuals called underwriters, who are members of Lloyd's, and with whom the insurance is placed by Lloyd's brokers. The name underwriter arose because the insurer wrote his name under the contract.

Intercursus magnus: the 'Great Intercourse', signed 24 February 1496, between Henry VII of England and Burgundy, providing freedom of trade between the two countries and protecting the English wool trade. It was directly of great benefit to merchant ships and their owners.

International Call Sign: *see* IDENTIFICATION MARKS.

International Code of Signals: a code of letters and numbers internationally agreed and suitable for transmission by every means of communication. The code covers principally situations relating to safety of navigation or persons. Before the coming of radio, flags were used for passing messages between ships and from ships to shore. The first International Code was put out by the British government in 1857, and was adopted by most seafaring nations. Since that date there have been a succession of revisions, the last in 1969, with subsequent amendments, all agreed by the Inter-Governmental Maritime Consultative Organization. At sea the International Code of Flags, one for each letter of the alphabet, is used by most navies and all merchant ships. Messages can be spelt out or indicated by one, two or more flags according to the International Code. Some single flags carry a standard message, thus P, the Blue Peter, indicates the ship is about to sail, and Q indicates on arrival at a port that the ship is healthy. *See also* SIGNALS *and colour section.*

International Date Line: *see* DATE LINE.

International Regulations for Preventing Collisions at Sea: *see* RULE OF THE ROAD.

International Sea Scale: *see* SEA.

International Swell Scale: *see* SWELL.

'Investigator': 334-ton sloop in which Matthew Flinders made the first survey of a large part of the Australian coast (1801–3). One of his company was the young John FRANKLIN. Fifty years later, by one of the bitter ironies of history, Captain Robert MCCLURE sailed for the Arctic in another *Investigator* to search for Franklin.

'Invincible': 74-gun French ship captured by Anson off Finisterre (3 May 1747), taken under the same name into the British Navy and, because of her superior design, used as a model for a number of British 74s. In the actions of the Glorious FIRST OF JUNE and prior days (1794), the *Invincible*, commanded by the Hon. Thomas Pakenham, was severely damaged, losing her main top mast and having the main and fore masts 'wounded'. She made the signal that she was 'ready to engage the enemy but could not keep the line of battle'.

Another well-known *Invincible* was the 15,900-ton armoured cruiser (1907) which could attain the remarkable speed, for her day, of nearly 30 knots under service conditions. In 1916 a Jutland survivor wrote: 'I saw the *Invincible* . . . blow up . . . hardly a mile off: a great crimson cloud of flame a hundred feet high and perhaps two hundred broad, that rose leisurely, contemptuously, with an awful majestic dignity to a good four hundred feet.' That was the end of Sir Horace Hood's flag-ship, with the loss of the admiral and over 1000 men.

The latest H.M.S. *Invincible* was launched in May 1977, the largest warship built in Britain for over 30 years. This is the 19,500-ton anti-submarine cruiser that will operate five Harrier and nine Sea King aircraft and will join the fleet in 1980 when fitting is complete, her sister ships being *Illustrious* and *Indomitable*.

Of her launching by H.M. the Queen, a reporter wrote:

> The ship gathered speed rapidly and there was a tremendous roar as she entered the water and 1300 tons of restraining chains thundered into the water in a brown cloud of rust. The drag and weight of the chains pulled the ship up in the water in a distance less than half as long again as her 678 ft length.
>
> *Daily Telegraph* (4 May 1977)

Ionian Sea: part of the Mediterranean Sea between Greece and southern Italy. It connects with the Adriatic Sea by the Strait of Otranto, and with the Tyrrhenian Sea by the Strait of Messina.

Irish battleship (or **Irish man-o'-war**): one of the ballast lighters which worked on the Thames in the 19th century.

Irish hurricane: a flat calm with a slight drizzle.

Irish Sea: sea separating Ireland from Great Britain, with outlets to the Atlantic through the North or St Patrick's Channel and St George's Channel to the south. Storms in the Irish Sea can produce very rough conditions with short seas, which were a considerable hazard in the days of sail.

Ironclad: a wooden warship clad or armoured with iron. After various earlier experiments in armouring the 'wooden walls', the victory for iron was marked by the launching in 1860 of H.M.S. *WARRIOR*, the first true ironclad British warship. *See also* ARMOUR.

'Iron Duke': joyously rechristened the 'Tin Duck' by seamen. A 'super-dreadnought', she was Jellicoe's flag-ship at the Battle of Jutland (1916). Built in 1912, she served in both World Wars. An earlier *Iron Duke* distinguished herself in September 1875 by ramming her sister ship, H.M.S. *Vanguard*, off the coast of Ireland in fog. Fortunately the crew of about 400 were saved.

Irons: *see* IN IRONS.

Iron shipbuilding: the use of iron as the chief material in the construction of a ship. By the end of the 18th century iron barges had appeared on inland waterways, and in 1815 an experimental iron boat was launched on the Mersey. But it was not until 1820 that the first iron steamer, suitable for sea-going, was built. This was the *Aaron Manley*, which crossed the Channel in 1822. Thereafter for almost fifty years wood versus iron for shipbuilding was the subject of much debate. But though sea-going iron ships were built in increasing numbers as the extra strength and advantages of iron were demonstrated, the Royal Navy was tentative in experimenting and was loath to abandon faith in the 'wooden walls' which had served so well for so long. The *Dover*, a small iron packet-ship appearing in 1840, was the first iron ship of the Royal Navy. But it was not until after the launching of H.M.S. *WARRIOR* (1860) that all new naval ships were constructed of iron. Meanwhile Isambard Kingdom Brunel at Bristol in 1843 had launched the *GREAT BRITAIN*, the first large ocean-going ship built of iron, screw-propelled, 322 ft long and with a displacement of 3618 tons. In addition to her engines, she carried 15,000 square feet of sail on six masts. Her remarkable achievements during nearly 40 years of service were a convincing victory for iron. *See also* ARMOUR; IRONCLAD.

Isobar: a line on a meteorological chart joining all points with the same barometric pressure. Such a chart will indicate the areas of lowest and highest pressure, and with other information will enable the meteorologist to interpret the development of the weather, and so assist the navigator.

Isthmus: a narrow neck of land between two seas and joining two larger areas of land, e.g. the isthmus of Panama in Central America separating the Caribbean Sea from the Pacific.

J

Jack: (1) a national flag flown at the bow of a ship during day-time in harbour, and at sea only on certain ceremonial occasions. For the 'Union Jack', *see* UNION. (2) Colloquial name for a sailor: JACK TAR. (3) Old naval nickname for anyone surnamed Sheppard – evidence of the curious folklore which persists when the origin has been generally forgotten. Jack Sheppard (1702–24) was a notorious thief and prison-breaker who managed to escape four times before he was finally hanged at Tyburn.

Jackass barques: barques re-rigged in certain unorthodox fashions. The barque – square-rigged on the main and fore mast, fore-and-aft rigged on the mizen – was the chief trading vessel of the northern merchant fleets. When steam came into general use, many barques were re-rigged to economize on maintenance and reduce crews. Some unpleasant anomalies occurred, e.g. ships with a fore-and-aft sail on the lower main mast and square sails on the top-mast and top-gallant.

Jack-block: a block and tackle used for raising and lowering top-gallant masts.

Jack-crosstree: the crosstree at the head of the top-gallant mast.

Jack Dusty (or **Jack of the Dust**): in the old Navy, the purser's steward in the breadroom, or the rating in charge of provisions.

Jacket jobs: the best jobs, especially among the stewards, barmen, storekeepers etc., because of their uniforms.

'Jackie' (or **'Jacky'**): *see* FISHER, JOHN ARBUTHNOT.

'Jackie's Yacht': H.M.S. *Renown*, flagship of Admiral FISHER.

Jack-knife: the large clasp-knife beloved of the old sailor, especially with a horn handle.

> When first I went to sea as a lad
> A new jack-knife was all I had:
> And I've sailed for fifty years and three
> To the coasts of gold and of ivory:
> And now at the end of a lucky life,
> Well, still I've got my old jack-knife.
>
> Wilfrid Gibson, 'Luck'

Jack Nasty-face: *see* ROBINSON, WILLIAM.

Jack of Dover: a popular sea-dish in the Middle Ages and afterwards. Unfortunately (or fortunately?) its ingredients are no longer known.

Jack-staff: a staff at the top of the main mast, or, more usually, at the bow of a ship, on which the jack is hoisted.

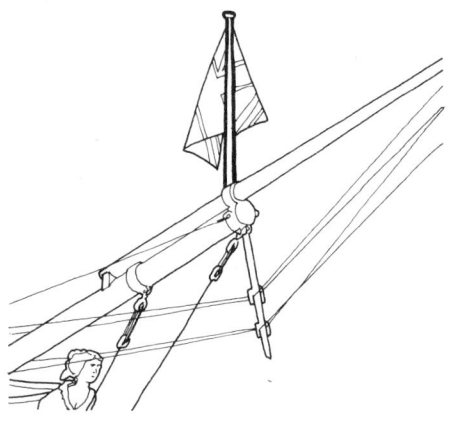

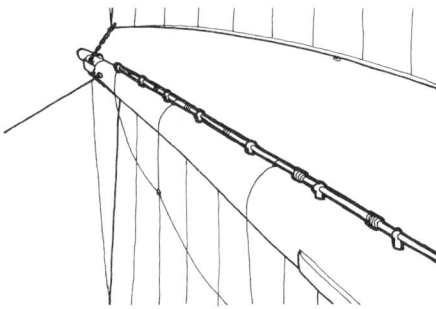

Jack-stay: (1) in a general sense, any rope or wire stretched taut for securing or holding something firm; (2) in a specific sense, a batten of iron or wood or a taut wire above a yard, and to which the head of a square sail is bent.

Jack Tar (or **Jack** or **tar**): old colloquial names for the common sailor. 'Tar' may be a shortening of TARPAULINS, the sailor's tarred canvas clothing, or it may refer to the tar from the ship's caulking and rigging, which marked a sailor's hands and clothes.

Jacob's ladder: a ladder with wooden rungs and rope sides, particularly one from a swinging boom to a boat, or running up a main mast.

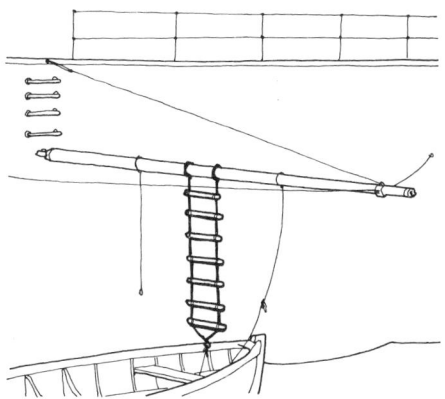

Jamaica: an island in the West Indies, lying south of Cuba. It was discovered by Columbus (1494) and became part of the Spanish Empire until 1655, when it was taken by the British, though for a time it

A posed group of British sailors taken at the time of the Crimean War, 1854.

remained a resort of buccaneers. The development of sugar plantations and the need for labour made Jamaica a mart for the notorious trade in negro slaves captured and bought in West Africa and shipped in terrible conditions across the Atlantic. In the naval wars of the 18th century the valuable trade and plantations of the West Indies gave Jamaica an important place in British strategy. Attempted invasions by the French and Spanish were thwarted by the victory of Admirals Rodney and Hood at the Battle of the Saints off Dominica (1782), and again in 1806 by Admiral Duckworth. Today Jamaica is an independent member of the Commonwealth.

Jamaica discipline: in pirate and buccaneer days, the articles of agreement under which booty was shared between the crew.

James I (1566–1625): king of England. His reign saw a number of developments in the design and appearance of ships. The use of the fourth mast (the 'bonaventure mizen'), increasingly common in the reign of his predecessor Elizabeth, continued till at least half the king's ships were four-masters; then, with the growth in the size of the mizen mast and additional sail power, this feature declined so rapidly that by 1640 there were almost no four-masters left. More lofty sail was carried with the general introduction of the top-gallant mast. A great vogue for carving and gilding began, and continued through much of the Stuart period. Chatham Dockyard was greatly developed under James I, so that it rivalled Deptford. Dry docks and large mast ponds were among the improvements.

James II (1633–1701): king of England, and Lord High Admiral (created 1660). In that capacity he reorganized the Navy Board and issued the FIGHTING INSTRUC- TIONS that substantially remained in force for more than a century and a half. In 1672, as Duke of York, he flew his flag in the *PRINCE* at the Battle of Solebay when the Dutch were defeated, but the ship was so badly damaged that James had to shift his flag. *See also* LOWESTOFT, BATTLE OF; YELLOW REGIMENT.

James, Dame Naomi (1949–): round-the-world yachtswoman who, on 8 June 1978, completed a 272-day single-handed circumnavigation – the first woman to do so. She set sail on 9 September 1977 and, when she came into Dartmouth after her 30,000-mile voyage in the 53-foot yacht *Express Crusader*, had knocked two days off the record established by Sir Francis Chichester in 1969. One remarkable feature was that Mrs James had formerly had no long-distance sailing experience; another was that she survived a capsize off Cape Horn.

James, William (*d.*1827): distinguished naval historian whose *Naval History of Great Britain from the Declaration of War by France in 1793 to the Accession of George IV*, first published in 1822, later expanded to carry it up to 1827, and reprinted many times, remains the standard work for the period. It has been described as 'one of the most valuable works in the English language' and 'the best Naval History of England'.

James, one of the most pertinacious of investigators, set a new example. He honestly did his utmost to satisfy himself of the absolute truth of every statement which he submitted to his readers . . . Never was there a man more painstaking, more indefatigable, more scrupulously conscientious.

Fortnightly Review (on James's death)

On one occasion, however, James received a thrashing for alleged inaccuracy by an indignant officer, Sir John PHILLIMORE.

'James Baines': one of a group of four famous clipper ships built by Donald McKay of Boston in the mid-19th century for the Black Ball Line of Liverpool, owned by James Baines; the other ships were the *Champion of the Seas*, the *Donald McKay* and (most famous of all) the *LIGHTNING*. Of 2275 tons, the *James Baines* made a record run on her maiden voyage from Boston, reaching the Rock Light, Liverpool, in 12 days, 6 hours. She made another record run to Melbourne, in 63 days.

During the Indian Mutiny the *James Baines* was chartered to take the 93rd Highlanders to Calcutta. She was destroyed by fire soon after in Huskisson Dock, Liverpool, and survives in one of the landing stages, which was partly constructed from the wreck.

See colour section.

'James Watt': the largest steamship of her times, 141·8 ft long and 47 ft wide over the paddle-boxes. The paddle-wheel was 18 ft in diameter. She also carried sail on three masts. She was used on the coastal service between London and Leith in the 1820s.

Jammed like Jackson: in an awkward predicament, usually through one's own fault. Who the original unfortunate Jackson was is lost in the mists of time.

'Jane's Fighting Ships': the standard reference book of the world's navies. It was founded in 1897 by Fred T. Jane, is currently edited by Captain John E. Moore, R.N., and is published annually by Macdonald & Jane's Publishers of London. No other book contains such a wealth of detailed information about the world's navies, their auxiliary vessels, research and survey ships and other special-purpose naval ships.

Jaunty (or **jauntie, janty** or **jonty**): naval slang for a Master-at-Arms.

Jay, John (*fl.*1460–80): Bristol merchant who, in the summer of 1480, sent an 80-ton ship to 'traverse the seas' in quest of the Island of Brazil. Jay at the time was already trading with Iceland and Portugal. Though the expedition was unsuccessful, it is interesting evidence of the enterprise of Bristol men before Columbus. In 1498 the Spanish Ambassador reported that 'for the last seven years the people of Bristol have sent out every year two, three, or four caravels, in search of the Island of Brazil and the Seven Cities'.

Jeer: tackle used for hoisting and lowering lower yards. *See p. 234.*

Jeffrey, Robert: *see* MAROONING.

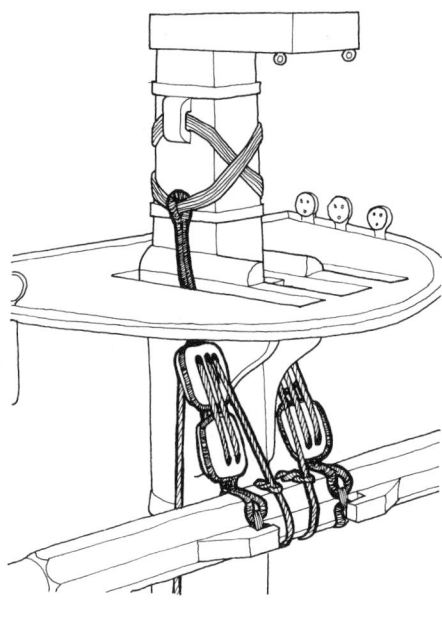

Jellicoe, Christopher Theodore (1903–77): nephew of Earl JELLICOE who became a rear-admiral and commanded several destroyers in the Second World War. In 1942 he had his ship sunk under him twice in one month; one of them, *Jackal*, having picked up survivors from two other destroyers after an air attack in the Mediterranean, was on fire from stem to stern when the flotilla leader came alongside and took off Jellicoe and 500 men. He won the D.S.O. and D.S.C. and bar for gallantry in a number of actions.

Jellicoe, John Rushworth, first Earl Jellicoe (1859–1935): Admiral of the Fleet. The son of a captain in the merchant service, he qualified as a gunnery lieutenant and served on the staff of H.M.S. *Excellent* gunnery school (1884–5). By 1905 he was Director of Naval Ordnance, having survived the wreck of the *Victoria* off Tripoli (1893) and been severely wounded at Peitsang (1900) after the Boxer rising.

Following a number of important commands and administrative posts, the outbreak of the First World War found him in command of the Grand Fleet. He also became First Sea Lord (1916) and Chief of Naval Staff (1917). His name will always be associated with the Battle of JUTLAND (1916), the chief naval engagement of the war, after which the German ships retreated and did not risk another encounter for the rest of the war. Jellicoe lies alongside Nelson and Collingwood in St Paul's Cathedral, a fitting tribute to a man of deep religious convictions, iron nerve and inspiring leadership, winning devotion from those who served under him.

Jenkins' Ear, War of (1739–41): war between Britain and Spain, which merged into the subsequent War of the Austrian Succession (1740–48). The war began with a minor incident in which Spanish coastguards were alleged to have cut off the ear of a British seaman, Robert Jenkins, when he was bringing home the brig *Rebecca* in 1731.

On reaching England Jenkins presented his grievance to the King, but the matter seems to have created little stir till, in 1738, the indignant mariner told his story all over again and displayed his severed ear to the House of Commons. Asked what his feelings were when the offence took place, Jenkins made the reply: 'I committed my soul to God, and my cause to my country' – sentiments which no right-minded Englishman could resist.

Jenkins subsequently commanded an East Indiaman and was appointed supervisor of the Company's affairs at St Helena.

. . . probably the only war on record which has taken its name from a part of the human body.

T. H. White, *The Age of Scandal* (1950)

Jenkinson, Anthony (*d.* 1611): sea-captain, traveller and merchant who between 1546 and 1553 covered an extraordinary amount of land and water, visiting, among other places, France, Germany, Italy, Spain, Portugal, Malta, Sicily, Rhodes, Cyprus, Greece, Turkey, Syria, the Holy Land and North Africa. In 1553 he was granted an interview with Suleiman the Magnificent and obtained permission to trade in Turkish ports. In 1557 he sailed with four ships to Russia as Captain-General and Agent for the Muscovy Company. He anchored in the White Sea on 12 July 1557, having sailed 2250 miles since leaving Gravesend on 12 May. He arrived in Moscow on 6 December and dined with the Tsar, Ivan the Terrible, on Christmas Day. His subsequent adventures included the navigation and mapping of the Caspian Sea, which he was the first Englishman to enter. For fifteen years he used his energies to develop good relationships between England and Russia. Among his other 'firsts' were the description of the eastern parts of Russia from personal observation, the surveying of the coasts of the Caspian, and the descent of the Volga as a Russian river.

And thus, being weary and growing old, I am content to take my rest in mine own house, chiefly comforting myself in that my service hath been honourably accepted and rewarded of her Majesty and the rest by whom I have been employed.

Quoted in C. R. N. Routh, *Who's Who in History* (1964)

Jervis, John, first Earl St Vincent (1735–1823): Admiral of the Fleet. The son of a civil servant, he ran away to sea as a boy. When he was brought back, his father told him he could make the Navy his career if he was prepared to accept that nothing could be done for him beyond a suit of

clothes and £20. His first coat hung down to his heels because he bought it second-hand (*see also* JEWING). His naval career is one of the longest on record, from 1747 to 1807, when he resigned at the age of 73; yet, despite unremittingly dedicated service, he was virtually unknown outside the Navy till he won immortal glory at the Battle of CAPE ST VINCENT (1797), when he captured four ships and disabled many others, after which he was created Earl (later Viscount) St Vincent and granted a pension of £3000 a year.

He was a severe disciplinarian (*see* HANGING JERVIS), believing that 'men must be made to fear their officers more than danger; the slightest loosening of discipline will lead to barbarization'. He was a deeply religious man, of high integrity, whose career owed nothing to favour and influence. Collingwood and Nelson were only two of the distinguished commanders who expressed admiration and gratitude to him for his leadership. George III referred to him as 'my old oak'. He was forthright, with a gift for a trenchant phrase. He once said that 1782 was a memorable year for him, because in it he committed three great faults: 'I got

235

knighted, I got married and I got into parliament.'

As a specimen of Jervis's epistolary powers may be quoted part of a letter to Evan Nepean, Secretary of the Admiralty, on the subject of Sir Charles Middleton (later Lord Barham), the new First Lord:

> That damned fellow Sir Charles Middleton, after making more money by sale of offices at the Navy Board than any of his predecessors, comes to the Admiralty with his cant, imposture, hoards of precedents and scraps of tape and buckram, and makes you all believe that he is the only man capable of regulating your proceedings when . . . he neither possesses a mind to direct great features, nor was ever in a situation as an officer to acquire knowledge or experience.

But Jervis had his softer moments. Betsy, wife of Captain Fremantle, recalled that when they went on board *Victory* soon after Jervis came out to the Mediterranean, the old gentleman 'desired that we should pay the tribute which was due to him on entering his cabin. This was to kiss him, which the ladies did very willingly.' And when a child asked him what was the Star of the Order of the Bath he was wearing, and where he had found it, he said: 'I found it upon the sea; and if you become a sailor, and search diligently, perhaps you will find just such another.'

'Jervis Bay': escort ship, commanded by Captain E. S. F. Fegen, which in November 1940 was escorting Convoy HX84, of 37 merchant ships, on the North Atlantic route, when the 'pocket battleship' *Admiral Scheer*, with her vastly superior armament, appeared. Fegen ordered the convoy to scatter, then made straight for the battleship, guns blazing. The *Jervis Bay* went down, but not before the convoy had dispersed so widely that 32 of the ships escaped.

The raider's guns were speaking
   and the ships were sorely pressed
(*Andalusia*, *Cornish City*, *Rangitiki*
   and the rest),
But the leader steamed to meet her in the
   setting of the sun,
Knowing, as she challenged, that her
   fighting days were done.
And she battled, flame-enveloped, in the
   closing of the day
Till, out-gunned and ensign flying,
   sank the gallant *Jervis Bay*.

Admiral Jervis, high in heaven,
   sat upon a headland's crest
(Watching *Varon*, *Emile Franqui*, *Hjalmar*
   Wessel and the rest),
And he smiled as Drake swore gruffly,
   looking down at smoke and flame,
'By the Host, St Vincent, she is worthy
   of your name.
With the *Hind*, *Revenge* and *Lion*
   let her ride at break o' day,
While the cannon of the ages
   roar salute to *Jervis Bay*!'

Grant Uden

Jesso: naval nickname for anyone surnamed Read or Reade.

'Jesus of Lübeck': royal ship lent by Queen Elizabeth, in the hope of much profit, to Sir John HAWKINS on two of his trading and slaving voyages. On the 1567–8 expedition the ship was captured by the Spaniards at San Juan de Ulloa. She had been purchased from the Hanseatic port of Lübeck by Henry VIII in 1544, and was a big vessel for those days, of some 700 tons and with an armament of over 60 guns, large and small.

'Jesus of the Tower': royal ship featuring in the accounts of the Keepers of the King's Ships in Henry V's reign. She is described as a vessel of 1000 tons, the largest known for the period. *See also . . . OF THE TOWER.*

Jetsam: any goods, gear or tackle cast overboard, especially to lighten a ship when in difficulties. If the jetsam sinks and is marked with a buoy it is known as LIGAN; if it floats or is washed up on shore it becomes flotsam and jetsam.

Jetty: any structure of stone or wood built out from the shore to give harbour protection, or to provide a landing pier, for ships to secure alongside.

Jewing: making clothes in the old Navy. The 'jewing bag' was the private bag in which the seaman kept his sewing gear. There was an officially issued 'housewife' ('hussif') or mending-kit, which was generally scorned. Even the great St Vincent (John JERVIS) made his own trousers as a youngster.

My father had a very large family, with limited means. He gave me twenty pounds at starting, and that was all he ever gave me. After I had been a considerable time at the station [Jamaica] I drew for twenty more, but the bill came back protested. I was mortified at this rebuke and made a promise, which I have ever kept, that I would never draw another bill, without a certainty of its being paid.

I immediately changed my mode of living, quitted my mess, lived alone, and took up the ship's allowance, which I found to be quite sufficient; washed and mended my own clothes, made a pair of trousers out of the ticking of my bed . . .

Jedediah Tucker, *Memoirs of Admiral the Right Hon. the Earl of St Vincent* (1844)

Jib: (1) a triangular sail before the fore mast; in small craft, a foresail. In a three-masted sailing ship there might be four such sails, the jib, inner jib, outer jib, and flying jib. *See also* SAIL. (2) As a verb, 'jib' is a variant of GYBE.

Jib-boom: a boom or spar extending the bowsprit and on which the jib is spread. *See also* RIGGING.

Jigger: (1) an old-fashioned fishing sloop; (2) a small square sail on the jigger mast (the aftermost mast of a four-masted sailing vessel); (3) small tackle consisting of a single and double block.

'Jimmy-the-One': the First Lieutenant; *see also* NUMBER ONE.

Job Captain: an officer given temporary command of a ship when its proper captain was otherwise employed. It frequently happened when naval officers were Members of Parliament, a common occurrence in the 18th and 19th centuries (e.g. Rodney, St Vincent, Pellew, Howe, Harvey, Hood, Hawke and many others).

John (?1167–1216): king of England, traditionally the worst she ever had – and a poor sailor too. He granted lands at Kepperton and Atterton in Kent to Solomon Attefield and his heirs on condition that, when the king should be pleased to cross the sea, one of them should accompany him to hold his head when he was sea-sick. John has, however, some claim to a place in English maritime history. He saw the value of a standing navy and appointed an administrator known as the Keeper of the King's Ports and Galleys, the holder of the office being William de Wrotham, Archdeacon of Taunton; and he was the first English king to demand the salute in the English Channel.

'John Biscoe': diesel-electric Royal Navy Research Ship, completed 1956; gross tonnage 2250, length 220 ft. On her maiden voyage she carried supplies and relief staff to Antarctic bases. . *See also* RESEARCH SHIP.

237

'John Company': *see* EAST INDIA COMPANY, BRITISH.

'John Wesley': composite clipper with an interesting history. Built in Aberdeen (1867) for the Australian trade, her internal framing was mostly iron, her external planking a mixture of teak and American elm. In 1873, rigged as a brig, she came into the hands of the Wesleyan Missionary Society and was used for their work for four years. She then returned to trading till she was finally laid up in 1899. In 1903 she was destroyed by fire at her moorings. An earlier *John Wesley* was launched at West Cowes in September 1846. The whole history of missionary ships would make an interesting addition to the saga of the sea, enshrining much hardihood and heroism.

'John Williams': the name of several missionary ships belonging to the London Missionary Society and named after the missionary John Williams (1796–1839), who proved a considerable seaman, building a ship for himself and making voyages to many islands, including Cook, Austral, Navigators' and the Society group. He was killed by the natives of Erromanga. The first *John Williams* sailing ship was launched at Harwich in 1844 and was wrecked on Danger Island 20 years later. The third (*c.*1870) was a 186-ton bark.

Jolly (or **Jollies**): nickname for a marine or for the Royal Marines.

> Sez'e I'm a Jolly – 'Er Majesty's Jolly – soldier and sailor too!
>
> Rudyard Kipling, 'Soldier and Sailor Too'

Jolly-boat: a small ship's boat. The name may derive from the Dutch *jol*, which also gave us 'yawl'.

Jolly Roger: a black flag with white skull and crossbones, formerly flown by pirates (though pirate flags were not restricted to this one design). In the Second World War the name was also given to a flag, flown unofficially, to indicate successes on patrol.

Jonah: a name given to anyone on board who is supposed to bring ill-luck to the ship or voyage. Jonah in the Old Testament story was sailing to Tarshish when a storm arose, and the sailors cast lots to decide who had brought upon them this misfortune. When the lot fell upon Jonah he was cast into the sea, where he was swallowed by 'a great fish'; but it threw him up again on the land.

Jones, Davy: *see* DAVY JONES'S LOCKER.

Jones, John Paul (1747–92): naval adventurer who was born in Scotland, the son of a Kirkcudbrightshire gardener, but became a hero of the American Navy. At the early age of 12 he was apprenticed to a shipmaster, and when he was only 19 he took command of a ship after the captain and first mate had died of fever. He was engaged in the slave trade at one period, and there are unsubstantiated stories that he also served on a pirate ship. He entered the American Navy in 1775 and the next year received his captain's commission, with command of the *Providence* and liberty to cruise as a free-lance for 'six weeks or two or three months' – a type of dispensation wholly to his liking which resulted, in the space of seven weeks, in the capture or destruction of some sixteen ships, brigantines, sloops and schooners. In 1778, commanding the RANGER and with permission to act as he deemed best 'for distressing the enemies of the United States', he attacked the forts commanding the harbour of Whitehaven, England, and

From a picture by John Collet, 1779, showing Paul Jones shooting a sailor who attempted to strike the colours.

four days later captured the British sloop *Drake*. His most famous adventure, however, was his encounter, while commanding the *Bonhomme Richard*, with the British *Serapis* off FLAMBOROUGH HEAD (1779).

In 1781 Jones was invited by Catherine the Great to command the Russian Navy. In his hurry to take up the appointment, he crossed the Baltic Sea in a 30-ft boat despite the floating ice. The jealousy of subordinate commanders and court opposition prevented him from showing his true powers and he returned to Paris, where, worn out by his exertions, he died at the early age of 45. In 1913 his body was taken back to America, honourably escorted by warships.

Jonty: *see* JAUNTY.

Jourdain, John: *see* SEYCHELLES.

Juan Fernandez Island: one of a group of small islands in the South Pacific about 400 miles west of Chile, discovered in 1563 by the Spanish navigator after whom the island is named. Alexander SELKIRK, the original of Robinson Crusoe, lived alone on the island from 1704 to 1709.

Judgements (or **Rules** or **Laws**) of **Oléron:** set of rules, dating from *c.*1194 (and based on earlier codes), governing the conduct of ships. They took their name from a small island off the coast of France which was formerly a great rendezvous for shipping, especially that engaged in the wine trade. The rules give many interesting glimpses of relationships between master and crew, e.g.:

If a man give the lie to another at table, where there is bread and wine, then he is fined four deniers; but if the master himself offend in any way, he is to pay a double fine . . . If any sailor impudently contradict the master, he is fined eight deniers, and if the master strike him he is required to bear that blow; but if the master strike more than one blow, the sailor may defend himself; whereas, if the sailor commit the first assault, he is fined one hundred sous or condemned to lose his hand.

See also NAVAL DISCIPLINE ACT.

'Judith': barque of 50 tons commanded by Drake on Sir John HAWKINS's 1567–8 expedition. For some reason never fully explained, Drake left his commander after the disastrous battle at San Juan de Ulloa and reached Plymouth on his own (20 January 1569). No more is heard of the *Judith*, and it has been suggested that Drake sold her in order to provide for his marriage in July of that year to Mary Newman at Plymouth.

Jumper: (1) the upper blouse-like garment worn by seamen and colloquially known as 'square rig' (*see* RIG (*2*)); (2) a rope used in keeping a yard in position.

Jump ship, to: to desert or abscond just before sailing.

Junk: (1) a general name for different sizes of Chinese trading vessels with square sails

made of reed matting, a high forecastle and
flattish bottom (*see also KEY-ING*); (**2**)
pieces of useless old cordage, rubbish
generally, and perhaps so applied to (**3**)
salted meat formerly supplied as part of a
ship's provisions.

'Juno': a famous name, perhaps best-
known as that of the 32-gun frigate that had
an amazing escape on a winter night in
January 1794. Unaware that the British
fleet had evacuated Toulon, leaving the
port in the hands of the French
Republicans, she sailed into first the outer,
then the inner, harbour, surrounded by
enemy vessels and troops and with the guns
from the forts able to catch her in a
withering cross-fire. For a time the French
did their best to conceal their identity and,
as a result of an order shouted from a brig,
caused the *Juno* to put her helm over and
run hard aground, thus adding to her
danger. While her commander, Captain
Samuel Hood, was trying to warp her off, a
boat came alongside and, apparently
speaking for the British admiral, ordered
him to another part of the harbour. At this
point a sharp-eyed midshipman, peering in
the moonlight, yelled: 'Sir! They are
wearing national cockades!'

The Republican sailors, seeing that they
could not keep up the deception, tried to
persuade Hood that he and his men were in
safe hands and would be honourably
treated. Meanwhile, Webley, the third
lieutenant, as a sudden wind whipped
across the harbour, told Hood he believed
they could get out if they could only
contrive to get under sail. The canvas
began to fill, the anchor cable grew taut,
and Hood gave the order to cut it. The ship
lurched and then was in clear water. The
boats were still over the side, and these too
were cut adrift. Guns from the surrounding ships and the forts ringed her in smoke

and flame, but, with most of her rigging
shot away and a 36-lb. shot in her hull, the
Juno gained the open sea without a man
lost.

She was built on the Thames in 1757, of
667 tons, 127 ft long and 34·3 ft in breadth.

Jury: temporary or makeshift, as in 'jury
rig' or 'jury mast', improvised when the
original has been carried away or broken.

Jutland, Battle of (31 May 1916): the
major naval battle of the First World War,
fought some 60 miles west of the Jutland
peninsula by the British Grand Fleet
(under Admiral Jellicoe), based on Scapa
Flow, and the German High Seas Fleet.
Judged by present-day standards, the size
of the two battle fleets is staggering.

British	German
24 Dreadnought battleships	15 Dreadnought battleships
4 Battleships	7 Pre-dread- noughts
9 Battle cruisers	5 Battle cruisers
8 Heavy cruisers	11 Light cruisers
26 Light cruisers	62 Destroyers
77 Destroyers	
148 ships	100 ships

Putting it another way, the British had 37
capital ships, 8 armoured cruisers, 26 light
cruisers and 80 flotilla leaders and
destroyers. They mustered a total of 344
turret guns. The Germans had 27 capital
ships, 11 light cruisers, and 63 flotilla
leaders and destroyers, with a total of 244
turret guns.

In the course of the hard-hitting action
Britain lost 3 battle cruisers (including the
INDEFATIGABLE), 3 cruisers (including
the *INVINCIBLE*), and 8 torpedo craft,
against German losses of 1 battleship, 1
battle cruiser, 4 light cruisers and 5 torpedo

Photograph showing the battle cruiser H.M.S. *Lion* hit on Q turret during the early stages of the battle.

craft. In terms of men, Britain lost 6097 against Germany's 2445. There would therefore seem to be some justice in the German claim of victory. But the fact remains that in the end the German fleet retreated to base under cover of night and left the British in undisputed command of the seas for the rest of the war. The German High Seas Command did, in fact, make two further attempts to go to sea. On the first occasion (19 August 1916) Admiral Scheer learnt that the British were advancing to meet him and thereupon returned to base. On the second, right at the end of the war, Scheer ordered the Fleet to sea in an effort to break the British blockade; but, dispirited and mutinous, the crews refused to weigh anchor and mutinied at Wilhelmshaven (29 October 1918). On 21 November 1918 Admiral Beatty received the surrender of the major part of the German High Seas Fleet.

K

'**Kaisow**': fine China trade clipper, built (1868) by Robert Steele of Greenock, a composite ship with iron frames and teak planking, 193·2 ft long, 32 ft beam and 20·3 ft depth of hold. She was well-known among sailors for several features, chiefly perhaps her magnificent crew quarters – a teak deck-house abaft the fore mast, quite unlike the more usual uncomfortable forecastle accommodation. She had a particularly splendid figurehead of a Chinese mandarin resplendent in flowing blue robes and red cap with a yellow tassel. She was remarkable for her ability to keep moving in the lightest of airs, the slightest flap of sail being sufficient to maintain her steerage way. She foundered off Valparaiso in 1890, her crew managing to get away in the boats.

Kamikaze: a Japanese word meaning 'divine wind', applied in the Second World War to the suicide aircraft squadrons and the pilots who flew their planes directly at American ships in the Pacific.

'**Kathleen and Mary**': the last of the British wooden trading schooners (1900), carrying coal and clay from the Mersey to Eire. Fore-and-aft rigged on three masts, she was built at Connah's Quay. Her master and owner was Captain Tom Jewell.

Kattegat: the 'Cat's Throat', the narrow sea between Denmark and Sweden, linking the Baltic with the North Sea via the Skagerrak at its northern end and The Sound, the Great Belt and Little Belt at its southern end. Winter storms can cause rough and dangerous seas in the Kattegat, and a surface current of relatively fresh water from the Baltic sets northwards through it.

Kayak: a canoe-like boat made by the Eskimoes for fishing and hunting. The kayak is constructed of seal-skin stretched and stitched over a wooden frame, no nails or metal being used. Different types of kayak are found along the Arctic from Greenland to Alaska, but the finest are from East Greenland. Once settled in the kayak's little cockpit the Eskimo ties the hem of his seal-skin coat round the opening, thus making all water-tight. This enables him to tip over for safety in rough water and take the break of the wave on the keel. The Eskimo hunts the seal from his

The moment of impact as a Japanese Zero fighter deliberately crashes into the side of an American warship.

kayak with a light harpoon or spear, and propels his craft with a short paddle. Other open types of kayak were used for hunting the walrus. Somewhat bigger but similarly constructed craft are the oomiaks (or umiaks) used by the Eskimo women.

Keats, Sir Richard Goodwin (1757–1834): admiral. A favourite commander of Nelson's, he was the first to hear the famous 'Nelson touch' – the plan for beating the French at Trafalgar – as the two friends walked in the gardens at Merton Place. Though Keats expected to be present at the battle, he in fact missed it and heard the news of Trafalgar and his friend's death from the schooner *Pickle* when she was on her way back to England with Collingwood's dispatches. His best-known command was the 74-gun *Superb* ('The Old Superb').

> I am very much pleased with the cheerfulness with which you are determined to share the fate of the Fleet . . . I will take care that the *Superb* shall have neighbour's share in everything.
>
> Nelson to Keats (8 May 1805)

> Four year out from home she was, and ne'er a
>   week in port,
> And nothing save the guns aboard her bright,
> But Captain Keats he knew the game, and
>   swore to share the sport,
> For he never yet came in too late to fight.
>
> Henry Newbolt, 'The Old Superb'

Kedge: (1) a small anchor taken out in a boat and laid away from the ship. It is then used for warping – that is, moving the ship over a short distance into the desired position by hauling against the anchor. **(2)** To 'kedge' is to perform this manoeuvre.

Keel: (1) the lowest longitudinal timber or iron in a ship, forming the base on which the framework of the whole vessel is built; **(2)** a name once in local use on the E. coast of Britain from the Tyne to the Norfolk Broads for a shallow-bottomed vessel used for river traffic; also applied to a type of coasting vessel. The keels of the Tyne once brought coal from the upper river to ships in Tynemouth harbour; they had a square sail and were manoeuvred by a heavy oar worked by men known as keel-bullies. *See also p.577 and* HUMBER KEEL.

Keelhauling: a punishment by which a man was hauled by ropes underneath the keel from one side of a ship to the other. He would be lacerated by the barnacles on the ship's bottom and sometimes drowned. This punishment was not inflicted after about 1750.

> . . . and if the offence be very fowle, he is alsoe drawne under the verye keele of the shippe, the which is termed keele haling; and while he is thus under the water a greate gunn is given fire righte over his head; the which is done as well toe astonishe the more with the thunder thereof . . . as to give warning untoe all others toe look out and toe beware by his harmes.
>
> Document in the Harleian MSS. on the punishment of seamen in the reign of Charles II

Keelson (or **kelson**): a line of timbers or plates running parallel with the keel and securing it to the upper framework and floor timbers or plates.

Keep hold of the land: keep close to shore.

Keeping the sea: mobilizing the sea-coast population for defence; or holding the sea approaches against all comers. For an example of the latter usage, *see LIBELLE OF ENGLISH POLICIE.*

Keith, Viscount: *see* ELPHINSTONE, GEORGE KEITH.

Kelp: the name given to certain varieties of sea-weed which can be collected and used commercially. The kelp or wrack is burnt in kilns, and from the calcined ashes iodine, bromine, potash and other substances are extracted.

Kelson: *see* KEELSON.

Kelvin, Lord: *see* THOMSON, WILLIAM.

Kempenfelt, Richard (1718–82): admiral. As well as having a distinguished record of service, he produced a numerary code of signals, combining the old and new methods in that each signal had both a number, a flag and a position for use; thus 'Engage the enemy' could be sent using the number 224, or by flying a red flag at the head of the fore topmast. 'Come to closer engagement' could be represented by either the numerary signal 171 or a horizontal-striped red and white flag at the main topmast head. In a letter of March 1781 Kempenfelt said: 'that [i.e. the code] which I would have adopted – though most evidently the best – I could not get any of the Admirals or Officers of note to approve

and countenance. I therefore followed in a great measure Lord Howe's mode, he being a popular character.' A seaman who knew him described him as 'a tall thin man who stooped a great deal'. He went down with the *ROYAL GEORGE*, while writing in his cabin.

> His sword was in its sheath,
> His fingers held the pen,
> When Kempenfelt went down
> With twice four hundred men.
>
> William Cowper, 'On the Loss
> of the *Royal George*'

Kenning glass: an old name for a telescope.

Kent: because of its position at the S.E. extremity of England, commanding both the narrowest part of the Channel and to the north the estuary of the Thames, the County of Kent has played a notable part in maritime history. Stone and Iron Age man settled here, to be followed by the Romans when Julius Caesar's expedition arrived near Deal (55 and 54 B.C.); and in A.D. 43 Claudius landed in Kent to begin the conquest of Britain. With the departure of the Romans, Jutes, Saxons and Danes in turn followed, fought and settled. After the Battle of Hastings (1066) Dover, because of its command of the Straits, was the first township taken by William. In these early times and in the medieval period the coastline was somewhat different from its appearance today. Three of the original CINQUE PORTS, Sandwich, Dover and Hythe, were in Kent and provided ships and men for defence. Naval dockyards were established at Chatham in Tudor times and at Sheerness in the reign of Charles II, who had landed at Dover on his restoration to the throne (1660). Seven years later Sheerness, Gravesend and Chatham were attacked and damaged by a

Dutch fleet. During the threat of invasion by Napoleon the fortifications at Chatham and Dover were strengthened, the Royal Military Canal between Hythe and Appledore was built, and so were the coastal forts known as Martello Towers. In the First and Second World Wars the ports of Kent were as important as ever for guarding the narrow seas; the Dover Patrol in 1914–18 and the Coastal Forces in 1939–45 played a distinguished part in our naval annals. Little ships and boats from all the harbours of Kent took a brave and considerable share in the evacuation of British and Allied troops from the beaches of Dunkirk in 1940. 'Kentish Men' (those living north and west of the Medway) and 'Men of Kent' (those living south and east of the Medway) have ever felt the call of the sea, not least those who man the lifeboats so often called out to ships in distress on the treacherous Goodwin Sands, which lie off the Kentish coast between the South and North Forelands.

'Kent': name shared by many ships through the centuries. The 74-gun H.M.S. *Kent*, launched on the Thames in 1798, was Duncan's flag-ship in the actions off the Dutch coast which led to the ignominious surrender of the Dutch fleet (1799), and she lasted in one capacity or another for a further 80 years, being finally broken up at Devonport in 1881. The County class armoured cruiser of 9800 tons displacement was built in 1901. The East Indiaman *Kent*, of 1350 tons, was built at Blackwall in 1820. In 1825, bound for China with several companies of the 31st Regiment of Foot aboard, she caught fire in a gale in the Bay of Biscay, with a loss of 82 lives, the rest being rescued by the brig *Cambria*. The clipper ship *Kent* of 1852 was built and owned by Money Wigram of Blackwall and was a pioneer of the Melbourne trade.

In 1875 she was serving as a coal hulk at Chile and was still afloat in the 1930s.

Kent, Alexander: pen-name of Douglas Reeman (1924–), novelist, naval historian and naval technical adviser for films etc. He has written many fine sea-tales, of which the best-known are those of the Navy of Nelson's time with Richard Bolitho as hero. Amongst these are *Enemy in Sight* (1970), *The Flag Captain* (1971), *Sloop at War* (1972), *Command a King's Ship* (1973), *Signal – Close Action!* (1974) and *Richard Bolitho – Midshipman* (1975).

Kentish Knock, Battle of (28 September 1652): battle fought off a sand-bank near the mouth of the Thames between an English fleet under Blake and a Dutch force under de With, who had taken over from Tromp. The Dutch were defeated, though not decisively, and Tromp was soon back to turn the tables (*see* ANGLO-DUTCH WARS).

Kentledge: pig-iron ballast laid permanently in a ship's hold along the keel to give her increased stability. The word is of unknown derivation.

Keppel, Augustus, first Viscount Keppel (1725–86): admiral. He entered the Navy in 1735 and four years later went round the world with Anson – a voyage which Professor Michael Lewis has pointed out 'proved . . . a remarkable school for future admirals'. Keppel reached flag rank in 1762 and was subsequently a Lord Commissioner of the Admiralty, Commander-in-Chief of the Grand Fleet, and First Lord. All this did not prevent him from being court-martialled (1779) for the indecisive action off USHANT (1778), but his judges pronounced the charges 'malicious and ill-founded'; *see also* COURT-MARTIAL.

Keppel, George, third Earl of Albemarle (1724–72): *see* HAVANA, CAPTURE OF.

Keppel, Sir Henry (1809–1904): admiral, son of the fourth Earl of Albemarle. As well as serving with some distinction, especially in the Baltic campaign of 1854, he contrived to live to be 95, despite a somewhat exacting friendship with Edward VII. He served under four sovereigns and told the story (or at least the professional part of it) in a three-volume autobiography (1899).

Kerr, Lord Mark Robert (1776–1840): admiral. His career began as midshipman of the *Lion* (64 guns) in Lord Macartney's expedition to China (1792). He is best remembered for his pre-Trafalgar initiative when, while his frigate *Fisgard* was refitting at Gibraltar, he sighted Villeneuve's fleet, eleven battleships with a company of frigates and brigs, making out into the Atlantic. Kerr hired a brig, put one of his officers in command, and sent him scurrying eastward in search of Nelson with hastily scribbled information. Then he so hustled the *Fisgard*'s crew that in four hours the frigate was at sea, leaving a great part of her equipment on the quay, including twenty-two tons of water, a launch, a barge and an anchor.

Ketch: a strong two-masted vessel, fore-and-aft rigged, but sometimes carrying square sails on the main mast. Early types were used for coastal trading and in the Navy. *See also* BOMB-KETCH.

Kevel: an uncommon word for a cleat, peg or bollard, to which a rope is secured.

Key (or **cay**): a small island or reef, particularly such as those found off the southern tip of Florida and the many small islets of the Bahamas.

Keyes, Roger John Brownlow, first Baron Keyes (1872–1945): Admiral of the Fleet. He is remembered chiefly for his planning of naval operations and army landings during the First World War and for his work in the submarine service.

'Key-ing': a Chinese war-junk that visited London in 1848, providing a rare sight in home waters, having crossed from Boston to St Aubin's Bay in 21 days. According to report, such large junks, sometimes over 1000 tons and carrying 20 or more guns of varying dimensions, were unpredictable as to their intended destination and where they actually arrived. Another visitor to the West was the *Whang-ho*, which started on an exhibition tour of the world at the beginning of this century, left San Francisco for New York and London, via Cape Horn, pursued an erratic course to Tahiti, the Torres Straits and Batavia, and was finally abandoned (1909) because, according to her captain, 'She will not hold together much longer . . . The beams are not fastened to the hull of the vessel, but lie loose in her.'

Kidd, William (*c.*1645–1701): pirate. Born in Scotland, he went to sea as a boy and later settled in the American colonies. He commanded a privateer and in 1695 was given a special commission, under the Great Seal, to seize and hang pirates in the eastern seas. In 1699, when he returned to Boston, he was himself arrested on charges of piracy, the chief charge being that he had seized a French ship, the *Queda Merchant*, and £70,000 worth of treasure. He was sent to England for trial and was hanged at Wapping Old Stairs, though the sentence was for the murder of one of his crew. The beautiful Queen's House at Greenwich was bought by the Commissioners of Greenwich Hospital with part of the recovered treasure.

Kiel: West German town with a fine port lying at the W. end of the Baltic. In medieval times the town was a member of the HANSEATIC LEAGUE and has ever since owed much to its magnificent harbour, especially during the First and Second World Wars, when it was an important naval base. Just north of Kiel lies the eastern entrance to the KIEL CANAL.

Kiel Canal: canal in the *Land* of Schleswig-Holstein (West Germany) connecting the Baltic with the North Sea, where it terminates at the mouth of the River Elbe. It was built between 1887 and 1895, and its enlargement was completed just before the First World War, after which it was in effect made an international waterway. In 1936 Hitler repudiated the conditions imposed, but after the Second World War it again became open to ships of all nations. Many merchant ships favour this short, easy and cheap passage to and from the Baltic.

Killick: a small all-purpose anchor. The word is also used colloquially for a leading hand of any branch in the Royal Navy, because his badge is an anchor or killick; to 'ship the killick' is to be promoted to this rank. To 'up killick' is to run away or desert ship; in other words, to up anchor.

King, Sir George St Vincent: *see* KING, SIR RICHARD.

King, James (1750–84): naval captain who sailed with Captain Cook as astronomer and second lieutenant (1776). He prepared the journal of Cook's third voyage for the press, and published his own *Astronomical Observations* in 1782, in

The German battleship *Admiral Scheer* passing through the Kiel Canal.

which year he became a Fellow of the Royal Society.

King, Philip Gidley (1758–1808): naval officer and colonial governor. He was with the 'first fleet' which sailed for Australia in 1787 and was Governor of Norfolk Island (1790) and New South Wales (1800–1806).

King, Philip Parker (1793–1856): admiral. The son of Philip Gidley KING, he was born on Norfolk Island and became a distinguished naval surveyor, surveying the coast of Australia (1817–22) and the southern coast of South America (1825). Later he surveyed the western coasts of Australia. He published many charts and *Sailing Directions to the Coasts of Eastern and Western Patagonia*.

King, Sir Richard (1774–1834): admiral. He commanded the *Achilles* (74 guns) at Trafalgar and was rewarded with the gold medal, the thanks of Parliament and a sword of honour from the Patriotic Fund. His father, another *Admiral Sir Richard King* (1730–1806), had distinguished himself in the Mediterranean and the East Indies; and his son, *Admiral Sir George St Vincent King* (*d.*1891), served in the Crimean War and was Commander-in-Chief, China.

King, Richard (?1811–1876): traveller. Trained as a surgeon, he accompanied Commander (later Admiral) George Back on an exploring expedition to the Great Fish River (1833–5). He published his *Narrative of a Journey to the Shore of the Arctic Ocean* in 1836, and was assistant surgeon on the *Resolute* in the 1850 expedition to find Franklin. He received the Arctic Medal and wrote works on the natives of Vancouver Island, the Eskimoes and the Laplanders. His interest in the origins and varieties of the human race led him to found the Ethnological Society, of which he was the first secretary.

King, Thomas (1835–88): seaman and prize-fighter. He served in both the Royal Navy and the merchant service, then took to the ring, his most famous fight being his defeat (1863) of John Camel Heenan ('the Benicia Boy'), the American champion.

King George V Dock: one of the great wet docks of London. It lies on the N. bank of the Thames in North Woolwich and is entered through huge hydraulically operated steel gates from Gallion's Reach. It is 4300 ft long and 38 ft deep, with berths for as many as fourteen large ships, and was opened in 1921, being the last of the great Inner London docks to be constructed. Close by are the Royal Albert and the Royal Victoria Docks.

'King of Prussia': nickname of a celebrated 19th-century Cornish smuggler, John Carter. On one occasion the revenue officers found one of his caches of contraband goods and carried it off in triumph to the Customs House store. That night Carter broke in and took it all back, scrupulously confining himself to his own goods.

King post: *see* SAMSON POST.

King's Bencher: old naval term for a seaman who was better at talking than doing a job of work; probably from the old Court of Law, which saw a great deal of speech-making.

King's Letter Boys: a somewhat scornful name given to young gentlemen who entered the Navy as 'Volunteers-per-Order' under a system introduced in 1676 by Samuel Pepys. The King's Letter came from the Board of Admiralty, and therefore had royal authority; it entitled the young gentleman to be taken on the strength of a ship, whose captain was responsible for training him in his profession. The number of such youngsters, whose upper age limit was 16, was specified for each rate or class of ship, and each was to be paid £24 a year. If satisfactory, the King's Letter Boy would become a MIDSHIPMAN, and ultimately be given a commission; but it was only one of several routes to the quarter-deck. The system lasted for some 60 years; the future Admiral Rodney, who went to sea in 1732, was the last of the King's Letter Boys. After 1733 young gentlemen were nominated for training at the new Naval Academy at Portsmouth, but the numbers who entered the Navy by these routes were always quite small; most midshipmen had gone direct to sea for their training.

Kingsley, Charles (1819–75): clergyman, reformer, critic, poet and novelist who turned his pen to a variety of subjects. Among his novels is *Westward Ho!* (1855), a long sea story of intrigue, adventure and naval enterprise in the times of Queen Elizabeth I. Towards the end of the book there is a gripping account of the fight against the Armada in 1588.

Of Kingsley's father, another Charles, it was said that his parishioners at Clovelly, Devonshire, respected him because he was 'a man who feared no danger, and could steer a boat, hoist and lower a sail, shoot a herring-net, and haul a seine as one of themselves.'

King's Parade: old naval name for the quarter-deck, normally reserved for officers.

King's Regulations: *see* REGULATIONS.

Kingston, William Henry Giles (1814–80): writer of many boys' stories about the sea, of which *Peter the Whaler* (1851) is the best remembered. Altogether he wrote over 100 tales, and has been called 'the boys' Marryat'.

King's yarn: coloured thread interwoven into a rope to show that it had been made in one of the Royal Navy ropewalks and was therefore, theoretically, at least, for use only on Royal Navy ships. In practice, dishonest storekeepers, especially abroad (where supervision was often lax), often sold it to merchant skippers who, with the aid of an application of tar, not only preserved the rigging but covered up the betraying thread.

Kipling, Rudyard (1865–1936): poet, short-story writer and novelist. His long list of works shows great variety and originality, based both on experience and on a rich imaginative power. His pride in the imperial achievement of Britain was deeply felt, even if today some of his expressions of it are outmoded; nevertheless that pride was ordered by a sense of Britain's responsibility. With such an outlook Kipling could hardly fail to be conscious of the place and importance of the sea in the British story, and from his early days its appeal and mystery led him to write about the sea and ships in both verse and prose. Some of his best-known sea poems appeared in *The Seven Seas* (1896) and *The Five Nations* (1903), whilst his first long story about the sea was *Captains Courageous* (1897), a tale of the fishermen on the Grand Banks off Newfoundland. Further sea stories appeared in *The Day's Work* (1898) and *Traffics and Discoveries* (1904). During the First World War his books *Fringes of the Fleet* (1915) and *Sea Warfare* (1916) gave vivid accounts of the Royal Navy and merchant service and of the men who served in them. He won the Nobel Prize for Literature (1907).

Kissing the gunner's daughter: *see* FLOGGING.

Kite: a fore-and-aft topmost sail; also a sail carried above the royal in a square-rigged ship.

Kitty: naval nickname for anyone surnamed Wells.

Knee: a naturally bent strong piece of TIMBER used for joining the beams and ribs in old wooden ships; also a shaped piece of wood for securing the thwart to the side of a boat. In ships of iron and steel construction

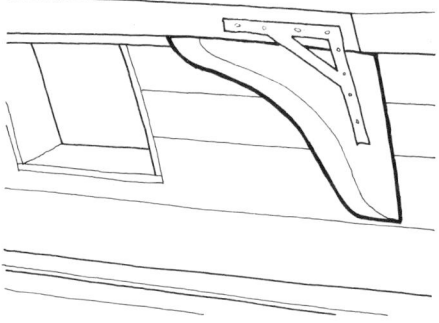

the name is given to an angular iron used for similar purposes (*see* SNODGRASS, GABRIEL).

Knightheads: strong timbers in old sailing ships on each side of the upper stem and to which the bowsprit was secured. The name may derive from the early custom, observed in a number of examples, of incorporating a man's head in the carving at the top.

Knights of Malta: name, after 1530, of the Knights of St John of Jerusalem, Knights Hospitallers or Knights of Rhodes. They wore a black habit with a

white cross, offered a life of hard endeavour and became particularly associated with the care of the sick and aged. At times they took to the sea in fine style. Soon after they settled at Malta they acquired the great *Santa Anna*, built for them at Nice, a ship of over 1700 tons burden and with six decks, two of them under water. She is recorded as having 50 heavy guns and a great number of lesser pieces of ordnance. The Order's normal sea-going strength seems to have been some seven GALLEYS, the flag-ship black, the rest painted crimson. At the siege of Malta in 1565 by the corsair fleet of Khair-ed-Din Barbarossa, the garrison put up a magnificent fight. 'Under the gallant, grim, bigoted old Grand Master, Jean de la Valette, a grand fighter still in spite of his seventy years, the garrison put up a defence unequalled in history' (Bowen, *The Sea, Its History and Romance*, 1924–6), and finally drove off the Turkish horde, who are said to have reached home with only 5000 survivors from their original 30 or 40 thousand.

The Order attracted many noble-minded men, Englishmen among them. The sad thing was, as with other great military Orders, the outlets for their courage and energies became more limited as the years passed, and at times their ideals and knightly oaths were forgotten. But we

Knightheads.

catch a moving glimpse of them in action in the late 18th century:

The last expiring token of the old spirit in the old forms which I have found, is in the records of the Knights of Malta . . . when the news of the great earthquake in Sicily, in 1783, arrived at Malta. Then these poor feeble-minded sybarites remembered for a moment their manhood and their knighthood, and their vows as Hospitallers; they manned their galleys, and, with food and clothing and medicines, and the consolations of their faith, were speedily seen, in their half-military, half-priestly garb – the armour covered by the black robe with the white cross, at the bedsides of the wounded and the dying, as they lay amid the still tottering ruin of their devastated houses.

Sir Edward Strachey, Introduction to the Globe edition of *Le Morte d' Arthur* (1891)

Knock: *see* NOCK.

Knot: the unit of measurement of a ship's speed. One knot is an advance of one nautical mile in one hour, an international nautical mile being 1852 metres or 6076·115 ft. The name arose from the early method of assessing a ship's speed by the use of the LOG-LINE. *See also* SPEED.

Knots: when generally used, the word 'knot' means the fastening or tying of rope, cord or twine to make something secure; but in strict nautical usage knots should be distinguished from bends and hitches, for 'knot' generally implies a permanent fastening, whilst a bend unites two rope ends or makes a loop or bight for a special purpose, and a hitch makes ropes fast to other objects. Moreover, bends and hitches should be capable of being undone at once. By these definitions the well-known reef knot is really a bend, and the fisherman's bend is actually a hitch! Because all three words are really synonymous, and to avoid confusion, we use the word knot to cover all

purposeful complications of rope or cord.

Knots have, of course, been used from the very earliest times and evolved to serve the particular purposes of different skills and crafts from primitive weaving to modern mountaineering, but the sailor by the nature of his calling has surely contributed most to the many hundreds of known knots. Their development and application undoubtedly reached the highest level during the 19th century, when the sailing ship was at the zenith of her glory. Knots are not only functional but can also be used decoratively, and in sailing-ship days much fancy work was done with SENNET, a kind of flat braided cordage formed by plaiting rope and cord together. With this the sailor made his ship and his own gear look smart; he made handles for chests, for buckets and barricoes, he made different kinds of lanyards, covered handrails and stanchions, wove mats and decorated cases and small boxes.

It was the working of the ship day and night at sea, or loading or unloading in port, that demanded so many special knots. The following are the names and uses of some of the best-known:

1. *Half-hitch:* the basis and simplest of all hitches.

2. *Round turn and two half-hitches:* a useful knot for securing a line to a buoy or ring bolt. Does not jam and is very easy to release.

3. *Fisherman's bend:* really a hitch; similar to a round turn and two half-hitches, but more secure. Used for bending a warp to the ring of an anchor.

4. *Figure of eight knot:* a stopper knot used to prevent a rope running out through a block, a fairlead or a cleat.

5 and 9. *Crown knot* and *wall knot:* used singly or in combination to prevent the end of a rope from unlaying. A crown knot can also be used to decorate the top of a

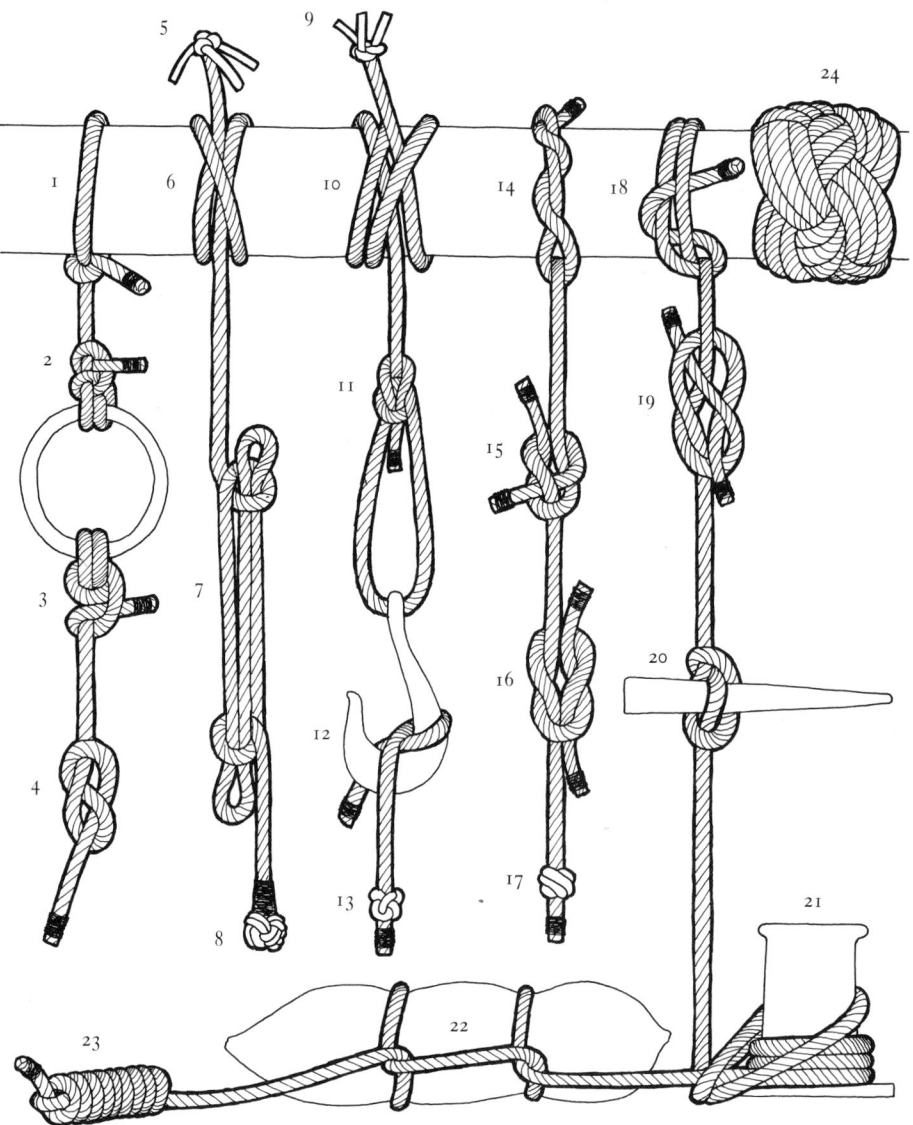

stanchion. A double wall knot can be used as a stopper knot for preventing a rope running through a block.

6. *Clove hitch:* a form of two half-hitches which hold by jamming. Used for securing a rope athwart another or to a rail; one of the most frequently used knots, it is quickly made and does not jam.

7. *Sheepshank:* not really a knot, but a means of shortening a rope to take up slack, or to lessen the strain over a weak or frayed part. It is formed by double bights with eyes made by half-hitches on the end of the doubled sections.

8. *Manrope knot* or *double wall and crown knot:* wall and crown knots

developed to finsh off neatly the end of a MANROPE.

9. *Wall knot;* see 5 above.

10. *Rolling hitch:* similar to a clove hitch but with an additional round turn to make it more secure. It is a quick and secure hitch, useful for securing a rope to a spar, chain or to a thicker cable.

11. *Bowline:* a bend of which there are several varieties – running, on a bight, double and french. All provide a loop or double loop which does not jam, used for securing, lowering or hauling.

12. *Blackwall hitch:* for securing a rope to a hook. Can be single or double.

13. *Diamond knot:* single or double; also used at the end of a rope by unlaying and relaying the rope's strands.

14. *Timber hitch:* for securing a rope to a spar or baulk of timber.

15. *Sheet bend* or *becket bend:* for joining two ropes of unequal size, or for securing to the eye of a cable or hawser. Can be single or double.

16. *Reef knot:* the most commonly used. Really a bend for joining two small ropes of the same or similar size. So named because it was used for tying the reef-points of sails when taking in a reef. It is simple, secure and easily undone.

17. *Matthew Walker knot:* a simple decorative knot similar in kind and purpose to a wall knot. Can be single or double.

18. *Stunsail bend:* not really a bend, but a hitch dating from the days of sail, generally useful for securing a rope to a spar.

19. *Carrick bend:* for joining two ropes or hawsers by looping and lacing the ends together. Can be single or double.

20. *Marline spike hitch:* not for securing, but used with a marline spike to obtain purchase on a rope for hauling taut.

21. *Thames* or *tugboat hitch:* a mooring hitch used by lightermen for securing craft to a post or bollard.

22. *Marling hitch:* for securing bundles, especially for lashing up hammocks.

23. *Heaving line knot* or *monkey's fist knot:* used for giving weight to the end of a heaving line.

24. *Turk's head:* the general name for several varieties of knot. The most common is that used for running round a stanchion or hand-rail, both to provide a grip and for decoration.

See also SWORD-KNOTS.

'Kon Tiki': *see* PACIFIC.

Kozhikode: *see* CALICUT.

Kraken: a huge and fabulous sea-monster which was believed to appear in the ocean off Norway, and to drag ships down in its arms as it descended to the depths. The legend perhaps had its origin in the appearance of a giant squid.

Kuro Siwo Drift: a relatively warm current, the counterpart in the Pacific of the Gulf Stream or North Atlantic Drift in the North Atlantic. It sweeps north to the southern coasts of Japan and then turns N.E. across the North Pacific Ocean, warming the prevailing westerly winds and moderating the coastal climate of British Columbia.

Kwangchow: *see* CANTON.

L

Labrador Current: a cold, southward-flowing current moving from Davis Strait and along the coasts of Labrador and Newfoundland. It brings with it icebergs and often causes fog when the cold air above it meets the warm, moister air over the Gulf Stream or North Atlantic Drift, which it helps to deflect north-eastwards. Its cold waters, interposed between the coast and the Gulf Stream, greatly affect the climate of the N.E. United States and the Maritime Provinces of Canada, and where the two currents meet, the differences in the appearance and colour of the sea and in the temperature of the air, are most marked.

Lace: (**1**) the gold braiding worn on the cuffs of blue uniform or on shoulder straps, to indicate an officer's rank; (**2**) to lace an awning, sail etc. is to lash it with rope or cord to mast or stay.

Ladder: any set of steps, permanent or temporary, inboard or outboard. *See also* COMPANION LADDER, JACOB'S LADDER etc.

'Ladies' Resolution': mid-18th-century privateering vessel, affording interesting evidence that London ladies were not averse to increasing their pocket-money: a group of them fitted out the ship from their own resources in 1758.

Lading: *see* BILL OF LADING.

Ladrone: a robber, thief, rogue or pirate; hence the name of the Ladrone (or Mariana) Islands in the West Pacific, reputed to be a haunt of thieves.

'Lady Nancy': remarkable craft constructed by the officers and crew of the *Stromboli* for the bombardment of Taganrog by the Anglo-French fleet (1855). A raft was made of 29 casks placed in six rows and cradled in a framework of heavy spars. Part of the raft was planked over and, with the aid of tackles, she carried a long 32-pounder gun weighing over two tons, 100 rounds of ammunition and a crew of 18. The construction took 12 hours and the *Lady Nancy* apparently acquitted herself well.

Lady of the Gunroom: the gunner's mate in charge of the after scuttle where the gunner's stores were kept. The store was sometimes known as the Lady's Hole.

Lagan: *see* LIGAN.

Laggers: barge men who lie on their backs when their craft are going through narrow tunnels and push the barges along with their feet on the roof or sides. In the old days the term was sometimes applied to convicts being taken overseas (hence 'old lag' for an ex-convict).

Lagoon: name generally applied to an enclosed area of seawater; more especially such an area behind a barrier reef or within the atoll of a coral island.

We passed through the Low or Dangerous Archipelago, and saw several of those most curious rings of coral land, just rising above the water's edge, which have been called Lagoon Islands. A long and brilliantly-white beach is capped by a margin of green vegetation; and the strip, looking either way, rapidly narrows away in the distance, and sinks beneath the horizon. From the mast-head a wide expanse of smooth water can be seen within the ring.

Charles Darwin, *The Voyage of the 'Beagle'* (1840)

Lagos (or **Lagos Bay**), **Battle of** (18 August 1759): an amazing encounter between Admiral Boscawen and a French fleet under Admiral de la Clue, off the seaport of Lagos in southern Portugal. Compelled to raise his blockade of Brest because of damage to his frigates and lack of supplies, Boscawen fell back on Gibraltar, but took the precaution of leaving a frigate on watch in the Straits. The frigate reported that the French had followed hard on Boscawen and, under cover of night, had reached the Atlantic. For an account of the subsequent action, *see* BOSCAWEN, EDWARD.

La Hogue, Battle of: *see* BARFLEUR AND LA HOGUE, BATTLES OF.

Laid up: retired from active service either temporarily or permanently and, in the latter case, stripped of equipment and fittings.

Laird, Sir John (1805–74): shipbuilder. He built in 1829 a 60-ton lighter for use on canals and lakes in Ireland, one of the first iron ships, and in 1834 the *John Randolph* for Savannah, probably the first iron ship

seen in America. Another of his famous ships was the *Birkenhead*. His younger brother, *Macgregor Laird* (1808–61), was one of the promoters of the British and North American Steam Navigation Company in 1837. He fitted out private expeditions to Africa, established trading depots, and published a narrative of an expedition to the Niger.

'Lake' ships: group of sailing ships ordered in the 1860s to be built on the Clyde for the newly formed Canada Shipping Company and the regular emigrant service to the St Lawrence. The first three took their names from the Great Lakes, the tonnage varying according to the size of the lake. The largest was therefore the *Lake Superior* (1868), with a gross tonnage of 1274, the others being the *Lake Erie* and *Lake Ontario*. Historically, they formed the nucleus of the enterprise that was to develop into the great Canadian Pacific fleet of ships.

Lammy coat: a short, thick woollen coat with a hood; another name for a duffle coat.

... the smell of the wet 'lammies' and damp wardroom cushions ...

Rudyard Kipling, *Sea Warfare* (1916)

Lancaster, Sir James (?1554–1618): seacaptain and trading pioneer. He commanded the *Edward Bonaventure* against the Spanish Armada (1588) and on the first English voyage to the East Indies (1591–4). In spite of terrible hardships and losses of men (of the 198 who set out with him, only about 25 returned), this expedition broke the Portuguese monopoly of trade with the East Indies, and Lancaster came home with rich booty.

In less than six months he went to sea again and returned with more wealth, having captured Pernambuco (Brazil) and

255

taken more booty than his ships could carry (1594). In 1601 he was put in command of five ships which sailed to the East Indies as the first venture of the East India Company. He visited the Nicobar Islands, then went on to Sumatra, where he captured Portuguese ships, set up a trading station, and loaded his ship with a rich cargo of spices, with which he returned home to be knighted (1603). Nearly half of the crews of the other ships had died of SCURVY, but Lancaster had kept his own crew healthy by dosing them daily with lemon juice (a lesson which was afterwards for long forgotten).

He devoted most of the rest of his life to the organization and administration of the East India Company's affairs. Most of his accumulated wealth was left to charities, some of which are administered to this day by the Skinners' Company of London, the Company of which Lancaster had become an apprentice in his youth.

Land breeze: an off-shore wind, often rising at night with the cooling of the air over the land relative to the temperature of the air over the sea; frequent off tropical coasts and occurring in fine, warm weather elsewhere.

> A land breeze shook the shrouds
> And she was overset;
> Down went the *Royal George*
> With all her crew complete.

William Cowper, 'On the Loss of the *Royal George*'

Landfall: approach to land after a voyage. It can be a good or bad landfall according to the accuracy of the navigator's calculation.

Landing craft: specially designed craft for amphibious operations, particularly in war-time, when they can land anything from a small group of men to heavy tanks and other equipment. One type can be used for flying men in by helicopter. Among the more modern types are the L.S.T. (landing ship tank), able to carry 20 tanks, 700 troops and a crew of over 100; the L.S.M. (landing ship medium) of 1095 tons; and the L.C.U. (landing craft utility) of only 360 tons displacement. Another variety is the American dock landing ship, a parent vessel able to land smaller craft as well as being provided with a helicopter deck. The Royal Fleet Auxiliary *Sir Geraint*, known as a logistics landing ship, is designed for combined operations and carries several hundred soldiers and their vehicles.

Landlocked: almost or completely surrounded by land. The word is applied not only to seas: a ship is said to be landlocked if it cannot reach open water.

Landlubber: a landsman, ignorant of ships and the sea. To call a seaman a 'lubber' is a serious reflection on his skill. The word probably derives from the old word 'lob', meaning a clumsy, stupid fellow.

Landman: *see* LANDSMAN.

Land-mark: *see* SEA-MARK.

Land's End: the extreme S.W. point of the mainland of England, forming a dramatic and dangerous rocky headland.

Landsman (or **landman**): (1) a rating for a man who had no sea experience and no special skill, introduced at the end of the 18th century and continuing till the middle of the 19th. *See also* RATING OF MEN; WAISTERS. (2) The word 'landsman' is also used generally for 'landlubber'.

Lanes, sea (or **shipping**): the most frequented tracks for shipping, sometimes made obligatory in narrow waters, e.g. the busy English Channel.

Langrace (or **langrage**, **langrel** or **langridge**): *see* SHOT.

Lantern: the casing of a light or lamp either for navigation or for signalling. Before the coming of electricity the care and maintenance of the ship's lanterns was an important duty. Port, starboard and mast-head lights are housed in lanterns. The chamber containing the lights in a lighthouse is known as the lantern.

Lanyard: a small length of cord, often ornamentally knotted, to fasten something or to act as a handle. A seaman's lanyard originally secured his knife or a whistle about his neck. The lanyard on a gun moved the percussion lock and gave safer clearance to the gunner.

Larboard: old name for the left-hand side of a ship when looking towards the bows; the opposite of 'starboard', and now superseded by PORT.

La Rochelle, Battle of (22 June 1372): the third major sea-fight of the Hundred Years' War. The English were severely defeated by the Castilians, who were helping France. The chief cause of the defeat seems to have been the unsportsmanlike behaviour of the enemy in dropping iron bars and heavy stones from their higher 'castles', rather than fighting hand-to-hand.

Lascar: an oriental seaman, generally Indian or East Indian, employed as a member of the crew of merchant ships. The word has its origin in the Urdu language.

Lash, to: to make fast with a rope or cord. To lash down gear is to make it secure; to lash a hammock is to lace it up in a neat bundle; to lash together is to join.

Lashing: any rope used for securing things; or the action of doing so.

Lateen: from the French *voile latine*, meaning 'Latin sail'; a triangular sail once commonly used in small, especially Mediterranean, craft. The name is also applied to the type of sail used in Arab dhows and Chinese junks. *See p. 258; see also* RIG; YARD.

Latitude: angular distance north or south

Lateen.

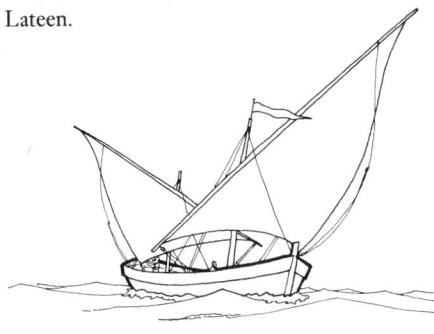

of the Equator measured on the meridian in degrees, minutes and seconds. In a general sense the word means a locality or region, e.g. 'in tropical latitudes'.

Launch: (1) large boat belonging to a man-o'-war, often sloop-rigged, i.e. with one mast rigged fore-and-aft; (2) an open pleasure boat mechanically propelled, e.g. steam launch, electric launch.

Launch, to: to send a ship down the slipway into the water, ready for fitting. Launching a vessel has sometimes presented problems. Usually a ship is launched stern first, to slow her up sufficiently when she takes to the water. The *GREAT EASTERN*, because of her size, had to be launched sideways and stuck several times.

'Laurentic': British steamer sunk in the First World War by a German torpedo off the coast of Donegal in 20 fathoms (120 ft) with £5,000,000 in gold on board. The gold was recovered by Captain G. C. C. Damant and an Admiralty team of divers between 1917 and 1924.

Lawrence, James (1781–1813): U.S. naval captain, hero of the *Shannon* and *Chesapeake* battle (1813) outside BOSTON, when he was killed. He had previously won fame on the sloop *Hornet* when, in February of the same year, he sank the R.N. brig *Peacock* at the Demerara River.

Lay: a word with many different maritime uses as verb and noun: (1) to lay up a rope is to twist its strands together; the lay of a rope is the way in which its strands are so twisted; (2) to lay up a ship is to keep her in reserve; (3) to lay in stores is to bring food and gear into a ship; (4) to lay aboard is to bring a ship alongside the enemy's; (5) to lay a gun is to aim it by elevating the barrel; he who does so is a 'gunlayer'; (6) to lay aft, forward, aloft etc. is to go to the position indicated; (7) to lay a mine or a buoy is to place it in position; (8) to lay on one's oars is to bring the oars out of and horizontal to the water, keeping them at right angles to the bow line. For 'laying down' *see* MOULD LOFT.

Lazaret (or **lazaretto**): from the name Lazarus; originally a pest-house or hospital for contagious diseases, but in ships the name was formerly applied to a small store between decks and in the stern of the vessel.

Lead (pronounced 'leed'): (1) guide or path for a rope, as in 'fairlead'; (2) navigable passageway through sea ice; (3) any narrow sea route through rocks or reefs.

Lead (pronounced 'led'): the weight or plummet of between 7 and 14 lb. tied to the end of a rope (the 'lead-line') and heaved by the LEADSMAN into the sea to sound the depth of water. The traditional hand lead-line used in relatively shallow water up to 25 fathoms (1 fathom = 6 ft) was marked at intervals as follows:

at	2 fathoms	2 strips of leather
	3 fathoms	3 strips of leather

at 5 fathoms	a strip of white linen canvas ('duck')
7 fathoms	a piece of red bunting
10 fathoms	a square of leather with a hole in it ('washer')
13 fathoms	a piece of blue serge
15 fathoms	a piece of white linen canvas
17 fathoms	a piece of red bunting
20 fathoms	a piece of cord with two knots in it

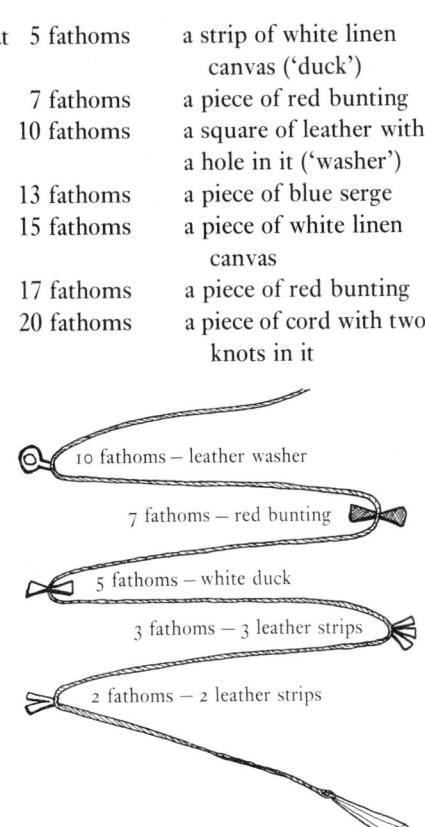

10 fathoms — leather washer

7 fathoms — red bunting

5 fathoms — white duck

3 fathoms — 3 leather strips

2 fathoms — 2 leather strips

These distinctive marks could easily be identified by the leadsman not only by day but also by feel at night. The lead was heaved somewhat ahead of the ship so that it was immediately below when the lead struck the bottom and the leadsman called the depth according to the mark on the line then near the surface. The unmarked fathoms were called deeps. Thus the leadsman would call out the number of fathoms preceded by the words 'By the deep' (or 'Deep') or 'By the mark'. (Samuel Clemens, author of *The Adventures of Tom Sawyer* and *Huckleberry Finn*, chose 'Mark Twain' as his pen-name because he remembered this cry from his time as a pilot on the River Mississippi.)

There were different kinds of lead – the lighter, shorter boat's lead, the hand lead, and the deep-sea heavy lead, formerly used in surveying. The bottom of the lead could be greased to show the nature of the sea-bed by the sand, mud or shingle clinging to it. The lead has now been largely replaced by devices such as the ECHO-SOUNDER.

For England when, with favouring gale,
Our gallant ship up Channel steered,
And scudding under easy sail,
The high blue western lands appeared,
To heave the lead the seaman sprung,
And to the pilot cheerly sung,
'By the deep – Nine.'

anon., 'The Leadsman's Song'

Leading Hand: *see* LEADING SEAMAN.

Leading Seaman: a rating in the seaman branch of the Royal Navy immediately below a petty officer. In other branches a Leading Hand is the equivalent rating. Colloquially called a KILLICK.

Leading strings: yoke lines on a ship's rudder.

Leadsman (pronounced 'ledzman'): the man who heaved the LEAD and called out the depth of the water in fathoms. He stood in the CHAINS, and leant against an apron, a band of canvas stretched across the rigging, keeping him safe and dry and leaving both his hands free to heave the lead.

Leake, Sir John (1656–1720): Admiral of the Fleet, son of Richard LEAKE. Of comparatively humble origins, he rendered distinguished service in the relief of Gibraltar and the capture of Minorca. He was governor and commander-in-chief at Newfoundland, commanded in the Mediterranean and was a Member of Parliament.

Leake, Richard (1629–96): gunner who

rose by his ability to become Master Gunner of England, after a varied career in which he served in the Parliamentary Navy, in the Dutch army and as captain of a merchant ship.

'Leander': after the Battle of the Nile (1798), H.M.S. *Leander* (50 guns), commanded by Captain Thomas Boulder Thompson and carrying Captain Edward BERRY with Nelson's dispatches, fell in with a French survivor from the battle, the 74-gun *Genereux*. All the circumstances dictated that Thompson should avoid an encounter, not only because of the dispatches, but because of the odds – a French broadside of over 1000 lb. against the *Leander*'s 432 lb., and the enemy crew of 936 against only 282. Nevertheless, with the *Genereux* overhauling him, Captain Thompson decided to stand and fight. He held out for six and a half hours till, with heavy casualties and his ship hopelessly incapacitated, he had no alternative but to surrender.

The *Leander* was now totally ungovernable, having her lower yards on the booms, and no stick standing, save the bowsprit and the shattered remains of the fore and main masts: the ship's hull was also cut to pieces and her decks were strewed on every side with killed and wounded.

William James, *The Naval History of Great Britain* (1822)

The captives received unusually inhumane treatment at the hands of the French, but the *Leander* was eventually restored to the British Navy, and both Thompson and Berry were knighted for their gallantry. In the words of the court-martial verdict:

The court having heard the evidence brought forward in support of Captain Thompson's narrative of the capture of the *Leander*, and having maturely and deliberately considered the whole, is of opinion, that the gallant and almost unprecedented defence of Captain Thompson, of his majesty's late ship *Leander*, against so superior a force ... is deserving of every praise his country and this court can give ... and the court does therefore most honourably acquit Captain Thompson.

Leatherneck: a slang name for a marine or soldier, originating in the leather stock once worn by marines.

Leddy (i.e. 'lady'): old seaman's name for the ship's figurehead, irrespective of its sex. The veneration of the sailor for the 'leddy' (female or male) is well illustrated by an incident on board H.M.S. *Brunswick* during the battle of the 'Glorious FIRST OF JUNE' (1794), when enemy chain-shot knocked the hat from the figurehead of the Duke of Brunswick.

Then a solemn deputation from the
    Brunswick's fo'c'sle came
With the news to Captain Harvey: 'Sir! Your
    Honour! 'tis for shame,
And in no ways right or proper, for our Royal
    Duke to go
With his noble head uncovered in the face of
    any foe.'
At a word, the Captain's coxswain fetched a
    hat superbly laced,
Which the captain of the fo'c'sle on the oaken
    temples placed,
Nailed secure, and passed a lashing fit to
    stand the hardest strain,
And the happy deputation scampered off to
    fight again!

Ten o'clock the battle started; close on two
    before they'd done,
With the gallant *Vengeur* sinking and the
    Brunswick's mizen gone;
But the noble Duke came through it, like a
    fighter born and bred,
With his hand upon his sword-hilt and his hat
    upon his head.

R. A. Hopwood, *The Figureheads* (1916)

Lee: on the side away from, or sheltered from, the wind. The word is practically synonymous with 'leeward' and is used in many nautical combinations, e.g. 'lee gage', the position of a ship or ships to leeward of others; 'lee line', a line of ships to leeward (*see* WEATHER); 'lee shore', a shore on to which the wind is driving from the sea; 'lee tide', a tide or tidal stream flowing in the same direction as the wind; 'leeway', a drift to the side caused by the wind.

Leeboards: heavy fan-shaped blades hinged at both sides of a ship and lowered to resist sideways movement by vessels under sail with little or no definite keel.

Leech: the free edge of either a square or a fore-and-aft sail. The leech was dragged inwards when furling sail. *See also* SAIL.

Which three will furl their sail first and come
    down?
Out to the yard-arm for the leech goes one,
His hair blown flagwise from a hatless crown,
His hands at work like fever to be done.

        John Masefield, 'Dauber'

Leeward (pronounced 'looard'): on the side away from the one from which the wind blows; the opposite of 'windward'.

Leeward Islands: (1) a chain of islands which with the WINDWARD ISLANDS make up the Lesser Antilles of the West Indies. The names of the two groups came from their position in relation to the prevailing Trade Winds. From the time of their discovery by Columbus (1493) the islands have been subject to the maritime and colonial aspirations of the European nations; first the Spanish, then the Dutch, British and French came, claimed and left their mark. Today many of the islands, e.g. Montserrat, Antigua, St Kitts, Nevis, Anguilla and some of the Virgin Islands, are within the British Commonwealth, but enjoy varying degrees of local autonomy; others, such as the Guadeloupe group, are an overseas department of France, whilst some of the Virgin Islands are American, and the Dutch have a presence in a few small islands. English Harbour in Antigua was once the main naval base for the British fleet in the Caribbean, and still has much that recalls the times of Nelson and his unremitting pursuit of the French.

(2) *See* SOCIETY ISLANDS.

Leeway: *see* LEE.

Le Fanu, Sir Michael (1913–   ): admiral who was Third Sea Lord and Controller of the Navy (1961–5) and later Commander-in-Chief, Middle East, and First Sea Lord. He was one of the modern eccentrics and, in the words of one commentator, 'that he rose above the rank of commander seems not much short of a miracle' in a service where it is highly risky not to stick to the book. Among his less usual accomplishments were a facility for writing verse, doing embroidery and throwing bars of chocolate as rewards to those who pleased him. He earned the nickname 'Dry Ginger', not only because of the colour of his hair, but because the Navy's rum ration was finally abolished under his authority.

Leg: distance covered by a sailing ship in one tack. *See also* SHOW A LEG.

'Lenin': *see* NUCLEAR-POWERED SHIPS.

Les Espagnols sur Mer: *see* ESPAGNOLS SUR MER.

Lestock, Richard (?1679–1746): admiral; a central figure in a discreditable affair in February 1744 during the War of the Austrian Succession. Admiral Thomas Mathews was endeavouring, off Toulon, to engage a Franco-Spanish fleet according to the Fighting Instructions, i.e. van to van, centre to centre and rear to rear. Apparently despairing of forming the conventional line, he turned in to attack the French rear with his centre squadron. His van engaged the French centre, leaving Lestock, commanding the rear, to take on the empty sea. It was a classic case of muddle and stupidity, with some captains intent on obeying Mathews and others on observing the Fighting Instructions. Thirteen courts-martial followed. Seven captains were convicted and two acquitted. Mathews was broken and, after a trial of extraordinary length, was dismissed the service for not observing the Fighting Instructions. Lestock was acquitted because he obeyed them rather than his commander-in-chief. The result was that British naval captains got the impression that it would be unwise to depart from the rule book, and so for some years afterwards initiative and originality in fighting tactics were not much in evidence (*see also* LINE AHEAD).

Letters of Marque: official licences, signed by heads of state or their representatives, giving limited protection to PRIVATEERS, who attacked in a 'private' capacity ships of nations at war with their own country. The letters gave them some legal protection, saving them from being dealt with simply as pirates if they were captured. In early times letters of marque took two forms – those granted to any adventurer out for a quick profit (usually on the understanding that he shared it with the government), and those issued to merchants and traders who had suffered loss and wished to recoup themselves with goods to the same value. By the 18th century the privateer was almost always a pure fortune hunter and the government, at least in England, had practically renounced its claim to a share. Beginning in the 13th century, the issue of these licences continued almost unbroken (with an interval in James I's reign) till 1856. During the French Revolutionary and Napoleonic Wars some 4000 were issued.

Many East Indiamen took out letters of marque for rather different reasons from the ordinary privateer. They did not wish to cruise in search of prizes, but the letters enabled them to fire first if necessary, gave them some protection from the press-gang, and enabled them to dodge some of the annoying convoy regulations.

'Leucadia': famous late-19th-century clipper, built in Aberdeen, commanded at one period by an equally well-known skipper, Captain J. W. Holmes, who, though he 'may not have looked the popular figure of the clipper ship-master, with his shortness, limp, and high-pitched voice ... was a sailor to his finger-tips' and 'could be a holy terror if the necessity arose.' He was a keen gardener with a fondness for geraniums, which he ranged round the hatchway and poop skylight. There was one unfortunate voyage when the fo'c'sle hands took on board an Australian opossum which turned out to have a great fondness for geranium leaves.

The *Leucadia* was noted for her fine figurehead – the poetess Sappho with her lyre, strung with gilt wire. When the ship was in port the lyre and the figure's arms were taken off and kept in safety till she sailèd again.

Levant, to: to desert ship.

Levant Company: company trading with the Near East through Syria. Earlier known as the Turkey Company, it became the Levant Company in 1592.

Levanter: (1) a moist easterly wind blowing over the Strait of Gibraltar and (in summer especially) often alternating with the prevailing westerly wind; (2) a ship trading to the Levant, i.e. the countries of the eastern Mediterranean.

Leveson, Sir Richard (1570–1605): Vice-Admiral of England, appointed in 1604. He was a volunteer against the Armada (1588), took part in the Cadiz expedition (1596), and destroyed a Spanish fleet off Ireland (1601).

'Leviathan': 74-gun ship at Trafalgar, commanded by Captain (later Admiral) Henry William Bayntun. The ship was built at Chatham in 1789 and commissioned in 1793. She saw a great deal of action, including the 'Glorious FIRST OF JUNE' (1794). At Trafalgar the *Leviathan* sustained 26 casualties, killed and wounded, took eight shots between wind and water, suffered severe damage to masts, rigging and canvas, and had three guns knocked out. From 1816 to 1844 she served as a convict hulk at Portsmouth, and then as a target till she was broken up in 1848, having earned in the more glorious part of her career the naval medal with two clasps.

Among other ships that have borne the name was the Drake class armoured cruiser of 1901.

Leyte Gulf, Battle of: *see* PHILIPPINE ISLANDS.

'Libelle of English Policie, The': an anonymous work, perhaps by Adam de Molyneux (Moleyns or Molins), Bishop of Coventry, which appeared *c*.1437. The writer was one of the earliest people to appreciate the advantage to England of being an island, and of the straits both as a means of defence against invaders and as a highway for our merchant shipping.

> Keepe then the sea about in special,
> Which of Englonde is the town wall:
> Keep then the sea, that is the wall of
>   Englonde,
> And then is Englonde kept by Goddes hand.

That he was a thinker ahead of his time is evidenced by the fact that the Naval Estimates of his period averaged less than £5. Molyneux was killed in a riot over the payment of sailors at Portsmouth (1450). *See also* ALFRED.

Liberty men: those about to go ashore on short leave or liberty; also those already ashore and those returning from leave. A 'liberty boat' takes liberty men to and from the shore.

Lie off: keep a ship away from but not far from something.

Lie to: stop a ship and remain stationary.

Lieutenant: officer rank in the Royal Navy between sub-lieutenant and lieutenant-commander. The making of the professional qualified officer as the modern naval lieutenant has a long history; in the past the ways by which he attained his status and the conditions he had to fulfil have varied considerably. *See also* FIRST LIEUTENANT.

See colour section.

Lieutenant-at-Arms: in the old Navy, the junior lieutenant who helped the Master-at-Arms with the small-arms drill.

Lifeboat: simply, any boat used to save lives; more properly, a craft specially designed for that purpose, operating from shore. The first such boat built in England was the *Original*, built by Henry Greathead of South Shields and launched in 1790; but Lionel Lukin of Essex had earlier converted a Northumberland coble and sent it up to Bamburgh, where it served as the first craft in the world specially adapted for saving life at sea. Another contender for the title of inventor of the lifeboat is William Wouldhave of South Shields, who conceived the idea of the self-righting boat and built a model in 1789. Lukin also designed a lifeboat to work among the sand-banks on the east coast, the forerunner of the great line of Norfolk and Suffolk lifeboats. In the fourteen years after the launching of the *Original*,

Greathead built another 31 lifeboats, eight of which went to stations abroad.

The man chiefly responsible for organizing a lifeboat service all round the coasts of England was Sir William Hillary (1771–1847), founder of the ROYAL NATIONAL LIFEBOAT INSTITUTION for the Preservation of Life from Shipwreck (1834). Hillary himself shared in the saving of over 300 lives from shipwreck and three times won the Gold Medal of the Institution, the highest recognition it can offer and one rarely conferred.

It is one of the most moving coincidences of history that in August 1940 the Margate lifeboatmen saved from the sea a blinded and badly burnt pilot who had baled out of his blazing Spitfire above the Channel. He was Richard Hope Hillary, great-great-great-great-nephew of Sir William.

It [the lifeboat] drives on with a mercy that does not quail in the presence of death, it drives on as a proof, a symbol, a testimony, that man is created in the image of God, and that valour and virtue have not perished in the human race.

Sir Winston Churchill

For ships' lifeboats *see* BOATS, SHIPS'.

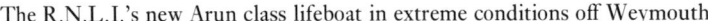

The R.N.L.I.'s new Arun class lifeboat in extreme conditions off Weymouth.

Life-buoy: a float to hold up a person in the water till a boat can reach him.

Life-jacket: an essential piece of equipment for all seamen, professional or amateur, designed to keep afloat anyone thrown into or having to take to the water. In its most sophisticated form it is an inflated sleeveless jacket, equipped with whistle or other means of attracting attention. A less satisfactory form is the life-belt. Amateur sailing associations and clubs very sensibly impress on their members the desirability of wearing life-jackets at all times. Professionals too carry out regular drills for crew and passengers.

Life-line: a rope thrown to save life; or one provided as a safeguard in a hazardous spot.

Ligan (or **lagan**): goods or gear thrown overboard and marked with some sort of buoy so that they can easily be found again. It was a favourite device of smugglers to sink contraband and mark it unostentatiously. A contrivance discovered in Langston Harbour in 1835 was so craftily arranged that the floating mark above a weighted line of barrels was just visible on the ebb tide but covered on the full tide.

Light buoy: a buoy showing a light to aid navigation.

Lighter: large open, usually flat-bottomed, craft used in loading and unloading ships; hence 'lighterage', 'lighterman' etc. *See p. 266.*

Lighthouse: a special building or structure on the coast or on a rock in the sea designed to give a powerful light as an aid to navigation. Around Great Britain there are more than 600 major and 1000 minor lights to warn ships of dangerous headlands, reefs and shoals. The most important of these are the great lighthouses, many of whose names are well-known, such as Bishop's Rock, Longships, Wolf and Eddystone, marking dangerous reefs in the southwestern approaches to England; many others, e.g. the lighthouses on the Lizard, Beachy Head and North Foreland, are familiar sights on the mainland. The Great Pharos at Alexandria, built *c.*280 B.C., in whose tower a bright fire was kept burning, was one of the Seven Wonders of the Ancient World, and lights and beacons have been used throughout the ages. Today for England and Wales the lights and seamarks around the coast are the responsibility of the Corporation of Trinity House, London, presided over by the Elder Brethren. The Commissioners of Northern Lights look after the lights around the coasts of Scotland, and for Ireland there are the Commissioners of Irish Lights. The first off-shore lighthouse was erected in 1696–8 and was the first of the five lighthouses which have been built on EDDYSTONE. From that time there has been steady development in the building and technical efficiency of lighthouses. After the use of fires came candles and oil-lamps, then vaporized acetylene gas, and in 1862

Two lightermen rowing a lighter in the Pool of London.

there was the first installation of electric carbon arc lamps at Dungeness. In 1922 the South Foreland light was the first to use electric filament lamps. Today, what are known as xenon high pressure arc discharge lamps and mercury arc lamps are used to give most powerful and reliable beams. At the same time technical skill has vastly improved the reflectors and refractors and the apparatus was made to swivel easily by floating it on a bed of mercury.

Lighthouses can each be identified by their 'characteristics', the distinctive form and duration of their lights, which can be divided into six classes:

1. Fixed – showing a continuous light.
2. Flashing – with a dark period longer than the light.
3. Isophase – equal dark and light.
4. Group flashing – two or more flashes at regular intervals.
5. Occulting – light as long as or longer than the dark period.
6. Group occulting – groups of two or more periods of light, followed by equal or shorter periods of dark at regular intervals.

Thus, as an example, Eddystone will be shown on the chart as GP.FL(2) (W) 10 sec., which means it gives two white flashes at ten-second intervals. Today lighthouses are also equipped with radio, radio beacons, radio-telephone and radar, and send sound signals in fog and bad visibility.

The history of the lighthouse service is full of heroism and devotion to duty, not only by the men who serve in them, but by those who man the boats carrying their reliefs. Heroines too are part of the story, and all should remember Grace DARLING, whose father was keeper of the Longstone lighthouse off the Northumbrian coast. A great mystery of the lighthouse service was the unlit lamp and missing keepers on Flannan Isle, told in Wilfrid Gibson's poem which begins:

Though three men dwell on Flannan Isle
To keep the lamp alight,
As we steered under the lee, we caught
No glimmer through the night.

Lighthouse tender: a small ship, generally specially designed, engaged in the lighthouse service for carrying supplies and relieving crews of isolated lighthouses and light-ships. The lighthouse tender also services navigation buoys and automatic beacons.

'**Lightning**': name given optimistically to a number of ships, e.g. the first Post Office steam packet, of 205 tons and 80 horsepower (1821); the early Royal Navy steamer of 1823; the 'first real TORPEDO BOAT' (1876), whose speed of $18\frac{1}{2}$ knots was thought by many to have reached the limit in terms of safety; and the 1894 destroyer which rejected their fears by doing another nine knots. But the most celebrated *Lightning* was the great clipper, built (1854) by Donald McKay for the Black Ball Line, reputed to have been the fastest vessel of all these ocean greyhounds. On her maiden voyage from Boston to Liverpool she made a run of 436 miles in 24 hours, a record never surpassed by a sailing ship. Among her commanders were 'Bully' FORBES and Captain Anthony Enright, an equally brilliant seaman with the unexplained nickname of 'Yankee', who had her till 1857. Enright is described as a kindly but rather severe-looking man who looked as if he would have made a good bishop. He 'stuck to his canvas' just as much as 'Bully' Forbes did, and on *Lightning*'s fourth voyage she returned the remarkable figures of 2188 miles in six days. Many incidents concerning her are chronicled. On one occasion a drunken woman passenger set fire to her bonnet and was clapped in irons. On another a carpenter fell over the side but was able to hook his hatchet over the foresheet and hold on till rescued. Enright was known to stop his passengers' food if they disobeyed orders about lights. The ship went out to India with troops during the Mutiny and kept her record for speed to the last. In October 1869, when loading wool in Geelong harbour for the London sales, she went up in flames, probably from internal combustion from ignited wool.

Her life was a short one – only a little over fifteen years from start to finish. But still in the imagination of man she goes plunging on her way through the Roaring Forties, her own special realm of achievement, with royals and stunsails set, the knots reeling out behind her; a sight no more to be seen while the seas endure ...

Cecily Fox Smith, *A Book of Famous Ships* (1924)

Lightning-conductors: slang name for naval full-dress trousers, resplendent with the broad gold stripe down the seams.

Light-room: *see* POWDER MAGAZINE.

Lights, navigation: international maritime law requires ships at night to show distinctive lights. First, there are the most important steaming lights, which vary somewhat with the size of ship and differ for a small sailing vessel. A ship over 45 metres long shows a white light on her fore mast 6 to 12 metres above her hull, visible ahead and $22\frac{1}{2}°$ (or two points) abaft either beam; a similar white light is also shown on her main mast at least $4\frac{1}{2}$ metres higher than the forward light. Then there are the red and green side or bow lights on port and starboard sides respectively. These are set lower than the mast-head white lights and must show ahead and for two points abaft either beam. Vessels under 45 metres long show a single mast-head white light. Small sailing vessels may use a combined three-colour lantern on the mast-head or a combined port and starboard light on the bow and a white stern light. If the sailing vessel is under power these lights will have the addition of a white mast-head light, but the arcs of visibility must conform to the rules. In addition there is a whole series of

267

light regulations for special kinds of ship and for ships engaged in particular activities or in particular situations. Lights for a trawler differ from those for other types of fishing vessel with gear down; lights for vessels towing or under tow vary with the length of tow; hovercraft have distinctive lights, and so do ships not under command and ships at anchor (*see* RIDING LIGHT). There are many combinations of lights of which the sailor must be aware.

See colour section.

Light-ship: a specially designed ship anchored in dangerous waters, manned by a small crew, and serving the same functions as a lighthouse to aid navigation. There are numerous light-ships round the British coasts, especially in shoal waters, e.g. the North, East and South Goodwin light-ships, the first of which was placed there in 1795; the first light-ship to be placed in English waters was at the Nore (1732). The number of light-ships is decreasing, because of their costliness; they are being replaced by automatic beacons.

Ligurian Sea: part of the Mediterranean Sea between the islands of Corsica and Elba and the coast of the Italian Riviera. Its northern part forms the Gulf of Genoa, on which lie the great commercial port of Genoa and the Italian naval base of La Spezia.

Lime dust: a barbarous missile used in early naval engagements. Arrows were fired carrying containers of unslaked lime which burst on impact and, carried on the wind, entered the eyes, causing blindness, temporary or permanent.

Lime juice: *see* SCURVY.

Limey (or **lime-juicer**): American name for the British seaman, an interesting reminder of the days when lime juice was issued as a preventive of scurvy.

The North Goodwin light-ship, from a blacklead sketch by E.W. Cooke, 1875.

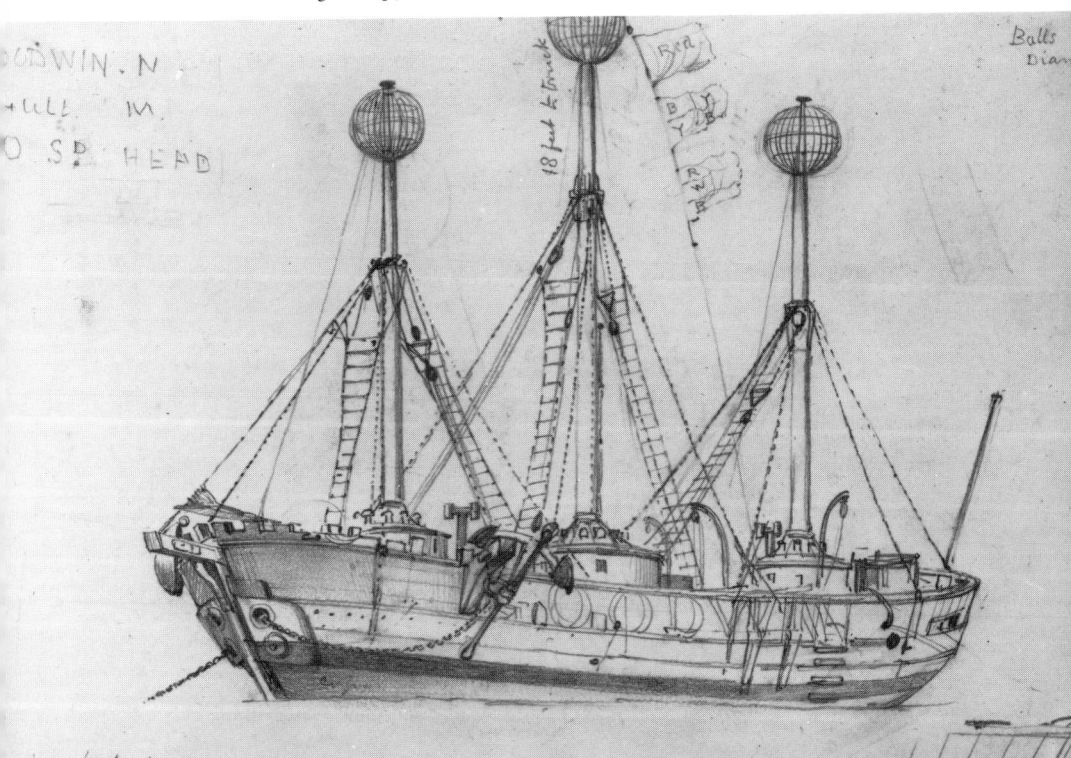

Lind, James (1716–94): naval surgeon and author of medical books. His chief place in naval history lies in his strong advocacy, if not the actual first discovery, of the strong preventive and curative effects of lemon juice on scurvy.

Line, the: (1) the Equator (*see also* CROSSING THE EQUATOR); (2) *see* SHIP OF THE LINE.

Line abreast: the formation and positioning of ships so that they are abeam of one another. Line abreast was the usual formation of the early fighting galleys in Roman and medieval times because they relied on ramming and boarding, attacking on a broad front and so protecting their oarsmen on their sides. When guns came to be placed along the length of the ship, and when the broadside developed, line abreast gradually gave way to LINE AHEAD as the essential battle formation.

Line ahead: the formation and positioning of ships so that they follow one another stem to stern, in other words in single file. The doctrine of line ahead as a battle formation gradually but naturally evolved during the latter part of the 17th century; it was incorporated in the early FIGHTING INSTRUCTIONS and enshrined in the Permanent Fighting Instructions which held so rigid a grip on naval tactics throughout the 18th century. The admiral endeavoured to get to windward of the enemy and then, preserving his line ahead, to bring his ships' broadsides to bear and destroy his opponents. Many of the 18th-century engagements so fought tended to be indecisive (there was no complete and utter defeat of the enemy between the Battle of Barfleur in 1692 and the Battle of the Saints in 1782); and there was controversy between the formalists and those who thought differently, though sometimes those who broke the rules and did not succeed brought disastrous results to themselves. When combined with the GENERAL CHASE, the line ahead could bring success, but it was not until Admiral Rodney at the Battle of the Saints (1782) 'broke his own line, the enemy's line and all the formal rules' that a clear-cut victory was won. His example was soon followed by others, notably by Howe at the Battle of the FIRST OF JUNE (1794) and later by Nelson. Although the shackling effect of the necessity of preserving the line ahead was broken, it survived as a battle formation because of the advent of the rotating gun turret, and it was used in the Battle of Jutland (1916).

Line of battle: the formation and positioning of ships for a naval engagement. From the mid-18th century, when Admiral Anson was at the Admiralty, the line of battle was composed only of ships of the first three rates (*see* RATING OF SHIPS), and for this reason ships so rated came to be known as 'ships of the line'.

Liner: large ship, usually built specifically to carry passengers, belonging to a recognized shipping company (or line) and often operating on fixed routes, though these may change with the season, etc.; e.g. a cruise liner may run to Scandinavia and the Baltic from early June to September and switch to Mediterranean cruises in late summer. Some of the largest and most luxurious ships in the world have been 'liners', e.g. Britain's *QUEEN MARY* and *QUEEN ELIZABETH*, and the French *NORMANDIE* (*see p. 270*).

For 'cargo liner' *see* TRAMP.

Line squall: a sudden violent storm occurring with a rapid change of air-stream

The first-class dining room from the liner *Normandie*; 285 ft long and 33 ft high, it was the largest single room space ever to be put afloat.

and an unusually strong cold front. The squall occurs along a line, sometimes marked by a long roll-cloud looking in the distance like a black arch. It arrives with squalls of cold wind and heavy showers, and within it violent whirlwinds, called waterspouts over the sea, may occur.

'Lion': as might be expected, a name carried in British naval history by a long succession of ships, great and little, noble and not so noble: from the Scottish pirate ship under Andrew Barton, harried to destruction off the Goodwins in Henry VIII's reign, to the 58-gun ship that in 1745 tried to intercept Prince Charles Edward on his way to Scotland and fought the escorting French man-o'-war *Elizabeth* to a standstill; from the merchantman that sailed from Portsmouth for the Gold Coast

in 1553 to the 64-gun royal naval vessel that helped capture the *Guillaume Tell* in 1800; from the privateer cutter of 1803 to Beatty's flag-ship in 1916.

The lion is also among the most common figureheads of early Royal Navy ships: for a long period it was used on all men-o'-war below second rate.

List: the inclining or heeling of a vessel to one side, caused by unequal loading, shifting of the cargo, or the intake of water after damage.

Lists, Navy: *see* NAVY LISTS.

'Little Edward': perhaps the earliest sea-going vessel belonging to London for which documentary evidence survives. In 1315 John Brand is recorded as taking the ship from London to Antwerp with 120 half-sacks of wool.

Liverpool: the great port and city on the Mersey which overcame its original natural disadvantages to become second only to London in the nation's sea-borne trade. The opening up of trade with the Americas in the 18th century gave Liverpool her first great opportunities, and much of her early prosperity was based on the SLAVE TRADE. In the 19th century the Industrial Revolution, and the growth of Lancashire's industries in particular, made Liverpool the great outlet for British manufactured goods; the docks were extended and the population increased rapidly. Liverpool's position on the N.W. approaches to Britain has been of the greatest maritime importance.

Liverpool packet: a ship operating out of Liverpool at regular intervals carrying mail, goods and passengers.

Now the *Dreadnought*'s a-sailing up Long
    Island Sound,
With the flags all a-flying and boats all
    around.
With our wives and our sweethearts, oh, soon
    we shall be,
Drinking luck to the *Dreadnought* wherever
    she may be.

Chorus:
Bound away, bound away where the wild
    waters flow!
She's a Liverpool packet – oh Lord, let her
    go!
            From an old sea song

Lizard: (1) a short rope with an eye at the end to enable it to run along another rope or stay; (2) *see* LIZARD POINT.

Lizard Point (or **The Lizard**): the most southerly point of Cornwall, a formidable

headland which was once the scene of many wrecks. Its name means in Gaelic 'the point of the high fort'. On the Lizard Peninsula at Poldhu Marconi sent and received the first transatlantic radio messages (1901). The Lizard lighthouse is one of the biggest in England, stands 230 ft above the sea, and flashes white once every three seconds.

LL sweep: *see* MINESWEEPER.

Lloyd's (of London): corporation and ancient institution where all forms of insurance except life assurance can be arranged. The corporation does not itself subscribe policies, but each of its members, whose reputation and financial standing must be impeccable, can sign for a specified sum for which he is responsible. The security of a Lloyd's policy is virtually impregnable. A particularly important part of the corporation's business, recognized throughout the world, is the collection and diffusion of information about the sea and its affairs. Its stations and agencies all over the globe exist not only for this purpose, but to give assistance when casualties occur, to assess cargo values etc. *See also* A1 AT LLOYD'S; LUTINE BELL; INSURANCE.

The history of Lloyd's goes back to Edward Lloyd (*fl.*1688–1726), whose London coffee-house, first in Tower Street, then in Lombard Street, became a centre for shipbroking business, marine insurance and shipping intelligence. *Lloyd's News* on these subjects was issued

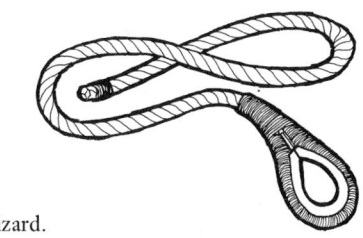

Lizard.

1696–7; it was revived in the 18th century as *Lloyd's Lists* and still continues.

It is an interesting example of the deep roots of Lloyd's maritime business that its present-day policy of marine insurance can be traced to a type of transaction found in Florence in 1523. Lloyd's possesses a policy in the name of the *Golden Fleece*, insured in 1600 for a voyage from Lisbon to Venice for £1200 at 4 per cent. Another extraordinary document treasured by the corporation is a policy effected at Lloyd's on the life of Napoleon:

> In consideration of three guineas per one hundred pounds, and according to that rate for every greater or lesser sum received of William Dorrington, we have hereunto subscribed our names, and do for our respective heirs and ourselves, executors, administrators, and assigns of the other or others of us, assume, engage, and promise that we respectively, or our several respective heirs, executors, administrators or assigns, shall or will pay or cause to be paid unto the said William Dorrington, the sum and sums of money which we have hereunto respectively subscribed our names: without any abatement whatsoever, in case Napoleon Bonaparte shall cease to exist, or be taken prisoner on or before the 21st June, 1813.

> £100 R. Heath
> £150 Anthony Finn Kemp
> £150 B. I. Mitchell

Loadlines (or **Plimsoll marks**): markings which by international convention must be made conspicuous on each side of the hull of every merchant ship. They consist of a circle with a horizontal line through it; this line, which is parallel to the ship's upper deck, marks the depth to which the ship may legally be loaded for the open sea. The distance between that line and the upper deck is the freeboard. The circle has the letters L R against it, standing for Lloyd's Register, by whom the marks are assigned. Other lines close by the

circle give different permitted loading levels according to different circumstances, for a ship will float at different levels according to the kind of water and its specific gravity. Thus different loadlines are marked by T F for Tropical Fresh Water, F for Fresh Water, T for Tropical Salt Water, S for Summer Salt Water, W for Winter Salt Water and WNA for Winter North Atlantic. So a ship is said to be 'down to her marks' when fully laden for the voyage she is making or about to make. *See also* PLIMSOLL, SAMUEL.

Loadstone: *see* LODESTONE.

Loblolly-boy: sick-bay attendant. Loblolly was the seaman's name for gruel or porridge, a diet perhaps associated with the sick-bay.

Locker: general name for any enclosed space for stowing gear; specifically used when designed for a particular purpose, e.g. ammunition locker, flag locker, kit locker, cable locker.

Locker, William (1731–1800): Royal Navy captain and (from 1793) Lieutenant-Governor of Greenwich Hospital. His chief claim to fame is that he gave Nelson his first command, a small captured vessel that Nelson renamed *Lucy* in honour of Locker's daughter (1777); and that, according to Nelson himself, he first taught the young officer how to fight a Frenchman.

> I have been your scholar; it is you who taught me to board a Frenchman ... it is you who always told me, 'Lay a Frenchman close and you will beat him.'
>
> Nelson to Captain Locker

Lodestone (or **loadstone**): iron ore that shows polar magnetism; hence figuratively something that guides.

Lofoten Islands: an archipelago of mountainous and mainly bare islands off the N.W. coast of Norway and forming the western arm of the Vest Fjord. Though well within the Arctic Circle the islands are able to support a few farming settlements because of the moderating effects of the North Atlantic Drift, but the main activity is fishing. In late winter and early spring the islands' fishing boats and many from the south catch the great shoals of cod which arrive to spawn in the surrounding waters. The taking of the fish, preparation, drying, extraction of cod-liver oil, freezing and dispatch occupy thousands of the islanders.

Log (book): daily record giving, when kept fully, a detailed account of a ship's movements and speed, weather encountered, signals, duties carried out, encounters etc. Some logs were official and obligatory, e.g. the Captain's log in the Royal Navy, which was handed in at the end of the cruise and remained as an invaluable historical record. Other officers often maintained them for their own and their families' pleasure and it was part of a midshipman's training to keep a good log, regularly examined and signed by one of the officers. Many of these are beautifully illustrated with water-colour drawings of foreign ports, track charts, diagrams of equipment etc. and are much prized by collectors. There are important collections of ships' logs at the Public Record Office and the National Maritime Museum, London, much used by students of naval history. Some have been published, notably *Logs of the Great Sea Fights 1794–1805* (2 vols., Navy Records Society, 1899–1900).

A good, though fictionalized, account of the keeping of the log on H.M. ships in Nelson's time occurs in Dudley Pope's *Governor Ramage, R.N.* (1973):

> He went down to his cabin again, found he'd forgotten to collect the master's log and sent his steward for it. Irritating how much paperwork was needed to keep a ship afloat, but at least the log served an obviously useful purpose. Every two months a parcel of documents had to be prepared for dispatch to the Admiralty and the Navy Board, and in every third parcel, among other lists and reports, were the captain's journal and the master's log.
>
> They were usually almost identical, which was hardly surprising since they were both based on the same source: the large slate kept in the binnacle box, and which was used to record wind direction, courses steered and speed and distances made good, either every hour or when any of them changed. An hourly diary of the ship's life, in fact.
>
> Southwick [the Master] took the slate down to his cabin every day, copied the details into his log and added other items of information concerning the ship and her crew, wiped the slate clean, and returned it to the binnacle, where the quarter-master could reach it easily. Every day, like every other captain of a King's ship, Ramage took the master's log as the basis for his journal entry, adding any other information likely to be needed for reference or required by regulations.

Log-line: line attached to the LOG-SHIP, for centuries the chief method of determining a ship's speed. The log-line, often 150 fathoms in length, was unreeled over the stern for a fixed period of time, measured by a sand-glass. At first the line runout was carefully measured; later it was marked with knots at calculated intervals. The length between knots had to be the same fraction of a nautical mile (formerly 6080 ft) as the sand-glass was of an hour; then counting the number of knots run out in the time taken by the sand to run from top to bottom would give the number of nautical miles run per hour. This is the reason why a ship's speed is still given in 'knots'. *See also* INSTRUMENTS.

Log-ship (or **log-chip**): the piece of wood used with the LOG-LINE. It was the shape of the sector of a circle and was weighted along the arc so that it always floated point upwards when thrown overboard.

London: *see* LONDON RIVER; PORT OF LONDON.

'London': of the many ships, merchantmen and Royal Navy, that have carried this name, perhaps the best-remembered are the vessel that blew up off the Nore (1665), replaced a year later by the equally ill-fated *Loyal London*; Parker's flag-ship at Copenhagen (1801), from which he gave the famous signal that Nelson could not see with his blind eye; the 90-gun battleship at the bombardment of Sevastopol in 1854; and the ill-fated emigrant ship which was lost in the Bay of Biscay in 1866 on her way from Plymouth to Australia. Among the more than 200 lost were the captain, six stowaways, and the well-known Shakespearean actor Gustavus Vaughan Brooke, who laboured heroically at the pumps in an effort to save the ship. A major cause of the disaster was that the hatches were so inefficiently protected that, as the vessel rolled, water ran into the engine and boiler rooms and extinguished the fires. Designers thereafter paid much more attention to this danger.

London River: mariners' name for the River Thames, its docks, pools, reaches and all its estuary used by shipping. *See* PORT OF LONDON.

The broad inlet of the shallow North Sea passes gradually into the contracted shape of the river; but for a long time the feeling of the open water remains with the ship steering to the westward through one of the lighted and buoyed passage-ways of the Thames, such as Queen's Channel, Prince's Channel, Four-Fathom Channel; or else coming down the Swin from the north.

Joseph Conrad, *The Mirror of the Sea* (1906)

London waggon: the tender that, in the days of the press-gang, took the victims down river from the Tower of London to receiving ships.

Long-boat: the largest boat carried by a sailing ship.

Long Island: the large island off the E. coast of the U.S.A. on which stands part of New York city; separated from the mainland by Long Island Sound, the Narrows of New York Bay and the East River. It was first settled by the Dutch and English and became English in 1664.

Longitude: angular distance, measured in degrees, minutes and seconds, between the meridian of Greenwich and the meridian at the point of observation. The accurate determination of longitude was a great difficulty for the early sailors, and was not really satisfactorily solved until the development of the chronometer in the 18th century.

Long sea (more correctly **long swell**): waves formed by past wind or wind at a distance. A swell is said to be long when the distance between each successive top of the swell is large.

Long ship: type of sea-going ship used during the VIKING period. How 'long' they could be at maximum is still a matter for debate. The 9th-century GOKSTAD SHIP was 79 ft long, and the OSEBERG SHIP was 70·5 ft. Olaf Trygvason's *Long Serpent*, built at Trondheim in A.D. 99 was about 140 ft over-all (114 ft in the keel), but seems to have been a failure; and a long ship belonging to King Canute and described as about 250–300 ft must be classed with the Norse legends. It should be remembered that 19th-century shipbuilders, with much greater facilities, rarely built wooden ships beyond about 250 ft. *See also* RUM (2).

A Viking gravestone from Gotland illustrating a contemporary long ship.

Longships, the: famous lighthouse on a very dangerous reef about a mile offshore from Land's End. The present lighthouse stands 117 ft above the sea and is an occulting light, that is, the duration of the light is longer than the dark phase; it shows white to seaward and red to landward every fifteen seconds.

Longshoreman: a landsman employed on the shore, e.g. at fishing, stevedoring etc. The word is an abbreviation of 'along the shore man'.

Loom: part of the OAR near the grip and inboard from the rowlock.

'Lord Clyde': steam frigate built in the 1860s, one of the last armour-plated wooden ships. At the same time, she was the first vessel in the British Navy to mount an armour-plated bow battery on the main deck. Her armour was nowhere less than $4\frac{1}{2}$ in. and at the waterline was $5\frac{1}{2}$ in.

Lord High Admiral: later form of the title Lord Admiral or High Admiral; it came into use in the 14th century.

'Lord's Own, The': nickname for H.M.S. *Vengeance*, from the Biblical text 'Vengeance is mine. I will repay, saith the Lord'.

Lorient: *see* ST NAZAIRE.

Louis, Thomas: *see MINOTAUR.*

Louisburg (or **Louisbourg**): a town at the N.E. end of Cape Breton Island, Nova Scotia, Canada. It was built as a strongly fortified port by the French to command the entrance to the St Lawrence when they had to cede Newfoundland and Acadia to the British by the Treaty of Utrecht (1713). For half a century Louisburg was a key town in the long struggle of the British and

French in North America. In the War of the Austrian Succession it was captured by a force from New England (1745) but was returned to the French at the Treaty of Aix-la-Chapelle (1748). During the Seven Years' War it was recaptured (1758) by Colonel (later General) Amherst helped by naval forces under Admiral Boscawen. The fortifications were destroyed and the French population moved, so that Louisburg ceased to be a threat to the British in the north-east of the continent.

Lower deck: formerly the general naval name for all members of the ship's company who were not officers, so named because the lower decks were where they were quartered; antithesis of 'upper deck' or 'quarter-deck', meaning those of officer rank.

Lower mast: the lower part of the MAST; it carried the lower sails and was inserted ('stepped') in the bottom of the ship.

Lowestoft, Battle of (3 June 1665): first important naval action of the Second Dutch War (1665–7). At least twelve Dutch ships were destroyed and fourteen captured. It is alleged that the Duchess of York, concerned for the safety of her husband, the Lord High Admiral (later JAMES II), caused him to break off the pursuit instead of following up and inflicting even greater damage.

'Loyal London': second-rate ship of 96 guns built at Deptford by Captain John Taylor and launched in 1666, as a gift from the City of London to replace the earlier *London*, which blew up off the Nore (1665). A notable feature of the *Loyal London* was the lavish gilding and carved work. She was burnt by the Dutch in the MEDWAY (1667). A splendid contemporary model of her is

owned by the Elder Brethren of Trinity House.

L sweep: *see* MINESWEEPER.

Lubber: *see* LANDLUBBER.

Lubber's hole: a space through which a 'lubber' wriggled at the top of the lower mast of a sailing ship, thus avoiding a more difficult movement round the futtock shrouds.

I was afraid to venture, and then he proposed that I should go through the lubber's hole, which he said had been made for people like me. I agreed to attempt it, as it appeared more easy, and at last arrived, quite out of breath, and very happy to find myself in the main-top.

Captain Marryat, *Peter Simple* (1834)

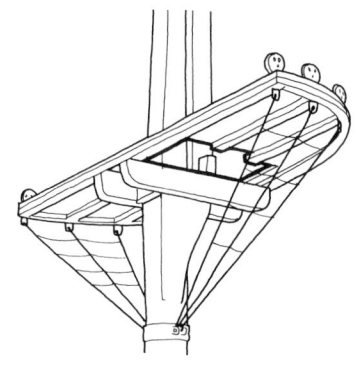

Lubber's line: a line or pointer on the steering compass marking the position of the ship's head.

Lübeck: city and port on the Baltic coast of West Germany, close to the border with East Germany. It was one of Europe's most important trading towns in the Middle Ages and played a leading role in the HANSEATIC LEAGUE.

Lucas, Charles Davis (*fl.c.*1854): admiral. When serving as mate on the paddle steamer H.M.S. *Hector* during the attack on Bomarsund (June 1854) in the Crimean War, he picked up a live shell that had fallen on deck and hurled it overboard. For his heroism he was awarded the first Victoria Cross ever granted. By a coincidence, his commander on that occasion, Admiral Sir William Hutcheon Hall (?1797–1878), has a memorial in the same church as Lucas, at Mereworth in Kent.

Luff: to sail a ship nearer to the wind by putting the tiller to the lee side. As a noun the word is used in many phrases, and can also mean the leading edge of a SAIL or the broadest point of a ship's bows before they narrow to the stern.

'Luff now, all you can, quarter-master,' cried the captain. 'Send the men aft directly. My lads, there is no time for words – I am going to club-haul the ship, for there is no room to wear. The only chance you have of safety is to be cool, watch my eye, and execute my orders with precision.'

Captain Marryat, *Peter Simple* (1834)

Lugger: a small fast sailing vessel with two masts, and sometimes a small mizen, carrying lug sails and a triangular jib. The

lugger was useful for carrying stores and was favoured by smugglers. 'Once aboard the lugger and the girl is mine' is a popular misquotation from *The Gypsy Farmer* by John Benn Johnstone (1803–91).

But, even some thirty years back, a share or two in the *Tiger*, *Early Morn*, *Fly*, or *Hawk* lugger was a nice little property for a retired pilot or widow... Each lugger has her own capstan, with a little black wooden shed near it on the beach, where the leading men of her crew keep their sea-armour, with one or two spyglasses, lanterns, etc. In summer, a bird-cage gives a homelike look to these watch-houses; and I fancy years ago the boatmen almost lived in such huts, and thus got the name of hovellers.

A woodcut of Lübeck from the *Nuremberg Chronicle*, 1493.

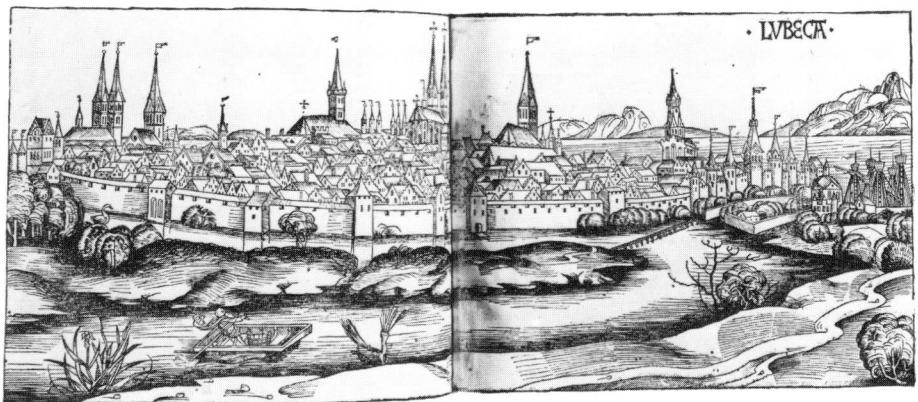

The crews only sail the lugger, sharing two-thirds of her earnings; the owners receiving the other.

R. C. Leslie, *A Sea-Painter's Log* (1886)

Lug sail: a type of four-sided sail slung from a yard at a third or a quarter of its length from the forward end so that it hangs obliquely.

'Lusitania': a CUNARD passenger liner sunk off Ireland (7 May 1915) by a German submarine with a loss of 1198 lives. The world-wide outrage caused by this act of barbarism was a potent factor in bringing America into the First World War.

Lutine Bell: bell in the Underwriters' Room at LLOYD'S, rung once upon the announcement of a ship being lost, and twice when an overdue ship is reported safe. The bell was taken from H.M.S. *Lutine* (32 guns), which was wrecked off Vlieland in 1799 with the total loss of her crew. She was carrying upwards of £1,000,000 in bullion and money, some of which was still being salvaged in the 1870s. She was formerly *La Lutine* and had been captured by Admiral Duncan.

Lyme Regis: small town on the Dorset coast, today a tourist resort, but once an important port. The jetty of the harbour, known as the Cobb, was the scene of the Duke of Monmouth's landing before the Battle of Sedgemoor (1685), which ended his attempted rebellion.

Macassar, Strait of

Macassar, Strait of: a long channel between Borneo and Celebes in the East Indies, named after the town of Macassar in the latter island. Macassar oil, once much favoured for dressing the hair, led to the introduction of the Victorian anti-macassar for protecting the backs of chairs. In the Second World War the Macassar Strait was the scene of a five-day attack (January 1942) by American and Dutch air and naval forces on a Japanese force carrying troops who landed and occupied Borneo.

McClintock, Sir Francis Leopold (1819–1907): admiral. From 1848 to 1852 he was in the Arctic with Ross, Ommaney and Belcher. In 1859, commanding the *Fox*, a small ship fitted out by Lady Franklin, he finally established the fate of Sir John FRANKLIN. His book describing that discovery, *The Voyage of the 'Fox' in Arctic Seas*, first published in 1859 and dedicated to Lady Franklin, has been reprinted many times and is a classic of polar exploration. He served in other naval spheres for half a century.

I am commanded by my Lords Commissioners of the Admiralty to acquaint you that, in consideration of the important services performed by you in bringing home the only authentic intelligence of the death of the late Sir John Franklin, and of the fate of the crews of the 'Erebus' and 'Terror', Her Majesty has been pleased ... to sanction the time during which you were absent on these discoveries in the Arctic Regions, viz., from the 30th June, 1857, to the 21st September, 1859, to reckon as time served by a captain in command of one of Her Majesty's ships.

> W. G. Romaine, Secretary to the
> Admiralty, to McClintock
> (24 October 1859)

McClure, Sir Robert John le Mesurier (1807–73): admiral, chiefly associated with Arctic voyages and exploration, though he also served in the West Indies, on the China station etc. Commanding the *Investigator* in the search for Sir John Franklin, he proved the existence of the NORTH-WEST PASSAGE (1850); but after many hardships the ship had to be abandoned in the ice in Mercy Bay (1853). For this McClure was court-martialled on his return to England (1854) but was honourably acquitted.

McFee, William (1881–1966): writer of stories and essays about the sea. Having trained as a mechanical engineer, he went to sea and became a Chief Engineer; and a Chief Engineer is the main character in several of his stories, some of which were *Casuals of the Sea* (1916), *Captain Macedoine's Daughter* (1920), *Sailors of Fortune* (1929) and *The Beachcomber* (1935).

McKay, Donald (1810–80): most famous of American shipbuilders, especially of clippers. Born near Shelburne, Nova Scotia, he worked as a shipwright in a number of yards, gradually building up a reputation as a designer, until Enoch Train, owner of a line of packet ships running between Boston and Liverpool, persuaded him to open a yard at Boston, where he became famous. F. W. Wallace tells us that 'he designed and built more wooden clippers than any other constructor, and almost every vessel he fashioned made a name for herself.' Among them were the *FLYING CLOUD*, the *Sovereign of* *the Seas*, the *LIGHTNING*, the *JAMES BAINES*, the *Champion of the Seas*, the *Donald McKay*, the *GREAT REPUBLIC* and the *GLORY OF THE SEAS*. In all, McKay designed and built 42 ships.

His bust is enshrined in the Louvre, his designs are the admiration of naval architects, but the story of the ships he built and their wonderful passages are golden pages in the history of shipping destined to live for all time.

Frederick William Wallace, *Wooden Ships and Iron Men*

Mackenzie, Daniel Tremendous (*b.*1794): baby born on board H.M.S. *Tremendous*, his mother being present at the Battle of the 'Glorious' FIRST OF JUNE (1794). In 1848 Mackenzie received the Naval General Service Medal with the appropriate clasp, rated 'Baby'.

McKenzie, Captain George (1798–1876): sometimes termed 'the Father of Nova Scotia shipping'. Physically strong, of limitless energy and daring, he became famous not only as a shipbuilder but as a magnificent seaman. Scorning to 'snug down' at the threat of heavy weather, 'he hung out his canvas' to the last minute and drove his ships under all the sail they could carry, night or day, storm or shine. But he was such a good seaman that in all his voyaging he never lost a man overboard. On one occasion he was a passenger in the paddle liner *Atlantic* when her machinery broke down and she tried to battle on under sail to Halifax in the teeth of westerly gales. Her captain eventually accepted McKenzie's advice, chopped off the paddles to make the ship more manageable, swung her round for Liverpool and brought her safely in after being given up for lost.

McLeod, John (?1777–1820): naval surgeon who packed a good deal into a short life. In his early years he served on a slaver and was tried for piracy. More respectably, he was surgeon on the royal yacht *Royal Sovereign* (1818–20), and, having accompanied MAXWELL, he contributed to the annals of discovery with his *Narrative of a Voyage in His Majesty's late Ship 'Alceste' to the Yellow Sea, along the coast of Korea* (1817) and *A Voyage to Africa* (1820).

McMurdo Sound: a great channel leading off the Ross Sea and running between Ross Island and the Antarctic coast. It features prominently in the story of Antarctic exploration from the days of Sir James Clark Ross, who discovered it (1841), to modern times, when Sir Vivian Fuchs completed his crossing of the continent at McMurdo (1958). Here Captain Scott and Sir Ernest Shackleton made bases, and here the Americans established an important Antarctic research station (1955).

'Macquarie': famous iron sailing ship, built (1875) at Greens' Blackwall yard. She began life as the *Melbourne* and finished as the *Fortuna*, a coal hulk. In her pride she was a full-rigged ship, 269·8 ft by 40·1, with a depth in the hold of 23·7 ft. As well as her considerable loading capacity, she could carry 60–70 passengers under her 69-ft poop and even offered bathing facilities. In 1887 she was bought by Messrs Devitt & Moore and renamed *Macquarie*. Among her commanders was Captain Goddard, a well-known character who was always sea-sick going down Channel, even in mild weather, was a stickler for religious observances and never allowed washing to be hung out on Sundays. The *Macquarie* was converted into a cadet sail-training ship and enjoyed much success in that capacity. Many

stories are told of a petty officer named McGregor who would go into the cadets' quarters at the beginning of the day, remove his cap and courteously ask the young gentlemen to turn out. He then carried out an elaborate ritual of resettling his hat at the right angle, by which time every cadet was supposed to be out and about; otherwise his manner changed with remarkable abruptness. He once fell down the main hatch and broke his arm but rejected all offers of help from the cadets with the stern exhortation: 'Who the hell told you to knock off work? Get back to your jobs and come back at twelve. I can wait.' The ship was bought by the Wallarah Coal Company in 1909 for use as a coal hulk in Sydney Harbour.

'Mad Charlie': *see* NAPIER, SIR CHARLES.

Madras: town and port, once a chief post of the East India Company, on the E. coast of India. Formerly known as the Coromandel Coast, this area was the scene of great commercial and maritime rivalry between Britain and France during the 18th century. During the War of the Austrian Succession (1740–48) Madras was taken by the French in 1746 but was returned at the Treaty of Aix-la-Chapelle two years later. Thomas Griffin, and later Edward Boscawen, were the admirals operating the British squadrons off the coast at that time. The struggle with the French was renewed during the Seven Years' War (1756–63), when Madras was again besieged, but the arrival of reinforcements under the future Admiral Kempenfelt caused them to retire. At the same time Admiral Charles Watson, whose brilliant naval tactics are little remembered, was giving splendid naval support to Robert Clive in maintaining a British hold on India.

Britain's control was again challenged by the famous French admiral Suffren off the Coromandel Coast during the War of American Independence (1776–83). Suffren was opposed by Admiral Sir Edward Hughes, whose dogged fighting, although not crowned with great victories, was sufficient to withstand the French until the declaration of peace.

281

Maelstrom: an often dangerous strait to the south of the LOFOTEN ISLANDS. The word means a whirlpool, and swirling currents occur when wind and tide are at variance. It was much feared in earlier times, and its supposed dangers were the subject of many a sailor's yarn.

Magazine: *see* POWDER MAGAZINE.

'Magdelayne': vessel named by Chaucer as belonging to the shipman of DART-MOUTH, who

knew alle the havenes, as they were,
Fro Gootlond to the cape of Fynystere,
And every cryke in Britaigne and in Spayne.

> Prologue to *The Canterbury Tales* (*c*.1387)

There are records that there was a ship from Dartmouth called the *Magdelayne* in the late 14th century.

Magellan, Strait of: a winding, treacherous and stormy passage linking the Atlantic and the Pacific at the southern extremity of South America and separating Tierra del Fuego from the mainland. It is named after Ferdinand Magellan, who discovered it in August 1520. A year previously Magellan had set out with five ships on the King of Spain's commission to find a western route to the Spice Islands of Asia as an alternative to the eastern route round Africa, which was under the control of the Portuguese. The strong tides and tidal streams, the mists and fogs and the contrary winds caused Magellan's remaining three ships to take 38 days to force the passage, although it is only about 320 miles long (*see also* CIRCUMNAVIGATION). The forbidding nature of the Strait for sailing ships made it greatly feared, and in later years many preferred to go further south and sail round Cape Horn. With the advent of the steamer the Strait of Magellan was more easily navigated and was frequently used until the opening (1914) of the PANAMA CANAL.

Magellan jacket: old name for the watch-keeping coat with a hood. Tradition has it that it was first used by Captain Cook's crews.

Maggie Miller: mythical laundress on the old sailing ships who did the washing when the dirty clothes were towed through the sea on a line.

Magnetic poles: positions on the earth's surface which are centres of its magnetism and to which a magnetic compass points rather than to true north and south. The magnetic poles lie in northern Canada and in Antarctica and are themselves variable over the years. There is thus an angular distance between magnetic north, shown by a magnetic compass, and TRUE NORTH. This is known as the variation of the compass or magnetic variation and is shown on charts for various parts of the world; it has to be allowed for in setting a true course.

Magnetic variation: *see* MAGNETIC POLES.

'Magnificent': one of the battleships which in name and style typified late Victorian naval supremacy. Completed in 1895, she had a belt of 9-in. steel armour, increased to 10–14 in. for her main guns. With a coal capacity of 2200 tons, she exceeded her designed speed of $17\frac{1}{2}$ knots. Her great height of superstructure added to her imposing appearance.

Mahan, Alfred Thayer (1840–1914): American admiral and naval historian. An officer with active experience, a well-known lecturer, a student of immense energy and powers of memory, he produced several works which commanded world-wide respect and greatly influenced naval policy. The most famous is *The Influence of Sea Power upon History, 1660–1783* (1890), followed in 1892 by *The Influence of Sea Power upon the French Revolution and Empire, 1793–1812* and in 1897 by *The Life of Nelson*. He served for 40 years in the United States Navy, beginning with the Civil War, when he designed a 'mystery ship'. He saw the surest hope of world peace in Anglo-American understanding and naval supremacy. One of his biographers called him 'a deeply religious man, high-minded, chivalrous and unassuming. As an exponent of sea power he had no peer in the annals of literature' (Charles Carlisle Tay). His most quoted passage describes the blockade of the French ports by the British Navy during the Napoleonic Wars; *see* BLOCKADE.

Mahogany: *see* TIMBER.

Mail: *see* PACKET-BOAT.

Main: adjective of frequent occurrence in nautical terminology, e.g. 'main brace', rope attached to the main yard; 'main course', the mainsail of a square-rigged ship; 'main deck', deck below the spar deck in a man-o'-war; 'main mast', the principal mast; 'main-stay', the stay from the main top to the foot of the fore mast; 'main top', platform above the head of the lower section of the main mast; 'main yard', yard or spar on which the mainsail is extended. 'Mainsail' is often pronounced 'mainsl'.

Main, the: old term, often poetical, for the ocean or high seas. The Spanish Main was the N.E. coast of South America and the adjacent Caribbean Sea.

And the little *Revenge* herself went down by
  the island crags
To be lost evermore in the main.

Tennyson, 'The *Revenge*'

'Maine': U.S. armoured cruiser (described as a second-class battleship), authorized in 1886 and sent to Havana for political reasons in 1898. There, with a loss of 265 lives, she blew up at her moorings. The cause of the explosion was never finally established: it was widely attributed to the Spaniards, but an investigation in 1911 is said to have revealed its origin in the ship's magazines. The disaster was a contributory cause of the Spanish-American War of 1898–9.

Mainwaring, Henry (*fl*.1610–20): pirate. In a burst of courage, he cut up the Newfoundland fishing fleet in 1614. Later, he plundered the Spanish and Portuguese coasts. Acting on the principle of setting a thief to catch a thief, James I granted him a pardon and he was sent in command of a squadron against the Barbary corsairs. Mainwaring, however, betrayed his trust and joined up with the pirates.

Make: a verb used in many nautical phrases, e.g. 'make sail', to get under way; 'make water', to take in water because of a leak in the hull; 'make fast', to secure; 'make way', to move through the water; 'make one's number', originally to identify one's ship by hoisting her identifying letters, now used colloquially meaning to report one's presence or arrival. For 'make heavy weather' *see* WEATHER.

Make and mend: an afternoon free from duty, originally to allow men to make and mend their clothes and given once a week; now sometimes allowed twice a week or occasionally to compensate for extra work.

283

Malacca, Straits of: a long strait lying between the Malay Peninsula and the island of Sumatra, taking its name from the port of Malacca. For centuries this waterway has been a focal point for the sea-borne trade to and from Asia. The Portuguese were the first of the western maritime nations to establish themselves in the Straits. In the latter half of the 17th century they were replaced by the Dutch, and then in the next two centuries by the British. During the period of great rivalry between the Dutch, French and British East India Companies the command and protection of the Straits called for great maritime effort. Malacca, the chief port, was superseded by the development of Singapore, which today is one of the world's greatest trading harbours, commanding the southern entrance to the Straits.

Malaga, Battle of (13 August 1704): the only fleet action of the War of the Spanish Succession, fought off Malaga, an important port on the Mediterranean coast of southern Spain, soon after the capture of Gibraltar by Admiral Sir George Rooke (23–4 July). Louis XIV, intent on its recapture, sent out the French Mediterranean fleet under the Comte de Toulouse, who managed to interpose his ships between Rooke's Anglo-Dutch fleet and the Rock. Rooke, short of ammunition, dinted the line but failed to break through, resolving to try again the next day. He was spared the necessity: under cover of night, the enemy, despite all their advantages, slipped away, leaving Rooke with Gibraltar and his reputation intact. But, although no ships had been captured, there were many casualties and much damage on both sides in the battle.

Malta: a small, but historically famous, island south of Sicily in the Central Mediterranean, occupied in turn by the successive maritime powers of the Mediterranean and by the KNIGHTS OF MALTA. The island's splendid Grand Harbour at Valletta grew into an almost impregnable fortress; but Napoleon on his way to Egypt in 1798 captured and garrisoned the island. For two years Malta was blockaded and besieged by the British, but surrendered in September 1800. Thereafter the island remained British, being formally annexed at the Treaty in 1814, after which it became an important base for the Mediterranean Fleet. The vital role of the island was demonstrated in the Second World War when, in spite of devastating air attacks, Malta held out and was awarded the George Cross for its valour. Sustaining Malta between 1939 and 1945 was costly in ships and men, and the passage of the relieving convoys was achieved at great sacrifice. Malta achieved independence in 1963; its commanding position still makes it important for the navies of the North Atlantic Treaty Organization (*see also* MEDITERRANEAN SEA).

Man, to: to furnish with a proper crew, or to take the fore-ordered place of duty, e.g. at the helm, the capstan, the guns, the hawser, the SIDE, the sheets, the YARDS, the ship's boats etc.

Manaccan: village south of Falmouth, Cornwall, near Helston River. It has no claim to seafaring history except for a delightful story of an unknown sailor who spoke up boldly from one of the church pews on a matter of professional concern to him.

The parson was dealing with the story of Paul's shipwreck at Malta, including the words: 'Then fearing lest we should have fallen upon rocks, they cast four anchors out of the stern, and wished for the day.' He was somewhat startled when a robust voice from the pews said: 'All wrong! Bad seamanship!' In the sailor's experience, anchors should have gone from the bows, so that the ship would not foul the cables.

Manger: roughly triangular space aft of the ship's stem, with a bulkhead or movable partition designed to keep water from the hawse-holes from running over the deck. 'It masqueraded at times as the ship's farmyard, pigs and other animals being kept in it' (Nepean Longridge, *The Anatomy of Nelson's Ships*, 1955).

Manifest: the detailed list of a ship's cargo, presented to customs officers etc.

Manila: (1) capital and chief port of the PHILIPPINE ISLANDS, part of the Spanish Empire from 1564 to 1898 (*see* MANILA GALLEONS). In 1762, during the Seven Years' War, Manila was captured by a British fleet, but in the following year, at the signing of the peace, it was returned to Spain. In 1898 a Spanish fleet of eight ships was destroyed in Manila Bay by the Americans under Commodore Dewey, and the city was occupied.

(2) A type of ROPE made from plant fibres, taking its name from the town. Manila rope is made in three qualities or grades and does not need tarring as it is not affected by seawater.

Manila galleons (also called ACAPULCO GALLEONS): Manila was the point at which the Spanish gathered their galleons to ship treasure and valuable cargoes across the Pacific to Acapulco in Mexico for onward transmission to Spain.

During the struggle with Spain in the War of the Austrian Succession, ANSON captured one of these great treasure ships

off the Philippines (20 June 1743). By the time of the fight, the six ships with which he had set out were reduced to one, the *Centurion*, but in a ninety-minute battle he overcame the great Spanish galleon *Nuestra Señora de Covadonga* and captured a fortune. Anson's share of the prize money made him rich for life.

By this time the particulars of the cargo of the galleon were well ascertained, and it was found that she had on board 1,313,843 pieces of eight, and 35,682 oz. of virgin silver, besides some cochineal, and a few other commodities, which, however, were but of small account in comparison of the specie.

Richard Walter, *A Voyage Round the World* (1748)

Man-of-war (invariably shortened to **man-o'-war**): a warship. It is one of the idiosyncrasies of the English language that men-o'-war continue to be 'she'.

Manrope: a rope secured along a gangway or companion ladder etc., to be grasped like a bannister to give a safe hold. For the manrope knot *see* KNOTS.

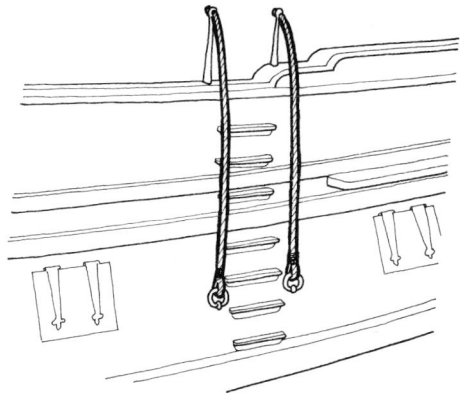

'Marco Polo': famous clipper-type vessel laid down by James Smith at St John, New Brunswick, about 1850; registered tonnage 1625, length 185 ft, breadth 38 ft, depth of hold amidships 30 ft. Though often described as a clipper, she was built as a timber drogher (normally a fairly slow coaster), but was very sharp under the water and, though lofty and box-like, hollow-bowed and very fast. Her first run was to Liverpool with timber, made, it is said, in 15 days. After being bought by 'Paddy McGee ... rag man and marine store dealer' of Liverpool, she was taken over by James Baines of the Black Ball Line of Australian packets and refitted for passengers. On Sunday, 4 July 1852, commanded by the famous Captain 'Bully' FORBES, she left for Melbourne with a crew of 60 and 930 emigrants. Before Forbes left he boasted that he would have her back in the Mersey within six months, and he made good his promise, being 5 months and 21 days on the round voyage. Over one spell of four days she covered 1344 miles, averaging 336 miles a day. Visitors to Salthouse Dock were confronted with an enormous banner slung between fore and main mast, with the legend 'THE FASTEST SHIP IN THE WORLD'. The strange thing is that she was in the nature of a fluke, for though a number of attempts were made to build duplicates, none of these matched her for speed. On the *Marco Polo*'s second voyage to Australia Forbes is said to have told his passengers: 'Ladies and gentlemen, last trip I astonished the world with the sailing of this ship. This trip I intend to astonish God Almighty!'

'Maria Reigersgergen': Dutch 36-gun frigate captured in the Batavia Roads (18 October 1806) by Captain Peter Rainier in the *Caroline* and taken into the British Navy under the name *Java*.

'Maria Rickmers': *see FRANCE*.

'Marie Celeste': *see MARY CELESTE*.

Marine insurance: *see* INSURANCE.

Marines: soldiers trained for service at sea and on land. In the Middle Ages fighting at sea was considered the business of soldiers; they manned the fore- and aftercastles, from which they fought while the seamen managed the ship. But the origin of the modern marines more certainly dates from the time of Charles II, when in 1664 the Duke of York and Albany's Maritime Regiment of Foot (the YELLOW REGIMENT) was formed, perhaps with secondary motives of strengthening and adding discipline to a fleet that was of uncertain quality at that time. The marines quickly established themselves as a force to be reckoned with; their tradition of bravery and steadfastness began to grow. They played a distinguished part in the capture and defence of Gibraltar (1704) and were prominent in all the long succession of wars in the 18th century. They had come under full Admiralty control in 1755, and by the end of the century marines might

A Royal Marine private from the early 19th century.

contribute between a quarter and a fifth of the complement of larger ships of the line. On board they formed part of the gun crews, acted as sharpshooters, made up landing and boarding parties and acted as sentries. In 1802, in recognition of their services, they became the Royal Marines, and from 1804 to 1923 they were divided into two branches, the R.M. Artillery and the R.M. Light Infantry. In the era of the turreted battleship the marines always had charge of one main gun turret, also continuing their traditional duties about the ship. The long story of their service cannot be told briefly, but the marines have played a distinguished and important role from the capture of Gibraltar to the raid on Zeebrugge in 1918, from the defence of Crete in 1941 to the assaults on the beaches of Europe in 1944, and again in Korea in 1950. They serve in commando and landing craft and act as an amphibious force linking army and navy. Rightly the globe is their badge and their motto *Per Mare, Per Terram*, 'By Sea and by Land'.

There never was any appeal made to them for honour, courage or loyalty that they did not more than realize my expectations.

Admiral Lord St Vincent (1735–1823)

Marine Society: a philanthropic society founded (1756) by Jonas HANWAY. The work of the Society was to take in destitute boys, including some sent by the magistrates, to clean, feed and clothe them, and, after a measure of instruction and discipline, to send them to sea. They went to the merchant ships in peace-time and to the Royal Navy in war-time. On the warships the boys were either apprenticed to learn the sailor's skills or became servants to officers. Considerable numbers entered the Navy in this way, and they were generally looked upon as a very acceptable type of volunteer, though in fact

they probably had little or no choice. These boys entering the ships from the Marine Society were between 13 and 17 years of age, but some older volunteers were also sponsored, who joined the Navy as 'landmen', no doubt so called because they had no knowledge of the sea on enlistment.

Mark: a piece of leather, bunting, or a knot attached to a lead-line to show the depth of water; *see* LEAD.

Mark, by the: *see* LEAD.

Marks: *see* LOADLINES.

Marline: a two-stranded line used for lashing.

Marline spike: heavy pointed iron pin for forcing open the strands of a rope when splicing etc. For the marline spike hitch *see* KNOTS.

Marmara, Sea of: a sea some 170 miles long and 50 miles wide lying in N.W. Turkey between the mainlands of Europe and Asia Minor. It is connected with the Black Sea to the east via the Bosporus, and with the Aegean Sea to the west via the Dardanelles.

Marooning: the putting ashore and abandonment of an offender on a desert island or coast. The most famous case in history is that of Alexander SELKIRK, whose story was later used by Defoe as the basis for *Robinson Crusoe* (1719). The practice was common among pirates and buccaneers, but a *cause célèbre* occurred in the Royal Navy in 1807 when Captain the Hon. Warwick Lake, of the 18-gun sloop *Recruit*, put ashore Robert Jeffrey, accused of theft, on the small deserted island of Sombrero, west of the Virgin Islands and at the northern end of the Leewards. When Admiral Sir Alexander Cochrane, commanding in the West Indies, heard of the punishment, he immediately sent Lake back to pick up the offender; but when the *Recruit* arrived, nine weeks after Jeffrey had been put ashore, there was no sign of him. It was not until some three years later that his fate was known, after questions in Parliament and so much popular indignation that ballads were sold on the street. In fact, after suffering considerable privations for eight days on Sombrero, he was taken off by an American schooner, the *Adams*, whose skipper, John Dennis, landed him at Marblehead, Massachusetts, where he took up his old trade as a blacksmith. Eventually Jeffrey presented himself at the Admiralty on 22 October 1810, having been brought home by the Royal Navy schooner *Thistle*; he received all his arrears of pay and was discharged from the service without any stain on his character. Lake had been court-martialled on 5–6 February 1810 and dismissed the service for 'behaving in a scandalous, infamous, cruel, oppressive or fraudulent manner, unbecoming the character of an officer'.

Marryat, Frederick (1792–1848): novelist and Captain R.N. Though famous for his novels, Marryat should also be remembered as a distinguished and intrepid naval officer. After trying to run away to sea, he entered the Navy at the age of fourteen, and had the good fortune to serve in a most efficient and active frigate, the *Impérieuse*, commanded by the dashing and brilliant Captain Lord Cochrane. The fighting and adventures he experienced during this time made a deep impression on him and were to become material for his tales of the sea. He rose to be a Commander, and in that rank was in command of the guard-ship at St Helena in 1821 when Napoleon died. By the time he was 30 he had been awarded 27 life-saving certificates, and had published a code of signals advocating what was later to become the International Code. He saw much further exciting sea-service in the East Indies and Burma before retiring in 1830 to devote his time to writing. Many of Marryat's novels were about the sea, and of these *Peter Simple* (1834) is considered the best. The other sea stories were *The Naval Officer; or Frank Mildmay* (1829), *The King's Own* (1830), *Newton Forster; or the Merchant Service* (1832), *Jacob Faithful* (1834), MR MIDSHIPMAN EASY (1836), *The Pirate and the Three Cutters* (1836), *Poor Jack* (1840), *Percival Keene* (1842), and *The Privateer's Man* (1846).

Marrying the gunner's daughter: *see* FLOGGING.

Martha's Vineyard: an island off the coast of Maine in New England. It was for long in the 19th century a great centre of the old-time whaling trade, but today it is a popular holiday resort. Herman Melville, in *Omoo* (1847), described leaving Tahiti in the *Leviathan*, a New England whaler:

I had seen the captain, and liked him ... He was a Vineyarder, or native of the island of Martha's Vineyard (adjoining Nantucket), and – I would have sworn it – a sailor, and no tyrant.

Martin, Sir Thomas Byam (1773–1854): admiral. He began his sea life in 1786 as 'Captain's Servant' on the *Pegasus* (28 guns) commanded by Prince William (later William IV). By a combination of good luck and good management in his later career he captured an extraordinary number of privateers and other vessels, including the French *Immortalité* (42 guns). In 1808 he added the Russian 74-

BALTIMORE CLIPPER: the *Rambler*, American privateer brigantine.

BAYEUX TAPESTRY: part of the tapestry showing Duke William's flag-ship.

'BRENDAN': the *Brendan* at sea under full sail, 1976.

CAMOUFLAGE: a First World War merchantman in 'dazzle paint'.

CLIPPER: the American clipper *Hurricane*, from a painting by Shillet.

CLOTH OF GOLD, FIELD OF THE: detail from the painting by Vincent Volpe.

COOK, JAMES: from a painting by N. Dance.

FIGUREHEAD: the figurehead of a French merchantman.

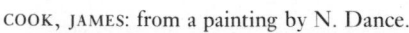

'ENDEAVOUR': the *Earl of Pembroke* leaving Whitby, from a painting attributed to Thomas Luny.

FIRE-SHIPS: the launch of the fire-ships against the Spanish Armada at Calais.

FIRST OF JUNE: the painting of the action by de Loutherbourg.

GALLEASS: from a design for a tapestry, showing a galleass in the Spanish Armada.

GOKSTAD SHIP: view from the bow.

ICE-BREAKER: the Russian nuclear-powered ice-breaker *Lenin*.

'JAMES BAINES': embarking passengers at Liverpool: litho by S. Walters, 1854.

INTERNATIONAL CODE OF SIGNALS

Letter	Meaning	Letter	Meaning
A ALFA	I AM UNDERGOING A SPEED TRIAL	K KILO *	YOU SHOULD STOP YOUR VESSEL INSTANTLY
B BRAVO	I AM TAKING IN OR DISCHARGING EXPLOSIVES	L LIMA *	YOU SHOULD STOP— I HAVE SOMETHING IMPORTANT TO COMMUNICATE
C CHARLIE	YES (AFFIRMATIVE)	M MIKE	I HAVE A DOCTOR ON BOARD
D DELTA	KEEP CLEAR OF ME — I AM MANOEUVRING WITH DIFFICULTY	N NOVEMBER	NO (NEGATIVE)
E ECHO	I AM DIRECTING MY COURSE TO STARBOARD	O OSCAR *	MAN OVERBOARD
F FOXTROT *	I AM DISABLED— COMMUNICATE WITH ME	P PAPA *	IN HARBOUR:— ALL PERSONS ARE TO REPAIR ON BOARD AS THE VESSEL IS ABOUT TO PROCEED TO SEA. *AT SEA:— YOUR LIGHTS ARE OUT OR BURNING BADLY
G GOLF	I REQUIRE A PILOT	Q QUEBEC	MY VESSEL IS HEALTHY, AND I REQUIRE FREE PRATIQUE
H HOTEL	I HAVE A PILOT ON BOARD	R ROMEO *	THE WAY IS OFF MY SHIP—YOU MAY FEEL YOUR WAY PAST ME
I INDIA	I AM DIRECTING MY COURSE TO PORT	S SIERRA	MY ENGINES ARE GOING FULL SPEED ASTERN
J JULIETT	I AM GOING TO SEND A MESSAGE BY SEMAPHORE	T TANGO	DO NOT PASS AHEAD OF ME

ALPHABETICAL FLAGS AND SUBSTITUTES		NUMERAL PENNANTS
U UNIFORM *	YOU ARE STANDING INTO DANGER	ONE
V VICTOR *	I REQUIRE ASSISTANCE	TWO
W WHISKEY *	I REQUIRE MEDICAL ASSISTANCE	THREE
X XRAY	STOP CARRYING OUT INTENTIONS AND WATCH FOR MY SIGNALS	FOUR
Y YANKEE	I AM CARRYING MAILS	FIVE
Z ZULU *	TO BE USED TO ADDRESS OR CALL SHORE STATIONS	SIX
1st SUBSTITUTE	USED TO REPEAT THE FIRST FLAG OR PENNANT IN THE SAME HOIST	SEVEN
2nd SUBSTITUTE	USED TO REPEAT THE SECOND FLAG OR PENNANT IN THE SAME HOIST	EIGHT
3rd SUBSTITUTE	USED TO REPEAT THE THIRD FLAG OR PENNANT IN THE SAME HOIST	NINE
CODE AND ANSWER	USED TO ACKNOWLEDGE A SIGNAL. ALSO FLOWN BY A WARSHIP WHEN MAKING A FLAG SIGNAL FROM THE INTERNATIONAL CODE TO DISTINGUISH IT FROM THE NAVAL CODE	ZERO

USED ON ALL OCCASIONS WHEN IT IS REQUIRED TO REPRESENT NUMBERS IN FLAG SIGNALLING

INTERNATIONAL CODE OF SIGNALS.

MIDDLE GROUND.

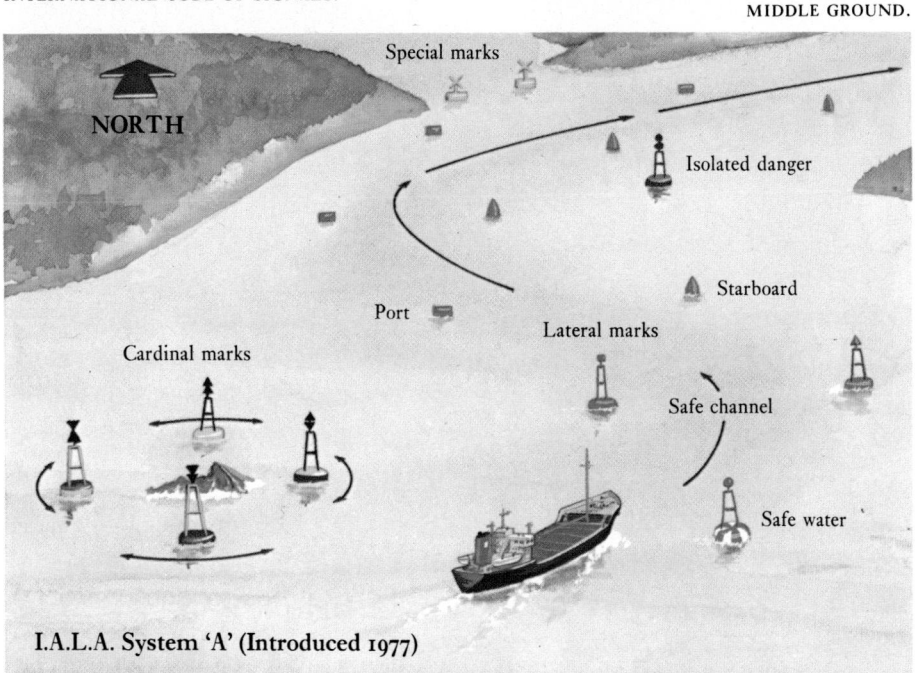

Special marks

NORTH

Isolated danger

Starboard

Port

Lateral marks

Cardinal marks

Safe channel

Safe water

I.A.L.A. System 'A' (Introduced 1977)

MISSILES: launches fitted with Sir William Congreve's explosive rockets, 1814.

'NELSON CHEQUER'.

'TEMERAIRE': from the painting by
J.W.M. Turner.

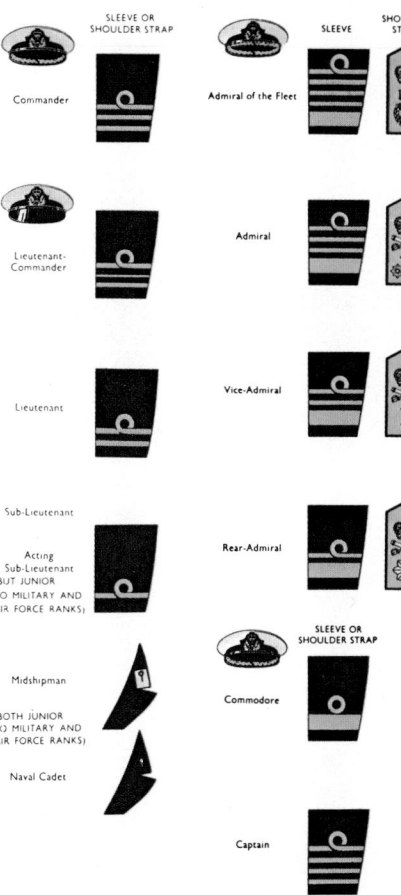

Commander

Lieutenant-Commander

Lieutenant

Sub-Lieutenant

Acting Sub-Lieutenant (BUT JUNIOR TO MILITARY AND AIR FORCE RANKS)

Midshipman

(BOTH JUNIOR TO MILITARY AND AIR FORCE RANKS)

Naval Cadet

SLEEVE OR SHOULDER STRAP

Admiral of the Fleet

Admiral

Vice-Admiral

Rear-Admiral

Commodore

Captain

SLEEVE

SHOULDER STRAP

SLEEVE OR SHOULDER STRAP

OFFICER.

MOTOR torpedo boat.

RALEIGH: attributed to the monogramist 'H', 1588.

'OLD WHITE HAT': John Willis, shipowner.

TRAFALGAR: from the painting by J.W.M. Turner.

SHIPBUILDING: a shipyard on the Thames, by
J. Clevely, 1762.

'VICTORY': in dry dock at Portsmouth.

SUBMARINE: H.M.S. *Valiant* at speed.

gun *Sewolod* to the tally. He was Comptroller of the Navy (1818–31), and when he was 76 became Admiral of the Fleet. *See also IMPLACABLE.*

Martin, Sir William: *see* PINCHER.

Martingale: a lower stay for the jib-boom or flying jib-boom.

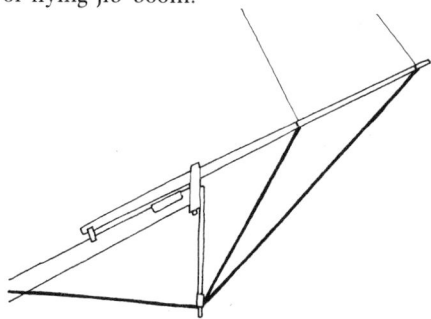

Martinique: a fertile volcanic island, an overseas department of France, in the Windward Islands, West Indies. It was one of the many Caribbean islands the possession of which was constantly contested between the British and French during the Seven Years' War, the Revolutionary and the Napoleonic Wars. Occupied by Admiral Rodney and General Monckton in 1762, Martinique was returned to the French a year later, only to change hands several times in the renewed wars before finally being returned to France in 1814.

'Mary': because of its religious associations, probably the most common ship name in all Christendom, either by itself or in combination (e.g. *Mary Fortune, Mary Rose, Mary Galley*). Apart from the *Mary*s mentioned below, it is worth noticing here the vessel that Charles II received as a present in 1660 when, as Sir Anthony Deane told Samuel Pepys, 'the Dutch gave his Majesty the yacht called *Mary*, from

whence came the improvement of our present yacht; for until that time we had not heard of such a name in England.' Probably Deane was not quite accurate, in that the word yacht was known earlier; but the important fact remains that the *Mary* was the first yacht to appear on the English Navy List, where she remained till she was wrecked in 1675 on the Skerries, near Holyhead (*see also* ROYAL YACHTS).

At the Restoration Charles the Second left Holland in a yacht which the Dutch had placed at his disposal... In an account of the proceedings published by Adrian Vlackett at the Hague, in 1660, the narrator relates that the yacht, in which the King embarked, had formerly belonged to his brother-in-law, the Prince of Orange, who died in 1650. At that time she belonged to the Board of Admiralty, of Rotterdam... The King's yacht had been brought to a state of high perfection. The interiors of the cabins were decorated and gilded, whilst some of the best artists of the time had been engaged in making beautiful paintings and sculptures with which to embellish them. The King appeared so pleased with the vessel that the burgomaster of Amsterdam begged to be allowed to present His Majesty with a ship of the same style and elegance. Two months later this yacht was sent to England, and was named the *Mary*.

C. M. Gavin, *Royal Yachts* (1932)

This *Mary* was a ship of 100 tons, 52 ft long in the keel, carrying eight guns and 30 men. Her figurehead was a unicorn. In general lines she was rather like a Thames barge, though she was larger and lavishly decorated, the royal state-room being superimposed aft on the upper deck, with ornate side windows.

A second royal yacht *Mary*, 66 tons larger, was built by Phineas Pett at Chatham in 1667.

'Mary and John': ship in which some 140

colonists from Dorsetshire, England, sailed from Plymouth to settle at Dorchester, Massachusetts, U.S.A. (1630).

'Mary Celeste' (often wrongly called **'Marie Celeste'**): the centre of one of the most famous unsolved mysteries of the sea. The 282-ton brig left New York on 5 November 1872 with a cargo of crude alcohol. On board were the master, B. S. Briggs, his wife and small daughter, and a crew of seven. The last contact with the shore was a letter from Briggs in which he wrote 'We are enjoying our melodion and have some good songs.' A month later she was found by the brigantine *Dei Gratia* 600 miles west of Gibraltar, completely abandoned with every sign of an un-premeditated and hasty departure. The vessel was in excellent shape, having only some slight weather damage. The lifeboat was missing. Though many possible explanations have been advanced (at least two in the form of novels), it is improbable now that the truth will ever be known. The most popular theory is that the master opened the hatches, was blasted by escaping alcohol fumes and immediately took to the boat with the whole company; and that the lifeboat, clumsily lowered in the general panic, capsized before they got away from the ship.

'Mary of Guildford': ship sent out by Henry VIII in 1527, along with the *Sampson*, commanded by John Rutt of Radcliffe, to explore the American main-land. The *Sampson* was lost and the voyage achieved little.

'Mary Rose': one of Henry VIII's ships. Built in 1509, she heeled over and sank off Portsmouth 36 years later. Unsuccessful attempts were made to raise her at the time, and to this day she has been a subject of underwater research. In 1836 a number of her guns were recovered. They revealed interesting evidence of a transitional period in ships' guns – old iron breech-loaders mixed with fine brass cannon; or, putting it another way, iron serpentines, slings and stone-throwing guns side by side with cannon-royal, demi-cannons, and cul-verins. *See also* ANTHONY, ANTHONY.

Masefield, John (1878–1967): best re-membered as a poet, but also writer of plays, short stories and novels; he became Poet Laureate in 1930. Much of his best work is inspired by the sea. After training on H.M.S. *Conway* he sailed as an apprentice on a square-rigged ship round Cape Horn, and later was a junior officer on an Atlantic liner. He left the sea and turned to writing, publishing in 1902 *Salt Water Ballads*, in which the language of the sea is used with original skill. His reputation grew with further poems, short stories and novels, many of which had a salt-water setting. Some of the best-known of these are the stories in *A Main-sail Haul* (1905) and *A Tarpaulin Muster* (1907), *Dauber* (1913, a narrative poem), *The Bird of Dawning* (1933, a story of the tea clippers), and *Victorious Troy* (1935). He also wrote *Sea Life in Nelson's Time* (1905, a history), *The Everlasting Mercy* (1911), *Sard Harker* (1924) and *Odtaa* (1926). His best-known poems are 'Sea Fever' ('I must go down to the sea again') and 'Cargoes' ('Quin-quereme of Nineveh from distant Ophir'), but in many other poems the call of the sea is echoed in the lilt of Masefield's verse.

Clean, green, windy billows notching out the sky,
Grey clouds tattered into rags, sea-winds, blowing high,
And the ships under topsails, beating, thrashing by,
And the mewing of the herring gulls.

'Cardigan Bay', from *Salt Water Ballads*

Massachusetts Bay: the great Atlantic bay off the coast of the state of Massachusetts, U.S.A. Its coastline is full of Anglo-American history. Here the Pilgrim Fathers landed (1620), here BOSTON harbour was the scene of the celebrated 'Tea Party' (1773) before the American War of Independence, here were the harbours which became centres of the old-time whaling trade and a nursery of great American naval and mercantile marine tradition.

Mast: originally a tall strong pole of wood erected vertically to carry sails, being stepped into the keelson and supported by shrouds and stays. As ships increased in size and carried more sail the single trunk of a tall tree was not strong enough, and so the lower part of the mast was sometimes made up of several timbers joined to give strength. This was known as the lower mast; above it was the top mast and above that the top-gallant mast, these last two being pole masts, that is single tree trunks (*see also* RIGGING; TIMBER).

The names of a sailing vessel's masts are:

Fore: the foremost mast in a vessel with three or more masts, also in a two-masted vessel when the after mast is the main mast.

Main: the chief mast of a two-masted vessel (in which it can be the foremost mast), the centre mast of a three-masted vessel, and the second from forward in vessels with more than three masts.

Mizen (or mizzen): the aftermost mast of a three-masted vessel, or of a two-masted vessel where the foremost mast is the main mast.

Jigger: the aftermost mast in a four-masted vessel. In five-masted vessels the aftermost mast was given a variety of names, such as driver, after-jigger, after-spanker and pusher.

With the coming of steam, masts did not disappear, for they serve many other purposes such as giving height for signal halyards, for navigation lights and for radio aerials and radar; but wood has given way to metal, and the form of the mast has changed, especially in warships, in which there appeared lattice and tripod masts evolving into structures which can no longer be recognized as, or called, masts.

Master: (1) the officer responsible for sailing and navigating the ship in the old-time Royal Navy. He was subordinate to the Captain for fighting the ship. He was appointed by warrant up to 1843, when he became a commissioned officer. By the 1860s he had become a Navigating-Lieutenant and the title disappeared from the Royal Navy, except as an abbreviation for MASTER-AT-ARMS.

(2) The commanding officer of a merchant ship, who holds a Master's certificate for which he qualifies by experience and examination. The title dates from earliest times and may be an abbreviation of 'Master Mariner'.

Master-at-Arms: a Chief Petty Officer, appointed by warrant, with a special standing and seniority; his position makes him responsible for the good order and discipline of the ratings. His name derives from former days, when he was called upon to give the crew instructions in the use of small arms; his distinctive importance is marked by wearing a sword on formal occasions. He is familiarly known as a 'jaunty'.

Master Mariner: a Merchant Navy officer who has passed the examination for a

Master's or Extra Master's certificate of competency. Such certificates are issued by most maritime nations.

Mast-head: the topmost part of the mast; also used to indicate a position high up on the mast, as in 'mast-head look-out' or 'mast-head lights'.

Mastheading: a punishment for minor offences in the old Navy. It was given to junior officers and midshipmen and consisted in being sent up to the top mast crosstrees and made to stay there for anything up to 24 hours without food or drink – unless a sympathetic friend smuggled something up. The punishment was generally ordered by the First Lieutenant, and although after the middle of the 18th century it apparently disappeared, there is an instance of the mastheading of an erring midshipman during the First World War!

Mast pond: an enclosed salt-water basin in a dockyard in which floated a supply of mast timbers for shipbuilding and repair.

Mat: *see* COLLISION MAT.

Matapan: *see* CAPE MATAPAN.

Mate: (1) in the old-time Royal Navy, a Petty Officer assisting the MASTER with sailing and navigation, and known as a Master's Mate. In Nelson's time the position was on the line of advancement to the quarter-deck for promising ratings, but midshipmen also added to their pay by qualifying as Master's Mates while waiting for promotion to Lieutenant. The word 'Master's' was dropped and Mate later became a substantive rank between Midshipman and Lieutenant; but in 1861 the name Sub-Lieutenant was substituted.

(2) An assistant, as in 'Gunner's Mate' (former title for a gunnery instructor), 'Boatswain's Mate' etc. (3) The name for Merchant Navy deck officers assisting the Master. They were formerly called the Mate, Second Mate, Third Mate etc., according to their seniority by appointment and qualifications (the certificates held after examination); but today officers of the Merchant Navy are generally known as Chief Officer, Second Officer, Third Officer etc.

Mathews, Thomas (1676–1751): admiral. Described by one writer as 'a crabbed and conceited man', he pursued a not unmeritorious career until the inglorious battle of Toulon (February 1744), where he attacked bravely but not strictly according to the Fighting Instructions (*see* LESTOCK, RICHARD).

'Matthew': one of the most famous ships in history, which carried John CABOT on his voyage to Newfoundland (1497). The 50-ton ship was one of the first English vessels to cross the Atlantic.

'Mauretania': famous CUNARD transatlantic liner, in her time a magnificent record-holder. Of 31,938 gross tonnage and with four-screw propulsion, she reigned from 1907 to 1935. *See also* RADIO; SPEED.

Mauritius: former British Crown Colony, now independent, in the Indian Ocean to the east of Madagascar. Discovered by the Portuguese early in the 16th century, colonized by the Dutch in the 17th century, Mauritius became an important base for the French in their rivalry with the British East India Company, and from it sailed many of the French privateers who had numerous successes against shipping in the

Indian Ocean. One of the most famous and successful French privateers was Robert Surcouf who, between 1796 and 1809, did much damage by capturing or destroying East Indiamen. The British tried blockading Mauritius, but this had to be broken off. Finally, in 1810, the British mounted an expedition which captured the island, but only after some severe losses, among their ships. The French had called the island Ile de France; Mauritius was the name previously given by the Dutch in honour of Prince Maurice of Nassau.

Maxwell, Sir Murray (1775–1831): naval captain who enjoyed an adventurous career not confined to normal service duties. He took Lord Amherst to China to protest to the Emperor about the wrongs suffered by British merchants there; then, after landing him at Pei-ho (1816), explored the Gulf of Pechili, the west coast of Korea and the Loo-Choo (or Lu-chu) Islands. Having re-embarked Amherst at the conclusion of his mission, Maxwell wrecked his ship, the *Alceste*, on a sunken rock in the Gaspar Straits (Malay archipelago) in 1817, but managed to ensure that his distinguished passenger and all the crew were saved. He was acquitted at his subsequent court-martial, and was knighted a year later. *See also* MCLEOD, JOHN.

'Mayflower': one of the most famous ships in history, the vessel that carried the Pilgrim Fathers from Plymouth to New England in 1620. Unfortunately, considering the burden of history she carried, little authentic detail has survived; the various descriptions, models etc. (*see*

Mayflower II under sail for the first sea trials off Brixham, 1957.

MAYFLOWER II) are largely conjectural, based on contemporary or near-contemporary manuscripts on shipbuilding, rigging etc. Undoubtedly the *Mayflower* was an ordinary small merchant ship of about 180 tons burden, rigged with the three masts of the period and, probably, with a simple sail plan of main and fore courses, lateen sail on the mizen and a spritsail under the bowsprit. Since she had already made voyages to Bordeaux and Rochelle, the ship was not new. Possible dimensions: length of keel, 64 ft; stem to stern-post, 90 ft; breadth, 26 ft; depth in hold, 11 ft.

'Mayflower II': full-size replica of a typical 17th-century merchant vessel, approximating as closely as possible to the original *MAYFLOWER*. Built at Brixham, Devon, in 1957, she was sailed across the Atlantic to Plymouth, Massachusetts, with Alan Villiers as master.

Mean: an average, worked out after a long series of observations and records; thus, 'mean high water', 'mean sea level' etc. *See also* GREENWICH MEAN TIME.

Medals: pieces of metal, often in the form of a coin, struck to commemorate long service, individual gallantry or some important event. They occur in England from Tudor times, though little is known about the earliest medals, apart from the fact that they were probably symbols of royal favour. Examples are the famous Armada medal, struck in gold and silver, and the so-called 'Ark in Flood' medal also issued by Queen Elizabeth. As the 17th century progresses, many more examples and details become known. In 1649 Lieutenant Stephen Rose of the *Happy Entrance* destroyed one of Prince Rupert's best ships, the *Antelope*, and was rewarded by the Commonwealth Council of State

with £50, part of it in the form of a gold medal. Other members of the crew received medals of lesser value. In 1650 Captain Robert Wyard, commander of the *Adventure*, received a gold medal worth £50 for fighting off six Royalist frigates when he was convoying a small fleet of merchant ships from Hull.

An extraordinary exploit occurred in May 1695, when William Thompson, master of a Poole fishing smack, with only one man and a boy on board, was attacked by a French privateer with sixteen men. Thompson, with two small guns and a few muskets, managed to disable the captain and half the crew of the privateer, which gave up the fight and made off. Not content with his victory, Thompson went in pursuit and, after another two-hour battle, boarded her and brought her into Poole harbour. The Admiralty gave him a gold chain and medal and allowed him to keep the privateer. Awards continued for single-ship and fleet actions, and for individual heroism, but spasmodically; for example, none seems to have been granted during the reign of George I, and, although the nation was heavily and continuously engaged, no medals for naval service were awarded in George III's long reign till Howe's victory off Ushant on 1 June 1794 (the 'Glorious FIRST OF JUNE').

The first instance of a medal given by a private person being accepted and worn in the Royal Navy is that struck after the Battle of the Nile (1798) by Alexander Davison, a friend of Nelson's. He presented every man engaged in the battle with a medal, graded from gold to bronze according to rank, at a cost of nearly £2000. For the most glorious victory of the period, the Battle of Trafalgar, the junior officers, seamen and marines received no official medal or other reward; but private enterprise again stepped in to compensate for this government meanness, and Matthew Boulton of the Soho Works, Birmingham, received permission to strike his own medals. At his personal expense, he presented medals in silver to the captains and in pewter to the junior officers and men. It is recorded that many of the recipients of the latter either threw them overboard or returned them in disgust.

A naval medal for long service and good conduct for seamen and marines was granted by an Order in Council of 24 August 1831. It was awarded, to nominated men, for 21 years' blameless service. A medal for conspicuous gallantry was instituted by another Order, on 13 August 1855, but was superseded by the Victoria Cross (January 1856), though of course this is not exclusively a naval medal. By the end of the century some 50 Victoria Crosses had been won by naval personnel and marines of all ranks, the first being awarded to C. D. LUCAS.

Among other medals for seamen may be mentioned the rare Naval Engineers' Medal of 1842, presented to 'Engineers of the first class, serving in Her Majesty's Navy, who by their good conduct and ability deserve some special mark of notice'. On the obverse is a two-masted paddle steamer, with a trident. In its short existence of about five years, only six or seven were granted. In January 1855 the Arctic Medal was instituted for all officers and men who had been engaged in the search for the North-West Passage between 1818 and 1855. Other special polar medals followed. The Albert Medal was instituted by warrant of 7 March 1866 for saving life at sea. The Royal National Lifeboat Institution has its own coveted medals; see LIFEBOAT.

See also PATRIOTIC FUND.

Mediterranean Sea: the great and almost totally enclosed sea between southern Europe, S.W. Asia and the northern coast of Africa. Its only exit to the ocean is through the narrow Strait of Gibraltar at its western extremity; at its eastern end it extends into the Black Sea via the Sea of Marmara.

In *The Mirror of the Sea* (1906) Joseph Conrad wrote of it: 'The cradle of oversea traffic and of the art of naval combats, the Mediterranean, apart from all the associations of adventure and glory, the common heritage of all mankind, makes a tender appeal to the seaman ... The first impulse of navigation took its visible form in that tideless basin freed from hidden shoals and treacherous currents, as if in tender regard for the infancy of the art'. Certainly the Mediterranean was the cradle of navigation and the nursery of the western world. The coast-hugging craft of the earliest sailors gave way to bolder voyagers reaching out of sight of land. Here there evolved the fighting galleys of the ancient world; here the Greeks fought their great sea battle at Salamis against the Persians (480 B.C.), and spread their sea-linked colonies throughout the Mediterranean. Then Roman power dominated and in 260 B.C. overcame the strong fleet from Carthage, a colony of those trading sailors the Phoenicians, whose ships had sailed to Spain, to the Scilly Isles and far down the west coast of Africa. In 31 B.C. the Mediterranean saw the sea battle of Actium, when Octavius and Mark Antony struggled for mastery of the Roman world. Centuries later Venice and Genoa rose as maritime powers controlling the sea and its trade, but with the discovery of the New World and the route to the East round Africa there arose the new sea-going powers of Spain and Portugal; for a time the Mediterranean declined in importance and many of its coasts became the haunt of pirates.

During the period of England's struggle, first with Spain and then with France, British warships were in evidence in countless engagements, which culminated in Nelson's great victory at the Battle of the Nile (1798). For 150 years afterwards a strong British fleet was maintained in the Mediterranean, particularly after 1869, when the opening of the Suez Canal linked it with the Red Sea and the sea route to India. It was then that the Grand Harbour at Valletta in MALTA became the main base of the British Mediterranean Fleet. It was to play a part in both World Wars. In 1939–45 air power was added to submarines as a serious threat to the warship, and the heroic story of the convoys nourishing Malta and our forces in North Africa cannot be forgotten, nor the eventful story of the British fleets operating from Gibraltar and Alexandria. Today in place of a strong British fleet in the Mediterranean American and Russian ships watch each other warily in this most famous setting of maritime and naval history.

Medway: a river with a broad estuary on the N. coast of Kent leading into the Thames estuary. On the Medway lie the ancient naval base of Chatham and, nearer open water, Sheerness, a former naval base. In June 1667 during the Second Dutch War (1665–7) the Dutch admiral de Ruyter sailed into the Thames with a fleet of over 80 ships. Having stormed and captured Sheerness the Dutch entered the Medway with a division of warships, having broken through a chain boom at Gillingham. They sailed up to Chatham, burnt five English ships (including the *Great James*, the *Loyal London* and the *Royal Oak*) and captured two others. The English fleet had not been fitted out that year for lack of money, many of the sailors had deserted (some to the Dutch), and the low state of morale and

efficiency brought about an ignominious defeat. For some weeks de Ruyter blockaded the Thames and brought London's sea-borne trade to a standstill, until England was forced to make a humiliating peace with the Treaty of Breda.

This brilliantly conducted Dutch victory – one of the most disgraceful episodes in English naval history – created great despondency throughout England, as, amongst others, the diarists John Evelyn and Samuel PEPYS recorded. From this low point Pepys was to begin his great work of reforming naval administration.

No sooner up but hear the sad news confirmed of the *Royall Charles* being taken by them, and now in fitting by them – which Pett should have carried up higher by our several orders, and deserves, therefore, to be hanged for not doing it . . . Late at night comes Mr Hudson, the cooper, my neighbour, and tells me that he come from Chatham this evening at five o'clock, and saw this afternoon the . . . *James*, *Oake*, and *London* burnt by the enemy with their fire-ships: that two or three men-of-war come up with them, and made no more of Upnor Castle's shooting than of a fly . . . of worse consequence is . . . many Englishmen on board the Dutch ships speaking to one another in English . . . 'We did heretofore fight for tickets; now we fight for dollars!'

Pepys, *Diary* (13–14 June 1667)

On the 28th I went to Chatham, and thence to view not onely what Mischiefe the Dutch had don, but how triumphantly their whole Fleete, lay within the very mouth of the Thames, all from North-foreland, Margate, even to the Buoy of the Noore, a Dreadful Spectacle as ever any English men saw, and a dishonour never to be wiped off.

Evelyn, *Diary* (28 June 1667)

Melbourne: capital of Victoria, Australia, and a great seaport which figures prominently in British maritime history, not least because of its role in the wool races of the clipper ships. 'Hell or Melbourne', the famous expression of one hard-driving captain ('Bully' FORBES), typified the spirit of the period. With its many miles of wharfage and highly developed facilities for warehousing and trading, Melbourne has witnessed over the years some of the most majestic concentrations of shipping ever seen.

'Melbourne': *see* MACQUARIE.

Melville, Herman (1819–91): American writer of sea romances. Shipping first as a cabin-boy and crossing the Atlantic to Liverpool, he then joined a whaler bound round Cape Horn for the whaling grounds of the South Pacific. Here Melville and another sailor deserted and lived for a time amongst natives of the Marquesas Islands, eventually returning home in a U.S. frigate. Using, but embellishing, his experiences at sea, he settled down to write, and between 1846 and 1851 had a number of tales published in quick succession. These were *Typee* (1846) and *Omoo* (1847) – tales of the South Seas – *Redburn* and *Mardi* (1849), and *White Jacket* (1850), a tale of life on a naval frigate. His greatest work was *Moby-Dick; or, The Whale* (1851), which drew on his time in the whaler and tells of Captain Ahab's demoniac and vengeful pursuit of the Great White Whale. At the end Ahab himself, his ship the *Pequod* and his crew are destroyed by Moby-Dick, and the final scenes are an awe-inspiring conclusion to a remarkable book. Melville wrote a number of other less successful tales, but *Billy Budd*, written towards the end of his life and based on the press-gang and the harsh life in the Navy at the time of the Napoleonic Wars, is remembered as the tale on which Benjamin Britten's opera of the same name (1951) is based.

The harpoon was darted; the stricken whale flew forward; with igniting velocity the line ran through the groove; – ran foul. Ahab stooped to clear it; he did clear it; but the flying turn caught him round the neck, and voicelessly as Turkish mutes bowstring their victim, he was shot out of the boat, ere the crew knew he was gone. Next instant, the heavy eye-splice in the rope's final end flew out of the stark-empty tub, knocked down an oarsman, and smiting the sea, disappeared in its depths.

Moby-Dick (1851)

Mercantile (or **merchant**) **marine:** the merchant shipping of a country.

Mercator: the Latin name by which the great Flemish geographer and map-maker Gerhard Kremer (1512–94) is known. The basis of his fame was the production in 1569 of a world map on which parallels of latitude and the lines of longitude cut each other at right angles. This is known as Mercator's Projection; its great advantage was that on it a constant compass course appears as a straight line, known as a RHUMB-LINE. This was to be of great assistance to navigators, but although Mercator continued to amplify his work with further productions of maps until his death in 1594, it was not until the middle of the 17th century that charts based on Mercator's projection became widely used and accepted as the basis of navigation.

Merchant Adventurers: association of English merchants, particularly active, though not exclusively, in the cloth trade from the 15th to the 17th century. Though their origins may well have been earlier, they appear as an organized body in the 1400s; they received their English charter in 1505. Thereafter, with their head-quarters overseas, generally in the Low Countries, the Merchant Adventurers dominated trade across Europe to the

Baltic, building up a virtual monopoly in the export from England of fine cloth, white and coloured, and trading from many ports, particularly London. Their chief rivals were the Merchant Staplers and the HANSEATIC LEAGUE, but they succeeded in defeating both. Though the organization was by no means tightly knit, their trading arrangements were so efficient that they were the largest and wealthiest association until the Civil War of 1642–9, after which their power declined. In the reign of William III and Mary their monopoly of cloth export to north and central Europe was broken; but the Adventurers remained active overseas and were still in business in Hamburg at the beginning of the 19th century.

Merchantman: ship used for trading or commerce.

Merchant marine: *see* MERCANTILE MARINE.

'Merchant Royal': 400-ton merchant ship, one of the 163 mustered by Elizabeth I from her subjects to reinforce the 34 royal ships against the Armada.

'Mercury': ship which carried James COOK as Master in the expedition against Quebec (1759).

'Mere Honour' (or **'Merhonour'**): Lord Thomas Howard's ship in Essex's attack on Cadiz (1596). The ship appears in the Navy List of 1602 as the longest (not the largest) then in service – 110 ft in the keel and over 150 ft from stem to stern-post.

Meridian: *see* PRIME MERIDIAN.

Mermaid: legendary figure, common to the folk-lore of many countries, possessing the head and body of a woman (usually beautiful) but, below the waist, the fashion of a fish, with fins and scales. Less popular in the public imagination is her male counterpart, the merman. The innumerable stories and poems about mermaids, their appearance in heraldry and inn-signs, testify to the popularity of the myth, which, despite all efforts to prove the contrary, has no foundation in fact. The showman Phineas T. Barnum's famous Feejee Mermaid was an orang-utan stuffed into the body of a fish.

'Mermaid': of the many ships named *Mermaid*, sometimes most incongruously, may be selected for mention the small iron steamer of 164 tons, built at Blackwall in 1842. At her trials in May 1843, her 153-revolutions-a-minute screw drove her at something over $10\frac{1}{2}$ knots, or over 12 m.p.h. The Admiralty had promised to take her over if she reached this speed, and did so, thus acquiring their first iron screw steamer, renamed *Dwarf*.

'Merrimac' (or **'Merrimack'**): one-time steam frigate burnt and sunk in Norfolk harbour, Virginia, by the Union forces when they retired; raised by the Confederates and converted into an ironclad armoury with a casemate of thick oak beams reinforced with plating and lengths of railroad iron. She also had a ram of cast iron. It was to counterbalance her that the Union built the *MONITOR*. The historic encounter between the two monsters took place on 9 March 1862 in the Hampton Roads, the *Monitor* having arrived from New York after the *Merrimac* had taken heavy toll of the wooden fleet of the Federals. As the first battle between ironclad vessels, it was something of an anticlimax, since neither seriously damaged the other and there were almost no

An Allegory, oil painting attributed to F. Franken, 1618.

The *Merrimac* firing on the *Monitor*.

casualties. But the encounter opened the era of the armoured warship and may therefore be regarded as an important seamark. Within a few months both vessels had disappeared from the scene, the *Merrimac* being sunk in the James River. It is not often noticed that the *Merrimac* was renamed *Virginia* when she was reconstructed; history prefers to remember her by her maiden name.

Mess: (1) a group of men or women, usually of the same rank, on board ship or in a shore establishment, who live and eat together; (2) a part of the ship etc. where the group is accommodated. A 'messmate' is a sailor in the same mess or messdeck as another; but a 'messman' is a rating engaged in the homely duties of looking after the needs of a mess.

Messenger: a continuous rope passed around the capstan and through blocks forward of the capstan. As the messenger turned with the capstan so the anchor cable was bound and attached to it by a NIPPER.

Messina, Strait of: the narrow strait between Sicily and the toe of Italy. In ancient times the fierce currents and whirlpools of the Strait were the origins of the legends of Scylla and Charybdis, the former a monster on a rock enticing sailors to their destruction and the latter a terrible ship-devouring whirlpool. Odysseus's encounters with the two terrors are related in Book XII of Homer's *Odyssey*. During the Second World War the bulk of the German and Italian forces in Sicily escaped to the mainland in a brilliantly conducted

Messenger.

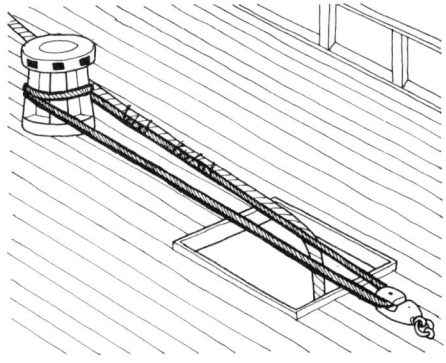

withdrawal by crossing the Strait of Messina (August 1943). A fortnight later General Montgomery and his 8th Army crossed the same waters in pursuit.

Meteorology: *see* WEATHER.

M.G.B.: *see* MOTOR GUN BOAT.

'Michel': the last German armed merchant-ship raider operating on the ocean routes in the Second World War. After leaving Germany in March 1942 she accounted for 94,342 tons of shipping in the South Atlantic and Indian Oceans before she was sunk in October 1943 by the U.S. submarine *Tarpon*.

Michelborne, Sir Edward (*fl.*1590–1610): adventurer who accompanied the Earl of Essex on his unsuccessful expedition to the Azores (1597) and later became a subscriber to the newly formed East India Company, in which respectable guise he became a virtual pirate, sailing to the East in 1604 and plundering Chinese ships before he returned.

Middle ground: a sand-bank, shoal or reef lying in the middle of a channel or fairway. It will normally be marked by distinctive buoys indicating whether it is to be passed by the channel to the right or to the left or to either side, and the buoys have distinctive top marks to indicate the inner and outer ends of the middle ground.
See colour section.

Middle passage: the passage across the Atlantic by ships carrying slaves, so called because it was the middle leg of the triangle sailed by ships starting from Britain; *see* SLAVE TRADE.

Middleton, Charles, first **Baron Barham** (1726–1813): admiral. After service at sea on convoy work and in the West Indies, he rose to administrative distinction, becoming Comptroller of the Navy, a Lord Commissioner and, when he was nearly 80, First Lord. It was he who received the news, sent by Nelson by the fast brig *Curieux*, that the French admiral Villeneuve was heading for home from the West Indies and would therefore make landfall in preparation for the inevitable final struggle against Britain; and it was Barham who, as a result, issued the fleet orders that, a few months later, culminated in the victory at Trafalgar (1805). *See also* EVANGELICALS.

Middleton, Sir Henry (*fl.*1600–1613): merchant captain and trade pioneer. He served as a captain in the first voyage organized by the East India Company (1602) and commanded the second and sixth (1604–6 and 1610–13), thus playing an important role in the establishment of the rich trade with India and South-East Asia. It is said that the first cargoes carried home, of cinnamon, pepper and cloves, brought about 95 per cent profit to the Company. After an adventurous career, which included escape from imprisonment at Mocha, the S.W. Arabian seaport, Middleton died in Java.

Middle watch: the period of duty or time from midnight to 0400 hours.

Midget submarines (officially known in Britain as **X-craft**): miniature submarines, used by both sides in the Second World War for attacking ships in harbour. The idea of underwater attack of this kind had long been thought of, but was really pioneered by the American David Bushnell, whose primitive one-man midget submarine and other early developments

Midget submarine *X51* hanging on slings.

are described under SUBMARINE. In the development of the large sea-going submarines the possibilities of midget submarines were not forgotten. A distinction must be made between the 'human' torpedo and the later four-man midget submarine or X-craft. The former was 'ridden' by two frogmen and was pioneered by the Italians, who at the end of the First World War sank an Austrian warship in Pola harbour, and again in the Second World War used such 'chariots' (as the British called their own version) in attacking shipping. Their best-known success was the crippling of the British battleships *Queen Elizabeth* and *Valiant* in Alexandria harbour (December 1941). In the same month in their attack on Pearl Harbor the Japanese had employed five midget submarines, but, unlike the rest of the attack, these were not successful. The best-known use of the four-man midget submarine by the British was in September 1943, when the *Tirpitz* was damaged by charges laid on her hull by two of the six midget submarines that had set out on the mission, only one of which returned. Another instance of the use of midget submarines was by the Italians in an attack on Valletta harbour in July 1941; and a Japanese midget submarine seriously damaged the battleship *Ramillies* in Diego Suarez harbour in May 1942.

Midshipman: the lowest rank of officer (but non-commissioned) in the Royal Navy, immediately junior to sub-lieutenant; also a junior officer under training in the Merchant Navy. The origins of the name are obscure, but the earliest midshipman surely worked amidships and may have been a kind of petty

302

officer. However, the clearest starting-point for the midshipman's story lies in Restoration times with the introduction in 1676 of the system of officer recruitment known as KING'S LETTER BOYS. Young gentlemen of suitable standing were given a letter from the Crown to a ship's captain, who was bound to take the youngster on board and train him in his profession, the first step being to become rated as midshipman. But the great majority of those who rose to be commissioned officers in the 18th century obtained their entry to the Navy by personal recommendation, by the claims of relationship or by influence otherwise exercised. These young boys, normally about the age of 13 but often younger, were entered on the ship's books, frequently before they had in fact joined, under a variety of headings. They were the captain's protégés, and after two years' service were rated as midshipmen and in due time recommended for examination and commission as lieutenants. This method continued for a long time and was

indeed Nelson's mode of entry when his uncle Captain Suckling offered to take him on board. Nelson was just three months over 12 when in 1771 he was rated midshipman. A number of other midshipmen entered via the NAVAL ACADEMY, which had been set up at Portsmouth in 1733, but this establishment was never thought much of by sea-going officers, in spite of occasional attempts at reform and a change of name (1806) to the Royal Naval College.

Training was transferred to a ship in Portsmouth harbour in 1857, and this was the forerunner of the present-day ROYAL NAVAL COLLEGE, DARTMOUTH, though the future midshipmen no longer begin their training at the early age of 13, as was the custom for so long in the past. Today an intensive education and training are provided for the midshipman both ashore and afloat in a training ship, followed by time in a ship of the fleet, after which he takes his examination for promotion to sub-lieutenant.

From *The interior of a midshipman's birth* [*sic*].

And oh, the little warlike world within!
The well-reeved guns, the netted canopy,
The hoarse command, the busy humming din,
When, at a word, the tops are manned on
    high:
Hark to the Boatswain's call, the cheering cry!
While through the seaman's hand the tackle
    glides;
Or schoolboy Midshipman that, standing by,
Strains his shrill pipe as good or ill betides,
And well the docile crew that skilful urchin
    guides.

Lord Byron, *Childe Harold's Pilgrimage* (1812)

Midshipmen's parade: lee side of the quarter-deck in an old man-o'-war, the weather side being reserved for the midshipmen's seniors.

Midway, Battle of (4–7 June 1942): one of the decisive naval battles of the Second World War, fought between the Americans and Japanese. The battle was remarkable for being the first ever fought between opposing fleets without the ships coming within gun range of each other, all the attacks being conducted by carrier-borne aircraft. Midway Island lies in the Central Pacific and was the objective of an intended Japanese invasion, but their fleet and transports were spotted and attacked. The early stages of the battle favoured the Japanese, but aircraft from the three American carriers *Enterprise*, *Hornet* and *Yorktown* concentrated on the Japanese carriers, four of which and a heavy cruiser were sunk during a long series of attacks. The *Yorktown* was damaged and later sunk by a Japanese submarine, but the Americans had destroyed the core of the Japanese naval air strength, both in pilots and in planes, a blow which handicapped their future operations in the Pacific and from which they never fully recovered.

Mile: *see* NAUTICAL MILE.

Milford Haven: a fine deep-water estuary and harbour on the coast of Pembroke in S.W. Wales. Its enclosed and sheltered waters have long been recognized as offering great advantages for the naval protection of the south-western approaches. Milford Haven in the past saw the arrival and departure of several English kings; from it in 1171 Henry II's army sailed to Ireland; in 1399 Richard II landed here before succumbing to Henry of Lancaster, who became Henry IV; and here Henry Tudor landed from France in 1485. During the Napoleonic Wars a French invasion of Ireland was once again feared and in 1809 a naval dockyard was established. In the Second World War the Navy made great use of Milford Haven; and today it has developed as a great oil port and sees the arrival and departure of huge modern tankers. *See also* PEMBROKE.

Military mast: fighting-top or platform, usually of hollow steel, introduced into sea-going turret warships for mounting machine guns or other quick-firing small guns. Sometimes it was equipped with a searchlight.

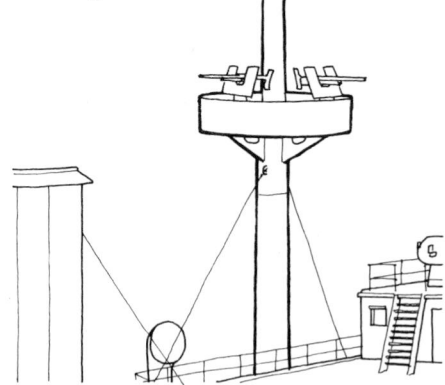

Miller, Patrick (1731–1815): interesting name in the history of steam navigation. A successful Scottish merchant and banker, he devoted his later life to agricultural improvements and experiments in ship-building, among them a vessel with two or three hulls and paddle-wheels between, worked by men at the capstans. In 1788–9 he tried a double boat fitted with a Symington engine; but he got no encouragement from his more successful compatriot James Watt and lost heart.

Millwall: a part of London dockland, at one time celebrated for the fine sailing ships built there.

'Miltiades': clipper ship built (1871) by Hood of Aberdeen and for long owned by the White Star Line. She was intended for the emigrant trade but, although she often carried a few passengers, she came to fame in the wool fleet. In 1873, despite poor N.E. Trade Winds, she was out to Melbourne in 63 days and made many other fine runs in the next 20 years. One of her most famous races was with the *Cimba* in the late 1880s. The two clippers left Sydney on the same day. *Miltiades* caught up her rival at the Antipodes Islands and went ahead as far as the Horn, where *Cimba* overtook her and held the lead till the South Atlantic. After that, the two lost sight of each other but came into London on the same day. With the great days of the wool clippers over, *Miltiades* carried coal and grain before being sold to the Norwegians. One admirer said 'She was as beautiful as she was good, and as good as she was beautiful.'

Mine: explosive container placed in the water and so devised that detonation (effected in a variety of ways) will sink or at least seriously damage a ship. Although experiments with underwater explosives had been tried earlier (*see* SUBMARINE), the prototype of the mine as we know it today was used (with little success) by the

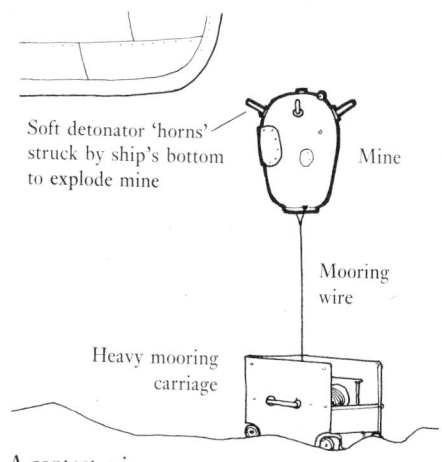

Soft detonator 'horns' struck by ship's bottom to explode mine

Mine

Mooring wire

Heavy mooring carriage

A contact mine.

Russians in the Baltic in 1855 during the Crimean War. As with other weapons, rapid technical developments were made, and mines were extensively laid by both sides during the First World War. Already by 1918 a mine that would explode in reaction to a ship's magnetism was being developed, and by the beginning of the Second World War (1939) mines had become both more powerful and more varied in the devices by which they were caused to explode. In addition to these contact and magnetic mines, there appeared the acoustic mine and the pressure mine, which were detonated respectively by a ship's vibrations and by the change of water pressure caused by the hull. Sometimes a combination of these methods of detonation was used, and the newer types of mine could be used in shallow water, especially in river estuaries. For defence, controlled mines could be laid in the entrance to a harbour or off the coast, and detonated only from the shore.

Minelayer: a vessel designed or adapted for laying mines. During and after the First World War many navies built minelayers. Minelaying submarines were also constructed because of their ability to lay minefields in secrecy. In the Second World War British minelayers were powerfully engined to allow a speedy completion of mine sowing, but a very great number of mines were laid by aircraft, a method found to be satisfactory and cheaper. The result has been the virtual disappearance of the specially designed minelayer.

Minesweeper: a vessel designed or adapted for sweeping or destroying mines at sea or in river estuaries. The different types of MINES which have been developed require different types of sweeping gear and different types of vessel. Contact mines can be swept by towing a sweep which cuts their mooring so that they surface and can then be destroyed. Magnetic mines can be

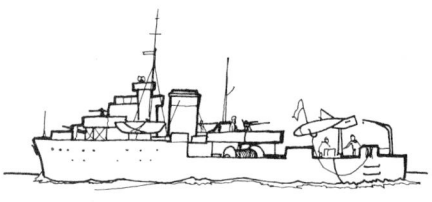

destroyed with an electromagnetic device known as the 'LL' or 'L' sweep, but require ships with wooden or glass-fibre non-magnetic hulls. Acoustic mines can be destroyed by artificial vibrations, but pressure mines are more difficult to locate and deal with. During the First and Second World Wars many ships, especially trawlers, were turned to minesweeping duties. *See also* SWEPT CHANNEL; OROPESA SWEEP.

> Dawn off the Foreland – the young flood making
> Jumbled and short and steep
> Black in the hollows and bright where it's breaking
> Awkward water to sweep.
> Mines reported in the fairway,

> Warn all traffic and detain.
> Sent up *Unity*, *Claribel*, *Assyrian*, *Stormcock* and *Golden Gain*.

> Rudyard Kipling, *Sea Warfare* (1916)

Minorca: one of the Balearic Islands which lie in the western Mediterranean off the coast of Spain. It was captured by the British in 1708 during the War of the Spanish Succession and remained in British hands till 1756, when it was lost to the French at the beginning of the Seven Years' War, a loss for which Admiral BYNG was blamed and shot. Byng, with an undermanned and poorly equipped fleet, had fought an indecisive action with a French fleet off Minorca, and by deciding to return to Gibraltar he failed to prevent French troops from landing and capturing the chief town and harbour, PORT MAHON, where the British garrison was forced to surrender. Minorca was restored to the British at the treaty in 1763, but it was retaken by the Spanish towards the end of the War of American Independence (1775–83). The island was again in British hands from 1798 to 1802, and during the Napoleonic Wars Port Mahon was once more secured as a naval base by Collingwood for his blockade of Toulon. After the defeat of Napoleon in 1815 Minorca finally reverted to Spain.

'Minotaur': the most famous ship of this name was the 74-gun vessel built at Woolwich in 1793 and commissioned in 1794 by Captain Thomas Louis, one of Nelson's great 'Band of Brothers'. She was implicated in the 1797 mutiny of the fleet at Spithead, but more than redeemed her reputation at the Battle of the Nile (1798), when she sustained 23 killed and 64 wounded and Louis received a personal tribute from Nelson: 'Your support has prevented me from being obliged to haul out of the line'. After many other actions, including Trafalgar (1805), she was convoying sixty sail from the Baltic to Yarmouth when she became detached in a severe gale and was wrecked on the Haak Sands at the mouth of the Texel (22 December 1810) with a loss of 370 lives. A figurehead believed to be hers is preserved at Sheerness.

'Miranda Guinness': 1540-ton beer carrier which sailed for her sea trials at the end of 1976; a good example of the modern specialized carrier. She was the last ship to be built in the Bristol City Docks before Charles Hill & Sons, the last remaining shipbuilding company in the docks, decided to close their business.

Missiles: general name for a range of offensive weapons mostly depending on their own propellant rather than on the initial discharge of a gun. An early form of missile was the explosive ROCKET developed by Sir William Congreve and first used in 1806. Another missile was the self-propelled TORPEDO, first produced in 1867. But today missiles of great sophistication have been designed in association with electronic devices which, either from the ship or from their own mechanism, guide their flight to the target. The intercontinental ballistic missile (I.C.B.M.; see POLARIS) with a nuclear warhead, a fearful weapon, is capable of being fired by submarines below the surface. Other missiles used on warships are surface-to-surface and surface-to-air projectiles; guided-missile cruisers, destroyers and other ships so equipped are found in most of the world's navies. There are many types designed for medium-, long- and short-range attack. For anti-submarine warfare, missile launchers have patterns of depth charges, and torpedoes have been fitted with homing devices. Development of new missiles and counter-measures continues and this form of weapon is tending to replace the previous reliance on the gun.

See colour section.

Mister: the form of address given by the master of a sailing ship to his mate, and also much used formerly in the Royal Navy in addressing junior officers and certain senior ratings (see, for example, Captain Marryat's *Mr Midshipman Easy*).

'Mr Midshipman Easy': a well-known sea story (1836) by Captain Frederick MARRYAT. It tells of the adventures and tribulations of Jack Easy, who goes to sea as a midshipman and is involved in many exciting scrapes and incidents, which, like the varied naval characters in the story, owe much to Marryat's own experience.

Mistral: an unpleasant northerly or north-westerly wind originating in the Rhône valley and sometimes in winter and spring causing fierce gales in the Gulf of Lions in the Mediterranean. During the Napoleonic Wars British ships watching or blockading the French fleet in Toulon were sometimes blown off their stations by the mistral.

Mizen (or mizzen): *see* MAST.

Mnemonics: aids to memory; the word derives from the Greek for 'mindful'. This example was used by East Coast colliers:

First the Dudgeon, then the Spurn;
Flamborough Head comes next in turn.
Whitby Castle stands out to sea
Twenty-seven miles right northerly.
Sunderland town lies in a bight
Thirty-six miles from Whitby High light:
The Old Man says, 'If all goes right
We'll all get drunk in Shields tonight.'

307

Mnemonics served a useful purpose for youngsters, but it is difficult to imagine that an old salt straining his eyes for landmarks would be desperately mumbling a mnemonic the while.

Model ships: the making of model ships dates back to very early times, often as votive offerings to the spirits controlling wind and tide or to assist the passage of the soul to the next world. Centuries-old rites were chronicled recently of toy boats being floated in Cornwall, Guernsey and Eire on Good Friday to mark the beginning of another fishing season and, doubtless, to placate the gods of shoal and breeding-ground.

Models fall into various groups and types. Most precious to the historian are actual shipbuilders' ('dockyard') models, made to show the design and construction details of a projected new vessel. The earliest we know of in England is that produced by Phineas Pett in 1607 to demonstrate the lines of the PRINCE ROYAL (launched 1610). The most famous model surviving from the 17th century is that of the PRINCE, a first-rate launched in 1670; only some half-dozen models have survived from the century and the *Prince* is the more precious in that it is one of the very few that have been positively identified with an actual ship, in this case from unmistakable evidence afforded by a drawing by Van de Velde in the Rijksmuseum at Amsterdam and from contemporary tapestries of the Battle of Solebay (1672), in which the *Prince* was the English flag-ship. The model, now preserved at the Science Museum, London, is on a scale of 1:48, and was meticulously re-rigged in 1925 from ship-plans and details

A contemporary shipyard model of the *Royal George* undergoing rigging overhaul.

in the manuscript of Sir Anthony Deane's *Doctrine of Naval Architecture* (1670).

As some guide to the labour involved in making a precise model of this kind, it may be recorded that C. Nepean Longridge, who constructed the 20th-century model of the *Victory*, also now in the Science Museum, took some 12,000 hours to build the hull; this excluded all the carved work.

As time went on, doubtless for reasons of economy, the detailed anatomical model often gave place to the type cut from the solid, and what is called the 'half-block' version, fitted to a backboard.

Side by side with the highly finished models from the hands of anonymous dockyard craftsmen or of highly skilled amateurs are the 'sailor' models, fashioned more crudely but with great depth of knowledge by the roughened hands of men who lived in, and sailed, the ships. In a sense, they portray even more vividly than their patrician sisters the hazards and labour of the sea. A particular fancy of the seaman was the ship in the bottle, with all its mystery of construction. In modern commercial manufacture the tricks and infinite patience required for the genuine article have been largely circumvented.

In a special category came the prisoner-of-war models from the Napoleonic period, made of bone, instead of the more usual boxwood. This unlikely material (obtained from the mutton joints with which the prisoners were fed) was manipulated with extraordinary skill by Frenchmen with their long tradition of craftsmanship in ivory. The fashioning of these beautiful pieces was at once a way of beguiling the tedious hours of imprisonment and a very profitable occupation, since the captives had easy access to the public and sold them readily. There are good grounds for thinking that bone models were also made by the ordinary British sailor in his spare

time at sea, but it is customary (and doubtless more rewarding economically in the antique market) to label all such creations as French prisoner-of-war work. Among the prisons and prison hulks which produced bone models were Norman Cross, Colchester, Tonbridge, Dartmoor, Perth, Chatham and Portsmouth.

Other, even more difficult, materials used in these prisons were fine wood shavings, and straw, trimmed into tiny cylinders and then split into even tinier flat pieces. The fragile and perishable nature of straw has meant that very few examples of such models have survived.

There is still ample scope for the recreational model-maker, though it is devoutly to be hoped that some of the horrendous Spanish galleons, Golden Hinds and Mayflowers, owing more to their creators' nightmares than to historic fact, will go to oblivion without delay. First-class kits, based on authentic ship-plans, are readily available in varying degrees of size and complexity.

You most truly told us years ago that 'Take it all in all, a ship of the line is the most honourable thing that man, as a gregarious animal, has ever produced.' I shall not therefore hesitate to ask you to put on your best spectacles and look for a moment at the enclosed photograph, which I have had taken for you from a model of the *Temeraire*, which we have here now in a sort of museum. The model is nearly three feet long, and belonged to an old naval man; it was made years ago by the French prisoners in the hulks at Portsmouth out of their beef-bones! Even if we were at war with France, and had the men and ships likely to do it, it would be impossible to catch any prisoners now who could make a ship such as this out of anything, much less of beef-bones; and I foresee that this lovely little ship must soon, in the nature of things, pass away ... and that there will be no one living able to restore a rope or spar rightly once they are broken or displaced in her.

Robert Leslie to John Ruskin (1884. The model may still be seen in the Tudor House Museum, Southampton, restored, contrary to Leslie's gloomy expectations, in 1949 by Laurence Pritchard)

'Mohawk': destroyer built by White at Cowes (1907) which upset many calculations about speed and fuel consumption. The Admiralty's wish for a speed of 33 knots produced gloomy prophecies that such demands would make a ship with an enormous fuel consumption and liable to buckle in a rough sea or founder if she put her nose in a big wave. In the event, *Mohawk* attained $34\frac{1}{2}$ knots in her six-hour trials in fairly rough November weather and used $64\frac{3}{4}$ tons of oil. With a capacity for 148 tons, this gave her a range of 1500 miles at a cruising speed of 14 knots.

Mole: stone or concrete structure acting as a breakwater and helping to form a harbour; it may be joined to the land at one end and give berthing to ships, or be an island structure acting solely as a breakwater. The mole at ZEEBRUGGE was the scene of a gallant diversionary attack in April 1918.

Monck (or **Monk**), **George**, first Duke of Albemarle (1608–70): naval commander and general. Trained as a soldier, he was appointed an admiral, at the age of 44, in the First Dutch War. Though his ignorance of nautical language was at first a joke, he proved himself a skilled commander in action, with a number of successes to his credit, including the Battle of the GABBARD (1653) and, later in the same year, the action off Scheveningen in which Tromp was killed. He achieved less in the Second Dutch War (1665–7). Although an amateur at sea, he was a notable innovator, for he was no means averse to breaking away from the formal line of battle and attacking the enemy in a general mêlée of the type that was to prove so successful in later British naval history.

He was of a very comely personage, his countenance very manly and majestic, the whole fabric of his body very strong, his constitution very healthful and fitted for business, before his sickness; he was never known to desire meat or drink till called to it, which was but once a day . . . I have known him fast from eating and drinking above thirty hours many times upon the obligation of necessary and important affairs . . . four hours sleep was to him sufficient and full satisfaction.

Thomas Gumble, *Life of General Monck, Duke of Albemarle* (1671)

Monitor: shallow draught type of ironclad warship, dating from the 1860s, chiefly intended for bombardment purposes. The idea may be traced back to the bombketches of the 17th century. The most famous vessel of the type was the one that gave her name to the class: the 1861 *Monitor* designed by the Swedish engineer John Ericsson and ordered by the Union, during the American Civil War, as a counterblast to the Confederate *MERRIMAC*. Ericsson's ship was a strange construction, with the hull in two parts – an underwater body 124 ft long, 34 ft wide and 5·8 ft deep, and, above, an armoured teak hull 48 ft longer, $7\frac{1}{2}$ ft wider and about 5 ft high. The rotating gun tower was equipped with two 11-in. guns positioned amidships (*see also* GUN TURRET). She was never a safe sea-going vessel, having nearly foundered on her way to the historic encounter with the *Merrimac*, and soon after that fight she went down in a gale off Cape Hatteras, with a loss of 16 men.

The impregnable and aggressive character of this structure will admonish the leaders of the Southern rebellion that the batteries on the banks of their rivers will no longer present barriers to the entrance of the Union forces. The ironclad intruder will prove a severe monitor to those leaders. But there are other leaders who will also be startled and admonished by the booming of the guns of the impregnable iron turrets. Downing Street will hardly view with indifference this last Yankee notion, this monitor.

> John Ericsson, writing to the Secretary, U.S. Navy

Monk: *see* MONCK, GEORGE.

Monkey: (1) a small wooden tub or cask in which rum was carried to the messes after issue; later applied to the metal mess kettle used for the same purpose (*see also* SUCKING THE MONKEY). **(2)** The first element of several compound words, sometimes with a connotation of small: e.g. 'monkey-block', a swivel block for running rigging; 'monkey-boat', an old type of small river and coastal vessel; 'monkey-engine', a type of steam engine; 'monkey-gaff', a small gaff; 'monkey-rail', a light rail; 'monkey-rope', a securing rope round a seaman's waist; 'monkey-wheel', a wheel in a block over which a hoisting rope runs. (See also the entries below.)

Monkey-jacket: the everyday jacket worn by officers and petty officers.

Monkey-pump: a straw inserted through a small hole in a cask to draw out liquor illegally. *See also* SUCKING THE MONKEY.

Monkey's fist: a form of round knot which

gives weight to the end of a heaving line.

'Monmouth': a name occurring in some great passages of British naval history. One *Monmouth*, of 54 guns, added the famous *FOUDROYANT* of 84 guns to the English Navy List (1758). Just over 150 years later another *Monmouth* fought heroically in the Battle of CORONEL (1914), when the German battle cruiser *Gneisenau* sent her to the bottom, crippled and on fire.

Monson, Sir William (1569–1643): admiral, a distinguished seaman whose service stretched over half a century: he went to sea in 1585 and was still there in 1635. He commanded a ship to the Azores and Canaries (1589), was held prisoner in Spain (1591–3), was knighted by Essex for his part in the action at Cadiz (1596), exterminated a nest of pirates at Broad Haven in Ireland (1614) and, a little off course, got himself deprived of command for suspected complicity in the murder of Sir Thomas Overbury. Apart from his battle record, he will always be re-membered for his command in the Narrow Seas where, in 1604, he was sent to enforce the proclamation for keeping the peace; for his restoration of the sovereignty of those seas to the English; and for his *Naval Tracts*, one of the best authorities for the naval history of the early 17th century:

> I went on board the Admiral of Holland, who had been my old and familiar acquaintance by reason of many actions and services we had been in together. I told him that after twenty years spent in the wars, I was now become a watchman with a bill in my hand to see peace kept and no disorder committed in the Narrow Seas. (1604)

In July 1605, he put into Calais, and found there six Dutch ships newly arrived to join the Dutch squadron... One of these was the Admiral's ship. On Sir William's approach this

Dutch admiral dipped his flag thrice. Sir William sent him a message to take it in altogether. The Dutchman refused, asserting that he had struck his colours thrice, and that was acknowledgment enough. Sir William assured him that it was not, and added that if he did not promptly salute as he was told, the British admiral would at once weigh anchor, fall down to him, and settle the question with powder and shot: 'for,' as he put it, 'rather than I would suffer his flag to be worn in view of so many actions as were to behold it, I resolve to bury myself in the sea.'

The Dutch Admiral, however, was convinced at last. He took down his flag, fired a gun for the rest of the fleet to follow him, and stood off to sea in a huff.

'And thus,' Sir William winds up very drily, 'I lost my guest the next day at dinner as he had promised.'

Sir Arthur Quiller-Couch (ed.), *The Story of the Sea* (1898)

Monsoon: an Arab word meaning 'season', but generally and specifically denoting the S.W. monsoon wind and rainy season of India and the Indian Ocean, though also occurring in northern Australia and the China Sea. Such winds are caused by the intense heating of the land mass creating a low-pressure area which draws in air in the form of wind from over the ocean, bringing heavy rainfall. The S.W. monsoon of India is of this kind and occurs approximately from May to September. When it begins to blow it is said to 'break' and is often accompanied by thunderstorms. From October to April it is followed by a wind flowing in the reverse direction, which is the N.E. monsoon, caused by the relative cooling of the land and the creation of a high-pressure area from which the air flows outward towards low pressure. Only where the N.E. monsoon has crossed the sea does it bring rain to the land in S.E. India and Sri Lanka. On moving across the Equator the N.E. monsoon is deflected by the earth's rotation and becomes a N.W. monsoon over northern Australia.

When Vasco da Gama discovered the route to India round Africa (1498) it was the following wind of the S.W. monsoon which enabled him to cross the ocean from Malindi on the African coast to Calicut in India in 23 days.

Moodie, Captain George (*fl.*1870–73): sailing ship commander, well-known especially as the first master of the great clipper *Cutty Sark*. Though he was never such a hard driver as some of his fellow-captains, he was an extremely skilful seaman and navigator. It was during his command of the *Cutty Sark* that the famous race occurred between her and the *Thermopylae* (1872), an occasion marred by the former losing her rudder in a heavy gale when she was 400 miles ahead. The owner's brother, who was on board, tried to order Moodie into the Cape for repairs; but

Moodie, by a splendid piece of seamanship and with the help of Henry Henderson, the ship's carpenter, and the blacksmith, made a jury rudder from spare parts, the necessary ironwork being forged while heavy seas still swept the deck, and brought the ship safely into London only seven days after the *Thermopylae*. Unfortunately Moodie had been so angered by the owner's brother that he resigned his command and went into steam.

Moonlit (or **Moonlight**) **Battle** (or **Battle of St Vincent**; 16 January 1780): action off Cape St Vincent in which Admiral Rodney attacked a Spanish fleet, which lost seven ships, including the flagship of Admiral Don Juan de Langara. The battle began in the late afternoon and continued, in a storm, until 2 o'clock the next morning.

For the more famous battle in the same area *see* CAPE ST VINCENT, BATTLE OF.

Moonraker (or **moonsail**): light sail sometimes carried above the sky-sail; one of the more fanciful names for sails ('cloud cleaner' is another example). The moonraker was also known as a 'sky gazer'. *See also* SAIL.

'Moonshine': 35-ton ship which, in company with the *Sunshine* of 50 tons, was used by Captain John DAVIS in two of his expeditions in search of the North-West Passage. In 1586 he reached Labrador in her, catching a great deal of cod which he salted and brought home.

Moor: to secure a ship or boat by anchor, cable, ropes or chains.

Moored all fours: moored fore and aft instead of able to swing.

'Mora': ship associated with the best-known date in English history, the arrival of Duke William of Normandy in 1066. The *Mora* was the Duke's flag-ship, presented by his wife Matilda. It is shown in the BAYEUX TAPESTRY.

Moresby, Sir Fairfax (1786–1877): admiral. Though he lived to be over ninety, O'Byrne tells us that in 1823 'to such an extent had his health become impaired while in command of the *Menai*, particularly in the extensive surveys he made of the Ethiopian archipelago and of the African coast, that for five years he was subject to attacks which reduced him each time to the lowest state of debility.' He is best remembered for his period of command at Mauritius (1821–3), when he was successful in suppressing the slave trade there and also arranged a treaty with the King of Madagascar for the cessation of the trade in his dominions.

Morgan, Sir Henry (?1635–1688): buccaneer, originating from Glamorgan, who combined courage and powers of leadership with a black streak of treachery and unscrupulousness. His adventurous nature

313

took him to the West Indies and the Caribbean where, in 1668, he was chosen 'admiral' of the buccaneers and led his horde on a series of brutal and daring raids. In the same year they sacked Panama, the base for the Spanish silver galleons, and took away 250,000 pieces of eight. They plundered the shores of Lake Maracaibo in 1669 and two years later captured Panama, plundering the surrounding countryside for many miles. In 1672 Morgan was sent home to England under arrest but, after a short period of disgrace (more theoretical than real), he won the favour of the unpredictable Charles II, received a knighthood and was sent out to Jamaica as Lieutenant Governor and commander-in-chief. He reverted to type (if he ever forsook it) and occupied most of his last years in gluttony and gambling. The physician Sir Hans Sloane, in *Voyage to the West Indies* (1707), has left us with an unpleasant picture of an unpleasant character at the age of 53:

Sir Henry Morgan... lean, swallow-coloured, his eyes a little yellowish and belly jutting out or prominent, complained to me of want of appetite to victuals; he had a kicking or reaching to vomit every morning and generally a small looseness attending him, and withal was much given to drinking and sitting up late, which I supposed had been the cause of his indisposition.

'Morning Light': for nearly twenty years the largest ship built in North America. Constructed by W. and R. Wright of St John in 1855, she was 264 ft long, 43·8 ft beam and of 2377 tons, composite wood and iron and two-decked. Taken over by the Black Ball Line, she made a run of 73 days from Liverpool to Melbourne in 1856, being beaten that year only on an outward run by the famous *Lightning*. *Morning Light* was afterwards sold to a German

firm, was renamed *J. W. Wendt* and foundered in March 1889 at Barnegat, New Jersey.

Morse code: a system of communication developed by Samuel Finley Breese Morse (1791–1872), American painter and inventor who in 1844 demonstrated before Congress his electric telegraph by sending the famous message 'What hath God wrought' over the wire from Washington to Baltimore. The Morse code is based on combinations of dots and dashes as sound signals to represent the letters of the alphabet and the numerals, the dash being three times the length of the dot. The code was the most generally used as the commercial telegraph, and later radio-telegraph systems, came into use. Slightly altered to become the International Morse Code, it is still widely used, although other systems have developed. With long and short flashes from a lamp, or by hand-flag movements, the Morse code is also used for visual signalling.

Mortar boats: small, shallow draught powerful ships carrying short pieces of ordnance and capable of engaging enemy batteries at short range. They proved particularly useful in, e.g., the Crimean War.

Mostyn, Savage (*fl.*1734–57): admiral. Not a very distinguished figure (he was court-martialled at one stage for failing to engage two French ships); but a letter of his among the Admiralty papers is worth quoting as showing the quality of some of the men from whom the naval service was miraculously fashioned:

I don't know where they come from but whoever was the officer who received them, he ought to be ashamed, for I never saw such except in the condemned hole at Newgate. I was

Mortar boats.

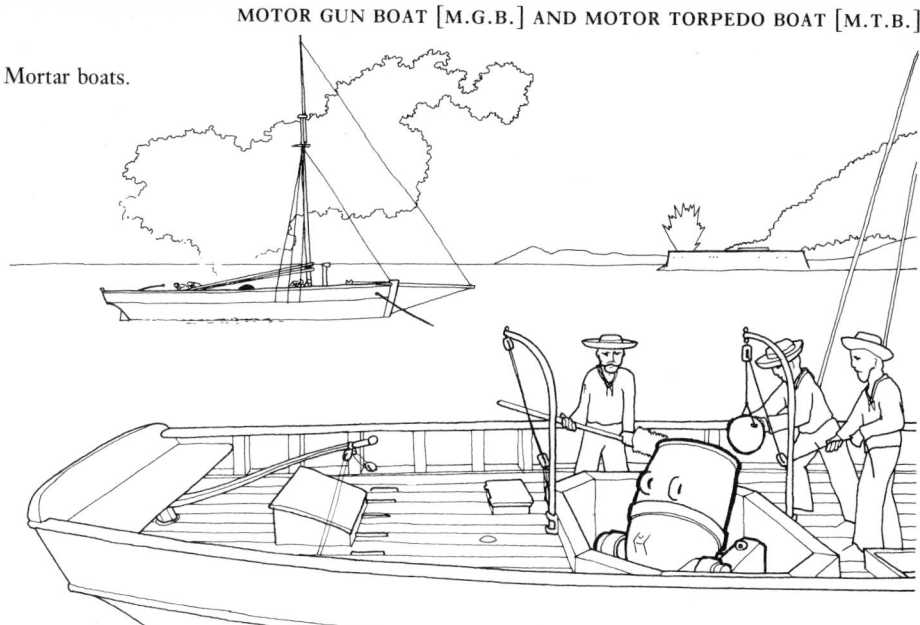

three and a half hours mustering this scabby crew, and I should have imagined that the scum of the earth had been picked up for this ship.

(1759)

Mother Carey's Chickens: sailor's name for the STORMY PETREL; 'Mother Carey's Goose' is the great petrel or fulmar. The name is thought to be a corruption of the Latin *mater cara*, 'dear mother', i.e. the Virgin Mary. A superstition among sailors was that the appearance of the bird foretold storm or disaster.

'Mother of the Navy': Agnes Elizabeth Weston (1840–1918), so-called for her philanthropic work among seamen. She corresponded with them, published a monthly letter for distribution to ships' companies (from 1871), and organized 'Sailors' Rests', the first of which opened at Devonport in 1876. She was often affectionately known as 'Aggie'.

Mother-ship: a depot ship intended to serve a group of particular warships such as submarines, destroyers or coastal craft. The mother-ship will carry special equipment and stores for maintaining warships; she will have special derricks or cranes for lifting heavy machinery in need of repair; she will carry a special complement of officers and men and have facilities to meet most of the needs of her attendant ships.

Motor gun boat (M.G.B.) and **Motor torpedo boat (M.T.B.):** small, fast, engine-driven boats designed for offensive action in coastal waters. During the Second World War British coastal forces included considerable numbers of such craft, which were driven by powerful petrol engines and had speeds of up to 40 knots. They were active in numerous encounters with the enemy in the Channel and the North Sea, where they were often opposed by their counterpart, the German E-boats. The M.T.B. carried two torpedoes in tubes on the upper deck, and both types were

315

equipped with various light and heavy machine guns. Today these boats have been developed into a general class of fast patrol boats, engined with gas-turbines giving speeds of over 50 knots in some types. Some carry two or four torpedo tubes and missile launchers. *See also* TORPEDO BOAT.

See colour section.

Mould loft: large shed in dockyards, on the floor of which the master-shipwrights drew the plan of a new vessel full-size. The walls were high enough for them to mark out the side elevations. This was the process known as 'laying down' the ship.

Mountbatten, Louis Francis Albert Victor Nicholas, first Earl Mountbatten of Burma (1900–79): admiral, Supreme Allied Commander in S.E. Asia (1943–6), First Sea Lord (1955–9) and Chief of U.K. Defence Staff (1959–65). He was Viceroy of India when the dominions of India and Pakistan were established (1947).

Mr: *see* MISTER.

M.T.B. (Motor torpedo boat): *see* MOTOR GUN BOAT.

Mud pilot: the pilot who takes a ship from Gravesend Reach in the Thames to her dock entrance.

Mulberry harbour: code name for the artificial harbours created off the Normandy coast to supply the Allied forces for Operation 'Overlord', the invasion of France (June 1944). The harbours consisted of various elements, moles and breakwaters being formed by scuttled ships, by huge constructions of concrete and steel towed across the Channel and sunk in position, and by different kinds of floating piers, the whole being known as 'Mulberry', though each part had a separate code name.

The whole project was majestic. On the beaches themselves would be the great piers, with their seaward ends afloat and sheltered. At these piers coasters and landing-craft would be

Air photograph showing the western entrance.

able to discharge at all states of the tide. To protect them against the wanton winds and waves breakwaters would be spread in a great arc to seaward, enclosing a large area of sheltered water. Thus sheltered, deep-draught ships could be at anchor and discharge, and all types of landing-craft could ply freely to and from the beaches. These breakwaters would be composed of sunken concrete structures known as 'Phoenix' and blockships known as 'Gooseberries'.

Winston Churchill, The Second World War, Vol.V (1952)

Thus does Churchill describe the evolution of the idea, but in the event the stormy weather which accompanied the landings created great difficulties.

'Mumble bees': small type of Brixham fishing craft, cutter-rigged and about half the size of the better-known ketches.

Mundy, Peter (*fl.*1600–1637): seaman and traveller. Beginning as a cabin-boy on a merchant ship, he rose to comfortable circumstances and travelled widely, visiting India, China, Japan, Denmark, Russia and Prussia. On many of his journeys he kept interesting journals.

Muscovy Company: company which developed from that organized to finance the 1553 expedition of Willoughby and Chancellor to seek markets for English cloth along the north coasts of Asia, which succeeded in penetrating the White Sea and Russia itself. The company later developed a prosperous business with Persia by the overland route through Russia. Its charter gave it exclusive rights in all exploration north of English latitudes, including the North-East and North-West Passages, which some of the more far-seeing and energetic members wished to open up (*see* JENKINSON, ANTHONY). Muscovy was an early name for Russia, especially from the 14th to the early 18th century, when the grand duchy of Moscow (Muscovy) was the dominant power.

Muster: a ship's company. The muster-book or roll was the official record of the officers and crew. To muster is to assemble the company.

He is to keep a Muster Book in which are to be inserted the names of all persons forming a part of the Complement of the Ship, with every circumstance relating to them... being particularly accurate in the account of their age, and the place of their nativity ... The number under which a man is entered in the original Muster Book, is to be continued in all following Muster Books ... He is to furnish the Clerk of the Cheque or Muster Master with a perfect Muster Book, signed by himself and the other signing Officers ... He is to present himself at all musters of the Ship's Company.

Instructions to Captains of
H.M. Ships (1808)

'Mutine': 16-gun brig at the Battle of the Nile (1798), commanded by Captain Thomas Masterman Hardy. He had earned the command when, in 1797, he was the lieutenant in charge of the boats that cut her out in the bay of Santa Cruz in the face of heavy fire, and transferred her from the French to the British Navy.

Mutines have busied around in many other actions, including those at Copenhagen with Lord Gambier (1807) and Algiers (1816), when Sir Edward Pellew bombarded the forts and shipping so devastatingly. The 1844 12-gun brig *Mutine* was in the Experimental Squadron which took part in extensive sailing tests.

Mutiny: a concerted refusal to obey legitimate orders from a superior officer. 'Mutiny' applies to such a refusal not only by men in the armed forces, but also by the crew of a merchant ship. In the Royal Navy mutiny was at one time considered the most serious crime after treason, and was for long punishable with death by hanging at the yardarm, this punishment being within the captain's power to administer. This is, of course, no longer so, and properly constituted courts-martial follow the offence (except for merchant seamen, who are tried in the civil courts).

Of mutiny in individual ships numerous instances are on record. One of the best-known is the mutiny on the *Bounty* under the irascible, though undoubtedly able, Captain BLIGH. Perhaps foreshadowing the later fleet mutiny at Spithead was the refusal of duty by the men of H.M.S. *Culloden* in 1794. In this single-ship mutiny the crew refused duty until they either got a new ship or the *Culloden* was dry-docked for repairs. When the mutiny was over, five of the leaders were hanged, although it was widely believed that they had been promised immunity.

Three years later, in April and May 1797, occurred the mutiny of the Channel Fleet at Spithead. This resulted from a culmination of grievances, poor pay and delay in a promised increase, bad and short victuals and other harsh conditions of service. It began in, and was organized from, H.M.S. *Queen Charlotte*, and was

Three American mutineers hung from the yardarm.

supported by crews throughout the fleet. At first only the question of pay was raised by the mutineers in their 'Humble Petition to the Right Honourable the Lords Commissioners of the Admiralty'. If ever it is permissible to say that a mutiny was 'well conducted' by the mutineers, this is an instance. For the greater part of its duration the men acted with moderation and restraint, though there was some violence in the later stages due to tactless words and actions by certain officers. The men refused to weigh anchor, but were otherwise prepared to obey orders and even sail if 'the enemy were at sea and a convoy wanted'. The naval authorities were slow to realize the serious and widespread nature of the mutiny, which before long spread to the ships at Plymouth also. There was much coming and going of admirals and other officers trying to restore obedience, but the men were carefully organized and they stood firm. In their later petitions they increased their demands to include better victuals and better sick pay. When their requests were agreed to they said they would not submit until they had received the full pardon of His Majesty with a promise of no punishment for the offenders. This was at last obtained, and the mutiny ended. There was agreement that the men were justified in their complaints; pay and conditions of service were improved, and no scapegoats were sought; there was not even a court-martial.

Towards the end of the Spithead affair, on 12 May 1797, a mutiny broke out in the fleet at the Nore, where the mutineers were led by Richard Parker · of H.M.S. *Sandwich*. This spread to Admiral Duncan's squadron lying at Yarmouth, and some of his ships left to join the mutineers at Sheerness, though he himself acted with admirable firmness on board the *Venerable* and the *Adamant*. The men at the Nore acted foolishly and truculently and at first, in spite of appeals from the men at Spithead, they failed to react to the fact that all the men's demands there had been met and the mutiny settled. The Admiralty stood firm. Gradually discontent with the mutineers' leaders grew, and when Parker proposed to take the rebellious ships across to Holland, fighting broke out amongst the crews. Though a few succeeded in making an escape to the Continent, the mutiny gradually collapsed and one by one the ships surrendered unconditionally to the authorities. By 13 June all was over; Parker and 28 other ringleaders were tried, found guilty and hanged, whilst others were flogged round the fleet.

One other sad outbreak should be mentioned. In the great depression of 1931 the seamen in the fleet at Invergordon on the Cromarty Firth were suddenly faced in September with a 10 per cent cut in their pay; they were driven to desperation and refused to weigh anchor. The pay cut was retracted a few days later and the mutiny subsided, but a number of the ringleaders were dismissed the service.

See also BANTRY BAY; *HERMIONE*.

Muzzle-loading: loading a gun with its ball or shot from the forward end of the barrel or the muzzle. The very earliest guns employed a primitive form of breech-loading (that is, loading from the rear end of the gun), but the difficulties encountered and the slow rate of fire made the gunmakers turn to muzzle-loading. Thus, at least from the time of the Armada and for nearly 300 years, the guns in British warships were muzzle-loading. Nelson's guns were in principle the same as Drake's but more powerful and effective. The modern breech-loading gun evolved in the 19th century with the great improvements made by Sir Joseph Whitworth and Sir William ARMSTRONG, the latter's breech-loading principle being finally adopted, after delays and changes, in 1880. *See also* ARMAMENT.

Myngs, Sir Christopher (1625–66): admiral. The son of a shoemaker, he was still only about 23 years of age when he was promoted captain and captured a fleet of Dutch merchant vessels (1653). He was mortally wounded leading the van on the fourth day of the FOUR DAYS' BATTLE (1666).

'Myrtle Holme': a good representative of the little barques which traded from England to Tasmania in the old days. She was a semi-clipper of 945 tons, built (1875) at Sunderland for the firm of Hine's and loading at the West India Dock.

Like all Hine's ships ... she had a good deal of elaborate and very finely carved teak on deck, not only scrolls but also texts and moral precepts which, it is to be feared, gave rise to a good deal of ribaldry among the apprentices. It was a firm which, in prosperous days at least, took the greatest pride in its ships and it expected all hands to do the same; there was trouble if any of them were seen in port without the masts being beautifully stayed and the yards squared, the usual thing being to hoist the upper topsail yards in order to improve their appearance.

Frank Bowen, *Sailing Ships of the London River*

A survivor from happier days, she met her end at the hands of a German submarine off the S.W. coast of Ireland (4 September 1915).

Mystery ships: general name for ships whose true nature and purpose are concealed with the intention of deceiving the enemy. Under this heading comes first the ruse used in the times of the sailing Navy by which a ship would pretend to be in trouble or trying to escape, but in reality intended to attract an enemy ship which could then be overcome, especially if separated from any consorts. All sorts of ways of decoying ships into a trap were employed. An exciting account of a Russian frigate pretending to be British occurs in Captain Marryat's *Mr Midshipman Easy*, when Captain Wilson in the *Aurora* comes up with a ship of which he is very suspicious. He has his suspicions confirmed when she opens fire, but to no avail, as the *Aurora* overcomes and captures her.

Perhaps the best-known use of mystery ships was during the First World War when, in order to help combat the German submarine menace, the British sent to sea a number of apparently harmless tramp steamers. They were decoys, known as Q-ships, which carried concealed armament and employed every *ruse de guerre*. The idea relied on the belief that U-boats would not expend a torpedo on destroying an apparently harmless merchant vessel, but would surface and destroy her by gunfire. This had already happened in the Channel,

and the incident suggested that ships, made to appear unarmed but carrying concealed guns and torpedoes, and even proceeding under false colours, might lure the submarine to the surface for a supposedly easy victim. Winston Churchill, who was then at the Admiralty, put the idea into effect, and the Q-ships began to operate. By these means eleven U-boats were destroyed in the two years 1915 and 1916, but the last success of this kind was in September 1917. The name of Commander Gordon Campbell is particularly associated with the story of the Q-ships, and it was he who was in command of H.M.S. *Dunraven* on 8 August 1917 when she engaged in a long and eventually unsuccessful duel with *U61* in the approaches to the Bristol Channel. The *Dunraven*, disguised as a merchant ship, tried every ruse to draw the submarine to close range. In the first encounter only the Q-ship's lighter gun was used, and her concealed 4-in. gun was held on stand-by. Smoke and steam were made so as to pretend she had boiler trouble, fake signals in plain language were sent out, and a false panic and abandonment of the ship were tried. But still the U-boat's shells continued to damage the *Dunraven*, and before she could bring her 4-in. gun to bear, the gun and her crew were blown up in an explosion. This clearly indicated to the U-boat's captain that he was dealing with a Q-ship, and his submarine dived but kept her periscope in view. The *Dunraven* foundered after her remaining crew had been taken off. For his bravery and leadership during this engagement Commander Campbell was awarded the V.C.

At the beginning of the Second World War there was an experiment with a few similarly disguised merchant ships, but it was not considered a success and was abandoned.

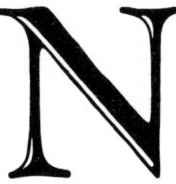

Nabob: originally a prince or deputy governor under the Mogul Empire in India; hence, a rich man who had amassed a fortune in India, and, in the old Navy, an affluent passenger in an East Indiaman.

Nail one's colours to the mast: refuse to surrender. If the colours are thus fixed, they cannot be hauled down in the traditional token of submission.

Names, ships': a fascinating subject which deserves a book to itself. Some, for example the name of a proud owner or some fair lady to whom it was wished to pay tribute, occur only once and pass from the pages of history. Others, especially in the Royal Navy, resound through the centuries. There have been a score of *Dragons* since 1512, almost as many *Lions* and more like thirty *Fortunes* since the early 16th century. Names such as *Revenge*, *Warspite* and *Victory* are, like Henry V's paladins, familiar in our mouths as household words. Cromwell named a ship after the fight he called his 'crowning mercy', his victory at Worcester (1651); in 1942 the eighth *Worcester* gained glory in her fight against the German *Scharnhorst* and *Gneisenau*. Some names have had to yield to political pressures and the shift of events and loyalties. Thus, when Charles II was restored to the throne in 1660, there was a quick change of name for nearly all those ships that had been called after Parliamentary victories and towns with Commonwealth sympathies. Whims of fashion or the personal predilections of an Admiralty official have produced some batches of names. Thus, the fourth Earl of Sandwich (1718–92), twice First Lord of the Admiralty, is generally held to have been responsible for a rash of classical names, such as *Ajax*, *Juno*, *Agamemnon* and *Jupiter*. Understandably, the seaman resolutely refused to twist his tongue round some of these outlandish introductions. *Amphitrite* became 'Am and Tripe', *Psyche* was better known as 'Pisky' or 'Sitch' and the stately Iphigenia, daughter of Agamemnon, would doubtless not have relished her rechristening as 'Niffy Jane'.

Since tradition rules strong in the Royal Navy, it is not surprising that there is less variety of name than is found in the merchant fleet. In the former, long periods go by with very few new names being added to the list; in the latter, there are few inhibitions. The Second World War period, for example, saw a number of trawlers named after famous football teams.

Certain superstitions have become attached to ships' names, for example that a snake name is unlucky. Captain Davys Manning, an authority on the subject of ships' names, traced 53 vessels named after snakes, eleven of which were lost by accident.

Not a very high proportion when one considers the risks of the days of sail, but three disasters in modern times have turned naval opinion against the names. The losses of the *Serpent*, *Cobra* and *Viper* were, I believe, the cause of the superstition, but that it still exists is proved by the outcry that arose about thirty years ago when a submarine was given the name *Python*. The name was changed to *Pandora* before she was launched.

Lecture to the Society for Nautical Research (1956)

Looking back over the centuries, one

cannot help feeling that some of the glory and imagination has departed from the naming of ships. Where are the *Cloud in the Sun*, the *Falcon in the Featherlock*, the *Due Repulse* and the *Lion's Whelp*; the *Peter Pomegranete*, the *Shruce of Dawske* and the *Ostrich Feather*; the *Flower de Luce*, the *Double Rose* and the *Bark of Bullen*?

'Nancy Dawson': a popular ship name, originating from a dancer of the name (?1730–1767) who danced her way into the public heart by her rendering of the hornpipe in *The Beggar's Opera*. The tune became a great popular success and, the ultimate tribute, was frequently used to summon seamen for their grog ration. Hence the rum itself was often called 'Nancy Dawson'.

Nantucket: harbour and town on the northern side of Nantucket Island, which lies off the coast of Massachusetts. Discovered in 1602 by an English sailor named Gosnold, the island was bought from the Indians and settlement began in the mid-17th century. In the 18th century Nantucket became a famous base for whaling ships and continued so for 150 years. Today its whaling days are commemorated in the town museum.

Nantucket! Take out your map and look at it. See what a real corner of the world it occupies; how it stands there, away off shore, more lonely than the Eddystone Lighthouse. Look at it – a mere hillock, and elbow of sand; all beach without a background... What wonder then, that these Nantucketers, born on a beach, should take to the sea for a livelihood!

Herman Melville, *Moby-Dick* (1851)

Napier, Sir Charles (1786–1860): admiral. A difficult and somewhat eccentric man who acquired the nicknames 'Black Charlie' and 'Mad Charlie', he was a distinguished sailor, and his service to the sea spanned some 60 years from the time he entered the Royal Navy in November 1799 as a first-class Volunteer on the sloop *Martin*. By the end of his career he had been decorated, not only by Britain, but by the Emperors of Austria and Russia and the King of Prussia. He was ennobled in the Portuguese peerage as Viscount Cape St Vincent, after taking command of the Portuguese fleet in 1833 and, on behalf of the young Queen of Portugal, destroying the fleet of the usurping Don Miguel. This was all part of a Byzantine and Mediterranean policy of keeping the balance between Russia and Turkey and, at the same time, upholding the small and oppressed against powers intent on wielding the big stick.

Napier took a great interest in steam navigation. In 1828 he submitted to the Admiralty a ship model that was placed in the United Services Museum, and in 1846 he worked on the construction of the *Sidon*, a steam frigate of 560 h.p. The choice of name reflects another Napier exploit, in 1839:

On 10 Sept. in that year he there [on the coast of Syria] effected a landing at D'journie, at the head of a body of 1500 Turks and marines; and ... he displayed such indefatigable zeal and activity as to elicit the particular praise of his Admiral. In the course of the same month he defeated a body of the enemy at Kelbson, and on 27, in the execution of a judicious and excellent plan he had previously formed, he bombarded and successfully stormed, with a force of not more than 900 allies and 500 Turks, the strong town of Sidon, protected by a fort and citadel and a line of wall defended by 2700 men, all of whom were made prisoner. On that occasion, at the head of the British marines, he broke into the enemy's barracks, and then obtained possession of the castle.

William O'Byrne, *Naval Biographical Dictionary* (1849)

Napier, David (1790–1869): marine engineer who in 1818 introduced steam packets for the Post Office service and established regular steam communication between Liverpool, Greenock and Glasgow, and between Greenock and Belfast. His cousin, *Robert Napier* (1791–1876), supplied engines for the East India Company and the Cunard Company. Afterwards he took to shipbuilding and constructed iron ships for many nations.

Napoleonic Wars: general name for the wars of 1803–15 fought by France against coalitions of European powers, following, with only a brief interlude, the French Revolutionary Wars, the interval being provided by the Peace of Amiens (1802). So far as the Navy was concerned, the renewed wars were marked by the threatened invasion of Britain by the fleet assembled by Napoleon at Boulogne, the devastating victory at Trafalgar (1805), which finally established British supremacy over all the maritime theatres of war, and the economic BLOCKADE. *See also* FRENCH WARS; CONTINENTAL SYSTEM; PENINSULAR WAR.

Narrow boat: small English canal boat, so called because its beam is not more than about 7 ft. It is often picturesquely painted with traditional decorations of long standing and serves as a floating home for a family who cherish the way of life and have followed it for generations. The typical craft were some 72 feet long, were horse-drawn and carried 25 tons. Some were owned by individuals as skippers ('Number Ones'), but ownership tended to pass to large carrying companies who, nevertheless, carried on the highly distinctive colour schemes; even government control, in the shape of the Docks and Inland Waterways Executive, failed to subdue this native form of art. Though much of this pulsing way of

life has disappeared with the development of other forms of transport, its evidences are much prized by collectors, including the magnificent teapots associated with Measham on the Ashby Canal, the painted tea-caddies, the rose-decorated feed bowls of the horses and the distinctive dress often adopted by the boat-folk.

Narrow seas: traditionally the English Channel and the southern North Sea, over which England, as soon as she became a maritime power, claimed sovereignty. In the Narrow Seas England sought the right to regulate fishing and for English warships to receive a salute. Later, international agreement on a three-mile limit as the extent of TERRITORIAL WATERS brought a change to these claims.

Narvik: seaport on the northern coast of Norway, the railhead outlet for ore from the Swedish ironfields at Gällivare. Narvik figured prominently in the early stages of the Second World War during April and May 1940. The British Navy had laid minefields in Norwegian waters and had for some time been planning a landing at Narvik, ostensibly to aid Finland and to deny the Swedish iron to Germany; but by a lightning and highly successful invasion of Denmark and Norway, Germany forestalled the British plans. Narvik was the most northerly of the Norwegian ports seized by the Germans and was occupied on 9 April 1940 by ten of their destroyers and supply ships. A British force of five destroyers under Captain B. A. W. Warburton-Lee on the following morning entered the fjord on which Narvik lies and sank two of the German destroyers and damaged three others. On returning down the fjord the British ships met a further German force of five destroyers. On both

sides damage was considerable, but two British destroyers were sunk, and Captain Warburton-Lee was killed, being awarded the V.C. posthumously. A second naval engagement was fought a few days later when H.M.S. *Warspite* and nine destroyers arrived in the fjord and sank the remaining German destroyers and a U-boat, with only relatively light damage to themselves. Late in May, Allied forces retook Narvik from the Germans, but in spite of superior numbers the Allied campaign in Norway crumbled, and on 7 June the last troops were withdrawn, leaving the whole of Norway in the hands of the Germans.

Nasty-face, Jack: *see* ROBINSON, WILLIAM.

National Maritime Museum: housed at GREENWICH, and established in 1934 by Act of Parliament as a repository for the illustration of the maritime history of Great Britain through archaeological survivals, paintings, prints, models, maps, instruments, written records, relics of celebrated commanders etc. The collections are housed in the beautiful Queen's House, which was transferred to the new museum in 1934 and opened in 1937 after extensive restoration, and in the adjoining Caird Galleries. The Museum absorbed the collections formerly maintained in the old Greenwich Hospital, and in 1960 it added to its unique facilities the Old Royal Observatory, which now houses a planetarium. The famous clipper ship *Cutty Sark* lies nearby. The collections, unrivalled in this country, are enhanced by fine display, by regular exhibitions featuring special aspects of maritime history, and the provision of facilities for schoolchildren as well as adult researchers. The strong associations with the Royal Naval College

The National Maritime Museum, Greenwich.

and the Hospital have inevitably meant great emphasis on the Royal Navy through the centuries; but the equally important part played by the merchant service is being increasingly established as accommodation and finances permit.

NATO (North Atlantic Treaty Organization): a combination of states set up for defence and security against aggression. The treaty was signed in 1949 and at first included the U.S.A., Canada, Great Britain, France, Belgium, Luxembourg, the Netherlands, Norway, Denmark, Iceland, Italy and Portugal. Greece and Turkey signed the treaty in 1951, and West Germany in 1954. The headquarters of NATO were at first in Paris, but when France decided on a more independent role (1966) they were moved to Brussels (1967). Combined exercises by both the land and sea forces of the signatories are regularly held, but standardization of equipment and methods remains an outstanding problem between the various members.

Nautical Almanac: an annual publication which gives tables of information about all the heavenly bodies needed for celestial navigation. The best-known Nautical Almanac is published jointly by the British and American governments, but commercially produced Nautical Almanacs with additional and local information for coastal navigation are also published regularly.

Nautical mile (or **sea mile**): for long generally reckoned as 6080 ft, compared with the land mile of 5280 ft. The terms 'sea mile' and 'nautical mile' have often been confused, and matters were brought to a state of greater confusion by the introduction of metric equivalents. For a precise and accurate definition of the position one can do no better than quote verbatim the explanation of David Haslam, the present Hydrographer of the Navy:

The basic unit of distance measurement at sea is ... still the 'Sea-Mile' which is defined as 'the length on the spheroid that subtends a minute of Latitude at the centre of the radius of curvature'; its length varies because the earth is not a perfect sphere and because of the various mathematical figures of the earth's shape that may be used. For example, the length of a Sea-Mile at the Equator is approximately 1842 international metres and at the two Poles is of the order of 1861 international metres.

325

Until 1970, the length of a 'Nautical Mile' used in the United Kingdom was 6080 ft, or 1853·18 international metres; this is the length of a Sea-Mile in about Latitude 48°. As announced by Admiralty Notice to Mariners 1518/70, the United Kingdom adopted, in 1970, the 'International Nautical Mile' which is precisely 1852 international metres and is the same length as a Sea-Mile in Latitude 45°.

As far as mariners are concerned, the adoption of the 'round' value for the 'Nautical Mile' was purely academic since they will always be taught to measure distances from the Latitude scale printed on charts; this caters for the variations in length at different Latitudes. Although such distances, are often, and incorrectly, referred to as 'Nautical Miles', they are really 'Sea-Miles'.

Letter to *The Times* (10 August 1978)

'Nautilus': name famous in both fact and fiction, originating from the early Greek word for 'seaman', though it is a far cry from the biremes and triremes of the Greeks to the American nuclear-powered submarine *Nautilus* (1954), which in 1958 made the first voyage under the North Pole, having navigated without benefit of star, compass or radar. An earlier submarine *Nautilus* was designed by Robert Fulton and tried out in the Seine in 1800; a later model was egg-shaped, iron-ribbed and copper-sheathed, and fitted with a hinged mast and bat-wing sail, so that it could also be used on the surface. This type was tried against British warships at Brest, but failed to inflict any damage. One *Nautilus*, a 16-gun ship, was engaged against the Americans who attacked the British at Fort Penobscot in 1779; another was a training brig for young seamen, paid off in 1904; and one must not forget the little steamer *Nautilus* which in about 1820 began work as the first American commercial tow-boat, bringing up the packets from Sandy Hook.

Naval Academy: a school for intending young naval officers set up at Portsmouth in 1733. Its establishment had been proposed by an Order in Council four years previously, 'For the better education and training of up to forty young gentlemen for H.M. Service at sea'. In its early years it was not a great success, and the number of entrants to the Royal Navy by this route was always small, for most MIDSHIPMEN had gone direct to sea for their training. It was reformed after a visit by King George III in 1773 and again in 1806, when it was renamed the Royal Naval College, but had to close in 1857. It was, however, a forerunner of the modern Britannia ROYAL NAVAL COLLEGE, DARTMOUTH, for instruction and training were continued at Portsmouth, first in H.M.S. *Illustrious* and later in H.M.S. *Britannia*.

Naval architecture: the science and art of building ships.

Naval bases: ports, harbours and anchorages from which warships operate and are serviced. All maritime countries with their own warships have naval bases, many of which have been strongly protected with forts, gun emplacements, booms and other defences. In Britain the main bases for the Royal Navy are Portsmouth, Plymouth with Devonport, the Medway (Chatham) and Rosyth.

Defensive harbours were built by the Admiralty at Dover and Portland as minor naval bases, and following the outbreak of war in 1914 and again in 1939, many ports became additional naval bases temporarily; for example, Harwich and Immingham on the Humber were important bases for light naval forces, as indeed were many other small ports. Fleet anchorages such as Invergordon at the mouth of the Cromarty Firth and Scapa Flow in the Orkneys, important in both World Wars, must also be included in any definition of naval bases.

The sea-links of the British Empire were formerly secured by a great chain of naval bases running round the world from Gibraltar and Malta to Singapore and Hong Kong; for a fuller account of these and the passing of nearly all of them into different hands *see* ROYAL DOCKYARDS.

Naval brigade: a force of naval officers and men who fought on land; generally applied to the two naval brigades which were sent to assist the Belgians in the defence of Antwerp in the first week of October 1914. Winston Churchill, at that time First Lord of the Admiralty, dispatched these barely trained and inexperienced naval volunteers to join a brigade of regular marines already aiding the Belgian defence of Antwerp, a port of vital importance to the Allies, as Churchill had been at pains to point out. These brigades were known as the Royal Naval Division. Antwerp fell to the Germans on 10 October, and, apart from losses in killed and wounded, nearly 1000 of the Naval Division were made prisoners, and 1500 men, crossing into Holland in the retreat, were interned for the rest of the war. Churchill was much criticized in some quarters for this episode; but his concern about the safety of Antwerp and the Channel ports was justified, and his dispatch of the naval brigades had helped to delay the German advance and so give a little more time for the Allies to organize their lines in Flanders when Belgium was overrun.

'Naval Chronicle, The': a periodical publication that ran from 1799 to 1818 in 40 volumes, recording the personalities, exploits, ship movements etc. of the Royal Navy.

Naval Discipline Act: a statutory series of rules and regulations governing the powers of naval officers and giving them authority to command and administer discipline. The first Act under this title dates from 1661, but before that there had been regulations embodied in the ancient JUDGEMENTS OF OLÉRON, introduced into England by Richard I and later embodied and codified in the Black Book of the Admiralty in 1336. The basis of the modern Naval Discipline Act is that passed by Parliament in 1866, revised in 1956. That part of the Act which is particularly concerned with disciplinary matters is known as the ARTICLES OF WAR.

Navarino, Battle of (20 October 1827): battle fought off Greece during the Greek War of Independence in which the British intervened in support of Greece and, with the French and Russian fleets, shattered the Turkish-Egyptian fleet. At home, Wellington's cabinet disapproved of the action, since Codrington, commander of the combined fleet, had been ordered to avoid battle; he was recalled to London but later cleared of blame.

Nave: the main part of a church, used by the lay members of the congregation. The reason for the derivation from the Latin *navis*, 'ship', is not entirely clear. One early writer attributes it to the resemblance between the keel of a ship and the vaulted roof of a church; but it may have been because one of the early symbols of the church was a ship. *See also* NEF.

Navel pipe: the tube or pipe through which the anchor cable runs from the forecastle deck to the cable locker. *See p. 328.*

Navicert: consular certificate confirming

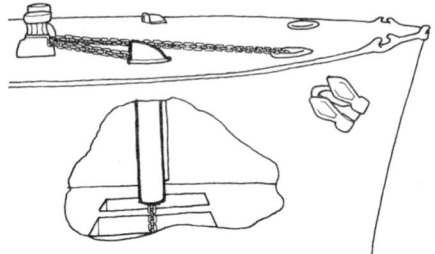

Navel pipe.

the list of a neutral ship's cargo (manifest) in time of war, thus exempting her from search or seizure. The word is a combination of 'navigation' and 'certificate'.

Navigation: the art of guiding a ship accurately from one place to another. The earliest form of navigation at sea was coastal: ships did not sail out of sight of the land but proceeded from one known feature of the coast to another. Very soon, however, sailors learnt to read their direction from the position of the sun, from the stars, especially the Pole Star, and from their knowledge of the prevailing winds and currents. It is fairly certain that this was the way in which the earliest ocean voyagers, the Phoenicians and the Norsemen, made their long journeys.

Modern navigation was born in the Middle Ages with the coming to northern Europe of the compass, the use of the astrolabe and primitive charts (*see* SURVEY-ING). The following centuries saw a gradually increasing skill in the art of navigation; for a fuller account of the various means by which this was achieved *see* INSTRUMENTS. In the past a very high proportion of the losses of ships was due to faulty navigation, but these decreased with knowledge of the deviation and variation of the compass, and by more accurate celestial observation achieved with the sextant and reliable nautical tables, by accurate time-keeping with the chronometer, and by accurate charts. Today navigation has become highly scientific, relying less on observation of the heavenly bodies for fixing position, for the coming of radio and electronics has transformed it. Large areas of the sea are covered by electronic navigation systems by which the ship's position can be quickly and accurately plotted; radio time signals make the chronometer of less importance, and the gyro-compass has increased accuracy in bearings and direction.

Science has taken navigation even further with what is known as inertial navigation. By this highly developed electronic system, which gives a continuous reading of position, nuclear submarines are enabled to make very long voyages submerged without the need for celestial navigation and with a minimal and negligible error over hundreds of miles. Because of its expense the inertial navigation system has not yet been fitted into many surface ships.

Navigation Acts: laws in England devoted to the privileges of English, or British, ships and laying down conditions under which foreign ships were permitted to trade. Thus, in 1381/2 Richard II prohibited the use of foreign vessels in carrying goods to or from England; and there were later enactments concerning the wine trade. It is, however, in the 17th century that various Navigation Acts assumed particular prominence and received the special name. The First Navigation Act (1651) forbade the importation of goods into England except in English vessels or those of the country producing the goods carried. This was specifically intended to hit the Dutch carrying trade and was a main factor in bringing about the Dutch Wars. Among the provisions of a Second Act (1660) was one ordering that all colonial produce should be exported in British ships and, even more restricting, another insisting that various types of produce should be sent only to British ports and those of her dependencies. In 1663 it was enacted that the colonies should receive no trade in foreign ships, and nine years later came the stringent Navigation Act of Charles II prohibiting the introduction of all the principal articles of commerce (known as 'enumerated articles') to the colonies except in English ships with crews at least three-quarters English. Again war, in the shape of the American rebellion, was one of the ultimate results of punitive Acts of this nature. Retaliatory measures followed, and, despite the views of some economic theorists, such as Adam Smith, free-trade legislation gradually superseded restrictive regulations, though the issues are not entirely dead even in the 20th century.

Navy blue: the colour traditionally associated with the seaman. Historically, the association is of very long standing. Henry I (1100–1135) gave blue woollen cloth to Cinque Ports seamen. When the future James II was Lord High Admiral, there is mention of blue shirts at 3s. 6d. each and blue suits at 5s. to be sold to sailors. But this was a long way from regulation or standardized uniform. There is a well-established story that Admiral John Forbes (1714–96) was summoned by the Duke of Bedford and asked to select an appropriate colour for the Navy from a range on display. Forbes opted for 'red and blue' or 'blue and red' as the national colours; but the Duke replied: 'No, the King has determined otherwise, for, having seen my duchess riding in the park a few days ago in a habit of blue faced with white, the dress took the fancy of His Majesty, who appointed it for the uniform

of the Royal Navy.' There still exists in the Bedford family records a bill for a blue-and-white riding habit that belonged to the daughter of the duchess who caught George II's eye. *See also* UNIFORM, NAVAL.

Navy Board: administrative body which emerged in Henry VIII's reign and, with various reorganizations and modifications, continued to manage the affairs of the Navy up to the early 19th century. Its chief officials were the Comptroller (or General Manager), the Treasurer, the Surveyor (responsible for technical details), and the Clerk of the Ships (or Clerk of the Acts), who virtually ran the office side. Under them came to flourish a whole body of lesser officers, such as the Storekeeper, the Clerk of the Cheque (equivalent to a modern time-clerk), the Master Shipwright, the Clerk of the Ropeyard etc.

Navy Commissioners: *see* COMMISSIONERS OF THE NAVY.

Navy Lists: printed lists of naval officers (sometimes including marines), published in various forms and in varying degrees of completeness since the mid-17th century. Under Samuel Pepys, lists of flag-officers and sea officers were drawn up for the period 1660–88. Confusion is very easy here, since at that time our now familiar ranks, e.g. admiral, captain, lieutenant, were not ranks at all but simply the designation of temporary jobs or appointments. From 1780 to 1815 the London publisher Steele issued valuable annual lists from his 'Navigation Warehouse'; then from 1814 the Admiralty began to produce its own official lists. These were divided into (1) that showing rank and seniority and (2) the alphabetical list. Since they are official and, barring occasional error, complete, they are much more reliable and easier to use, for purposes of research, than the earlier examples, some of which are very rare. The present-day list names all officers in the British and Commonwealth navies, and provides much other information, including naval and civil officers serving in various capacities ashore and afloat, at home and abroad.

Navy Records Society: society established in the 1890s 'for the purpose of printing rare or unpublished works of naval interest . . . rendering accessible the sources of our naval history and . . . elucidating questions of naval archaeology, construction, administration, organization and social life'. Many distinguished naval historians, seamen and scholars have served it as patrons, council members, editors and authors. Its list of more than 100 volumes now published includes *State Papers relating to the Defeat of the Spanish Armada*, *Naval Accounts and Inventories in the Reign of Henry VII*, *Logs of the Great Sea Fights, 1794–1805*, *A Descriptive Catalogue of the Naval MSS. in the Pepysian Library*, *Fighting Instructions, 1530–1816* and *The Papers of Admiral Sir John Fisher*.

Naze, the: (1) a low-lying promontory on the Essex coast south of Harwich; (2) a promontory at the southern extremity of Norway, correctly known as Lindesnaes; during the French Revolutionary and Napoleonic Wars it was a favourite point for French privateers to lie in wait for British shipping entering the Baltic, and in spite of an extensive convoy system the British suffered many losses of merchant ships and their cargoes right up to 1815. By derivation 'Naze' is connected with 'nose', suggesting the shape of the promontory.

Neap tides: tides occurring during the first and third quarters of the moon when the sun and moon are at right angles or in opposition to each other, and so their tide-producing effect is reduced. The result is that at neap tides high water is lower and low water is higher than when sun and moon exert their gravitational pull in conjunction as they do at spring tides. *See also* TIDES.

Needle, sailmaker's: a large needle, triangular in cross-section, used for sewing canvas. It can be pushed through stiff material with the aid of a sailmaker's PALM.

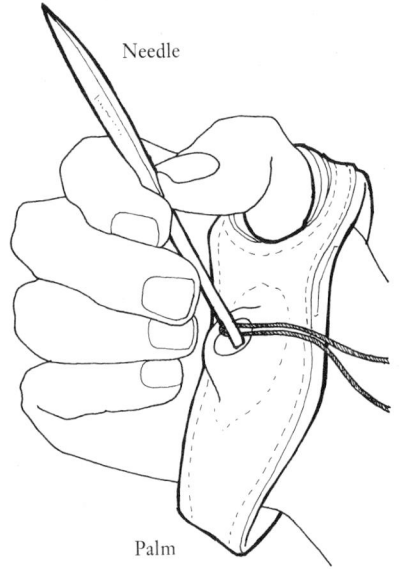

Needle

Palm

Needles, the: the three chalk stacks at the most westerly point of the Isle of Wight. The Needles lighthouse lies on the seaward side of the chalk stacks and assists shipping coming up Channel to the main deep-water passage to the western Solent.

Nef: ornamental table-piece of plate or precious metal, shaped like a ship and frequently used by the wealthy to hold salt-cellars, napkins etc. Nefs were also found in churches as incense carriers. It was sometimes the old name for the NAVE of the church.

Nelson, Horatio, Viscount Nelson (1758–1805): admiral, England's greatest naval hero, who set the seal on his immortality by dying in the heat of action at his supreme victory. Full biographical details may be found in innumerable books, and all his major actions are described elsewhere in this dictionary. By way of summary, he was born at Burnham Thorpe, the son of a Norfolk clergyman, went to sea at the age of 12, and was post-captain at the age of 21. He lost his right eye at the siege of Calvi in 1794, and his right arm at Santa Cruz in 1797. His most celebrated victories were at the Nile (1798), Copenhagen (1801) and Trafalgar (1805). Measured on the promotion list, his career was:

Lieutenant	10 April	1777
Commander	8 December	1778
Captain	11 June	1779
Rear-Admiral of the Blue	20 February	1797
Rear-Admiral of the Red	14 February	1799
Vice-Admiral of the Blue	1 January	1801
Vice-Admiral of the White	23 April	1804

It is one of the enigmas of Nelson's personality that although his physical endowments and appearance were unimpressive he commanded a devotion and loyalty accorded to very few in our long history, and that not only from his officers and men but from the general public. There are few more moving scenes than that of the crowds at Portsmouth cheering, weeping, praying, some of them on their knees, as the slight one-armed figure walked through the street to board *Victory* for the last time – a scene which led Nelson

From a litho by Couzens.

(who had a fair but forgivable share of vanity) to say to Hardy: 'I had their huzzas before, I have their hearts now.' The best account of him is in the words of some of the people who knew him.

Captain Nelson appeared to be the merest boy of a captain I have ever beheld. He had on a full-faced uniform; his lank, unpowdered hair was tied in a stiff Hessian tail of extraordinary length; the old-fashioned flaps of his waistcoat added to the quaintness of his figure ... There was something irresistibly pleasing in his address and conversation, and an enthusiasm when speaking on professional subjects that showed he was no common being.

Prince William Henry (later William IV)

It may reasonably be supposed, that among the number of thirty, there must have been timid souls as well as bold. The timid he never rebuked; but always wished to show them he desired nothing that he would not instantly do himself. And I have known him say: 'Well, sir, I am going a race to the mast head, and I beg I may meet you there.' No denial could be given to such a request.

Lady Hughes, wife of Admiral Hughes, who

was a passenger on board Nelson's frigate *Boreas*, on a voyage to the West Indies

... one of the most insignificant figures I ever saw in my life. His weight cannot be more than seventy pounds, and a more miserable collection of bones and wizened frame I have never yet come across. His bold nose, the steady eye and the solid worth revealed in his whole face betray in some measure the conqueror... He was almost covered with orders and stars.

> An onlooker at Dresden in 1800

Nelson is covered with stars, ribbons and medals more like a Prince of an Opera than the Conqueror of the Nile. It is really melancholy to see a brave and good man, who has deserved well of his country, cutting so pitiful a figure.

> Sir John Moore, during a
> visit to Palermo

... having left nothing to achieve on earth, and bequeathing to the English fleet a legacy which they alone are able to improve.

> Lady Londonderry, stepmother of Lord
> Castlereagh, the Secretary for War

'Nelson': Royal Navy battleship built (1927) to the regulations laid down by the Washington Conference of 1922. She was 710 ft long, 106 ft wide, draught 30 ft, with a displacement of 33,950 tons (38,000 fully loaded). Nine 16-in. guns were mounted in three triple turrets on the fore-deck, and the armour plating was 14 in. thick. Speed was 23 knots. *See also* QUEEN ANNE'S MANSIONS.

The first H.M.S. *Nelson* was a 120- gun ship launched at Woolwich in 1814. Forty-five years later she was converted to screw propulsion. She was transferred to the Colony of Victoria, Australia, as a training ship, based at Melbourne, and was eventually broken up in 1898.

'Nelson chequer': style of external painting of ships favoured by Nelson – black sides and port-lids, with yellow

streaks to mark each deck of guns. Originally used by those ships that fought at the Battle of the Nile, it became almost standard pattern throughout the Navy. *See colour section.*

Nelson Column: one of London's best-known landmarks, in Trafalgar Square, completed in 1843. The famous lions by Landseer were added later and uncovered in 1867. They were made in part from metal from the salvaged guns of the *Royal George*.

Nelson touch, the: the name given by Nelson to the famous 'General Memorandum' circulated to his captains before the Battle of Trafalgar, setting out the general lines of his plan for the battle (though leaving a good deal of discretion for individual initiative). Thus, Nelson's private journal for 9 October 1805 has the note: 'Sent Collingwood the Nelson touch.'

Since then the phrase has taken on a different meaning – the flair, the courage, the devotion to duty, that characterized Nelson and the thousands of seamen subsequently inspired by him. Thus, in *'Minora Sidera'* Newbolt wrote:

Whether their fame centuries long should ring
They cared not over-much,
But cared greatly to serve God and the king,
And keep the Nelson touch.

The original memorandum, in Nelson's own hand and spreading over eight pages, has had an amazing history. After Trafalgar it disappeared for a century and was eventually sent to Sotheby's, the London auctioneers, by a bus driver who used to drive his vehicle between Clapham Junction and Raynes Park.

The driver, William Jackson, was asked by a passenger if he had ever been to Merton, where Nelson used to live.

Jackson apparently hadn't but said he knew something about him since his father had been a sailor who, when he gave up the sea, became an admiral's servant. The admiral took a fancy to him and gave him an old desk with some letters in it, one of them something to do with Trafalgar.

'If you show me that,' said the passenger, 'and I like it I will give you £10 and a suit of clothes for it.'

Jackson, however, was a cautious type and sought advice from someone else, who told him to send it to Sotheby's. It fetched £3600 and later found its way to the British Museum.

Neptune: the Roman god of the sea, son of Saturn and brother of Jupiter and Pluto. In legend, he was married to Salacia, goddess of salt water. The Romans later identified him with the Greek Poseidon. A festival of Neptune, accompanied by games, was celebrated on 23 July.

'Neptune': an obvious and inevitably popular ship name. The Trafalgar *Neptune* (98 guns), built at Deptford in 1797, was the third ship in the weather column. She took nine shots between wind and water and lost 44 killed and wounded in the action. She afterwards towed *Victory* into Gibraltar. She continued in service for some years and was eventually broken up at Plymouth in 1818.

The Science Museum in London has a beautifully restored model of a 90-gun ship on the 1706 Establishment, probably the *Neptune*, being the Navy Board model formerly belonging to Daniel Finch (1647–1730), Earl of Nottingham and Winchilsea, holder of many important posts including that of First Lord of the Admiralty. Robert Dodd (1748–*c*.1816), the marine artist, has left us a splendid aquatint of the 1780 East Indiaman *Neptune*, finely built despite the Royal

Navy's clamour for any timber then on the market. A later representative (the eighth in the Royal Navy) was the 9310-ton ironclad launched at Poplar in 1873, built for the Brazilian government and purchased into the British Navy in 1878.

Elaborations of the name included *Neptune's Car* and *Neptune's Favorite*, well-known American clippers in their day.

Ness, Battle of the: *see* DUNGENESS, BATTLE OF.

Net: a screen constructed of crossing wire or rope, used for a variety of purposes, the most obvious of which is for fishing (*see* FISHING CRAFT). Huge wire nets are suspended from booms to protect a harbour entrance from underwater attack, and have also been used suspended round large ships to protect them from torpedo-attack. A scrambling net is a large rope net lowered over the side of a ship to allow rapid descent into smaller assault craft, or for ascent by men in the water. *See also* NETTINGS.

Nettings: a network of rope arranged along the upper decks of sailing warships to give day-time stowage for hammocks. When the crew's hammocks were lashed up and stowed in assigned positions in the nettings several purposes were served: the cramped spaces between decks were cleared, the hammocks got an airing, and in the case of disaster a well-lashed hammock

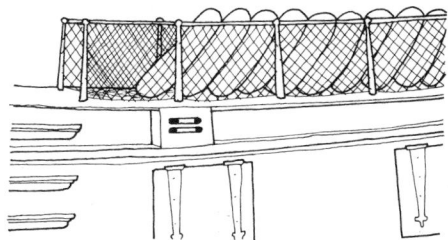

would float and support a man in the water for some time. But a more important value of this practice was the protection provided by the hammocks against the enemy's musket-fire and against case-shot and flying splinters.

Netting in another form was also used by being rigged horizontally across and above part of the upper deck. This was a kind of safety-net to prevent spars and tackle shot away in battle from crashing on those below, and it also broke the fall of men from the rigging.

Net tonnage: *see* TONNAGE.

Neutrality: the state of not taking the part of either side in a dispute, especially in a war. Throughout history what constitutes acceptable neutrality has been disputed, and in spite of international agreements its interpretation has varied according to the viewpoint and circumstances of those involved. In sea warfare maritime nations have constantly disagreed over the transport in neutral ships of goods belonging to a nation at war. Can the other side seize the goods or the ship for departing from neutrality and helping the enemy? From the time of the Anglo-Dutch Wars in the 17th century, throughout the wars of the 18th century, during the Napoleonic Wars and the First and Second World Wars, the matter of enemy goods in neutral ships was a constant problem. The British maintained that such goods were lawful prize everywhere at sea and persisted in the right of search. Only a few examples can here be given of the many instances of quarrels enlarged, of alliances formed and broken, of the difficulties and complications encountered, and of the ruses and deceptions which have been employed by belligerents to disguise their ownership of goods carried in neutral ships.

In 1800, under pressure from Napoleon, Russia, Sweden, Denmark and Prussia revived an earlier League of Armed Neutrality to resist the customary rights of search and seizure claimed by Britain. This challenge threatened the British blockade of France and an interruption of trade to the Baltic, the source of essential naval stores. There followed the dispatch of a fleet under Admiral Sir Hyde Parker, and the destruction of the Danish fleet by Nelson, Parker's second-in-command, at the Battle of Copenhagen (1801).

A chief cause of the war with the United States in 1812 was the refusal of the British to give up their practice of stopping American ships on the high seas in order to take off any deserting British seamen found on board. Yet another instance of a quarrel over strict neutrality occurred in 1862 during the American Civil War. A fine ship, the *Alabama*, had been built at Birkenhead for the Confederate States, and by a ruse managed to sail, although, in view of Britain's declared neutrality, belated attempts had been made to stop her. The *Alabama* wrought considerable damage to Federal shipping, and after the war the United States successfully sued the British government for damages for this breach of neutrality.

In the First and Second World Wars the problem of the transport of enemy goods in neutral ships was eased by the issue of NAVICERTS, which gave clearance for ships to pass unmolested by the Allied blockade. In December 1939, after the Battle of the River Plate, the German 'pocket battle-ship' *GRAF SPEE* sought refuge in Montevideo, the capital of neutral Uruguay, for refuelling and repairs. By international law she was permitted a stay of 24 hours, but Uruguay extended this by a further 72 hours. When this expired the *Graf Spee* had to sail and was scuttled outside the three-mile limit because it was believed that a superior British force was awaiting her. In 1940 and 1941 the United States, which had not yet entered the war, exhibited a supreme example of friendly neutrality towards Britain and her Allies. This was marked by 'Lend-lease' and many other favourable arrangements beyond the demands of strict neutrality.

New Bedford: seaport in Massachusetts on the estuary of the River Acushnet, once a leading shipping and whaling port and notable for its active part in the Revolutionary War against Britain. Herman Melville, in *Moby-Dick* (1851), gives a graphic description of the old port:

In thoroughfares nigh the docks, any considerable seaport will frequently offer to view the queerest-looking nondescripts from foreign parts. Even in Broadway and Chestnut Streets, Mediterranean mariners will sometimes jostle the affrighted ladies. Regent Street is not unknown to Lascars and Malays; and at Bombay, in the Apollo Green, live Yankees have often scared the natives. But New Bedford beats all Water Street and Wapping. In these last-mentioned haunts you see only sailors; but in New Bedford, actual cannibals stand chatting at street corners; savages outright.

Newbery (or **Newberry**), **John** (*fl.*1579–85): merchant and voyager. For a man of his intrepidity and accomplishments, too little is known, not even his ultimate fate. Apparently he tired of his respectable life as a London merchant and, 'desirous to see the world', made three remarkable voyages in five years. The first occupied him from March to November 1579, during which time he visited Tripolis, Jaffa and Jerusalem. Now thoroughly bitten with wanderlust, he took off again on 19 September 1580 and this time was away almost two years, taking in Aleppo, Baghdad, Basra, Hormuz, Shiraz,

Isfahan, Kashan, Tabriz, Erzingan, Constantinople and Danzig, and becoming the first Englishman to travel down the Euphrates valley, to cross southern Persia, to reach Constantinople via Asia Minor and to sail on the Black Sea.

Since he had learnt to speak Arabic and was already on friendly terms with some of the local dignitaries, Newbery was chosen by the New Turkey Company to lead a commercial enterprise with Ralph FITCH aimed at reaching Cathay via Hormuz and India. Carrying letters from Queen Elizabeth to the ruler of the Mogul Empire and the Emperor of China, the expedition left London on 13 February 1583 in the ship *Tiger*. Their adventures and misadventures brought some of them eventually, via Tripoli, Aleppo and Baghdad, to India, to Bijapur, Golconda and Agra, near which they came to the court of Akbar (1542–1605), the greatest emperor of the Mogul period, and presented their letter from the Queen. In September 1585 Newbery separated from Fitch and set out for home, but he disappeared en route.

There is a curious echo of Newbery's third voyage in Shakespeare's *Macbeth* (I.3), written over twenty years later; the First Witch says:

A sailor's wife had chestnuts in her lap . . .
Her husband's to Aleppo gone, master o' the
   Tiger.

Newbolt, Sir Henry John (1862–1938): author and poet with a special feeling for the sea and the British naval tradition. His best-known poem is DRAKE'S DRUM, which appeared in 1896 and in the following year was included with other verse in *Admirals All*. Amongst his other writings connected with the sea are verse and songs published in *The Sailing of the Long-ships* (1902), *Songs of the Sea* (1904) and *Songs of the Fleet* (1910). Newbolt was knighted in

1915, and after the First World War he wrote the final two volumes of an official history of the war at sea, the first three volumes of which had been completed by Sir Julian Corbett before he died.

Newcastle: large industrial city and port on the Tyne in Tyne and Wear. From Elizabethan times onwards Newcastle shipped coal to the south of England, and 'carrying coals to Newcastle' soon became a popular phrase for an unnecessary effort or journey. A great shipbuilding industry grew up in the 19th century and the famous yards on the lower reaches of the Tyne produced many ships, from the largest warships to small colliers. Many other industries, of which the engineering and chemical industries are the chief, developed in Newcastle and along the Tyne, and although shipbuilding has declined in output the area remains a great industrial centre.

'Newcastle': *see* BLACKWALL FRIGATE.

New England: the name given to that region of the N.E. U.S.A. which comprises the states of Maine, New Hampshire, Vermont, Massachusetts, Rhode Island and Connecticut. This area of early settlement from the British Isles is particularly associated with the Pilgrim Fathers, who landed at what is now Plymouth, Massachusetts, in 1620. The early history of the New England colonies, shaped by the Puritan tradition, is marked by hard endeavour rewarded by increasing prosperity. But New England was also a gathering ground of resistance to British rule, and it saw the opening phases of the American War of Independence in 1775, of which the celebrated Boston Tea Party (1773) was one of the forerunners. When the war broke out, in addition to the cessation of the profitable colonial trade, a valuable source of timber and masts was cut off from the British Navy, which was fully stretched in blockading the coast, supporting the military, and attacking American harbours and shipping in numerous engagements. At the same time American privateers wrought great damage to British shipping. One of the most successful of American naval commanders was John Paul JONES.

After the war the maritime prosperity of New England proceeded apace, favoured as it was with good harbours, rich fishing grounds and natural resources. It was a great centre for the whaling trade, and its shipbuilding became renowned for the famous clippers which were so graceful and fast, breaking many sailing records in the 19th century. During the war with America in 1812–14 the renowned engagement between the *Shannon* and the *Chesapeake* was fought off BOSTON.

Newfoundland: large island and, since 1949, one of the Provinces of Canada. It lies in the Atlantic off Canada's eastern coast, at the entrance to the Gulf of St Lawrence. Recently it has been suggested that the rich cod fisheries off the coasts of Newfoundland were known to the fishermen of the West Country even before the voyage of John Cabot (1497), who is generally credited with their discovery. It is possible also that Newfoundland may have been reached by the Norsemen sailing from Greenland and Iceland some 500 years previously. It was formally annexed to the English crown by Sir Humphrey Gilbert in 1583, but for long the fishing grounds were the scene of rivalry between English, French, Basque and Portuguese fishermen. Three times (1697, 1705 and 1708) the French attempted to take Newfoundland, but by the Treaty of Utrecht (1713) at the end of the War of

Spanish Succession, British sovereignty was recognized. Nevertheless the surrounding seas continued to be the scene of fighting during the wars with the French in the 18th century. The fisheries continued to be valuable but many other industries, especially timber and mineral, have been developed. In the Second World War Newfoundland was of particular concern for the defence of the U.S.A. and Canada. St John's, the island's chief port and capital, became a Canadian naval base and gathering ground for the dispatch of Atlantic convoys. The U.S.A. established other bases and developed airports, including Gander, now of international importance.

Newport: *see* RHODE ISLAND.

New South Wales: one of the States of Australia and the area of earliest colonization. It was named by Captain Cook in 1770 on his first voyage (1768–71). He and his men, having charted the coasts of New Zealand, sailed up the eastern coast of Australia and landed in Botany Bay, so called because of the wealth of plants. Proceeding up the coast Cook narrowly escaped disaster on the Great Barrier Reef, and then, as he was about to leave New Holland (as Australia was then known), he recorded the occasion in his journal in the following words:

As I was now about to quit the eastern coast of New Holland, which I had coasted from latitude 38° to this place (Cape York), and which I am confident no European had seen before, I once more hoisted English colours, and though I had already taken possession of several particular ports, I now took possession of the whole Eastern coast, from latitude 38° to this place, in the right of His Majesty King George the Third, by the name of New South Wales.

Eighteen years later the first settlement was made, not at Botany Bay, which was found unsuitable, but at Port Jackson to the north, where the great city of Sydney now stands.

New World: the name given early in the 16th century to the newly discovered continent of America. After the voyages of Columbus, Amerigo Vespucci, the Cabots and many other sailors, the reports brought back to Europe caused great wonder and excitement, so that it did indeed appear that a New World lay across the Atlantic. Thus the phrase passed into common parlance; *see also* OLD WORLD.

New York: America's greatest seaport and city, with an extensive deep-water harbour lying at the mouth of the Hudson River. The first European to enter this magnificent harbour was Giovanni da Verrazzano, an Italian sailing for the French king (1524); the first Englishman was Henry Hudson, sailing for the Dutch East India Company (1609). The first settlement of the present site of New York City was made by the Dutch early in the 17th century; they called it New Amsterdam.

In 1664 the settlement was taken by the English and it was renamed New York after James, Duke of York, Charles II's brother. Although retaken by the Dutch nine years later, New York reverted to the English by the treaty which ended the Third Anglo-Dutch War.

By the mid-18th century New York and the surrounding area had become a centre of resistance to the royal authority, largely because of the Stamp Act of 1765, other taxation demands, and the impressment of men for the Royal Navy. When the War of Independence broke out (1775) New York was held by the Americans, and Washington made it his headquarters. In 1776, with the arrival of the British fleet under Richard, Admiral Lord Howe, and an army under his brother, General William Howe, New York was recaptured, and it remained in British hands for the rest of the War. The landing of troops from the transports on this occasion was the largest combined operation hitherto undertaken.

When war with America again broke out (1812) New York was blockaded by the British. The latter half of the 19th and the early part of the 20th century saw New York grow into the vast and busy city of today.

New Zealand: independent Commonwealth country of two large and other smaller islands lying in the South Pacific Ocean over 1000 miles to the S.E. of Australia. New Zealand had been earlier settled by Polynesian Maoris when it was first discovered by a European. This was the Dutch navigator Abel Tasman (c.1603–1659), who in 1642 sighted the coast of the South Island of New Zealand but believed it to be part of the mainland of Australia. Tasman then sailed north and passed through the strait between North and South Islands and into the Pacific.

In the 18th century Captain James Cook visited New Zealand and made very careful coastal charts of the islands on his first voyage to the Pacific in 1769, before again visiting New Zealand on his two later voyages between 1772 and his death in 1779. In 1840 Edward Gibbon Wakefield led the first permanent British settlement at Wellington, which became the new nation's capital. New Zealand became self-governing in 1852 and an independent member of the British Commonwealth in 1931.

Nicholas of Lynn (*fl.c.*1360–1380): a scholarly Carmelite monk who lectured in theology at Oxford and is reputed, on very vague evidence, to have made a voyage into the Arctic.

Nicobar Islands: a group of islands lying in the Indian Ocean N.W. of Sumatra. James LANCASTER, one of the great Elizabethan sea-captains, was the first to bring English ships to the Nicobar Islands when he landed there on 9 April 1602. French, Danes and British at various periods laid claim to the Nicobar Islands, but in 1869 the British rights were recognized. During the Second World War the islands were occupied by the Japanese, but after the war they became part of India when that country received her independence (1947).

Nicol, John (*fl.*1776–1802): one of the few 18th-century ordinary seamen whose reminiscences have survived. He was found destitute, wandering the streets of Edinburgh, by John Howell, a bookseller, who patiently wrote down his recollections, though they were not published till 1937. Nicol had volunteered in 1776 and served the sea for 25 years, circumnavigating the globe twice, visiting China and Egypt, fighting in the American War, at St Vincent and the Nile, and, after all that, failing to obtain a pension.

Old as I am, my heart is still unchanged and were I young and stout again I would sail upon discovery; but, weak and stiff, I can only send my prayers with the tight ship and her merry hearts ...

Nile, Battle of the (or **Battle of Aboukir Bay**; 1 August 1798): the first fleet action in which Nelson was in command, one which displayed all his particular genius – inspiring leadership, meticulous planning allied with brilliant improvisation, and delegation of initiative to individual captains when the opportunity presented itself. The battle was fought in the wide bay of Aboukir on the Mediterranean coast of Egypt. Of the thirteen French ships, only two escaped. The essence of the success was that Brueys, the French admiral, in the 120-gun flag-ship *L'Orient*, thought he had his line so anchored that nothing could pass between it and the treacherous shoals and rocks off Aboukir Point. Led by Foley in the *GOLIATH*, however, five ships managed it, so that the leading French vessels were hopelessly caught between two merciless barrages. *See also* BERRY, SIR EDWARD.

Strangely enough, the best-known piece of literature about the action, beloved by earlier generations, was written by an Englishwoman about a French ship, or, rather, one of the people lost on the flag-ship *L'Orient*, the young son of the captain, Commodore Casabianca, immortalized in Felicia Hemans's much-parodied poem beginning 'The boy stood on the burning deck, Whence all but he had fled'. There is much conflict of evidence about what actually happened to Casabianca and his son. One story has it that both left the ship but drowned before they could be picked up. Midshipman John Theophilus Lee of the *Swiftsure* wrote:

> The son of Casabianca had lost a leg, and was below with the surgeon, but the father could not be prevailed upon to quit the ship even to save his own life, preferring to die beside his son rather than leave him wounded, and a prey to the flames.

Nipper: a short length of rope used to bind the anchor cable to the MESSENGER. In large sailing ships, when the anchor cable was too thick to go round the capstan, a continuous rope known as a messenger was passed round the capstan and round blocks forward of the capstan. As this turned with the capstan, so stage by stage the anchor cable was attached to it by nippers and then released as it came in to be passed down to the cable locker. The task of nipping the cable to the messenger and then releasing it

was often performed by the younger deck hands, who were also called 'nippers', a slang phrase for young boys which passed into common speech, as in 'a smart nipper'.

Nock (or **knock**): the upper fore-corner or throat of a fore-and-aft sail.

Nombre de Dios: an early fort and settlement on the Spanish Main, situated on the eastern side of the Isthmus of Panama. Nombre de Dios is particularly associated with Francis Drake and his daring adventures on this coast in 1572–3. It was Drake's first big enterprise in independent command when he sailed from Plymouth in May 1572 with two ships, the *Pascoe* (70 tons) and the *Swan*. With him were two of his brothers and John Oxenham; another English ship joined him when he reached the coast of the isthmus. He had brought with him three pinnaces in sections, and when they were put together, he and his small force set out in them to make a surprise night attack on Nombre de Dios. The town was captured, but when Drake was badly wounded his men felt compelled to return to the boats. In the ensuing months Drake had some failures as well as successes as he harried the coast and Spanish shipping, but what he was planning was an attack on the mule-train with which the Spanish carried their treasure from the Pacific coast across the isthmus to Nombre de Dios, where their fleet was waiting to carry the hoard to Spain. During his march inland Drake and Oxenham climbed a high tree and from it saw for the first time the Pacific Ocean, whereupon Drake besought the Almighty that he might sail in an English ship in that sea. Eventually Drake and his men were in position to attack the mule-train, but the folly of a drunken seaman caused his plan to fail and he had to return to the coast. One final attempt was planned and, with the help of some Frenchmen who had joined him, Drake set out overland once again. At last he and his men lay in ambush behind and above Nombre de Dios when the mule-train bearing gold and silver approached. The attack was sudden and successful. Taking as much gold as they could carry, Drake and his men got back to their ships and sailed for Plymouth, arriving on 'Sunday about Sermon-time, August the ninth 1573'.

On his last voyage Drake again sacked Nombre de Dios, but died and was buried at sea in the waters close by (January 1596).

Drake he's in his hammock an' a thousand
   mile away,
(Capten, art tha sleepin' there below?),
Slung atween the round shot in Nombre Dios
   Bay,
An' dreamin' arl the time o' Plymouth Hoe.

Sir Henry Newbolt, 'Drake's
Drum' (1896)

'Nonpareil': Armada ship, commanded by Captain Thomas Fenner, who, following a cruise along the French coast earlier in 1588, had brought Drake news of the Spanish preparations. The *Nonpareil* was also with the unsuccessful Cadiz expedition of 1589.

The name crops up in many other periods and settings, e.g. the American schooner of 210 tons and 12 guns seized by the British in 1808, and the well-known clipper owned by Thomas Richardson & Company, New York.

Nore, the: a sand-bank in the Thames estuary lying off the approach to the River Medway; the site of the first light-ship placed in English waters (1732). The area for long provided an anchorage for ships based on Chatham and Sheerness. The Nore was the name given to this area of naval command.

The Nore sand remains covered at low-water, and never seen by human eye; but the Nore is a name to conjure with visions of historical events, of battles, of fleets, of mutinies, of watch and ward kept upon the great throbbing heart of the State.

Joseph Conrad, *The Mirror of
the Sea* (1906)

For the mutiny at the Nore (1797) *see* MUTINY.

Norman Cross: *see* PRISONERS OF WAR.

Norman ships: most of our knowledge of Norman ships of the mid-11th to the mid-12th century is derived from such sources as the BAYEUX TAPESTRY and from seals to documents concerning ports such as Sandwich, Dover and Winchelsea. There seems to have been little difference in design between the English and Norman ships and those Scandinavian examples, e.g. the GOKSTAD SHIP, which have been preserved. They were clinker-built with a steering paddle on the starboard quarter, and with high figureheads and sterns. The mast was secured fore and aft and carried a single square sail. Shields were ranged along the gunwales.

See colour section.

Norris (or **Norreys**), **Sir John** (?1547–1597): primarily a military commander but, like so many soldiers of the time, adaptable to the sea. He helped in the preparations against the Armada and, with Drake, took command of the expedition to Spain in 1589.

Norris, Sir John (?1660–1749): admiral. His distinguished career embraced the Mediterranean and Channel commands, and service at Lagos (1693), Malaga (1704), Barcelona (1705) and the Baltic (1715–27).

Norsker: old sailors' term for a Norwegian.

North Atlantic Drift (or **North Atlantic Current** or **Gulf Stream Drift**): an extension of the Gulf Stream; a movement of relatively warm water north-eastwards across the Atlantic. It is part of a complex circulation of the world's oceanic waters, though the prevailing south-westerly winds undoubtedly influence this drift of water north-eastwards across the Atlantic. The drift moves to the seas round Iceland and N.W. Europe and northwards towards the Arctic; it has an important moderating effect on climate and keeps harbours as far as the North Cape in Norway ice-free when more southerly harbours in the St Lawrence and the Baltic are icebound. The

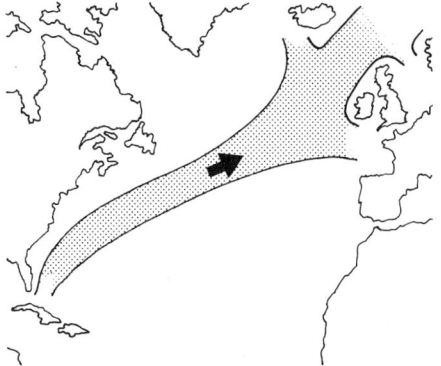

air above the North Atlantic Drift is cool in summer relative to that over the land, and so it reduces extremes of temperature in maritime N.W. Europe in summer as well as in winter.

North Atlantic Treaty Organization: *see* NATO.

North-East Passage: the name given to the sea-route from the Atlantic to the Pacific round the northern coasts of Europe and Asia. After the southern routes round Africa and South America to the Spice Islands of the East had been discovered and largely monopolized by the Portuguese and Spanish, the belief began to grow in the countries of northern Europe that a northern sea-route to Cathay (China) might be found. In 1527 Robert Thorne wrote to Henry VIII urging upon him this possibility, since, 'of the foure partes of the worlde, it seemeth three partes are discovered by other Princes', and 'because the situation of this your realm is thereunto neerest and aptest of all other'. In 1553 a company of merchant venturers, which became known as the Muscovy Company, had been formed under the auspices of the ageing Sebastian Cabot, and the first English expedition was sent out under the command of Sir Hugh Willoughby and Richard Chancellor, their destination being 'Cathay, and divers other regions, dominions, islands and places unknown'. Passing north of Norway their ships became separated and Willoughby was never seen again. Though Chancellor had not got very far, he managed to return and brought back valuable information. In 1556 Stephen Borough, who had been master of Chancellor's ship, sailed to the farthest point yet reached on the Kola Peninsula. Further expeditions were undertaken by James Bassendine (1568), Arthur Pet and Charles Jackman (1580), and Henry Hudson (1607 and 1608), but though knowledge of these northern waters increased, none of the voyages penetrated more than a little way to the distant entry into the Pacific.

At the same time the Dutch were also seeking to test the possibility of a northern route to the East. The greatest of the Dutch navigators to make the attempt was Willem Barents in his three voyages (1594, 1595 and 1596). On the last of these he reached the Kara Sea, but, his ship being fast in the ice, he and his men were compelled to winter in a hut ashore built from driftwood. The journey home was begun in open boats, and Barents died before his men made contact with the other Dutch ship, which had left them the year before and which returned with the survivors to Amsterdam in November 1597. 274 years later the hut in which Barents and his men had passed the winter was discovered, and in it was Barents' last letter and other relics, which may be seen in the naval museum at The Hague.

After these famous early voyages ships of the Muscovy Company did trade to the north, but beyond Novaya Zemlya little was known of the coasts and seas further east. In the following centuries, however, knowledge was gradually extended, particularly by the Russians themselves, and by the end of the 18th century it was known that a North-East Passage did in fact exist, though the ice was still a barrier. The North-East Passage was at last achieved in 1878–9 by the Swedish-Finn Nils Nordenskiöld in the *Vega*, which wintered only a hundred miles from the Bering Strait leading into the Pacific. The first ship to make the passage in one season was a small Russian ice-breaker, the *Sibiriakov*, in 1932. Since then these northern waters have seen much activity. During the Second World War a number of ships

made the passage, and today ice-breakers and other ships are fast opening up trade and tapping the riches of Siberia.

Northern Confederacy: confederacy instigated by Napoleon to frustrate the British naval blockade of enemy ports by resisting the right of search of vessels suspected of carrying goods of value to the other side; and, conversely, to prevent the delivery of vital supplies, such as timber, rope and sail cloth, to Britain. The combination of Russia, Sweden, Denmark and Norway posed a serious threat, but the Battle of Copenhagen (1801) caused the capitulation of Denmark and, with it, the collapse of the confederation.

Northern lights: *see* AURORA BOREALIS.

North Foreland: a bold chalk cliff, 100 ft high, on the N.E. coast of Kent. It has a distinctive lighthouse whose flash is visible for 20 miles. *See also* FOUR DAYS' BATTLE.

Northiam Ship: ancient ship found in 1822 in a field near the River Rother, Sussex. Northiam lies just below Bodiam Castle, built in 1386, and the vessel was probably employed bringing up stone. Laird Clowes described her as

double-ended and rather wall-sided, decked fore and aft, while amidships lay a long open hold, crossed by only two heavy deck-beams. The construction is by no means primitive, and all details seem to have been well finished ... It is difficult, therefore, to escape from the conclusion that this vessel represents a type which was at one time employed in the English coasting trade, and that the type did not differ substantially from the recent Humber keels ... with their primitive rig of one large square sail and a square topsail.

Sailing Ships ... as Illustrated by the ... Ship-Models in the Science Museum (1932 etc.)

Northing: the distance in latitude made northwards from the last point of reckoning.

North Sea: the shallow sea lying between England and Holland and Scandinavia. From earliest times the North Sea has been the scene of maritime endeavour. Across it sailed the Angles, Saxons, Danes and Norsemen, at first to maraud and then to conquer and settle in England. On it countless actions have been fought with the French, the Dutch and the Germans, from the Battle of Sluys in 1340 to the Second World War of 1939–45. The mightiest clash of powerful fleets that it has seen was the Battle of Jutland in 1916. Command of the North Sea has always been vital to the defence of Britain, and its rich fishing grounds have been a source of food for the countries of N.W. Europe. It is a grey and often stormy and rough sea that has played a vital part in British history, and may do so again with the discovery of oil beneath its floor; today oil-rigs dot and break its grey horizon. Tankers and merchant ships of every kind make it one of the busiest of the world's seas, for it provides the access to the Baltic and to many great ports such as London, Antwerp and Rotterdam.

North Star: *see* POLE STAR.

'Northumberland': perhaps the best-remembered ship of this name is the one that witnessed the Navy's farewell to an arch-enemy. On 7 August 1815 the ex-Emperor Napoleon transferred from the *Bellerophon* to the *Northumberland*, a 74-gun third-rate, and on Sunday 15 October the ship dropped anchor before St Helena with Napoleon studying the island, without any visible emotion, through his telescope. Since no doctor was available on the island, Doctor Barry Edward O'Meare

(1786–1836), surgeon on the *Northumberland*, agreed to share Napoleon's exile and later wrote an account of his experiences.

A later *Northumberland* was an excellent example of the British Admiralty's enduring belief in the necessity of sail. Built 1865–9, she was a ship-rigged armoured first-class cruiser with five masts and 28 guns, with $5\frac{1}{2}$-in. thick armour, backed up with 9 in. of teak. Not surprisingly, she did not handle very well.

Earlier ships of the name included the 74-gun *Northumberland*, under Captain Thomas Watson, captured by the three French ships *Mars*, *Content* and *Venus* in May 1744 off Lisbon Rock. The captain was mortally wounded, and before the other officers could get on deck, the Master struck the colours. For this action he was sentenced to the Marshalsea prison for life, the other officers being honourably acquitted by the court-martial.

North-West Passage: the name given to the sea-route from the Atlantic to the Pacific round the north of Canada. Like the search for the North-East Passage, the earliest voyages were motivated by the hope of an alternative route to the riches of Cathay (China) and the East Indies. The modern map of the seas, coasts, and islands to the north of Canada is studded with the names of the early explorers, and bears witness to the fact that the English were foremost in attempting to find the North-West Passage. The first attempts were made by one of the great Elizabethan navigators, Martin Frobisher, who undertook three voyages (1576, 1577 and 1588). He was followed by John Davis, who also made three voyages (1585–7). The last of Henry Hudson's voyages ended tragically in 1611 when his crew mutinied. Twenty years later Luke Fox added further knowledge of these unknown waters and showed that it was not from Hudson Bay that a North-West Passage would be found.

In the 18th century further voyages were made, and though none got very far the knowledge of northern Canada was extended by a number of overland journeys encouraged by the HUDSON'S BAY COMPANY. The 19th century saw the greatest effort yet made to find and chart the sea-route to the north of Canada, and James Ross, his nephew James Clark Ross, and William Parry all made memorable voyages which were promoted by the influence of Sir John Barrow at the Admiralty until his retirement in 1845. It was in that year that he sent out Sir John FRANKLIN's ill-fated expedition in yet another attempt to find the North-West Passage. Franklin sailed with two ships, *Erebus* and *Terror*; after being sighted in Baffin Bay they were not heard of again. Expedition after expedition, 39 in all, were sent out to search for them; their fate was finally established by Leopold MCCLIN-TOCK in 1859.

By this time and after all these voyages the charting of the North-West Passage was almost complete. Robert McClure in 1850 had shown its existence, but its conquest had to wait another fifty years for a Norwegian to achieve what had eluded so many ships and sailors from the British Isles. This was Roald Amundsen, who between 1903 and 1906 successfully and safely took the first ship from the Atlantic to the Pacific by the North-West Passage. His ship was the *Gjöa*, a small fishing vessel of only 47 tons and shallow draught. The next transit of this icy and dangerous route did not occur until 1940 (*see ST ROCH*), after which four more passages were made by Canadians, the later voyages being in an ice-breaker. The first commercial cargo was carried in 1969, when the *Manhattan*

brought oil from the Alaskan wells to the east coast refineries. For many years the North-West Passage had been looked upon only as a geographical challenge to man's ingenuity and endurance; and it is doubtful whether the route will ever be used regularly and profitably.

Nova Scotia: one of the Maritime Provinces on the eastern coast of Canada. Possibly it was visited by the Norse and Icelandic voyagers in the 10th and 11th centuries and by the Cabots in 1497–8. It was first settled by the French, who named it Acadie, the English calling it Acadia. It was an area of dispute between the two nations, both of whom made settlements during the 17th and 18th centuries; possession of the land alternated as the struggle continued. In 1749 Halifax, the modern great port of eastern Canada, was founded to counter the French fortress of Louisburg on Cape Breton Island. In 1763, at the end of the Seven Years' War, France lost her colonies in North America, and the whole area became British. At the time of the War of American Independence many loyalists moved north to settle in Nova Scotia; farming, fishing and shipbuilding continued to develop.

Novaya Zemlya: a long, narrow and forbidding archipelago lying athwart the Arctic Ocean off the northern coast of Russia. On its west lies the Barents Sea and on the east the Kara Sea. Novaya Zemlya had perhaps been reached by the Norsemen, but for long it was a barrier to the many voyagers seeking the NORTH-EAST PASSAGE.

Nuclear-powered ships: ships propelled by atomic energy. The application of this new form of power to ships has been limited by the expense, though the

344

The Japanese nuclear merchant ship *Mutsu*.

advantages are considerable. With it ships can remain at sea for very long periods without refuelling, and this is of particular importance to warships, especially SUB-MARINES, which with nuclear power can not only stay submerged almost indefinitely but can also proceed below the surface at speeds considerably faster than by the previous methods of propulsion. In 1954 the first nuclear-powered submarine, *Nautilus*, was completed for the American Navy, and this form of power is now used also in Russian, British and French as well as American submarines, particularly those carrying I.C.B.M.s (Inter-Continental Ballistic Missiles). The United States have gone further in adding to their fleet a number of nuclear-powered surface ships, including aircraft carriers, missile cruisers and missile frigates. The first merchant ship ever powered by nuclear energy, the *Savannah*, was also built by the Americans (1959), and in the same year the Russians launched the *Lenin*, a nuclear-powered ice-breaker. Germany and Japan have nuclear-powered cargo vessels, but the building of other merchant vessels with this type of propulsion has not proceeded as fast as might have been expected.

Number One: colloquial name for the First Lieutenant. He is generally the second in command and executive officer of a ship or establishment, but if a Commander is the executive officer, 'Number One' will be the next senior officer of the seaman branch. He may properly be addressed as Number One by fellow officers. In lower-deck slang he is known as Jimmy or Jimmy-the-One.

Number Ones: a sailor's best uniform, worn for special occasions, going ashore, etc. What is to be worn is often piped to the ship's company; thus 'Rig of the day: Number Ones'.

Numerary signals: signals by flags each

345

of which represents a number. Messages can be conveyed in two different ways: (a) one flag is assigned to each of the numbers 1–9 and 0, and by combining flags any desired signal number may be represented; (b) the more complicated tabular method, when a table like a chessboard is ruled out, the number of squares not being fixed, but perhaps consisting of 64, 100, etc. A corresponding number of flags are selected and laid in order along the top and down the side, starting at the top left-hand corner. Thus, in a 16-square table the arrangement might be:

	Red	White	Blue	Yellow
Red	1	5	9	13
White	2	6	10	14
Blue	3	7	11	15
Yellow	4	8	12	16

It is clear from this that each number will have two flags, one at the head of the vertical column and the other at the left of the horizontal column; so that, for example, the figure 9 would be represented by a blue flag over a red, and 15 by a yellow flag over a blue. Each captain in a fleet, or squadron, would of course have a copy of the signal book setting out the precise message conveyed by each number, e.g. 'Anchor' or 'Engage the enemy more closely'.

In the British Navy the numerary system began to be used c.1778, but the French had invented the method some 40 years before. See also SIGNALS.

Nun buoy: a buoy which has the shape of two cones base to base.

Oak: *see* TIMBER.

Oakum: loose fibre made by unpicking old rope. Oakum was used for caulking the decks and sides of wooden ships; it was driven between the planks with a caulking iron struck with a hammer, and was then covered with hot pitch. Picking oakum (the process of teasing it out of the strands of old rope), a tedious task and very cruel on the hands, was once demanded of the inmates of workhouses and gaols, and in the Navy it was formerly used as a punishment for sailors condemned to the cells.

Add to this that with labouring so long and severely some of the ship's seams began now to open and shut and discharge the oakum, which is terrible to the bravest seaman.

Charles Reade, *Hard Cash* (1863)

Oar: a pole with a blade for pulling a boat through the water by the action of rowing. The broader blade thins to the shaft, which ends with the loom, the rounded part on which the rower pulls. The oar evolved from the primitive paddle, and from very early times in the Mediterranean warships were propelled by oars, becoming the great galleys with banks of oars or sweeps used by the Romans and later maritime powers throughout the Middle Ages and even down to the beginning of the 18th century. Today a race between well-trained and disciplined rowing 'eights' excites admiration. Equally impressive in a different way is a naval crew pulling a ship's boat and smartly obeying the coxswain's orders:

'Give way together' and his crew start rowing; 'Oars' and they cease pulling and bring up their oars, blades uppermost, so that they are all at the same horizontal level and at right angles to the line of the boat; 'Toss your oars' and the oars come smartly to a vertical position with the blades fore and aft and the loom on the bottom of the boat between the rower's feet; 'Oars down' and the crew is ready again to give way together unless the coxswain says 'Lay on your oars', when they can relax by resting the oar lightly on the water and holding it steady.

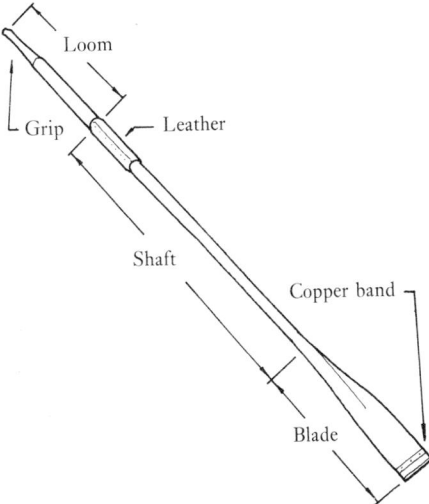

O'Byrne, William Richard (1823–96): compiler of *A Naval Biographical Dictionary* (1849). Naval historians will for ever be in his debt for this book, 'comprising the Life and Services of every Living Officer in Her Majesty's Navy, from the Rank of Admiral of the Fleet to that of Lieutenant'. Running to 1400 pages, it includes detailed accounts of nearly 5000 officers, for which O'Byrne searched with the utmost assiduity both official accounts and private sources.

Occident: *see* ORIENT.

Occulting light: a light on a lighthouse, beacon or lighted buoy which shows as long as, or longer than, the dark period. *See also* LIGHTHOUSE.

Ocean: the whole expanse of open deep sea, as opposed to inland and partly enclosed seas. For the Greeks, Oceanus was the name of the deity of mariners and of the great river supposed to encircle the earth, the surrounding waters as opposed to the inland sea, the Mediterranean.

The waters of the earth cover seven tenths of its surface, and their greatest expanses are called the oceans; of these there are strictly four, namely (in descending order of size) the Pacific, Atlantic, Indian and Arctic Oceans. The Antarctic, though called an ocean, is not recognized as separate by the International Hydrographic Bureau, for it merges with, and has no distinct boundaries from, the southern areas of the Pacific, Atlantic and Indian Oceans.

'Ocean': as might be expected, a name of frequent occurrence in merchant and Royal Navy shipping, from ships of the line to small trading schooners. In the Second World War the *Oceans* were a well-known standard type of American-built cargo ship, characterized by a split superstructure. In Australian history the transport *Ocean* will be remembered: in 1803, convoyed by H.M.S. *Calcutta*, she carried 299 convicts to Port Phillip, Victoria. For the French *L'Océan*, *see* CENTRAL BATTERY BATTLESHIP.

Oceania: a general name for the greater part of the PACIFIC Ocean and its numerous islands, which are said to number over 10,000. The precise limits of Oceania are ill-defined, but they exclude such island groups as Japan, the Aleutians and Indonesia. Oceania is subdivided into Melanesia (New Guinea to Fiji), Micronesia (Mariana, Caroline, Marshall and Gilbert Islands), and Polynesia (the islands of the eastern Pacific).

Oceanography: the scientific study of the sea in all its aspects, its plant and animal life, its depths, tides, currents, winds and temperatures, and the contours and nature of the ocean bed. Modern oceanography reflects the mass of knowledge accumulated by observations made not only by thousands of ships in the course of their ordinary voyages, but also by ships specially equipped for research and survey. One of the first of such ships was H.M.S. *CHALLENGER*, whose voyage of 1872–6 added greatly to knowledge of the sea and established oceanography as a precise science. Today RESEARCH SHIPS are differentiated from survey ships and are operated either by government departments or by authorities such as the National Environment Research Council, whose Royal Research Ship *Challenger* carries on the tradition of her earlier namesake. SURVEY SHIPS, on the other hand, are specially designed and operated by the Royal and other navies primarily for recording all features of the sea which are necessary for making accurate charts and sailing directions for safe navigation.

Octant: an early navigational instrument for taking the altitude of heavenly bodies; it had a graduated arc of 45°, one eighth of a circle. The reflecting quadrant invented by John HADLEY was really an octant.

O.D.: *see* ORDINARY SEAMAN.

Off: adverb and adjective used in a number of nautical expressions, e.g. 'off-shore', away from the shore; 'off-wind', a wind coming from the shore. To 'sail off the wind' is to sail freely with the wind on or before the beam, not close-hauled. *See also* BEAR; LIE OFF; PAY OFF.

Officer: one who holds authority in the Navy conferred by commission; midshipmen do not receive a commission until promoted, but they are of officer status. Some historical retrospect is necessary to understand the complex route by which the status of the modern naval officer evolved.

In the medieval Navy it was considered that it was for soldiers to do the fighting at sea and for sailors to look after the ship. So in time of war a ship was fitted with forecastle and aftercastle on which bowmen and other fighting men were placed to engage in combat. With them came their feudal or semi-feudal lord, who was in command of them as their captain, and with them was his second-in-command or lieutenant. The captain held the king's commission giving him this authority. Thus it is that we have two purely military titles for naval ranks. But the ship to which these fighting men went was already in being, with her own master responsible for

A wooden octant by G. Adams, 1753.

navigation, and her boatswain responsible for the general working of the ship. The master and the boatswain were, however, considered as having inferior social status to the captain, who anyway had the king's commission and in the accepted precedence of those times took command, even though he left nautical matters to the master and the boatswain, who were what we may call the seamen officers as opposed to the fighting officers. When the war was over the captain's commission was completed; he returned to the land and the ship to her normal duties. This sort of arrangement continued until the days of the early Tudors, but when Henry VIII began to build his own fighting ships it was necessary to maintain them in peace as well as in war-time. Therefore a permanent or standing master and boatswain had to be appointed, and this was done by warrant, thus confirming them as seamen officers standing by in readiness for their fighting commanding officers. The distinction was not always quite so sharp, as we may see in Elizabethan times, when Francis Drake was both a fighting and a seaman commander. Nevertheless, throughout much of the 17th century the king's commission to command usually went to those of some social standing ashore, and many of the great sea captains of this era were men of many parts, being both soldiers and sailors; such were 'Generals at Sea' George Monck and Robert Blake. There was thus an impermanence about the Navy's senior officers which was evidently unsatisfactory.

It was during Restoration times that a more permanent officer corps began to evolve, and much of the credit for this must go to Samuel PEPYS. His numerous reforms had lasting results in shaping the nature of the Navy during the next century, creating what gradually became a professional corps of officers, and leading to the eventual disappearance of the gentleman amateur. One of his reforms was the introduction of the KING'S LETTER BOYS, young gentlemen placed with experienced captains who were called upon to train them in their profession. However, in spite of this, for the next 150 years at least, the majority of young gentlemen who aspired to becoming officers went direct to sea by the patronage of a captain willing to sign them on as 'servants' or midshipmen, as they became. But even so the late-17th-century naval officer was still part-time in that he held his post as captain or lieutenant only for the duration of the ship's commission; when that was finished he was unemployed, with technically no naval status, until he received another commission. To retain such men a system of HALF-PAY was introduced, and in the 18th century this had to be half the pay received in the post last held. The result was that this in turn began to establish the idea of rank, and later the principle of seniority within that rank.

In addition to the commissioned captain and his lieutenants, there were on board other officers entitled to walk the quarter-deck who were also members of the lieutenants' wardroom mess. The master, who, as we saw earlier, was responsible for navigation, maintained his standing and was a warrant officer of wardroom rank by the end of the 18th century. In 1843 he became a commissioned officer, and his title disappeared (except as the name for the captain of a merchant ship) when in the 1860s he became a navigating lieutenant. The master's mate, which had been a position for bright young seamen with aspirations to the quarter-deck, at the same time became a sub-lieutenant, which was also the next stage for the young gentleman midshipman.

Other warrant officers of the old sailing Navy were the surgeon, the purser and the chaplain, all of whom had become commissioned officers in 1843. The surgeon became an officer in what today is the Medical Branch, and the purser part of the modern Supply and Secretariat Branch, each with gradations in rank according to promotion, but the chaplain, though a commissioned officer, by reason of his vocation bears no distinction of rank.

Again, in former times there were other warrant officers of importance though not of wardroom rank. Some have disappeared; others are found at the level of petty officer; others again have their modern counterparts in commissioned rank. One of these, the boatswain, who was responsible for all sailing matters and for discipline, lost ground with the coming of steam, and though the title is still used in the Navy, the boatswain was in fact succeeded by the new engineer officers, who were given commissioned rank in 1847 though they were not seamen officers. The gunner was a most important warrant officer, for upon his efficiency the success of the ship in battle largely depended; for this he had to know something of seamanship too, so in a sense he was one of the first officers to combine the old fighting and seaman functions. The gunner was also in charge of the young gentlemen midshipmen and shared the gunroom with them and his mates. When the 19th century brought a necessary specialization in duties the gunner became part of the corps of commissioned officers. Warrant officers, however, continued until quite recent times, for the rank was a major step on the ladder of promotion from the lower deck. The carpenter in the days of wooden ships had an important place as a warrant officer, but as wood gave way to iron, his status declined, his title was changed to shipwright, and as a separate class he disappeared from the hierarchy of officers. There is one other group of officers in the modern Navy not so far mentioned, namely the Instructor Branch; see the entry under that heading for an outline of the rise of the very humbly placed schoolmaster to the highly qualified commissioned instructor officers of today.

The evolution of the modern officer has therefore been a long process, marked by the coalescence of the originally separate fighting and seaman branches, brought about by the development of naval warfare and by continual reforms by the Admiralty, especially over the last hundred years. Today all officers are commissioned; they enter Britannia Royal Naval College, Dartmouth, either direct from school or after university. Those who begin life in the Navy as young ratings may be selected early if suitable for a commission so that they enter Dartmouth of an age with the others, and those so doing amount to one in three of all officers. Other ratings after longer service may also gain commissions as Special Duties Officers. After promotion to sub-lieutenant the paths of officers diverge according to whether they are to specialize as Seamen, Supply and Secretariat or Engineer Officers.

See colour section.

For officers of the Merchant Navy, *see* MASTER; MATE.

Officer of the Day: the officer on duty who is responsible for the routine work and general management of a ship in harbour, or of a shore establishment.

Officer of the Watch: the officer in charge of a ship when the captain is below or absent. At sea he keeps his watch on the bridge, and in harbour he may be additional to the Officer of the Day and

responsible for the ship's safety at anchor or at moorings, etc.

Offing: a safe navigational distance from the shore. 'In the offing' means the distance a ship can be seen from the land.

'... of the Tower': suffix attached to many early ship names (e.g. *JESUS OF THE TOWER*), signifying that they were in royal ownership, the Tower of London being the chief armoury. A grim story is told of William de la Pole, Duke of Suffolk (1396–1450), who was assured in a prophecy that he would be safe if he escaped the Tower. Accused by the Commons of having betrayed the realm to the French, he was making his escape to France by sea when his vessel was intercepted by another on which he read the words *...of the Tower*. He was beheaded at sea.

Ogle, Sir Chaloner (?1681–1750): admiral. He made a reputation as a frigate captain in the Mediterranean and was knighted in 1723 for capturing a gang of pirates off Cape Lopez. After a number of important posts, he became Commander-in-Chief in 1749.

Oil-carrier (or **tanker**): specialized type of bulk carrier that now forms one of the most important parts of the merchant fleets of the world and, since it is more economical to carry large cargoes, provides some of the largest ships the world has seen. Oil-carriers can generally be distinguished by a long low hull, three 'islands' (forecastle, bridge and poop) connected by light 'cat-walks', and engines aft. Transverse and longitudinal bulkheads are used to divide the ship into many tanks, each with water-tight hatch and ventilator, thus reducing the risk from fire, and another safety feature is the so-called

351

'coffer dam' inserted in several positions – a double bulkhead providing both a narrow air-space and additional strength.

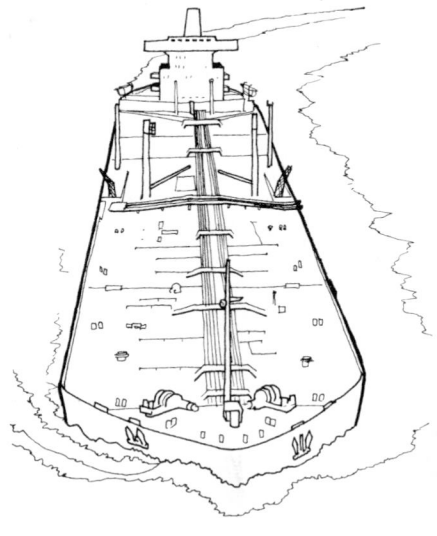

Oil slick: an area, great or small, of oil spilled from a ship. Large oil slicks from damaged or wrecked tankers cause pollution of beaches and death to sea-birds. The effect of oil on a rough sea was long known to reduce the force of the waves, and a device known as an oil bag was used for this purpose; hence the saying 'to pour oil on troubled waters', meaning to produce calm in a quarrel by the use of tact.

Old Glory: the colloquial and affectionate name for the national flag of the United States, the Stars and Stripes.

'Old Grog': *see* VERNON, EDWARD.

'Old Ironsides': *see CONSTITUTION*.

'Old Man, the': familiar term for the captain in a merchant ship. In the Royal Navy 'Father' is used for the commanding officer.

Old Man of the Sea: in the story of Sinbad the Sailor (from *The Arabian Nights Entertainments*), the sea monster who climbed on to Sinbad's back and refused to be dislodged till Sinbad made him drunk and threw him off.

Old salt: a sailor of long experience, obviously so called because he has been salted and preserved by the sea.

'Old Stormy': *see* OLD WHITE HAT.

'Old White Hat': nickname for John Willis, the Scottish seaman and shipowner for whom the *Cutty Sark* was built. The name derived from his habit of wearing a white top-hat. His father, another John Willis, was the original 'Old Stormy' of the sea chanty *Stormalong*.
See colour section.

Old World: the name given to Europe, Asia and Africa, in contrast to the NEW WORLD of North and South America; the eastern hemisphere compared with the western hemisphere. 'I called the New World into existence, to redress the balance of the Old', said George Canning in 1826 in reference to his foreign policy of supporting the independence of the countries of South America.

Oléron: *see* JUDGEMENTS OF OLÉRON.

Ommanney, Sir John Ackworth (1773–1855): admiral. Having had his name on the books of H.M.S. *Ajax* at the tender age of seven or eight, Ommanney 'soon obtained a high character for activity'. The activity included accompanying Lord Macartney on an embassy to China (1793), helping to put down the mutiny at the Nore (1797), and causing a Swedish fleet of merchantmen, accompanied by a frigate, to be searched for contraband of war (1799). He was flag-captain at Newfoundland and was decorated by several countries, including his own, for his services at Navarino (1827), subsequently being knighted.

One-gun salute: the single gun fired to announce a naval court-martial.

'One hand for the ship, the other for yourself': the traditional advice to the inexperienced, especially to those going aloft.

Onker: old Thames-side name for a ship in the Baltic timber trade.

Onslow, Sir Richard (1741–1817): admiral, knighted for his services at the Battle of Camperdown (1797), when, in the *Monarch*, he opened the British attack with such concentrated broadsides that the Dutch suffered heavy casualties at the outset.

Oomiak: *see* KAYAK.

Operation Drake: *see EYE OF THE WIND*.

Opium clipper: clippers are usually thought of in connection with the wool and tea trades, but some were engaged in less savoury affairs, including opium-running. Such vessels needed to be very swift to outsail the Chinese preventive vessels. One of the best-known was the 351-ton *Falcon*, built (1824) as a yacht for the Earl of Yarborough. In 1835 she was sold and was subsequently acquired by Jardine, Matheson & Co. for the opium trade. Despite her small size, she looked like a man-o'-war, was ship-rigged and originally carried 22 small guns. Other well-known opium ships were the *Sylph*, *Lady Hayes* and

Powasjee Family, and the Americans joined the racket with such vessels as the *Anglona*, *Ariel* and *Zephyr*. Opium ships often sailed in convoy as a protection against pirates and were usually heavily armed.

Opium Wars: in the early 19th century, despite protests from the Chinese authorities that importation of opium was illegal, large quantities were being introduced into the country from India by British traders. In 1839 some cargoes were confiscated and burnt, an act which led to war between Britain and China (1839–42). At the conclusion of peace, Hong Kong was thrown open to European traders, together with five other ports, and China paid an indemnity of 21,000,000 dollars, partly in compensation for their effrontery in burning the opium.

Fifteen years later a second war broke out, after which the importation of opium from India was legalized. Since 1900 there has been considerable international action to control and suppress traffic in opium, of which in the late 18th century the Directors of the East India Company wrote: 'If it were possible to prevent the use of the drug altogether except strictly for the purpose of medicine, we would gladly do it in compassion to mankind'; and which Lord Ashley in 1843 declared in Parliament to be 'utterly inconsistent with the honour and duty of a Christian kingdom'.

Opposite number: someone placed in a similar position of duty in another ship or in a mess, a watch, or other responsibility in the same ship. The abbreviation 'oppo' in lower-deck slang has come to mean also a messmate, a pal.

Orde, Sir John (1751–1824): admiral. He assisted at the reduction of Philadelphia in 1778 and Charleston in 1780, and was created a baronet for his services in Dominica, of which he was made governor in 1783. A very touchy officer, he complained to St Vincent about being superseded by Nelson and quarrelled with Nelson himself over a number of grievances, real or imaginary. In return, Nelson complained bitterly that Orde, in command of a squadron off Finisterre (1804–5), did not watch or report on the course of the Combined Fleets in the months that led up to Trafalgar. Orde was relieved of this command at his own request.

Order of battle: the positions taken up by ships for an engagement with the enemy.

Order of sailing: the positions taken up by ships when sailing together or in convoy. It is not necessarily the same as ORDER OF BATTLE, though for Nelson they were to be one and the same in his written instructions to his captains before Trafalgar.

Orders: *see* SEALED ORDERS; STANDING ORDERS.

Ordinary, in: formerly, a term for ships laid up in reserve. Ships were said to be in ordinary when they were not fully manned or equipped, as opposed to ships in commission. The phrase is a very old one, probably dating from early Tudor times, when the cost of fighting ships was borne by the king. He could not afford to keep

them always in commission, so they were referred to as being in their ordinary condition. In the 17th century many ships were laid up 'in ordinary' for the winter and brought into commission in the spring.

Ordinary Seaman: naval rating between Junior and Able Seaman, abbreviated O.S. Ordinary seamen are so rated at about the age of 18, and when basic training is finished, men of the seaman group begin to sub-specialize in particular skills demanded for working and fighting the modern warship. There are ratings equivalent to ordinary seaman in the other non-seaman branches, e.g. communications, catering, marine and electrical engineering, etc. In the old sailing Navy a man with some experience of the sea, whether volunteer or conscript, would be rated Ordinary Seaman before being made Able Seaman.

Ordnance: cannons, big guns and gun armament in particular, but also meaning in a general sense equipment and material for fighting. *See* ARMAMENT.

Orient: the East, especially the countries of eastern Asia. The word derives from the Latin for 'rising' (of the sun); 'Occident', used as a general name for the West, is from the Latin for 'setting'.

Orientation: the position of anything in relation to points of the compass; the taking of one's bearings.

'Orion': the most distinguished ship of the name was built on the Thames in 1787. In the actions of 28 May–1 June 1794 (the 'Glorious FIRST OF JUNE'), commanded by J. T. DUCKWORTH, she suffered a number of casualties and severe damage to masts and spars. She was subsequently at the

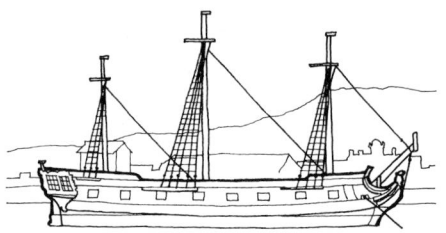

battles of Cape St Vincent, the Nile and Trafalgar, at all of which she played a brilliant part; and towards the end of her career she was with Gambier at Copenhagen and Saumarez in the Baltic. When she was broken up at Plymouth (1814) she had seen hard service for 26 years and earned five clasps to her war medal.

Orkneys: a group of some 70 islands and islets separated by the Pentland Firth from the north-east of Caithness in Scotland. The islands have many remains of prehistoric settlement; a Roman fleet reached them; and they were raided by the Norsemen in the 8th and 9th centuries. For long the Orkneys were under the kings of Norway and Denmark, but they became part of Scotland in 1472 as dowry when James III married the Danish king's daughter. The islands enclose a great stretch of water known as SCAPA FLOW.

Orlop: the lowest true DECK in the old sailing warship; the word comes from the Dutch *overloop*. It was generally below the water-line and was dark and airless. In its various parts were to be found the sleeping quarters for gunners, boatswains and carpenters, and for the young midshipmen, whose home was the after cockpit. Other parts of the orlop deck were used for stores and for stowing the anchor cable (*see* TIER).

Oropesa sweep: a long wire, towed astern of a minesweeper and held in position by an

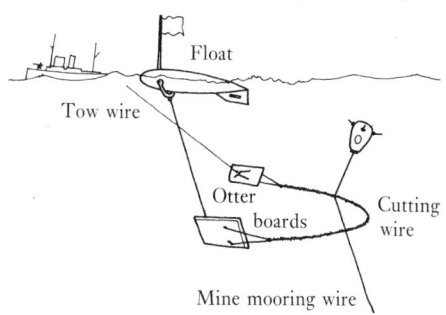

otter board, for cutting the cables of moored mines. The name comes from H.M.S. *Oropesa*, which in 1919 first used this method for clearing mines in the North Sea.

Oseberg Ship: Viking ship found (1903) near Oslo Fjord, dating from *c.* A.D. 850. She was 70·5 ft long and pulled 15 oars a side. With her elaborate carvings and light design, she was probably used for pleasure purposes in sheltered waters.

Detail of the stern decoration and steering oar.

Otter board: a board at the end of a long wire, used in minesweeping in order to extend the wire sideways (*see* OROPESA SWEEP and PARAVANE) and in fishing to keep open the mouth of a TRAWL net.

Outboard: on or towards the outer side of a ship, as opposed to 'inboard'. An outboard engine is one secured outside the hull of a small craft.

Out-port: a sea or river port some distance from the main city port. Thus Tilbury can

355

be described as an out-port of London, and Avonmouth of Bristol.

Outrigger: (1) a balancing log or beam secured by projecting spars and in line with the hull of a sailing or paddling canoe, thus giving additional stability. Outriggers are a feature of various types of native fishing craft in the Pacific and Indian Oceans. (2) an extension for stays in larger types of sailing ships. (3) a temporary beam from a ship's side rigged to give extra support to the masts when a ship was careened. (4) a metal stay with a rowlock at the end projecting from a rowing boat.

Overboard: over the side of a ship or a boat.

Overfall: *see* TIDES.

Overhaul: (1) to examine, repair and clean a ship, boat, engine, etc.; (2) to overtake from astern and pass a ship under way.

'Owen Glendower': East Indiaman (built 1838–9) which (along with the *Earl of Hardwick*) marked a departure from the old type of vessel. Of 852 tons, she was without the characteristic poop and had only a single tier of stern and quarter windows, thus providing a much more efficient and workmanlike design that soon spread to the larger ships.

Owling: old term for smuggling wool out of England to the Continent without payment of official dues.

Oxenham, John (*d.*1575): sea captain who sailed with Drake on his 1572 expedition (*see* NOMBRE DE DIOS) and in 1576–7 led his own venture against the Spaniards. He and his crew were the first to sail on the Pacific. He crossed the Isthmus of Panama and captured several Spanish vessels with their treasure. He had plans for occupying the Isthmus permanently, thus cutting the Peru–Spain treasure route, but the Spaniards captured and hanged him at Lima. Charles Kingsley introduced a somewhat imaginative account of this expedition into *Westward Ho!*.

P

Pacific: the world's largest ocean, bounded by eastern Asia, Australia and the Americas, and extending from the Arctic to the Antarctic. This vast area of water covers about a third of the earth's surface and contains the greatest ocean depths in various 'deeps' or trenches. Of these the Mindanao Trench off the Philippines has revealed a depth of over 7 miles, which would more than cover Mount Everest were the world's highest mountain sunk there. The ocean is studded with hundreds of islands, many of which are of volcanic origin, though many others are coral islands or mere coral atolls rising only a few feet above sea level. The Pacific islands are somewhat loosely grouped according to their peoples into Melanesia, Micronesia and Polynesia (*see* OCEANIA). How these islands came to be peopled across thousands of miles of sea is a matter of debate, but in spite of Thor Heyerdahl's famous Kon-Tiki expedition showing that it was possible for the islands to be reached by primitive craft from South America, the generally accepted view is that the islands were peopled from Asia. Voyages in open canoes across such vast distances remain one of the wonders of early navigation.

The Spaniard Nuñez de Balboa is credited with having been the first European to sight the Pacific when in 1513 he saw its waters from a peak in Darien in the Isthmus of Panama. The first European to sail into the Pacific was Magellan, who in 1520, after his long and stormy passage through the Straits named after him, was then met with such fair weather that he gave the new-found ocean its present name. But it is by no means always calm, and large areas are subject to fierce tropical storms – HURRICANES or TYPHOONS.

Like Balboa, Sir Francis Drake also sighted the Pacific from the Isthmus of Panama, and his prayer that he might one day sail an English ship on that sea was granted during his great circumnavigation of the globe in the *Golden Hind* (1577–80).

The succeeding centuries saw the Pacific become an area of trading rivalry and territorial acquisition between the maritime nations. After the Spanish and Portuguese came the Dutch in the 17th century and the English in the 18th. Knowledge of the ocean and its lands was greatly increased by the detailed observations made during the voyages of James Cook between 1768 and 1780. Annexation of most of the islands as colonies continued apace in the 19th century, and Britain, France, Germany, Japan and the U.S.A. all laid claim to various island groups. After the First World War Germany's influence in the western Pacific disappeared when the Caroline, Marshall and Mariana Islands became Japanese mandates and N.E. New Guinea passed to Australian administration. In December 1941 the attack without warning by the Japanese on the American fleet and naval base at Pearl Harbor in the Hawaiian Islands brought the U.S.A. into the Second World War. It was thus on the vast waters of the Pacific that the great naval battles between the Japanese and U.S. fleets were fought. Such were the Battles of the Coral Sea and Midway (1942) and the Battles of the Philippine Sea and Leyte Gulf (1944); the latter was the greatest naval battle in history in terms of the size of the opposing forces.

Packet-boat (or **packet**): a vessel used for

The packet-boat *Shelldrake* off Falmouth, from an oil painting by N.M. Condy.

carrying mail. In the late 18th and first half of the 19th centuries packet-boats were designed to give speed in carrying mail on such important routes as those to India and America. They also carried important people and goods, and some were armed. Today overseas surface mail is carried under contract by a variety of merchant and passenger liners. *See also* LIVERPOOL PACKET; NAPIER, DAVID; SMACK.

'Packet of Woodbines': the British sailor's name for the famous five-funnelled Russian cruiser *Askold*, Woodbines being a popular cheap cigarette sold in packets of five.

Packet rat: a seaman on the old transatlantic packet ships, often a Liverpool Irishman.

Paddle ship: steam vessel propelled by paddle-wheels – large wheels with long boards projecting at right angles from the circumference. It is believed that there were experiments with paddle-wheels as early as Roman times, but the first paddle steamers appeared early in the 19th century. If the wheels were on each side of the ship she was called a 'side-wheeler'; another type was the 'stern-wheeler', which proved more economical to run. Björn Landström, in *The Ship* (1961), records that 'the stern-wheeler was for a long time the ugly duckling of the Mississippi, the swans being the large, fast side-wheelers ... The captains of these side-wheelers called the others "wheelbarrows".' However, from about 1815 onwards, after the stern-wheeler *George Washington* was built, more than 5000 similar ships came into use on the Mississippi.

The first passenger steamship, the *Comet*, built on the Clyde in 1812, was propelled by a four-horsepower engine driving two pairs of paddles (later reduced to one pair). The *GREAT EASTERN* (1858) left nothing to chance, having a screw, paddles, six masts and sails, and five funnels. Paddle steamers began to disappear from the high seas by the middle of the 19th century (*see* PROPELLER), but they long continued in use for short crossings and for shallow harbour and inland water work.

See also CHARLOTTE DUNDAS; PHOENIX; SAVANNAH; STEAMSHIPS.

'Paddy's milestone': nickname for Ailsa Craig, more or less exactly halfway between Belfast and Greenock on the packet route.

'Pageant of Richard Beauchamp': an important manuscript in the British Library, considered to be the work of a priest named John Rous, of Guy's Cliffe, near Warwick, and carried out *c*.1485–90. The MS. is intended to depict the pilgrimage of Richard, Earl of Warwick, to the Holy Land earlier in the 15th century. The drawings give a valuable picture of ships at the time they were made. From them, at least one fine model of an English ship of *c*.1485 has been made – a three-masted cog type – and can be seen at the Science Museum, London.

Painter: a short length of rope running from the bows of a boat and used for securing it in a moored position. A 'lazy painter' is a longer line securing a boat to a boom set out from a ship's side and with which the boat may be hauled in for use.

'Pallas': a famous fighting 32-gun frigate much in action in the 18th and early 19th centuries, e.g. off the Isle of Man (1760), off Ushant (1795), with Lord Cochrane in the Isle of Aix (1801) and Gambier in the Basque Roads (1809). To confuse the issue a little, the French had a slightly larger frigate of the same name.

Palliser, Sir Hugh (1723–96): admiral. Entering the Navy in 1735, he rose to occupy a number of important sea-going and administrative posts, at one time directing a survey of the coasts of Newfoundland. In 1778, while serving under Keppel, he disobeyed an order during the action off USHANT, perhaps because he misunderstood a signal, but probably deliberately. At his subsequent court-martial he was acquitted, with no credit to himself, and was not reinstated in the offices he had resigned before the trial. He was fortunate enough, however, to receive a consolation prize, the governor-ship of Greenwich Hospital.

Palm, sailmaker's: a strip of leather with a thumb hole and running across the palm of the hand. It has a hardened part in the centre which is used in a similar way to a thimble for pushing the NEEDLE through the canvas being sewn.

Panama Canal: a waterway, linking the Caribbean and Pacific Oceans, cut through the narrow Isthmus of Panama in Central America. The earliest Spanish explorers had seen the possibility of such a canal, but its fulfilment had to wait for nearly four hundred years. After the French engineer Ferdinand de Lesseps had successfully completed the Suez Canal (1869) he became in 1879 the head of a company set up to cut a canal at Panama. But the company got into difficulties and through corruption and general financial mis-management it failed after ten years. In 1894 excavation began again, but the new company was little more successful, one of its most serious problems being the ravages of yellow fever amongst its workers. The need for the United States to have warships in both the Atlantic and Pacific Oceans was shown during the Spanish-American War of 1898, and the Americans realized the value of a canal that would avoid the long journey round South America in transfer-ring ships from one ocean to the other, and linking the centres of population and trade on the east and west coasts of South America. Subsequently, after long but abortive negotiations with Colombia, to whom the isthmus belonged, the in-dependent republic of Panama was set up, and within it the United States obtained sovereignty over a strip of territory some 10 miles wide running across this narrow neck of land. Work on building the canal was begun by the Americans in 1904 and four years later was taken over by the U.S. Army's engineers, who completed the task. The canal was opened to shipping in 1914. In addition to the problems of health, other difficulties in construction had to be overcome. The differences in the levels of the two oceans and the height of the land necessitated construction of a series of locks, of which there are twelve in twin flights through which ships are towed by engines. The total length of the canal is just over 40 miles, and it takes about eight hours for a ship to pass through.

Over recent years the United States and Panama have been negotiating a new treaty, and in 1974 reached agreement on general principles. By this new treaty (finalized in 1978) the U.S. will surrender its jurisdiction over the canal and the Canal Zone on 31 December 1999, and both the U.S. and Panama will participate in the maintenance and protection of the canal.

P. & O.: the familiar abbreviation for the Peninsular and Oriental Steam Navigation Company, founded by the London firm of shipowners Willcox & Anderson as the 'Peninsular Service' in 1834 and changing its name in 1840. It grew to become the largest shipping group in the world, forming a vast combination of shipping and shipowning companies, transport and forwarding agencies and marine engineering concerns.

Pangbourne: village on the Thames in Berkshire, site of a nautical college founded in 1917 (*see* DEVITT & MOORE). Today Pangbourne College is an independent school for boys aged 11 to 18, providing the usual secondary school courses and activities, but its nautical traditions are to

some extent continued and, except for the younger entrants, boys are gazetted by the Ministry of Defence (Navy) as Cadets Royal Naval Reserve and wear the uniform of that service, though on leaving they enter a variety of careers.

Pantaloons: type of tight trousers, blue or white, worn by midshipmen and officers. At first unauthorized, they appeared as an alternative to breeches in the official dress regulations of 1825.

We were considered a crack ship and the midshipmen dressed in cocked hats, tight white pantaloons and Hessian boots with gilt twist edging and a bullion tassel.

Captain John Harvey Boteler (1815, when he was appointed as Lieutenant to the *Antelope*)

Paper Blockade: term sometimes used to describe Napoleon's 'Continental System', by which, though he could not seal off British ports with warships, he instituted an army of port-officials from the Gulf of Finland to the Dardanelles, whose job was to prevent the British trading into European ports.

Paravane: a device formerly used for countering moored mines. First used in 1916, the paravane consisted of two wires extending like an arrowhead from the bows of a ship, the wires being held at an angle outwards by otter boards. As the ship's bow wave pushed the mine outwards its mooring wire was caught and cut by the wire of the paravane; the mine then floated to the surface and was destroyed by gunfire.

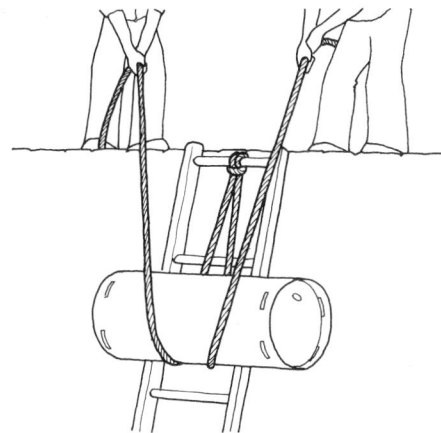

Parbuckle: an arrangement of rope for raising or lowering a heavy object, e.g. a cask or large spar. The middle of a length of rope is secured at an appropriate level and the two ends are passed under and back over the object so that they can be hauled or lowered away, allowing it to roll up or down as required.

Parcelling: *see* WORM, TO.

Paris, Declaration of (1856): an important declaration on international law after the Crimean War. The powers agreed that (1) privateering should be abolished; (2) except for contraband of war, a flag of neutrality covered even enemy goods; (3) blockades, if they were to be effective, must be maintained by sufficient forces to stop access to the enemy coasts involved. The United States, one of the participating powers, did not agree to the first point.

Paris, Treaties of: a number of treaties affecting Britain and her navies have been concluded with this title. Among the most important were (1) that of February 1763, concluding the Seven Years' War, with France ceding to Great Britain Canada, Nova Scotia, Cape Breton Island, Grenada, Dominica, St Vincent, Tobago,

Minorca and Senegal, and Spain ceding important fishing rights off Newfoundland; Britain made less important concessions to both France and Spain, including certain towns in India, Cuba and the Philippines; (2) that of May 1814, which consisted of seven separate treaties signed by the individual powers of the Fourth Coalition and France after Napoleon's abdication and banishment to Elba; (3) that of 20 November 1815, concluding the Napoleonic Wars, which in general imposed very much more severe terms on France and banished the Emperor to St Helena.

Parish rig: kit given to needy or ill-clothed man sent to sea by the parish in the old days. The term was especially used in Canada and Eastern America. Sometimes it was transferred to a poorly-found, badly conditioned ship. *See also* SLOPS. Compare SNAPPER-RIGGED.

Parker, Sir Hyde (1739–1807): admiral. His chief claim to fame is that he was the commander-in-chief concerned when, at the Battle of COPENHAGEN (1801), Nelson turned his 'blind eye' to Parker's signal to withdraw.

Two other Hyde Parkers, father and son of the above, became admirals. For some reason the name Parker figures with unusual prominence in the Commissioned Officers List over the period 1660–1815. There were some 40 of them; at least eight attained flag rank.

Parker, Sir Peter (1721–1811): admiral. He was in command of the squadron that attacked Charleston and was beaten off with the loss of three frigates (1775). He reached the highest rank in the Navy, however, and added to his distinction by being an early patron and supporter of Nelson. His grandson, another *Sir Peter*

Parker (1785–1814), was killed in a skirmish in Chesapeake Bay during the Anglo-American War.

In your grandson Peter, you possess everything which is amiable, good, and manly.

Nelson to Admiral Sir Peter Parker
(July 1804)

Parker, Richard (?1767–1797): mutineer. Having been imprisoned for debt, he obtained his release by volunteering for service in the Navy. He led the dissidents at the Nore MUTINY (1797) and was hanged after its collapse.

Parliament heel: strange term used when (as in the case of the *ROYAL GEORGE*) a vessel was tilted to one side to make a hull repair.

When the hull of a ship is damaged in any part which can be got at by making her lean on one side, they adopt this plan of removing some of the heavy furniture to the opposite side of the vessel; by this means, the ship is heeled up till the damaged part is above water. This heeling of the ship on one side is called the parliament heel.

George Mogridge, *The Old Sea-Captain* (1853)

'Parliament Joan': name given to Mrs Elizabeth Alkin, who selflessly nursed the wounded during the Civil War of 1642–9 and, at the outbreak of the Dutch War, transferred her services to the sailors at Portsmouth, often paying out of her own pocket and in the end selling her own bed. She finished broken in health and impoverished and appealed to the government for a bed in a London hospital. She seemed to have regarded the Dutch prisoners as generously as she did her own countrymen, saying: 'Seeing their wants and miseries so great, I could not but have pity on them, though our enemies.'

Parrel: *see* TRUSS.

Parry, William (*fl.c.*1600): traveller by sea and land about whom little is known except that he accompanied Sir Anthony SHIRLEY on his adventures and published an account of them in *A New and Large Discourse of the Travels of Anthony Sherley* (1601).

Parry, Sir William Edward (1790–1855): admiral and Arctic explorer. He commanded three expeditions in search of the North-West Passage (1819–25) and in 1827 tried to reach the North Pole by sledge-boats over the ice from Spitsbergen. Though conditions defeated him, no higher latitude was reached for another 50 years. He was Hydrographer to the Admiralty 1825–9.

Part brass rags, to: a slang phrase meaning to break off a friendship, to quarrel. It probably derives from the days when messmates would have to spend a long time cleaning the ship's brightwork, which was generally brass. To quarrel when doing this was therefore to part brass rags.

Pasco, John (1774–1853): officer, who, though he later attained the rank of admiral, achieved immortality in a junior rank, when, as Signal Lieutenant on *Victory* at Trafalgar, he transmitted the most famous signal in British history – a signal whose wording he was partly responsible for. In his own words:

His lordship came to me on the poop and at about a quarter to noon said:
'I wish to say to the Fleet, ENGLAND CONFIDES THAT EVERY MAN WILL DO HIS DUTY'; and he added: 'You must be quick, for I have one more to make, which is for Close Action.' I replied: 'If your lordship will

permit me to substitute *expects* for *confides*, the signal will soon be completed, because the word *expects* is in the vocabulary, and *confides* must be spelt.'

His lordship replied, in haste, and with seeming satisfaction: 'That will do, Pasco, make it immediately!'

When it had been answered by a few ships in the Van, he ordered me to make the signal for Close Action and to keep it up; accordingly, I hoisted No.16 at the top-gallant mast-head, and there it remained until shot away.

Pasco was severely wounded in the right arm and side during the action, and received an Admiralty pension of £250 per annum as well as a grant from the Patriotic Fund. *See also* PROMOTION.

Passage: (1) any sea journey between port and port; hence the phrase 'to work one's passage' meaning to be employed in the ship in return for a free passage; (2) an opening or channel, e.g. into a bay or between rocks or shoals. An ice-breaker forces a passage through the ice.

Patriotic Fund: fund administered by the Patriotic Committee established (20 July 1803) at a meeting of merchants, underwriters and other subscribers to Lloyd's. It was resolved:

That to animate the efforts of our defenders by sea and land, it is expedient to raise, by the patriotism of the community at large, a suitable fund for their comfort and relief; for the purpose of assuaging the anguish of their wounds, or palliating in some degree the more weighty misfortune of the loss of limbs, of alleviating the distress of the widow and orphan, and of granting pecuniary rewards, or honourable badges of distinction, for successful exertions of valour or merit.

By the end of August 1809 some £425,000 had been subscribed and over £330,000 expended in gratuities and annuities, of which £21,274 had gone in payment for

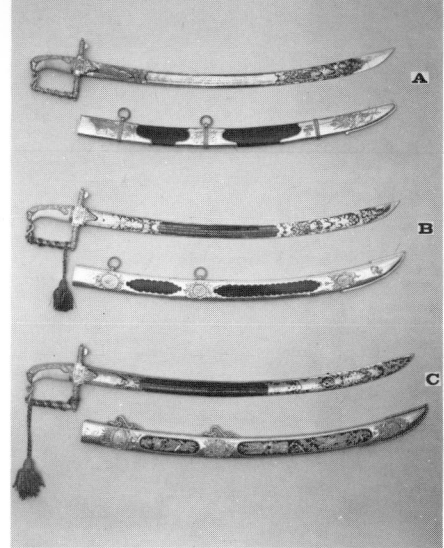

Presentation swords made for the Patriotic Fund.

special swords and plate to distinguished officers. In 1810 this type of award was discontinued, the Committee having reached the decision that the Fund should be used, not for merit alone, but merit and distress combined. Ultimately, after the Napoleonic Wars, the Fund ceased its grants (1825) and the remaining sum was put in trust for any future war.

Patronage: the power to influence appointments, particularly prevalent in the 18th and 19th centuries, when having 'interest' (i.e. knowing the right sort of people) was often very important for those seeking a naval career as an officer. At one end, it simply involved knowing a captain who would take a boy to sea; at the other, acquaintance with a noble family or powerful administrator could ensure rapid promotion and attainment of high rank. Sir William Dillon recorded that when he was 13 Lord Hawke said to him:

Let me explain my intentions towards you. When there is a general naval promotion, I am always allowed to provide for one friend, to get him made a Lieutenant, a Commander or a Post Captain. Therefore, when your time is up, let me know, and you shall be my Lieutenant. In short, you are as sure of the commission as if you had it in your pocket.

One of the most notorious cases was that of John Rodney, son of the famous Admiral Lord Rodney. John was taken to sea at $14\frac{1}{2}$ years of age. Before he was 16 his father made him a lieutenant and, just over a month later, promoted him first to commander and then to post-captain. The appointments were all confirmed by the Admiralty. The career of Sir Thomas John Cochrane makes equally interesting reading:

Born: February 1789
At sea, as a First Class Volunteer: 1796 (at the age of 7)
Lieutenant: 14 June 1805
Commander: 24 September 1805
Captain: 23 April 1806 (when he was 17)

Paulet, Harry (*fl.*1750–1800): master mariner and Hampshire smuggler who is reported to have been on board Hawke's *Royal George* at the Battle of Quiberon Bay (1759). According to the story, Paulet was running an illicit cargo across the Channel when he spotted the French Admiral Conflans escaping from Brest and making south-east. On his way back to England he came up with Hawke's squadron and went on board to inform the Admiral, who told him that, if the information were true, he was in a fair way to make his fortune; if not, he was likely to be hanged at the yard-arm. Hawke sailed in pursuit, with the smuggler, apparently at his own request, still on board. After the subsequent victory, Paulet came home with letters of recommendation from Hawke and enough money to keep him in comfort for the rest of his life.

The *Dictionary of National Biography* tends to discredit the story; but the fact remains that Paulet settled in Cornhill; and William Parson, a comic actor of the day, used to say that he would rather spend a crown to hear Paulet tell the story of Quiberon Bay than listen to the greatest orator.

There was a manner in his heart-felt narrations that was certain to bring his auditors into the very scene of action; and when describing the moments of victory I have seen a dozen labouring men at the Crown public house rise together and, moved by an instantaneous impulse, give three cheers while Harry took breath to recite more of his exploits.

Pax Britannica: literally, the Peace of Britain; the predominant role played by Britain in the 19th century in establishing the freedom of the seas and maintaining the peaceful use of them by all nations.

Pay, seamen's: money paid in return for service in the Navy or in merchant ships. Pay and food have always been two most important matters to seamen, and yet over a long period in the old sailing Navy they were far from satisfactory. Because of the changes in the value of money over the centuries and because of the complexities of the subject, no more than a few points can be made here. Michael Lewis in *The Navy of Britain* tells us that Henry VIII's seamen had their pay raised to 6s. 8d. a month and they were at least paid regularly, but it is difficult to know just what this sum meant without a study of the prices of those times. By Elizabeth's time seamen were receiving 10s. a month, but the value of money had declined and so had the regularity of payment. In the Stuart period pay rose to 14s. and then 15s. a month, but it is believed that a strong contributory reason for Charles I's Navy not supporting him was his failure to pay them over long periods, sometimes running to years. Under the Commonwealth there was a further rise to 19s. a month for ordinary seamen and 22s. 6d. a month for able seamen. Pay then remained around this figure for a considerable time, in fact until the end of the 18th century, when pay was one of the grievances of the men in the mutiny at Spithead (1797), which achieved an improvement. One of the hardships seamen had to bear in the 18th century was that wages were not paid until they were six months overdue, and sometimes longer when they were not paid until a ship finished her commission. Even then the men were frequently paid with 'tickets' which could be exchanged for cash at the Navy Pay Office at Tower Hill in London. As a result of this, much sharp practice grew up at the naval ports, where swindlers bought the pay tickets at a discount from the sailors and cashed them at the full rate, for naturally only a few seamen would have the opportunity or wish to go to London, and they wanted ready money quickly.

By the end of the Napoleonic Wars there had again been a small improvement in pay, but the cost of living had risen also. During these years pay varied of course with the rating of the seaman, whether landsman, ordinary or able seaman, and it varied for certain officers, petty officers and some others with the rate of the ship in which they served; there was thus a scale between the highest paid in a first-rate ship and the lower paid in ships of sixth rate and under. In 1825 the ship's purser became also a paymaster, and paid the men a proportion of wages due. Pay in itself was not much of an inducement to join the Navy, but there were certain allowances and the hope of a share in PRIZE MONEY, whilst food and accommodation was assured. Even more complex are the variations in officers' pay and HALF-PAY

before the latter was abolished as we enter the modern period. Today seamen's pay is computed to give equivalence to comparable civilian occupations, and of course still varies with a man's rating; it is also affected by length of service and increased with allowances for special qualifications and for service in submarines and in flying duties.

Pay, to: in a general sense, to cover, coat or smear with pitch, tar or other waterproofing and preserving substance. In a particular sense, to pay is to pour pitch on the oakum used for caulking a vessel's decks or sides; to pay the vessel's bottom is to cover it with a compound made to stop fouling by weed or barnacles.

Pay off, to: (1) to fall away to leeward, especially when a sailing vessel is tacking and her head turns away from the wind; (2) to pay and discharge the crew of a ship at the end of a voyage; to end a commission. To 'pay off all standing' is to pay off a ship leaving her fully equipped and ready for the new crew, without any dismantling.

Pay out, to: to slacken and gradually let out a rope or cable.

'Peace with honour': 'Lord Salisbury and myself have brought you back peace – but a peace I hope with honour', announced Disraeli to the House of Commons in July 1878, following the Congress of Berlin, which concluded the Russo-Turkish War. The chief factor in bringing about a settlement had been the Royal Navy, which, led through the Dardanelles to Constantinople by Admiral Sir Geoffrey Phipps Hornby, remained resolutely off the Golden Horn for more than a year – a wonderful demonstration, as the naval historian Geoffrey Callender pointed out, of the truth of Nelson's dictum that 'A fleet of British ships-of-war are the best negotiators in Europe.'

Peak: (1) the outer, upper corner of a fore and aft SAIL extended by a gaff; (2) the narrowed part of either the bow (fore peak) or stern (after peak) of a ship, often forming a small compartment or store.

Pearl Coast: the name given by early Spanish explorers to part of the coast of northern Venezuela westwards from Trinidad; it was famous for its pearl-fishing, and the islands were known as the Pearl Islands.

Pearson, Sir Richard (1731–1806): Royal Navy captain in the celebrated fight of the *Serapis* against the *Bonhomme Richard*, commanded by John Paul Jones, off FLAMBOROUGH HEAD (1779). With nearly two thirds of his crew lost but his convoy saved, Pearson surrendered and was given wine in his cabin by his opponent, who returned his sword to him in tribute. George III knighted Pearson for his gallantry, and Jones is reputed to have said that if he ever met Pearson in combat again he 'would make a lord of him.'

'Pelican': the original name of Drake's famous *GOLDEN HIND*.

Pellew, Sir Edward, first Baronet and first Viscount Exmouth (1757–1833): admiral; one of the greatest frigate captains of his time, and an exceptionally brave officer. He began life so puny that he seemed unlikely to survive and was accordingly baptized on the day he was born. This seems to have had a restorative effect, for at school he developed unusual stature and strength with a formidable reputation as a fighter and swimmer. A Cornish clergyman, the Rev. Richard

Polwhele, wrote of him rather plaintively: '. . . with his high spirit he had a very kind heart. Pellew would never suffer the weak to be trampled upon, but would fight their battles. But I think he once thrashed me.' He ran away to sea at the age of 13, joining the frigate *Juno*, and from then on his life was packed with action and adventure. On one occasion, when he was serving on the *Blond*, a soldier passenger was amazed to see a midshipman standing on his head on the yardarm. Captain Pownall, the commanding officer, said it was nothing to worry about. It was only young Pellew, and if he happened to fall overboard he would undoubtedly go right under the ship and come up safely on the other side. He was a splendid swimmer and saved many lives. He commanded the respect and admiration of his crews because he would never ask them to do what he was not prepared to tackle himself, however dangerous. In 1799 he prevented a general mutiny in the

Sir Edward Pellew, from a painting by Beechey.

Bantry Bay squadron by leaping among the mutineers and seizing the ringleader with his own hands. Three years earlier, when arriving to dine with a clergyman at Plymouth, he heard that the *Dutton*, a transport ship, was ashore in circumstances of great peril. He jumped from his coach, ran down to the shore, took charge of the rescue operations (having been hauled aboard by rope, still in his frock coat and with his sword on) and got everyone safely ashore before the ship finally broke up. One of the greatest of his later exploits was his bombardment of Algiers (1816), which compelled the Dey (ruler) to release thousands of Christian slaves – a feat for which Pellew received honours from all over Christendom and was made a viscount. *See also INDEFATIGABLE*; TROUBRIDGE, SIR THOMAS.

It is sad that his son Fleetwood, although he too achieved flag rank, was not so adept in handling men. Three mutinies broke out under his command and, though not dismissed, he was virtually relieved of further service.

Pellew, Sir Israel (1758–1832): admiral, brother of Sir Edward PELLEW. While not attaining quite the reputation of his brother, he was an equally intrepid officer, reaching his peak at Trafalgar, where, in command of the *CONQUEROR*, he captured the French flag-ship *Bucentaure*.

Pelorus: a ring with sights on a compass bowl, used for taking bearings.

Pelorus Jack: the fond name for a dolphin which was said to guide ships through the narrow strait between the mainland and D'Urville Island at the northern extremity of South Island, New Zealand. For long in the 1890s and early years of this century Pelorus Jack accompanied ships using this passage; he became a great favourite and was protected by the New Zealand government.

Pembroke: town and port on the southern shore of MILFORD HAVEN. Pembroke Dock was opened as a royal dockyard in 1814; it was closed in 1926, but in the Second World War Pembroke was in use again as one of the smaller naval bases.

Pendant (pronounced 'pennant') and **pennant**: more modern terms for the old 'streamer', a long and fairly narrow flag flown from mast-head top or yardarm. Records of the 13th and 14th centuries show that streamers were often 30 ft or more in length. 'Pendant' is really a more official form of 'pennant'.

'Penelope': 46-gun frigate, built as a sailing vessel, which created a sensation in shipping circles at home and abroad when in 1843 she suffered a major transformation, being cut in half and lengthened to accommodate engines and 600 tons of coal. Independent of the wind, despite her increased size and weight she managed to sail faster than before.

The *Penelope* of 1867 was the first twin-screw ocean-going ironclad in the Royal Navy, carrying ten 12-in. guns.

Peninsular War (1808–14): part of the Napoleonic Wars, fought in the Iberian Peninsula by Britain, Spain and Portugal against France. Just emphasis is usually placed on the land exploits of Wellington, but it must always be remembered that it was ships that formed the supply-line and brought to the Peninsula every man, gun and piece of equipment, except for the minor contribution of the native guerrillas.

Penn, Sir William (1621–70): admiral

The *Penelope* in heavy seas, just after conversion, from a litho by T.G. Dutton, 1843.

and 'General at Sea'. He served in the Parliamentary Navy and distinguished himself in the First Dutch War (1653), being rewarded with posts as General of the Fleet and Commissioner of the Admiralty. Afterwards his career fluctuated considerably, as did the opinions of those who knew him. After an expedition in 1654–5, which took Jamaica but failed to capture Domingo, he was imprisoned for a short time (ostensibly for returning without leave) and retired in disgrace to his Irish estates. At the Restoration he was knighted and restored to favour, though he ran into trouble and censure again at the Battle of Lowestoft (1665). He was probably responsible for the famous 'Duke of York's Sailing and Fighting Instructions'. Samuel Pepys considered him at one time 'a merry fellow and pretty good natured, and sings very loose songs', but in time he became 'a very villain'. He was the father of the great Quaker William Penn, founder of Pennsylvania.

Pennant: *see* PENDANT.

Pennant number: *see* IDENTIFICATION MARKS.

Pennon: word used at sea in early times to denote a short, as opposed to a long, 'streamer'.

Pensions, seamen's: payments from a common fund to the wounded and disabled, to elderly seamen of long service, or to the widows of those killed in action. The earliest such fund was the CHATHAM CHEST, founded in 1590. The money given out for the wounded was for long known as 'smart money'. The next form of pension was that arising from the founding of the GREENWICH ROYAL HOSPITAL, which began to receive old, disabled or frail seamen in 1705. The pensioners were well looked after and there was much demand for places, for in addition to getting free board and lodging, there was a small allowance of pocket money and some essential clothing and bedding were provided. All active seafarers contributed 6d. a month (warrant officers a shilling), deducted from their pay, towards the GREENWICH CHEST, which was amalgamated with the Chatham Chest in 1814 (*see* SIXPENNY OFFICE). In addition to the many hundreds of pensioners who lived in at Greenwich, there were also out-pensioners who lived at home but received small pensions. Among the methods of providing for the widows and dependants of seamen killed in action was the curious arrangement known as WIDOWS' MEN. These arrangements of former years were gradually replaced by the better-organized pensions systems prevailing today. *See also* REGISTER OF SEAMEN.

Penzance: town and harbour at the S.W. extremity of Cornwall. Like many other coastal towns of Devon and Cornwall its men were seafarers and fishermen, though at one time the tin trade was also important. But it was smuggling that

became a way of life for many, especially in the 18th century, towards the end of which there was even a mayor of the town who had a reputation as a successful smuggler.

Pepys, Samuel (1633–1703): famous for his *Diary* and for his service in improving the administration of the Navy. Pepys owed much to his patron and relation Edward Montagu, who had served the Commonwealth as a 'General at Sea' but who turned to the royalist cause and was instrumental in the restoration of Charles II. The King made Montagu Earl of SANDWICH, and he in turn obtained for Pepys the Clerkship of the Acts to the Navy Board, a body which was responsible for the civil administration of the Navy. Pepys was a scholarly and gifted man who entirely justified his appointment by tackling the corruption and maladministration which marked the management of the Navy at

The Greenwich Pensioner, from a print by George Cruikshank.

Samuel Pepys, from a portrait by Godfrey Kneller.

that time. The Second Dutch War (1665–7) severely tested his performance in office. After Admiral de Ruyter had captured and burned several ships of the English fleet in the MEDWAY and blockaded London, an attempt was made to lay the blame on the Navy Board, but Pepys was able to justify its actions. In 1673 he became First Secretary to the Admiralty and again introduced many beneficial reforms. Seven years later he was falsely accused of being involved in the Popish Plot; he was deprived of his office and briefly imprisoned. After being set free, and after a voyage to Tangier with Lord Dartmouth, Pepys was reappointed Secretary to the Admiralty, and there he continued to serve under James II until the King was deposed in 1688, and he was again falsely accused and forced to resign and retire. During his time at the Admiralty, however, Pepys had greatly improved naval affairs and laid the foundations for a more efficient and regular Navy which was to stand the nation in good stead in the ensuing century. He served

also as a Member of Parliament, was President of the Royal Society and Master of Trinity House.

Pepys's *Diary*, which remains with his other books and manuscripts in a special library at Magdalene College, Cambridge, is a wonderful record of his times. It is written in a cypher, or kind of shorthand, and though versions of it have previously appeared, the full transcription has only recently been published. Pepys had hoped to write a history of the Royal Navy, but did not in fact do so, though he produced in 1690 *Memoirs Relating to the State of the Royal Navy*, which gave an account of the work of the special commission set up in 1686 to produce an efficient fleet.

In face of the difficulties of his times the achievement of Pepys was remarkable, and the nation and the Navy owed much to his work. *See also* EDUCATION; OFFICER.

'Peregrine galley': sixth-rate ship of 20 guns, built at Sheerness in 1700, but in 1716 converted into a royal yacht and renamed *Carolina*. In 1733 she was completely rebuilt and suffered another change of name, this time to *Royal Caroline*. When a new royal yacht was commissioned with this name (1749), the old ship again became the *Peregrine*, this time as a 16-gun sloop, which continued in general service till she foundered on a voyage to the West Indies in 1762. She may thus serve as a warning to the aspiring historian on ships' names.

Perier (or **cannon-perier**): an early type of short-barrelled gun, used in 15th- and 16th-century ships. It fired a 24-lb. stone shot and was a formidable weapon at close range; but its maximum range was less than that of the cannon and the culverin.

Periscope: a pillar-like optical device of mirrors and lenses for observation at a level

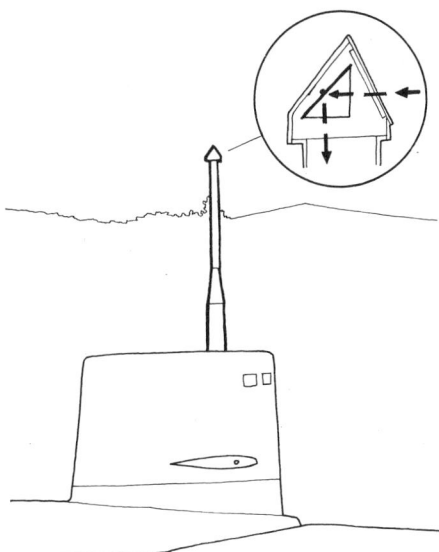

above the observer, used particularly in submarines. While the submarine's hull is hidden just below the sea's surface, the periscope is raised above it to give a view of the surrounding area.

Permanent Fighting Instructions: *see* FIGHTING INSTRUCTIONS.

Persian Gulf: the great shallow arm of the Arabian Sea with Iran lying on its eastern side and Saudi Arabia and the Gulf States on its western. Famous in ancient times for its trade and ports, the Persian Gulf has in the present century become synonymous with oil, and is the world's major supplier of this essential source of energy. The presence of bituminous oil was certainly known long ago, and where it welled to the surface it was used for caulking and building, but it was in 1908 that a major oil field in Iran (or Persia, as it was then known) began to be developed. Since the Second World War off-shore oil has also been tapped and oil-rigs have become a common feature. Saudi Arabia, Kuwait and other states of the Persian Gulf today

draw enormous revenues from their oil and as a result no region in the world has developed so fast, almost leaping at a stride into the modern technological age. Nevertheless the ancient pearl fisheries and the Arab dhow are still to be seen, though the pirates who menaced the coast, and with whom the Royal Navy had many an encounter in the 18th century, are no longer the threat they once were.

Peruvian (or **Peru**) **Current:** *see* HUMBOLDT CURRENT.

Peter I, called 'the Great' (1672–1725): Tsar of Russia, given a place in this dictionary because he had the good sense to work in an English dockyard. His favourite boyhood pastimes were the building and sailing of ships. He saw the sea for the first time at Archangel in 1683 and in 1694 launched a ship there. Among his chief ambitions was to build a formidable Russian Navy and to give Russian entry to the Black Sea and the Baltic. At times he served as a sailor, calling himself 'Peter Mikhailov' and 'Captain Peter Alexeyevich'. In the course of his apprenticeship to the sea, he came to Deptford (1697) and rented the fine house of the diarist John Evelyn, who had cause to regret it: one of the Emperor's amusements at Sayes Court was to ride in a wheelbarrow along the top of a dense holly hedge specially planted by Evelyn.

Petrel: *see* STORMY PETREL.

Pett: a famous family which did great service to the English Navy in the 16th and 17th centuries. *Peter Pett* (*d*.1589) was master shipwright at Deptford. His son *Phineas* (1570–1647) was master shipwright at Deptford (1605) and Woolwich (1607) and later was Commissioner of the Navy. He designed the famous

SOVEREIGN OF THE SEAS, laid down by his son, another *Peter* (1610–70/72), then master shipwright at Woolwich, later Commissioner of the Navy but superseded because of the 1667 disaster on the MEDWAY. Another *Phineas* (1628–78) designed the equally splendid *PRINCE* (1670); *see also MARY*.

Petticoat: short garment of tarred sail-cloth worn by sailors in earlier times in rough weather (TARPAULINS). The petticoat was finally discarded *c*.1820.

Petty Officer: a naval rating whose status is above a Leading Seaman and below a Chief Petty Officer. Petty Officers (from the French *petit*, meaning 'little') carry important responsibilities and are similar in standing to N.C.O.s such as sergeants in the army. Though the name was long used in a general sense to describe certain key ratings, it did not become an official rate and title until 1853. Petty Officers when suitably qualified and recommended, whether in the seaman group or other specialist categories, are generally promoted in their mid-twenties, after which they may proceed to Chief Petty Officer and finally to Fleet Chief Petty Officer, which is the highest rating of all.

Petty warrant: term given to the reduced rations allowed to the skeleton crews who looked after a ship laid up 'in ordinary'.

. . . a little brown bread made of the worst of their wheat, a little small beer, which is as bad as water bewitched . . . and a little old, tough beef . . . and a little fish.

Barlow's Journal (*c*.1650; 1934 edition)

Pevensey: town in Sussex, about 6 miles east of Beachy Head, once a seaport on the coast, but now a mile from the sea. Before its harbour silted up Pevensey was an important entry point to Britain; the Romans protected it by building a large fort, and the stretch of coast on which it stood was known as the Saxon Shore. It was in Pevensey Bay that William the Conqueror landed unopposed in 1066, and the Normans built a castle to guard this important part of the coast. For long Pevensey was associated with the CINQUE PORTS, contributing men and ships, but it declined as the harbour silted up. The new land was reclaimed gradually and was known as the Pevensey Levels, but this part of the coastline remained open to the threat of invasion. It was guarded at the time of the Armada (1588); in 1803 small forts about 40 ft high, known as martello towers, were built along the coast because of Napoleon's threatened invasion, and in 1940, when Hitler was planning to invade England, concrete pill-boxes and other defences were constructed.

'Phaeton': one of the last arguments of the die-hards who treasured the days of sail in the Royal Navy. Built in 1897, she was one of the last cruisers to be supplemented with square sail. To the ill-concealed glee of the sail school, she broke down on her commissioning trials and would have been completely disabled without her canvas.

Pharos: a lighthouse. The name was that of an island near Alexandria in Egypt on which, during the reign of Ptolemy Philadelphus (285–246 B.C.), was built a huge lighthouse tower, over 400 ft high, in which a constantly burning fire was used to guide ships. It was reckoned as one of the Seven Wonders of the Ancient World.

Philadelphia catechism: version of the Commandment said to apply to the old hard-driven American sailing ships:

On six days shalt thou labour and do all that
thou art able,
And on the seventh holystone the deck and
scrub the cable.

Philippine Islands: a large archipelago of
many islands lying off South-East Asia in
the S.W. Pacific Ocean. The first European
to land in the Philippines was Magellan
(1521), but although at first well-received
he foolishly became involved in fighting
against one of the island chiefs and died of
his wounds, leaving one of his captains, Del
Cano, to complete the first circumnavigation of the globe. The islands were
occupied by the Spanish in 1564 and
thereafter, except for a brief English
occupation in 1762–4, they remained part
of the Spanish Empire until 1898, when
they passed to the United States after the
Spanish-American War. MANILA, the
capital of the Philippines, was the port for
the dispatch of Spanish treasure ships
(MANILA GALLEONS). Transition to independence began for the Philippines in
1935, but during the Second World War
the Japanese captured the islands (1941);
they were retaken by the Americans in
1944–5. In June and October 1944 two
great naval battles, the Battle of the
Philippine Sea and the Battle of Leyte
Gulf, were fought, the latter being the
biggest naval battle ever fought in terms of
the size of the opposing fleets. The
Philippines became a republic in 1946.

Phillimore, Sir John (1781–1840): Royal
Navy captain. He entered the Navy in 1795
and was promoted to post rank in 1807. He
will be remembered most for his action,
while commanding the 38-gun frigate
Eurotas in 1814, against the 40-gun French
Clorinde. The latter was eventually taken as
a prize after the intervention of H.M.S.
Dryad; but, though the historian William
JAMES gave an account of the fight on the
whole flattering to the courage of
Phillimore, who was dangerously wounded
and fainted three times on deck, he took
exception to James's accusation of indifferent gunnery on the part of *Eurotas*
and, when the opportunity occurred, he
gave the chronicler a thrashing. In a later
edition of his *Naval History of Great
Britain*, James justified his criticism in
great detail, and concluded:

We trust that we have now completely
established the accusation of our former
statement, that the guns of the *Eurotas*, in her
action with the *Clorinde*, did not perform so well
as they ought; and that the fault lay, not in the
guns themselves, but in the manner in which
they were handled.

Phillimore was knighted in 1815.

Phillip, Arthur (1738–1814): admiral,
chiefly remembered for his contribution to
the history of Australia. In 1787 he took
command of the first ships to carry convicts
to Australia; and in 1788 he founded
SYDNEY; he was the first governor of New
South Wales and led it through its early
privations before, himself broken in health,
he returned to England in 1792.

Phipps, Constantine John, second
Baron Mulgrave (1744–92): naval captain
and explorer. In 1773 he commanded the
Racehorse on a polar expedition, of which
he wrote an account. Had he lived a little
longer, he would doubtless have related
with pride that one of the midshipmen on
that expedition was the 15-year-old
Nelson.

Phipps, Sir William: *see* SALVAGE.

Phoenicians: a Semitic seafaring people
who settled in Phoenicia *c.*3000 B.C. with
their chief centres at Tyre, Sidon and
Biblos. At the height of their power

(*c*.1200–800 B.C.) they exported timber, glass, metalwork, spices, amber, dyes and perfumes and traded not only through the Mediterranean but into the Atlantic; some of their vessels have been described as 'the East Indiamen of the ancient world'. As some evidence of their wealth, one Greek historian says that even their anchors were sometimes made of silver.

They are said to have reached Britain, though the nearest point may have been the Scilly Islands, where they traded for tin.

> There runs a road by Merrow Down –
> A grassy track today it is –
> An hour out of Guildford town,
> Above the river Wey it is.
>
> Here, when they heard the horse-bells ring,
> The ancient Britons dressed and rode,
> To watch the dark Phoenicians bring
> Their goods along the Western Road.
>
> Rudyard Kipling, 'Merrow Down'

'Phoenix': the name of two 17th-century vessels of interest in the history of shipbuilding. The *Phoenix* of 1612 marks the complete change in the style of decoration from that of Tudor times. James I's ship exemplifies the love of elaborate carving and gilding as the main style of ornament beloved in the 17th century, coming to a peak in the *Sovereign of the Seas* (1637) but continuing long after. The fourth-rate *Phoenix* of 1670 was sheathed in milled lead, holding in place a layer of tar, tallow, hair and sulphur, designed to preserve the ship's bottom when going to sea for considerable periods.

Another *Phoenix* was the steam vessel built (1807) by Robert Fulton for traffic on the River Delaware. Since she had first to travel from New York to Philadelphia, she has a fair claim to be the first sea-going steamship.

Phosphorescence: light produced by minute marine organisms and by various fish when the sea is disturbed by a ship, a wave or any other cause.

While sailing a little south of the Plata on one very dark night, the sea presented a wonderful and most beautiful spectacle. There was a fresh breeze, and every part of the surface, which during the day is seen as foam, now glowed with a pale light. The vessel drove before her bows two billows of liquid phosphorus, and in her wake she was followed by a milky train. As far as the eye reached, the crest of every wave was bright, and the sky above the horizon, from the reflected glare of these livid flames, was not so utterly obscure as over the vault of the heavens.

Charles Darwin, *The Voyage of the 'Beagle'* (1840)

Physician: naval grade established in the 18th century to organize and oversee the ordinary ships' surgeons. Generally speaking, physicians served only on first-rate and hospital ships. By 1820, a Senior Physician was almost as well-off financially as a Rear-Admiral.

Picket boat: a vessel specially stationed to act as a look-out against attack or to carry out other given duties.

'Pickle': schooner of 10 guns, formerly the *Sting*, which was sent home with Collingwood's dispatches announcing the victory of Trafalgar. Commanded by Lieutenant John Richards Lapenotiere, she was the smallest vessel in the battle, though, stationed to windward of the weather column, she took no part in the actual action. In January 1807 she boarded and captured a French privateer of 14 guns, but she was wrecked in July 1808 when entering Cadiz.

Pieces of eight: old Spanish silver coins, known as *pesos* and marked with an eight, being in value eight *reals* or one dollar.

They were much used in the 17th and 18th centuries, and were often part of the treasure taken in captured ships.

Pier: any structure of wood, iron or stone, jutting out into water and designed for vessels to come alongside; a jetty. To 'make a pier-head jump' is a figure of speech meaning to be appointed or to join a ship at the very last moment before sailing.

Pigot, Hugh (1769–97): Royal Navy captain with an inglorious reputation. His cruelty while commanding the *HERMIONE* drove the crew to mutiny, kill most of the officers, and hand over the ship to the Spaniards.

Pig-tail: popular hair-dressing style in the old Navy, one explanation being that a long heavy pig-tail was some protection against a cutlass. Often the pig-tails were doubled up during the ordinary working day and let out in their full glory only on Sundays and special occasions. The seamen took great pride in their tails and regularly cleaned and dressed each other's. The last recorded instance of a pig-tail being worn was apparently in 1823.

The term was also used for a length of tobacco twisted in a similar form.

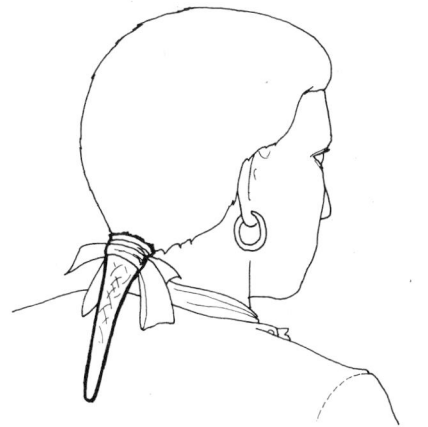

Pilgrim Fathers: *see MAYFLOWER.*

Pilgrim trade: a thriving business in the Middle Ages, involving some of the most uncomfortable sea journeys imaginable. Pilgrims required transport not only to Palestine but to such famous shrines as that of St James of Compostella in N.E. Spain. William Wey (?1407–1476) went to both, and wrote an interesting travel guide for the benefit of others. Among his recommendations was a berth in the upper part of a ship, because lower down was 'ryght smolderyng hote and stynkynge'. Travellers were also advised to lay in a good stock of private provisions, since the fare, even at the captain's table, was poor and needed to be supplemented by bread, cheese, eggs, fruit, bacon, wine 'and other' to make a decent meal.

> Men may love all gamys
> That saylen to Saint Jamys:
> For many a man hit gramys [upsets]
> When they begyn to sayle.
> For when they have take the sea,
> At Sandwyche or at Wynchylsee,
> At Bristow, or where that it bee,
> Theyr herts begyn to fayle.
>
> Old ballad (*c.*1445)

Pilot: (1) one who directs the navigation of a ship through a difficult course, channel or harbour approach. Many maritime nations require ships over a certain size to take on pilots at specified points of entry to their ports. Pilots are themselves generally experienced seamen, but have a special knowledge of the waters of their pilot station. Thus in the days of sail, ships bound for London, for example, would pick up a pilot in The Downs at the entrance to the Thames. The pilot would wait either on shore or in a pilot cutter, and when the ship requiring him hoisted the Pilot Jack (originally a Union flag surrounded with a white border) the pilot would go on board. Today the flag indicating 'I require a pilot' is letter G in the International Code of Signals, and has three blue and three yellow vertical stripes (though requests for pilots are nowadays mainly made by radio). Letter H, a flag with white and red vertical halves, means 'I have a pilot on board'. TRINITY HOUSE is the English authority for licensing pilots. Some masters of merchant ships may also be licensed pilots for waters they sail frequently, but if they employ a pilot then his directions must be followed, though the master remains responsible for the safety of his ship.

(2) The navigating officer of a ship is often called 'Pilot' as a friendly form of address.

(3) The various volumes of SAILING DIRECTIONS are colloquially known as 'Pilots'.

Pilot Jack: *see* PILOT.

Pilot's Grog: in the days of the East Indiamen, an extra allowance of grog served out to the crew as some encouragement for the extra hard work involved in beating up the Hooghly (the western arm of the Ganges delta) to Calcutta, with the pilot on board.

'Pincher': the invariable nickname for all seamen surnamed Martin, after Admiral Sir William Martin (1801–95), a strict disciplinarian who was likely to 'pinch' anyone for a minor offence.

Pink: type of vessel with a very narrow stern, chiefly used in the Mediterranean; thus 'pink-sterned' has nothing to do with colour. A variation is 'pinkie'.

Pinnace: (1) a flat-sterned small schooner-

rigged vessel, formerly used in both commerce and warfare; (2) a man-o-war's boat, with six or eight oars. Shakespeare several times uses the word in its first sense.

Pin rail: a rail positioned in the bulwarks but below the top-gallant rail and pierced to hold belaying pins.

Pipe, boatswain's: *see* BOATSWAIN'S CALL.

Pipe down and **pipe the side:** *see* BOATSWAIN'S CALL.

Pirates: men who illegally attack and plunder ships, and in so doing commit piracy. What qualifies a man to be labelled as a pirate has often been a matter of dispute: to the Spanish, Francis Drake was a pirate; to the English he was a hero. BUCCANEERS distinguished themselves

A pink.

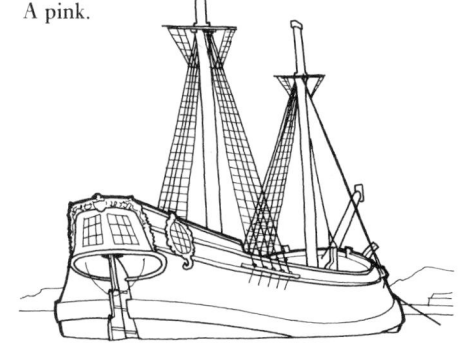

from pirates in that they did not attack ships of their own nation; they looked upon themselves as PRIVATEERS, but generally they lacked any authority for that role and were often indistinguishable from pirates. So pirate, buccaneer, corsair, picaroon, filibuster, freebooter, are all words which have been loosely used to describe sea-rovers illegally marauding at sea.

Pirates have existed from the earliest times amongst maritime nations, and almost every sea and ocean has at one time or another suffered from their depredations, though to most people they are associated particularly with the Spanish Main. It was in the Mediterranean, however, that pirates continued to be a menace down to their suppression in the 19th century. As Venetian, Genoese and Spanish maritime power declined, the Algerine pirates of the Barbary coast of North Africa, known as BARBARY CORSAIRS, grew in strength and boldness. They plundered ships and attacked coastal towns to carry off captives into slavery and service at the oars of their galleys. The 18th century saw the height of their power, which was not broken until ALGIERS, their chief stronghold, was bombarded (1816) and later occupied by the French (1830).

It was the Spanish Main and the West Indies that became the haunt of some of the most notorious pirates. The many lonely islands and their creeks and bays provided ideal concealment for pirate ships, crewed and commanded by men of different nationalities, but all turned pirate in the hope of quick riches or often, no doubt, to escape the arm of the law. The West Indies became the setting for many pirate tales, of which R. L. Stevenson's *Treasure Island* is the supreme example. Undoubtedly many of the pirates were ruthless men who practised vile cruelties while their ships flew the pirate's flag, the JOLLY ROGER.

The woman pirate Anne Bonny.

One notorious pirate was Captain William KIDD, hanged in London in 1701; another rascally pirate of the time was Edward TEACH, known as 'Blackbeard', the model for all pirates of frightening appearance. Starting as a privateer, he turned pirate, but was eventually hunted down by the English Navy and shot dead by the captain of the sloop which boarded the pirate's ship. There were many other pirates who harried shipping in the West Indies and off the Atlantic coast of America at this time; amongst them was Jack Rackham, known as 'Calico Jack', who was married to the woman pirate called Anne Bonny. With them was another woman pirate called Mary Read. They were all captured at Jamaica in 1720; Rackham was hanged, but the two women were spared though imprisoned. Just as little mercy was shown by the pirates to their victims, so when they themselves were captured they were generally hanged and their bodies exposed as a warning to others. In London they used to meet their fate at Execution Dock at Wapping.

Gradually, however, international law and order prevailed upon the high seas and the old-time pirate disappeared, though instances of piracy still occur occasionally, especially in eastern seas. For some years in the first half of the present century the China Seas were subject to a form of piracy which caused much concern. Pirates would come aboard a vessel as apparently harmless passengers, but would later produce arms which they had concealed, capture the ship and profit from the sale of the cargo at some secret rendezvous.

We'd a long brass gun amidships, like a well-
conducted ship,
We had each a brace of pistols and a cutlass at
the hip;
It's a point which tells against us, and a fact
to be deplored,
But we chased the goodly merchant-men and
laid their ships aboard.

John Masefield, 'A Ballad of John Silver'

There were other dangers in the China Seas to be reckoned with besides indifferent pilots, rocks, shoals and dangerous currents. Pirates swarmed along the coast. For protection against these, every tea-clipper was provided with an armoury of muskets, pistols and cutlasses, besides two cannons, which were capable of more than ornamental or saluting duties.

Basil Lubbock, *The China
Clippers* (1914)

Pitcairn Island: a tiny island of volcanic origin, only $2\frac{1}{2}$ miles long and a mile wide, set in the Pacific Ocean about halfway between Australia and South America. It was to this remote island that the remaining mutineers of the *Bounty* (*see* BLIGH, WILLIAM) sailed from Tahiti in 1790.

When the ship arrived at Pitcairn she had on board nine Englishmen with their nine Polynesian wives, six Polynesian men, three of whom had wives with them, and an infant girl ten months old. Thus there were 28 who began the settlement on Pitcairn. Terrible strife and the violent death of seven of the Englishmen marked the early years. By 1800 only one of the original mutineers, Alexander Smith, later known as John Adams, remained alive, but he fortunately introduced a measure of order and education for the children of these families. No other ship visited the island until 1808, when an American vessel, the *Topaz*, chanced upon the settlers. No further notice was taken of the islanders until 1814, when H.M.S. *Briton* and H.M.S. *Tagus* arrived at the island, but though John Adams feared that retribution had caught up with him, no charges were made and he was left in peace. By 1831 the community numbered 87 people who were in that year removed to Tahiti by order of the British government because of fear of drought. However, they soon returned and the community thrived and multiplied, but once again the whole population, now about 200, were removed to Norfolk Island in 1856. Again, after a short while, several families returned to Pitcairn, where their descendants are to be found today.

The names of the nine mutineers who reached the island in the *Bounty* were:

Fletcher Christian	Master's Mate
Edward Young	Midshipman
John Mills	Gunner's Mate
Matthew Quintal	Able Seaman
William M'Coy	Able Seaman
Alexander Smith,	
alias John Adams	Able Seaman
John Williams	Able Seaman
Isaac Martin	Able Seaman
William Brown	Gardener

Pitch: (1) compound of tar, turpentine etc., used for sealing a ship's seams etc. (*see* CAULKING); (2) *see* PITCHING.

Pitching: one of the six 'freedoms of motion' of a ship: her ability to rotate about her transverse horizontal axis, or, to put it more simply, tilt forwards and backwards.

'Pitt': former coal-depôt at Portsmouth which serves as a good example of the complexities and, sometimes, eccentricities of the Royal Navy in naming its ships. In 1820, a new three-decker, H.M.S. *Trafalgar* of 104 guns, was built at Chatham. She was not, however, commissioned under that name, and was renamed *Camperdown*. Much of her life was spent 'in ordinary' and it was not till she was 21 years old that she was at last commissioned, to serve as flag-ship of the Commander-in-Chief, Woolwich, for four years. She was then again retired, to Portsmouth, where she served for 40 years as a coal-depôt before being sold out of the service in 1904. In 1882, when a new *Camperdown* was laid down, she was renamed *Pitt*. As a footnote to all this, the ship to which she yielded up her original name of *Trafalgar* was not completed for 14 years, and both were first commissioned in the same year (1841)!

An earlier *Pitt*, a fine frigate, was the first ship ever built in India for H.M. service.

Plain sailing: a corruption of 'plane sailing', that is navigating on the assumption that the world is a flat surface or plane. The earliest charts were drawn on this principle and were used by navigators for their simplicity and in spite of the resulting errors in calculating longitude. 'Plane sailing' was often written as 'plain sailing' and the phrase has therefore come to mean anything easy and without problems.

Plane, to: a boat is said to plane when it reaches a speed sufficient to lift its bows so that it rides up on the surface of the water. When this occurs its speed is further increased. Planing occurs only in small fast sailing or power-driven craft.

Plankton: the collective name given to the many kinds of microscopic plant and animal life which drift in the oceans and seas and which form an important element in the food-chain of marine life. The word comes from Greek and means 'wandering', for these countless minute forms of life drift about in the water layers at all depths between the sea surface and the bottom. They are, however, most numerous in the cooler and colder waters of the world where the seas are fairly shallow, and it is for this reason that such areas provide rich feeding and spawning grounds for vast shoals of fish such as cod and herring. The importance of plankton in the pattern and economy of sea-life can hardly be over-estimated. Sometimes they are so numerous as to add a distinct tinge to the colour of the water, a fact which the experienced fisherman will observe before casting his nets.

They are exceedingly minute, and quite invisible to the naked eye, only covering a space equal to the square of a thousandth of an inch. Their numbers were infinite; for the smallest drop of water that I could remove contained very many. In one day we passed through two spaces of water thus stained, one of which alone must have extended over several square miles. What incalculable numbers of these microscopical animals!

Charles Darwin, *The Voyage of the 'Beagle'* (1840)

Plate, armour: *see* ARMOUR.

Plate, River: *see* RIVER PLATE, BATTLE OF THE.

Pleasure steamer: as the name implies, a small steam vessel used mainly for short crossings and cruises in holiday seasons. Typical early examples were the *Prince Coburg* in the 1820s, crossing twice daily from Southampton to Cowes in the Isle of Wight, and the *Rose* in 1845 offering voyages westward to Lyme and eastward to Southampton. Nothing ashamed of their comparatively humble role, their names can rank with the most illustrious, *Britannia, Conqueror, Emperor of India, Jupiter, Majestic, Monarch* and *Nelson* among the rest. In both World Wars they did wonderful service, many being re-quisitioned as minesweepers etc. In the 1914–18 war, the *Duke of Devonshire*, accustomed to excursions round the south coast, got as far as Mesopotamia and back under her own steam. In 1940 pleasure boats were conspicuous in the heroic evacuation at Dunkirk with the rest of the 'little ships'.

Strangely enough, a number of Royal Navy vessels finished up, not ingloriously, as pleasure steamers. The sloop H.M.S. *Bitterne* became an Admiralty yacht and was bought in 1946 for conversion, though in this case the venture was not a success. The 800-ton paddle minesweepers *Atherstone* and *Melton*, after being laid up by the Admiralty for years, were purchased in the 1920s and gave pleasure to thousands of holidaymakers as the *Queen of Kent* and *Queen of Thanet*. There were many others.

It is a tribute to their builders that some survived an extraordinarily long time. *Premier* put in 91 years' service, surviving a collision with H.M. Submarine *Weymouth* in 1932. She had been built in 1846 for the Glasgow–Dumbarton run and was among the vessels which escorted Queen Victoria into Greenock in 1847. She operated out of Weymouth for some 85 years and was the oldest passenger steamer in the world.

Pledget: a wad or roll of oakum ready to be used for caulking the deck or sides of a ship.

Plimsoll, Samuel (1824–98): called 'the Sailors' Friend' because of his zeal for their welfare in Parliament. He did much to expedite the passing of the 1875–6 Merchant Shipping Acts, which gave the government greater powers against un-scrupulous owners and unseaworthy ships, and his name is perpetuated in the so-called 'Plimsoll line' or 'mark', which began as a simple line on the ship's side indicating the safe depth to which she could be loaded and has now developed into a whole series of marks (*see* LOADLINES).

There was in the House a whimsical Radical – Plimsoll by name – a curious mixture of philanthropy and self-advertisement. He had for some time been collecting and accumulating evidence as to malpractices of certain ship-owners who, he asserted, deliberately sent out ships ill-found, unseaworthy, and risked and not infrequently lost the lives of their employees and made money out of the transaction. The influence of the shipowners in the House of Commons was strong, for the vast majority were upright and honourable men, though, as a body, they were opposed to more severe measures of inspection and loading. Plimsoll heard that the Merchant Shipping Bill was to be withdrawn and he seized his opportunity with consummate skill and assurance.

As soon as the announcement was made in the House by the Prime Minister, he rushed into the gangway between the two sides of the House, gesticulating and flourishing his fists, and shouting out strong language. In vain the Speaker called him to resume his seat and obey the rules of order. He openly defied the Chair, walked up to the Government Bench, looked as if he was about to assault the Prime Minister, and, finally yielding to the persuasion of his friends, left the House shouting: 'Scoundrels, scoundrels, scoundrels!'

Lord George Hamilton, *Parliamentary Reminiscences and Reflections, 1868–1885*

Plum-duff: *see* DUFF.

Plush (colloquially **plushers**): the name given to any grog left over after the daily issue. Officially any spirits remaining were supposed to be poured away over the side, but as may be imagined there were instances when this was craftily circumvented and the plush divided amongst those in the deception.

Ply: among its other meanings, (1) to go to and fro, to sail regularly; (2) to use vigorously, as in 'plying' oars; (3) to beat or work to windward.

Plymouth: town, seaport and major naval base in South Devon. Guarding the western entrance to the Channel, Plymouth has played a historic part in our maritime history. The height of its fame was perhaps in Elizabethan times, when so many seamen came from Devon and Cornwall, and Plymouth became the starting point for many of the great enterprises of the time. Sir John Hawkins, his son Sir Richard, his cousin Sir Francis Drake, Sir Humphrey Gilbert and his half-brother Sir Walter Ralegh all sailed from Plymouth. In the waters of Plymouth Sound the English ships awaited the Armada in 1588, while ashore Lord Howard of Effingham, the Lord High Admiral, and Sir Francis Drake, his second in command, took counsel and considered the right moment to sail in pursuit. From Plymouth in 1620 the Pilgrim Fathers set out in the *Mayflower* to land at Plymouth in New England. The town continued to develop as a chief base for the Royal Navy, and around its dockyards grew up the adjoining town of DEVONPORT.

For merchant ships, both sail and steam, Plymouth was also important as a first and last port of call on their homeward and outward journeys, but the coming of air-travel has led to a decline in passenger ships, and so those standing on the famous vantage-point of Plymouth Hoe see fewer liners come and go than in the past.

Plymouth cloak: sarcastic term in the old days for the cane carried by officers and warrant officers.

'Pocket battleships': the name given to three heavily armoured warships built by Germany in the 1930s. By the Treaty of Versailles (1919) Germany was prohibited from building any warship larger than 10,000 tons. The first 'pocket battleship' built was the *Deutschland*, later renamed the *Lützow*; she was heavily armed and fast, as were the *Admiral GRAF SPEE* and the *Admiral Scheer*, the other two so-called 'pocket battleships' built on similar lines. Though nominally of 10,000 tons they were in fact somewhat larger, and had been designed for surface raiding in the event of a war. When war broke out in 1939 both the *Graf Spee* and the *Deutschland* sailed into the Atlantic to threaten British shipping. The *Deutschland* achieved little and returned to Germany after two and a half months, but the *Graf Spee* was more daring and successful, sinking several ships including one during a feint visit to the Indian Ocean. She was finally cornered at the Battle of the RIVER PLATE (December 1939). *See p. 382.*

Point, compass: one division of the 32 points into which the compass card is divided, each point being $11\frac{1}{4}°$ ($32 \times 11\frac{1}{4}° = 360° =$ the circumference of a circle). The four cardinal points are N., S., E. and W., and the four inter-cardinal or half-cardinal points are N.E., S.E., S.W. and N.W. The eight intermediate points are N.N.E., E.N.E., E.S.E., S.S.E.,

The 'pocket battleship' *Deutschland* in the Straits of Dover, 1939.

S.S.W., W.S.W., W.N.W. and N.N.W. The sixteen by-points are named by the nearest cardinal or inter-cardinal, thus N. by E., N.E. by N., etc. Each of these 32 points is sub-divided into half and quarter points. To 'box the compass' is to repeat in order the points, half and quarter points in a clockwise direction from N. through S. and back to N. again; the term derives from a Spanish word meaning 'to sail round'. In former times the helmsman of a sailing ship would be given a definite compass point on which he was to keep the ship's head, but gradually degrees came to be used, each of the four quadrants of the compass rose being divided into 90°, so the helmsman was given an order to sail so many degrees between two cardinal points, thus E.S.E. would be E.$22\frac{1}{2}$° S. As the gyro-compass came into use the course came to be indicated by use of the full 360° of the compass rose, thus 090° = E., 180° = S., etc. *See also* COMPASS.

The word point is still occasionally used to indicate a bearing in relation to the ship's head, beam or stern: e.g., another ship may be said to bear four points on the port bow. But even this has given way to the use of degrees with the words green (starboard) and red (port), so that a ship bearing four points on the port bow is now said to bear Red 45.

> 'There she blows' was sung from the masthead.
> 'Where away?' demanded the captain.
> 'Three points off the lee bow, sir'.
>
> J. Ross Browne, *Etching of a Whaling Cruise* (1846)

Point-blank: aimed directly at the target without making any allowance for the trajectory. A gun or firearm is fired point-blank when it is so close to the target that it cannot miss. The word probably comes from the blank or white circle of old archery targets. *See also* RANGE.

Polacca (or **poleacre**): large square-rigged Mediterranean merchant ship with two or three single-piece masts. Their capture is frequently mentioned in British log-books of the 18th and 19th centuries.

Polar exploration: the story of polar exploration, in both the Arctic and the Antarctic, is a long history of heroic endeavour over the centuries by sailors and explorers of many nations. Only a bare outline can be given here. The existence of the Arctic regions was certainly realized by the Greeks in ancient times. The fringes of the Arctic were reached by the Norsemen who made settlements in Iceland and Greenland between the 8th and 10th centuries. After them it was not until the 16th century that there began the great series of voyages to find a northerly route to Cathay (China) by way of both the NORTH-EAST and NORTH-WEST PASSAGES.

Nelson was a young midshipman on board H.M.S. *Carcass* when he had his encounter with the polar bear during an unsuccessful naval expedition to sail to the North Pole in 1773, though before being turned back by the ice the expedition had reached a latitude of over 80° N. The 19th century was an era of great Arctic exploration by sea, and the names of Franklin, Ross, Clark Ross, Parry, McClure and McClintock are amongst the many British pioneers. But Americans, Russians and others were active also in numerous journeys. By the end of the century expeditions under the great Norwegian explorer, Fridtjof Nansen, and

under the Italian Duke of Abruzzi, had reached furthest north to a point only some 220 miles from the North Pole, which was now the specific objective. Finally in 1909 the American Robert Peary, after several earlier attempts, led the first party to reach the North Pole. Since then many further expeditions have added to our scientific knowledge of the area. In 1926 the North Pole was flown over by the American Admiral Byrd, by the Italian Nobile in an airship, and again in an aeroplane by the Australian Hubert Wilkins. In 1958 and 1959 two voyages under the ice of the North Pole were made by American nuclear-powered submarines, and a British expedition under Wally Herbert crossed the Arctic, passing over the North Pole, from Alaska to Spitsbergen in 1968–9.

In the Antarctic the history of polar exploration begins later than in the Arctic, but has similarities in that knowledge of the ice-covered continent was gradually built up as a result of a long series of voyages by men of many nations, followed by attempts to reach the South Pole, and then by the modern period of scientific observation and discovery. For long there was a belief that there was an unknown southern land, or TERRA AUSTRALIS INCOGNITA, as it was called, lying in the seas at the southern extremity of the known world. It was the second voyage of Captain Cook (1772–5) that showed conclusively that no such land existed where it was believed to be, for Cook in making his circumnavigation sailed further south than any previous sailor and he sighted no land. But he did discover the island groups of South Georgia and South Sandwich on the fringes of Antarctica.

By the end of the 18th century British and American seal hunters were frequenting these waters and perhaps kept to themselves knowledge of what lay beyond.

However, in 1819 a British sealer reached the South Shetland Islands, and the first sighting of the Antarctic peninsula was made in the following year. At the same time the Russian explorer Bellingshausen completed a second circumnavigation which added further knowledge of Antarctica, as did other voyages undertaken to find new sealing grounds. The early 19th century saw further expeditions under British, American and French leadership; amongst the best-known were those led by James Weddell (1822–3), the Frenchman d'Urville (1840), and James Clark Ross (1840–43) in the two famous ships H.M.S. *Erebus* and H.M.S. *Terror*, which were later to be lost in the Arctic in Sir John Franklin's ill-fated voyage. By the end of the century the hunt for whales and the desire for discovery led other nations, Norway, France, Belgium and Germany, to send ships to Antarctic waters.

Gradually the shape of the ice-covered continent was being charted and its interior explored by sledge journeys, amongst the first of which was that made by Captain Robert Falcon Scott in 1901–4. But the furthest point reached by Scott was surpassed by Sir Ernest Shackleton who in 1907–9 took his sledges to within 100 miles of the South Pole. The climax came three years later when Captain Scott, hoping to be first at the Pole, reached it in January 1912 only to discover that he had been forestalled a few weeks earlier in December 1911 by the Norwegian Roald Amundsen. The heroic story of how Scott and his four companions perished on the return journey, revealed when their bodies and diaries were discovered, is one of the great tales of Polar exploration. Mention must also be made of the work of the Australian explorer Douglas Mawson, and of Shackleton's expedition of 1914–17, during which, when his ship was crushed in the ice, he made one of the bravest and most hazardous open-boat journeys over 300 miles of wild and icy sea to South Georgia to organize the rescue of the rest of his men left on Elephant Island.

As in the Arctic, the coming of the aeroplane made it much easier to supply expeditions and to carry out surveys. The American Admiral Byrd first reached the Pole by aeroplane in 1929, and his compatriot Lincoln Ellsworth flew across Western Antarctica in 1935. The British Graham Land Expedition of 1934–7 under J. R. Rymill, and the Commonwealth Trans-Antarctic Expedition of 1957–8 under Fuchs are two further expeditions which added greatly to our knowledge of the South Polar regions.

Polaris: (1) the POLE STAR; (2) the intercontinental ballistic missile with a nuclear warhead mounted in American and British nuclear-powered submarines. It can be fired while the submarine is submerged and is believed to have a range of over 2000 miles. *See also RESOLUTION.*

Poleacre: *see* POLACCA.

Pole mast: *see* MAST.

Poles, the: the two extremities of the axis of the earth; the North and South Poles, the northernmost and southernmost points of the world, where all meridians or lines of longitude converge. The North Pole is covered by a mass of ice, varying in depth according to the season, but going up to 30 ft deep; beneath the ice-cap lies the Arctic Ocean, which immediately below the North Pole reaches a depth of 1500 fathoms. The South Pole, however, is in the middle of a great ice-cap which rests on the continental land-mass of Antarctica. *See also* MAGNETIC POLES; POLAR EXPLORATION.

Pole Star (also known as **Polaris**, the **North Star** and sometimes as **Stella Maris**): star in the constellation of Ursa Minor or the Little Bear. It lies approximately over the North Pole, and its orbit around that position is so slight as to make it very reliable for navigation and the calculation of latitude. Its value as a direction indicator is believed to have been recognized by the Phoenicians in the first millennium B.C.; *see also* NAVIGATION.

Polperro: town and narrow harbour on the south coast of Cornwall. Particularly in the 18th century, it was notorious for smuggling and was one of the chief centres for this illicit trade along the whole of the south-western peninsula.

Pompey: sailors' nickname for Portsmouth. Its origin is unknown.

Pondicherry: town and port on the Coromandel Coast of Southern India, lying to the south of Madras. It was a chief centre of French power and influence during the long 18th-century struggle between France and Britain for the command of India and its trade. Pondicherry was blockaded in 1747–8 by British warships under Admiral Thomas Griffin and then under Rear-Admiral Boscawen. In the Seven Years' War (1756–63) the seas off Pondicherry again saw engagements with French warships and the port was again blockaded, but in 1761 it was forced to surrender to the British, only to revert to French control at the peace in 1763. Once more, when France joined the Americans during the War of American Independence, Pondicherry was besieged and captured by British land forces (1778). Each time France and Britain renewed hostilities Pondicherry was taken by the British and was restored when peace was signéd. At the end of the Napoleonic Wars, Pondicherry was yet again returned to the French, under whose control it remained until it was rejoined to India in 1954.

Pontoon: a floating bridge, either of special construction or supported on a flat-bottomed boat, barge or lighter.

Poole: largest town in Dorset, situated at the head of an extensive and land-locked harbour. Poole is an ancient town and its harbour, though not developing into a large port, has always been important, especially during the 17th and 18th centuries. Its creeks were once much favoured by smugglers, who in 1747 even made a raid on the town's Customs House and captured a fine cargo of tea.

Poop: (1) a raised deck on the stern or after-part of a ship. The aftercastle of the medieval ship evolved into the poop. It was on the poop that three great poop-lanterns were carried by sailing warships so that they could be clearly seen by ships following astern at night. *See also* DECK. (2) A vessel is said to be 'pooped' when a wave overtakes her and breaks over her stern.

Popham, Edward (?1610–1651): admiral; one of the three 'Generals at Sea' chosen by Cromwell (the others being Blake and Deane). He was the only one with any previous experience in a ship of war, having held a command in 1639.

Popham, Sir Home Riggs (1762–1820): admiral. Though he had an adventurous career, his greatest service to the Navy was his development of a new code of signalling – the code used in the most famous signal in British maritime history: 'England expects that every man will do his duty'.

It may be that in this matter, as in so many other inventions, the first to make some practical use of an idea got that idea at second hand. However this may be in Popham's case, it is clear that the labour of perfecting the invention and what is perhaps equally important, of persuading others that it was really worth a trial, was undertaken by Popham alone. For twelve years the books which he produced were privately printed by him, and from the free-handed way in which he gave them to his brother officers when urging them to try this code, it is probable that he carried out his propaganda at some pecuniary expense to himself. The idea that dominated it was to provide parts of speech and let users make their own sentences whenever those in the signal book did not suffice. It was the step from a 'Traveller's Manual of Conversation' to a dictionary of the language.

W. G. Perrin, *British Flags* (1922)

The first edition of Popham's code, *Telegraphic Signals, or Marine Vocabulary* (1800), consisted of almost 1000 words chosen from the ordinary English dictionary as being those of most use for naval purposes. In 1803 he added a second 1000 words, almost as useful, and nearly 1000 sentences, 'sentences most applicable to military or general conversation'.

He later enlarged and improved the code even further in various ways, so that, e.g., 11,000 different signals could be sent using only a three-flag hoist in different combinations; with a four-flag hoist 223,675 signals were possible. Among the examples given by Popham himself (and no one seems to know whether his sense of humour was equal to his ingenuity) was:

BOE = Your
AC8 = sister
852 = married
85F = to
C87 = a Lord of the Admiralty.

Poppenruyter, Hans (*fl. c.* 1515): inventor and gunsmith of Mechlin (Malines) who enters the annals of the British Navy because Henry VIII was so impressed with his new heavy-shotted muzzle-loaders – capable, said Poppenruyter, of demolishing a town – that the King insisted on installing them in his new ship the *Great Harry* (*Henri Grâce à Dieu*), breaking, in the process, all the old traditions by locating guns on the cargo deck (instead of in the fighting 'castles') and cutting gunports in the hull.

Port: (1) a harbour where ships berth, load and unload (e.g. the Port of London). A 'port of call' is a port at which a ship stops before continuing to her destination. (**2**) An opening in the side of a ship for taking in or discharging cargo or passengers. The opening may consist of hinged, sliding or lifting doors, which are closed when the vessel is at sea. Gunports were square holes cut in the sides of ships through which the guns were fired; they were hinged at the top and closed when the ship was not prepared for action and when a rough sea made it unsafe to have them open. (**3**) The left-hand side of a vessel when looking from the stern towards the bows; the opposite of 'starboard'. Before the middle of the 19th century this was generally known as the larboard side, but it was changed to 'port' because of the danger of confusion with the similar-sounding word 'starboard'. It was a logical change, because in the earliest ships the larboard side was brought alongside when in port to avoid damaging the 'steer board' or large guiding oar on the other or starboard side. There had also been some earlier usages of 'port' to mean the left-hand side. Port's associated colour is red, the colour of the port navigation light. *See p. 577.*

Portable soup: mid-18th-century innovation on ships, of considerable benefit to the sick. Consisting of cubes from which good broth could be made, it was invented

(1756) by a Mrs Dubois and was at first supplied by a Plymouth apothecary called Cookworthy, a wholly appropriate name. An actual specimen has survived from one of Captain Cook's voyages.

Port admiral: admiral chiefly engaged on administrative duties, securely based on a port in comfortable quarters, thereby sometimes incurring the wrath of those whose lives he controlled; witness a long poem by Frederick Marryat called 'Port Admiral', one verse of which runs:

Who ever heard in the sarvice of a frigate made
    to sail
On Christmas Day, it blowing hard, with sleet
    and snow, and hail?
I wish I had the fishing of your back that is so
    bent,
I'd use the galley poker hot unto your heart's
    content.
  Here Bet and Sue
  Are with me too,
    A-shivering by my side;
  They both are dumb,
  And both look glum,
    And watch the ebbing tide.
  Poll put her arms a-kimbo,
    At the admiral's house looked she,
  To thoughts that were in limbo
    She now a vent gave free.
  'You've got a roaring fire, I'll bet,
    In it your toes are jammed:
  Let's give him a piece of our mind, my Bet,
    Port Admiral, you be damned.'

Porthole: the landsman's name for a

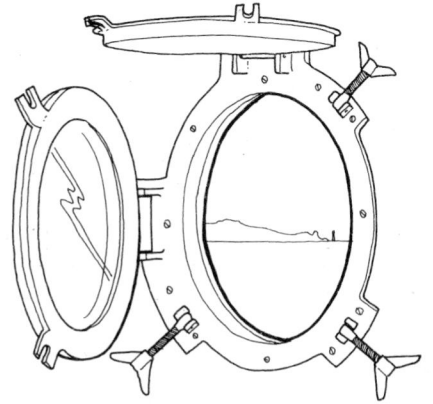

circular opening in a ship's side to let in light and air. The correct nautical name is SCUTTLE.

Portland: (1) town and harbour on the Isle of Portland, a peninsula on the coast of Dorset, England. The Admiralty began to build the present enclosed harbour in 1847, and from time to time it has been used as a base by the Royal Navy, which has an important establishment there today. Portland Bill is the southernmost point of the Isle of Portland; for the battles, see below. (2) City and port on the coast of Maine, U.S.A. As with many of the ports on the N.E. American coast, Portland's prosperity was based on fishing and shipping, followed by commercial development. The city made an important contribution in shipbuilding and as a naval base in both World Wars.

Portland Bill, Battles of: (1; 23 July 1588) part of the Spanish Armada saga, when Martin Frobisher became becalmed and fell under the attack of four Spanish ships. He fought them off with great gallantry until a timely wind brought some other English ships to his rescue. (2) Portland also witnessed a major action in the First Anglo-Dutch War when (18–20 February 1653) Blake intercepted Tromp and harried his convoy of nearly 300 ships for three days, from Portland to the Straits of Dover. After having lost something like 60 vessels, the Dutch admiral eventually escaped under cover of darkness. Blake's subsequent dispatch said that 'If it had pleased the Lord in His wise Providence . . . that it had been three hours longer to night, we had probably made an interposition between them and home.'

Port Mahon: port and chief town on the

387

eastern side of Minorca. Because of its position and desirability as a strong-point and harbour in the Western Mediterranean, Port Mahon frequently figured in 18th-century naval history; *also see* MINORCA.

Porto Bello: town and harbour on the Caribbean coast of the Isthmus of Panama, an important trading centre in the days of the Spanish Empire in the New World. Its name, meaning beautiful harbour, was given by Columbus, but it was not until the 17th century that Porto Bello became a stronghold of Spanish wealth and power. It was captured in 1671 by the English buccaneer Sir Henry Morgan and again in the first year of the War of Jenkins' Ear (1739–41), by a small British squadron under Vice-Admiral Edward VERNON. Porto Bello's prosperity gradually declined, and today it is no more than a small settlement.

Port of London: the port of Britain's capital city, situated on the River Thames. The long history of London as a port goes back to Roman times. Its steady growth thereafter received a great impetus with the rise of British sea-power in the 18th century and the consequent increase in mercantile trade. By the beginning of the 19th century the number of ships entering, discharging and loading was so great that there was evident need to increase the area of docks and wharfage. Consequently there began the building of basins, each tending to specialize in particular kinds of trade, entered at high tide through dock gates which, when closed, left the ship inside to discharge or load independent of the rise and fall of the tide.

The London and St Katharine Docks, the East India and Millwall Docks, the Surrey Commercial Docks, the Royal Victoria, Royal Albert and, most recent, the King George V Docks are all part of the complex which put London at the head of the world's ports. Since the Second World War, however, the pattern of trade has changed, and though still an important port, London's dockland has seen a decline; many of the docks are in process of being closed, possibly to be redeveloped for other purposes. There has been a move of shipping nearer to the mouth of the Thames, to out-ports such as Tilbury. The decline of trade in London's docks has also been due to the development of cargo handling in containers, which can be quickly moved by special equipment, and to the revival of many smaller ports around the British Isles, which have drawn away trade from London.

In 1909 the Port of London Authority (P.L.A.) was set up to be responsible for the general oversight of all London's docks and wharves and of all the water-borne traffic from the open sea to Teddington.

Port of Spain: capital city and chief port of TRINIDAD in the West Indies. The good sheltered harbour at Port of Spain and the rich island of Trinidad itself were constantly in dispute between the Dutch, French and English during their early rivalries in the West Indies when Spanish power in the Caribbean began to decline. Today Port of Spain is an important centre of trade and shipping.

Portolan (or **portulan**) **chart:** an early form of chart, originating in the Mediterranean. From compass roses on the chart a mass of lines drawn to numerous points on the coast indicated the direction in which the navigator had to head his ship. Such charts were often included in a PORTOLANO.

Portolano: an early handbook for navigators. It consisted of navigational information or sailing directions and often contained a portolan chart. Portolanos were compiled and used in the Mediterranean between the 12th and 15th centuries.

Port Said: town and seaport at the northern end of the Suez Canal. It grew in size and importance after the opening of the canal (1869) and remained a busy port of call for 100 years until the canal was closed after the war between Israel and Egypt in 1967. In the renewed short war of 1973 Port Said was much damaged and practically deserted, but with the reopening of the Suez Canal it is being rebuilt and beginning to revive.

Portsmouth: town and chief base for the Royal Navy and Royal Marines, on the coast of Hampshire. It is really an island linked to the mainland and is flanked by two stretches of water forming a fine harbour. Known affectionately as 'Pompey', Portsmouth owes much of its importance as a naval base not only to its harbour and position facing France, but also to its approaches: Spithead and the Solent, sheltered by the Isle of Wight, provided ideal riding ground for ships in the days of sail. Though in use much earlier, Portsmouth began to develop in early Tudor times when Henry VII and Henry VIII constructed docks for the royal ships, and oak from the Weald and New Forest was used to build new vessels. The town and naval dockyards continued to grow with British naval power in the 18th and 19th centuries, and it was strongly fortified. In Portsmouth and across the harbour at Gosport there are many naval establishments, both barracks and centres of specialist training. Much of the town was severely damaged by bombing during the Second World War, but has now been rebuilt.

In a dry dock in Portsmouth harbour lies H.M.S. *VICTORY*, Nelson's flag-ship at Trafalgar, and in a nearby museum are many relics of him and his times.

Portulan chart: *see* PORTOLAN CHART.

Poseidon: (1) the Greek god of the sea (known as NEPTUNE to the Romans); (2) the name given to a later American version of the nuclear-headed intercontinental ballistic missile POLARIS, fired from submerged submarines.

Post-Captain: a definite rank in the sailing Navy of the 18th and 19th centuries, applied to those captains who were 'posted', i.e. given command of a 'post-ship', which was any rated ship from sixth to first-rate. In such ships the post-captain was entitled to carry a master responsible for the navigation. In smaller ships the appointment was as master and commander, and though the officer appointed was captain of that ship, he might be only of lieutenant's rank: his post as captain was for the duration of the commission only, and when it ended he would revert to lieutenant. However, this situation led to the introduction of the rank and title of Commander by the end of the 18th century. Post-Captain was equivalent to the modern rank of Captain in the Royal Navy, where the word 'Post' referring to such a promotion is still sometimes used colloquially. Nelson was made commander at the age of 20 and post-captain before he was 21 – a very rapid and fortunate promotion.

Post-ship: *see* POST-CAPTAIN.

'Poultice walloper': as might be deduced, someone connected with the medical life of the ship; in general, a sick-bay attendant.

Poverty Corner: a reminder of the grimmer days of seafaring: the corner of Fenchurch Street and the railway station approach, where out-of-work seamen could often be found.

Powder (or **black powder**): the general name for the explosive material used as a propellant for guns. It is not known exactly when gunpowder was invented, but it was probably first used on ships in the west towards the end of the 14th century or early in the 15th. Powder was a mixture of saltpetre, charcoal and sulphur and was the main explosive for naval guns for over 400 years before the invention of more powerful explosives. The quality of the powder and the amount to be used for the different kinds and sizes of guns were important matters for the gunner and his mate in the days of the sailing Navy.

Powder magazine (or **magazine**): store-room for gunpowder and ammunition, generally situated in a safe position well below the upper deck, either on the orlop deck or below so long as it was dry. In the old sailing Navy the powder was made up into cartridges or charges, being encased in silk, and later flannel jackets, ready for insertion into and down the barrel of the gun.

The magazine was the most hazardous place on board ship and was always controlled with stringent regulations, being guarded day and night.

[The Gunner] is never to go into the Magazine without being ordered to go there. He is never to allow the doors of the Magazine to be opened but by himself; he is not to open them until the proper Officer is in the Light-room; and he is to be very careful in observing that the men who go into the Magazine have not about them any thing which can strike fire, and he must take care that no Person enters the Magazine without wearing the leather slippers supplied by the Ordnance.

Regulations and Instructions Relating to His Majesty's Service at Sea (1808)

(This is one of the many paragraphs in the Regulations covering safety precautions in handling powder. *See also* FIRE PRE-CAUTIONS. The 'light room' was the small compartment immediately outside the magazine, shut off from the powder by heavy windows.)

Powder monkeys: the name for boys who carried the charges from the powder magazine to the ship's guns during battle. They were sometimes assisted by women if any were on board, as they sometimes were in the 18th and early 19th century.

Prahu: *see* PRAU.

Pram (or **praam**): a flat-bottomed boat or lighter, much in use in Holland and the Baltic. In time of war it often served as a floating battery.

Pratique: licence to a ship, after quarantine, to communicate with a port; or certifying that she had not come from an infected place.

Prau (or **prahu** or **proa**): Malayan name for a canoe-like sailing boat fitted with a lateen triangular sail and an outrigger to give stability. It is also equipped for rowing.

Prayer books: one of the seamen's names for the HOLYSTONES.

Presentation sword: *see* PATRIOTIC FUND.

Press-gang: the best-known, but often misunderstood, former method of recruit-

Manning the Navy by Collings: the press-gang at work on Tower Hill, 1780.

ing seamen. In times of stress the Navy required as many as 40,000 extra men a year. Thirty or forty recruiting stations round the coasts attracted some volunteers; individual commanders sometimes published posters and hand-bills in an effort to tempt recruits; and the government tried special remedies, e.g. the QUOTA ACTS, which compelled counties and major towns to supply a stated number of men on a proportional basis. But the method best-known to the public was the press-gang, a detachment of men who raided taverns and homes in seaports (and sometimes further inland) and forced men into the service. Merchant ships were also raided.

There are a number of wild misconceptions about the subject. To start with, there is a fundamental distinction between a 'prest man' and a 'pressed man'. A 'prest man' was one who received a 'prest' or 'imprest', a small sum of money paid in advance as an inducement to join the service, whereas a 'pressed man' was one forced to come in against his will. And,

although novels, plays and popular ballads give a very different impression, the number of seamen 'pressed' by force was surprisingly small. Admiral Sir Cyprian Bridge spent a great deal of time examining ships' muster-books, in which the method of entry is recorded, and, writing in 1900, he came to the conclusion that, spread over the whole Navy at that time, the number of seamen forced in by the press-gangs was less than two in a hundred. In 1803, for example, when 39,600 men were needed to bring the service up to strength, more than 37,000 were volunteers and less than 2000 were pressed.

There were many regulations controlling 'pressing', and a whole list of exemptions: to quote only a few, the crews of colliers enjoyed special exemption, as did, by various Acts, all persons under 18 and over 45, foreigners serving in ships belonging to British subjects, and such numbers of a ship's crew as were necessary for safe navigation. These regulations were sometimes conveniently forgotten or over-

391

looked by captains in desperate need of men; on the other hand, many ruses were devised to protect and hide men ashore when a 'hot press' was in action.

At least one pressed man became an admiral. John Campbell (?1720–1790) was the son of a Scottish minister with a large family and a small stipend, so that the boy had to fend for himself and while still very young bound himself apprentice on a coasting vessel. In 1736 or 1737 the coaster was boarded by a press-gang who took everyone on board except the master and his apprentice, young Campbell. The mate, who had a wife and family at home, was so distraught that Campbell implored the officer leading the gang to take him instead. The officer agreed, saying: 'I would much rather have a boy of spirit than a blubbering man. Come along.'

Preventer: a general name for any extra length of rope or wire used as a stand-by safety measure in case a brace or a stay parted.

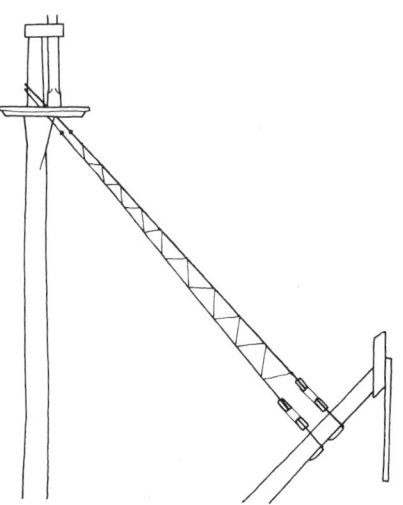

Preventive men (or **revenue men**): members of the Preventive Service, whose duty was to prevent SMUGGLING. The Preventive Service was equipped with fast and armed REVENUE CUTTERS and, though they had their successes, the smugglers used every kind of trick to outwit them, for it was very profitable to avoid the duties on spirits, tobacco and other valuable imported goods.

Prime meridian: a line of longitude reckoned as 0° and used as the starting point for calculating longitudinal position eastwards or westwards. Formerly various maritime nations chose their own prime meridian, generally making it pass through their chief city. This led to considerable confusion, particularly in calculating time, and it was not until 1880 that an international agreement was signed by which the nations accepted the meridian passing through Greenwich in London as the prime meridian; *see also* GREENWICH MEAN TIME.

'Prince': the best example of the ships of this name is probably the first-rate of Charles II's reign, the contemporary dockyard model of which is one of the prides of the collection at the Science Museum, London. It is one of the finest MODEL SHIPS in existence. The *Prince* was designed by Phineas Pett and launched at Chatham in 1670. She carried a maximum crew of 780 and, on war service, 100 guns. She was equipped with three boats and nine anchors. Her dimensions were: length of keel, 131 ft; beam, 45·8 ft; depth in hold, 19 ft; tons burden, 1463. The *Prince* was broken up in 1692 and some of her timber used in building a new ship, the *Royal William*, then on the stocks. *See also* JAMES II.

'Prince of Wales': a *Prince of Wales* can be found in many actions and incidents from the 17th century onwards; but recent memory will turn to the British battleship which, newly commissioned and with gun-trials not fully completed, took part in the hunting of the German *BISMARCK* in May 1941, sustaining very heavy damage and loss of life. But one of her 14-in. shells had penetrated *Bismarck*'s No. 2 oil tank, and because of this all the tanks became contaminated with seawater, reducing her capacity to stay at sea and contributing to her eventual defeat. The *Prince of Wales*, without air cover, was, along with *Repulse*, tragically sunk off Singapore by Japanese dive-bombers in December 1941.

'Prince Royal': designed by Phineas Pett and built in 1610, the first three-decker in England. She is described as one of the most beautiful ships ever built in this country, with a wealth of decoration, elaborately garlanded ports and stem carving; but she was a royal prestige ship rather than an effective vessel of war. *See also* MODEL SHIPS.

. . . most sumptuously adorned within and without, with all manner of curious carving, painting and rich gilding, being in all respects the greatest and goodliest ship that was ever built in England.

Contemporary account

'Princeton': vessel that an American historian claims 'dictated the reconstruction of the navies of the world'. A screw warship ordered by the U.S. government in 1841, she was the first vessel to have her machinery built in completely below the water-line and therefore out of reach of any direct shot from the enemy guns.

Prisoner-of-war models: *see* MODEL SHIPS.

Prisoners of war: persons who have surrendered or been captured by force during a war. For centuries there was no recognized treatment for prisoners of war, and in early times immediate slaughter or enslavement was often the result. The payment of ransom for the return of important captives later became a common practice, but this disappeared in the mid-17th century. Thereafter general principles for dealing with war prisoners gradually evolved among civilized countries. These culminated in a series of international agreements, known first as the Hague Convention and then as the Geneva Convention, the latest of which was made in 1949. Not all countries signed these agreements, and even amongst those who did there was considerable disparity in the treatment of prisoners during the two World Wars and the Korean War. There is a history of many cruelties and barbarities in modern times no less than in the past.

It is interesting to note that the increasing numbers of prisoners captured during the Napoleonic Wars gave rise to the building of Dartmoor Prison (1806). To the French sailors among the prisoners at this time we owe many fine MODEL SHIPS. Many models were also made at a French prisoner-of-war camp at Norman Cross in Cambridgeshire, near which may be seen a monument commemorating no fewer than 1800 French soldiers and sailors who died in captivity there.

Prison hulks: old dismantled ships used as prisons in the 18th and early 19th centuries. Under the harsh penal code of those times the death sentence or transportation to the colonies were imposed for many offences which today would earn far less severe punishments. As the few larger prisons on land became full, hulks were used to contain the prisoners awaiting transportation across the Atlantic to work in the plantations, though they

The prison hulks at Portsmouth, from a painting by Garneray.

would also be made to labour on public works; those from the two prison hulks at Woolwich were put to work in the arsenal and dockyard. After the War of American Independence transportation to the plantations was no longer possible and so from 1787 new outlets were found in Australia and Van Diemen's Land (Tasmania).

Apart from the hulks at Woolwich there were others lower down the Thames, in the Medway and at Portsmouth. Conditions on them were terrible and mortality was high. To be condemned to the hulks was greatly feared, for the chances of avoiding either death or transportation were slight. Transportation was abolished from British law in 1853, and the last prison hulk was taken out of service in 1859.

Privateer: merchant ship or captain carrying a commission to attack vessels of nations in a state of war with his own country. He was on the look-out for a quick profit and was provided with LETTERS OF MARQUE. Among the best-known and most successful privateers were Captain Woodes ROGERS and Captain George SHELVOCKE. It was not unknown for a Royal Navy officer, out-of-work in peacetime, to take to privateering. An example was Lieutenant Bartholomew James (first commissioned 1779), who took a 40-ton vessel to the West Indies and brought a number of prizes into

Jamaica. He lost the lot to the British government, however, because he had failed to take the precaution of sailing with letters of marque.

Prize: a ship and its cargo captured in war either by a warship or by a privateer. Such captures were traditionally the right of the Crown and had to be adjudicated by the High Court of Admiralty to assess the legitimacy of the capture and the value on sale of the prize (*see* PRIZE COURT).

Prize bounty: money paid for the destruction or capture of enemy warships. It was similar to PRIZE MONEY but was never as profitable as the capture of a merchantman with a valuable cargo. The warship prizes taken at the Battle of the Glorious FIRST OF JUNE (1794) brought each of the captains £1400.

Prize court: a court of law which sits to examine all matters concerned with a prize captured in war. The former High Court of Admiralty which dealt with prizes is now part of the High Court of Justice known as the Probate, Divorce and Admiralty Division, which hears all cases concerned with maritime matters.

Prize crew: a crew placed on board a

captured enemy vessel to sail it to a port for adjudication as a prize.

Prize money: money which derives from the sale of a ship and its contents captured in time of war. It was formerly distributed to those ships making the capture, but after 1914 it was paid into a common fund for distribution to the whole service. After the end of the Second World War it was announced that in future no prize money would be paid.

In the sailing Navy of the 18th and 19th centuries the prospect of prize money was undoubtedly a considerable inducement to both officers and men. Prizes had originally been the Droits (or Rights) of the Crown, but in 1708, under what was known as the Cruizers and Convoys Act, it was decreed that the captors should share the prize money according to a scale duly laid down. The whole value of the prize when it had been assessed at the High Court of Admiralty was divided into eighths. The captain of the successful ship received three eighths, but one of his eighths went to his flag-officer, even if the latter had taken no part in the action and might have been ashore or miles away. Another three eighths was divided equally amongst the officers, warrant officers and certain men of petty-officer status, while the remaining two eighths were divided in equal shares amongst the rest of the crew. In 1808, however, a new order decreed a slightly different distribution, still in eighths, but giving an increased share to junior officers, petty officers and the rest of the crew, on a sliding scale from boys to midshipmen. In 1834 another graduated scale for the distribution of prize money was introduced.

Those who were lucky enough to share in big prizes sometimes made fortunes by

A Sailors Prayer before Battle, a cartoon by Williams: a wry comment on the distribution of prize money in Nelson's Navy.

the action of a single day, not least the flag-officers, who had a right at first to an eighth of the whole value and then to a third of the captain's share. Admiral Sir Edward Pellew, Viscount Exmouth, is said to have made over £300,000 during his career. At the other end of the scale the seaman's share would often be quite small, no more than a pound or two, though occasionally seamen received what was for them considerable sums. Sometimes there was a very long wait before prizes were adjudicated and the prize money paid, while at one time there were instances of the charges made by the agent acting for the captain being greater than the sum he was to receive in prize money.

Proa: *see* PRAU.

Promotion: in earlier days a very unusual honour for a man on the lower deck. Professor Michael Lewis estimated that the chances of such promotion to the quarter-deck (i.e. commissioned-officer rank) were about one in 2500. Of those who made the grade, most never rose higher than lieutenant, and less than three in a hundred of them attained flag rank. There were some notable exceptions. Admiral Benbow began life as a master's mate, and Captain Cook had the same rating. John QUILLIAM, First Lieutenant in *Victory* at Trafalgar, began his career on the lower deck, and was promoted Captain. His shipmate John PASCO, Signal Lieutenant, did even better, becoming Captain of *Victory* in 1847 and retiring as rear-admiral. For other examples *see* BOWEN, JAMES and PRESS-GANG; *see also* HAWSE; TARPAULIN CAPTAIN.

Propeller: the bladed and rotating screw which drives a ship. The first steam vessels were PADDLE SHIPS. When the propeller was introduced in the 1830s there was much debate about its effectiveness; in 1845 a famous test was arranged between two sloops, H.M.S. *ALECTO* and H.M.S. *RATTLER*. But even though the screw-driven *Rattler* won, some expert opinion still backed the paddle against the propeller for haulage power, and ten years after the test the Admiralty was still ordering new paddle-wheel tugs.

At first the ship propeller was large and two-bladed, then it was steadily improved in efficiency, with differently shaped and additional blades; some large ships of today have five- and six-bladed propellers. Another improvement of modern times has been the controllable pitch propeller with three or four blades, each of which can be turned to an angle to give maximum efficiency for the prevailing conditions, and with which the ship can go astern without reversing the rotation of the propeller shaft. Some ships have also a reversible propeller near their bows to assist in manoeuvring in docks and other confined spaces, and for the same purposes some have a special kind of vertical propeller in the bottom of the hull. *See also* SCREW.

Provant clothes: ready-made clothes formerly sold on board to ill-equipped seamen, one object being the hygienic one of avoiding 'nasty beastliness which many men are subjected to by continual wearing of one suit of clothes.' *See also* SLOPS.

Prow: the forepart of a vessel, the bow.

Public Record Office: in London, the chief repository of national records since the Norman conquest, assembled from the various departments of government. It has innumerable documents of maritime interest, including Admiralty records, log-books, muster rolls, letters etc. Not all have been closely studied and a lifetime of research awaits many specialist students.

Puerto Rico: West Indian island at the easternmost end of the Greater Antilles in the Caribbean. The island was discovered by Columbus (1493) and became the Spaniards' first permanent settlement in the New World. The island had great strategic importance as they extended their conquests, and it was consequently strongly defended with fortifications. These were sufficient to drive off an intended attack by Drake (1595), though soon afterwards George Clifford, Earl of Cumberland, managed to capture and hold one of the forts for a short while. Over the succeeding century the island's defences were further strengthened, and it remained in Spanish possession until taken by the United States in the Spanish-American War of 1898. Today this densely populated island has full local self-government, though it remains under the aegis of the United States, and its people, many of whom have emigrated to New York, are American citizens.

Pumps: devices for raising and removing water or other fluids. In modern ships there are many different mechanical pumps, used for a variety of purposes, but the cry 'Man the pumps', often met with in tales of the sea, refers to the hand pumps which were fitted to sailing ships to clear water from the bilges. Wooden ships are prone to take in a certain amount of sea-water, which collects on the lowest part of the hull or the bilges. It was part of the ship's carpenter's duties to check the level of this water daily by sounding the well, which is an apartment in the ship's hold, serving to enclose the pumps. The well was sounded by dropping down a sounding rod, an iron measuring rod on a line. If the ship sprang a leak or was damaged in a storm or in

battle, the water might rise to a dangerous level, making the ship unmanageable and in jeopardy of capsizing or sinking. The only hope was to see whether the pumps could gain on the rising water and the leak be plugged. Very often when ships were in distress men had to work on the pumps for hours on end until they dropped with fatigue.

Thus while he spoke, around from man to
   man
At either pump a hollow murmur ran:
For, while the vessel through unnumbered
   chinks,
Above, below, th'invading water drinks,
Sounding her depth they eyed the wetted
   scale,
And lo! the leaks o'er all their powers prevail:
Yet at their post, by terrors unsubdued,
They with redoubling force their task
   pursued.

     William Falconer, *The Shipwreck* (1762)

Punishments: in the old Navy, punishment took many barbaric forms. Among the least objectionable were MASTHEADING (a spell on the top mast crosstrees without food or drink) and GAGGING with a marline spike between the teeth as a penalty for bad language or arguing with an officer. Another minor punishment was the use by petty officers of the STARTER to encourage quicker attention to duty. The more brutal forms of punishment included FLOGGING with the cat-o'-nine-tails, KEELHAULING, RUNNING THE GAUNTLET and MAROONING. *See also* IN IRONS.

Among the Harleian Manuscripts in the British Library is a document giving a picture of retribution in the reign of Charles II:

A capstan barr being thrust through the hole of a barrell, the offenders armes are extended to the full length, and soe made faste untoe the barr croswise, having sometimes a basket of bullets, or some other the like weighte, hanginge abowte his necke, in which posture he continues until he is made either to confesse some plotte or cryme whereof he is pregnantly suspected, or that he have received such condigne sufferings as he is sentenced to undergoe by command of the captaine.

The punishment of the bilboes is when a delinquent is putt in irons, or in a kinde of stocks used for that purpose, the which are more or lesse heavy and pinching as the quality of the offence is proved against the delinquent. The ducking att the mayne yarde arm is when a malefactor, by having a rope fastened under his armes and about his myddle . . . is thus hoysted upp to the end of the yarde; from whence hee is againe vyolentlie lett fall intoe the sea, sometymes twise, sometimes three severall times . . .

Purchas, Samuel (?1575–1626): editor and compiler of works of exploration and travel.

Purchas, Samuel (?1575–1626): editor and compiler of works of exploration and travel. He held several church livings and was chaplain to the Archbishop of Canterbury – occupations which seem to have left him leisure to devote much time to the study of the wider world. Although his work was not always careful and reliable, his books contain much information about early travel and exploration that cannot be found elsewhere. They include *Hakluytus Posthumus, or Purchas his Pilgrimes, contayning a History of the World in Sea Voyages and Lande Travells, by Englishmen and others* (4 vols., 1625). Of the sea he wrote:

It is . . . an Open Field for pastimes of peace; a Pitched Field in time of warre . . . matter of Contemplation to the minde, of Action to the bodie: . . . it yeeldeth all parts of the World to each part, and maketh the World . . . knowne to itself.

Purse net (or purse seine):

Purse net (or purse seine): a bag-like fishing net which can be drawn together to trap the fish as in a closing purse. It is used when the fish are in shoals and are caught

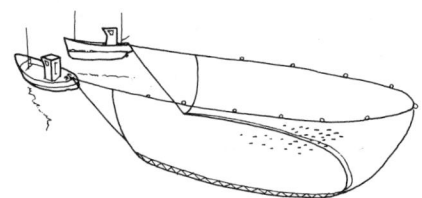

by a method known as ring netting. The fish are enclosed in the purse net and not caught by their gills as they are in a drift net.

Purser:

Purser: a variant of 'bursar', from the Latin *bursa*, meaning a purse. Purser was formerly the name of the officer on board H.M. ships responsible for keeping accounts, for the issue of victuals and other stores, particularly slops (ready-made clothing for seamen). Whilst the title has disappeared from the Royal Navy, except in its slang form PUSSER, it survives in the merchant service, where the officer responsible for payments, stores and the administrative needs of passengers is still called the purser.

In the old sailing Navy the purser had an unsavoury reputation, for reasons which were not entirely of his own making. The origin of his appointment lay in the clerk assigned to the king's ships in the earliest days. When in course of time he became a purser, he was generally appointed by warrant and had to lay out money as a surety for his position. In return he received a small emolument and was allowed to take commission on the purchase and sale of victuals and clothing. It was tacitly accepted that he would issue fourteen instead of sixteen ounces to the pound, and make other profits on the sale of tobacco, stores and slops. In the 17th and 18th centuries the opportunities for abusing these customary practices were undoubtedly frequently taken, and many pursers made themselves wealthy. Gradually, however, the purser's status improved and he became an officer of wardroom rank. By the 19th century he had acquired other important administrative duties, including that of paymaster (*see* PAY). In 1842 his title was changed to Purser and Paymaster, and a year later he became a commissioned officer. The old abuses, which had often caused much discontent, were eliminated, and in 1852 he was paid on a regular scale, at the same time dropping the title of purser to be called Paymaster, and able to rise by ranks equivalent to those of executive and other officers. In 1944 the name of the Paymaster branch of the Navy was changed to Supply and Secretariat, and the modern Supply officer controls the feeding, clothing and payment of the ship's company. He issues, replenishes and accounts for equipment, spare parts and the immense variety of other stores that are needed on board H.M. ships. He also acts as secretary and legal adviser to senior officers at sea and ashore.

Pusher: *see* MAST.

Pusser: slang form of PURSER. Though the latter is no longer an official title in the Royal Navy, 'pusser' is still occasionally used colloquially in referring to an officer of the Supply and Secretariat branch. More frequent is the use of the word to describe anything that is issued or obtainable from naval stores: thus 'a pusser's dirk' is lower-deck language for a clasp knife. A 'pusser's medal', however, is slang for a food-stain on clothing.

Put about: change a ship's course and go in another direction.

Put into: go into a harbour or bay; call at a port.

'QE 2': *see QUEEN ELIZABETH II.*

Q-ship: the name given in the First World War to ships which appeared to be harmless merchantmen but carried concealed armament. *See* MYSTERY SHIPS.

Quadrant: (1) the general name for a quarter of a circle on a compass card when each quarter is divided into 90°; (2) an old navigational instrument, forerunner of the modern sextant, but only measuring up to 90°. John Davis, the famous navigator and explorer of Elizabethan times, invented a quadrant (*c.*1594), the BACK-STAFF, which was used until HADLEY produced his reflecting quadrant (1731).

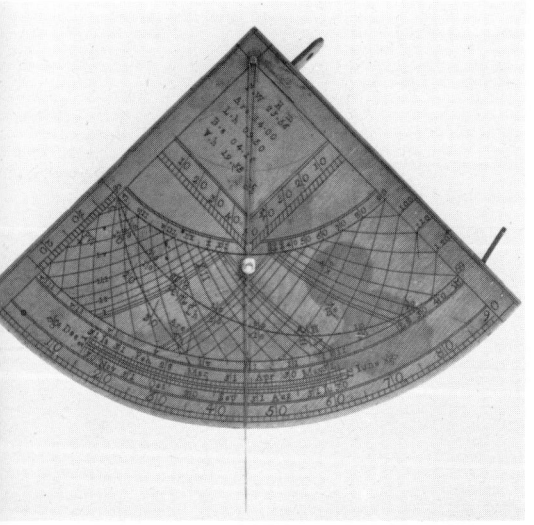

A quadrant in boxwood.

Well, that Ahab's quadrant was furnished with coloured glasses, through which to take sight of that solar fire. So, swinging his seated form to the roll of the ship, and with his astrological-looking instrument placed to his eye, he remained in that posture for some moments to catch the precise instant when the sun should gain the precise meridian.

Herman Melville, *Moby-Dick* (1851)

Quaker: an imitation gun, generally made of wood, mounted on a merchantman in the hope of frightening off privateers and other marauders. Miserly owners using such devices frequently paid the price in men and ships.

Quarantine: restriction placed on a ship or travellers infected with disease or coming from an infected port. By derivation the word means a period of 40 days, which was the time a ship and its passengers were isolated at the port of arrival to prevent the spread of any infection or contagion. This was particularly important in the days when plague and smallpox were prevalent and deadly. When a ship arrives at a port she must declare whether she is healthy or not. If healthy she flies a square yellow flag (or Yellow Jack); this is letter Q in the International Code of Signals, and means 'My vessel is healthy. I request free pratique'. If there is a case of infectious disease on board then Q9 is hoisted, meaning 'My ship is suspect'.

Quarter: (1) a fourth part of the circle of the compass rose, used to indicate a general direction, as in the next two meanings: (2) a relative bearing on either side of the after part of a ship; thus another ship or object is said to lie on the port or starboard quarter; (3) a direction from which the wind blows; thus a gale may blow from the north-easterly quarter and so on. (4) Mercy or clemency; to 'give no quarter' is to spare no man.

Quarter-deck: originally the after-part of the upper deck before the poop (*see also* DECKS). Close by were the captain's quarters, and on the quarter-deck he would meet his other officers and give his commands. The quarter-deck was normally reserved for officers, and only they could walk the quarter-deck. The name therefore came to mean 'of officer status' as opposed to 'lower-deck' meaning those who were not officers, for it was on the lower decks that the seamen messed and slept.

On boarding and leaving one of H.M. ships, officers and men salute the quarter-deck, a custom which dates from medieval times when this part of the ship contained a religious shrine before which all doffed their caps.

Quarter-gallery: a small gallery external to the cabins on either quarter of the stern of the larger sailing ships; it linked with the stern gallery. A kind of quarter-gallery was incorporated into the design of some ships for a long while after the age of sail.

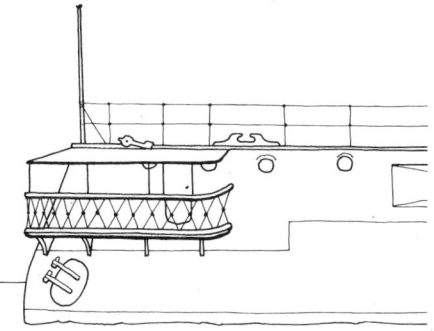

Quartermaster: in the sailing Navy, a trustworthy seaman and kind of petty officer acting as mate to those in charge of various parts of the ship. An official table of 1807 shows that first-rates bore thirteen quartermasters compared with four in a sixth-rate. Today the name is given to a senior rating responsible as chief helmsman and for other duties about the bridge, under the officer of the watch.

Quarters: (1) living accommodation.

(2) The places on board ship to which men were assigned for fighting duties. These were set out in a quarter bill. The marine drummers would 'beat to quarters' on their drums with the tune HEART OF OAK as a signal for the men to go to their battle stations, or 'action stations', as they are known today.

(3) 'Evening quarters' is a muster of men at the end of the day.

(4) 'At close quarters' means in close proximity.

Quebec: famous city and port on the north bank of the ST LAWRENCE RIVER, capital of the province of Quebec, Canada. It features in naval history as the target of one of the most successful and brilliant of combined operations between the army and the Navy. During the Seven Years' War (1756–63) and as part of the grand strategy for overcoming French power in North America, a carefully organized expedition was dispatched in 1759 to capture the French stronghold of Quebec. The force was commanded by General James Wolfe and Vice-Admiral Charles Saunders, and consisted of an army of some 5000 men in 200 transports protected by twenty-two sail of the line as well as frigates and sloops under Saunders. Leaving Louisburg, recently taken from the French, early in June 1759 the fleet sailed 300 miles up the St Lawrence to Quebec, a magnificent feat of navigation in an uncharted and dangerous river (*see* COOK, JAMES). The French had believed such a sea-borne approach to be impossible and had failed to block the river, so Quebec might easily have been surprised had not French ships under Bougainville been able to reach the town ahead of the British with captured details of the coming attack. The French quickly made new dispositions of their garrison, and when Wolfe and Saunders arrived they found Quebec almost impregnable, protected as it was by cliffs and hills. For some weeks the British tried various movements to find a weak point in the defences. On the last day of July Montcalm repulsed a probing attack, but the French forces had been extended by the passage of a British squadron higher up the St Lawrence, though an attempted landing there was again repulsed by Bougainville early in August. Saunders's squadron threatened on another side of Quebec where Montcalm expected a landing and had massed his forces. Meanwhile Wolfe and the pick of his troops had sailed a few miles above Quebec, whence on 12 September they dropped down river on the ebb tide in the ships' boats quietly and secretly to climb the heights of the river bank at a point virtually undefended because the French forces had been over-extended. At dawn on the next day Wolfe's army was drawn up on the Plains of Abraham. There after several steady volleys and a charge they defeated Montcalm's forces, which were superior in numbers but not in quality. Both Wolfe and Montcalm were killed in the course of the battle, but Quebec, now helpless before the besieging army, was surrendered to the British on 28 September. As winter set in, the occupying British garrison suffered terrible privations from scurvy and shortage of food until they were relieved in the spring of 1760 by supply ships.

With the capture of Quebec, followed by the capitulation of Montreal, Canada passed into British hands. Wolfe's great achievement at Quebec was but one of the British successes in 1759, which became known as the 'Year of Victories' or WONDERFUL YEAR.

Queen Anne's Free Gift: an annual sum of money granted in former times to surgeons in the Navy in order to supplement their earnings.

Queen Anne's Mansions: name bestowed by sailors on the high combined control tower and fore-bridge of H.M.S. *Rodney* and *Nelson*, after the (then) tallest block of flats in London.

'Queen Elizabeth': a Cunard liner, once the largest passenger ship in the world, carrying in her heyday 2300 passengers. Her gross tonnage was 83,673; overall length 1031 ft; breadth 118 ft 7 in.; normal service speed 28·5 knots (or 32·8 m.p.h.).

She was completed after the beginning of the Second World War and was at once put into service as a troop-ship, carrying thousands of troops across the Atlantic. It is said that the German leader Hitler offered the equivalent of £10,000 and the Iron Cross decoration to any U-boat captain who could sink her.

With the decline of the great passenger liners, she was sold off in July 1969 to serve as a floating hotel and centre for conventions. After an unsuccessful period at Fort Lauderdale, Florida, she moved to Hong Kong, where, from causes not yet fully explained, she was completely burnt out in 1972.

Friendly competition between the famous 'Queens' (*Queen Elizabeth* and *Queen Mary*) and the rival U.S. liners was naturally intense. On one occasion, as the *United States*, flag-ship of the United States Lines Company, slowly overhauled the *Queen Elizabeth* the American captain

The *Queen Elizabeth* in the Solent.

signalled: 'Sorry to have to pass you!' He received the reply: 'Think nothing of it. A real lady never likes to be seen in fast company.'

For H.M.S. *Queen Elizabeth, see WARSPITE.*

Queen Elizabeth class: *see WARSPITE.*

'Queen Elizabeth II' (or **'QE 2'**): a worthy, if smaller, successor to the *Queen Elizabeth*, completed in 1969, with a gross tonnage of 66,851 and over-all length of 963 ft. She achieved her own sort of record, making a 'turn round' for the homeward voyage of only 8 hours, 3 minutes, at New York in May 1972.

'Queen Mary': a Cunard ship, one of the largest and most famous liners formerly on the North Atlantic run (from 1936). With a gross tonnage of 81,237, she was 1019·5 ft in length and carried 2040 passengers. *See also* ATLANTIC GREYHOUND; TROOP-SHIP.

In the Royal Navy, the *Queen Mary* of 1912 was one of the largest and fastest capital ships till then laid down, and one of the first battle cruisers with 13·5-in. guns.

She won battle honours at Heligoland (1914) and at Jutland (1916), where she was sunk.

Queen's Regulations: *see* REGULATIONS.

Quiberon Bay, Battle of (20 November 1759): sea battle of the Seven Years' War in which Admiral HAWKE in the *Royal George* decisively defeated the French fleet threatening the invasion of England. The French admiral Conflans tried to escape a full-scale battle and made for the supposed safety of Quiberon Bay (N.W. France) through the entrance made hazardous by shoals and rocks. Although Hawke, unlike Conflans, had no local pilots to guide him through, he ordered 'General chase' and plunged after the enemy ships so close that the leading ships were able to benefit from their rivals' chosen courses, and one French ship, the *Formidable*, had her gunports wrenched off by her pursuer. Before night fell, the French had already lost four ships, two sinking and two striking their colours. The turmoil and confusion in the November dusk, which finally drove the fleets to anchor, is shown by the fact that, when the next day broke, Conflans found his flag-ship, the *Soleil Royal*, fast in the middle of the English ships. He cut his cables, only to grind on the rocks, then fired his own ship before he escaped ashore. Seven others tipped overboard their guns and heavy equipment in an effort to ride over the sand-banks into one of the rivers feeding the bay; of these, four were stranded and broke their backs, and the other three remained out of action for the rest of the war. Two English ships were lost.

In attacking a flying enemy, it was impossible in the space of a short winter's day that all our ships should be able to get into action, or all those of the enemy brought to it. The commanders and companies of such as did come up with the rear of the French on the 20th behaved with the greatest intrepidity, and gave the strongest proofs of a true British spirit. In the same manner I am satisfied would those have acquitted themselves whose bad-going ships, or the distance they were at in the morning, prevented from getting up . . .

When I consider the season of the year, the hard gales on the day of action, a flying enemy, the shortness of the day, and the coast they were on, I can boldly affirm that all that could possibly be done has been done.

From Hawke's dispatches to the Admiralty

See also GENERAL CHASE; PAULET, HARRY; WONDERFUL YEAR, THE.

Quick-match: a quick burning fuse made of cotton-thread packed with gunpowder and used for exploding a charge. For firing cannon, however, a slow-match was attached to a linstock (an iron-pointed staff) and this applied fire to the touch-hole of the primed and loaded cannon.

Quilliam, John: native of the Isle of Man who began his career on the lower deck,

was commissioned Lieutenant in 1798 and had the distinction of serving as First Lieutenant on H.M.S. *Victory* at Trafalgar, being promoted Captain immediately afterwards (24 December 1805). Previously, as a junior lieutenant on the *Ethalion* (1799), he had picked up the tidy sum of £5000 as his share in the capture of a treasure ship. In 1813, when commanding the *Crescent*, he seized an American privateer.

Quoin: a wedge. Quoins of wood were placed under the cannons used in the sailing Navy to give elevation and thus increase the range of the shot. Crowbars and handspikes were used to raise the cannon before inserting the quoin.

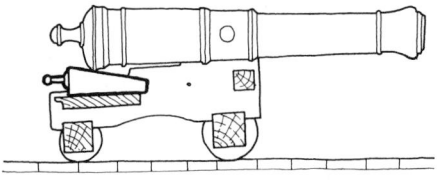

Quota Acts: measures put through by William Pitt the Younger in 1795 to supplement the supply of seamen by levying quotas (almost entirely of landsmen) on the counties and principal towns. Such recruits were known as 'Quota Men'. The scheme was in general a failure, since local authorities saw it as a great chance to get rid of jail-birds and other undesirable characters. Apart from the abject quality of the men, the plan worked against naval discipline because the quota included a few well-educated and intelligent ne'er-do-wells who could stimulate and organize lower-deck protest against poor conditions.

R

'R': *see* RUN (7).

Race: a rapid current, especially in the sea or a tidal river, sometimes produced by the meeting of two tides or near a headland separating two bays. The term may be applied to the channel or sea area where the phenomenon occurs, e.g. Portland Race, the Race of Alderney.

Rack, to: to hold two ropes together by means of binding with other smaller rope; generally a temporary device, but it can be made permanent with a 'racking seizing', an under-and-over taut kind of bind.

Radar: a word made up from the initial letters of '*r*adio *d*etecting *a*nd *r*anging'. Radar is an electronic device transmitting radio waves which, meeting an object within range of the set, are reflected and recorded at the point of transmission. The reflection of wireless waves was early known in the history of radio, but it was not until the 1930s that the application of this characteristic began to be developed. In its earliest form radar was known as R.D.F. ('radio direction finding'), and at this stage it was not particularly successful. Developments took place in Great Britain, Germany, France and the U.S.A. almost simultaneously. The development of the British system owed much to Robert Watson-Watt (1892–1974), and by the outbreak of war in 1939 a chain of radar stations had been set up on the eastern coast of England to give early warning of aircraft. The great advance came in 1940 with the invention of the magnetron and the use of micro-waves, which led to modern radar.

Independent of the state of atmospheric visibility radar can indicate with precision the bearing and range and can measure the speed of the object when picked up on the radar screen. Its application to navigation had already been foreseen, and its rapid development in war-time saw its use for detecting enemy ships, even for picking up a submarine's periscope, and for gunnery to provide accurate aim and range and general gunfire control. Problems of identification of radar signals, of counter-measures, and of extended use were overcome, and technically British and American radar became superior to the German. Since the Second World War radar has been further refined and adapted for many uses in navigation, gunnery, missiles and early warning systems. Airborne radar, also highly developed during the war, has likewise become further developed; and in the co-operation of ship and aeroplane for detection and surveillance radar holds an important and vital

place. Today all ships of any size, whether warships or merchant ships, carry radar, and its importance in navigation and the control of busy shipping lanes and port entrances cannot be overestimated.

Radio: the transmission and reception of electromagnetic waves through space as a means of communication. Radio, or wireless telegraphy as it was first called, owes much to the work of Guglielmo Marconi (1874–1937), an Italian who came to work in England at the end of the last century. The earliest use of wireless telegraphy for communication was by interrupting the signal waves with a key on which messages in the Morse code could be sent, and this is still the basis of a great deal of radio traffic, though of course with vast improvements in range and accuracy. The maritime application of this means of communication was soon seen to be important after Marconi in 1901 had sent signals from Cornwall to Newfoundland. In the next ten years warships and merchant ships were fitted with radio transmitters and receivers, and for the first time were in touch with the shore and with each other at considerable distances. When in 1912 the *Titanic* sank on her maiden voyage, her wireless messages brought other ships to her aid, though too late to save more than about a third of her passengers in the ship's boats. The first English merchant vessel to be equipped with a radio direction-finder to aid navigation by cross-bearings was the *Mauretania* (1911). By 1914, when the First World War broke out, radio was playing an important part in the control of shipping and the giving of tactical orders to warships, which, of course, had to be passed in codes or ciphers. At the same time progress was made with the sending of and reception of speech by radio waves.

Two-way radio-telephony was established between ships by 1916, and in 1929 a radio-telephone service from the shore to big liners became available. The inter-war years saw the great development of broadcasting and the refinement and application of radio to a multitude of uses, in police work, in the armed services and in public and commercial communication. At sea, apart from radio communication, perhaps the most important modern application of radio has been the development of radio navigational systems. First used early in the Second World War for fixing the position of aircraft, radio navigation is now used by an increasing number of ships, and with the appropriate equipment, of which there are various types, a ship can quickly and accurately fix her position from radio waves emanating from special shore stations. Already large areas of the ocean are covered by such systems, both short- and long-range, and soon every portion of the world's oceans may be so served.

In war-time, radio has been used to deceive the enemy by the transmission of false messages, as when, in 1939, the captain of the German 'pocket battleship' *Graf Spee* was led to believe a large force of British ships lay in wait for him off the River Plate. The interception of a warship's radio transmissions can not only give her position away, but if the code or cipher has been broken vital information may be revealed.

Today orbiting satellites are used to extend the power and range of radio communication, and radio is also used for the control of a range of new missile weapons. RADAR is a further extension of the use of electromagnetic waves or radio.

Raffee sail: one of several names given to small sails set above the skysails in square-rigged ships when the breeze was very light.

Raft: a flat, buoyant structure, generally of timber, used: (**1**) as an emergency measure to support men after a shipwreck instead of a boat; it may be previously built and lashed on deck for such an occasion, or it may be improvised from planks, barrels etc.; (**2**) as a floating stage or catamaran for small boats to come alongside; or placed against a ship to allow work on her hull.

'Rag, the': nickname for the Army and Navy Club; the 'rag' is the flag under which both services fought.

Rail: continuous bar of wood or metal, with supports at regular intervals, running round a ship's deck, usually at about waist height, to safeguard crew and passengers against falling overboard.

'Rainbow': 40-gun ship, carrying some 250 men, which shared in Drake's great Cadiz expedition (1587) and the defeat of the Spanish Armada. At the latter she was commanded by Lord Henry Seymour and, when Drake took up the chase of the defeated ships, was left behind to guard the approaches. Seymour disliked the duty and wrote to Walsingham 'from on board the *Rainbow*, this 1st of August, 1588, at anchor at three in the afternoon':

I pray God my Lord Admiral do not find the lack of the *Rainbow* and that company; for I protest before God and have witness for the same, I vowed I would be as near or nearer with my little ship to encounter our enemies as any of the greatest ships in both armies.

Rainier, Peter (?1741–1808): admiral. His reputation was made principally as Commander-in-Chief in the East Indies 1793–1804, a period which saw the capture of Amboyna, Trincomalee and Banda Beira. *See also MARIA REIGERSGERGEN.*

Rake: (**1**) the projection of the stem or stern of a vessel beyond the length of the keel; (**2**) the backward slope of the masts for additional speed; hence 'rakish', meaning smart-looking, fast. (**3**) To 'rake' a ship etc. is to sweep her with shot from end to end.

Ralegh (or **Raleigh**), **Sir Walter** (?1552–1618): sailor, naval commander, soldier, historian and poet. He remained at Elizabeth's court for many years, much favoured and knighted in 1584; but his eyes were increasingly set on further horizons. Over the years 1583–9 he sent out six expeditions to plant colonies in America and followed with others. None of them produced permanent results, save for the introduction of the potato and tobacco into England and Ireland. In 1594 he sent ships to reconnoitre the South American river Orinoco and a year later he himself led an expedition in search of the fabulous EL DORADO. In 1616 he tried again, after thirteen years' imprisonment at the hands of James I for alleged high treason. This expedition too was a disaster; but, true to the agreement he had made with his unworthy king, though he knew he was almost certainly returning to his death, he came home and, largely at Spanish instigation, was executed (29 October 1618).

Ralegh was in many ways a typical Elizabethan, though of exceptional intellect. He was ambitious, at times unscrupulous, arrogant, fearless, open-handed, bitter of tongue, deeply religious (although accused of atheism). His name was probably pronounced 'Rawley' and he himself is never known to have used the modern spelling 'Raleigh'. His family contrived to spell the name in more than 70 different ways.

407

He was a tall, handsome, and bold man; but . . . damnable proud . . . Old Sir Thomas Malett . . . knew Sir Walter; and I heard him say that, notwithstanding his so great mastership in style and his conversation with the learnedest and politest persons, yet he spake broad Devonshire to his dying day.

John Aubrey (1626–97), *Brief Lives*

And then putting off his doublet and gown, [Ralegh] desired the executioner to show him the axe; which, not being suddenly granted unto him, he said:

'I prithee let me see it. Dost thou think I am afraid of it?'

So, it being given unto him, he poised it in his hand, and felt along the edge of it with his thumb, to see if it was keen; and, smiling, spake unto Mr Sheriff, saying:

'This is a sharp medicine, but it will cure all diseases.'

. . . And there being some dispute that his face should be towards the east, he made answer and said:

'So the heart be straight, it is no matter which way the head lieth.'

Contemporary account of his execution
See colour section.

Ram: (1) the act of running the bows of a ship into another vessel or into a jetty etc.; (2) a strengthened projection from a ship's bows when ramming was employed offensively to sink or disable the enemy. Roman war galleys had an iron beak on their bows for this purpose; it was called *corvus*, the Latin for crow, because of its likeness to the bird's beak. This kind of ram was for long employed in the rowed fighting galleys of the Mediterranean. The idea of ramming as a method of successful attack revived with the coming of the ironclad, and during the 19th century many warships were built with ram bows. Ramming by accident had not infrequently shown what disastrous results might follow when one ship rammed another. One such

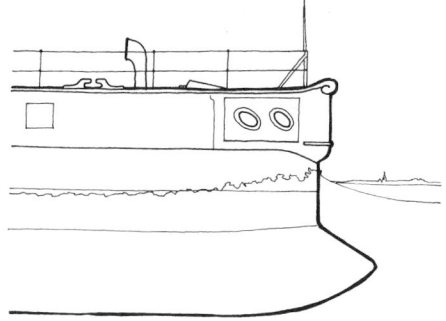

naval catastrophe occurred in 1875 when H.M.S. *Vanguard*, a battleship of over 6000 tons, was accidentally rammed and sunk by H.M.S. *IRON DUKE*. Ramming as a deliberate offensive action was successfully employed against a number of enemy submarines during the two World Wars.

'Ramillies': of the ships that have carried this battle-name, perhaps the most curious story attaches to the third, a 74-gun ship, while she was engaged in the war with America. In 1814, in Chesapeake Bay, several attempts were made by means of a 'diving boat' to pass right under her and fasten a clockwork mine to her hull. These attempts continued till the British commanding officer collected all his American prisoners on board the harassed ship and informed the American government that if his ship was blown up the prisoners would go up too. This unconventional ruse seems to have been successful.

In 1813 the *Ramillies* had lost eleven men who had boarded a captured American schooner that was deliberately laden with casks of gunpowder, concealed under innocent-looking stocks of flour and set to blow up by a clockwork device.

Ramsay, the Hon. Sir Alexander Robert Maule (1881–1972): admiral. His reputation was made chiefly with the air service. He was Rear-Admiral, Aircraft

Carriers (1933–6), and Chief of the Naval Air Service (1938–9).

Ramsay, Sir Bertram Home (1883–1945): admiral. After a distinguished career, he retired in 1938 but came back to serve brilliantly in the Second World War, organizing the Dunkirk evacuation (26 May–4 June 1940) and acting as allied naval commander-in-chief for the Normandy invasion. He was restored to the active list and promoted to flag rank in 1944, being killed the following year in an air-crash.

Randan: the arrangement of three oarsmen pulling a boat by which stroke and bow pull a single oar and the centre man pulls a pair of oars, thus giving an even pull of two oars on each side.

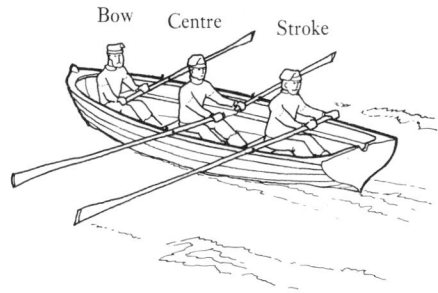

Bow   Centre   Stroke

Random range: extreme RANGE for the guns of the old sailing Navy, i.e. about two miles; so called because at such a distance the chance of hitting the target was slight. Broadsides were generally fired by British sailing warships only when the enemy was closed to a range of about 200 yards or less.

Range: the distance to which a gun will fire its projectile, as in 'extreme range'; also the distance between a gun and its target, as in 'a range of 10,000 yards'.

In considering the range of guns used in the old sailing Navy a distinction must be made between extreme or RANDOM RANGE,

which is the longest distance the projectile will carry with the gun elevated, and POINT-BLANK or effective range, which is the distance a projectile will carry with the gun's barrel in a horizontal position, straight to its target before beginning to fall. Range will also obviously vary according to the calibre of the gun, the weight of the shot fired, and the type and amount of the charge used.

It is difficult to be precise about the range of guns in Tudor times, when the broadside was beginning to develop. Though it was to be a long while before gunfire alone would sink a ship, it seems that the most effective gun in range used by the English ships against the Armada (1588), the culverin, fired a 17-lb. shot to a random range of about $1\frac{1}{4}$ miles, with an effective range of about 350 yards. The bigger guns of those times, the cannon and demi-cannon, firing 50-lb. and 32-lb. shot respectively, reached about a mile at random and about 280 yards at point-blank range.

During the next two and a half centuries the muzzle-loading gun firing a solid shot was to remain the chief weapon of the British Navy, and though there were improvements there was as yet no great increase in range. From 1779 the introduction of the carronade increased the destructive fire-power of British ships, but its lack of range eventually saw its disappearance. Thus in the days of Nelson's Navy, though gunnery was more efficient than in the past, point-blank range had increased only to about 400 yards. In any case, except for bombardment of shore batteries, range did not greatly matter to British naval gunners because during the 18th and early 19th centuries, they held their fire until the enemy was at 'half-musket range', that is about 100 yards, when the effect of a broadside could often be devastating to the other ship. The French, however, often fired at greater range in the hope of so damaging the sails, masts and rigging of the English ships that they could be approached and attacked at close quarters.

The enormous improvements in ARMAMENT that began in the mid-19th century revolutionized the range of guns, which steadily increased as bigger and bigger guns were made. In 1875 a 9-in. gun would fire a shell of 250 lb. to a distance of over $5\frac{1}{2}$ miles. In 1905 the defeat of the Russians by the Japanese fleet at the Battle of Tsushima showed the world's navies the much increased ranges at which big guns could be fired with effect. At the Battle of Jutland (1916) firing in the opening phase was at 14,500 to 16,000 yards, and later at 18,000 to 20,000 yards; the 13·5-in. guns fired shells of 1400 lb. By 1939 a 16-in. gun could throw a shell of over a ton to a distance of over 20 miles. The battleships with the biggest guns ever installed in a ship were the Japanese *Yamato* and *Musashi*, each with nine 18-in. guns firing to a range of 27 miles, though both ships were sunk by American carrier-borne aircraft towards the end of the Second World War without having fired their enormous guns at enemy ships. Although range-finding by RADAR and automatic control greatly increased the accuracy of fire at long range, the coming of the aeroplane exposed the battleship's vulnerability to bombing or attack by aerial torpedo, and the big-gunned ship has become a part of history.

'Ranger': ship commanded by John Paul JONES. She can claim a unique distinction in naval history: while lying in the French port of Quideron, she received the first national salute given the American flag in Europe (1778).

Rank: *see* OFFICER.

Rank keel: a very deep keel.

Ransome, Arthur (1884–1967): British author who made a great and deserved reputation with his stories for the young about the young enjoying boats, sailing and adventure. He had written several books while working as a journalist in Russia, Egypt and China, but it was after his return to England to recover from illness that he began the series of children's books on which his reputation rests. He had always been interested in sailing and he owned and sailed his own boats. The knowledge so gained was reflected in the details and incidentals of his stories, which are convincing and accurate; even the imaginary adventures were sometimes tested for the practical details, as when he sailed his own boat across the North Sea and used the experience as a basis for one of his later stories, *We Didn't Mean to Go to Sea* (1937). His best-known, though not perhaps his best, book was *Swallows and Amazons* (1930). This was followed by a succession of books which became immensely popular with young readers. Amongst them were *Swallowdale* (1931), *Peter Duck* (1932), *Coot Club* (1934), *Pigeon Post* (1936), *Secret Water* (1939) and *Great Northern?* (1947).

Rastell, John (*fl*.1517–20): brother-in-law of Sir Thomas More and author of a play called *A New Interlude and a Merry of the Nature of the Four Elements*, which gives the earliest literary description of America in our language. Rastell was not a seaman by training, but in 1517 he emerged as the leader of an expedition, supported by Henry VIII, apparently intended for the further exploration and colonization of America. He carried an open letter from the King 'addressed to all Christian princes and adjuring them of their friendship to assist John Rastell and his associates engaged upon a voyage to distant countries' (J. A. Williamson, *The Ocean in English History*, 1941). The voyage seems to have been a fiasco; Rastell could not control his seamen, who had no intention of crossing the Atlantic, put him ashore at Cork and sailed the ships home again. In his play Rastell condemns the faint-hearts,

Whiche wolde take no paine to saile farther
Than their owne lyst and pleasure;
Wherfore that vyage and dyvers other
Such kaytyffes have distroyed.

Despite his failure as a leader of men, Rastell ranged wide in his thought and imagination, speculating on all the boundless opportunities offered by colonization, especially of America, including the extension of the King's dominions, the conversion of the heathen, 'who as yet knew neither God nor the Devil, heaven nor hell', and such considerable practical advantages as sources of supply for pitch, tar and fish.

Ratcliff Highway: famous thoroughfare in East London, much frequented by seamen and running near many of the docks, e.g. Regent's Canal, Shadwell and Eastern. Among its other features was its amazing number of taverns to lure the unwary, some of them mentioned in an anonymous ballad of *c.*1840:

The Old Three Crowns I anchored in,
Oh such a jolly crew,
There's rough and smooth from every
clime,
And copper colour too.
Such lasses there, so neat and fair,
With hair both grey and red,
Some with no nose and some no teeth,
And damaged figurehead . . .

Rates: *see* RATING OF MEN; RATING OF SHIPS.

Rating: (1) the classification of ships according to their size or the number of their guns; *see* RATING OF SHIPS. (2) The classification of men into different grades; *see* RATING OF MEN. (3) A 'rating' is a member of a ship's company, other than an officer, who holds the grade or rate assigned to him, e.g. Able Seaman, Petty Officer etc.

Rating of men: classifying men into different grades or rates, equivalent to the ranking of officers. In the Navy of the 18th century everyone had to be rated in the ship's books according to their capabilities and duties, for the rate at which they were paid depended on their status. (For some it also depended on the ship in which they served, pay being higher in the bigger ships of the line.) The backbone of the crew were the Ordinary Seamen, the Able Seamen and the Petty Officers in charge of the various parts of the ship. But there were other ratings, such as the boys, and at the end of the 18th century the rating of LANDSMAN was introduced; he was below the grade of Ordinary Seaman, for, as his name implies, he had no nautical experience and in time of war he was often a victim of the press-gang. Gradually the need was seen for the proper preliminary training of men entering the Navy as ratings, and in 1853 regular service engagements were introduced. At the same time the new rates of Leading Seaman and Chief Petty Officer were introduced.

Today in the Royal Navy the ratings are Junior Seaman, Ordinary Seaman, Able Seaman, Leading Seaman, Petty Officer, Chief Petty Officer and Fleet Petty Officer. Within each rate a rating will hold additional titles according to his category and specialization (e.g. Leading Radio Operator or Petty Officer Cook), and he wears a badge to indicate the category within which he is rated.

411

Rating of ships: in the old Navy, ships were officially classified ('rated') according to the number of their guns. The original classification (introduced by Admiral Anson in the mid-18th century) was:

First-rates	100 guns or more
Second-rates	84–100 guns
Third-rates	70–84 guns
Fourth-rates	50–70 guns
Fifth-rates	32–50 guns
Sixth-rates	up to 32 guns

The figures for each rate were later raised (e.g. to 90–110 guns for the second rate). Some guns were disregarded in reckoning the classification: carronades, for example, were not included for almost 40 years after they were first introduced (1779).

Only ships of the first three rates were considered suitable for the LINE OF BATTLE. Fifth- and sixth-rates were generally frigates. There were many smaller ships, carrying a variety of armament, which were not rated: brigs, sloops, cutters etc.

Terms such as 'first-rate' and 'fourth-rate' have passed into common speech as indicators of quality; but this gives a false impression of their original significance, which had only to do with the *quantity* of guns. A swift-sailing frigate of light armament could well be a better-*quality* ship than a lumbering first-rate.

Ratlines: the pieces of rope secured horizontally across the shrouds of a ship so that they acted as the rungs of a rope ladder. They were seized to the outermost shrouds and passed round each intervening shroud with a clove hitch.

Rats: once one of the common HEALTH hazards in ships. The *Universal Directory for Taking alive, or Destroying, Rats and Mice* (1788) by Thomas Swaine, ratcatcher to His Majesty's Royal Navy, gives us a unique and somewhat horrifying picture of ship conditions in the 18th century. His list of rats destroyed on H.M. ships of war includes:

Victory	171
Achilles	704
Diligente	665, 140 and 141
Prince of Wales	1015
Duke	415 and 2475

Rattenbury, Jack (*b*.1788): most famous of the band of Devonshire smugglers, whose exploits became legendary and earned him the nickname of 'Rob Roy of the West'. Born at Beer, he was by turns fisherman, pilot, pressed man and privateer, but principally a skilful and daring smuggler from about the age of 16. He was captured by both French and Spanish privateers, but managed to escape. In his many encounters with government excise men he showed remarkable ingenuity, on one occasion climbing up a chimney to elude them. On another, having been taken on board a government revenue cutter, he managed to get ashore and return at night to rescue his imprisoned comrades. On the lighter side, he was once betrayed to the

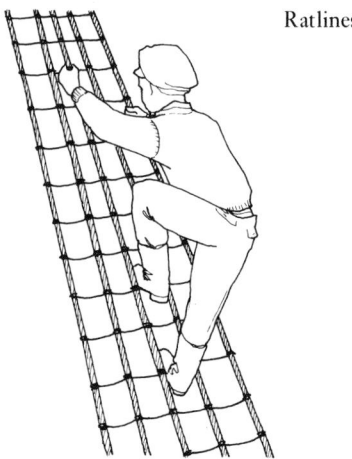

Ratlines.

412

coastguard by the indignant braying of a sleeping donkey over which he tripped while climbing the cliff at Seaton Hole with an illicit cargo. By his own standards (and, indeed, by those of many responsible citizens) he was a decent and honourable man. One of his friends, Lord Rolle, gave him a pension in his later years. Once he gave evidence before a court for his own son, another well-trained smuggler. Said Jack: 'I have always trained him up in an honourable way, larnt him the Creed, the Lord's Prayer, and the Ten Commandments.'

'Rattler': *see ALECTO.*

Razée: a vessel cut down to fewer decks than when she was originally built. Thus in 1831 the 74-gun ship *Eagle* (built 1804) was 'razéed' to a 50-gun frigate. In 1813, three 74-gun ships, *Goliath*, *Majestic* and *Saturn*, along with several other vessels, were cut down into frigates. This cutting down, not always successful, took various forms, including reducing the quarterdeck and forecastle to provide a complete and fully-armed upper gun-deck. Others retained a waist without guns.

Reach: (1) a stretch of water along a river or estuary. The word may be used in a general sense, as in 'the upper reaches of the Thames', or it may refer to a particular or straight stretch, e.g. Gallion's Reach, one of the many reaches of the lower Thames with individual names.

(2) A sailing term, either as noun or as verb: 'reach' is the position when a vessel is sailing free with the wind on or just before the beam. 'A broad reach' is when she is so sailing with the wind on or just abaft the beam. To 'reach across the wind' is to sail free between these positions of the wind.

Rear-Admiral: lowest rank of ADMIRAL.

Recall: a ship is recalled to base or to some other point when a mission is cancelled or further duties are to be given. Boats from a ship are generally recalled by a flag signal indicating either a particular boat or all boats; the latter signal is known as the general recall.

Receiving ships: old ships for the reception of recruits to the Navy, especially those brought in through impressment. They were usually to be found at the larger ports, decrepit and foul hulks with a bad reputation, often fully justified from the descriptions that have survived. Charles Reece Pemberton, who was caught by the press-gang at the age of 17, in 1806, and served six years at sea, describes the receiving ship at Plymouth as 'a human washing-tub on a grand scale where we were carried for the purpose of purification, fumigation, washing, scrubbing, and scraping'. It is a moot point whether these attempts to clean up the recruits, some of whom were verminous and dirty in the extreme, were not more than cancelled out by the insanitary conditions of the ships themselves.

Reciprocal: a bearing precisely opposite, that is, by 180°; e.g. the reciprocal of 090° is 270°, the reciprocal of 135° is 315° etc.

Reckoning: the calculation and recording of a ship's position. *See also* DEAD-RECKONING.

Reclamation dredger: scarcely a ship at all, being merely a pontoon carrying the pumping machinery and suction pipes for conveying the 'spoil' to a waiting hopper or suitable nearby area of land. *See also* DREDGER.

Recoil: the resulting backward movement of a gun when it is fired. The recoil of the cannon in the old sailing Navy was for long checked by ropes called breechings, secured both to the gun and the ship's sides. As the guns were muzzle-loading, the recoil had the advantage of bringing them back inboard for reloading, though the breechings sometimes parted dangerously and the strain on the ship's sides was tremendous. Improvements to check recoil by the use of steel springs and of corrugated wedges placed behind the truck-wheels were introduced by a great gunnery enthusiast, Rear-Admiral Sir Charles DOUGLAS, who was Rodney's flag-captain at the Battle of the Saints (1782). As the gun developed into its modern form, hydraulic recoil cylinders were introduced.

Red: the colour of the navigation side light shown on the port side; 'red' is used to give a quick bearing on the port hand, e.g. 'red zero four five', meaning 45° on the port bow.

Red, Admiral of the: *see* ADMIRAL.

Red Duster: *see* RED ENSIGN.

Red Ensign: the traditional flag of the British Merchant Navy, a red ENSIGN with the Union Flag in the top corner next the staff. For a long period, from the reign of Charles I, the Royal and Merchant Navies shared the red ensign, but by an Order in Council of 9 July 1864 it became the exclusive flag of the mercantile marine, affectionately known as the 'Red Duster'.

Red flag at the mast-head: an expression meaning distinctly in earnest, usually signifying trouble ahead for someone; from old single-flag signals ordering 'Close action' or 'No quarter'.

'Red Jacket': Nova-Scotian-built White Star clipper which made some remarkable runs to Australia in the 1850s. She achieved a record voyage to Liverpool from Boston, including one day's run of 436 miles, said to be the biggest ever accomplished by a sailing ship.

Red Marines: the old Royal Marine Light Infantry. After the First World War they were amalgamated with the Artillery and given blue tunics; but the old name stuck for a long time.

Red Sea: a long, narrow sea with the coasts of Arabia on its eastern side and of Egypt, Sudan and Eritrea on the western side. It is called the Red Sea because of floating algae which from time to time give the waters a reddish tinge. It is a sunken or rift valley in

Red Jacket.

origin; part of the great rift continues northwards along the line of the River Jordan and Dead Sea and south-westwards through the lakes of East Africa. The Red Sea was once a great highway for the Arab world, and still carries tens of thousands of pilgrims making the journey to the holy city of Mecca. But it was the opening of the Suez Canal (1869), linking it with the Mediterranean, that made it one of the busiest sea routes in the world until the closing of the canal after the war between Israel and Egypt in 1967. Since the reopening of the Suez Canal in 1975 the Red Sea has recovered as an important sea route, but not to its previous extent, because the size of many giant tankers and bulk-carriers prohibits their passage through the canal, and for many ships it is cheaper to take the longer route round South Africa.

The Red Sea, I suppose, will never be a popular resort. No pleasure, as it is commonly defined, may be found where the shade temperature may rise to 110°, where rain rarely falls, where there is either no wind or a malicious stern wind, where the enclosing shores have no rivers but only beaches of radiant sand and precipices of glowing metal . . .

H. M. Tomlinson, *Tidemarks* (1924)

Reef: (1) a ridge or shelf of rock or coral which may or may not show above the surface of the water, but is always a hazard to navigation.

(2) A part of a sail that can be taken in, rolled up and secured by reef-points, i.e. short lines attached direct to a sail or to reef-bands, which are extra strips of canvas running horizontally along a square sail for strengthening the hold of the reef-points. Thus to 'take in a reef' or to 'reef' is to shorten the area of sail by one or more reefs.

For the reef knot *see* KNOTS.

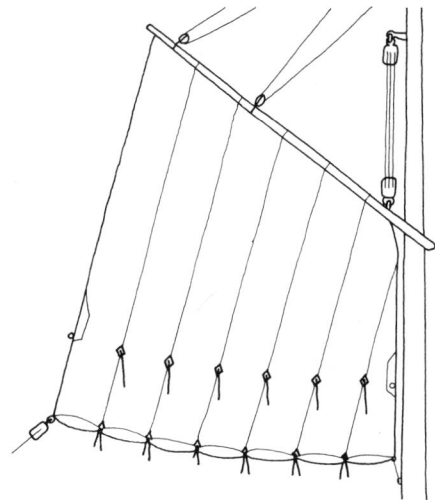

Reef (2).

Reefer: (1) an old name for a midshipman under sail, since it was part of his duties to superintend topsail reefing; (2) REFRIGERATED SHIP.

Reeming iron: an iron tool with a wedge-shaped edge used for opening up the planking of a ship so that it can be caulked with oakum and pitch to make it water-tight.

Reeve, to: to pass a rope through any opening such as that of a block, a thimble or a ring-bolt. When the action is completed the rope is said to be rove through the opening.

Refit: to renew damaged or worn-out gear, or to modernize. After an engagement a ship might require a refit, the duration of which would depend on the extent of the damage; it might require dockyard help or be completed by the crew. Older ships often undergo an extensive refit when they are modernized, and sometimes are completely altered in type.

415

Refraction: the bending or deflection of light rays due to the varying density of the atmosphere through which they pass. When a navigator takes a sight to find the altitude of a heavenly body, his observation will be subject to refraction; so to obtain the true altitude he must apply a correction, for which he will rely on the Nautical Almanac and appropriate tables. Refraction can play some curious tricks depending on the state of the atmosphere; it can have a mirage effect, making objects appear nearer than they really are, and it can have a similar effect in certain kinds of mist or fog, when a ship or other object will loom large.

Refrigerated ship (or **refrigerator ship**; sometimes called **reefer**): ship specially equipped to transport perishable goods, e.g. meat, fruit, fish and dairy produce, the hold being partly or wholly built as a refrigerator, with insulated walls. In the nature of their work, such craft are usually designed as fast ships and, because the insulating materials are both expensive and easily damaged, they are not generally used for other cargoes.

'Regent': one of Henry VII's great ships, built in 1487 and recorded as being of 1000 tons. She was the first four-master we know of in English history, carrying top-masts and topsails on main and fore masts. She was equipped with some 180 guns in her fighting castles. (Geoffrey Callender put the total number of guns at 225.) Her great size may well have been an important factor in Henry's decision to build the new dock at Portsmouth. She met her end when she blew up in 1515.

Register of Seamen: a list of men trained and suitable for service at sea. It was always realized that men already trained to the sea were the best reserves for manning the Navy, although in times of war the numbers forthcoming were never sufficient, necessitating the use of impressment, the Quota Acts and, in modern times, conscription. However, to know what trained reserves were available, compulsory registration of seamen was introduced by Parliament as early as 1696. The Act embraced men in both the Royal and the Merchant Navies, and they had to contribute 6d. a month to the finances of

The modern refrigerated ship *San Joaquin Valley*.

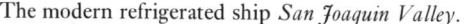

the Chatham Chest and later to Greenwich Hospital. In return the men called up were promised benefits in promotion, prize money and pay. But the Act was never properly implemented and was repealed in 1711. The Navy continued to rely on volunteers, and in time of war pressed and Quota Men, until the reforms of 1836, when proper service engagements with pensions were introduced. A modern register is kept by the Registrar General of Shipping and Seamen, who maintains records of British ships, the men serving in them and their qualifications.

Register ships: an old name for Spanish treasure ships, perhaps because when they were brought home their contents were carefully listed and officially valued before there was any division of the spoils. For example, when Sir Francis Drake captured the *San Felipe*, the Queen's representatives were at Plymouth for many weeks and reported 'here will be travail . . . to occupy us a long time.' In this case, a certificate was signed by responsible witnesses, the less valuable parts of the cargo were sold locally and the most precious items were stowed aboard other ships and brought round to London. The inventory totalled £97,610.

Regulations, Queen's (or **King's**): regulations issued under the authority of the Sovereign which, together with Admiralty Instructions, govern the organization and discipline of the British Navy (and Army). Up to 1731 every commander-in-chief had issued his own code of instructions to his ships, but in that year there appeared the first set of King's Regulations and Admiralty Instructions, to be followed by many others as they were periodically revised. For long they were known by their initial letters as 'K (or "Q") and A.I.', but

the correct title today is 'Queen's Regulations for the Royal Navy' ('Q.R.R.N.').

Relieving tackle: a name applied to two kinds of tackle rigged for special purposes. (1) When a ship was careened on a beach to clean and repair her bottom, relieving tackle enabled the crew to heel the ship over, to prevent her from heeling too far, and to right her when the job was finished. (2) Another form of relieving tackle was formerly used on either side of the tiller to give more control when heavy seas put such great strains on the rudder that steering by the wheel was too difficult for man-power alone.

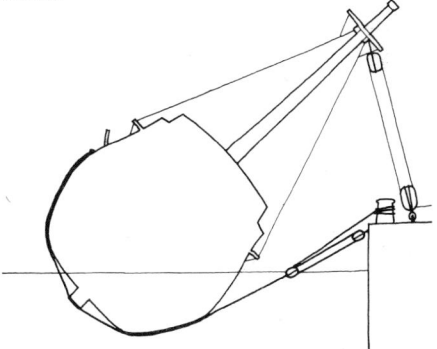

Research ship: vessel specially refitted and equipped to carry out research into, e.g., polar conditions, marine life, oceanographic problems etc. For examples *see CHALLENGER; JOHN BISCOE; and p. 418; see also* OCEANOGRAPHY.

Reserves: men in reserve to join and supplement the Royal Navy in time of war. Before the amalgamation in 1956 there were two main bodies of naval reserves, the Royal Naval Reserve (R.N.R.) and the Royal Naval Volunteer Reserve (R.N.V.R.). The officers and men of the R.N.R. were all experienced seamen drawn from the Merchant Navy, while the

The British Antarctic Survey research ship *John Biscoe*.

members of the R.N.V.R. were drawn from all walks of life, some with experience of boats and the sea, many without. All were enrolled voluntarily and undertook to do a stipulated amount of training annually with the R.N. Both the R.N.R. and the R.N.V.R. officers wore distinctive gold lace on the cuff of their uniform and on shoulder straps, intertwined for the R.N.R. and wavy for the R.N.V.R., which in consequence came to be known as the 'Wavy Navy'. In 1956, however, both bodies came under one organization known as R.N.R., and officers now wear the same straight gold lace markings of rank as the R.N. The R.N.R. is organized in territorial divisions with bases in maritime centres of population such as London, Severn, Clyde, Forth etc. All come under the Admiral Commanding Reserves, with headquarters in H.M.S. *Discovery*, moored in King's Reach, London. Certain R.N.R. and other officers, listed in the Navy List, are entitled to fly the Blue Ensign. All do an annual period of training with the Royal Navy.

In a broad sense the R.N.R. (and R.N.V.R.) can be traced back historically to medieval times when merchant seamen were called to man the king's ships and 'gentlemen' captains came on board with their fighting men to command for the duration of the war. Even when the Royal Navy had evolved into a full-time professional fighting service, the merchant service was always looked upon as the source of first reserves of seamen, as was recognized at the end of the 17th century (*see* REGISTER OF SEAMEN). When numbers of volunteer reserves fell short of demand in time of war, recourse was had to the press-gang, which was sometimes ruthless in taking merchant seamen off their ships as well as pressing into service landlubbers quite ignorant of the sea.

The R.N.R. as a distinct and separate named reserve was formed in 1859 of ratings only; sub-lieutenants and lieutenants were added two years later. The R.N.V.R. was inaugurated in 1903. Both these reserve forces were enormously extended and did valiant service in the First World War and again in the Second. It is interesting to note that by 1945 the composition of the executive officer branch of the Royal Navy was: R.N. 14 per cent, R.N.R. 12 per cent and R.N.V.R. 74 per cent, and though many of the R.N.V.R. group had entered as conscripts, they were volunteers as officers.

Two forgotten historical reserves forces were the R.N. Coast Volunteers, in existence between 1853 and 1873, whose duties were concerned with coast defence, and the R.N. Artillery Volunteer Reserve, which was formed in 1873 to provide a reserve of trained gunners, but was disbanded in 1892. Mention must also be made of the present-day Royal Marine Reserve, the Women's Royal Naval Reserve, and the R.N. Auxiliary Service, which is a small body of civilians with special and various war-time duties in ports and harbours (not to be confused with the ROYAL FLEET AUXILIARY SERVICE).

'Resolute': vessel which performed a

unique feat in 1854–5. One of the ships that Sir Edward Belcher took with him when he set out in 1852 to search for Sir John FRANKLIN, she became locked in the ice off Melville Island in the North-West Territory of Canada and was abandoned after two winters. In 1855, Captain Buddington in the American whaler *George Henry* was in Davis Strait when, on 17 September, he encountered a perfectly sound, empty ship. It was the *Resolute*, which had made a journey of 1000 miles without any crew, probably through Barrow Strait, Lancaster Sound and Baffin Bay, over a period of 474 days. She had shipped a little water in the hold, but was otherwise in perfectly good trim. She was taken back to America, faithfully refitted and presented to Queen Victoria for further service – a generous gesture which was ill rewarded, since the Admiralty allowed her to deteriorate till she was no longer fit for the element she had triumphed over so signally.

'Resolution': a name carried by many

Resolute in the ice off Melville Island with the *Intrepid*, 1851: from a litho by McDougal.

The revenue cutter *Vigilant* towing the barge *Charlotte* off Greenwich, 1845: from a litho by T.G. Dutton.

ships, one of the best-known being the vessel that sailed with Captain Cook on his second and third voyages (1772–5 and 1776–9). In our time it has been given to Britain's first Polaris submarine, with a range of 3000 miles and a terrifying potential of mutilation and destruction (*see also* SUBMARINE).

'Retribution': one of the more awe-inspiring ship names in use through the centuries from Tudor times onwards. The paddle frigate *Retribution* (launched at Chatham 1844) was sent to Sevastopol in 1854 to demand the release of a number of engineers taken prisoner at the Battle of Sinope, her armament of 28 guns being of 'a very persuasive size'. *See also* HERMIONE.

'Revenge': among all the line of ships carrying this distinguished name from Tudor times onwards, pride of place will always go to the small ship in which Sir Richard GRENVILLE fought a single-handed action against 53 Spanish ships for

fifteen hours (1591). At the Armada, the *Revenge* had flown Drake's flag as Vice-Admiral.

Revenue cutters: fast R.N. ships employed to prevent smuggling. A typical cutter of the 1830s was of about 130 tons, 70 ft long in the deck, 20 ft wide and carrying two guns.

Revenue men: *see* PREVENTIVE MEN.

Rhode Island: smallest state of the U.S.A., one of the original thirteen colonies of New England, its full name being Rhode Island and Providence Plantations. Narragansett Bay, a great arm of the sea, deeply penetrates the coast, and at its entrance lies the large island which gave the state its name, with the town of Newport guarding the entrance to the magnificent anchorage of the bay. Further inland at the head of the bay lies Providence, the other chief town. Rhode Island enters into British naval history at the time of the American War of Independence. But even before that began the men of Providence had shown their dislike of taxation and rule by Britain when in 1772 they boarded and burnt H.M.S. *Gaspée*, which had grounded while on a mission to enforce the law. After the war broke out a British force of 6000 men occupied Rhode Island and Newport without opposition in December 1776, for the Royal Navy needed the fine harbour. When the French joined the Americans as allies, a French fleet under d'Estaing was dispatched and threatened the British hold on Rhode Island. French ships trapped four British 32-gun frigates and two other small vessels within the enclosed waters, and in face of a vastly superior enemy the British ships were run aground and burnt by their captains, whilst other ships were scuttled to try to block the entrance to the harbour of Newport itself. Three days later the French fleet under d'Estaing entered Narragansett Bay intending to land reinforcements for the Americans. But Admiral Lord Howe had sailed to counter this move, and the French, not wishing to be trapped in the harbour, came out to engage the British. After much manoeuvring, with Howe trying to gain the advantage of the weather gage, a storm dispersed the two fleets and there was no battle. The French ships retired to Boston to refit, and Newport was occupied by the British until the following year, when on the withdrawal of the garrison it became a temporary base for the French fleet.

Cannon and other objects from H.M.S. *Cerberus*, one of the British frigates which was run aground and burnt, have recently been recovered from the sea-bed. One of her cannons, on loan from the State of Rhode Island, can be seen in the National Maritime Museum at Greenwich.

Rhumb-line: a line (of a ship's course) which crosses all meridians, and also parallels of latitude, at the same angle.

Ribs: the timbers of a wooden ship or frames of an iron ship which rise upwards and outwards from the keel to give the shape of the hull. At an early stage of building they suggest the appearance of ribs on a skeleton.

Rich, Sir Robert, second Earl of Warwick (1587–1658): privateer, colonizer and Lord High Admiral. After a period of court life, he obtained a commission which enabled him to rove as a privateer in the East Indies. A later licence led him to harry the Spanish fleet, but he missed his greatest intended prize, the treasure galleons from Brazil. He played an important part in various colonizing schemes and companies, involving Bermuda, Massachusetts, Connecticut, New Plymouth and Rhode

Island. Against the King's wishes, he was appointed Admiral in 1642, becoming Lord High Admiral in 1643 and again in 1648. Although a loyal Parliamentarian and close friend of Cromwell, he openly opposed the execution of Charles I. *See also* RUPERT, PRINCE.

Ride: in its general nautical sense 'to ride' means to sustain a position, thus a ship rides to an anchor, or rides to the wind and tide; a ship rides out a storm in various ways to avoid being overcome by it. A rope is said to ride when in hauling it wrongly passes over another part of the same rope.

Riding hawse full: at anchor in a roughish sea and pitching bows under, so that water is slopping through the hawse-holes.

Riding light: a light required to be shown when a vessel is riding at anchor. Vessels less than 45 metres (150 ft) in length carry a single white riding light visible all round; larger ships carry an additional white all-round near the stern, but lower than the forward light.

Rig: (1) the way in which a sailing vessel's masts, spars and sails are fitted and arranged. It can refer to the type of ship, e.g. 'schooner rig', 'barque rig' etc., but the first general distinction is between square rig and fore-and-aft rig. In the former four-sided sails carried on YARDS lie square to the mast, whilst in fore-and-aft rig the sail's leading edge or luff is secured close to the mast or to a stay, the sail lies and is trimmed abaft the mast and is either triangular or four-sided. Over the centuries a very great number of different rigs, square, fore-and-aft, and combinations of the two, have been evolved. Each was adapted for a particular purpose, and to meet the conditions on the seas they sailed, but often a new rig was introduced to increase speed.

The history of square rig goes back to earliest times. Egyptians and Romans used boats with a square sail on a single mast; so did the Norsemen in their long ships and later the sailors of the Middle Ages in their round ships. As ships increased in size and additional masts were stepped, square rig was to be seen on the caravels, carracks, galleons and sailing galleys, and likewise on the bigger warships of the 17th and 18th centuries. By the end of the 19th century the acme of square-rig perfection was reached in what is known as the full-rigged ship with square sails on three or more masts. Many of the famous clippers, such as the *Cutty Sark*, which achieved such high speeds, were of this kind. These ships also carried a number of fore-and-aft sails; but they were square-rigged ships, because this was the nature of their main driving sails.

Fore-and-aft rig is not so old as square rig, though the lateen sail – a compromise

Square rig – a brig   Fore-and-aft rig – a schooner

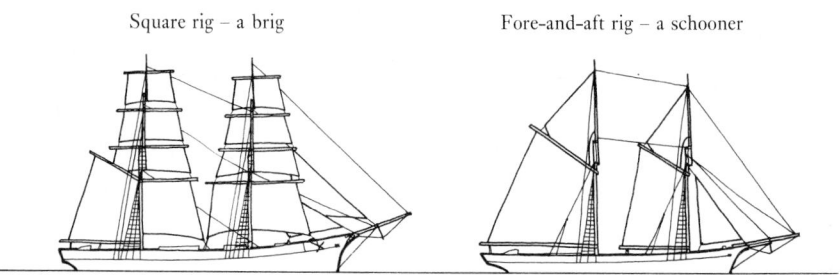

between the two – is of ancient origin. Over the centuries there evolved a very great number of different fore-and-aft rigs, many of them carrying both square and fore-and-aft sails in different combinations. Thus the barque was a three-masted vessel, square-rigged on the fore and main masts, and fore-and-aft rigged on the mizen mast, while a barquentine was square-rigged on one mast but fore-and-aft rigged on the other two. Many of the smaller sailing ships, both fighting and trading vessels such as the sloop, lugger and ketch, were fore-and-aft rigged. Today a great variety of different fore-and-aft rigs may be seen in the sailing yachts used for cruising and racing.

(2) By derivation from the above meaning, 'rig' is used for the uniform or dress worn by officers and men, e.g. 'rig of the day', meaning the dress to be worn for the day's duties. Colloquially the jacket and peaked cap of the officer and petty officer are often referred to as 'fore-and-aft rig', in contrast to 'square rig', the seaman's jumper, collar and round peakless cap.

(3) To rig a vessel is to fit her with masts, spars, sails, and running and standing RIGGING. The verb is also used for setting up a device or contrivance, e.g. to rig a life-line, a tackle etc.

Rigging: the entire system of ropes, wires and chains used to maintain a ship's masts, yards and other spars in position, including ropes and wires required for managing a ship's sails and other gear such as derricks and davits. According to its nature and duty a ship's rigging is of two general kinds, standing rigging and running rigging, the former being permanent in position and the latter being used for movement and control of sails or other gear.

Over the centuries the evolution of the sailing ship, from a single mast and sail to the full-rigged ship, such as the *Cutty Sark*, in the late 19th century, saw the growth of great complexity in rigging. Yet each part of the rigging serves a necessary and specific purpose and each part has its special name. There are two main tasks: first, to support the masts, yards and spars against the tremendous strains they are under when carrying sail, and secondly to hoist and lower sail and adjust the position of any moving spars. Standing rigging does the first job. The masts are supported athwartships by shrouds which are crossed and joined horizontally by ratlines; fore and aft the masts are supported by stays running from the various parts of the mast. Each is named after the mast and the part of the mast supported, e.g. 'main shrouds', 'main top-mast stay'.

Running rigging consists of the ropes which are moved in working ship, making sail and hoisting or striking (lowering) yards or spars. The sails are hoist by halyards and the yards by jeers. Buntlines are used for reefing or furling sail; bowlines and sheets trim the sails, and braces trim the yards to adjust the angle of the sail to the wind. These are but a few of the many elements of standing and running rigging, which have a common principle and purpose in all sailing ships, but which have differences from ship to ship and between use for square sails and fore-and-aft sails.

The art of rigging reached a very high level in the great days of the sailing ship, but though many of the intricacies and technical names may have disappeared, it is the experience of the past that is drawn upon for the rigging of modern sailing yachts and for much of the rigging that remains necessary, though reduced, in many modern engine-driven ships.

See pp. 424–5.

Standing rigging – Full-rigged ship

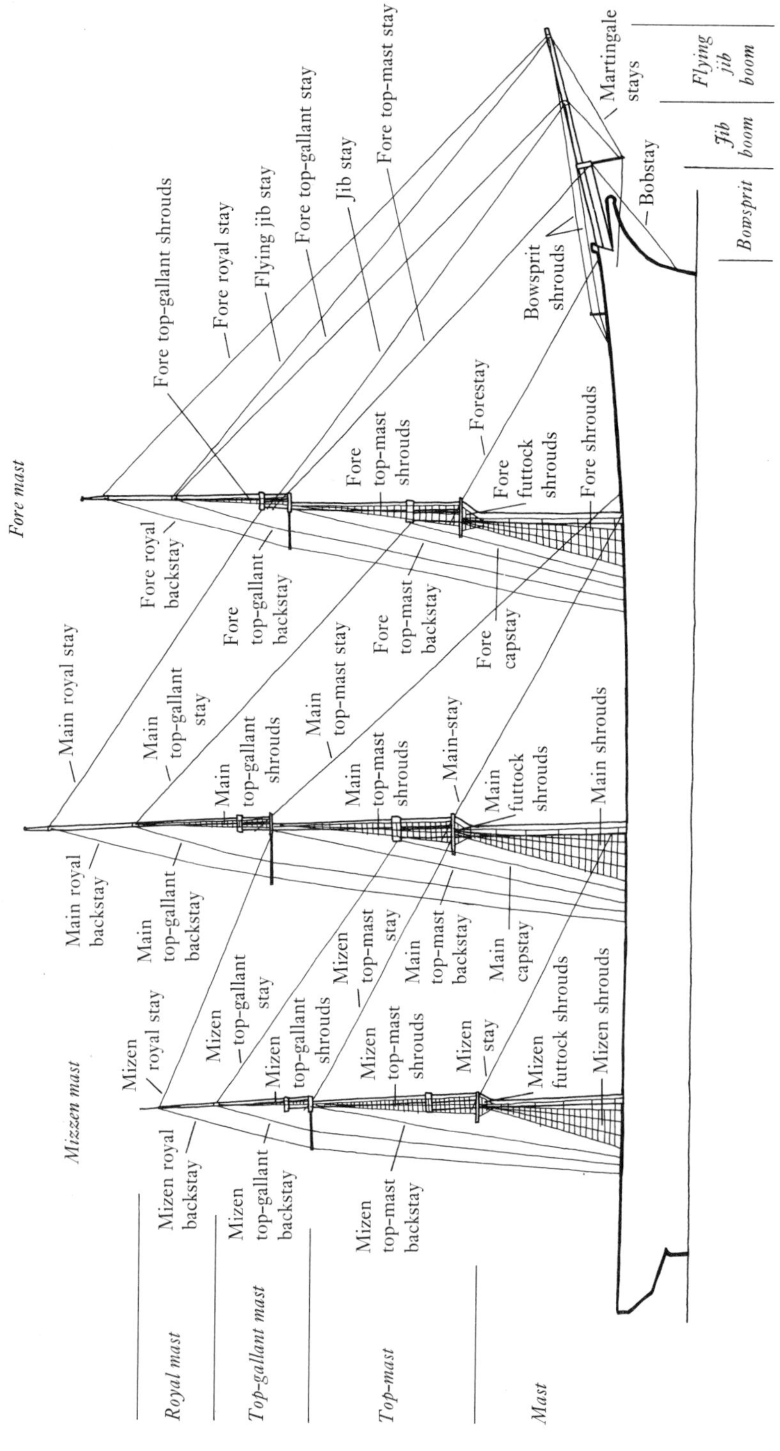

Fore mast

Main mast

Mizzen mast

Martingale stays

Flying jib boom

Jib boom

Bowsprit

Bobstay

Fore top-mast stay

Jib stay

Fore top-gallant stay

Flying jib stay

Fore royal stay

Fore top-gallant shrouds

Bowsprit shrouds

Forestay

Fore top-mast shrouds

Fore futtock shrouds

Fore shrouds

Fore capstay

Fore top-mast backstay

Fore top-gallant backstay

Fore royal backstay

Main royal stay

Main top-gallant stay

Main top-mast stay

Main top-gallant shrouds

Main top-mast shrouds

Main futtock shrouds

Main-stay

Main shrouds

Main capstay

Main top-mast backstay

Main top-gallant backstay

Main royal backstay

Mizen royal stay

Mizen top-gallant stay

Mizen top-gallant shrouds

Mizen top-mast stay

Mizen top-mast shrouds

Mizen futtock shrouds

Mizen stay

Mizen shrouds

Mizen top-mast backstay

Mizen top-gallant backstay

Mizen royal backstay

Royal mast

Top-gallant mast

Top-mast

Mast

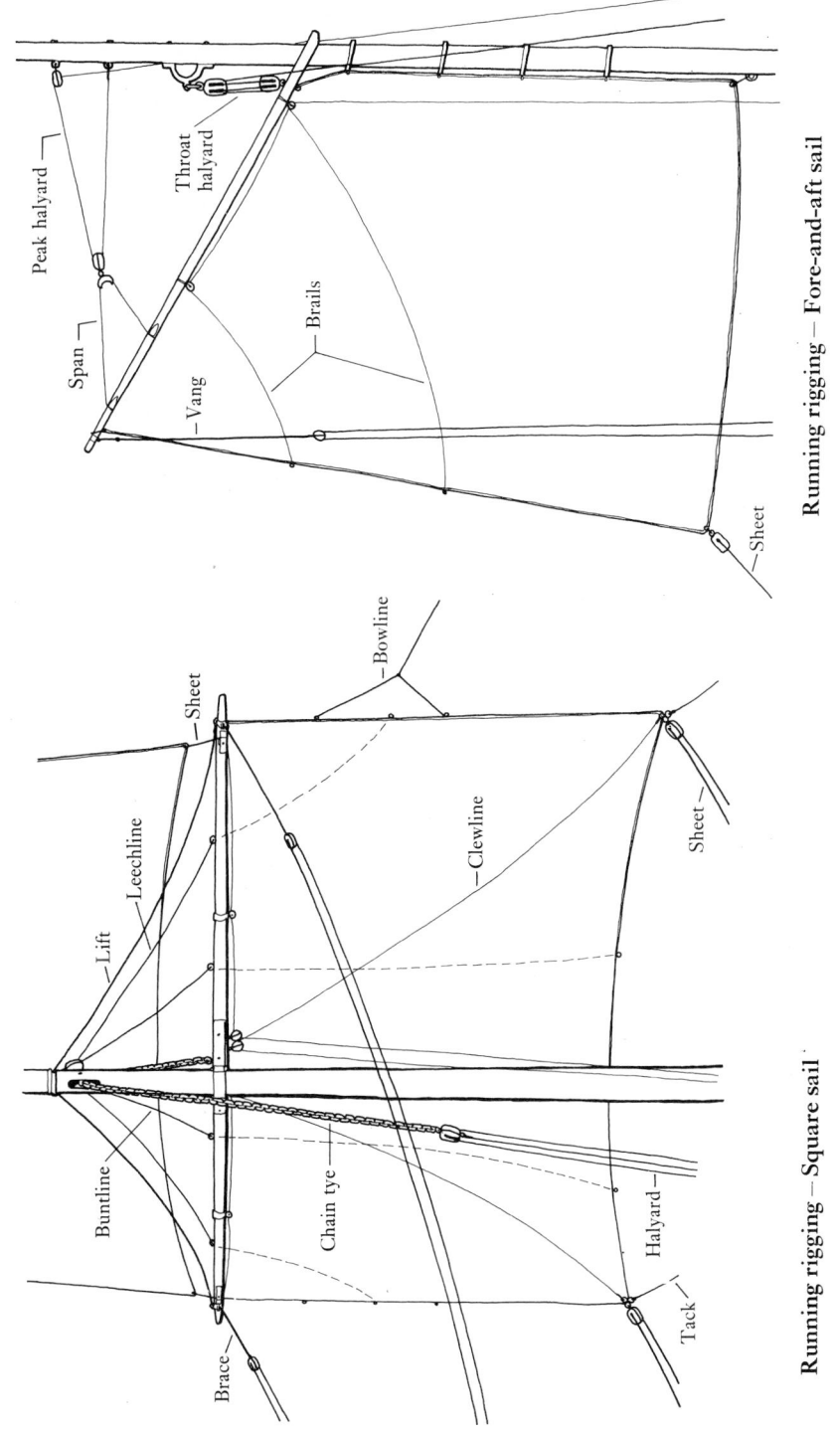

Running rigging — Fore-and-aft sail

Peak halyard

Throat halyard

Span

Brails

Vang

Sheet

Running rigging — Square sail

Sheet

Bowline

Leechline

Lift

Clewline

Sheet

Buntline

Chain tye

Halyard

Brace

Tack

425

Right of search: claim made by warring nations at various times to search neutral vessels suspected of carrying war supplies etc. Thus, in the Napoleonic Wars much of Britain's sea supremacy depended on her right to search the ships of Norway, Sweden and Denmark and to confiscate maritime supplies such as sailcloth, rope and timber.

Right of way: the right of a vessel to maintain her course and speed on the approach of another. The conditions under which a vessel has right of way are laid down in the International Regulations for Preventing Collisions at Sea (*see* RULE OF THE ROAD). The vessel with the right of way is known as the privileged vessel; the other is known as the give-way or burdened vessel. But even when a ship has right of way, she must take avoiding action if a collision seems imminent.

Riley, Mary Ann: *see* TOWNSHEND, JANE.

Ring-bolt: a bolt with a ring at the end for securing a rope or tackle.

Ring off: indicate that the ship's main engines are no longer required by moving the lever of the engine room telegraph on the bridge rapidly to and fro. This indication is given when a ship has berthed, anchored or moored, and all is secure, but it is not an officially recognized signal.

Ringtail: an extension fitted to a fore-and-aft sail to provide a greater spread of canvas. *See also* SAIL.

Rip: *see* TIDES.

'Rising Star' (sometimes mistakenly called **'Rising Sun'**): ship built at Rotherhithe by Lord COCHRANE, later

tenth Earl of Dundonald, when he was engaged by the Chilean government to command (and virtually create) the Chilean Navy. Though Cochrane intended the vessel to give additional weight to Chile against Spain, a series of delays resulted in her not arriving in time to join in the war. Begun in 1820, she reached Valparaiso in April 1822. Of curious design, she seems to have been at one time equipped with paddles and paddle-wheels, but she left England propelled by jets of water forced through apertures in the hull below water-level. At the same time, a contemporary picture shows her as fully rigged, without royals, but carrying oddly shaped square-headed staysails between her masts.

Ritchie, Sir Lewis: *see* BARTIMEUS.

River Plate, Battle of the (13 December 1939): attack on the German 'pocket battleship' *Graf Spee* by the cruisers *Ajax*, *Achilles* (Royal New Zealand Division) and *EXETER*, under Commodore Henry Harwood, commanding 'Force G'. The attack took place off the mouth of the River Plate (or Río de la Plata), the estuary of the

Ringtail.

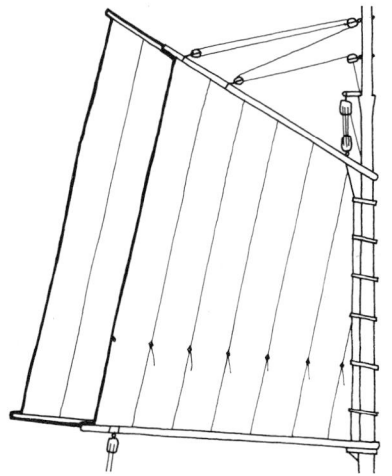

426

Rivers Paraná and Uruguay, between Uruguay and Argentina. After inflicting heavy damage, the German commander, Langsdorff, made for Montevideo; for the subsequent events, *see GRAF SPEE.*

R.M.: *see Royal* MARINES.

R.N.: Royal Navy.

R.N.R.: Royal Naval Reserve. *See* RESERVES.

R.N.V.R.: Royal Naval Volunteer Reserve. *See* RESERVES.

Roach: the curvature of the foot of a square sail, designed to keep the sail clear of the stays etc.

Roadstead: a stretch of water, generally outside a harbour but providing an area where ships may ride in safety. Spithead is an example of a roadstead.

Roaring Forties: those areas of the ocean which lie between latitudes 40° and 50° S., where the north-westerly winds blow regularly with considerable force. Between these latitudes, except for the southern-most parts of South America and New Zealand there are no land masses to break the force of the winds. The Roaring Forties were often sought by sailing ships, in spite of not infrequent gales, in order to make a fast passage between Africa and Australia and New Zealand.

Roberts, Bartholomew (?1682–1722): seaman who was captured by pirates in 1718, joined their company and became a formidable pirate leader. He was killed four years later in action with a man-o'-war off Cape Lopez.

Roberts, Richard Francis (*fl. c.*1805): an inconspicuous midshipman on *Victory* at Trafalgar who left the service the following year, but made some interesting notes on the battle. He recorded, e.g., that '*Victory* tellegraphed [sic] to the *Africa* to paint the hoops of her mast yellow.' The same signal was also made to the British *Belleisle*, since Nelson knew that the French ships usually had their mast-hoops painted black, and he wished to have no identification problems when firing began.

A human touch is added in Roberts's *Remark Book* when all preparations for battle were complete: 'At 11 – Dinner and grog.'

'Robertson's Golly': for obvious reasons, seamen greatly outnumber seawomen in this book, though women were frequently present, with official knowledge, in men-o'-war and sometimes fought a gun with the best of them. Wives often accompanied their skipper husbands on clippers and other merchantmen, not always to the pleasure of the crew. A popular song once recorded the popularity of a certain Captain Mack with the ladies from 'Frisco to Perim', who suddenly ceased their pursuit when he married and Mrs Captain

Crossing the line, Newport, Rhode Island, 1976.

Mack became Mistress of the Seas. A special cap must be raised to Clare Francis, standing 5 ft 2 in. and weighing $7\frac{1}{2}$ stone, who, in 1976, took her 38 ft sloop *Robertson's Golly* single-handed on the 3000-mile run from Plymouth to Newport, Rhode Island, in the Singlehanded Transatlantic Race of that year. In a fleet of more than 120 vessels, she survived gales, fogs, near-collisions with ships and icebergs, gear failure, sickness and depression, but battled on to finish in 29 days.

Robinet: an early type of small gun, firing a ball of between a half and one pound. It was in use during the 15th and 16th centuries and was aimed as a man-killer, not as a ship-destroyer.

Robinson, William ('Jack Nasty-face'; *fl.*1800–1810): seaman who fought at Trafalgar and in 1836 published an account of lower-deck life and conditions in the Navy called *Nautical Economy, or Forecastle Recollections of Events during the last War, dedicated to the Brave Tars of Old England, by a Sailor politely called by the Officers of the Navy, Jack Nasty-face*. Robinson volunteered as a landsman and eventually deserted in 1811. His book has nothing good to say about the officers under whom he served (except Nelson) and gives a fearsome picture of some aspects of ship's life; yet paradoxically, and despite his desertion, he is able to write:

... there is no profession that can vie with it; and a British seaman has a right to be proud, for he is incomparable alongside those of any other nation.

The name 'Jack Nastyface' is occasionally now used for someone with a constant grievance.

'Robinson Crusoe': a famous novel by Daniel Defoe (?1660–1731); the first great sea story. Its full title is *The Life and Strange Surprizing Adventures of Robinson Crusoe, of York. Mariner: Who lived Eight and Twenty Years, all alone in an uninhabited Island on the Coast of America, near the Mouth of the Great River of Oroonoque; Having been cast on Shore by Shipwreck, wherein all the Men perished but himself. With An Account how he was at last strangely deliver'd by Pyrates. Written by Himself.* The book was first published in 1719 and was immediately successful, being followed by two sequels written by Defoe and then, over the years, by a seemingly endless succession of tales on the same theme of a castaway upon an island. The real-life story of Alexander SELKIRK was evidently the basis of Crusoe's adventures on his island, but Defoe changed many of the details and interpreted it freely. It is not known whether he ever met Selkirk; probably it was the written accounts of his story that inspired Defoe's creation of Robinson Crusoe, one of the characters of fiction whose name has become universally known.

'Rob Roy of the West': *see* RATTENBURY, JACK.

Rochefort: town and port on the west coast of France. During the long struggle with France in the 18th century, Rochefort was an important French naval base and arsenal and was one of the ports blockaded by English cruisers. In 1757, during the Seven Years' War, when the French threatened an invasion of England, an expedition was dispatched to capture Rochefort, but it was a complete failure: Nothing was achieved except for the initial capture of the fortified island of Aix at the mouth of the River Charente on which Rochefort lay. It was at Rochefort that

Napoleon on 15 July 1815 surrendered to the commander of H.M.S. *Bellerophon* after his defeat at Waterloo and abdication.

Rock, the: colloquial name for GIBRALTAR.

> We passed Europa Point with a fair wind, and at sunset we were sixty miles from the Rock, yet it was distinctly to be seen, like a blue cloud, but the outline perfectly correct.
>
> Captain Marryat, *Peter Simple* (1843)

Rocket: basically a firework projected into the air by the thrust to the rear given by the combustion of explosive material. The rocket has long been known, but it is uncertain where it originated, perhaps in China. It was certainly used by the Moors in their attacks on the Iberian Peninsula in the 13th century, and as an offensive weapon was thereafter sporadically used in war. At the end of the 18th century, Tipu Sahib in India had a corps of rocket gunners, and at Seringapatam in 1792 Europeans were surprised by their range of a mile to a mile and a half. It was perhaps this which led to the military rocket, produced by Sir William Congreve (1772–1828), which was used with considerable effect when fired from ships in an attack against the French at Boulogne in 1806, and against the Danes at the siege of Copenhagen in the following year. Rockets were also used by Admiral Sir Edward Pellew during the bombardment of Algiers (1816). But with the great improvement of guns during the latter half of the 19th century, the rocket was little further developed as a weapon until the Second World War. It had, however, been adapted for carrying a line to a ship in distress, by means of which a breeches buoy could be rigged and run from shore to ship, or from ship to ship. In addition rockets were, and still are, used for signals of various kinds, particularly distress signals. Thus a boat in distress off-shore might fire red parachute rockets which, when observed by the life-saving station ashore, would be answered by three white star rockets at one-minute intervals.

The Second World War saw a great development of the rocket as an offensive weapon; first, by the use of more powerful explosives, which led to a whole range of new rocket-propelled weapons, and, second, by the use of liquid and gas explosive propellants, which aided the development by the Germans of the V.1 and V.2 flying bombs. Both were rocket-driven in principle. The first, known as the

A rocket ship firing a salvo.

'buzz bomb', was a rocket-propelled aeroplane with a range of about 150 miles, and the second was a huge rocket-driven projectile with a range of about 200 miles. Since the war we have seen further advance in rocket weaponry, of which the most awesome is the intercontinental ballistic missile (*see* POLARIS), fired from submarines as well as from shore, and the enormous rockets built to put satellites into space and to land men on the moon.

Rodney, George Brydges, first Baron Rodney (1718–92): admiral, chiefly remembered for his victories at the MOONLIT BATTLE, MARTINIQUE and the Battle of the SAINTS, for which services he was raised to the peerage (1782). In the course of his career he was also governor of Newfoundland, governor of Greenwich Hospital, and a Member of Parliament.

His person was more elegant than seemed to become his rough profession. There was even something that approached to delicacy and effeminacy in his figure; but no man manifested a more temperate and steady courage in action. I . . . have often heard him declare that superiority to fear was not in him the physical effect of constitution; on the contrary, no man being more sensible by nature to that passion than himself; but that he surmounted it from the considerations of honour and public duty . . . He . . . dealt his censures, as well as his praises, with imprudent liberality; qualities which procured him many enemies, particularly in his own profession.

Sir Nathaniel William Wraxall, *Historical Memoirs of My Own Life* (1815)

'Rodney': Royal Navy battleship built (1927), according to the agreements reached at the Washington Conference of 1922. Her displacement was 33,950 tons (38,000 fully loaded), the heavy guns consisted of nine 16-in. in three triple turrets on the fore-deck, and her armour was 14-in. thick. *See also* QUEEN ANNE'S MANSIONS.

'Roebuck': Royal Navy ship supplied by the Admiralty to ex-buccaneer William DAMPIER in 1699 for a voyage of discovery in and around Australia. In the *Roebuck* Dampier became the first Englishman to visit Australia and, in the words of Professor Christopher Lloyd, 'he might have anticipated Cook's discovery of the more attractive part of that continent had it not been for a rotten ship and a mutinous crew, who resented having an ex-buccaneer as their captain.'

Rogers, Woodes (*d.*1732): privateer captain whose chief claim to fame is that he rescued Alexander SELKIRK, the original of Robinson Crusoe. This was in the course of a privateering expedition that took Rogers

H.M.S. *Rodney* after refit, in camouflage paint.

round the world (1708–11). In 1712 he published *A Cruising Voyage Round the World*, which included a description of the rescue and gave Selkirk's own account of his life on the island. Woodes Rogers was later captain-general and governor-in-chief of the Bahama Islands. *See also* DAMPIER, WILLIAM.

Rogue's yarn: a coloured yarn laid up in and running through one or more strands of rope to identify it. At one time there was much purloining and stealing of rope from naval stores because of its good quality. Rogue's yarns of different colours were then introduced to identify the ropeyard from which the rope originated. In modern cordage different colours of rogue's yarn are used to identify several kinds of rope.

Roller: a long heavy wave, which may originate from a distant storm. The roller will increase in height as it reaches shallow water and break as a wave.

Rolling: the motion of a ship about its horizontal fore-and-aft axis, one of the six 'freedoms of motion'; more simply tilting from side to side.

Rolling hitch: *see* KNOTS.

Roman ship: part of a third-century A.D. Roman vessel was discovered on the south bank of the Thames in 1910, when the London County Council offices were being built. The ship was carvel-built, with numerous ribs, probably with a length of 40–50 ft, a beam of 14 ft and a depth of 7 ft. It was perhaps a type of barge used for carrying cargo and passengers, and was not in any sense a war-vessel.

Rooke, Sir George (1650–1709): admiral whose career, though not of unbroken success, included the capture of Gibraltar (23–4 July 1704). He is described as 'a careful, conservative fighter', though he could on occasion act with daring, as at La Hogue (1692; *see* BARFLEUR AND LA HOGUE). He was involved in politics too much for his own good and this brought about his eventual loss of command and lack of employment in the last years of his life. *See also* FIGHTING INSTRUCTIONS; MALAGA, BATTLE OF.

Room: *see* RUM (2).

Roos: *see* ROS.

Rope: a strong intertwining of fibres or wires in flexible lengths an inch or more in diameter. Rope is made of vegetable fibres, man-made fibres or steel wire. The various vegetable fibres used are hemp, manila, sisal, coir and occasionally cotton. Each had its particular characteristics and special uses, though today on board ship ropes of man-made fibre or steel wire are often found where vegetable-fibre ropes were formerly used. Hemp is employed for hawsers and running rigging, for it is very flexible and at its best can also be very strong. Manila rope is also strong and will take great strain in lowering and lifting, as in a boat's falls or heavy tackles. Sisal has a hairy appearance and is not so strong and reliable as manila and hemp, while coir rope is even less strong, though it has the advantage of floating on water.

Of the various kinds of man-made or synthetic fibres the strongest is nylon. The great advantage of synthetic-fibre rope is that it does not get water-logged and rot as do the vegetable fibres; it has come much into favour in recent years as it has been improved in quality.

WIRE ROPE is made of a varying number of small steel wires in strands which are

431

then laid up into rope. The heart of steel-wire rope will generally have a thin fibre core inserted to give the strands something to bind on when they are laid up. Steel-wire rope is of various kinds offering either flexibility or strength, or a combination of both. It can be very dangerous if a steel-wire rope snaps under strain, for it will whip back with tremendous force and cause great injury to anyone in its way.

Ropewalk (or **ropehouse**): a long shed or kind of alley for spinning rope-yarn into strands and making them up into rope. There were once ropewalks in all the dockyards; the one at Chatham may still be seen. A hand-worked spinning machine twisted the fibre into strands by means of rotating hooks, and then by an additional device the strands were laid up into lengths of rope, with the rope-maker moving down the ropewalk hauling on the rope to give an even lay. Today the making of rope is entirely mechanized. *See also* KING'S YARN.

Ros (or **Roos**), **John de** (*d*.1338): one of the earliest recorded admirals in English history. Son of William de Ros (at one time a claimant to the crown of Scotland), he was a joint admiral of fleets in the Thames and northwards.

Ross, Sir John (1777–1856): admiral. Entering the service of the East India Company in 1794, he transferred to the Royal Navy and soon made his reputation as surveyor and navigator in the Arctic regions, going in search of the North-West Passage in 1818 and 1829–33, when valuable survey work was completed in the Boothia Peninsula and Gulf, and in King William Land. He also went on a private expedition in search of Sir John Franklin (1850). He published accounts of his various voyages and on other nautical subjects, and was honoured by a number of learned societies for his contributions to geography.

Rosyth: town and port in Fife, on the north shore of the Firth of Forth. It was in 1909 that a naval base was begun at Rosyth, and though it was not until 1916 that the first warship was dry-docked there, the port played a considerable part in both World Wars The capital ships of the British Grand Fleet returned to Rosyth after the Battle of Jutland (1916), and after the German fleet had surrendered in 1918 and been scuttled at Scapa Flow, many of the raised hulks were brought to Rosyth for breaking up. Between the wars the naval base was closed down, but it was reopened in 1938 and saw a great expansion between 1939 and 1945. In 1963 Rosyth became a base for nuclear-powered submarines.

Rotherham, Edward (?1753–1830): naval captain. He was Flag-Captain to Collingwood on the *Royal Sovereign* at Trafalgar, after which he received the gold medal and a sword from the Patriotic Fund. Apart from his distinguished naval career, he is remembered for his reply when it was suggested his costume made him a conspicuous target for the enemy.

Captain Rotherham had on his gold-laced hat (rather a remarkable one) and gold epaulets. He was asked why he exposed himself so much to the enemy's sharp-shooters in that conspicuous dress. With the same spirit that animated the bosom of his heroic chief, he replied:
'I have always fought in a cocked hat, and I always will.'

Archibald Duncan, *The Life of the Right Honourable Horatio Lord Viscount Nelson* (1806)

Rotherhithe: a part of London's dockland

on the south bank of the Thames and largely occupied by the great complex of docks known as the Surrey Commercial Docks. The Thames sweeps round Rotherhithe in a great bend from the Pool of London southwards into Limehouse Reach, from which lies the entrance to Greenland Dock, the oldest wet dock in London (built 1700). Other docks are named Norway, Russia, Baltic and Quebec, all recalling the great trade, especially in timber, of which Rotherhithe was the centre. It was to Rotherhithe that H.M.S. *TEMERAIRE* was towed for breaking up (1838), and some of her timber was used for chairs in the sanctuary (and perhaps also for the altar table and rails) in St Paul's Church, Rotherhithe, which was being built at the time. Today this once great area of dockland is a ghost of its former self, with the docks largely unused and the whole district awaiting redevelopment.

Rotor ship: an experimental type of ship developed in the 1920s by Anton Flettner, a German engineer. The principle involved was the increased propulsive power of the wind when meeting a rotor revolving at three or four times the speed of that wind. A ship was converted to test the idea; she had two tall vertical, funnel-like cylinders on the upper deck which were rotated by small petrol engines, and to which the wind gave additional power greater than that provided by an equal area of sail. The experimental ship successfully crossed the Atlantic, survived several gales, achieved a satisfactory speed, and was said to be cheaper to run than a comparable sailing ship because so few men were needed to man her. A few other rotor ships were built, but the disadvantages of the vibration of the rotors and reliance on the wind outweighed any advantages, and the idea of the rotor ship was dropped.

Roundhouse: originally the quarters occupied by the captain in merchant ships, especially East Indiamen, in the 18th and 19th centuries. The roundhouse was abaft the quarter-deck and below the poop deck, and was so named, not because of its shape, but because one could walk round it. The name was later applied to other deck accommodation in sailing merchant ships and to the heads (latrines) in naval ships.

Round jacket: short jacket, now worn usually by stewards but formerly by midshipmen.

Rounds: a formal and routine round of inspection, e.g. 'captain's rounds', when the commanding officer, attended by others, tours the ship to see that all is clean and in good order.

The *Barbara*, a poor photograph of one of the few ships fitted with Flettner rotors.

Round ship: a general name for the type of vessel built in England in the Middle Ages, so called because of their cumbersome lines. Though they were capacious they were so unmanageable that they could not sail into the wind, but must wait for a following breeze before they could lumber on with their cargoes. A model (now in the Science Museum, London) of a typical English ship of *c.*1426 shows her length on the deck about 60 ft and her breadth about 22 ft – i.e. she was less than three times as long as she was wide. This can be compared with, e.g., the clipper *Cutty Sark*, nearly six times as long as she is wide.

Round stern: *see* ELLIPTICAL STERN; SQUARE STERN.

Round turn and two half-hitches: *see* KNOTS.

Rous, Henry John (1795–1877): admiral. Having reached the rank of post-captain, he retired from active service in 1835 to devote himself to horse-racing and use his naval telescope to watch the races, becoming a steward of the Jockey Club and public handicapper. In view of this, it must remain one of the mysteries of naval administration that he managed to become a Lord of the Admiralty in 1846, Admiral of the Blue in 1863, and of the White in 1864.

Rouse and shine: the traditional call for waking the hands and getting them out of their hammocks in the morning; sometimes corrupted to 'Rise and shine'. *See also* SHOW A LEG.

Rowing: *see* OAR.

Rowlock (pronounced 'rollock'): an opening or a pair of pins in the gunwale of a rowing boat which provide the pivot or fulcrum for the oar. The word is also commonly used for the metal U-shaped crutch in which the oar of a small rowing boat is placed.

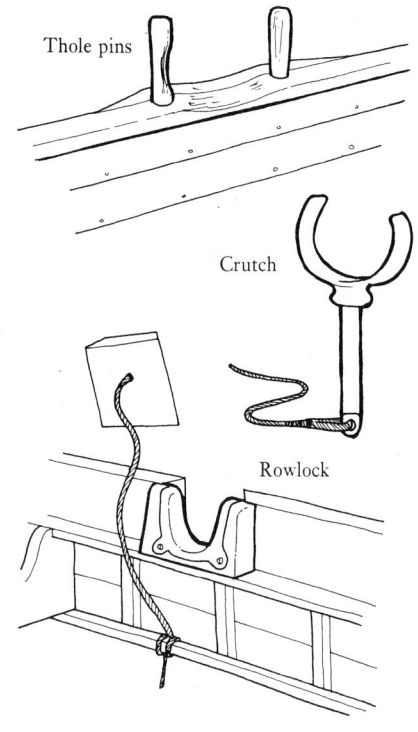

Thole pins

Crutch

Rowlock

Royal (mast or sail): *see* ROYALS.

Royal African Company: company (preceded by the Royal Adventurers to Africa) chartered by Charles II in 1672. Its main business was the supply of slaves to the sugar plantations of America.

Royal dockyards: dockyards developed and used by the Royal Navy. In 1496 Henry VII built the first royal dock at Portsmouth. It was further developed by Henry VIII, who made royal dockyards also at Deptford and Woolwich. Chatham and Plymouth came to the fore as royal dockyards in Elizabeth I's reign. Deptford and Woolwich were closed, but Sheerness, guarding the mouth of the Medway, was developed to add to the facilities at Chatham. In 1903 Rosyth, on the Firth of Forth, became another royal dockyard, whilst overseas the British Empire and the Royal Navy's world-wide commitment required the development of royal dock-yards at numerous key points on the sea routes, such as Gibraltar, Malta, Trinco-malee, Singapore, Hong Kong, Simons-town and Halifax. As the navies of the Commonwealth developed, and as coun-tries such as Malta and South Africa became independent, these former royal dockyards passed into other hands; Gibraltar is the only remaining royal dockyard outside the British Isles.

Royal Fleet Auxiliary Service: a service composed of men and ships giving vital logistic support to the Royal Navy. The ships include many different types such as large fleet tankers and smaller support tankers, trials and weapons research ships, water-carriers, tugs, tenders, mooring, salvage and boom vessels. In addition to carrying oil, stores, spare parts and cargo to supply ships of the Royal Navy at sea, some are designed to carry troops for combined operations. The Royal Fleet Auxiliary Service is manned by officers and men of the Merchant Navy, but some of its ships carry civilian research teams, and some are equipped with helicopters which are operated by officers and men of the Royal Navy.

'Royal George': with six British mon-archs and a fair sprinkling of princes bearing the name George, it was inevitable that a loyal company of ships should also carry it through the centuries. Their most famous representative is the 100-gun ship launched at Woolwich in 1756, 178 ft long on the main gun-deck and nearly 52 ft broad. She carried the tallest masts of any

ship then built in an English yard, her main mast soaring 114 ft 3 in. Her figurehead was composed of two white horses rearing on either side the bowsprit, with the 'G.R.' monogram on their flanks and bearing between them the royal arms. She carried Hawke's flag at the Battle of Quiberon Bay (1759), and thirteen years later, a victim of Admiralty neglect, she capsized and sank whilst under repair at Spithead, with the loss of Admiral KEMPENFELT and some 900 men, women and children, many of whom were visitors on board. *See also* COWPER, WILLIAM.

Over the years many guns and other relics have been recovered from the anchorage (*see* DURHAM, SIR PHILIP), but the injudicious use of explosives has left what a modern diver has described as 'no longer a ship, but rather a compost heap of mud, clay, shingle.' A more enduring memorial may be found in Trafalgar Square; *see* NELSON COLUMN.

Royal Marines: *see* MARINES.

Royal National Lifeboat Institution: institution founded on 4 March 1834 with the title 'The Royal National Life-Boat Institution for the Preservation of Life from Shipwreck'. The inaugural meeting was presided over by the Archbishop of Canterbury; George IV became a patron, and there was generous support from all over the country. In its first year nearly £10,000 was collected from subscribers, and the committee was able to announce in its first report that twelve lifeboats had been built for various stations on the coast and 39 more had been supplied by other societies and benefactors. *See also* LIFE-BOAT.

Unlike most other lifeboat services throughout the world, that in the British Isles is still entirely supported by voluntary

435

contributions, though there have been suggestions that it be brought under government control and given official financial support. Most people would applaud that such recommendations have so far come to nothing. Indeed, in an unusual burst of governmental modesty, the President of the Board of Trade declared in 1893:

No Government Department could ever do the work as well as the Royal National Life-Boat Institution. No Government Department would ever maintain that alacrity and alertness which the Governors of this Institute have always exhibited; and no Government Department could ever evoke that generous sympathy with heroism which has characterised the work of the Institution.

In 1897 a Select Committee of the House of Commons came to a similar conclusion, with the words:

There are many advantages in committing the control of this Service, as now, to a voluntary association of honourable men

Henry Freeman, cox of the Whitby lifeboat, photographed by Henry Sutcliffe.

. . . relying for funds on the beneficence of the people of these kingdoms, and for crews to man the boats on the unfailing courage and devotion of the maritime population.

Royal Naval Air Service: the original name of the Fleet Air Arm, dating from 1912 and lasting until 1918. The Royal Naval Air Service began when the naval wing of the Royal Flying Corps broke away to be independently operated by the Royal Navy, but in 1918 the Army's Royal Flying Corps and the Navy's Royal Air Service were merged to form the Royal Air Force, which thereafter controlled naval flying. Discontent with the state of affairs led to the formation (1924) of the Fleet Air Arm, which at first was under the aegis of the R.A.F., but became completely independent under the control of the Admiralty in 1937.

Royal Naval College, Dartmouth: the college on the Rivert Dart in south Devon where the general training for officers entering the Royal Navy is begun. Its official name is the Britannia Royal Naval College after H.M.S. *Britannia*, the ship which, in 1859, succeeded H.M.S. *Illustrious* as a training ship for naval cadets at Portsmouth. After a short time *Britannia* was transferred to Portland and then in 1864 moved to moorings at Dartmouth. In the early 1900s the R.N.C., Dartmouth, was built ashore and became the training centre for officer cadets. The old *Britannia* was broken up in 1916.

Royal Naval College, Greenwich: housed in the splendid buildings formerly used for the GREENWICH HOSPITAL. One of the chief glories of the buildings is the great painted hall, in which Nelson's body lay in state after Trafalgar, and nearby is the old Royal Observatory and the National Maritime Museum. The Hospital closed in 1869, and four years later the Royal Naval College, which had been established at Portsmouth for the additional scientific education of officers, was transferred to Greenwich. R.N.C., Greenwich, is today a centre for further naval education and training. Discipline and instruction are controlled by naval and academic staffs, and the whole is under the direction of an Admiral President. Over recent years numerous different advanced and war courses have been held there, many of them also attended by officers from Commonwealth and foreign navies. R.N.C., Greenwich, has been described as the university of the Navy; it is not only a centre for the advancement of professional knowledge, but at the same time a focal point of naval tradition and continuing history within the nation's capital.

Royal Naval College, Osborne: from 1903 to 1923, a naval college on the Isle of Wight, preliminary and supplementary to Dartmouth.

Royal Naval Division: *see* NAVAL BRIGADE.

Royal Naval Engineering College: *see* ENGINEER OFFICER.

Royal Naval Reserve: *see* RESERVES.

Royal Naval Volunteer Reserve: *see* RESERVES.

'Royal Oak': as might be deduced, a name deriving from Charles II's hiding-place and escape after the Battle of Worcester (3 September 1651) – a story which, it is alleged, his majesty repeated to the point of tedium. The first ship of the name suffered an inglorious end when the Dutch sailed up the MEDWAY (1667) and burnt her in home waters. Her captain, Archibald Douglas, heroically refused to retreat before de Ruyter, and perished with her. Another *Royal Oak*, a 74-gun ship, captured the *Glorieux* at the Battle of the Saints (1782). The sixth ship of the name, launched at Chatham in 1862, was a 35-gun ironclad; the 1892 version was a Royal Sovereign class battleship carrying seven torpedo tubes as well as her heavy armament. Thus Charles II's favourite story continues – without the tedium. *See also* SCAPA FLOW.

Royals: masts or sails above the topgallants; hence mizen-royal, main-royal, fore-royal. Royals on the fore and main masts are shown on a contemporary engraving of the *Sovereign of the Seas* (1637), and they are also mentioned in a document of 1640; but they did not come into general use till nearly 150 years later.

'Royal Sovereign': pride of place among all the *Royal Sovereigns* must surely go to Collingwood's ship that first broke the enemy line at Trafalgar (1805). A 100-gun ship, built (1787) in Plymouth, she was a heavy sailer and was jokingly known as the 'West Country Waggon'; but at Trafalgar, leading the lee column, she bore herself gloriously, sustaining 144 casualties, including 14 officers killed and wounded, and having her main and mizen masts shot away and her fore mast left tottering. Her general condition was such as to make her unmanageable, so that Collingwood, when he succeeded as commander-in-chief, had to shift his flag to the *Euryalus*. Her last service was in 1815–16. Then, with typical Admiralty insensitivity, she lost her name and ended up as *Captain*, a receiving ship at Plymouth, till she was broken up in 1841.

See how that noble fellow Collingwood carries his ship into action!

Nelson, on seeing the battle begin

What would Nelson give to be here!

Collingwood to Captain
ROTHERHAM, as he broke the line

Royal yachts: sailing or powered vessels used by royalty for pleasure, for racing or cruising, or for the performance of official duties. Though many kings before him had their private ships, it was Charles II who was really the first royal yachtsman; the word 'yacht' was barely known in the English language when the Dutch gave him the *MARY* in 1660 (and it was not until 1686 that the Navy List definitely classified yachts as different types of vessels). Charles II later had several other yachts, and he much enjoyed racing them, often for a wager. Nevertheless yachts were still looked upon mainly as vessels of state used for conveying princes and other important persons, and a number of royal yachts were built during the 18th century. With the coming of steam appeared the first royal yacht fitted with paddle-wheels, the *Victoria and Albert I* (launched 1843). Several other royal yachts were built during Victoria's long reign; one of the last

was the screw-driven *Victoria and Albert III* (1899). In 1893 Edward VII as Prince of Wales had a racing yacht built for him; this was the *Britannia*, a splendid cutter-rigged vessel which was also raced by George V until 1935. The name is continued by the modern royal yacht, H.M.Y. *Britannia*, designed to serve as a naval hospital ship in war-time, but in peace-time carrying the royal family on state visits. *Britannia* has a gross tonnage of 5769 and is capable of 21 knots; she has a range of 3000 miles at 15 knots, and carries a complement of 270 officers and men. In all there have been some thirty-five royal yachts since Charles II's *Mary*.

Rubber: (**1**) a metal tool used by sailmakers to rub and smooth the stitching on the joining seams of canvas; (**2**) an extra strengthening strip of wood running along the outside of the top strake of a boat; *see also* RUBBING-STRAKE.

Rubbing-strake: similar to a RUBBER (definition *2*). The rubbing-strake runs round a small boat just beneath the

Queen Victoria's yacht *Victoria and Albert III* leaving harbour. Her mizen mast is preserved at the National Maritime Museum, Greenwich.

gunwale; it is a strengthening of timber or other material to act as a protection or fender when the boat comes alongside.

Rudder: a flat vertical steering plate fitted below the water-line at the stern of a ship (though some modern ships also have a bow rudder to increase manoeuvrability). Before the 13th century ships were steered by a large oar pivoted on the quarter known as a steer board (*see* STARBOARD). When the rudder was first introduced it was moved by a tiller, a large bar of wood fitted to the head of the rudder. Small boats still have a tiller, but as ships grew in size the tiller became difficult to manage, and towards the end of the 17th century the steering wheel was introduced. Today, in ships of any size the movement of the rudder by the steering wheel is engine-assisted. As the rudder swings through its arc to one side or the other, the pressure of the water on its face swings the head of the ship in the direction required, while the stern is thrust in the opposite direction. Thus if a tiller is moved to starboard the rudder face will move to port, which will swing the bows to port and the stern to starboard. A steering wheel, however, is so contrived that a turn to starboard moves the rudder and the ship to starboard. *See p.577.*

Rule, Sir William: Surveyor of the Navy at a vital period, 1793–1813; as such responsible for the design of many important vessels, e.g. the brig *Cruizer* (launched 1797), whose pattern was followed by over 100 other naval brigs.

'Rule, Britannia': the famous British naval song and march. Like a number of other naval songs it was composed by a patriotic landlubber – the poet James Thomson, author of *The Seasons*. It was set to music by Thomas Arne and was first played in 1740 in a masque called *Alfred*,

written in honour of the birth of Princess Augusta. It was soon taken up by the Navy and, together with *Britons Strike Home*, was often played by the marine band when ships sailed into battle. The version of the words that is now familiar differs slightly from Thomson's original:

> When Britain first at Heaven's command
> Arose from out the azure main,
> This was the charter of the land,
> And guardian angels sung the strain:
> Rule, Britannia, rule the waves!
> Britons never will be slaves.

Rule of the Road: the colloquial name for a set of rules laid down in the International Regulations for Preventing Collisions at Sea, the latest version of which came into force in 1977.

Although the rules for lights, signals etc. represent a mass of accumulated experience, even so collision at sea is still all too frequent and is often as much due to human error as to any failure of machinery or equipment. Even if a vessel appears to have RIGHT OF WAY, avoiding action must be taken if a collision seems likely. The rules are too lengthy to be given here in detail, though a few general principles can be mentioned. When ships are approaching each other the general rule is to alter course to starboard; power-driven vessels should give way to sail, but sail gives way to a vessel fishing and to a hampered or deep-draft ship; an overtaking vessel must keep clear of the overtaken, even if she is under sail and the overtaken vessel is under power. For sailing vessels meeting each other there is a set of rules based on their position in relation to the wind, e.g. when two are on the same tack the windward vessel gives way; when on opposite tacks the vessel on the port tack keeps clear. Some of the rules can be conveniently summarized and remembered by rhymes, but the officer on the bridge must be

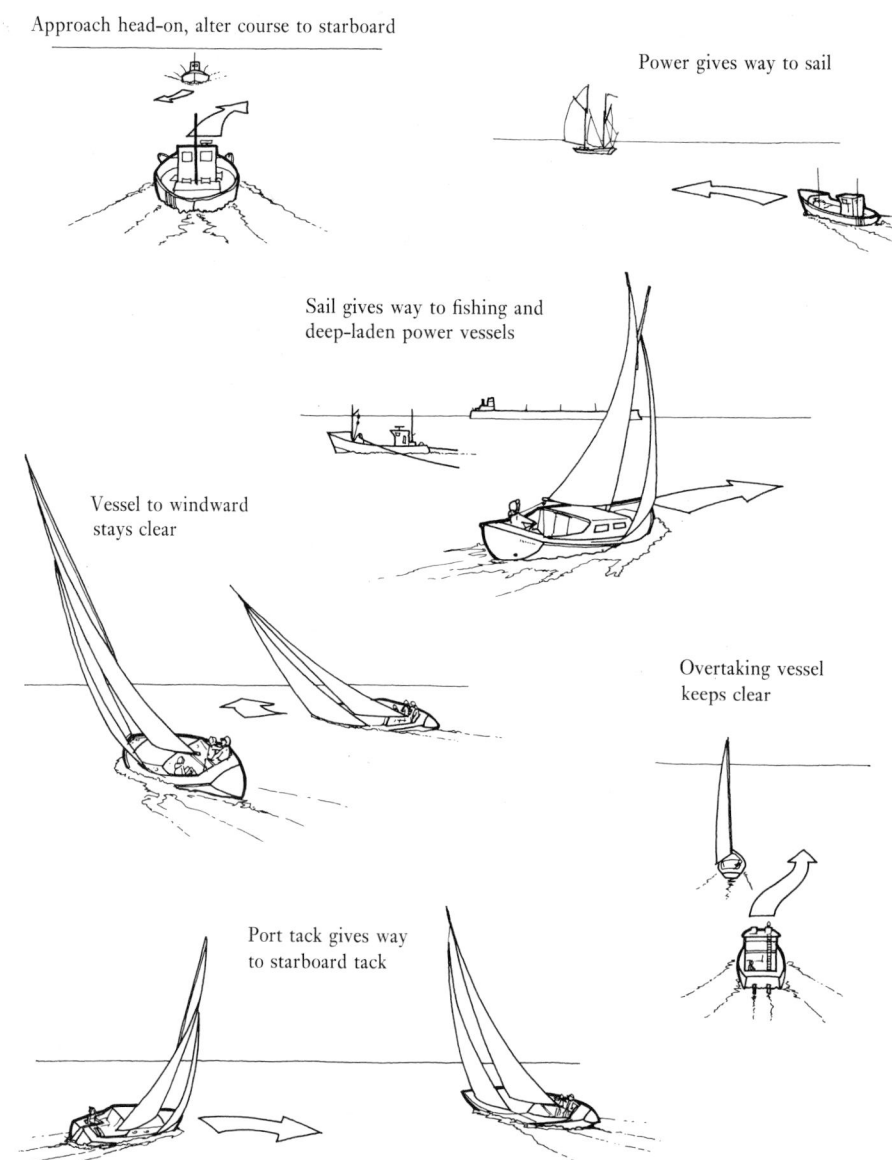

Approach head-on, alter course to starboard

Power gives way to sail

Sail gives way to fishing and
deep-laden power vessels

Vessel to windward
stays clear

Overtaking vessel
keeps clear

Port tack gives way
to starboard tack

familiar with all; navigation lights especially can tell him much about the course of
another ship, and knowledge of the
combination of lights, of shapes displayed
and of sound signals, tells him what the
other vessel is engaged in or intends to do.

Rum: (1) the traditional ration of spirit

formerly issued to the Royal Navy (more
familiarly known as GROG when diluted).
Rum first appeared in British ships after
the capture of Jamaica (1655) and
eventually became an official ration. It was
the cause of much drunkenness, since some
men hoarded their ration for special
'blinders' and the more sober traded theirs

The issue of rum at six bells: a photograph from 1898.

to the heavier drinkers (*see* HEALTH AND HYGIENE). The old ration was a half-pint daily, sometimes increased on the captain's orders at times of special stress or triumph. Admiral VERNON watered it down in 1740; but the issue of the spirit ration continued until 1970. 'Up spirits' was generally piped at 1100 hours for the formal issue of the 'tot'. Those who chose not to take their rum had a small monetary allowance instead.

(2) The 'rum' (or 'room') was the old Viking measure of a ship's size, the rum being the space between two successive frames, accommodating a pair of oars (one on each side). Thus a vessel of 30 rum pulled 60 oars (with, probably, more than one man to each oar). Olaf Trygvason's famous *Long Serpent* (A.D. 99) pulled 64 oars, i.e. she was a ship of 32 rum. *See also* LONG SHIP.

Rumbal (or **rumball**): an ancient feast kept on Christmas Eve by the fishermen of Folkestone, Kent, probably originally in honour of St Rumwold, who once had a chapel (long since demolished) between that town and Hythe.

They choose eight of the largest and best whitings out of every boat, when they come home from that fishery, and sell them apart from the rest; and out of this separate money is a feast made every Christmas Eve, which they call a rumball. The master of each boat provides this feast for his own company, so that there are as many different entertainments as there are boats.

Run: a word with many different nautical usages as noun and verb: (1) a voyage, as in 'the run to Gibraltar', but especially a regular voyage between two ports, as in 'the Southampton–New York run'.

(2) The distance sailed between two observations of the ship's position, as in 'the day's run' between one noon fix and the next.

(3) The after-part of a vessel's underwater hull where it rises and is shaped towards the stern, as in 'the clipper's design shows a good run'.

(4) To sail with the wind astern or from well abaft the beam. A ship is then said to be 'running free'.

(5) To smuggle or engage in the illicit carriage of goods by sea, as in 'the smuggler used to run brandy into England'. 'Gun-runners' are men who land guns and arms illegally.

(6) To break through, as in 'the ship tried to run the blockade'.

(7) To desert ship. A man was said to have run when he was missing from his ship and thought to have deserted, and 'Run', or merely the letter 'R.', was marked against his name in the ship's muster-roll.

(8) To flow, as in 'current was observed to run northwards'; also 'the sea was rough and running high'.

With a following preposition or adverb,

'run' has many other particular meanings, e.g.

(9) To approach or proceed, as in 'the ship had to run into harbour ' or 'the ship had to run along a dangerous coast'.

(10) To collide with another vessel head on, as in 'the steamer was seen to run down the yacht'. Also, when colliding, vessels are said to 'run foul' of each other.

(11) To pay out a line, as in 'the order was to run out a towing-line to the other ship'.

(12) To get ready, as in 'the crew began to run out the guns', that is to open the gunports and move the guns forward ready for action.

(13) To hoist, as in to 'run up a flag or signal'.

(14) To sail towards a desired latitude or longitude. A particular use of 'run down' in this sense is the phrase 'running the easting down', meaning to sail eastwards, especially in reference to the passage of sailing ships from the Cape of Good Hope to Australia within the latitudes of the Roaring Forties.

(15) To put a vessel on a reef or shoal etc. is to 'run aground'.

Running the gauntlet: punishment formerly inflicted by courts-martial or individual captains. The whole ship's company was formed in a line right round the main deck, and each man was armed with a knotted rope, which he used to flay the offender's back as he went by, either carried on a grating or prodded along at swordpoint.

Rupert, Prince, Count Palatine of the Rhine and Duke of Bavaria, afterwards Duke of Cumberland and Earl of Holderness (1619–82): nephew of Charles I of England, usually remembered as a dashing leader of cavalry. But he also took to the sea

at times, not without success. He was Admiral of the White at the Battle of Lowestoft (1665), was Vice-Admiral of England at the outbreak of the Third Dutch War (1672) and became Admiral of the Fleet a year later. For six years he was First Lord of the Admiralty.

He was brave and courageous even to rashness, and subject to certain eccentricities, of which he would have been sorry to correct himself . . . He was polite even to excess unseasonably; but haughty and even brutal when he should have been gentle and courteous.

Anthony Hamilton, *Memoirs of the Comte de Gramont* (1713)

An interesting situation arose when Rupert was given command of the royal ships during the Civil War, since the Earl of Warwick (Sir Robert RICH), appointed Lord High Admiral by Parliament in 1643 against the King's wishes, flew the royal standard by virtue of his office. This was thought to be highly discouraging to the royal ships, and Rupert too was authorized to fly the standard.

. . . since the Earl of Warwick wore a standard . . . whosoever commanded the fleet that was to fight against him, should wear one, lest the seamen be discouraged, and look upon the Earl as the greater person; so that it is the opinion of all that, when you are like to engage with the Rebel's fleet, your men may expect you should wear that ensign.

Sir Edward Hyde to Prince Rupert (27 January 1649)

Rupture: *see* HEALTH AND HYGIENE.

Ruse de guerre: from the French, meaning a trick of war or method of deceiving the enemy, such as sailing under false colours till the time of action (when it was obligatory to hoist one's true colours) or Duncan's stratagem at the Battle of

CAMPERDOWN, when he passed signals to an imaginary supporting fleet.

Russell, Edward, Earl of Orford (1653–1727): admiral. Enjoying strong patronage, he was a captain before he was 20 and by 1689–70 was Treasurer of the Navy and Admiral of the Blue. He was dismissed from command for failing to complete the destruction of the French fleet after the action off BARFLEUR (1692), but he was quickly reinstated and subsequently served three terms as First Lord of the Admiralty.

Rye: an ancient town, now about two miles inland from the East Sussex coast but until Elizabethan times an important port. Rye's value as a port in the 12th century enabled it to become, with Winchelsea, a member of the confederation of the CINQUE PORTS. In return for certain privileges Rye had to provide five ships and man some of the royal galleys in time of war. In the 15th century, after a period of some decline, the town revived as Winchelsea decayed, and it was an important port of passage to France. In 1545, when a French invasion of England threatened and was foiled by Henry VIII's Royal Navy, Rye provided seven boats and over 200 men for the defence of the realm. But although Queen Elizabeth when visiting the town (1573) had given it the name Rye Royal, its fortunes were declining as the harbour silted up, and great salt marshes were formed on its seaward side. In spite of much endeavour and expense to maintain a sea connection, the great days of Rye in maritime history came to an end.

Ryswick, Treaty of (21 September 1697): treaty which concluded the war which had broken out in 1689 between France and a coalition in which England, Spain, the Empire and Holland all played a part. As part of the conditions, William III was recognized as King of England, and Anne as his successor, and all assistance was to be withdrawn from the exiled James II.

Sag: (1) bend or curve downwards at the middle. A ship may sag if, in a long sea, her weight is borne by high waves or swell at bow and stern and there is little support of her hull by the water amidships. **(2)** To sag away to leeward is to drift away or to make leeway.

Sail: an area of cloth hoisted on a vessel by means of rigging to catch the wind and drive her forward. Canvas was the traditional material used for sails but modern, light, strong man-made fibres are now much used, especially for yachts. The cloths, that is the strips of canvas or other material, are cut as required and seamed together to form a sail of particular shape and size according to its intended function and position on the vessel (*see also* SAILMAKER).

Sails are of two general kinds, square and fore-and-aft. Square sails, roughly rectangular in shape, are set on yards running athwart the masts, whilst fore-and-aft sails are either triangular or four-sided, but are set in a fore-and-aft line by their leading edge or luff either from a mast or a stay. *See also* RIG.

The parts of a sail are known by different names. 'Head' and 'foot' are self-explanatory and apply to both square and fore-and-aft sails. The outer edge of a square sail is called the leech, while the belly or main body is the bunt. On a fore-and-aft sail the edge set against a mast or stay is the luff, with its upper corner known as the throat and the lower corner the tack. The aftermost edge is the leech; its upper corner is the peak, and its lower corner is the clew.

There are many different names for sails according to their position and function. In naming them the first element to remember is that in a ship of more than one mast a sail takes its name from the mast on which it is set; thus we have fore sails, mainsails etc. Thereafter a sail has a specific name. For example the normal six sails set on the main mast of a square-rigged ship with three or more masts are the main course, and above it the main lower topsail, the main top-gallant, the main royal and the main skysail. But such a ship in fine weather might also carry extra sails known as

Parts of a sail

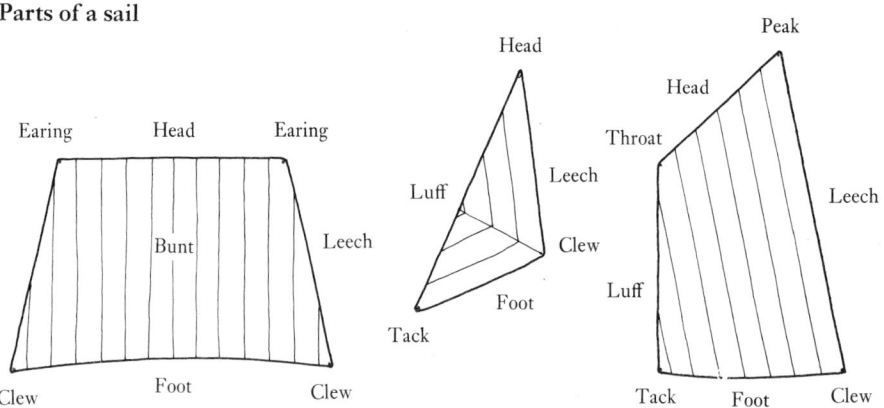

Sails – Full-rigged ship

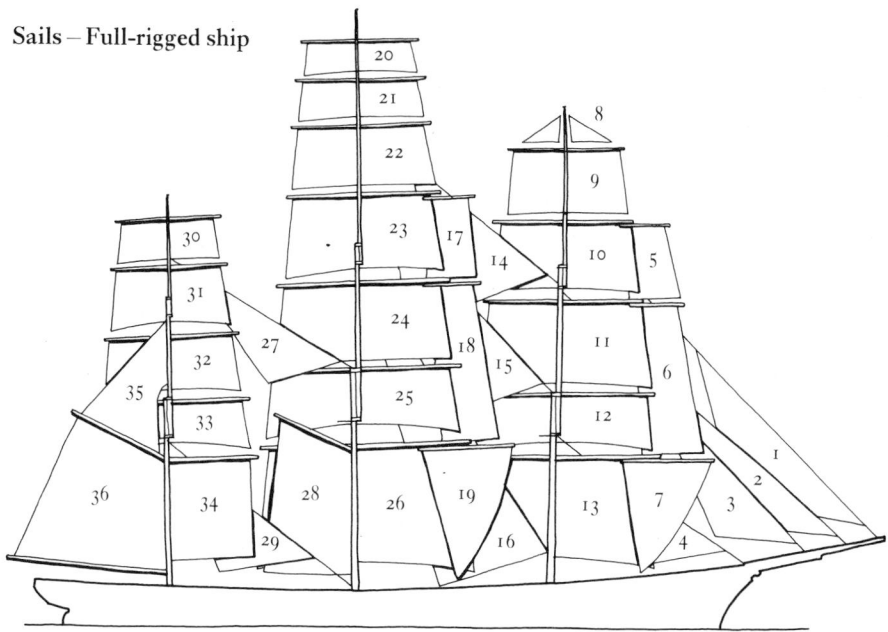

1 Flying jib	10 Fore top-gallant	19 Main lower stunsail	28 Spencer
2 Jib	11 Fore upper topsail	20 Moonraker	29 Mizen staysail
3 Fore top-mast staysail	12 Fore lower topsail	21 Skysail	30 Mizen royal
4 Fore staysail	13 Fore course	22 Main royal	31 Mizen top-gallant
5 Fore top-gallant stunsail	14 Main royal staysail	23 Main top-gallant	32 Mizen upper topsail
6 Fore top-mast stunsail	15 Main top-gallant staysail	24 Main upper topsail	33 Mizen lower topsail
7 Fore lower stunsail	16 Main top-mast staysail	25 Main lower topsail	34 Cro'jack
8 Skyscraper	17 Main top-gallant stunsail	26 Main course	35 Gaff topsail
9 Fore royal	18 Main top-mast stunsail	27 Mizen royal staysail	36 Spanker

Schooner

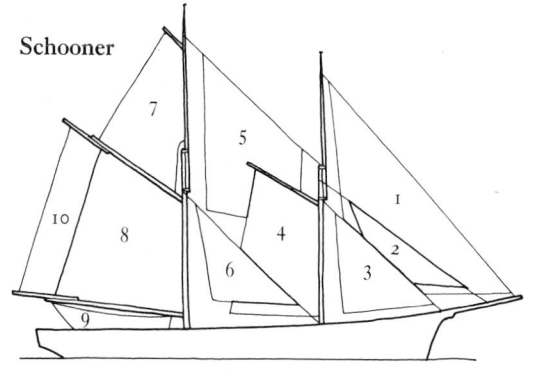

1 Ghoster	6 Main staysail
2 Jib	7 Gaff topsail
3 Fore staysail	8 Gaff mainsail
4 Gaff foresail	9 Watersail
5 Fisherman staysail	10 Ringtail

Bermudan Sloop

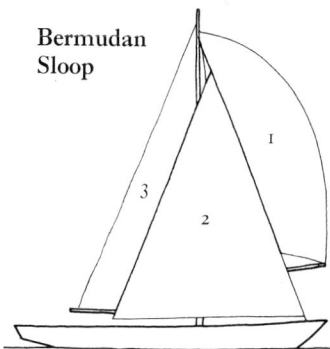

1 Spinnaker
2 Genoa
3 Bermudan mainsail

studding sails or stunsails. Again, such a ship would have fore-and-aft sails known as staysails; on her bowsprit she might carry flying, outer and inner jibs, whilst aft on her mizen mast she might carry a spanker. Smaller sailing vessels have lug sails and gaff sails; amongst many other names for particular sails are spritsail, cro'jack, spanker (or driver), spencer and spinnaker (all described in their separate entries).

The 16th-century *Victory* struggled along with about half-a-dozen sails. Nelson's *Victory* had over thirty. A good description of them occurs in Geoffrey Callender's *The Story of H.M.S. Victory* (1914):

She still set a spritsail on her bowsprit. She still set a great fore-and-aft sail upon her mizzen. She still used the word course to describe the sails that were nearest to the deck on fore mast and main. But here the re-semblance to her ancestress ended. Above the fore course rose the fore topsail. This was no longer a mere appendage. The fore course in area was more than 3,000 square feet. The fore topsail was more than 3,500 square feet. Above the fore topsail rose the fore top-gallant, and above that again the royal. Similar sails were set upon the main mast; but, each for each, they were bigger. The main topsail, the largest spread of canvas in the ship, measured 60 feet on either side, 55 feet along the head, and 90 feet along the foot. The main yard was 110 feet along. The mizzen mast, above its fore-and-aft sail, set canvas like the fore mast and main. In addition to these and other square sails, the *Victory* had at least a dozen that were triangular in shape. They were known to sailors as staysails, being set on the stays that supported the masts. Then there were stunsails, studding or steering sails. These were not included in the thirty-one. They were fair-weather sails, devices for extending the breadth of square sails when the wind was light.

By way of comparison, the clipper *Cutty Sark*, not a big ship, carried a total of 29 sails with an area, all set, of 32,000 square ft, or about three quarters of an acre. The five-masted German *Preussen* (1902) had 47 sails with a total spread of 50,000 square ft, or well over an acre.

The word sail was often used to indicate a ship in sight, as in the look-out's cry 'Sail ho!' or 'Twenty sail in sight!' Because of the importance of sail in maritime history it is not surprising that the word occurs in many phrases, e.g. to 'clap on sail' or 'crowd sail', meaning to put on all sail to make speed; to 'set sail', to set out on a voyage, a phrase still used in engine-driven ships; to 'shorten sail' to reduce the amount of sail taking the wind and so reduce speed; *See also* BEND; FURL; HOIST; STRIKE; WIND.

'Sailing Directions': the general name for a series of books, familiarly known as 'Pilots', giving navigational information and advice. Each volume covers the coasts and adjacent seas of a particular area, such as the Channel, the Mediterranean, etc. They are produced by the Hydrographic Department of the Royal Navy, and supplement the information given on charts.

Sailmaker: one who makes and mends sails. In the days of sailing ships the sailmaker was naturally an important member of the ship's company, and in the British Navy he was of officer status and had mates to assist him. He generally stayed with his ship unless promoted to one of higher rate. In both the Royal and Merchant Navies he was often familiarly known as 'Sails'. Sails were, of course, also made by sailmakers working ashore in dockyard sail lofts, large floor areas on which the canvas could be spread out and the sails cut and stitched to the pattern required. In making a sail the sailmaker cut out long strips of canvas, known as cloths, sewed them together with different kinds of stitching, using a sailmaker's PALM and NEEDLE, and then sewed rope round the edges to give strength and provide clews or securing points for the sail.

St Elmo's fire: the commonest of many names given to a luminous electrical discharge sometimes seen on the masts and yards of a ship. From ancient times it has been observed by many sailors and viewed with both religious and superstitious awe. Another name for St Elmo's fire is 'corposant', which derives from the Portuguese *corpo santo*, meaning 'holy body', for it was believed to emanate from the body of Christ. Some seamen, fearing that it portended death, would not dare to look on it. The name Elmo is perhaps a corruption of Erasmus, a 4th-century saint and patron of Mediterranean sailors. Charles Darwin in his voyage round the world in H.M.S. *BEAGLE* recorded how one dark night 'we witnessed a splendid scene of natural fireworks; the masthead and yard-arm ends shone with St Elmo's light; and the form of the vane could almost be traced, as if it had been rubbed with phosphorus'.

St Helena: a small island of volcanic origin situated in latitude 16° S. in the South Atlantic and 1,150 miles from the coast of Africa. The island was discovered (1502) by the Portuguese, who had recently made known the route to India round southern Africa. It was probably not visited by Englishmen until the voyages of Elizabethan adventurers such as Thomas Cavendish and James Lancaster revealed the advantages of St Helena as a watering and resting place for ships on the long haul to and from the East. The British East India Company formed a settlement there in 1659, but possession of the island was contested by the Dutch. However, from 1673 St Helena became an acknowledged possession of Great Britain. The prosperity of the island grew with the great increase of mercantile shipping in the 18th and 19th centuries, but its importance as a port of call diminished after the opening of the Suez Canal (1869). Nevertheless, during the two World Wars of the present century the strategic importance of St Helena and the neighbouring Ascension Island was recognized, and both islands played a valuable part in ocean surveillance, air and telecommunications.

St Helena is particularly remembered as the place chosen by the British government for the detention of Napoleon after his defeat and abdication (1815). The remoteness of the island ensured a measure of safety, which was strengthened by a garrison of troops and a guarding warship. Napoleon was taken to St Helena in H.M.S. *NORTHUMBERLAND*, and remained on the island until his death in 1821.

St Helena beef: according to a passenger on an emigrant ship to Australia in 1838, the name commonly given to the albacore, a species of tunny-fish caught by the sailors and served up to the passengers as a tough but not unpleasant dish.

St James's Day Fight (25 July 1666): name given to the last fleet action of the Second Dutch War, when the Duke of Albemarle (George MONCK), at the head of ninety sail, decisively defeated the Dutch, who lost twenty ships to our one.

St Kitts (properly called **St Christopher**): one of a group of three associated islands in the Leeward Islands, West Indies, the others being Nevis and

447

Anguilla. St Kitts was discovered and named by Columbus during his second voyage in 1493. Early in the 17th century the island was colonized by English and French settlers, who brought in African slaves to work the sugar plantations. After disputes between the settlers, and following the War of the Spanish Succession, the island was ceded to Britain at the Treaty of Utrecht (1713). But it once again, like other West Indian islands, became the subject of contention during the War of American Independence; its garrison had to surrender to the French in 1781, in spite of brilliant manoeuvres by Rear-Admiral Samuel Hood (1724–1816) in attempting to hold off the numerically superior French fleet under Vice-Admiral de Grasse. However, St Kitts was returned to Britain at the Peace of Versailles (1783). Today the islands are self-governing members of the Commonwealth in association with Great Britain, which remains responsible for defence and foreign affairs.

St Lawrence River: the great river and waterway of eastern Canada, leading from the Great Lakes in the heart of the North American continent to the Atlantic Ocean. It was the French explorer Jacques Cartier who in 1535 first ventured up the river to the point which he named Mont Réal, where the great modern city of Montreal now stands. Here his further progress was impeded by rapids. In 1608 the first permanent settlement was made by the Frenchman Samuel de Champlain at Quebec, and this town was to be the key to the conquest of Canada by the British. The St Lawrence was a formidable river to navigate, but in 1759, thanks to the excellent work of charting performed by James COOK, a British force sailed safely up it and accomplished the capture of QUEBEC and the defeat of the French.

The rapids above Montreal and the falls in the levels between the Great Lakes had to be overcome if full use was to be made of this magnificent waterway extending over

A Great Lakes ore-carrier about to enter the Iroquois lock.

2000 miles from the ocean to the head of Lake Superior. Gradually, from the 18th century, canals and locks were built to bypass rapids and extend navigation by overcoming the difference in levels. Much was achieved in the present century up to 1939, but improvements to allow larger vessels to use the waterway were still desired when in 1954 the St Lawrence Seaway project was begun. This great joint U.S.-Canadian scheme has, since 1959, enabled vessels of up to 27 ft draught and 730 ft long to proceed from the ocean to the head of the Great Lakes. During the winter months the St Lawrence freezes over, but this hindrance to navigation has been much reduced by the use of ice-breakers and merchant ships specially designed to cope with the conditions.

St Nazaire: the great French dockyard and naval base at the mouth of the River Loire. During the Second World War St Nazaire was the scene of a heroic exploit by the Royal Navy and Army Commandos. The naval base contained the only dock on France's western coast large enough to take the German battleship *Tirpitz* if she broke out from Norwegian waters into the Atlantic to raid Allied shipping. It was therefore decided to put the dock and its installations out of action. At the close of March 1942 H.M.S. *Campbelltown*, one of the fifty old American destroyers transferred to Britain, led a force of destroyers and light coastal craft to achieve this end. The *Campbelltown*, with three tons of high explosive in her bows, but with delayed fuses, rammed the dock gates, while the Commandos leapt ashore to destroy the dock machinery. The raiders were met by overwhelming opposition by the Germans, and only remnants of the force returned safely home, the others being killed or captured. The delayed fuses in the bows of the *Campbelltown* seemed to have failed, but next day while the ship was being inspected by a large party of Germans, she blew up, and the vast explosion jammed and wrecked the entrance to the dock, which was put out of action for the rest of the war. St Nazaire and Lorient, another great dockyard and base in Brittany, continued to be held by German forces until the end of the war.

'St Roch': not a British ship, but one which worthily represents centuries of endeavour by British and Commonwealth seamen. She was a Royal Canadian Mounted Police schooner, built in 1928, and in 1940, under Staff Sergeant H. A. Larsen, she became the second vessel to navigate the North-West Passage from west to east and then, on her return, the first to make the voyage in both directions. The 300-ton schooner, then manned by a crew of eight, is now in the Maritime Museum at Vancouver.

Saints, Battle of the (12 April 1782): important battle named after the group of islets (christened by Columbus) between Guadeloupe and Dominica, where Rodney, with Hood as his second-in-command, came up with the French fleet under de Grasse, who was making for Jamaica, and won a decisive and morale-boosting victory, capturing five ships, including the flag-ship *Ville de Paris*. Apart from the victory itself, the fight was notable because, for the first time for a century, the British ships broke the sacred line of battle and indulged in a stand-up mêlée.

St Vincent, Battle of: see MOONLIT BATTLE.

St Vincent, Battle of Cape: see CAPE ST VINCENT, BATTLE OF.

St Vincent, Earl: *see* JERVIS, JOHN.

Saker: a small cannon of the 15th–16th centuries. It was about 9 ft long and fired a 5-lb. shot.

Salamander: an ingenious heating device in the old Navy: a round shot, fitted with a handle, made red-hot and hung up to provide warmth in cabins and mess-decks.

Salcombe clippers: vessels typical of many trading out of West Country ports in the 19th century on the West Indian fruit trade etc. Schooner-rigged and deep-heeled, they were built for speed; *see* FRUIT CLIPPER. Salcombe is a small port in Devon.

Sallee pirates: pirates operating from the Moorish port of Sallee. A 'Sallee man' could be either the man or the ship.

Sally Port: (1) an opening in the side of a

ship, especially that built into sailing warships for entry on their port side; (**2**) the landing place in Portsmouth Harbour reserved for boats and men of the Royal Navy. Peter Simple (in Marryat's sea story of that name), on joining his first ship, packed up his clothes, paid his bill at the Blue Posts Tavern in Portsmouth, and 'the porter wheeled my chest down to the Sally Port, where the boat was waiting'.

Salutes: various actions performed as marks of respect. The naval hand salute is made to the quarter-deck on entering or leaving a British warship. This dates from the time when in medieval ships men doffed their caps on passing the religious shrine on the quarter-deck. Hand salutes are given by ratings to officers and by officers to seniors and to important persons; they are also made to the national flag in the daily hoisting and lowering of colours in the morning and at sunset. Another form of salute is 'piping the side', the ceremonial call on the boatswain's PIPE

The fast fruit schooner *Queen of the West*.

given to greet royalty, admirals, captains and distinguished visitors. On such occasions the salute may be accompanied by a guard, a band, or both, and guns may be fired according to the importance of the occasion and the rank of the visitor.

In the days of sail it was customary for an unarmed ship to salute a warship by striking her topsails. If the ship carried guns these would be fired as a salute. But from the end of the 17th century regulations laid down the number of guns, always an odd number, to be fired as a salute to admirals according to their rank, nineteen guns being fired for an admiral of the fleet. Saluting by guns is now used only for very special occasions, but the maximum number of twenty-one guns is still fired for royalty and certain royal anniversaries.

Modern custom decrees that a merchant ship salutes a warship at sea by dipping her ensign and keeping it dipped until the warship has similarly answered. Vessels in a foreign port may fly the flag of the nation being visited as a form of courtesy salute. On naval and other special occasions ships may be dressed overall, a kind of salute given by a continuous display of flags from the jack-staff via the masts to the ensign staff; there are regulations for the order in which the flags, which include signal flags, should be displayed.

There are also appropriate procedures for saluting by a warship's boats. If the boat is under sail, the sheets are let fly; if it is being rowed, the crew lay on or toss their oars; if under power, the engine may be eased or stopped, and in all cases the coxswain or officer in charge will give a personal salute.

Salutes have sometimes been the cause of much acrimony between nations: *see* HONOUR OF THE FLAG; MONSON, SIR WILLIAM.

Salvage: (1) things saved from a shipwreck etc., or the value paid for such goods; (2) to carry out such a rescue operation, which can on occasion involve salvaging a complete ship (e.g. *MARY CELESTE* and *RESOLUTE*). The most remarkable underwater salvage operation has been the raising, in a state of amazing completeness, of the Swedish warship *Wasa*, which sank off the quay at Stockholm in August 1628 and is now housed in a special museum. Much other salvage work has been less creditable, prompted more by commercial interests than any regard for preservation or historical evidence. The virtual destruction of the *ROYAL GEORGE* over the centuries is a case in point. Some famous salvage exploits in British history have been the recovery by Sir William Phipps of £300,000 worth of silver ingots, coins and jewels from a Spanish ship sunk off Puerto de la Plata, in the Bahamas (1687); the lifting of £5,000,000 in gold from the *LAURENTIC* (1917–24); the rescue of almost £1,000,000 in gold and coin from the P. & O. liner *Egypt*, lying in 70 fathoms 45 miles from Brest, by an Italian team (1929–35); and the bringing up of £2,500,000 worth of gold and silver bullion from the steamship *Niagara*, which struck a mine 28 miles out from Auckland, New Zealand, in the Second World War. *See also p. 452*; *ASSOCIATION*; *COLOSSUS*; *MARY ROSE*; TOBERMORY BAY;

. . . on the sea-bottom lies the greatest fleet of ships the world can ever know . . . True, the sunlight will never gild their sails; but it will gleam on other precious survivals and relics; on wet woodwork and encrusted metal breaking surface after many centuries; and artificial light, taken into ocean depths by man, will cut through the green silence and bring us greater understanding and knowledge of these ships of old renown.

Grant Uden, *British Ships and Seamen* (1969)

Salvage: details from a proposed scheme to lift the remains of the *Royal George*, sunk at Spithead, 1782.

Salvo: literally, a salute (from the Latin *salve*, 'hail'); a discharge of guns fired simultaneously as a salute (e.g. 'a salvo of twenty-one guns') or a simultaneous discharge of guns fired in a naval action.

Sampan: a light boat of the coastal waters, rivers and harbours of the Far East. Harbour sampans have a covering amidships and are moved by sculling over the stern; others on coastal waters use a small matting sail on a single mast.

Samson post (or **king post**): a strong, mast-like post fitted with a derrick and placed near the hatches for working the cargo. Samson or king posts are generally seen in pairs looking like goal-posts (by which name they are colloquially known).

Sand-bank: a bank or shoal of sand just below the sea's surface or at low tide appearing above it, always dangerous to navigation.

Sand-glass: an early device for measuring

the passage of time. It consisted of two glass bowls, one above the other, connected by a narrow neck through which fine sand trickled from the upper bowl to the lower. The time taken for the upper bowl to empty was of specific duration according to the size of the sand-glass, and when the bowl was emptied the sand-glass was reversed to repeat the process. Different sizes of sand-glass were used for different purposes. A half-minute glass was used in calculating the ship's speed by means of a LOG-LINE. Other sand-glasses recorded the passage of half-hour, hour and four-hour periods. These were used to mark the

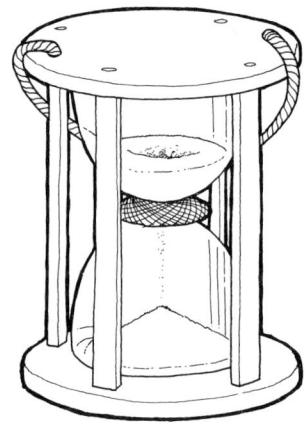

length of watches or periods of duty. The ship's bell was struck at every half-hour. When 'eight bells' was struck the four-hour glass was turned and counting began again

Samson post.

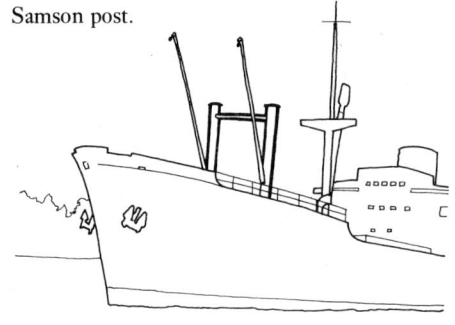

as the next watch took over. With the coming of the chronometer, sand-glasses disappeared from use, and we now perhaps see them surviving only as handy timers for boiling an egg!

Sandpapering the anchor: performing unnecessary work on board ship, perhaps in honour of an important visitor. There was an old story of a seaman, set to clean the cable, who so much preferred the work to his ordinary duties that he continued till every link gleamed like silver.

Sandwich, Edward Montagu, first Earl of (1625–72): admiral and 'General at Sea'. After distinguishing himself in the Parliamentary forces in the Civil War, including the Battle of Naseby and the storming of Bristol, he became General at Sea with Robert Blake in 1656. His naval service, though it had its ups and downs, was equally impressive, and he held a number of important commands, as well as diplomatic and administrative posts. He was eventually blown up in his ship when the Dutch surprised the English fleet at SOLEBAY, and was buried in Westminster Abbey. He is often mentioned in the diary of Samuel PEPYS, who was his secretary.

Sandwich, John Montagu, fourth Earl of (1718–92): soldier and naval administrator. As First Lord of the Admiralty (1748–51) he played a great part in correcting abuses and instituting reforms. But later the gamekeeper turned poacher and, after he came back to the Admiralty (1771–82), he used his office for bribery and political jobbery, bringing the Navy to the point of bankruptcy. The Sandwich Islands were named after him. *See also* NAMES, SHIPS'.

Sandwich Islands: former name for a chain of Polynesian islands in the North Pacific, today known as the Hawaiian Islands, which were formally annexed by the United States in 1898 and later became that country's fiftieth State. Whether the Sandwich Islands were discovered before Captain Cook visited them on his third great voyage in 1778 is doubtful, but he charted their true position and named them after the fourth Earl of Sandwich, First Lord of the Admiralty. When early in 1779 Cook returned after sailing north to the Alaskan peninsula, he was at first treated with great ceremony as a Polynesian god. After setting sail again Cook was forced to return only two days later for repairs to a mast in his ship *Resolution*. This time, however, the natives were suspicious and unfriendly, and thefts and misunderstandings resulted in an affray. Cook went ashore to take a hostage and demand restitution, but before his men could defend him he was attacked and stabbed to death.

'San Juan Baptista': *see* TOBERMORY BAY.

'Sans Pareil': ship name (meaning 'without equal') borrowed from the French. One *Sans Pareil* entered the Royal Navy after being taken by Lord Howe at the Glorious FIRST OF JUNE (1794) and continued on the Navy List till 1842. A new ship on the same lines was designed by Sir William Symonds and laid down at Devonport in 1845. Originally intended to be an 84-gun line-of-battle ship, she was in fact launched (1851) as a screw ship, 193 ft along the gun-deck and of 2242 tons burden. Another first-class battleship followed in 1887.

Santa Cruz: chief seaport and capital of Tenerife, one of the Canary Islands, possessions of Spain lying off the N.W. coast of Africa. Santa Cruz figures in British naval history in two bold and

453

exciting incidents, one successful, the other unsuccessful. In the first, Robert Blake, who was blockading Cadiz, heard in the spring of 1657 that a Spanish treasure fleet was lying at Santa Cruz. By the time his ships arrived the treasure had been landed and the Spanish ships were lying under the protection of the shore batteries. Nevertheless, Blake sent his rear-admiral into the harbour to attack the galleons and himself followed soon after with the rest of his fleet to engage the guns on shore. The attack was a magnificent success: five enemy ships were taken and eleven destroyed; the English lost only one ship, but 50 of their men were killed. Blake's fleet withdrew with difficulty, but managed to get clear. Returning·home because of ill-health and the effect of wounds, Blake died just before entering Plymouth in August 1657.

The second attack on Santa Cruz was made by Nelson in July 1797, also in the hope of capturing a Spanish treasure ship. Nelson's first attempt was repulsed, for the element of surprise had been lost and the weather was unfavourable. A renewed attack on the following day found the Spaniards well prepared, and, although landing parties managed to capture the mole and spike the guns, they were unable to break into the town. It was during the landing that Nelson was shot in the right arm as he was drawing his sword. The severity of his wound compelled him to return to his ship, H.M.S. *Theseus*, where his arm was amputated. The Spanish governor of Santa Cruz behaved magnanimously and under a flag of truce the landing party ashore was allowed to withdraw. Nelson's small squadron achieved no success, and after rejoining the main fleet he himself was sent home to recuperate from the loss of his arm. The failure at Santa Cruz was one of the few reverses he ever suffered in clashes with the enemy.

'**Sapphire**': a wooden corvette built in 1874, evidence of the extreme reluctance of the British Admiralty to abandon its old 'wooden walls' since it had already ordered its first steel ships.

Sargasso Sea: a vast area of weed-strewn sea lying in the S.W. quarter of the North Atlantic Ocean and forming a still centre to the anticyclonic circulation of the currents in these latitudes. Its name comes from Sargassum, a species of sea-weed with berry-like air-sacs found floating over great areas of the surface. Some of the huge quantity of this weed has no doubt drifted to the Sargasso Sea from the coasts of the West Indies and Florida, but it is probable that the greater part is a self-propagating community of floating marine plants, amongst which the sea-creatures have evolved some remarkable adaptations in shape, coloration and modes of survival. One of the most amazing migrations is the annual return of the eels of Europe and N. America to breed in the Sargasso Sea.

In earlier centuries the Sargasso gave rise to many stories of ships being trapped in the weed, becalmed and compelled to drift aimlessly to their doom. But few of these yarns had any basis in fact.

The Sargasso is a place forgotten by the winds, deserted by the strong flow of waters that girdle it as with a river. Under the seldom-clouded skies, its waters grow warm and heavy with salt. Separated widely from coastal rivers and from polar ice, there is no inflow of fresh water to dilute its saltiness; the only influx is of saline water from the adjacent currents, especially from the Gulf Stream or North Atlantic Current as it crosses from America to Europe. And with the little, inflowing streams of surface water come the plants and animals that for months or years have drifted in the Gulf Stream.

Rachel Carson, *The Sea Around Us* (1951)

Saumarez: a distinguished name in the British Navy in the 18th and 19th centuries. *Philip Saumarez* (1710–47) reached the rank of captain, captured a French ship in 1746 and was killed in action when serving with Hawke. His brother *Thomas* (*d.*1766) was also a captain and captured the *Belliqueux* in 1758, subsequently commanding her in the West Indies. The most famous of the family was their nephew, *James Saumarez*, Baron de Saumarez (1757–1836), who reached flag rank, became Vice-Admiral of the United Kingdom (1821) and was Commander-in-Chief at Plymouth (1824–7). When he was made General of Marines in 1832 he had given some sixty years' service all over the world, his actions including the Battles of Cape St Vincent and the Nile. He was one of Nelson's 'Band of Brothers'.

'Savannah': often said to have been the first steamship to cross the Atlantic; in fact, on her 1819 crossing from the River Savannah to Liverpool, she used her machinery very little. She was a full-rigged ship with a 'back-up' engine and a collapsible paddle-wheel. *See also* NUC-LEAR-POWERED SHIPS.

Save-all: (1) a small tray fixed below a scuttle to catch drips; (2) a small extra sail set below a studding sail, or an extra canvas attached to a square sail, to catch every small breath of wind.

Scandalize: to scandalize a sail is to reduce its area in a quick untidy manner, generally to reduce speed; but at one time scandalizing sails and yards, that is setting them awry, was a sign of mourning by the ship's company.

Scantling: in shipbuilding, the dimensions of a piece of timber, with regard to its breadth and thickness.

Scapa Flow: a great stretch of enclosed sea ringed by islands at the southern end of the Orkneys. During both World Wars Scapa Flow was an important anchorage and base for the Royal Navy. After the German surrender at the end of the First World War 70 German warships were ordered to Scapa Flow in November 1918 to be interned, but on 21 June 1919 they were scuttled within the anchorage on the orders of the German admiral in command, Ludwig von Reuter, who had mis-

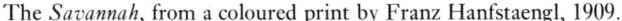

The *Savannah*, from a coloured print by Franz Hanfstaengl, 1909.

The German fleet interned at Scapa Flow, 1919.

understood the terms of surrender. The sunken ships were later raised and towed away to be broken up. On 14 October 1939, at the beginning of the Second World War, a German submarine, *U47*, daringly penetrated the defences of Scapa Flow by shadowing a ship as she entered, and sank the British battleship H.M.S. *Royal Oak*. The submarine afterwards made an escape; her captain, Günther Prien, became one of the most successful German U-boat commanders, sinking many Allied merchantmen until he died (1941) when his boat was sunk with all hands by a British destroyer. After the attack the defences of Scapa Flow were much strengthened, including the building of a causeway, and British warships continued to use this important anchorage and base.

Scarborough warning: a very ancient (and unexplained) phrase for no warning at all; thus, someone who lets something go on the run without cautioning others to stand clear is said to have given a Scarborough warning. One theory has it that the phrase originated in 1557, when Thomas Stafford took Scarborough Castle without the townsmen knowing of his approach.

The wind wos werry moderate, but that shifted an' come round strong from the norrowest, an' hove her ashore; 'twos a Scarboro' warnin'.

R. W. Emerson, *Wild Life* (1890)

Scarph (or **scarf**): type of joint or method of joining two lengths of timber firmly, e.g. when laying a ship's keel. Since in a big ship it was impossible to get a single piece of timber long enough for the whole keel, lengths were 'scarphed' together, the number of scarphs varying according to the size of the ship. Thus, seven were normal in the keel of a first-rate (about 175 ft). The scarph itself was at least 5 ft long, the pieces

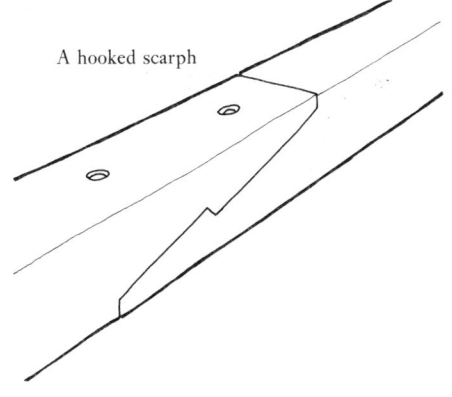

A hooked scarph

456

being strongly bolted together. There were many patterns, the most common being the plain, the hooked and the tabled (or coaked).

Scend (pronounced and often spelt **send**): (1) the upward lift of a ship caused by waves in a heavy sea; (2) the driving movement of waves surging forward.

'Scharnhorst': German 32,000-ton 11-in.-gun battle cruiser used as a convoy- and commerce-raider in the Second World War and sunk after a running fight with a mixed force under Admiral Fraser in the *Duke of York* (26 December 1943) off North Cape, Norway.

Scheveningen, Battle of (31 July 1653): the last battle of the First Anglo-Dutch War, fought off Scheveningen (two miles N.W. of The Hague), in which the Dutch fleet was routed by Monck and the great Admiral Tromp was killed by a stray bullet.

Schnorkel: the German name for a long tube fitted to U-boats in the later stages of the Second World War. It was a kind of

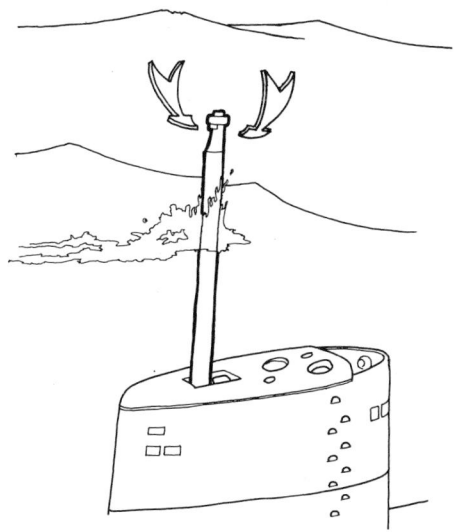

flexible funnel which could be raised to a vertical position to allow the submarine to take in air whilst remaining just below the surface, thus enabling her to run her diesel engines to recharge the batteries. When fitted to British submarines it was called a snort.

Schoolie: slang name for an officer of the Instructor Branch of the Royal Navy.

Schoolmaster, ship's: the title formerly given to men who were appointed to teach the young on board ships of the Royal Navy. The schoolmaster first appeared about the beginning of the 18th century when some captains felt that their young midshipmen ought to be trained in the theory of navigation and seamanship. His position was a lowly one and for long he himself was rated and paid as a midshipman. He might be appointed from men already on the lower deck, or from civilian applicants whose past and future were uncertain. Not all warships carried a schoolmaster, for much depended on the attitude of the captain, and the humble position and pay did not prove attractive to many. In 1812 the Admiralty recognized his unenviable position and his pupils were called upon to pay £5 a year to supplement his pay. Four years later his pay was again raised, and in 1836 he became a warrant officer with a uniform and was given wardroom status. In 1840 his title became Naval Instructor and Schoolmaster, and in 1861 he became a commissioned officer. From these beginnings the modern INSTRUCTOR BRANCH of the Royal Navy has evolved.

Schooner: originally a small vessel with sharp lines and two masts rigged fore-and-aft. If she carried square topsails on one or both masts, she was a 'topsail schooner'.

Later, vessels with up to six masts, similarly rigged, were constructed and were called 'three-masted schooners' and so on. Schooners first appeared in the British Navy List in 1764, when a number were purchased in America, of French-Canadian build. They carried small guns, often six a side.

The first schooner ever constructed is said to have been built in Gloucester, Massachusetts, about the year 1713, by a Captain Andrew Robinson, and to have received its name from the following trivial circumstance: When the vessel went off the stocks into the water, a bystander cried out, 'O, how she *scoons!*' Robinson replied, 'A *scooner* let her be'; and from that time, vessels thus rigged have gone by this name. The word *scoon* is popularly used in New England to denote the act of making stones skip along the water.

Webster's International Dictionary (1907)

Webster also quotes a letter of 25 September 1721 which says: 'This gentleman [Captain Robinson] was the first contriver of schooners, and built the first of that sort about eight years since.'

See also RIG and SAIL.

Scilly Isles: an archipelago of small islands, rocks and reefs lying some 30 miles S.W. of Land's End in Cornwall. The islands have been the scene of many shipwrecks, especially in sailing days, for in spite of their generally genial climate they are often shrouded in fog and mist, and in winter fierce seas break on the rocks and reefs. One of the most terrible disasters occurred in 1707 when Admiral Sir Cloudisley Shovell was returning with the Mediterranean fleet; *see ASSOCIATION.*

Scirocco: *see* SIROCCO.

Scotchman: (1) a protecting piece of leather or wood to prevent chafing and

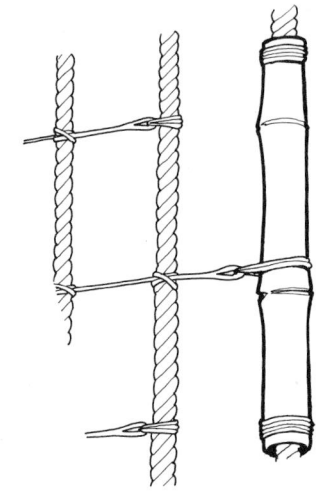

wear from the contact of standing and running rigging; (2) a metal protection of a wooden deck to prevent wear by the anchor cable.

Scott, Robert Falcon (1868–1912): Royal Navy captain, one of the greatest British heroes of Antarctic exploration. He led the National Antarctic Expedition in *Discovery* (1901–4), doing important survey work, discovering King Edward VII Land, and reconnoitring the ice barrier. In 1910–12 he led a new expedition, in the *Terra Nova*, and reached the South Pole on 18 January 1912, five weeks after the Norwegian Roald

Amundsen. On the return journey, owing to terrible weather conditions and lack of supplies, he perished with all his party. They were found by a search party eight months later, Scott's diary providing an imperishable record of heroism in the face of odds.

> Had we lived, I should have had a tale to tell of the hardihood, endurance, and courage of my companions which would have stirred the heart of every Englishman.
>
> Scott's 'Message to the Public'

Scow: large, square-ended, flat-bottomed boat.

Scrambling net: *see* NET.

Screw: a ship's rotating PROPELLER. In the early days of the steamship ships still placed their chief reliance on sails, and the engine was used only when the wind failed or when an emergency or a particular manoeuvre made it necessary. The reason for this was partly faith in sail and suspicion of engines, but mainly the problem of carrying enough coal for a long voyage. When the engine was employed the order 'up funnel, down screw' would be given, at which the funnel would be raised from its stowed horizontal position on deck and the propeller lowered from its housing in the hull and connected to the propeller shaft.

Scrimshaw: spare-time handicraft done by sailors, generally consisting of designs and pictures carved and incised on bones, teeth and tusks of sea mammals such as whales and walruses. The art probably began to flourish in the early whaling ships. The origin of the word is not known; it may derive from a surname.

Scud: (1) a light shower, quickly over; (2) to run before a gale with little or no sail spread.

Scull: a light oar, generally used by one or two people, each rowing with a scull in each hand (i.e. 'single sculls' and 'double sculls'). To scull means to row in this way, but it is also the action of propelling a boat by working a single oar to and fro over the stern.

Scupper: deliberately sink a ship by letting her fill with water (the same meaning as to scuttle a ship). As slang, to scupper can also mean to throw into disorder, to prevent; to defeat.

Scrimshaw: a sperm whale tooth decorated with a charming romantic picture of a sailor and his sweetheart.

Scuppers: openings cut in the sides of a ship's deck to allow any water shipped on board to run off into the sea.

Scurvy: for centuries the most serious disease to threaten seamen on long voyages, caused by the restricted diet (especially the lack of fresh vegetables) and marked by gum trouble, falling teeth, skin blotches and such general enfeeblement that a sudden movement could end life. Scurvy is recognizable in descriptions given earlier in other languages, but the first detailed account in English is provided by Sir Richard Hawkins on his voyage of 1593–4. Hawkins estimated that 10,000 men died of scurvy in the reign of Elizabeth I.

Only in the present century has the vital necessity of vitamin C from fruit and vegetables been fully understood. But probably the Portuguese Prince Henry the Navigator's captains in the 15th century used citrus juice, as supplied by limes, lemons and oranges; and their value was also known to some of the Elizabethan adventurers.

This is a wonderful secret of the power and wisdom of God, that hath hidden so great and unknown a virtue in this fruit, to be a certain remedy for this infirmity.

Sir Richard Hawkins

The juice worketh much better if the party keep a short diet and wholly refrain salt meat, which salt meat, and long being at sea, is the only cause of the breeding of this disease.

Sir James LANCASTER

But the Navy was slow to learn. In 1780, after a six-week cruise, 2400 seamen suffering from scurvy were landed at Portsmouth. A controlled experiment by Dr James Lind on H.M.S. *Salisbury* (1747) and his *Treatise of the Scurvy* (1753) had established the case beyond reasonable doubt, but it was not until 1795 that the Admiralty, under pressure from Sir Gilbert BLANE, ordered a regular issue of lemon juice. Ironically, it was the advice of Captain Cook, whose crews were remarkable for the good state of their health, that had delayed the action; he supplied his men with a variety of fresh food, but regarded lemon juice as unnecessarily expensive. For long the mistaken impression continued that the cheaper lime juice was an adequate substitute for lemon. However, the disease was effectively conquered by about 1800, though even in the present century the scourge has sometimes broken out again on voyages of polar exploration.

In view of the laggard attitude of the Admiralty to the health of seamen, it is interesting to note that the English housewife was better informed, or more concerned: here is a 1704 domestic recipe against scurvy:

Grass, one peck. Water-Cresses, 12 hand-fulls. Brooklime, 6 handfulls. English rhubarb, 6 ounces. Anniseeds & Carraway seeds, of each one ounce. Sena, two ounces. Polipody of the Oak, 4 ounces. Raisins stoned & Lent Figs, of each 8 ounces. New Ale, 5 Gallons.

Scuttle: (1) a 'porthole' or any other such hole in the side or deck to let in light and air, usually with a glazed and hinged metal frame backed by a solid hinged metal plate known as a deadlight. Scuttle and deadlight are made water-tight when closed with strong butterfly nuts.

(2) To scuttle a vessel is to make holes in the bottom or sides in order to sink her.

Scylla and Charybdis: the names, originating in Greek mythology, of a rock (Scylla) and a whirlpool (Charybdis) between Italy and Sicily, the scene of frequent shipwrecks as ships tried to take avoiding action. Hence, being 'between

Scylla and Charybdis' has come to mean being caught between two difficult situations.

Sea: the state or condition of the sea in relation to the weather immediately affecting it (compare SWELL). Assessment of the condition depends on the height of the WAVES from trough to crest, and is recorded by figures 0 to 9 as follows:

Code figure	State of the sea	Height of waves Feet	Metres
0	Calm (glassy)	0	0
1	Calm (rippled)	$0-\frac{1}{3}$	$0-0\cdot1$
2	Smooth (wavelets)	$\frac{1}{3}-1\frac{2}{3}$	$0\cdot1-0\cdot5$
3	Slight	$1\frac{2}{3}-4$	$0\cdot5-1\cdot25$
4	Moderate	4–8	$1\cdot25-2\cdot5$
5	Rough	8–13	$2\cdot5-4$
6	Very rough	13–20	4–6
7	High	20–30	6–9
8	Very high	30–45	9–14
9	Phenomenal	over 45	over 14

Sea anchor (or **drag anchor**): a sail or similar piece of material stretched between spars and thrown overboard to lessen the leeward drift of a vessel and assist her in keeping head to wind.

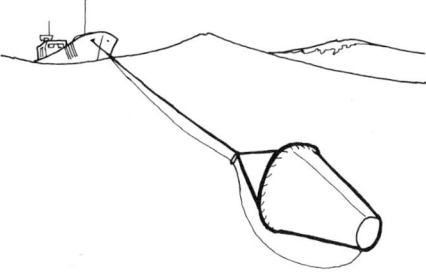

Seaboat: general name for a boat carried by a ship and kept ready for immediate launching to go over to another ship, or in an emergency etc.

Sea Fencibles: a force of men raised in coastal areas to protect England against threatened invasion during the wars against Revolutionary and Napoleonic France. 'Fencible' is a variant of 'defensible', and had earlier been applied to regiments of horse and foot, but the sea fencibles were men such as fishermen and boatmen who, as Nelson reported to St Vincent in 1801, would leave their employment only 'when the enemy are announced as actually coming to sea'. Men in the reserve of the sea fencibles were reckoned to be immune from the attentions of the press-gang.

Sea lawyer: a seaman knowing, or pretending to know, all the rules and regulations, and taking advantage of the fact to argue, criticize and avoid duty.

Sealed orders: orders placed on board a ship by higher authority which are to be opened and obeyed only when a certain position has been reached, or when a specified eventuality arises.

Sea-legs: to find or get one's sea-legs is to become accustomed to the motion of a ship, so that balance is preserved and sickness avoided.

Sealing: the killing and taking of seals for their fur, hides, blubber and oil. There are many different kinds of seal widely distributed over the oceans of the world, especially in their northern and southern limits, and almost all species are of commercial value. The Eskimoes, for whom the seal provided the necessities of life – food, clothing and fuel for heat and light – have no doubt hunted the seal from earliest times, but the commercial taking of these creatures began as an additional and easier catch for the whaling ships of the 17th century. Then sealing developed as a separate occupation, and by the first half of

461

the 19th century great numbers of ships and men were engaged in the trade, with the consequent slaughter of vast numbers of seals. It is recorded that in the one year 1831 nearly 700,000 seals were killed on the coasts and islands of Eastern Canada and Newfoundland.

Seals congregate in great herds (called rookeries) on the shore, on pack-ice and the edges of ice-barriers. In the northern hemisphere the chief sealing areas are the northern fringes of the Atlantic, the islands and pack-ice of the Arctic and the islands of the Bering Sea in the north Pacific Ocean. In the southern hemisphere it was the hunting of seal southwards from the coasts of South America to the Falkland Islands, and on to the islands of South Georgia and then to the South Shetlands that led to the discovery of Antarctica. In addition seals were at one time taken at sea during their migration in the Pacific, but this has now ceased by international agreement because it indiscriminately killed the breeding female seals ('cows').

By the second half of the 19th century the number of seals in both the northern and southern hemispheres, especially in the Bering Sea and in Antarctica, had become so seriously depleted that control of hunting and limitations of the catch were clearly necessary. The fur seals of Antarctica had almost disappeared, though elephant seals were still taken for their oil. International agreement among the nations concerned, mainly Russia, Norway, Denmark, U.S.A., Canada, Japan and Britain, has today done much to preserve the stock of seals, numbers having recovered from a figure which at one time appeared disastrous. The fur seal of northern waters, particularly Canada and the Bering Sea, remains commercially important and profitable, and even in Antarctica numbers are said to be recovering.

Sea-Lion, Operation: the code name given to Hitler's intended invasion of Britain in 1940. After the defeat of the Allied armies by the Germans, the evacuation of the British forces at Dunkirk and the capitulation of France, Hitler believed that Britain could not continue the war on her own and was bound to seek terms for peace. But gradually he came to realize that his hopes were futile, and on 16 July 1940 he gave orders for the invasion of Britain, christened 'Operation Sea-Lion'. Preparations were to be completed by mid-August, but the magnitude of the task, difficulties in raising adequate shipping resources, differences of opinion and the misgivings of the German Navy under Admiral Raeder caused inevitable postponements. A key to the situation was thought by the Germans to be mastery of the air, but the R.A.F. was still holding them at bay in spite of the high expectations of success by Field-Marshal Göring. The Battle of Britain fought in the air over the Channel and southern England in August and September, showed, in the culminating engagement of 15 September, that a sea-borne invasion of Britain was very doubtful of success. Two days later Hitler decided to postpone Sea-Lion indefinitely. On 12 October the invasion was called off until the following spring, by which time the Germans had turned to the attack on Russia, and in February 1942 Sea-Lion was totally abandoned.

The main plan for the invasion had been to establish a bridgehead on the south-east coast of England with subsidiary landings further west. This was to have been followed by a second wave of invasion forces exploiting their mobility to advance northwards and cut off London. Churchill's account in *The Second World War* (Vol. II) records that for the invasion the German naval authorites had requisitioned

168 transports (totalling 700,000 tons), 1910 barges, 419 tugs and trawlers, and 1600 motor boats – an armada which was under constant attack from the R.A.F. as the various craft began to assemble in the Channel ports of France and Belgium during the fateful days of August and September 1940 before the Germans decided not to proceed with Operation Sea-Lion.

Seals: not the amphibian mammals (for which, *see* SEALING) but the pieces of wax or lead attached to documents, which might seem to have rather slighter connections with the sea. But they are in fact an important source of information about early ships, though their restricted area inevitably leads to some obvious distortion of design and dimension. The 1588 seal of Southampton, for example, gives an accurate picture of a large Tudor warship, with small fore and main topsails and without the square mizen topsail or spritsail topsail, introduced later. An earlier seal (*c.*1426), probably used by John, Duke of Bedford, Lord High Admiral of England, Ireland and Guienne, depicts a heavily built ship with a straight

The second town seal of the city of Southampton.

vertical stern-post, from which hangs a rudder. She carries one mast, and both bow and stern-castles are comparatively low. The bowsprit carries no sail. The single mast is strong enough to support a large fighting 'top-castle', equipped with lethal-looking darts. The seal of another Lord High Admiral, the Earl of Rutland, shows a similar 'castle' (*c.*1397).

Sea-mark: originally any conspicuous object set up on shore to assist the navigator of a ship; this is now generally known as a land-mark. A sea-mark is more strictly a floating navigational aid, such as a buoy.

Sea mile: *see* NAUTICAL MILE.

Seams: (1) the small spaces between the wooden planks in the sides and decks of a ship or boat. These are caulked with oakum and pitch to make them water-tight, but have to be nicely judged and left in building to allow for the expansion of wood as it swells with exposure to water. The seams 'take up' as the wood swells and makes a vessel more water-tight; or they may 'work' and let in water if the planking is under strain from rough seas. **(2)** The stitched edges of joined canvas.

Searchlight: a powerful movable electric light mounted in warships to illuminate an enemy ship or a target on shore at night. The searchlight was also employed for relatively long-distance visual signalling. From the closing decades of the 19th century searchlights became an important aid in night actions and were part of a warship's standard equipment, but today the pinpointing of targets is accurately achieved by radar, which avoids the searchlight's disadvantage of revealing the user's presence.

463

Sea-room: plenty of open water within which to manoeuvre a ship without any navigational danger. A traditional toast once drunk by naval officers was 'A willing foe and sea-room'.

Sea-skimmer: a ship specially designed and equipped to skim the sea to take up escaped or spilled oil.

Sea-wall: a wall or embankment to protect low-lying land against the encroachments of the sea.

Sea-wolf: (1) a Viking, pirate or sea-robber; (2) a large fish found in the N.E. Atlantic; (3) the name given to the Royal Navy's highly sophisticated radar-guided anti-missile missile.

Seaworthy: fit for the sea, worthy of being entrusted with cargo or passengers.

Sebastopol: *see* SEVASTOPOL.

Second-rate: *see* RATING OF SHIPS.

Seiner: *see* FISHING CRAFT.

Seizing: any of various kinds of small cordage used to bind ropes together, i.e. to 'seize' them. When the job is done the result is known as a seizing. Different methods, known as flat, round and racking seizings, are used according to the strength and permanency required.

Selkirk (or **Selcraig**), **Alexander** (1676–1721): sailor whose adventures inspired Defoe's *Robinson Crusoe*. He came from Fife in Scotland and in 1703 shipped as sailing master in a privateer, *Cinque Ports*, commanded by Thomas Stradling. After a quarrel with Stradling, Selkirk, who believed that the ship was not seaworthy, was marooned at his own request on Juan Fernandez Island in the South Pacific (October 1704). Here he survived alone until February 1709, when he was taken off by two privateers, which were commanded by Captain Woodes ROGERS.

When Selkirk returned to England (1711) his story aroused great public interest. Woodes Rogers and the essayist Richard Steele published detailed accounts of his adventures, based on what they had heard from Selkirk himself, and Daniel Defoe brilliantly interpreted the story in his novel *ROBINSON CRUSOE* (1719).

See also DAMPIER, WILLIAM.

Selvagee: a coil of rope-yarn wound tightly together by lashing and forming a strop or sling for lifting or securing.

Semaphore: system or apparatus for signalling by means of movable arms, lights or hand-held flags. The term derives from Greek words meaning 'sign bearing'. A semaphore station was erected at the Admiralty Office in London in 1816; *see* TELEGRAPH.

Send: *see* SCEND.

Sennet (or **sennit**, **sinnet** and various other spellings): literally 'seven-knit': a braided cord, composed, in fact, of anything from three to nine strands and used for packaging, certain rope jobs, hats (see below) etc. *See also* KNOTS.

Sennet hats: plaited straw hats, worn for a long period in the past by British sailors. Sometimes they were imported from the West Indies, but were often made by the seamen themselves.

Every bum boat was expected to bring off a bundle of peculiar grass, and soon you would see the men at work at their sennet and in a very short time, with first rate hats.

Captain John Harvey Boteler,
Recollections (describing a scene in 1815)

The sennet hat did not finally disappear from the Navy till the 1920s.

Seppings, Sir Robert (1767–1840): naval architect and Surveyor of the Navy (1813–32). From humble beginnings as a shipwright's apprentice in Plymouth Dockyard, he rose to a knighthood and a Fellowship of the Royal Society, contributing many improved methods of shipbuilding. Among his inventions were 'Seppings blocks' for suspending vessels in dock, and a diagonal method of bracing and trussing frame timbers in ships.

Serang: leading hand or boatswain of a ship crewed by Indians or East Indians (known as LASCARS). The word is of Persian origin.

'Serapis': *see* FLAMBOROUGH HEAD.

'Serica': *see* ARIEL.

Serpentine: an early type of small gun, similar to a ROBINET and used in the same way, being fired from the top deck against men in the opposing ship.

Service, the: the Royal Navy; also known affectionately as the Silent Service, because it quietly performs its duties far from the ears of men, and as the Senior Service, because it takes precedence of the other fighting services on formal and ceremonial occasions.

Serving: *see* WORM, TO.

Set: (1) the direction in which a tidal stream or current flows; (2) the direction in which a vessel is moved by a current, or the distance it is so moved.

Sevastopol (or **Sebastopol**), **Bombardment of** (17 October 1854): naval action in the CRIMEAN WAR, part of the lengthy attempt to capture the heavily fortified city of Sevastopol, the Russian fleet's main base in the Crimea. The bombardment achieved little except to prove to the Admiralty that the future of the Navy lay with steam. The sailing battleships suffered the indignity of having to be pulled and pushed into position by steam tugs and were sitting targets for the Russian shore guns; and were thankful to be towed out of action by the same means. *See also ARETHUSA.*

Seven Seas: a somewhat literary name for the Arctic, Antarctic, North and South Atlantic, North and South Pacific and Indian Oceans.

Seven Years' War (1756–63): war fought in Europe, North America and India between a coalition of France, Austria and Russia on one side and Frederick the Great of Prussia on the other, with some assistance from Britain, already involved in a colonial war with France. British land troops played a secondary part, but, though it is often overlooked and underplayed, the Navy's role was all-important and led to Britain becoming the world's chief colonial power. There would have been no victory for Wolfe at Quebec without the Navy to bring the men and supplies by a unique feat of dangerous navigation; and, despite all the genius and courage of Clive, India would not have been added to the British crown without the naval supremacy established round the coasts. The war ended with the Treaty of PARIS (1763).

Sextant: a navigational optical instrument used for measuring vertical and horizontal

The first Englishman to give an account of the Seychelles was John Jourdain, who touched there on a voyage to India in 1608. For a long while the islands were a haunt of pirates, but in 1742 they were occupied by the French. After the wars against France the Seychelles, having been captured in 1794, came under British rule and were made a separate colony in 1903. In 1976 they became an independent member of the Commonwealth.

Shackle: (1) name for a device, of which there are various patterns, for joining or coupling, used for securing rigging, sails to halyards, anchors to cables, wires to mooring buoys, tow-lines, and for joining lengths of cable etc. The commonest form of shackle is U-shaped with a bolt which passes across the jaw or open end of the U and screws into the opposite lug. Shackles used in joining lengths of chain anchor cable are of different design and are secured with a locking pin.

(2) 'Shackle' is also the name given to the actual length of chain cable, $12\frac{1}{2}$ fathoms, between the positions of each joining shackle.

Shackleton, Sir Ernest Henry (1874–1922): Antarctic explorer. After service in the Merchant Navy, he went as a junior officer on Scott's National Antarctic Expedition (1901–4). Afterwards he left the sea for a while and made his own careful plans to reach the South Pole. He sailed in *Nimrod* in 1907, sending parties to the South Magnetic Pole and to the summit of Mount Erebus. In 1914, in *Endurance*, he set out in command of a trans-Antarctic expedition which, when the ship was crushed in the ice, culminated in his magnificent voyage of 800 miles (1916) in a small boat through stormy seas to South Georgia, in order to seek help for his

angles by reflection. The sextant consists of a metal frame, the lower part of which is an arc, finely graduated in degrees and minutes. The arc is one sixth of a circle, that is a sextant, or 60°. (Angles up to 120° can also be measured.) A sight is taken by looking through a telescopic attachment and moving the index bar, on which is a fixed mirror, until the sun, star or other object being observed is reflected from that mirror on to the mirrored half of the horizon glass on the frame. This reflection is then lined up with the horizon seen through the plain-glass half of the horizon glass. The position of the index bar on the graduated arc is then read off and the angle recorded. The finely made and very accurate modern instrument has evolved from the reflecting quadrant made by John HADLEY (1731).

Seychelles: an archipelago of numerous small islands in the Indian Ocean, lying about 700 miles N.E. of Madagascar. Fertile and blessed with a healthy climate, the islands were surprisingly uninhabited when discovered by the Portuguese (1505).

comrades. The last thirty-six hours were occupied in crossing the snow-fields and mountains on foot.

Shackleton set out for a third time (in *Quest*) in September 1921 but died off South Georgia Island in the following January and was buried there.

> Everybody at Stromness knew Shackleton well, and we were very sorry he is lost in ice with all hands. But we do not know three terrible-looking men who walk into the office off the mountainside that morning. Manager say:
>
> 'Who the *hell* are you,' and terrible bearded man in the centre of the three say very quietly:
> 'My name is Shackleton.'
>
> > Mansell, who witnessed the encounter
> > (R. B. James, *Of Whales and Men*, 1956)

> When I look back on those days, I have no doubt that Providence guided us, not only across those snow-fields, but across the storm-white sea that separated Elephant Island from our landing-place in South Georgia. I know that during that long and racking march of thirty-six hours over the unnamed mountains and glaciers of South Georgia it seemed to me often that we were four, not three. I said nothing to my companions on the point, but afterwards Worsley said to me:
>
> 'Boss, I had a curious feeling on the march that there was another person with us.'
>
> > Sir Ernest Shackleton, *South* (1919)

Shadwell, Charles (*fl.*1710–20): dramatist (and son of a dramatist) whose only claim to fame is a play, *The Fair Quaker of Deal*, which appeared in 1710 and was revived by Garrick more than sixty years later to coincide with a naval review to be held by George III at Spithead. In Garrick's revised version it provides us with interesting glimpses of naval life and of characters who were to become stock material for the stage: amongst them 'Flip, the commodore, a most illiterate Wapineer Tar, hates the Gentlemen of the Navy, gets drunk with his Boat's Crew, and values himself upon the Brutish Management of the Navy'; Mizen, 'a finical Sea-Fop, a mighty reformer of the Navy, keeps a Visiting Day, and is Flip's opposite'; Worthy, 'a Captain of the Navy, a Gentleman of Honour, Sence and Reputation'; Indent, the Purser; Cribbage the Lieutenant, and a dozen others.

> FLIP: I have served in every office belonging to a Ship, from Cook's Boy to a Commodore; and have all the Sea Jests by Heart from the forecastle to the Great Cabin; and I love a Sailor.

'Shah': in 1877 the light armoured cruisers *Shah* and *Amethyst* were detailed to search for *Huascar*, a turret ship of 1800 tons, built for the Peruvian government in 1865 at Birkenhead, whose crew had mutinied and taken to piracy. *Huascar* was eventually found off Ilo (South Peru) and the subsequent engagement was noteworthy because *Shah* discharged the first automatic torpedo ever used in war. It failed to reach its mark, but the pirate ship, though it sustained little major injury, was badly dented from some 70 shell hits and surrendered to the Peruvians.

Shallop: a light open boat. The term is often used poetically.

467

Shanghai, to: to make a man unconscious by drink, drugs etc. and take him on board to work in an out-going ship. The original phrase may have been 'take him to Shanghai', meaning send him on a long voyage (Shanghai being the famous trading port on the China coast). Shanghai-ing was used to man ships short of hands in the 19th century, especially in the ports of North America, and was usually carried out with the collusion of tavern-keepers and rogues ashore, who extorted a fee for the men delivered aboard.

Shank: the main shaft of an ANCHOR between the ring and the arms.

'Shannon': *see* BOSTON.

Shanty: *see* CHANTY.

Shark: the general name for a great group of voracious fishes dangerous to man; used by derivation for anyone dangerous to sailors. Pirates were sometimes referred to as 'sea-sharks'; those who swindled sailors ashore were also known as 'sharks'.

Sheathing: *see* COPPER SHEATHING.

Sheave: the grooved and revolving wheel in a block round which the rope runs. It is made either of metal or of very hard wood such as lignum vitae.

Sheepshank: *see* KNOTS.

Sheer: (1) the upward curve of the lines or deck of a ship from amidships to stem or stern as viewed from abeam; (2) a deviation from the proper course of a ship; (3) to 'sheer away' or 'sheer off' is to move away, especially when a ship turns away at an angle from another. *See also* SHEER-LEGS.

Sheer-hulk: *see* SHEER-LEGS.

Sheer-legs (or **sheers**): two or three long spars lashed together at the top and spread out at the bottom like a pair of shears. The top supports a tackle used for lifting heavy weights, especially masts, in and out of ships. Sometimes an old dismasted ship fitted with sheer-legs, known as a sheer-hulk, was used for this purpose.

Sheer pole: a spar or bar of iron secured horizontally across the bottom end of a ship's shrouds in a comparable position to, but below, the ratlines.

Sheers: *see* SHEER-LEGS.

Sheer strake: the uppermost line of planking on the sides of a wooden vessel and of plates on a steel hull. The sheer strake runs round the ship just below the gunwale.

Sheet: a line or purchase running and secured to the clews of a sail so that the sail's position can be adjusted in relation to the wind. When the sail is drawing fully it is said to be 'sheeted home'. To 'let fly the sheets' is to let them run free, which may be done either to prevent an accident or as a form of salute. For the sheet bend *see* KNOTS.

Sheet anchor: an extra anchor carried on the bows of large ships in addition to the starboard and port bower anchors. Its purpose is to provide an additional measure of security in case the other anchors fail to hold. The name has therefore come into general use as a metaphor for someone or something that provides reliability and safety.

Shell: (1) the main body of a block inside which are the wheels or sheaves over which the rope runs.

(2) An explosive projectile shot from a

gun; so called because the earliest shells, developed on land, were produced by filling the shell of a hollowed-out iron ball shot with explosive. Although in 1787 Lieutenant Shrapnel of the Royal Artillery had demonstrated the effectiveness of his exploding shell, it was some years before this new form of weapon was taken up by the Royal Navy. However, in 1839, in spite of opposition from the diehard advocates of Nelsonian gunnery, part of the gun complement in ships of the Royal Navy was made shell-firing. The next half-century saw the great increase in accuracy and range with the introduction of the 'long' or cylindrical shell, the rifling of guns, the development of the breech-block and new, more powerful explosives.

Shellback: an old sailor, a tough nut.

Shelve: dip, slope or incline gently, as in a shelving shore or coast.

Shelvocke, George (*fl.*1690–1728): privateer who, after service in the Navy, was given command by a group of London merchants of the privateering *Speedwell*. His adventurous career included the capture of a Portuguese ship off the coast of Brazil, being wrecked on Juan Fernandez, the building of another ship and the seizure of several other treasures. But perhaps his chief claim to fame (though unknown to him) is that an incident in which he figured inspired one of the greatest poems in the English language. When rounding Cape Horn he caused a black albatross to be shot – an incident related by Wordsworth to Coleridge, who thereupon wrote 'The Ancient Mariner', his most famous work.

'And a good south wind sprung up behind;
The Albatross did follow,
And every day, for food or play,
Came to the mariners' hollo!

In mist or cloud, on mast or shroud,
It perch'd for vespers nine;
Whiles all the night, through fog-smoke white,
Glimmer'd the white moonshine.'

'God save thee, ancient Mariner,
From the fiends that plague thee thus'. –
Why look'st thou so?' – 'With my crossbow
I shot the Albatross.'

'The Ancient Mariner', *Lyrical Ballads* (1798)

Sherley, Sir Anthony: *see* SHIRLEY.

Shetland bus: light-hearted name given to boats engaged during the Second World War in secret passages between Shetland and Norway. Fishing boats, manned by Norwegians, were used at first but were replaced in 1943 by American-built submarine chasers. Eight of the fishing boats and 50 men were lost out of 94 trips made, but the three submarine chasers made 129 trips and suffered no casualties. Secret agents and stores were landed by the Shetland bus, and refugees and returning agents were brought away.

Shetland Islands: a group of one large and many small islands and islets lying N.E. of the Orkneys and northern Scotland. The islands are the most northerly part of the British Isles and are in the same latitudes as the southern tip of Greenland. They have a strong Scandinavian tradition, and until recently their people have relied almost solely on fishing, crofting and raising sheep. Today the development of the Brent oilfield in the North Sea, about 100 miles N.E. of the Shetlands, has brought new activities to the islands and given them further strategic importance. Sullom Voe, a long and deep inlet on the north of Mainland, the chief island, may develop as a great oil-port capable of handling modern tankers of the largest size. During the First World War the huge anchorage at Sullom Voe was used by the Royal Navy, and in the Second World War it also served as a base for R.A.F. flying-boats patrolling northern waters.

Shift: any change in the direction of the wind, covering both veering (in a clockwise direction) and backing (in an anticlockwise direction).

Ship: despite the great variety of vessels that the word now covers, and the even greater variety of words derived from or associated with it, 'ship', to be technically accurate, means a sea-going vessel with three or more square-rigged masts; and that is also the definition of the term 'ship-rigged'.

Ship, to: to take or send on board (cargo, gear, etc.); also to take in water from a heavy sea or from a leak (to 'ship it green' is when a solid unbroken wave comes inboard). Other meanings are: to engage for service in a vessel; to place something in its proper position (thus to 'ship a mast' or 'ship the tiller'; to 'ship oars' is to remove them from the rowlocks and place them inboard); to embark and sail, as in 'we were due to ship from London on the next day'.

Shipbuilding: considering that this is one of man's most ancient crafts, beginning in the dawn of history with primitive man hollowing out a log or simply sitting astride a piece of driftwood, it remained strangely imprecise for centuries, and it is little short of miraculous that epic exploits and voyages were accomplished with vessels fashioned so haphazardly. Only a few years before the beginning of the 18th century, Paul Hoste, a mathematician, wrote:

It cannot be denied that the art of constructing ships, which is so necessary to the state, is the least perfect of all the arts. The best constructors build the two principal parts of a ship, viz. the bow and the stern, almost entirely by eye; whence it happens that the same constructor, building at the same time two ships after the same model, most frequently makes them so unequal that they have quite opposite sailing qualities.

In 1862, Lord Robert Montagu, M.P. for Huntingdonshire, had to plead in the House for better advice on shipbuilding. That he was amply justified is proved by the fact that eight years later the *Captain*, a new ironclad still rigged as a sailing ship, turned over in a moderate gale as a result of serious instability and was lost in three minutes. Things had not improved all that much since, over two centuries before, the new Swedish warship *Wasa* tilted over in about 100 ft of water before she had cleared the harbour at Stockholm.

Nowadays mathematician, scientist, naval architect and craftsman have come together as never before to solve the manifold problems of design, speed, buoyancy, equilibrium, stress and strain; and the law has imposed such strict standards that many, or most, of the old errors can be avoided. But nothing can ever be completely taken for granted, for the old saying still holds: 'It is not yet known what the sea requires.'

See colour section.
See also SHIPWRIGHT.

Ship-money: ancient method of providing and financing the fleet, first by a levy of ships and then by commutation into money payment. Although it can be traced back to pre-Conquest days, it is always chiefly associated with Charles I and the Civil War (1642–9), of which it was one of the causes. In 1634, the necessity of raising a fleet led

Charles to impose a levy on the coast towns. Despite some opposition, this was generally submitted to; but subsequent writs, involving the inland towns and counties, brought fierce opposition. It found its most famous expression in John Hampden (1594–1643), whose county, Buckinghamshire, was required to provide either a ship of 450 tons, manned and equipped for six months, or the sum of £4500. Hampden was brought to trial in respect of the 20 shillings levied on the parish of Stoke Mandeville. After much legal argument, seven of the judges decided for the Crown, two for Hampden on technical grounds and three for him on every count. An act annulling 'the business of ship-money' was passed in 1641.

And ... it was at last (upon the refusal of a private gentleman to pay twenty or thirty shillings as his share) publicly argued with great solemnity before all the judges of England in the exchequer-chamber, and by much the major part of them, the king's right to impose asserted, and the tax adjudged lawful: which judgment proved of more advantage and credit to the gentleman condemned ... than to the king's service.

Edward, Earl of Clarendon, *The History of the Rebellion and Civil Wars in England* (1702–4)

Ship of the line: a sailing warship capable of lying in the LINE OF BATTLE.

You truly told us years ago that 'Take it all in all, a ship of the line is the most honourable thing that man, as a gregarious animal, has ever produced.'

Robert Leslie, in a letter to John Ruskin (1884)

There has been, perhaps, no such beautiful thing on earth, the work of man's hands, as an old 74 under sail.

John Masefield, *Sea Life in Nelson's Time* (1905)

Shipping his land face: a phrase used of some of the old-time tough skippers when they went ashore, polite and all smiles, to greet the owners and merchants. On sailing day, some made a ceremony of sending for a bucket of seawater to 'wash off their land face' – a fair promise of what lay ahead. *See also* SHORE SAINTS.

Ship-rigged: *see* SHIP.

Shipshape and Bristol-fashion: all in good order, trim and neat. 'Bristol-fashion' had its origin in the time when Bristol was the chief west-coast port and enjoyed its greatest commercial prosperity. The great increase in shipping and commerce, caused by the SLAVE TRADE, led to a high respect for the good nautical standards set by the ships and sailors of Bristol.

Ship's husband: the agent of a ship-owner who in port superintends all matters connected with the ship's seaworthiness, business, trade and other activities outside the scope of her officers and crew.

Ship-worm: *see* COPPER SHEATHING.

Shipwrecks: the number of wrecks through the centuries and round the world is naturally beyond any computation. In 1800 Lloyd's of London estimated that the loss of merchant and other ships 'by wreck upon lee-shores, coasts, and disasters in the open sea' was about an average of 365 ships yearly (Haydn's *Dictionary of Dates*, 1885). In 1830 *Lloyd's Lists* gives 677 British vessels totally lost. Later in the century there were 49,322 wrecks in the 25 years 1854–79. The comparison between the loss of sailing ships and steamships becomes increasingly striking as the years go on (though the numbers of ships operating in each category are not easy to come by and

must affect the situation): in 1848, 501 British sailing vessels were wrecked against 13 steamers; in 1851 600 sailing ships and 11 steamers.

For some famous shipwrecks in English history, *see ASSOCIATION*; DARLING, GRACE; *MARY ROSE*; *ROYAL GEORGE*; *TITANIC*; *TORREY CANYON*. *See also* SALVAGE.

Shipwright: the ancient and honourable term for a shipbuilder, 'wright' coming from the Anglo-Saxon word for 'worker'. The shipwright looks back to Noah for his ancestry.

> The sea that is above the sky
> Low on it like a load did lie,
> The skies grew green and black and nigh
> And broke: and the Flood came.
> But through the inky violet sea
> A candle-lighted ship went she
> Whose master made our Mystery
> With Noah for his name.
>
> > G. K. Chesterton, 'The Shipwrights'
> > from 'For Five Guilds'

In England, the Company of Shipwrights dates back to *c*.1605, though various offices, e.g. of Master Shipwright, existed from Tudor times. It is one of the City Guilds or Livery Companies (so called from the distinctive dress or livery worn by members on ceremonial occasions). Despite the honour of their craft, shipwrights long had a name for pilfering (*see* CHIPS). Kipling's poem 'King Henry VII and the Shipwrights' tells a pleasant story of Henry VII coming 'in an old jerkin and patched hose that no man might him mark' to 'Hamull on the Hoke in the Countie of Suthampton' to see if his shipwrights working on the *Mary of the Tower* were doing him wrong. He found them stripping the ship, even to the extent of heaving the main mast overboard, sawing it up into

planks and making beds for their wives and children, as well as stealing the pots and pans from the galley. This incensed Robert Brygandyne who, though he firmly believed in the shipwright's traditional 'perks', could not tolerate thieving. He caught the ringleader, Slingawai, and threw him overboard in the mud.

> 'I have taken plank and rope and nail, without the King his leave,
> After the custom of Portsmouth, but I will not suffer a thief.
> Nay, never lift up thy hand at me – there's no clean hands in the trade.
> Steal in measure,' quo' Brygandyne. 'There's measure in all things made!'

According to the story, Henry was so pleased with the shipwright's 'honest' attitude that he made Bob Brygandyne his Clerk of the Ships; and there was a real Robert BRYGANDYNE who held this office in Henry VII's time.

Shirley (or **Sherley**), **Sir Anthony** (1565–?1635): Elizabethan adventurer who, after attaining a fellowship of All Souls College, Oxford (1581), turned his talents to roving over land and sea, with fluctuating fortunes. He commanded an expedition against the Portuguese settlement of San Thomé (1596), took Santiago (Cape Verde Islands), landed in Dominica and Venezuela, and came back to England via Newfoundland. He went on political and commercial commissions, received a fine mixture of decorations, foreign titles and prison sentences, and finished up in poverty in Madrid. He published a narrative of his travels in Persia in 1613. *See also* PARRY, WILLIAM.

Shivering: (1) the state of a sail shaking or fluttering in the wind, neither full nor aback; or of a whole vessel caught in some phenomenal wave action.

The water, I suppose, hitting the naked form of the ship simultaneously throughout a large area, naturally struck her with immense force. The effect was to bring the craft up 'all standing', and the blow would be followed by an almost human shivering, which was apt to make one think that the hull had not been able to withstand it.

Admiral Sir Christopher Cradock,
Whispers from the Fleet (1907, describing
his destroyer's behaviour in a
China Seas typhoon)

(2) To 'shiver' can also mean to break into pieces as would the timbers of a ship when striking a reef or running into a rocky shore; hence the supposedly old nautical exclamation 'Shiver my timbers!', much used in fiction.

Shiver my timbers: *see* SHIVERING.

Shoal: a shallow stretch of water, often associated with sand-banks.

Shoe an anchor: improve the holding power of an anchor by fitting 'shoes' (plates of timber or metal) to its flukes.

Shore: (1) the meeting of sea and land. The word has many specific nautical applications, and can mean ashore or on land, as in 'shore party', 'shore duty' etc. (*see also* INSHORE; LEE; OFF). (2) A strong timber beam used for supporting or strengthening. A ship in dry dock is 'shored up' with shores.

Shoreham: a seaport on the West Sussex coast, six miles west of Brighton. The original site of Shoreham harbour was further inland, but a shift in the position of the mouth of the River Adur, on which it lay, led to the development of modern Shoreham, which, though a minor port, has a busy trade in coal, timber, grain, cement etc.

Shore saints and sea devils: captains who were very decorous and polite characters ashore, especially when meeting owners and shippers, but underwent a mysterious and sudden transformation at sea. *See also* SHIPPING HIS LAND FACE.

Shot: the general name for various kinds of non-exploding projectiles fired from naval guns, but excluding bombs fired from mortars in bomb-vessels, and explosive projectiles or shells from the early incendiary carcass to the modern explosive shell. The most common form of shot in the old sailing Navy was the round, solid, cast-iron ball, which varied in weight and size according to the calibre of the gun, from the 2-lb. shot of the small falconet of the 15th and 16th centuries to the 66-lb. shot of the cannon royal. The Royal Navy in its great sailing days came to rely mainly on cannons firing 32-lb. and 24-lb. shot, but the carronade or 'smasher', introduced in 1779, fired a 68-lb. shot. Guns were referred to by the weight of the shot fired; the main heavy guns of ships of the line were the 32-pounders, which were on the lowest gun-deck, with the 24- and 18-pounders on the upper decks.

Other kinds of shot were chain-shot, two shots joined by a chain, and bar-shot, two half-balls joined with a bar, both of which were fired to cripple the enemy's masts and rigging. For the same purpose there was also a kind of shot known variously as langrage, langridge, langrel and langrace. This consisted of a kind of canister

Chain-shot.

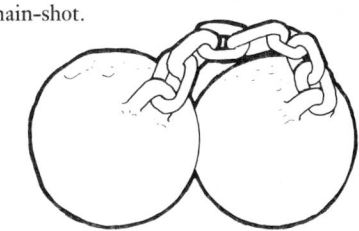

containing jagged pieces of iron which scattered when fired. It was, needless to say, devastating not only to sails and rigging but also to men on deck, and was once much favoured by privateers. Finally, there was case shot, which released from a container a spread of small iron bullets or stones amongst the crew on deck. Grape-shot was similar and, as its name suggests, was a cluster of musket-balls which flew in all directions from the container just like the later shrapnel from an exploding shell.

Shot across the bows, to put a: to fire a single round of shot or shell ahead of another ship, warning her that she must stop or take whatever action has been ordered. It is generally used only when the initial order has been ignored.

Shovell (or Shovel), Sir Cloudisley (or Clowdisley; 1650–1707): admiral who lost his life in particularly grim circumstances after a fine naval career, beginning at the age of 14. One story tells of him swimming under hot fire with dispatches in his mouth. He greatly contributed to the English victory at La Hogue (1692), and played a prominent part in the capture of Gibraltar and the action off Malaga (1704). On the homeward voyage after the destruction of the French Mediterranean fleet at TOULON in 1707, he was wrecked off the Scilly Isles (*see ASSOCIATION*). Described by Addison as 'a brave rough English Admiral', he was apparently cast ashore still alive but was then murdered by a woman wrecker, or by fishermen, for the sake of an emerald ring he was wearing. Later the ring was recovered, and the Admiral's body was buried in Westminster Abbey.

It is certainly a just observation, that virtue alone creates nobility. He who enjoys a title by birth, derives it from the virtue of his ancestors;

From a portrait by Dahl.

and he who raises himself into high rank, which is a sort of self-creation, supplies the wants of his ancestors by personal merit . . . His courage, and his sincerity, were alike unquestionable; and though this was not the most credulous age, yet there never was heard of such an infidel, as one who did not believe that Shovell had both.

Dr John Campbell, *Lives of the British Admirals* (1812 edition)

Shove off: to leave the shore in a boat, or to push or bear off another boat with a boat-hook; hence the slang expression meaning 'go away'.

Show a leg: a traditional part of the order, still used, for men to turn out of their hammocks and start the day's duties. It probably arose in earlier times when men were not allowed to go on shore when in harbour for fear they would desert, and so their womenfolk were permitted to stay on board. When the order to show a leg was obeyed it was presumably possible to differentiate between the hairy leg of a man

474

and the smooth leg of a woman. The practice of allowing women to stay on board as 'guests' was abolished long ago, but the old cry remains part of naval tradition.

Shrouds: standing rigging supporting the masts of a sailing ship laterally, that is on the port and starboard sides. Shrouds run from the mast-head to the deck abreast the mast, where they are secured to the chain-plates on the ship's sides. In larger sailing ships with top-masts another set of shrouds ran from the mast-head to the tops (the platforms at the head of the lower mast). Each mast had its shrouds, which were made of strong ropes joined horizontally by ratlines. With the coming of the steamship the complex of shrouds was replaced by wire ropes, and in many modern ships shrouds have almost completely disappeared. *See also* RIGGING.

Sicily: the largest island in the Mediterranean, lying between the 'toe' of south-western Italy and the coast of North Africa. From earliest times Sicily has been subjected to conquest and settlement as one Mediterranean power succeeded another. (e.g. CAPE PASSARO, BATTLE OF). In the Napoleonic Wars Sicily was one of the vital strategic points of the Mediterranean, especially after the French in 1806 had invaded the Kingdom of Naples and controlled the Italian peninsula. But in January of that year the British had landed a garrison at Messina in Sicily which became the British headquarters in the central Mediterranean. Napoleon was determined to conquer Sicily, and it was the task of Vice-Admiral Collingwood, in command of the British Mediterranean fleet, to thwart his further advance and any attack on Sicily by bringing the French fleet under Admiral Ganteaume to battle.

This he failed to do, but the far-ranging and enormous endeavours of Collingwood's ships, together with the strengthening of the defences of Sicily, prevented the expected invasion. The British fleet continued to hold sway in the Mediterranean.

Sicily again featured in British history during the Second World War when in July 1943 the Allies made their landings from North Africa and captured the island. Sicily then became the springboard for the invasion of the Italian mainland in the following September.

Sick and Wounded (or **Sick and Hurt**) **Board:** created in 1653, during the First Dutch War, to make provision for the casualties. Its aims, though their realization fell far short, were to appoint representatives in every port, rent sick quarters, provide necessary warmth, food and lighting, appoint surgeons and nurses etc. The Board continued through the Second and Third Dutch Wars, the most distinguished Commissioner being John EVELYN.

Side: the two halves of a vessel running from stem to stern, as in 'starboard side'. The word occurs in many compounds, e.g. 'side-lights', the green (starboard) and red (port) navigation lights; 'side ropes'; 'side party' etc. A 'side boy' is a young rating with duties at the gangway, e.g. tending boats coming alongside. 'Manning the side' means that those detailed for duty at the gangway assemble for the formal reception or departure of an officer or visitor; for 'piping the side' *see* BOATSWAIN'S CALL.

Side arms: arms worn at a man's side or on the waist, e.g. pistols, revolvers, bayonets etc.

Sight: an observation of the altitude of sun,

moon or star taken with a SEXTANT for the purpose of fixing a ship's latitude. When it is combined with longitude worked from a chronometer, a ship's position can then be fixed.

Signal letters: *see* IDENTIFICATION MARKS.

Signals and signalling systems: methods by which ships can talk to each other, to give information, transmit orders, send warning, direct manoeuvres and battle operations, etc. These ways of communication can be roughly grouped under four headings:

1. By voice, direct when near enough, or amplified by speaking-trumpet, megaphone, loud-hailer, etc. over greater distances; and, in modern times, by radio and telephone.

2. By personal messenger; thus, a fleet or squadron commander would often hoist a signal summoning a representative from each ship to come aboard the flag-ship to receive orders. This representative officer normally signed the centrally held order as proof that he had read or understood it.

3. By auditory signals to an established code, using guns, whistles, sirens etc.

4. By visual signals, also to a previously agreed code, using lights, rockets and – most of all – flags.

All such systems have their advantages and disadvantages. A voice, even the most stentorian and amplified, can carry over only limited distances. Personal messengers can be used only when ships are grouped fairly close at hand. Flags cannot be seen at night; and lights cannot be relied on in thick weather. Human frailty and misunderstanding were, and are, all too frequent.

Firing guns was a very old method of signalling. In *Treasure Island* Captain Smollett gives the crew of the *Hispaniola*

some hours of recreation ashore and says: 'I'll fire a gun half an hour before sundown.' Nathaniel Boteler, writing in about 1634, described how an admiral about to sail in 'hazie and darcke weather' could 'about two or three houres before he begin to waye his Anchors cause fire to be given to a single Piece of Ordinance.' A 'minute-gun', so called because it was fired at one-minute intervals, was a well-established signal of distress. Two-minute, three-minute guns etc. could convey other messages.

But, over the centuries, the most important signalling systems that evolved used flags of different colours (and sometimes shapes). Long experience proved that if flag signalling were to be reliable and effective the colours must be sufficiently bold and clear to prevent blurring or merging one into the other, and the designs must be simple. In practice the colours used (with the addition of black and white) reduced themselves to red, blue and yellow; and, to simplify matters even further, these basic colours were used only in certain combinations in a single flag, e.g. red/white, yellow/blue, blue/white.

Plenty of examples of signalling systems can be found as early as the 16th and 17th centuries, but it was not till the latter half of the 17th century that a really efficient code appeared in the British Navy. In 1673 a proper 'signal book' emerged, with the various flags drawn and coloured, and their positions and meanings fully explained.

By 1750 there were sixteen flags in use, their different positions and combinations making possible 144 different signals, and in another thirty years 50 flags could be used to make 330 signals, e.g. the Admiral's flag at the main top-gallant mast-head with a red flag beneath meant 'Prepare for battle', and a red flag at the foretop masthead signified 'Engage the enemy'.

The chief disadvantage about this system, even though it was much more efficient than the old, was that it was tied down to the official Fighting Instructions: the officer in command could only say what those Instructions allowed him to say. Thus the next great step forward was a flexible and lively code, a language in its own right, that could be used to say anything at all within reason, irrespective of the old hide-bound rules. This development came with the evolution of numerary codes and vocabulary signal books (*see* NUMERARY SIGNALS). Among the men who made great contributions to this evolution were Richard KEMPENFELT, Home POPHAM and Captain MARRYAT. *See also* INTERNATIONAL CODE OF SIGNALS; PASCO, JOHN.

Simonstown: harbour and chief South African naval base, between Cape Town and the Cape of Good Hope. Whilst South Africa was a member of the British Empire and, later, Commonwealth, Simonstown was used as a base by the Royal Navy, and its development began early in the 20th century; but when South Africa became an independent republic (1961) British ships withdrew. The importance of Simonstown for the defence of the Cape route was re-emphasized by the closure of the SUEZ CANAL (1967–75) and the continuing use of the route as an alternative to the Canal.

Simoon: a hot, dry wind of the Red Sea. Like the SIROCCO its heated air originates over the adjoining desert lands.

Singapore: island, city and independent republic within the Commonwealth, situated at the southern end of the Malay Peninsula. Founded (1819) by Sir Stamford Raffles, Singapore grew into an important entrepôt trading centre within the British Empire, and between the two World Wars a great naval base was built there. One of the serious British reverses during the Second World War was in 1942 when the Malay States were overrun by the Japanese and Singapore was surrendered. Since its independence this great free port has achieved very rapid growth and development, and has become one of the largest centres of trade and wealth in the Far East.

Single up, to: to cast off additional berthing ropes, generally leaving only head and stern ropes and two springs. The order to single up is given preparatory to leaving from alongside a berthed position.

Sinnet: *see* SENNET.

Siren: a hooter or whistle used in ships to give signals of their intended manoeuvre or in fog. It is operated by steam or air driven through a revolving perforated disc. Of warships' sirens those fitted in destroyers seem to have a most distinctive and penetrating sound.

'Sir Geraint': *see* LANDING CRAFT.

'Sirius': the first iron ship officially classed at Lloyd's (1837). She was originally intended for the Cork–London run but was chartered for traffic to America. She thus became the first ship to make the Atlantic crossing entirely under steam and, against strong winds, averaged 6·7 knots.

'Sir Lancelot': one of the most famous and beautiful of the clippers, built by R. Steele of Greenock and launched in 1865.

Sirocco (or scirocco): a hot, enervating wind originating in the Sahara and blowing from the south and south-east over the Mediterranean, most frequent in late summer and autumn. It is similar in character to the SIMOON.

'Sir Winston Churchill': *see* TRAINING SHIP.

Sisal: a vegetable fibre used for making ROPE. The name comes from Sisal, a port in Yucatan, Mexico, the home of the agave plant, whose leaves provide the fibre. Sisal is commercially cultivated in the countries of East Africa and in Indonesia, which produce the bulk of the world's supply. Sisal rope is hairy and light-coloured, but may be tarred.

Sister-ship: one built to the same specifications or in the same class, at approximately the same time.

Sixpenny Office: former government office responsible for the management of the monthly 6d. deducted from seamen's pay to support the two naval charities of the Chatham Chest and Greenwich Hospital. The Sixpenny Office was set up in 1695 when Greenwich was founded, but the two funds were not amalgamated until 1814. The Sixpenny Office disappeared in 1834 when a reformed system of naval PENSIONS was developed.

Sixteen bells: an old nautical custom of striking the ship's bell sixteen times at midnight to welcome the New Year. It is generally done by the youngest member of the crew.

'Skeered o' Nothing': once suggested by an American senator as an appropriate name for a new 30- or 40-gun warship, in answer to the British *Dreadnought*.

Skiff: a small light boat; according to an 18th-century writer, 'resembling a yawl,

also a wherry without masts or sails, usually employed to pass a river.'

Skilly: a thin oatmeal gruel mixed with some meat, served to sailors in former times, and also to prisoners, who often got little else.

Skim: to pass lightly and quickly over the water, a movement possible only for vessels and boats of very shallow draught.

Skipper: sea-captain, properly applied only to one commanding a small merchant ship. White-crested waves were sometimes known as 'skipper's daughters'.

Sky gazer: *see* MOONRAKER.

Skylight: a glazed overhead window let into and standing above the deck to allow light into the compartment below.

Skysail: sail carried above the royals, sometimes on all masts, sometimes (as in the case of the *Cutty Sark*) on the main mast alone.

Slack water: when the tide pauses at high water and low water. There is no marked run of the tide over a total period of about half an hour before and after the actual times of high or low tide, and the water is 'slack'.

Slave trade: the capture, transportation and sale of human beings to work in bondage. 'The slave trade' generally refers to the taking of negroes from West Africa for sale in the New World, a trade which existed from the 16th to the mid-19th centuries. Slavery has, however, existed from ancient times; during the long conflict between the Moslem and Christian worlds, captured Christians were carried off to row as slaves in the Mediterranean galleys, and for long the Arabs engaged in a profitable

478

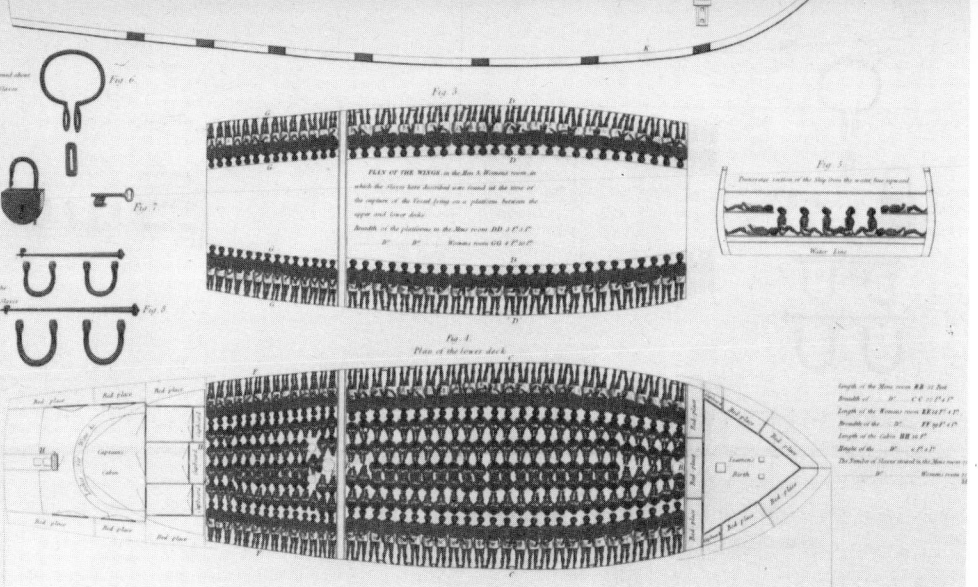

Plan of the French slaver *Vigilante*, captured on the African coast in 1822, showing the method of packing the 'cargo'.

trade in negro slaves in East Africa. Slavery is still heard of today in some of the more remote and less civilized parts of the world, although it is internationally condemned.

The West Indian slave trade was begun by the Spanish and Portuguese when the slaughter of the native inhabitants of their new dominions in the West Indies and South America left insufficient labour to work the plantations. Sir John HAWKINS may be said to have begun the British slave trade, from which flowed so much misery for many and wealth for others. He made three voyages between 1562 and 1568, taking slaves from the Guinea coast of West Africa and selling them in the West Indies, thereby bringing prosperity both to himself and to his home port of Plymouth.

By the mid-17th century the slave trade was well-established. The Dutch had ousted the Portuguese as the chief traders on the Guinea coast, and were selling slaves to the tobacco planters of Virginia. The right to supply slaves to the Spanish slave markets in the New World was known as the ASIENTO, a right disputed between

Dutch, French and English traders. By the Treaty of Utrecht (1713) the Asiento was transferred to Britain. Thereafter during the 18th century the slave trade steadily increased, and it was the merchants of Bristol and Liverpool who chiefly profited, sending their ships on the triangular run from Britain. The first leg of the run was from Liverpool, Bristol or London to the coast of West Africa; there cotton and other fabrics, rum, firearms and trinkets were exchanged for slaves, often captured inland and driven down to the coast by harsh traders, both negro and European. The second leg, known as the middle passage, took the ship, loaded with slaves in crowded and appallingly unhealthy conditions, to the slave auctions in the West Indies and southern states of America. On the homeward journey the ships returned to Britain with cotton, sugar, tobacco and rum.

By the middle of the 18th century Liverpool had surpassed Bristol in the number of ships and men engaged in the trade, in which the Americans themselves were also taking a prominent part, many slave ships being based on the New England ports. So the trade in slavery continued until the Anti-Slavery Movement in England, led by Thomas Clarkson and William Wilberforce, succeeded in getting it declared illegal in 1807. In the same year the importation of slaves into America was outlawed, but the emancipation or freeing of the slaves was not achieved in British colonies until 1834, and in America not until 1865, at the conclusion of the Civil War between the northern (Federal) and southern (Confederate) states.

When the slaves were shipped from Africa they were systematically packed in the holds so close together that many died on the passage, although this was clearly to the disadvantage of the slave-trader. It is probable that over two million negroes were sold into slavery in the New World during the 18th century, and many hundreds of thousands more during the first half of the 19th century, for slaves were in demand and the trade was very profitable in spite of the penalties imposed on the traffickers. In 1824 Britain had declared slave trade piracy to be punishable by death; many ships of the British Navy

were dispatched on anti-slavery patrols and cruised off the coast of West Africa to intercept the slavers until the trade was finally put down with the agreement of all nations.

Sling one's hook (or **hook it**): slang for to go away, leave quickly etc. The origin is probably nautical, from the sense of taking one's hook, meaning to weigh anchor or depart.

Slip: (1) an alternative name for SLIPWAY. (2) The difference between the theoretical and the actual effect of a propeller in moving a ship. (3) As a verb, to slip is to let go, e.g. to 'slip from a mooring' or 'slip the cable'. (4) In 'slip-knot', 'slip-hook', 'slip-rope', the word 'slip' implies quick and easy release.

Slipway: slope or ramp leading into the water, on which vessels may be built, from which they can be launched, and up which they can be drawn. Some slipways are fitted with rails and a cradle for smaller craft to be launched or brought ashore. Lifeboat stations often have slipways for these purposes.

Sloop: commonly defined as fore-and-aft rigged vessel with one mast, but this is too easy, since the number of masts and the rig of the sloop varied a good deal. An 18th-century writer describes it as 'a small vessel furnished with one mast, the main sail of which is attached to a guff [gaff] above, to the mast on its foremost edge, and to a long boom below.'

Until about 1760 all British sloops-of-war were two-masted and were rigged as snows, ketches or brigantines. In 1760 heavier ship-rigged sloops were introduced carrying fourteen or sixteen guns. To add to the difficulties of defining the sloop accurately, the yacht-class sloop is a very different matter from a sloop-of-war. By the beginning of the 20th century, the latter had become an unarmoured ship of about 1000 tons with a speed of 14 knots.

Slops: ready-made clothes (stockings, shirts, canvas suits, breeches, etc.) sold on board ship to seamen. In later times the term also covered such commodities as tobacco and soap. In the 17th century the purser often took a shilling-in-the-pound profit on what he sold, and others took their cut. The cost of purchases was deducted from the men's pay. An order of 1663 set a list of prices to be charged: caps 2s. 6d., blue shirts 3s. 6d., yarn stockings 3d., cotton waistcoats 3s., canvas suits 5s. etc. It was customary to sell at the main mast in the presence of a senior officer. The practice represented no mood of philanthropy on the part of the Admiralty. Some such arrangement was necessary – as many officers were not slow to point out – in view of the deplorable condition in which many men joined the ship, dirty, ragged, unshod, a menace to the health and good working of the fleet. *See also* PROVANT CLOTHES.

Slow-match: *see* QUICK-MATCH.

Sluys, Battle of (24 June 1340): the first of the three important sea-fights of the Hundred Years' War: an attack on the French fleet of the harbour of Sluys, on the coast of Flanders. It was in fact more a case of landsmen fighting at sea rather than a naval battle, with Edward III in command, at the head of his knights and archers, who won the day and celebrated the victory with junketings on board, including 'great noises with trumpets and all kinds of other instruments'. There was clearly some attempt at a regular battle order and some provision for casualties, either ships or men:

The king then drew up all his vessels, placing the strongest in the front, and on the wings his archers. Between every two vessels with archers there was one of men-at-arms. He stationed some detached vessels as a reserve, full of archers, to assist and help such as might be damaged.

There were in this fleet a great many ladies from England, countesses, baronesses, and knights' and gentlemen's wives, who were going to attend on the queen at Ghent: these the king had guarded most carefully by three hundred men-at-arms and five hundred archers . . .

The battle then began very fiercely; archers and cross-bowmen shot with all their might at each other, and the men-at-arms engaged hand to hand: in order to be more successful, they had large grapnels, and iron hooks with chains, which they slung from ship to ship, to moor them to each other. There were many valiant deeds performed, many prisoners, and many rescues.

Jean Froissart, *Chronicles* (1350–90; quoted in Thomas Johnes's translation, 1803–5)

Smack: small sailing craft, usually single-masted and associated with inshore fishing, but formerly having a much wider commercial use. Before the coming of railways, smacks of between 150 and 200 tons were a popular means of transport round the coast, sometimes for long distances, e.g. from London to Scotland. These were strong vessels, cutter-rigged, transporting both cargo and passengers; and, at least till the end of the Napoleonic Wars, they carried a few guns. Steam packets gradually reduced the trade, but the London–Leith smacks went on till the 1840s, being for many people a more congenial mode of transport than the stage-coach or lumbering waggon on land.

Small stuff: general name for all small cordage under about an inch in circum-ference, e.g. spunyarn, marline, twine, etc.

Smart ticket: a certificate formerly given to seamen who had suffered a wound (or 'smart'), enabling them to secure payment or compensation as out-pensioners of Greenwich Hospital. Such payments were known as 'smart money'; *see also* PENSIONS.

Smasher: nickname for the CARRONADE.

Smith, John (1580–1631): not usually reckoned a seaman but, judging from his own accounts, fully deserving the descrip-tion, since many of his adventures were at sea, including sailing to Italy with a shipload of pilgrims from France, being thrown overboard as a Huguenot and rescued by pirates. He also made two voyages in 1608, exploring the coasts of Chesapeake Bay and the Potomac and Rappahannock Rivers. But he is best-known as 'Captain' John Smith, the virtual founder of the colony of Virginia and the hero of the well-loved story of his rescue by Pocohontas, daughter of the chief Pow-hatan, when he was about to have his Lincolnshire brains bashed by hostile Indian clubs.

Smith, Sir (William) Sidney (1764–1840): admiral. He entered the Navy at the age of 13 and spent the years of peace travelling or in the service of other countries (e.g. with Sweden against Russia). When hostilities with France began again (1793) he arrived in a small ship of his own off Toulon, but soon got an official command, lasting till 1796, when (characteristically, it might almost be said) he managed to get captured during an attack on Le Havre. He spent two years as a prisoner and escaped by a notable exploit which brought him back to England and the command of an 80-gun ship, the *Tigre*. He is perhaps chiefly remembered for his heroic defence of Acre against Bonaparte (1799), but his whole career was full of adventure; after his own active service was terminated, he turned up as a spectator at the Battle of Waterloo. A quarrelsome and vain character, always eloquent about his own exploits, he was an incredible mixture of conceit, insubordination, unpredict-ability, daring, resourcefulness and imagi-nation – almost, it might be concluded, born out of time and belonging, in spirit and action, more to the Elizabethan age than to his own more disciplined period.

Smoke: word occurring in a number of terms, usually contemptuous, used of steamships by old sailing men, e.g. 'smoke-boat', 'smoke-box'; also 'smoke stack' (funnel).

Smoke-screen: dense cloud of smoke from guns or chemicals deliberately put up to conceal ship movements from the enemy; hence the everyday expression meaning some manoeuvre intended to conceal one's real intentions.

Smugglers' loft: gallery in some sea-coast churches, openly used for worship by local smugglers and their families in a body. One such church was Dundonald, on the coast of Ayr. One suspects that, with the connivance of the parson, the use of the loft was not confined to religious observances.

Smuggling: the illegal carrying of goods in or out of a country, usually to avoid paying duty on them. Historically, smuggling was an activity usually associated with the coast, and even particular counties, and those actively engaged in it were often daring and skilful seamen. At certain periods it was looked upon by whole communities as a by no means discreditable or dishonourable business, even when it ran contrary to national policy and involved some succouring of the enemy. Napoleon, for instance, had a special camp prepared for the accommodation of British smugglers and said they took from France every year 'forty or fifty millions of silk and brandy'. At any one time there might be as many as 500 smugglers on French soil, having sailed their swift luggers under the noses of the Channel ships of the line. Some, however (e.g. Richard ETCHES and Harry PAULET), seem to have been outstandingly patriotic, despite their law-breaking; and some, according to their lights, were strictly honest (e.g. Jack RATTENBURY). Surprisingly, smuggling gear was sometimes openly advertised with other, above-board merchandise:

A very useful CART, fit for a maltster, ash-man, or a smuggler – it will carry 80 half-ankers or tubs; one small ditto that will carry 40 tuns; also two very good wooden Saddles, three Pads, Straps, Bridles, Girth, Horse-cloth, Corn-bin, a very good Vault, and many articles that are very useful to a Smuggler.

From a Suffolk newspaper (1785)

Along with courage went considerable ingenuity. An innocent-looking boat might have a stout iron bar suspended beneath her from which hung a dozen or so barrels. A cleverly-weighted mark, covered over at full tide, could be attached to a raft of tubs almost down on the sea-bed; and Thomas Hardy, in *Wessex Tales* (1888), tells of an amazing movable apple-tree: a riding-officer on the track of a cargo of brandy brought up from Lulworth Cove became suspicious of an orchard at Overmoyne, a village on the Dorchester–Wareham road.

The excisemen, having re-entered the orchard, acted as if they were positive that here lay hidden the rest of the tubs, which they were determined to find before nightfall. They spread themselves out round the field, and advancing on all fours as before, went anew round every apple-tree in the enclosure. The young tree in the middle again led them to pause, and at length the whole company gathered there in a way which signified that a second chain of reasoning had led them to the same results as the first.

When they had examined the sod hereabouts for some minutes, one of the men rose, ran to a disused porch of the church, where tools were kept, and returned with the sexton's pickaxe and shovel, with which they set to work.

The grass was so green and uninjured that it was difficult to believe that it had been disturbed. The smugglers . . . saw, to their chagrin, the officers stand two on each side of the tree, and, stopping and applying their hands to the soil, they bodily lifted the tree and the turf around it. The apple-tree now showed itself to be growing in a shallow box, with handles for lifting it at each of the four sides. Under the site of the tree a square hole was revealed, and an exciseman went and looked down . . .

The contraband brandy thus uncovered in this unconventional cellar was lifted out and the hiding-place smashed in; but, Hardy records, 'the hole, which had in its time held so much contraband merchandise, was never completely filled up, either then or afterwards, a depression in the ground marking the spot to this day.'

See also PREVENTIVE MEN.

Snapper-rigged: in the old days (especially in America and Canada), indifferently rigged or turned out. It could be applied either to ships or to seamen.

Snatch block: a block with a hinged part that can be opened to allow a bight of a rope to be passed inside on to the sheave on which it runs.

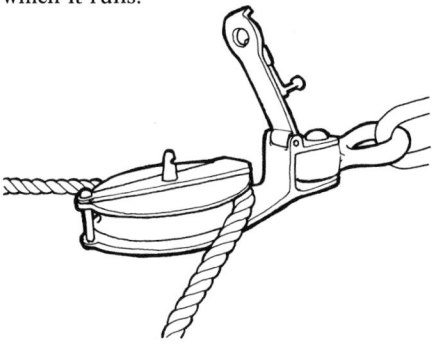

Snell, Hannah (1723–92): adventurous female who is chiefly remembered for disguising herself as a man and serving as a soldier, but is also said to have served with the fleet as a marine. Despite receiving many wounds, she was never detected until, when her ship came home, she revealed her identity. She received a pension but unfortunately died in Bedlam.

Snodgrass, Gabriel (*fl. c.*1790): sounding like a fictional character from Dickens, but in fact a Chief Surveyor to the East India Company and, as such, responsible for many modifications and improvements in ship design. For example, he proposed in 1791 the use of iron 'knees' (the angled structural pieces supporting the beams), and iron riders to strengthen the lower hull.

Snort: *see* SCHNORKEL.

Snotty: old nickname for a midshipman. The 'snotties' nurse' was the officer detailed to look after their general welfare, inspect their log-books etc.

Snow: formerly the largest type of two-masted vessel employed in European waters, often used for carrying dispatches etc., since it was very navigable. As so often in the old Navy, the term was used loosely, and it is difficult to pin down any precise method of rigging. One typical feature was that there was a small additional mast, called the snowmast, which was placed parallel to and behind the main mast. The alternative name 'snowbrig' is sometimes met with.

Snowbrig: *see* SNOW.

Snowflake: *see* STARSHELL.

Society for Nautical Research: society founded in 1910 'to encourage research into nautical antiquities, into matters relating to seafaring and shipbuilding in all ages and among all nations, into the language and customs of the sea, and into other subjects of nautical interest.' Its headquarters may be regarded as the NATIONAL MARITIME MUSEUM, Greenwich, one of whose officers normally acts as Secretary. Its quarterly journal is *The Mariner's Mirror*.

Society Islands: a cluster of islands in French Polynesia, in the centre of the South Pacific Ocean. Many of the islands are composed of old volcanic craters; others are low-lying coral or limestone atolls. The Society Islands are in two groups: the Windward Islands, of which TAHITI is the chief, and the Leeward Islands to the north-west. Though a number of the islands had been visited earlier by Dutch, French and English sailors, it was James Cook who in 1769 found and charted many others. He named the group after the Royal Society, which had sponsored his expedition to observe the transit of Venus from Tahiti. The Society Islands as a whole came under French rule and protection between 1842 and 1900, and today as part of an overseas territory of France they send representatives to the national assembly and senate in Paris.

Soft-ended: term applied to battleships which have the main weight amidships, the ends being comparatively unprotected.

Solebay, Battle of (26 May 1672): action in the Third Anglo-Dutch War, when de Ruyter surprised the English fleet, which was reinforced (if that is the word) by a French squadron. In the course of a muddled and indecisive action, the French managed to sail out of the fight. The hero of the battle was the Earl of Sandwich, who, with a small Dutch ship wedged under his bowsprit, became a sitting target for fire-ships. With the *Royal James* blazing from end to end, he remained on the quarter-deck with two steadfast young companions as she slowly burnt to extinction. *See also PRINCE.* 'Solebay' is an old name for Southwold Bay in Suffolk.

Somerville, Sir James Fownes (1882–1949): admiral. In his early career he was a wireless and signals specialist. He held important commands in the Mediterranean and East Indies before retiring with tuberculosis. Recalled at the outbreak of the Second World War, he served at the Dunkirk evacuation (1940), commanded the famous 'Force H' in the western Mediterranean (1940–42) and was Commander-in-Chief, Eastern Fleet (1942–4).

Sonar: an electronic device emitting ultra-sonic waves through the water for detecting underwater objects, particularly submarines, but also used for detecting mines, shoals of fish, wrecks etc. In its earliest form it was known as ASDIC and was first developed soon after the First World War. The sound wave is reflected or echoed by the underwater object and is recorded at the point of transmission, thus enabling bearing and distance to be automatically registered. At the same time a change of note in the echo indicates whether the range is closing or opening.

Son of a gun: born on board a warship. The phrase dates from the time when seamen's wives were allowed to live on board in harbour and sometimes at sea. A birth on board would most likely take place where the men and their wives lived, which was inevitably near the guns. To call anyone a son of a gun is now mildly abusive, though it was not originally so.

SOS: adopted internationally in 1908 as a Morse distress signal to be sent out by any ship requiring urgent assistance. The letters were chosen because of their simplicity in Morse code, three dots for S and three dashes for O: . . . − − − . . . They do not stand for 'Save our ship' or 'Save our souls', as popular belief has it. 'SOS' now also has the general meaning of a cry for help.

Sound: (1) a strait or channel between two areas of sea, e.g. The Sound, which gives entry to the Baltic between Denmark and Sweden; also an area of water mostly enclosed by land but with entry to the sea, e.g. Plymouth Sound. (2) To sound is to measure the depth of water in the sea etc. (*see* SOUNDING), or (3) to dive and swim deep; whales are said to sound when they do so.

Sounding: the act of measuring the depth of water by LEAD and line or any other device such as the modern ECHO-

SOUNDER; also the measurement of depth so recorded: thus taking a sounding gives a sounding of so many fathoms or metres. A ship is said to be 'in soundings' when she enters shallower waters of less than about 100 fathoms (*see also* STRIKE, TO). For 'sounding the well' *see* PUMPS.

Southampton: the great seaport at the head of the estuary of Southampton Water and lying on a tongue of land between the rivers Test and Itchen. Southampton has been helped in its development by the advantage of double high tides, thought to be caused by the position of the Isle of Wight, around which the second high tide arrives via Spithead some two hours after the earlier tide has reached Southampton via the Solent. Southampton's rapid development as a passenger and cargo port occurred in the 19th and 20th centuries. It became the main home port of many famous passenger liners, especially at the height of the transatlantic traffic before the aeroplane reduced the numbers travelling by sea. But the import and export trade of Southampton grew at the same time, and this has continued with the growth of container traffic and the development of other parts of Southampton Water for specialized maritime trade, e.g. at Fawley, where the modern huge tankers discharge at the oil refinery. *See also* SEALS.

Southern Ocean: another name for the ANTARCTIC Ocean.

South Foreland: a headland of chalk some 300 ft high on the coast of S.E. Kent. On it stand two lighthouses, one now disused, and the other exhibiting a triple-flashing white light every twenty seconds. The South Foreland is a particularly important light because off this coast lie the Goodwin Sands, the shoals and banks of which have

claimed so many ships and lives over the centuries, while between the Goodwins and the coast lies the deep water of The DOWNS.

Southing: difference in latitude south from the last point of reckoning; the distance made good to the south.

Sou'wester: (1) a strong wind blowing from the south-west. The south-westerly wind is the prevailing wind over the British Isles and is often associated with gales. (2) A waterproof hat with a broadish brim lengthened at the back to give protection from rain and spray. The modern oilskin sou'wester has evolved from the canvas hats coated with tar which sailors formerly made for themselves (*see* TARPAULINS).

'Sovereign of the Seas': the chief shipbuilding achievement in the reign of Charles I and indeed one of the finest ships in British history. Designed by Phineas PETT, she was laid down at Woolwich in 1636 by Phineas's son Peter. Throughout her career she was usually known just as *The Sovereign*. She first took the water on 13 October 1637, and both in size and in design she showed a marked advance on any predecessor. She was completely rebuilt at Chatham in 1659–60, and again in 1685; then, having been in action half-a-dozen times, was accidentally burnt out in 1696 while laid up at Chatham.

Her 1637 dimensions were: length of keel, 127 ft; length of gun-deck, 172·5 ft; over-all length, 232 ft; breadth, 46·5 ft; depth in hold, 19·3 ft. She was originally armed with 104 brass guns, ranging in size from 'demi-cannon drakes' weighing 53 cwt each to 'demi-culverin drakes' weighing 8 cwt.

The superb beauty of her carving, decoration and gilding (with her figurehead of King Edgar on horseback trampling down seven conquered kings) is known from one of the most famous ship-pictures in the world, an engraving by John Payne published in the spring of 1638; and Thomas Heywood, the poet, also celebrated her magnificence in a poem written the year before.

For the American clipper of the same name *see* SPEED.

Spanish Armada: *see* ARMADA, THE SPANISH.

Spanish Main: *see* MAIN, THE.

Spanish Succession, War of the (1702–14): struggle caused by the refusal of Louis XIV of France to abide by a settlement formerly agreed by him and William III of England on the succession to the Spanish dominions on the death of Charles II of Spain. Text-books normally, and understandably, concentrate on the great land campaigns of Marlborough, but the Navy's part must not be ignored, especially the capture of Gibraltar by Sir George Rooke (July 1704).

Spanker (or **driver**): fore-and-aft sail set by two spars on the after-side of the mizen mast.

Spar: pole or round piece of timber used for masts, yards etc.

Spar deck: the upper deck of a vessel, from stem to stern.

'Spartiate': the 1793 *Spartiate* was built for the French at Toulon and fought against the British at the Battle of the Nile (1798). After being dismasted she struck her colours and was added to the British Navy. At Trafalgar she was in the weather column, as one of the rearmost ships, but helped in the capture of the Spanish *Neptune*, suffering severe damage and 25 casualties, including five killed. She continued in service for another 50 years, finishing as a sheer-hulk at Plymouth and being broken up there in 1857.

Speak a ship: communicate with a ship at sea, either by hailing or signalling, or in modern times by radio-telephone or radio.

Speed: the rate of a ship's advance through the water. The speed of ships is measured in knots, one KNOT being an advance of one nautical mile in one hour.

In the days of sail a ship was dependent not only on favourable winds to make good speed, but also, of course, on her design and how she was rigged and handled. A skilful captain and an experienced crew could drive a ship to her limits and obtain her best speed. But for long the speed of sailing ships, both merchant ships and warships, was never more than a few knots. The great increase in speed under sail came with the building of the clipper, in which the Americans led the way. During the second half of the 19th century many clippers, both American and British, made some remarkably fast runs. The American clipper *Sovereign of the Seas* (built 1852) broke existing records for passages from New York to London and from London to Melbourne, reaching 22 knots at times. Great speeds under sail were also reached by the famous TEA CLIPPERS during their races home to London from China.

Meanwhile the steamship had arrived, and though the earliest machine-driven boats were slow, by the 1860s the last paddle steamer used by the Cunard Company on the Atlantic run had reached a speed of 16 knots. The screw-driven ship, however, had already demonstrated her

487

superiority, and there now began the building of the fast passenger liners which led to competition between Britain and other nations for the Blue Riband of the Atlantic. By 1897 the speeds of these liners had risen to over 20 knots; in 1907 the Cunarder *Mauretania* ran at 27 knots; in the 1930s the Atlantic was being crossed by the *Queen Mary* and French *Normandie* at over 30 knots; and in 1952 the American liner *United States* reached an average speed of over 35 knots. The speeds of the many different kinds of merchant ships vary from 7 or 8 knots for some small coasters up to 15 or 16 knots for many tankers and around 20 knots for many container and refrigerated ships.

Modern warships of the larger kind in the Royal Navy have speeds of up to about 30 knots. H.M.S. *Ark Royal* had a speed of 31·5 knots, cruisers and destroyers reach 30 knots, and some frigates 32 knots. Small fast patrol, gun or torpedo boats have speeds up to 40 or 50 knots; the fastest of these are propelled by gas-turbines giving a maximum speed of 52 knots. Now being developed as a submarine hunter for the U.S. Navy is a 3000-ton hovercraft frigate, known as 3KSES, which is expected to have a top speed of over 80 knots!

Spell: a word with two almost opposite meanings: (1) a period of activity or duty, as in 'a spell at the oars'; (2) a brief interval of rest, relief from duty, etc., as in 'He gave the man at the wheel a ten-minute spell'.

Spencer: a fore-and-aft sail set on the fore and main masts of a square-rigged ship, like a kind of spanker.

Spike: (1) naval nickname for anyone surnamed Sullivan; (2) to 'spike a gun' means to put it out of action by plugging the touch-hole; hence such common land

expressions as 'That'll spike his guns', i.e. stop his proposed course of action.

Spinnaker: a large jib-shaped SAIL carried opposite the mainsail on the main mast when running before the wind; usually associated with racing yachts.

Spirit-room: a compartment in the hold of the ship for the rum, wine and brandy casks.

Spithead: *see* MUTINY; PORTSMOUTH; WIGHT, ISLE OF.

Spitsbergen (or **Spitzbergen**; modern name **Svalbard**): a group of mountainous islands in the Arctic Ocean some 400 miles north of Norway. Though known to the Vikings, Spitsbergen was forgotten until the voyages in search of the North-East Passage. It was visited by the great Dutch explorer William Barents in 1596, and by Henry Hudson and William Baffin early in the 17th century. Whalers, sealers and fur-hunters were attracted to the islands, which feature frequently in the literature of polar exploration during the 19th century. Early in the 20th century various nations became interested in Spitsbergen's coal deposits, particularly the Norwegians and Russians. In 1920 the islands were assigned by agreement to Norway; the coal is now worked by the Norwegians and also, under concession, by the Russians. Early in the Second World War the Germans, having overrun Norway, were making use of Spitsbergen's coal, but when Russia entered the war (1941) an expedition under Admiral Vian landed a force to destroy the coal dumps and bring away the Norwegians who had been forced into German service.

Splice: the method of joining ropes,

Back splice   Long splice   Eye splice

making a loop or neatening the end of a rope by unlaying the strands and tucking them under and over other strands at the point of the splice. Wire ropes can also be spliced, and with both rope and wire different kinds of splice can be employed. A long splice will join two ropes and can, if required, be done without increasing the thickness of the rope, by thinning the strands. An eye splice forms a loop by turning the rope back and splicing it on itself. A back splice is a means of finishing off a rope to prevent it unlaying.

The slang phrase 'to get spliced', meaning to get married, is clearly of nautical origin.

Splice the main brace: provide a drink, usually to all hands, for some extra exertion. The origin of the phrase has never been satisfactorily explained.

Splinter mat: a tough, thick mat intended as a protection against splinters from, or caused by, shot and shell. In the days of wooden warships flying splinters of wood were often as dangerous as the shot itself.

Splinter netting: a stout rope netting erected above the quarter-deck in the old sailing Navy. It protected those below from falling spars or other parts of the rigging shot away during battle, and would also break the fall of any men shot out of the rigging above.

Sponson: a projection from the side of a vessel, sometimes used as a gun platform.

Spread-eagled: *see* EAGLED.

Spring: (1) name for a rope or wire used in

two particular ways in securing a ship alongside a quay or another ship. A forward or fore spring leads from the bows aft to a bollard ashore, whilst a back spring leads from the stern forward to the shore. These two lines in addition to the head rope and stern rope are necessary for the proper securing of the ship and, when the others are let go, can be used respectively for swinging out the stern by going ahead with the forward spring still secured, or for swinging out the bows by going astern with the back spring still holding.

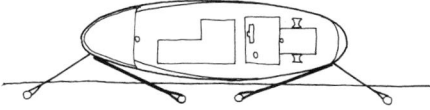

(2) To 'spring' is to come loose, e.g. when the planking or timbers of a vessel warp, split or crack. The part affected is then said to be sprung, as a result of which the vessel may spring a leak. A mast, a yard or spar is also 'sprung' when it is partially fractured.

Spring tides: tides occurring in the second and fourth quarters of the moon when the gravitational pulls of the moon and the sun are in conjunction (not in opposition, as in NEAP TIDES), so producing a higher high water and a lower low water than average. *See also* TIDES.

Sprit: a small spar set diagonally from the mast to the top outer corner of a sail; hence 'spritsail'. A spritsail could also be the sail carried by some vessels under the bowsprit; this type, then comparatively new, was carried by Columbus on the *Santa Maria*, a fact recorded in his log for 24 October 1492:

I let them set all sail, the main course with two bonnets, the fore course, the spritsail, the mizen . . .

Sprog: a slang name for someone newly entered in the Navy.

Sprung: *see* SPRING (*2*).

Spunyarn: loosely twisted fibres, sometimes from old rope, made up into line used for various purposes where no particular strength is needed, e.g. seizing and serving. To 'spin a yarn', meaning to tell a story, sometimes an exaggerated story, is a phrase of nautical origin, the idea coming from the lengthy entwining process of rope-making.

Spy-glass (or **glass**): a telescope. 'Spy-glass' and 'glass' were for long used in the Navy instead of the word 'telescope'. In Marryat's *Peter Simple* the young new midshipman whose name gives the novel its title is sent to fetch the master's night glass; not knowing what is meant, Peter brings a glass of grog, and gets cursed and laughed at for his ignorance.

Squadron: a main detachment or division of ships of war; in battle action in early British naval history normally one of three – the red, the white and the blue – each of which was capable of sub-division into three sections, the front (or van), the middle and the rear. This organization, and the associated squadronal colours, for several centuries formed the hierarchy of promotion for officers of flag rank (*see* ADMIRAL). The term squadron was also often used for a group of ships on some special duty, e.g. 'the inshore squadron' etc.

Squall: a sudden violent gust of wind, especially when accompanied by rain, hail,

sleet, etc. 'Look out for squalls!' has become a common expression when an outburst of anger is to be expected from a provoked person.

Square-rigged: having the principal sails extended on YARDS slung athwart the masts. *See also* RIG (*1* and *2*).

Square sail: four-cornered SAIL set on a yard suspended by the middle.

Square stern: a stern with a TRANSOM, as opposed to the round stern, which had no such transom.

Squid: the name given to an anti-submarine weapon introduced in the Second World War. It consisted of a sort of short-range mortar firing a pattern of three depth charges ahead of a destroyer or frigate, thus enabling the ship to maintain sonar contact with a submerged submarine.

S.S.: the normal abbreviation for 'Steam Ship'.

Stabilizers: projecting fins fitted to a vessel's side below the water-line in order to reduce the degree of rolling in rough weather. Modern stabilizers are automatic

and gyroscopically controlled ('gyro-stabilizers'); they can be retracted and stowed within the ship's hull when not required.

Staghorn: a metal bollard shaped like a cross and fitted both on ships and on quays and jetties to take berthing lines.

Stanchion: a prop or post acting as a support or strengthening for some part of the ship's structure.

Standard: in the meaning 'flag',the word has a very complex history. Gradually it seems to have become confined to a flag bearing the royal arms or the Cross of St George, and even to a special type, between a broad banner and a long streamer. Nowadays the word is almost always accompanied by the adjective 'Royal' and is confined, on board ship as elsewhere, to the royal arms.

Standing orders: rules and regulations laid down by the commanding officer of a ship.

Starboard: the right-hand side of a vessel when looking from the stern towards the bows; the opposite of 'port'. The word comes from 'steer board', a large paddle-like oar with which early ships were steered and manoeuvred before the coming of the RUDDER, and which was usually positioned on the starboard quarter. Starboard's associated colour is green, the colour of the starboard navigation light. *See p.577.*

Starshell: a type of shell used in a night attack to illuminate the enemy ship or ships. It was fired high into the air and on bursting released a powerful chemical flare, the descent of which was checked by a parachute. Starshell enabled gun crews to see enemy vessels silhouetted against the illuminated area. It was much used in the First and Second World Wars, especially in the latter when U-boats began to work in packs and make surface attacks against convoys. An improved form of starshell was known as snowflake, which gave a longer period of illumination; but the problem of visibility at night has been solved by the efficiency of modern radar and by special optical instruments.

Starter: short knotted cord formerly carried by boatswains, mates, etc. and used to encourage the men to more vigorous action (often unnecessarily) by belabouring them about the head and back.

Station: (1) an area of sea-command, e.g. 'the West Indies station'; (2) an assigned position either for a ship or for members of its crew. Thus a ship must 'keep station' in a convoy, a battle formation or an exercise; a light-ship must be 'on station' and not 'off station'; men have 'action stations' for engaging the enemy, 'harbour stations' for entering harbour etc.

Station bill: a detailed list giving the position or station of all men on board a ship for all normal duties, for emergencies and for fighting the ship.

Station pointer: an instrument used in the navigation of coastal waters, consisting of a circular protractor with one fixed and two pivoting arms. To it are transferred horizontal angles, taken by sextant, of three fixed points. When the station pointer is placed on the chart and its arms as set are made to correspond to the observed points on the chart, the position of the ship is shown at the axis of the arms.

Stave: (1) a curved piece of wood forming part of the sides of a wooden barrel or pail.

To 'stave in' is to break open a cask improperly, and is also applied to the planks or plates of a boat or ship when they are broken open by accident. To 'stave off' is to keep away or fend off one boat from another or from a jetty by using a boathook, oar etc., to prevent damage by too severe an impact. (2) A wooden pole, especially such as is used for a small flag.

Stay: (1) standing RIGGING which supports and runs from a mast to a securing point either forward or aft, and so called 'forestays' or 'backstays'. Each stay has its particular name according to the mast or part of the mast it supports, thus 'main-stay', 'mizen topmast backstay', 'fore top-gallant stay' etc. Large sailing vessels also had stays called martingale stays on the jib-boom, and bobstays on the bowsprit.

(2) 'Short stay' and 'long stay' are terms used of an anchor cable when it is taut. When the anchor is close below the bows and the cable is taut, it is at short stay; when it is at some distance from the bows, it is at long stay.

As a verb, 'stay' means (3) to support, and (4) to put a sailing vessel in a position to tack or go about. When the vessel hesitates in her reaction at this point she is said to be 'in stays', and when she fails to react to the helmsman's intention she is said to 'miss stays'.

Staysail: a triangular fore-and-aft SAIL extended on a stay.

Steamships: it often comes as a surprise to those who look upon the steamship as a 19th-century innovation to find that as early as 1783 the Marquis Claude de Jouffroy d'Abbans built a small steamboat called the *Pyroscaphe*, which gamely struggled upstream for a quarter of an hour on the River Saône, near Lyons. Three

years later the American John Fitch built a boat which made a brave show on the River Delaware with an engine energetically working twelve oars.

Great Britain was keeping pace. In 1785 Joseph Bramah, an Englishman, patented a device described as a 'wheel or fly' which could be fixed under water – 'when it would, being turned round either way, cause the ship to be forced backwards or forwards', its power being 'in proportion to the size and velocity of the wheel'. This sounds like the predecessor of the mighty propellers which later thrashed their way through the oceans of the world. For other developments *see* BRUNEL, ISAMBARD KINGDOM; *CHARLOTTE DUNDAS*; FULTON, ROBERT; *GREAT EASTERN*; *GREAT WESTERN*; MILLER, PATRICK; PADDLE SHIP; *PHOENIX*; *SAVANNAH*.

Steer: direct the movement and direction of a vessel, usually by control of the RUDDER by steering wheel or TILLER.

Steerage: inferior accommodation below deck provided for passengers paying the lowest rates. Steerage accommodation was commonly found in ships of the 19th century and was much used by emigrants to America and elsewhere. Conditions were often crowded and only lines of wooden bunks and cooking facilities were provided; otherwise steerage passengers had to look after themselves.

Steerage way: a vessel has steerage way when moving at a speed sufficient for her to answer to the helm. To lose steerage way means that the vessel can no longer be kept on her proper course.

Steer board: *see* STARBOARD.

Steeve: (1) the angle upwards from the

horizontal formed by the bowsprit. To steeve is to brace the bowsprit to form such an angle. (2) A spar with a block at one end formerly used in stowing cargo. To steeve in this sense is to use such a spar in stowing cargo; compare 'stevedore'.

Stella Maris: *see* POLE STAR.

Step: the socket in which the heel of the mast is set, normally a block of hard wood on the keel, the heel having a tenon and the step a mortice to hold the foot of the mast firm. To 'step the mast' is to set it into position.

Stern: the rear part of a ship. The word is related to 'steer', and it appears in many other ship words, e.g. 'stern-wheeler' (*see* PADDLE SHIP); 'stern-chase' (a pursuit in which one ship follows another, straight behind); 'sternmost' (furthest in the rear); *see* ASTERN etc. For 'stern gallery' *see* CLOSED GALLERIES; *see also* ELLIPTICAL STERN; SQUARE STERN; *p.577.*

Stettin oak: oak from central Europe, much used for shipbuilding in England during the 18th-century shortage (*see* TIMBER). It was a bad investment, since its sea-life proved to be only about a quarter that of English oak. Stettin, formerly a region of Germany, is now in Poland. The timber was floated down the River Oder.

Stevedore: dock worker engaged in loading and unloading ships. *See* STEEVE.

Stevenson, Robert Louis (1850–94): 'teller of tales', essayist and poet, whose great story *Treasure Island* ranks with Defoe's *Robinson Crusoe* in its appeal to almost everyone's imagination. If Stevenson had written little else (and he wrote many fine tales) he would be remembered

for *Treasure Island*, written during a rainy holiday in Scotland to entertain his stepson. Under the title *The Sea Cook* it first appeared as a serial in *Young Folks*, but when it was published in book form as *Treasure Island* (1883) it rapidly grew in popularity and established Stevenson's reputation, in spite of some critics who disapproved of the violence and the absence of explicit moral judgements. Here was a story full of the romance of the sea in the days of buccaneers and pirates, but with a young hero, Jim Hawkins, as the chief narrator. At the Admiral Benbow Inn, kept by Jim's mother, there arrives an old buccaneer who has with him a map of Captain Flint's buried treasure. His former confederates seek to get possession of the map, but Jim outwits them and passes it to Squire Trelawney and Dr Livesey. They sail for Treasure Island in the schooner *Hispaniola*, but on board as part of the crew are the redoubtable one-legged Long John Silver and some of the former buccaneers, whose plot to seize the ship is thwarted by Jim. Fights and adventures on the ship and on the island follow; the marooned pirate, poor Ben Gunn, is found, and with his help the villains are eventually defeated and the treasure secured. The pirates' haunting refrain had its gruesome note enhanced by the accidental omission of capital letters for 'Dead Man's Chest', which was really intended by Stevenson as the name of a small island in the pirates' haunts.

> Fifteen men on the dead man's chest
> Yo-ho-ho, and a bottle of rum!
> Drink and the devil had done for the rest –
> Yo-ho-ho, and a bottle of rum!

Stewards: on merchant ships, the name given to those who serve meals and look after the needs of the passengers; in the Royal Navy the name given to ratings who serve in the officers' mess.

Sticks: slang term for masts, met with in such expressions as 'shaking the sticks out of her', and 'two-sticker', 'three-sticker' etc. as terms for ships according to the number of masts. *See also* UNDER BARE POLES.

Stock: the wooden or iron cross-member to which the shank of an ANCHOR is attached.

Stockholm tar: a preservative extracted and distilled from the resin of pine trees; it was an essential commodity for treating rigging and ropes in the days of the sailing Navy. The chief source of supply was the BALTIC, where Stockholm, the capital and chief port of Sweden, was a great centre for the export of the tar, and it was also produced in Germany and Russia.

Stocks: the framework on which a ship rests when it is building. In the days of wooden ships they were normally of oak, set 4 or 5 ft apart.

Stone frigate: a colloquial name for a naval shore ESTABLISHMENT commissioned as one of H.M. ships.

Storm: a wind classed on the BEAUFORT SCALE as Force 10, blowing at 48–55 nautical miles per hour, or Force 11, violent storm, blowing at 56–63 nautical miles per hour.

The word storm is, of course, used more loosely in such words as thunderstorm, hail-storm, sand-storm, etc. A magnetic storm is a disturbance of the magnetic field, indicated by oscillation of the magnetic needle. The causes of magnetic storms are complex; they are associated with disturbances of the earth's upper atmosphere, brought on by solar flares (vast eruptions on the surface of the sun).

Storm cones (or **storm signals**): cones hoisted at coastguard stations and at other prominent shore points to warn of the approach within 100 miles and 10 hours of winds of Force 8 or above on the BEAUFORT SCALE. The positioning of the storm cones when hoisted indicates the direction from which the gale is expected. Thus, point of cone upwards indicates a northerly gale, point downwards indicates a southerly gale, whilst a south over north cone means the forecast of an easterly gale and a north over a south a westerly gale.

Storm sails: in the days of sail, ships often carried sails made of strong canvas but smaller in size to take high winds. When doing so the vessel was said to be under storm sails (or storm canvas).

Stormy petrel: a small sea-bird which appears to run lightly over the water and was thought by sailors to presage a storm. The name derives from the Italian *Petrello*, meaning 'Little Peter', recalling St Peter, who walked on the water with Christ. Figuratively, a stormy petrel is someone likely to cause trouble. *See also* MOTHER CAREY'S CHICKENS.

Stowage: (1) the art and practice of loading ships with their cargo and gear; (2) the place where cargo or gear is stowed; (3) the charge or cost of stowing.

The loading of ships is a matter of skill, judgement and knowledge. The cargo must be stowed so that it will not shift at sea and endanger the ship or give her a list; it must be so stowed that one kind of cargo will not damage or taint another. Many disasters have occurred because of faulty stowage, especially in the days of wooden ships. There was also the danger of spontaneous combustion with bulk cargoes of coal, and if a cargo of grain got wet it might swell so much that it would burst the ship's sides. Great damage could be done in a rough sea if heavy cargo broke loose and battered the bulkheads or sides with every roll of the ship. Today many ships are specially designed for the carriage of particular types of freight, e.g. oil, grain or timber, and refrigerated ships carry meat and fruit. Modern bulk carriers for ore, cement, phosphates, etc. are often huge and may be mistaken for oil-tankers. In recent years there has been a great development of container ships, on which cargo is quickly and safely stowed already packed in box units of standardized size, handled also by specially designed road vehicles, railway waggons and dockside equipment.

Stowaway: someone who hides himself on board a ship before sailing in order to get a free passage or escape to another country. Stowaways were perhaps more common in the past than they are today, though illegal immigrants still often attempt to enter countries either as true stowaways or with the connivance of someone among the ship's crew. If a stowaway is discovered while the ship is at sea he can be made to work his passage and must be handed over to the proper authorities at the port of arrival.

Strachan, Sir Richard John (1760–1828): admiral. He entered the Navy in 1772 and, after taking part in a number of actions, reached the summit of his career by capturing four French battleships which had escaped from Trafalgar in 1805.

Strait: a narrow channel of water connecting two larger, more open areas of sea, e.g. the Menai Strait between Anglesey and north Wales. The word occurs often in the plural, e.g. the Straits of Dover, the Straits of Gibraltar. 'The Straits' (sometimes spelt 'Streights') was once used colloquially in the Royal Navy to refer to the whole of the Mediterranean station.

Strake: a single breadth of planking or plating running continuously from stern to stem and forming part of a vessel's side. The garboard strake is the one next to the keel, while the sheer strake is the top strake of a wooden vessel.

Strand: (1) shore or beach. The street in London called the Strand runs parallel to what was once a shore of the Thames; (2) fibres twisted together to make up one of the strands (usually three) which are laid up into a rope; (3) to strand a ship is to run her aground or ashore; she is then 'stranded'.

Strategy: *see* TACTICS.

Straw House: old name for the Sailors' Home in Dock Street, London, where seamen lodgers slept on sacks of straw.

Stream: a word with several specific extensions of its common meaning of running or flowing out, e.g. 'tidal stream', 'Gulf Stream', 'stream-lined' etc. To stream a log or a sea-anchor is to pay them out on a line; to stream a buoy is to let it go to serve its particular purpose. A stream anchor is a spare anchor of medium size which can be streamed, and which is stowed at the stern of certain larger ships.

Streamer: *see* PENDANT.

Streights, the: *see* STRAIT.

Stretcher: a crosspiece of wood fitted athwart the bottom of a boat, against which the rower braces his feet.

Strike, to: (1) to lower or haul down. To strike a mast or yard is to lower it down on deck; to strike sails is to lower them. To strike a topsail was once a form of salute to a man-o'-war at sea. Striking or hauling down the colours was the customary signal of surrender by one warship to another.

About three p.m. many of the enemy's ships, having struck their colours, their line gave way.

> from Collingwood's Dispatches to the Admiralty after Trafalgar (22 October 1805)

(2) To run aground, as in striking a rock, reef etc.

(3) To 'strike soundings' is to come into shallower water which can be sounded by the lead, generally less than about 100 fathoms.

We'll rant and we'll roar, like true British
   sailors;
We'll rant and we'll roar across the salt seas;
Until we strike soundings
In the Channel of old England,
From Ushant to Scilly 'tis thirty-five leagues.

> Chorus of 'Spanish Ladies' (a famous old sea song of unknown authorship)

Stripey: slang for an able seaman who has earned three sleeve badges for good conduct and service of a certain length. The badges are worn just above the elbow.

Strongback: the strong steel hoop over a tug's after-part to keep her tow-lines clear of the deck.

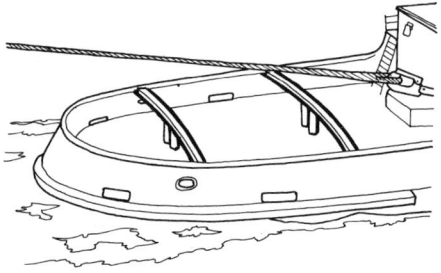

Strop: a band or ring of rope or wire. Strops are used for a variety of purposes on board ship, for slinging round bales or casks to lift them, for securing a hawser or anchor etc. Strop is also the name for the strengthening band of rope or wire passing round the shell of a block and giving an eye for attaching it to hook or shackle.

Studding sail (or **stunsail**; pronounced 'stuns'l'): mentioned as a recent invention by Sir Walter Ralegh in 1588, but not in general use, at least in English men-o'-war, for another hundred years. It was an extra SAIL set to catch light winds beyond the leech (or perpendicular edge) of a square sail, and was used on the topsail, as well as the lower yards of the fore and main masts.

Stunsail: *see* STUDDING SAIL.

Sturdee, Sir Frederick Charles Doveton (1859–1925): admiral. He entered the Navy in 1871 and became a torpedo specialist. He commanded the First Battle Squadron (from 1910) and later, at the outset of the First World War, won fame by his decisive victory at the Battle of the Falkland Islands (1914).

Sub-lieutenant: a rank in the Royal Navy between midshipman and lieutenant. Sub-lieutenant is the first substantive commissioned rank on the ladder of promotion. The title was used as early as 1804, but not as a rank, only as indicating the temporary holder of a post in certain smaller ships during the Napoleonic Wars. When in 1840 the former master's mates were given commissions, they were an accepted grade between midshipman and lieutenant, but the title of sub-lieutenant did not become official again until 1861.

See colour section.

Submarine: a vessel capable of being submerged and navigated below the surface of the sea. The evolution of the submarine can be divided into three periods: first, the historical period up to about 1900; then the years covering the two World Wars, when the submarine was steadily improved and became a vital naval weapon; and the period since 1954, when the first nuclear-powered submarine was launched, giving a vessel which was able to stay under the water almost indefinitely.

The idea of an underwater craft is very old, and there is a record of one of the earliest attempts to put it into practice when in 1624 a Dutchman, Cornelius van Drebbel, constructed on the Thames a wooden skin-covered submersible, propelled by oars through sealed ports. Then in 1775, at the beginning of the War of American Independence, David Bushnell made a hand-propelled, screw-driven submersible, the *Turtle*, with which Sergeant Ezra Lee attempted to place a bomb under the *EAGLE*. The attempt was a failure, since the mine drifted away, but the idea was further developed by Bushnell's compatriot Robert Fulton. The first fully successful submarine attack in time of war occurred in 1864 during the American Civil War, when the Federal ship *Housatonic* was sunk by a semi-submersible known as a 'David', built by the Confederates. This success was achieved by an iron steam-driven vessel armed with a spar torpedo, though the 'David' was itself sunk at the same time.

In the latter part of the 19th century the French, Spanish, German and American navies were steadily developing the possibilities of the submarine. Technological advance brought not only stronger metal hulls, but also the internal-combustion engine for surface propulsion, the electric motor for underwater power,

and controlled surfacing and driving with ballast tanks served by compressed air, and improved horizontal rudders or hydroplanes. Great advances were achieved for the American Navy by J. P. Holland, and at the turn of the century the first British submarines were based on his ideas. From then on development was rapid in the world's major navies, but it was the Germans who developed the much safer diesel engine to replace the petrol engine. The First World War demonstrated the power of the submarine as an instrument of war, and by 1917 the sinking of British and Allied shipping by torpedoes from German submarines reached such a level that an almost complete stranglehold seemed to be near. The danger point was passed, however, and when peace came the lesson was not forgotten, though it was perhaps inadequately acted upon before the Second World War broke out in 1939.

In the intervening years submarines and anti-submarine devices were improved. The range and speed of submarines were increased, and they were given more powerful guns and torpedoes, for they were intended to act as surface craft also. Some submarines carried an aeroplane, though this was a limited development. During the course of the Second World War the far greater range of submarines allowed their appearance in the furthest oceans, and the Germans refuelled their boats at sea, at first from carefully concealed supply ships and then, when these were steadily eliminated, from submarine tankers or 'milch cows', as they called them. The Germans also deployed their submarines with skilful tactics, hunting in packs, and sinking a great quantity of shipping in the early stages of the war. After 1943, however, the Allies began to gain the upper hand and losses from the enemy declined. In 1944, however, the Germans introduced the

497

schnorkel, which enabled the submarines to use their engines to recharge their batteries while remaining at periscope depth, but the war ended before full advantage could be taken of this. MIDGET SUBMARINES were also successfully used by both sides.

After the war came the nuclear-powered submarine, which in one sense is the first true submarine, for its development permitted almost unlimited navigation without surfacing. The first was the American *Nautilus* (launched 1954). Nuclear submarines have been built by other navies, British, French and Russian; armed with ballistic missiles, they are truly fearful weapons of war. The problem of fresh air in a submarine which rarely needs to surface is overcome by air-purifying machinery, and the difficulties of navigation are mastered by the system of inertial navigation, which gives a continuous reading of position.

The first British submarine used by the Navy at the beginning of the century could dive to only 100 ft and travel submerged at a mere 5 knots for 15 minutes, carrying two officers and five men. Modern nuclear-powered ballistic missile submarines of the Resolution class have a surface displacement of 7500 tons, can travel at 20 knots on the surface and 25 knots submerged, and carry crews of about 140 men. Nuclear-powered fleet submarines of the Valiant class can reach 30 knots. In addition to their missiles, these submarines also carry six tubes for homing torpedoes. Other British submarines, e.g. the patrol submarines of the Oberon class, are more of the traditional type, but even these can travel at 17 knots submerged and are armed with eight homing torpedo tubes.

Today the greatest submarine fleet in the world is that of the Russian Navy, which has some 400 boats, including 80 fleet submarines, nuclear-powered and torpedo-armed hunter-killers.

See colour section.

'Success': one of the 19th-century 'floating hells' in which convicts were held near Melbourne. When the rest were broken up, *Success* became a coal hulk and, afterwards, an exhibition prison ship.

Sucking the monkey: drinking from a coconut in which rum has been substituted for the milk. This stratagem was once much employed by sailors in the West Indies in the last quarter of the 18th century as a means of getting liquor on board without detection. 'Sucking the monkey' was sometimes also applied to stealing rum from a cask by means of a straw placed through a small hole bored in it (a 'monkey-pump'). A similar phrase was 'bleeding the monkey', which meant surreptitious drinking from the container, known as a monkey, in which rum was once issued to the messes.

Suez Canal: the ship canal linking the Mediterranean and the Red Sea by cutting through the narrow isthmus joining Egypt with the Sinai Peninsula. There had been earlier canals built by the Pharaohs and again by the Arabs in the 7th century, but these had linked the Red Sea with the Nile rather than with the Mediterranean itself. Napoleon saw the possibility of a canal through the isthmus, but the defeat of the French at the Battle of the Nile (1798) put an end to his plans. It was not until 1859 that, under the direction of the French engineer Ferdinand de Lesseps, work was begun on building the Suez Canal. Ten years later the great feat was completed, and the waterway, 100 miles long, making use of the intervening lakes and depressions, was opened to shipping. At first the

British had viewed the project with suspicion, fearing both the strategic results of the canal and the influence of the French in Egypt. The importance of the new route to the East soon became apparent, and the elimination of the long haul to India round the Cape of Good Hope was of great advantage to commerce. In 1875 Benjamin Disraeli, then Prime Minister of Britain, in a brilliant stroke secured nearly half the shares in the Canal Company from the bankrupt Khedive of Egypt, and thus gave a preponderant interest to Britain as the chief maritime nation.

Shipping passing through the Suez Canal increased steadily, and with the development of the oilfields of the Persian Gulf the canal became even more important for the passage of oil to the industrialized nations of Europe. Relations between Britain and Egypt had deteriorated when in 1956 President Nasser expropriated the Canal. At the same time as Israel also attacked Egypt, Britain and France landed troops to secure the Suez Canal. But the pressure of world opinion led to the end of military action and the withdrawal of forces. Ships had been sunk by the Egyptians to block the Canal, but these were quite soon cleared.

The Canal was again blocked, this time more effectively, during the Arab-Israeli War of 1967. It was not opened again until 1975. Though much traffic returned and the Canal remains one of the world's most important ways, it was no longer big enough for the giant tankers being used in increasing numbers to carry oil to the West from the Middle East; and other ships too, which during the closure had been compelled to use the route round the Cape of Good Hope, continued to do so if they found it more economic to avoid the charges made by the Canal authorities. Plans are afoot for deepening and improving this key waterway, which provides the shortest route from Europe to the East and to the oilfields of the Persian Gulf.

Sunderland: seaport, shipbuilding, marine-engineering and industrial centre at the mouth of the River Wear in Tyne and Wear. From the middle of the 18th century Sunderland grew into one of the great coal-exporting ports of the N.E. coast, and the many collier brigs from the Wear and Tyne for long had a prosperous trade in carrying coal to the south of England and abroad. In 1796 one of the wonders of the times, the great iron bridge across the Wear, with a single span of 236 ft, was completed. With the coming of the steamship the shipyards and engineering works developed and thrived until the great depression of the 1930s. The Second World War and new industries brought work again to Sunderland, where many splendid ships have been built, though the shipyards today are not as busy as they could be.

'Sunshine': *see MOONSHINE.*

'Superb': for the 'Old *Superb*' (the third ship of that name in the Royal Navy), *see* KEATS, SIR RICHARD GOODWIN. A 19th-century *Superb* was the last central battery battleship in the British Navy.

Supercargo: an old name for the cargo superintendent, an agent of the ship's owners who travelled with a merchant ship to attend to all the commercial business connected with the handling, transfer and sale of the cargo.

Superstructure: that part of the structure rising above the main deck.

Supply and Secretariat: the branch of

the Royal Navy responsible for pay and cash, naval stores, victualling, secretarial and certain legal duties. Officers of this branch also have very definite duties in the fighting and defence organization of a warship. The modern Supply and Secretariat Branch evolved from the old-time PURSERS, and the slang name 'pusser' is still applied to officers of this specialization.

Surf: the swell or foam of the sea breaking on the shore; hence 'surf-boat', one especially usable in such waters.

Surge: a large thrusting wave.

And they heard the merry murmur of the surges on the shore, as they tumbled in the moonlight all alone.

Charles Kingsley, *The Heroes* (1856)

For 'surging' (of a ship) *see* FREEDOMS OF MOTION.

Surgeon:

Whereas we have lately given you directions and commandments to imprest presently for our service a certain number of chirurgeons [i.e. surgeons] to be employed in our fleet, and that we understand you find opposition and hindrance in performing that service by colour of particular protections which they have obtained during the time of this parliament and otherwise. And therefore since it is in no way fit that the public service should be avoided and prevented by such particular pretences. Our will and pleasure is, as we do hereby authorise and require you, to imprest from time to time such and so many sufficient and experienced chirurgeons for our service as you shall have directions from us, notwithstanding any such protection whatsoever.

This direction from Charles I to the Master and Wardens of the Company of Barber-Surgeons gives a fair indication of the status of the ship's surgeon at the beginning of the 17th century, and the popularity of such service. The College of

Physicians regarded the Barber-Surgeons as an inferior breed and there was little or no co-operation between the two. The Barber-Surgeons were supposed to provide men on request, but nearly everyone tried to avoid the service. Eventually the Barber-Surgeons were ordered to press men and to present the candidates before a Board of Admirals, whose capacity to judge their qualifications must have been minimal. There was much ignorance on matters of ship hygiene and quite inadequate hospital provision for sick seamen.

A more efficient and adequate service was built up later in the 17th century with the appointment of James Pearce as Master of the Barber-Surgeons' Company and Surgeon-General of H.M. Navy, and with the founding of the Royal Hospital for seamen at Greenwich in 1694. Many other hospitals were established as time went on (e.g. HASLAR).

In the early 19th century the surgeon was a warrant officer of wardroom rank, with a cabin on the lowest true deck (the orlop), probably because it was in these lower regions that their chief duties lay. In battle, real or threatened, his station was in the after-cockpit, along with the surgeon's mates and the chaplain. By 1815, a surgeon with over 20 years' standing received £25 4s. a month, the scale descending to the junior with less than six years' service, who got £14. The haphazardness of methods of appointment is shown by the fact that at various times from 1800 to 1830 they were made by the Sick and Hurt Office, the Transport Office and the Victualling Office. Not until 1831 were surgeons appointed by the Admiralty. From 1787, though they then ranked beneath the Lieutenants, they were given a distinctive uniform.

See also PHYSICIAN; HEALTH AND HYGIENE.

Surveying, hydrographic (or **marine**): measuring, recording and plotting details of the sea and coastline for the purpose of making accurate charts for navigation. Hydrographic surveying employs many of the principles and methods of the land surveyor, but has additional problems and requirements, e.g. the recording of the depth and nature of the sea-bed, the set of tides and currents, and the plotting of isolated rocks and reefs out of sight of land.

The inaccuracy of the earliest charts was steadily reduced over the centuries by observations recorded in the logs of many thousands of voyagers and explorers, but the modern era of scientific survey may be said to have begun with Captain James Cook during the 18th century. The remarkable accuracy of his work in the St Lawrence River before the capture of Quebec, and afterwards on his voyages to the Pacific, set new standards of exactitude. As the accuracy of navigation improved with new instruments such as the quadrant, the sextant and the chronometer, so too did the associated science of cartography. France was the first nation to set up a special department for hydrographic surveying (1720); Britain did so in 1795, and because of the pre-eminence of the British Navy and mercantile marine during the 19th century, Admiralty charts eventually covered all the world's seas and came to be relied upon by other maritime nations, many of whom also established departments for hydrographic surveying and built special SURVEY SHIPS.

Log, compass, sextant, station pointer and chronometer all contributed, and still contribute, to marine surveying, but modern times have seen the advent of electronic devices such as the echo-sounder for depths, sonar for locating rocks and wrecks, radar, radio and various kinds of position-finding equipment. Because the sea-bed, especially in shallow waters, and the coastline itself are constantly changing, and because of wrecks and other hazards to navigation which appear from time to time, continuous work in hydrographic surveying is essential. *See also* HYDROGRAPHY.

Surveyor: official instituted, or at least first recognized at the highest level, by Henry VIII as the technical expert among the naval administration. As the years went on, his duties became more clearly defined and a small volume of orders, *The Œconomy of the Navy*, issued in 1717, indicates that he ranked third in dignity after the Treasurer and Comptroller. His chief functions were to report to the Lord High Admiral on the state of the ships, to prepare estimates of expenditure, including the provision of new ships and the repair of the old, and to check on the price and quality of all stores bought and issued.

Survey ship: a vessel built and equipped for SURVEYING. Most of the major naval powers build special survey ships, but of course any suitable vessel can be equipped to carry out the task. A famous name amongst British survey ships is the 19th-century H.M.S. *CHALLENGER*. Today the Royal Navy has eleven survey ships of different kinds, the largest being four ships of the Hecla class. H.M.S. *Hecla* is of 2000 tons displacement with a speed of 14 knots. She has the general design of a merchant ship, but has an additional propeller at the bows, a hull specially strengthened against ice, a helicopter landing deck, and a long cruising range. Inside she is equipped with electronic and other devices, with laboratories and workshops for the wide range of work she undertakes. The Navy also has four smaller survey ships, each of about 300 tons, and three smaller inshore survey craft of shallow draught. *See also* OCEANO-GRAPHY.

Swab: mop of old rope for cleaning and drying the decks. The word also has two usages in nautical slang: (1) swab or swabber can mean an unpleasant, clumsy person, and (2) swab can mean a naval officer's epaulet. After Peter in Marryat's *Peter Simple* has been promoted lieutenant he meets a former shipmate and says to him 'Oh! I understand you did not perceive before that I had shipped the swab. Yes, I'm lieutenant of the *Rattlesnake*, Swinburne, and hope you'll join us.'

Swaine, Thomas: *see* RATS.

Sweep: (1) a long heavy oar used for propelling smaller sailing vessels, and also for steering barges and lighters etc. In the days of sail sweeps were used when the ship was becalmed. (2) A steady irresistible flow, as in 'the sweep of the tide'. (3) A systematic search by ships or aircraft over a certain area, either to seek out the enemy or to carry out a rescue; also a search by sonar or radar for the same purposes; or a search for mines carried out by minesweepers.

He thrust out his sweeps, as they are called, huge oars requiring five or six men to each. These when properly handled, by a sufficiently numerous crew, in a small light vessel, give her the heels of a large ship, when so nearly calm as it now was with us.

> Captain Basil Hall, R.N., *Fragments of Voyages & Travels* (1831)

Sweeper: (1) a colloquial general name for any of the many types of ships used for sweeping mines (*see* MINESWEEPER); (2) a name for the rating responsible for keeping a particular part of the ship clean and tidy.

Swell: waves or undulations of the sea's surface caused by past winds or originating in a distant storm. A swell is different from a SEA. Different kinds of swell are classified by an International Swell Scale using the figures 0 to 9, and within that scale the swell can be either short or long, according to the distance between each successive top of the swell, and either low or heavy, according to the height between the lowest and highest part of the swell. Thus, on the International Scale, the code figure 2 indicates a long, low swell, 6 is a short, heavy swell, 9 a confused heavy swell etc.

Swept channel: any seaway or route which has been cleared of mines by MINESWEEPERS.

Dusk off the Foreland – the last light going
And the traffic crowding through,
And five damned trawlers with their syreens
    blowing
Heading the whole review!
Sweep completed in the fairway.
No more mines remain.
Sent back *Unity, Claribel, Assyrian,*
Stormcock and *Golden Gain.*

> Rudyard Kipling, *Sea Warfare* (1916)

Swifter: a rope passed round slots in the outer ends of capstan bars and rigged to give a kind of rim on which extra hands could haul when weighing anchor.

'Swiftsure': *Swiftsure* guns have thundered through four centuries of English history, and merchant ships of the same name have carried their commerce to every corner of the globe. Perhaps Benjamin Hallowell's *Swiftsure* at the Battle of the Nile (1 August 1798) can represent them all in storm and shine:

August 2nd.
A.M. . . . Carpenters employed stopping the shot holes. Found one of the cutters cut away and the other stove in in such a manner as rendered her quite irreparable; cut her adrift; the oars, masts, sails and everything washed out and lost. Received several shot in the hull,

masts, yards, &c., and a great part of the rigging cut in pieces.

P.M. – Moderate breezes and pleasant weather.

Swing a cat: *see* CAT.

Swing the lead, to: originally, to heave the LEAD when sounding the depth of water beneath the ship; now a slang phrase meaning to malinger, to find excuses for not working or doing a duty. Perhaps the phrase arose from the idea that this was a comparatively light duty which the seaman concerned made last as long as possible.

Sword, naval: up till the early 19th century the British naval officer wore whatever weapon he chose, so that it is difficult to identify any weapon before that time as definitely and exclusively naval. In the first half of the 18th century the preference seems to have been for short curved blades, very useful in hand-to-hand combat. By the middle of the century, judging from portraits, the fashion changed and many officers had more than one sword: the 'small' sword, with triangular or 'colichemarde' blade, reserved for dress and ceremonial occasions, and, for use in battle, either a fairly short, slightly curved weapon or a double-edged cut-and-thrust type hardly, if at all, distinguishable from the military sword. So matters went on, with the choice becoming even more varied, till the first years of the 19th century, when a definite official-pattern sword was introduced. An order of 4 August 1805 mentions two patterns, an ornamented type for flag-officers, captains and commanders and a plain sword for lieutenants and midshipmen. Regulations of 1825 laid down three types: (1) for ranks of lieutenant and above, a straight grooved blade, blued and gilt, 32 in. long, with a lion's-head pommel and ivory grip; (2) a similar sword as to the blade, but with plain pommel and black fish-skin grip, for masters and warrant officers (the blade being neither blued nor gilt); (3) a small sword to be worn by the 'civil' officers, i.e., the surgeon, secretary and purser. Midshipmen, volunteers and masters' assistants wore swords similar to type (2) but with a shorter blade.

A number of other changes, at fairly regular intervals, were introduced during the 19th century, sometimes major, often minor, e.g. the design of the crown, the nature of the grip and the width of the

A British naval officer's sword and scabbard, 1805.

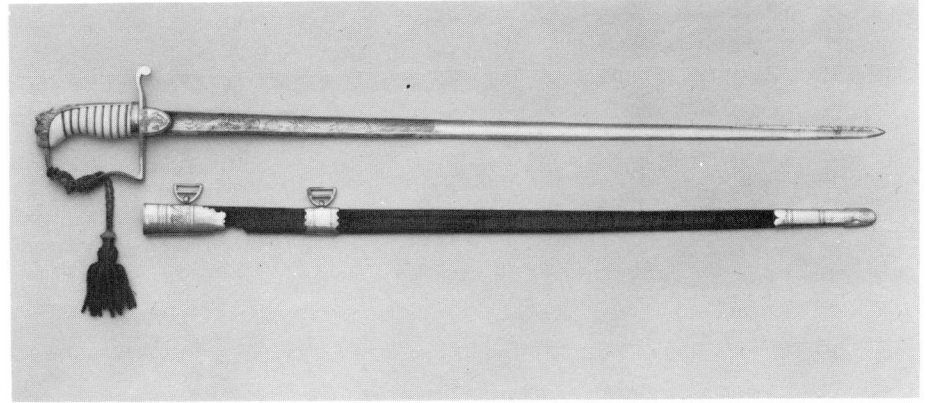

blade. Officialdom was at its best in the last, persistently dealing in eighths of an inch.

Individuality, however, continued to manifest itself, and various officers fitted favourite blades to official hilts, e.g. one mid-19th-century captain used the blade his father had in the Peninsular War.

See also SWORD-KNOTS. For 'Presentation sword' *see* PATRIOTIC FUND.

Sword-knots: ornamental knots attached to the knuckle guard on officers' swords. Judging from portraits, they first made their appearance in the 1740s. Patterns changed over the years, but basically they consisted of blue and gold tassels on cords or ribbons, often with an anchor embroidered on the side.

S.Y.: the abbreviation for 'Steam Yacht'.

Sydney: capital of New South Wales, Australia, with one of the finest harbours in the world. This great city and port owes its origins to Captain Arthur PHILLIP, who sailed from England in 1787 in command of the first fleet taking settlers and 700 convicts to Australia. The settlement had been intended for Botany Bay, but in January 1788 Captain Phillip preferred the splendid harbour site a few miles to the north, changing the name from Port Jackson to Sydney, after Viscount Sydney. There, in spite of many difficulties, this first settlement began to thrive under his firm but just rule. Today Sydney, with its famous bridge across the harbour, its distinctive opera house, its buildings and dockyards and its yacht-crowded water, is a thriving city and port of nearly three million people.

Symington, William (1763–1831): engineer who took out a patent for an improved steam engine (1787) and was responsible for the *CHARLOTTE DUNDAS*. Despite his skill and foresight, his talents were not properly recognized and he died in poverty.

Symonds, Sir William (1782–1856): admiral who, after a good deal of service, became Surveyor of the Navy (1832–47) and introduced some important structural changes, including the ELLIPTICAL STERN (*see also* EXPERIMENTAL SQUADRON). But a writer in the *Nautical Magazine* (1846) said of his ships 'for rolling, pitching, and lee-lurches, the Symondites beat the lot.'

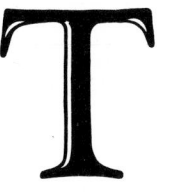

T: *see* CROSSING THE T.

Tabernacle: a wooden or metal socket on the deck of a vessel and in which a mast stands. A steel pin or bolt passing through the sides of the tabernacle and the foot of the mast secures it; when the pin is withdrawn the mast can be lowered aft.

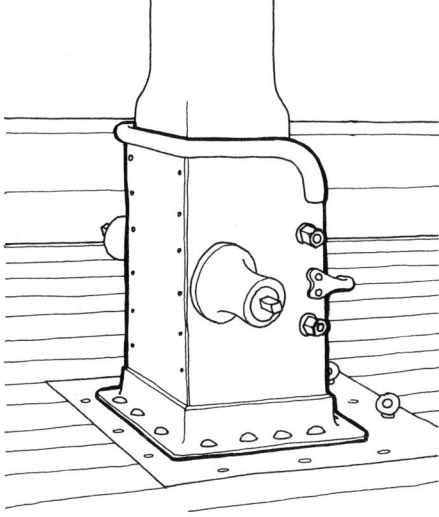

Table, to: (1) to sew strips of extra canvas on to a sail to add strength along the line of the reef-points, the strips being known as reef-bands; (2) to strengthen the edge of canvas by hemming.

Tack: (1) sailors' word for food or provisions (*see* HARD TACK); (2) the foremost lower corner of a three- or four-sided fore-and-aft sail; (3) the rope holding the lower corners of certain sails in square-rigged ships; (4) the ship's course in relation to the position of the wind and the sails, as in the phrases 'on the port tack' or 'on the starboard tack', i.e. with the wind coming from the port or starboard side.

Tack, to: to change a sailing vessel's direction by bringing a different side to the wind.

Tackle: (1) (pronounced 'tay-kl') a contrivance with ropes and blocks arranged so that there is a mechanical increase in the power of the pull on the rope. There are many different kinds of tackle according to the arrangement, number and kind of blocks employed. In sailing vessels tackles are extensively used for handling sails and spars, and they are needed for lifting and moving heavy gear, boats or cargo. Tackles range from the small handy billy to the large four-fold purchase; others with special names are luff, jigger, deck, sail and gun tackles. *See p. 506.*

(2) (pronounced 'takl') the equipment for some special occupation, e.g. 'fishing tackle'.

Tackline: a length of signal halyard bearing no flags and inserted between two signal hoists to separate the first message from the next on the halyard.

Tactics: the art of handling, disposing or operating ships in a naval encounter. Tactics are the immediate, short-term management of a ship or ships to achieve a desired result as opposed to strategy, which is the planned and long-term management and movement of naval forces to gain the initiative and win a war.

'Taeping': one of the most famous clippers, a composite ship built by R. Steele & Co. at Greenock: 279 tons register; length, 183·7 ft; breadth, 31·1 ft; depth in hold, 19·9 ft. She is best

Luff tackle   Two-fold purchase   Three-fold purchase   Four-fold purchase

Gun tackle

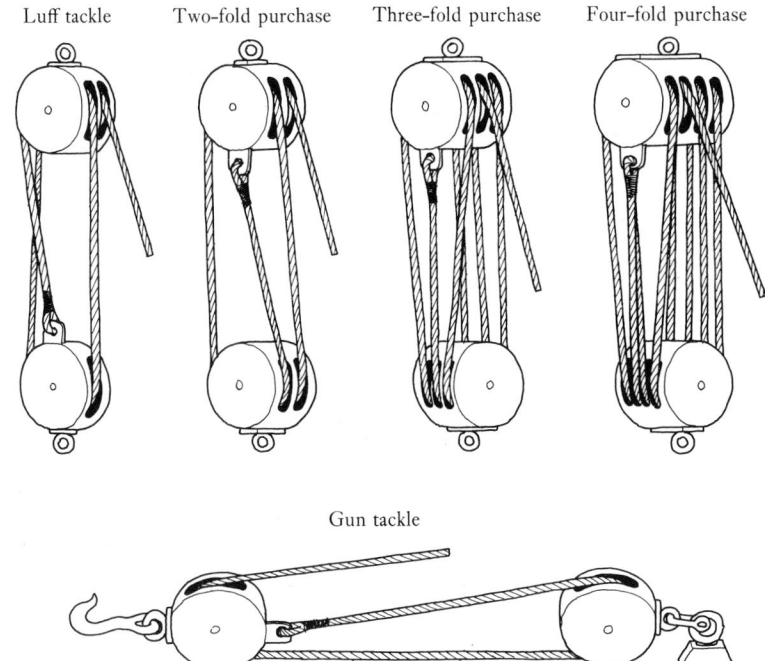

Tackle.

remembered for her part in the famous tea race of 1866: *see ARIEL.*

Taffrail: originally, the upper part of a wooden ship's stern timbers. Today the name is applied both to the rail and to the area of a ship's stern.

'Taffrail': pen-name of Captain Henry Taprell Dorling (1883–1968), writer and broadcaster about the sea and naval matters. Captain Dorling's service in the Royal Navy extended from 1900 to the Second World War. His knowledge of the Navy and his wide experience were reflected in his many books, amongst which were *Pincher Martin, O.D.* (1915), *Sea Ventures of Britain* (1929), *Endless Story* (1931), *Mid-Atlantic* (1936), *The Navy in Action* (1940), *Battle of the Atlantic* (1946), *Eurydice* (1953) and *Arctic Convoy* (1956).

Tahiti: an island in the eastern or Windward group of the SOCIETY ISLANDS. Tahiti was one of the many islands discovered in 1767 by Captain Samuel Wallis on his voyage round the world, but it became better-known when it was visited by Captain Cook (1769 and again in 1773 and 1777). It was from Tahiti that William BLIGH set out on the voyage that ended in the mutiny on the *Bounty* (1789).

'Take in your washing': unusually polite order to a careless boat's crew to bring its neglected fenders, ropes etc. inboard.

Take toko, to: inexplicable expression in the old sailing Navy, meaning to take the lashes from the cat-o'-nine-tails without crying out.

Talbot, Mary Anne (1778–1808): known as 'the British Amazon'. Having served as a drummer 'boy' in Flanders (1792), she took to the sea as a cabin-boy and was wounded at 'The Glorious First of June' (1794). These and her other adventures are recorded in the *Wonderful and Scientific Museum, or Magazine of remarkable and Eccentric Characters*, Vol. 2 (1804), published by her subsequent employer, Robert S. Kirby.

Tall ship: proud name – when properly applied – for the old square-rigged sailing ship with top-masts.

Tally: (1) a name-plate, label or tag of identification, used as slang in 'cap-tally' for a cap-ribbon, and 'purser's tally' for a false name; **(2)** a check by counting, hence 'tally-clerk', one who checks cargo being loaded or discharged; **(3)** to 'tally' also formerly meant to haul the sheets aft:

And, while the lee clue-garnet's lowered away,
Taut aft the sheet they tally, and belay.

William Falconer, *The Shipwreck* (1762)

Tampion: *see* TOMPION.

Tangier: ancient city and seaport in northern Morocco, commanding the western end of the Straits of Gibraltar. Tangier came into English possession as part of the dowry of Charles II's Portuguese bride, Catherine of Braganza, but it could not be maintained, and reverted to the Moors in 1684. In the following century Tangier became one of the centres of the notorious Barbary pirates, whose bases extended along the North African coast. During the 19th century, when France and Spain were both extending their influence in Morocco, Britain was anxious that neither power should gain control of this southern shore of the Straits of Gibraltar. After the French established a protectorate over Morocco (1912), there followed a long period of discussion, interrupted by the First World War, on the future of Tangier. Eventually in 1923 Tangier came under international control. It was occupied by Spain during the Second World War, but was restored to international control in 1945 and continued so until integrated with Morocco in 1956.

Tanker: *see* OIL-CARRIER.

Tapping the admiral: illicitly drawing off wine from a cask, often by means of a goose quill through a hole bored in the side. It often happened on the old East Indiamen carrying barrels of Madeira wine to mature it on the long voyages.

Tar: the thick, sticky black substance distilled from the resin of pine trees (*see* STOCKHOLM TAR), much used as a preservative for rigging in the days of sail. It was also used by sailors to waterproof their TARPAULINS, which may be the source of 'tar' and 'JACK TAR' as colloquial names for a seaman.

Taranto, Battle of (11 November 1940): *see ILLUSTRIOUS*.

Tarpaulin: (1) *see* TARPAULIN CAPTAIN; **(2)** *see* TARPAULINS.

Tarpaulin captain (or **tarpaulin**): experienced seaman who reached commissioned rank from the lower deck, usually having first served as boatswain, master or gunner. This type of promotion was fairly common in the 17th century, especially in Cromwell's day, but class distinction later made the opportunities much rarer; *see also* PROMOTION.

Now the Volunteers being grown mighty numerous and very chargeable to the Navy, and all the Commission Officers chosen out of them, there is no room left for the poor Seaman of any sort, Warrant Officers and others (out of whom many considerable officers have been produced, as namely Lawson, Harman, Kempthorne, Berry, Narborough, and Sir Cloudesley Shovell, to name no more) to hope for any preferment, which I take to be a discouragement to them.

Josiah Burchett (Harleian MSS., 1771)

Another famous 'tarpaulin' was Admiral Benbow.

Tarpaulin muster: a whip-round in the forecastle, usually for the purpose of buying liquor.

Tarpaulins: canvas coats and hats waterproofed by a coating of tar, formerly made by sailors themselves and worn in rough weather (*see* PETTICOAT and SOU'WESTER). This may be the source of the colloquial name JACK TAR.

Tarry breeks: old colloquial name either for a sailor or in particular for a naval officer who had come up from the lower deck (compare TARPAULIN CAPTAIN; *see also* TARPAULINS).

Tasmania: island and Australian state, separated from the mainland by the Bass Strait. Tasmania was discovered in 1642 by Abel Tasman, perhaps the greatest of Dutch explorers. He had been chosen by Van Diemen, the Dutch Governor of the East Indies, to lead an expedition to discover whether northern and western Australia, already known to voyagers, were part of the great southern continent which was believed to exist in this part of the world. Tasman sailed well to the south of Australia until he sighted the west coast of Tasmania, which he named Van Diemen's Land in honour of his sponsor. He sailed south about Tasmania, not realizing it was an island, and then turned east, later sighting New Zealand. Van Diemen's

Land was renamed Tasmania in honour of this great sailor and explorer (1853). *See also* PRISON HULKS.

Tattnall, Josiah (1795–1871): American commodore who, apart from his naval service, has passed into history for a remark he made following the Anglo-American attack on the Chinese forts at Peiho (1859), when he justified American participation on the grounds that 'blood is thicker than water'. In fact Tattnall was not the first to use the phrase: it had appeared, for example, in Sir Walter Scott's *Guy Mannering*.

Well worth recording is Tattnall's midshipman nephew, Joseph Tattnall, for his interview during an examination for promotion:

COMMODORE: Mr Tattnall, what would be your course, supposing you were off a lee shore, the wind blowing a gale, both anchors and your rudder gone, all your canvas carried away, and your ship scudding rapidly towards the breakers?

TATTNALL: I cannot conceive, sir, that such a combination of disasters would possibly befall a ship in one voyage.

COMMODORE: Tut, tut, young gentleman; we must have your opinion supposing such a case to have actually occurred.

TATTNALL: Well, sir – sails all carried away, do you say, sir?

COMMODORE: Aye, all – every rag.

TATTNALL: Anchor gone, too, sir?

COMMODORE: Aye, not an uncommon case.

TATTNALL: No rudder either?

COMMODORE: Aye, rudder unshipped . . . Come, sir, come; bear a hand about it! What would you do?

TATTNALL (at last and desperate): Well, I'd let the infernal tub go to the devil, where she ought to go.

COMMODORE (joyously): Right, sir; perfectly right: That will do, sir. The clerk will note that Mr Tattnall has passed.

Benjamin Park, *The New American Navy*

Taut: tight, no slack. A 'taut ship' was a trim vessel, in good order and efficiently officered.

Taut bowline, on a: sailing close-hauled; *see also* BOWLINE (*1*).

Teach (or **Thatch**), **Edward** (*d*.1718): pirate, familiarly known as 'Blackbeard'. Treacherous, brutal and unprincipled, he plundered friend and foe alike and became a byword for savagery in the West Indies and off Carolina and Virginia – his career sometimes aided by the connivance of land officials who benefited from his spoils. *See also* PIRATES.

Captain Teach assumed the cognomen of Blackbeard from that large quantity of hair which, like a frightful meteor, covered his whole face, and frightened America more than any comet that has appeared there a long time.

The beard was black, which he suffered to grow to an extravagant length; as to breadth, it came up to his eyes; he was accustomed to twist it up with ribbons, in small tails, after the manner of our Ramillies wigs, and turn them about his ears. In time of action, he wore a sling over his shoulders, with three braces of pistols, hanging in holsters like bandoliers; and stuck lighted matches under his hat which, appearing

on each side of his face, his eyes naturally looking fierce and wild, made him altogether such a figure that imagination cannot form an idea of a Fury from hell to look more frightful.

Captain Charles Johnson, *General History of the Pirates* (4th edition, 1726)

Tea-chest: the seaman's nickname for H.M.S. *Thetis*, because of its sound and also as a particular indictment of one of her captains, who is said to have ordered tea as a substitute for rum.

Tea clipper: clipper engaged in the Chinese trade in the mid-19th century. Tea quickly loses its flavour when carried in the hold of a ship, so competition was fierce and public interest high when the annual race took place to be first home with the earliest crop and thereby not only command high prices but win the prizes offered by London merchants. (For the famous race of 1866 *see* ARIEL.) After the opening of the Suez Canal (1869) and with the growing use of steamers, many tea clippers turned to other trades, especially the wool run: *see* WOOL CLIPPER. *See also* CHINA SEAS.

Teak: a tropical tree providing timber of excellent quality and durability. Teak grows in Burma, India, Thailand, Sri Lanka and Indonesia. One of its particular uses is for shipbuilding, but, although it is extremely hard, it is not impervious to the teredo worm. When in the 18th century there was a shortage of suitable oak, teak began to be widely used, especially for ships of the East India Company.

Tea waggons: name sometimes bestowed on the old East Indiamen, partly because of their cargo and partly because of their leisurely mode of sailing. They frequently anchored at night, whereas their suc-

509

cessors, the clippers, 'cracked on' for 24 hours a day.

Telegraph, manual: a device for rapid visual signalling, used by the Admiralty from 1796 to 1849 to communicate with the southern naval bases. When it was first set up it depended on the reading of coded messages based on the varying positions of shutters in a frame. The message was sent from Admiralty House and was repeated from hill-top to hill-top down to Deal and Sheerness, and similarly to Portsmouth, and in 1806 it was extended also to Plymouth. The system was replanned in 1816 when a new device, using the principle of SEMAPHORE, was introduced from London to Chatham, and a few years later to Portsmouth. Messages could be sent and acknowledged back to the Admiralty within a matter of minutes. The system could not of course be worked at night or in fog, but it was of vital importance to the control of the Navy during the Napoleonic Wars and later years until it was superseded by the electric telegraph.

Telescope: an extending instrument containing lenses which can be focused on a distant object for clearer observation. The telescope, formerly called a glass or spy-glass, was once much used in the Navy by officers and signalmen, but has largely been superseded by binoculars. It is still traditionally carried by captain, commander or officer of the watch when on formal duties in harbour.

Telltale: any mechanical or electrical repeater of information or orders. For example, the engine room telltale records the orders of the bridge telegraph, and the helmsman may have before him a telltale pointer to indicate the amount of helm he has on the rudder. Originally the telltale was a repeating compass in the captain's cabin, sometimes fixed on the deck-head, from which he could keep an eye on the ship's course.

'Temeraire': name occurring several times in the British Navy, but originating in France in 1668, when Louis XIV suggested it for a new ship. Three other French *Temeraire*s followed; the 1748 74-gun successor was captured by Admiral Boscawen in 1759 and added to the British Navy List. The most famous ship of the name, immortalized by the painter Turner as well as by her own actions, was the fifth, a 98-gun ship built at Chatham and launched in September 1798. At Trafalgar, under Captain Eliab HARVEY, she was the second ship in the weather line, immediately following *Victory* and at one stage nearly overhauling her, Harvey having to cut his studding sails and occasionally yaw a little in order to keep

From a broadsheet explaining the operation of the new telegraph, 1796.

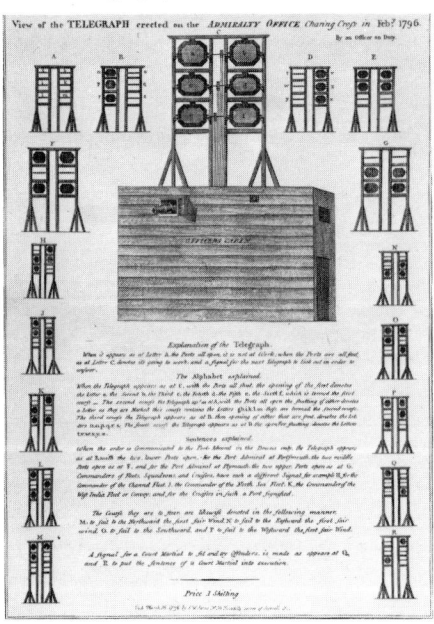

510

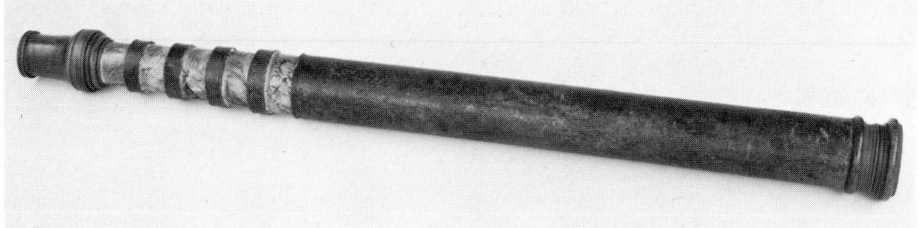

This telescope, signed M.R., is thought to be by Anton Schryle of Rheita, 1646.

station. At one stage in the battle the strange and perhaps unique sight was seen of two English ships and two French – *Victory*, *Redoutable*, *Temeraire* and *Fougueux* – locked side by side, till *Victory* lurched clear; *Temeraire* subsequently boarded both of the French vessels.

The rest of her career was comparatively uneventful and she was sold out of the service in 1838 for £5530 to the firm of Beatson, the ROTHERHITHE shipbreaker. Turner, who seems to have coined the name 'Fighting *Temeraire*', painted her passing up river on her last voyage.

See colour section.

Nothing could be finer. I have not words in which I can sufficiently express my admiration.

> Admiral Cuthbert Collingwood
> (after Trafalgar)

Surely, if ever anything without a soul deserved honour or affection, we owed them here.
> John Ruskin

> Now the sunset breezes shiver,
> And she's fading down the river,
> But in England's song for ever
> She's the Fighting *Temeraire*.

> Sir Henry Newbolt, 'The
> Fighting *Temeraire*'

Among the other notable *Temeraire*s was the ship launched in 1876, with her formidable combination of central battery guns and barbettes or turrets. Her fore turret armour was 10 in. thick, the rear turret 8 in.

Tender: (1) a vessel attending a larger one, or ferrying between ship and quayside, carrying goods, passengers, dispatches etc. (2) A ship is sometimes said to be 'tender' if she is in some measure less strong than she should be. Thus, the famous clipper *ARIEL* was considered to be 'tender' in stormy weather, so that her makers, Robert Steele & Co., made the equally well-known *TITANIA* more broad in the beam.

Tenerife: largest of the CANARY ISLANDS. *See also* SANTA CRUZ.

Teredo: *see* COPPER SHEATHING.

Terra Australis Incognita: Latin for 'unknown southern land'. The belief in the existence of a land mass in the southern half of the world was a relic of classical geography; it was a belief strengthened by the map of the world according to Ptolemy (*c*.A.D. 150) on which the southern limits showed a strip of land, named Terra Incognita, joining Africa to eastern Asia. During the Dark and Middle Ages the idea of a flat earth prevailed, but with the coming of the great age of sea exploration, after the Cape of Good Hope had been rounded (1487) and Magellan's men had circumnavigated the world (1519–22), belief in the unknown southern land

511

revived, and search for it began in earnest with the Spanish voyages of Quiros and Torres (1605–7). Important discoveries were made, and when Quiros found the island group now known as the New Hebrides, he believed the land to be part of the great southern continent. Then he was forced by his crew to return to Peru, but Torres sailed on to pass through the strait which now bears his name, between the northernmost tip of Australia and New Guinea.

At the same time the Dutch had been active in the East Indies and in all probability the actual discovery of Australia must be placed to their credit, in particular to William Janzoon who in 1606 had sailed into the Gulf of Carpentaria, though he believed the land to be connected with New Guinea, for he had no knowledge of the Torres Strait. In the following years other Dutch ships added piecemeal knowledge of the northern and western coasts of Australia. But the most important Dutch voyage was that of Abel Tasman in 1642. From Mauritius in the Indian Ocean he sailed well to the south until he discovered what is now called TASMANIA, which he named Van Diemen's Land. Thence he sailed eastward to find the eastern shores of New Zealand, which he named Staten Land, before turning northward and then westward to make his return through the East Indies to Mauritius. Tasman's achievements as an explorer of the South Pacific were not to be surpassed until the arrival of James Cook in the next century, but before that time other voyagers (amongst them in 1688 the English buccaneer William Dampier) had seen more of the north and western coasts of Australia, though they reported unfavourably on what they had found. As yet the whole of the east coast of Australia was unknown, and whether what had so far been discovered was in fact the great southern continent was still in doubt.

In 1768 James Cook was sent by the Royal Society to observe the transit of Venus from the Pacific, but with instructions also to make discovery of the southern continent. After completing his astronomical work in the Society Islands, Cook sailed south to make his circumnavigation of New Zealand. 'This land', he recorded, 'became the subject of much eager conversation; but the general opinion seemed to be that we had found the Terra Australis Incognita.' Cook's careful survey of the New Zealand coastline had shown that the country was not part of a larger southern continent, and the latter part of his voyage along the eastern coast of Australia and through the Torres Strait to the East Indies to reach England via the Cape of Good Hope in 1771 had revealed the limits of New Holland, as Australia had been known. But it was considered that his voyage had not yet disproved the possible existence of Terra Australis-Incognita, for there were large areas of the South Pacific not yet explored. French explorers, amongst them Bougainville, had been active in the South Pacific, but none had gone further than latitude 40° S. It was, therefore, to forestall the French and to dispel doubts about the existence of a southern continent that Cook set out on his second voyage (1772). He explored the southern limits of the Pacific in a zig-zag course which took him as far as 71° 10′ S. to the edge of the ice; and, though he discovered many other islands and had shown the absence of any land mass, his voyage led to the suggestion that Antarctica might exist, for he had seen the barren South Georgia and South Sandwich Islands.

Territorial waters: the area of sea

adjacent to any country and over which that country exercises control and sovereignty. In early centuries the sovereignty of the sea was often disputed and a cause of war, but at the beginning of the 18th century it was generally accepted by the European maritime nations that only those waters which could be guarded by a cannon from the land should be considered as under the control of the nation concerned. As the range of a cannon was then about three miles, there arose the convention of the three-mile limit as the extent of territorial waters. But claims were made by various countries that their territorial waters extended to various distances arbitrarily chosen up to as much as 200 miles. These extensions were often linked to the claim for an exclusive fishing zone, for which twelve miles off-shore was the most commonly accepted. In recent years, however, countries whose economy largely depends on fishing, such as Iceland, have declared a 200-mile limit. Some countries hold that territorial waters should extend to the limit of the continental shelf or the 100-fathom line. This idea is inspired not only by fishing rights, but also by the discovery of oil in the off-shore sea-beds. At the same time such claims do not deny the right of free and innocent passage on the waters of the high seas above the continental shelf.

A dispute between France and Britain as to the extent of territorial waters at the western end of the Channel has recently been settled by a compromise worked out by the European Court, but it was the prospect of oil that gave rise to these conflicting claims. International conferences have for long tried to settle the law of territorial waters, and the European Economic Community is much concerned with the question of the fishing limits and rights of their various members, but there is still great variation in what is claimed and what is accepted as the limit of territorial waters. *See also* COD WARS.

'Terror': of her line, probably the ugliest was the ship ordered for the Crimean War by an Admiralty convinced that ironclads were necessary to reduce the Russian forts. A floating battery, she was equally 'bluff' (i.e. broad or flattened) at both ends, so that it was difficult to tell whether she was moving forwards or backwards.
See also FRANKLIN, SIR JOHN.

Testing tanks: large indoor water-tanks in which scale models of ships are tested. Waves are produced in the tanks so that the strength and any weaknesses of the proposed design can be observed.

Texel, the: small island in the Netherlands West Frisian group, the scene of several naval actions. See below.

Texel, Battle of the (11 August 1673): the last action in the Anglo-Dutch Wars, between the Dutch Admiral de Ruyter and the French and British fleets under Prince Rupert. In the words of Geoffrey Callender, the French, who could have played a decisive part, 'sailed on serenely out of the picture, as if their presence in the battlefield had been a mere coincidence.' Rupert consequently had some difficulty, after a hard-fought battle, in extricating the British ships. For another action off the Texel, *see* CAMPERDOWN, BATTLE OF.

Thames: *see* LONDON RIVER; PORT OF LONDON.

Thatch: *see* TEACH, EDWARD.

'Thermopylae': one of the most famous of all the clippers: 'none was perhaps ever built more lovely and more swift'. Built by

Hood of Aberdeen and belonging to the Aberdeen White Star Line, she came off the stocks in August 1868, a composite ship with a hull made of the hard-timbered West Indian tree known as greenheart and teak upper works. A distinctive feature was the brass bulwark running the length of the ship. Her lines were so fine that, standing some 15 ft from either stem or stern, one could touch both sides of the ship with arms extended. After changing hands several times, she was bought by the Portuguese government and, as the *Pedro Nunes*, was used as a training ship for boys. In 1907 she was pronounced unfit for further use and, after being towed out to sea, was sunk by gunfire.

Like her rival the *Cutty Sark*, she began her career as a tea clipper, but most of her great work was on the Australian wool run. She made several records and on five consecutive days (of 24 hours) in the Roaring Forties made runs of 305, 310, 312, 330 and 326 miles.

It was not alone that she made astonishing passages. It was not alone that she achieved more than one record never beaten during the age of sail. There was in her some secret quality which moved the seaman's heart with an emotion of apprehended beauty . . . catching the breath, moving the heart, which the ship in her perfection can bring as surely as the poet's song or the artist's picture.

Cecily Fox Smith, *A Book of Famous Ships* (1924)

See also *CHARYBDIS*; CLIPPER; MOODIE, CAPTAIN GEORGE; WINCHESTER, CAPTAIN.

'Theseus': 74-gun Royal Navy ship (pierced for 70 guns), built (1786) at Blackwall. It was on *Theseus* that Nelson attacked SANTA CRUZ and lost his arm (1797). At the Battle of the Nile (1798), the ship was commanded by Captain Ralph Willett Miller, who wrote a very long and graphic account to Mrs Miller, including the damage he sustained:

We were now thus situated in the *Theseus*: our mizen mast so badly wounded that it could bear no sail; our fore and main yards, so badly wounded that I almost expected them to come down about our ears, without sail; the fore topmast and bowsprit wounded; the fore and main sails cut to pieces, and most of the other sails much torn; nine of our main and several fore and mizen shrouds, and much of our other standing and running rigging shot away, eight guns disabled, either from the deck being ploughed up under themselves, or carriages struck by shot, or the axle-trees breaking from the heat of the fire . . . In men we were fortunate beyond anything I ever saw or heard of; for though near 80 large shot struck our hull, and some of them through both sides, we had only 6 men killed and 31 wounded: Providence, in its goodness, seemed willing to make up to us for our heavy loss at Santa Cruz.

'Thetis': *see* TEA-CHEST.

Thick: as applied to weather, dense, cloudy, foggy.

Thick stuff: in a wooden ship, particularly strong planking about the water-line, reinforcing the main wale or strake.

Thimble: a shaped metal ring with an outside groove around which the rope runs for making an eye splice. The purpose of the thimble is to prevent excessive wear and strain on the eye of the rope.

Third Coalition: coalition formed by Pitt immediately before the Battle of Trafalgar, which finally destroyed Napoleon's hopes for an invasion of Britain. It included Russia and Austria.

Thirty Years' War (1618–48): series of political and religious struggles mainly brought about by Catholic-Protestant rivalry among the German princes and the intervention of interested foreign powers. Its chief importance from the point of view of the British Navy was that the government, in case Britain might become involved, instituted an inquiry into the state of the fleet and discovered a depressing state of affairs after the glory won by the Tudor ships. The eventual result was the raising of the SHIP-MONEY fleet, which safeguarded the country from external interference (e.g. from Louis XIII of France) in the Civil War of 1642–9.

Thole pins: upright short wooden pins set in pairs in the gunwale of a boat to provide a pivoting point for an oar, thus serving the same purpose as the more usual crutch or ROWLOCK.

Thomas Gray Memorial Trust: Trust founded in 1925 to commemorate Thomas Gray (1832–90), a distinguished Assistant-Secretary to the old Board of Trade. Among Gray's services was the formulation of the internationally recognized 'rule of the road' at sea. The Trust makes an annual award of a silver medal to a member of the British mercantile marine 'for a deed of outstanding professional merit performed at sea.' In 1977 the medal was awarded to Captain R. P. Blowers, master of the motor-vessel *Free Enterprise V*, for outstanding seamanship on 22 March, when he went to the rescue of the British coastal vessel *Tower Venture*, which

had a serious fire in her engine room. Since no adequate fire-fighting equipment was available on board, the only solution was the use of outside hoses.

For one and a quarter hours while the fire-fighting was accomplished, Captain Blowers kept his vessel exactly in position so that the connection between the ships could be maintained without parting . . . [He] not only had to judge distances, anticipate movements and control his ship, but also keep in mind all other aspects of the operation, such as watching over the safety of the working party on the foc'sle.

R.S.A. Journal (June 1978)

'Thomas W. Lawson': the only seven-masted schooner ever built, constructed by the Fore River Shipbuilding Company at Quincy, Massachusetts (1902). Each of the masts was the same height and consisted of a steel lower mast of 135 ft topped by a 58-ft mast of pine. She was steel-hulled and fitted with three steel decks along her whole length. Bilge keels were fitted amidships to increase her stability. The *Thomas W. Lawson* was employed successfully in the coastwise oil-trade between Texas and Philadelphia but came to a disastrous end in 1907 when, chartered for a transatlantic voyage, she ran into heavy weather, tried to ride out the storm among the Scilly Islands and turned turtle, with only one survivor. *See p. 516.*

Thompson, Edward (?1738–1786): naval captain and commodore, often called 'Poet' Thompson because of his fondness for writing verses, among the published specimens being a series of *Meretricious Miscellanies*. He was present at Quiberon Bay and took part in the relief of Gibraltar by Rodney. He was later court-martialled for the loss of the Guiana colonies but was honourably acquitted. Among his other literary work was an edition of the works of the 17th-century poet Andrew Marvell.

The *Thomas W. Lawson.*

Thompson, Thomas Boulder: *see LEANDER.*

Thompson, William: *see* MEDALS.

Thomson, William, Baron Kelvin (1824–1907): scientist and inventor who was responsible for many investigations and developments of great service to the seaman, including researches into gyrostatic problems, improvements to the mariner's compass, studies of wave motion, the invention of a tide-predicting machine, a sounding apparatus, and tables for determining the position of ships at sea. His brilliance was equalled only by his modesty and kindness to all who sought his guidance, and his influence as a teacher was profound.

Three-decker: a sailing warship with three gun-decks, upper, main and lower. The term does not refer to the total number of decks, but only to the number of decks on which an array of guns was carried.

Three-island ship: a ship, generally a merchant vessel, with three raised parts ('islands') above the ship's hull. These islands consist of a raised forecastle area, a bridge superstructure, and a raised area aft, or poop.

Three sheets in the wind: a phrase of nautical origin meaning drunk and unable to proceed steadily. Sheets are the ropes for trimming the sails; and if these are running loose they are said to be 'in the wind', and the sails would then flap wildly, whilst the vessel would be unsteady on her course, in fact careering and rolling like a drunken man.

Throat: (**1**) the upper fore corner of a four-sided fore-and-aft SAIL; (**2**) the channel of a gaff where it rides on the mast.

Thrum, to: to secure pieces of coarse rope

yarn to canvas to make a COLLISION MAT; or to take similar action on sail or rigging to prevent wear by chafing.

'Thunderer': along with *Orion*, *Monarch* and *Conqueror*, often regarded as inaugurating a new class of battleship. Built at Blackwall in 1911, she carried, as well as her 12-in. armament, ten 13·5-in. guns all mounted on the centre line of the ship. Her weight on launching was about 8000 tons, her estimated load displacement 22,500 tons, her engines developing some 27,000 shaft horsepower. It all sounds very different from Nelson's wooden *Thunderer* of 74 guns, also built on the Thames (1783), which was present at Trafalgar, earned the naval medal with three clasps and was broken up in 1814.

Thwart: the plank or bench fitted across a boat on which the rower sits.

Ticket: (1) certificate of professional competence, especially a merchant seaman's, given by the Board of Trade; e.g. 'mate's ticket'; (2) *see* PAY, SEAMEN'S.

Tiddley (or **tiddly**): sailors' slang for smart and neat; applied to a best uniform, to a caboose, cabin or any part of the deck made smart with extra touches of care.

Tide tables: printed tables, published each year, which list the data needed to predict the times of high and low water at the world's standard and secondary ports. Tide tables are published by the Hydrographic Department of the Navy and by maritime authorities of other nations.

Tides: the alternate rise and fall of the level of the sea. The tides are caused by the gravitational pull of the sun and moon. When the attractive forces of sun and moon

are in conjunction or working together, then tides are higher and lower than at other times; these are known as spring tides and occur twice in each calendar month, as do neap tides, which occur when sun and moon are in opposition (pulling at right angles to each other). At neap tides high water is lower and low water is higher than at other times. It is in fact the moon which has the greater influence on the tides, and just as the moon rises about 50 minutes later each day, so in most places is the time of high tide later by the same amount.

Though in theory, and in fact, every body of water has its period of oscillation, it is in the vast expanse of the Pacific, in its south-eastern quarter, that the pull of the sun and moon has a chance to build up its greatest effect and create a 'bulge' in the oceanic waters. From here the tidal 'bulge' or wave spreads out across the oceans and seas of the world, entering the Indian and Atlantic Oceans; it reaches and moves around the north and south of the British Isles 40–50 hours later. But this is to simplify what is a cosmic influence greatly complicated and varied by terrestrial influences such as the shape of the land masses, the form of the ocean bed and the depths and gradient of the off-shore sea floor, and the configuration of the land. Thus, in one area the rise and fall of the tide may be slight, whilst in another it may be very great, as in the Bay of Fundy in Nova Scotia, where the tide has a rise of some 50 ft. There is only a small variation between high and low tide in some enclosed seas, e.g. the Mediterranean, where the narrow entrance at the Straits of Gibraltar does not allow the tidal inflow from the Atlantic to have more than a small effect.

Where seas become shallower, as in the continental shelf around the British Isles, the tidal heave is constricted for space and therefore moves upwards to give good high

517

tides. Where these tides enter a narrowing and increasingly shallow estuary, they may appear as a moving and often rapid wave of water known as a bore or eagre, as in the lower reaches of the rivers Severn, Humber and Trent.

Local conditions off many coasts can increase the rate of the tidal stream to produce tide RACES and rips or overfalls which may make navigation hazardous for small craft. In the days of sail, tides as well as wind had to be used and reckoned with in the successful handling of ships, and today the state of the tide, its height and strength, remain important for power-driven vessels entering and leaving harbour, for anchoring and the many manoeuvres of ship-handling and good seamanship. *See also* TIDE TABLES.

Sailors talk about an ebb tide when the tide is falling, a lee tide when the tidal stream is flowing in the same direction as the wind, and half tide when the tide is at a level halfway between high and low water. *See also* FLOOD TIDE; SLACK WATER.

Tier: (1) a row (e.g. of oars or guns), especially one of several placed one above the other; **(2)** one of the windings of a cable when it is coiled; **(3)** the 'cable tiers' were the places on the orlop deck where the cables were stowed.

Tiffy: slang abbreviation of 'artificer', applied to skilled ratings engaged in the maintenance, repair and operation of mechanical and electrical equipment in ships and aircraft. It is also applied to ratings of the medical branch, e.g. 'sick berth tiffy'.

'Tiger': *see* NEWBERY, JOHN.

Tiller: the horizontal bar joined at one end to the head of the rudder and providing the

lever with which the rudder is moved. For its history *see* RUDDER.

Tilsit, Treaty of (July 1807): peace arranged between Napoleon, Russia and Prussia, one of whose chief objectives was the destruction of the maritime supremacy of England, both her fighting ships and her mercantile marine, counting on the support of neutrals such as Denmark. The most difficult problem was Napoleon's declared blockade of the British Isles by closing all European ports to her trading ships; England's reply, which, unlike Napoleon, she was able to back up with ships, was to declare in her turn a blockade of all the ports and harbours from which she was theoretically excluded. Fortunately the Continental ports themselves hated the Continental System; and Britain, despite some initial inconvenience (which, in fact, drove her to seek new and lucrative markets in the Far East and South America), stood the strain and in the end broke the bonds by the final defeat of Napoleon on land.

Timber: wood for use in building ships; or specifically any frame-member of a wooden vessel. Until the coming of the iron ship the supply of timber for shipbuilding meant the supply of oak, for oak was far and away the best wood, though elm was often used for building the keel and fir for masts and yards.

The oak used was of several kinds, all carefully chosen by surveyors, e.g. 'compass' timber with a natural curve, suitable for frames and ribs; 'thick stuff', planking more than 4 in. thick and anything up to 1 ft wide, much used in the lower parts of the ship, where the greatest strain occurred; and 'knees', either square or raking, being crooked timber used to secure and support beams.

English oak was considered best of all for shipbuilding. The oak forests of Kent, Surrey, Hampshire and especially Sussex were once extensive, and until the latter half of the 18th century were generally able to supply the needs of the Navy. But oak trees take a hundred years to grow to a maturity which makes them large and strong enough for shipbuilding, and the supply was not inexhaustible. The danger of a shortage was already seen in Tudor times, and special decrees were issued to encourage the preservation and planting of trees for shipbuilding. But it was the building of some two hundred ships for Cromwell's Commonwealth Navy that brought the danger to the fore. Even by that time many of the great royal and other forests were ceasing to provide suitable timber, but additional supplies were found in the woodlands of the sequestered estates of the Cavaliers. Attention to the importance of the supply of oak was further focused by the publication of *Sylva* (1664) by John EVELYN, which had considerable influence in increasing planting and improving the care of forests, and did much to stave off a real shortage of oak until a hundred years later.

Up to two thousand oak trees might be required to build a first-rate ship of the line, and by the second half of the 18th century much reliance had to be placed on oak from the American colonies, which had developed a fine shipbuilding trade of their own. Between the end of the Seven Years' War and the outbreak of the American War of Independence a serious shortage of suitable timber was felt, and American-built ships were added to the Navy. When during the war with the colonies this supply was cut off, German timber (*see* STETTIN OAK) and other types were tried as a replacement, but the quality was not satisfactory. The British Navy managed, however, to survive the crisis, partly owing to the long life of a well-built oak warship; Nelson's *Victory*, for example, was launched in 1765, remained in service until paid off in 1835, and then continued afloat at moorings at Portsmouth until 1922.

After the Napoleonic Wars the shortage of oak was again felt; TEAK, mahogany and other woods were increasingly imported and used for shipbuilding. Admiral Collingwood was to say that 'If the country gentlemen do not make it a point to plant oaks wherever they will grow, the time will not be very distant when to keep our Navy, we must depend entirely on captures from the enemy'. But the pocketful of acorns which he was in the habit of planting in the hedgerows and fields of his walks was not destined to be the answer, for by the time they had grown into mature trees the iron ship had supplanted the 'heart of oak' which was the essential framework of the old sailing warship.

Timmynoggy: a common 19th-century Royal Navy expression for almost any labour-saving or time-saving device.

Tin-clads: in contrast to the more heavily armoured warships, the lightly protected Federal gunboats used in the American Civil War.

Tin Duck: affectionate name for H.M.S. *Iron Duke*.

Tin fish: slang term for a torpedo.

Tiptaft, Captain W. E. (*d.*1878): one of the commanders of the clipper *Cutty Sark*, appointed in 1873. He was described as 'a quiet, modest man, a competent master and an excellent seaman, but lacking the qualities of a real hard driver.' In 1874, however, he made the year's fastest passage out to Sydney, 73 days. In November 1877 he narrowly escaped piling up on the Goodwins when in a hurricane that raged for two days the cables on both anchors parted and, out of control, the *Cutty Sark* drove through the rest of the huddled shipping, damaging two other vessels and sustaining considerable injury herself before she sent up blue flares for assistance and was brought into London River by two tugs. With cargo and freight the *Cutty Sark* was then valued at £85,000, and £3000 was paid out in salvage claims. The two ships damaged in the collision were not so lucky, since they were unable to prove that it was the *Cutty Sark* which had ripped by them. One indisputable piece of evidence, part of the name-boards of one of the ships struck, was conveniently dropped overboard by the *Cutty Sark*'s carpenter!

'Titania': graceful as befitting her name, yet able to 'make the run from London to Victoria in the teeth of the stormy westerlies in ninety to a hundred days', this was a composite clipper launched in 1866, built by Robert Steele & Co. of Greenock. She made a bad start, losing her fore mast – made of iron in the new fashion – on her first voyage to China; but she showed her mettle when she was 98 days out from Shanghai in 1869 and, in 1871, 93 days out from Foochow, overhauling the famous *Thermopylae* in the process. In the early 1880s she was bought by the Hudson's Bay Company for the Vancouver trade, then sailed the Mediterranean under Italian ownership till she was broken up at Marseilles in 1910.

'Titanic': White Star liner, at that time the world's largest ship, which, on her maiden voyage, went down in mid-Atlantic at about 2.20 a.m. on 15 April 1912 after colliding with an iceberg. Though the new medium of wireless soon brought a fleet of vessels to her aid, they could not reach her in time, and over 1630 people were drowned out of a total of 2367 crew and passengers. Full records are available in the reports of inquiries held in America and London.

The disaster provoked much class feeling at the time, partly incited by widely circulated statements that discrimination had been shown in saving the lives of first-class passengers, the *Daily Herald* quoting figures contending that 61 per cent of first-class passengers had been rescued, against 36 per cent second-class and 23 third-class.

Acrimony and recrimination set aside, there were many deeds of great heroism and unostentatious courage, both on the doomed ship and in the boats that got away; not the least moving being that of the orchestra (employed for the first-class passengers), who assembled on deck and played the hymn *Nearer My God to Thee* as the liner broke her back and went down.

Tobermory Bay: resting place, off the Isle of Mull, Scotland, of a Spanish galleon mysteriously blown up there in 1588 when she was struggling home after the Armada. Tradition held for a long time that the ship was the *Florencia*, a magnificently equipped ship provided by the people of Tuscany; but there is sound evidence now

The *Titanic* leaving Southampton on her maiden voyage.

for the belief that she is the *San Juan Baptista*. Whichever is the truth, it seems certain that the galleon carried considerable treasure. Archibald Miller, writing in 1683, told of 'a paper of Lattin' extracted from the Spanish records which stated that there were £30,000,000 in cash on board; and, having himself gone down in a diving bell, he claimed to have found 'a Crowne or Diadem'. He managed to hook it but 'being chained it fell among ye timbers.' The galleon is legally the property of the Dukes of Argyll, who from time to time have leased the rights to treasure-hunters. Already recovered have been a bronze cannon which stands in the grounds of the Argyll Castle of Inveraray, the ship's silver bell, swords, gold coins, cannon-balls, anchors, a capstan and a rudder.

Her sterne lyes into the Shore Norwest, and her Head to the Southwest. Shee lyes under ye Water at ye Deepest Nine fathom at a Low water, and twelve fathom at a full Sea or High water.

There is no Deck upon her Except on ye

Hinder part. There is one great heap of Timber, wch. I take to be the Steerage doore, and within that doore I did see a number of Dishes both great and small of a White blewish Colour, but whether they are pewter or plate I know not.

Archibald Miller (1683)

Miller adds somewhat wistfully:

Though I am an old man, I am willing yet to go alone after due consideration, for it is a pity that such a great business should be lost where it may be recovered by industry.

Toggle: a short, strong piece of wood fixed at right angles through the strands of a rope; it can then be passed through an eye, a bight of rope, or a becket to secure the two parts together and to provide a quick release. Small toggles are used as a means of buttoning certain types of coat, especially duffle-coats, but the main use of toggles was in the days of sail for securing parts of the rigging.

'Tom Bowling': *see* DIBDIN, CHARLES.

'Tom Cox's traverse': the equivalent of

521

another mysterious but colourful expression, 'all gas and gaiters but no threepenny bits': i.e. a great deal of talk and no effort. The identity of the original work-dodger, Tom Cox, is mercifully hidden in oblivion.

Tompion (or **tampion**): a disc or plug for stopping the mouth of a gun when it is not in use, to prevent water entering. The tompions used in ships carrying big guns often displayed a device or the ship's crest.

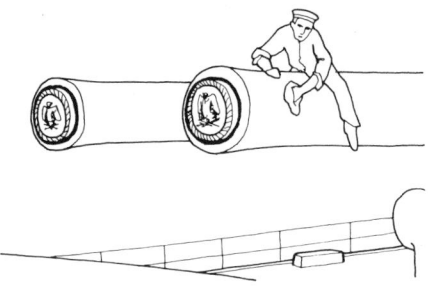

Tonnage: the measure of the weight of a ship or the measure of her capacity to carry weight. The tonnage of ships is very confusing, for many different ways of calculating it are used, and any comparison between the figures for two ships is meaningless unless the tonnages stated are reckoned by the same system of measurement and are clearly indicated.

The tonnage given for naval ships is usually *displacement tonnage*, that is tonnage by weight of water displaced when the vessel is fuelled, stored and ready for sea. A floating body displaces its own weight in water at the figure of 35 cubic ft per ton. Displacement tonnage is therefore actual weight and can be qualified as light or deep displacement: the former applies to a ship ready for sea but not fully fuelled and stored; when that is done she will have a deep displacement tonnage.

Merchant vessels also, of course, have a displacement tonnage, which again will vary between light displacement, when unladen, and deep or load displacement, when fully laden with cargo and down to the permitted summer load line marks. But it is the difference between these two, light and load displacement, which is called *deadweight tonnage*, and which gives for merchant ships the weight of all cargo, fuel and any other movables such as ballast and water. In stating a ship's deadweight tonnage the metric ton, or tonne, of 1000 kilograms or 2205 lb., is now increasingly used rather than the avoirdupois long ton of 2240 lb. But with merchant ships we are more concerned with capacity than with weight, and this is recorded or registered on the ship's Certificate of Registry as both *gross* and *net registered tonnage*. Gross registered tonnage is calculated from all permanently enclosed space above and below decks available for cargo, stores and accommodation, but with certain specified exceptions. Net registered tonnage is really an indication of the earning space of the ship, for it is calculated from the gross tonnage by deducting allowances for certain non-earning spaces occupied by crew, machinery or tanks.

The word 'ton' is a variant of 'tun', a cask for wine, and the modern measurement of a ship's capacity in tons has its origin in the Middle Ages when a ship's 'burthen' (or 'burden') was reckoned by the number of tuns of wine she could carry. As ships grew bigger and changed from wood to iron the maritime authorities employed different methods of calculating a ship's capacity in cubic feet and converting that volume to tons. Today in working a figure for a ship's tonnage as an expression of cubic capacity, 100 cubic ft or 2·83 cubic metres is reckoned as 1 ton.

'Tonnage' is sometimes used in a general sense for the total amount of a country's shipping calculated in tons, and is also applied to the fees payable in port or harbour or canal dues, as these are generally calculated on a ship's net registered tonnage.

Top: the platform at the head of the lower mast in sailing ships. Thus there were the fore, main, and mizen tops. In the sailing fighting ship men with muskets were stationed in the tops (*see* FIGHTING TOP) to fire down at those on the deck of the enemy ship; it was from such a French sharpshooter that Nelson received his mortal wound at Trafalgar.

Above the lower mast and the top was the top mast. This carried the topsails, either single or double (known as lower and upper topsails), in square-rigged ships. Above the top mast was the top-gallant mast carrying the top-gallant sails. Men who worked the sails and rigging in this part of the ship, known as 'topmen', were generally the best seamen in the crew. The petty officer in charge of them was known as 'captain of the top'. 'Top' is sometimes also used as an abbreviation form of 'topsail'.

As the modern Navy evolved, the original fighting top became a point for directing fire-control, and the word top continued in use, whilst topmen became a name given to a division or administrative unit of seamen.

To 'go up top' is used colloquially to mean to go on deck.

Top-gallant: *see* TOP.

Top hamper: all the superstructure and gear or cargo above the hull. A ship carrying too much top hamper is unstable.

Top mast: *see* MAST; TOP.

Topping lift: tackle for raising a derrick or other gear.

Topside (or **topsides**): strictly, the upper part of a ship's sides above the water, but also used to mean 'on deck'.

Torbay: a large bay on the coast of south Devon, with Torquay lying on the northern side and Brixham on the southern. Torbay provides waters which are well sheltered from westerly and south-westerly gales, and in the days of sail it was a much favoured anchorage for warships guarding the Channel or blockading the French ports. At Brixham William of Orange landed with his army in 70 warships and 400 transports (5 November 1688). During the Seven Years' War Torbay was a base for Hawke's Channel Squadron, and he sailed from here to his great victory at Quiberon Bay (1759). In the Napoleonic Wars Torbay was again a base and a haven for British ships conducting the blockade of Brest, and when finally Napoleon surrendered he was brought to Torbay as a prisoner in the *Bellerophon*. When the ship anchored off Brixham, he was heard to exclaim on the beauty of the bay.

Topping lift.

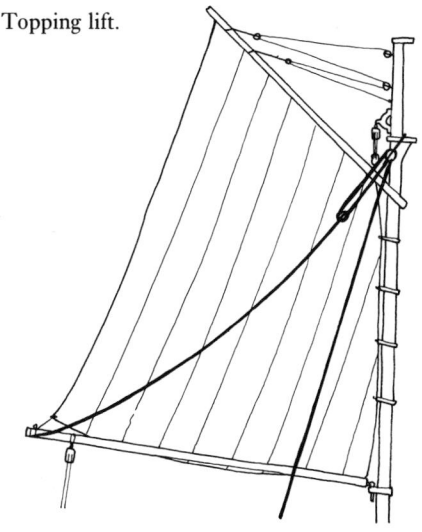

Tornado: a violent, revolving storm, of narrow dimensions and comparatively short duration. Tornadoes may be sudden and fierce, with very strong winds and a whirlwind-like cloud at their centre; they can appear in several parts of the world, but are commonest on the coasts of West Africa at the beginning and end of the summer rainy season, and also in summer in the southern U.S.A. *See also* WATERSPOUT.

Torpedo: a missile launched from ship, submarine or aircraft and self-propelled just below the sea's surface towards its target to explode upon impact. 'Torpedo' is also the name of a fish which numbs its prey with an electric shock; it was first borrowed to name what today would be called a mine, and was then used for an explosive device fitted to spars projecting from the bows of a small vessel which had to get near enough to the enemy ship to explode the spar torpedo under her hull. In 1871 there was also in the British Navy a kind of torpedo known as Harvey; this was a torpedo towed at an angle in order to strike the enemy's hull and explode on impact. But these early devices were soon to be completely replaced by the locomotive torpedo with which the name of the engineer Robert Whitehead (1823–1905) is particularly associated. In the middle of

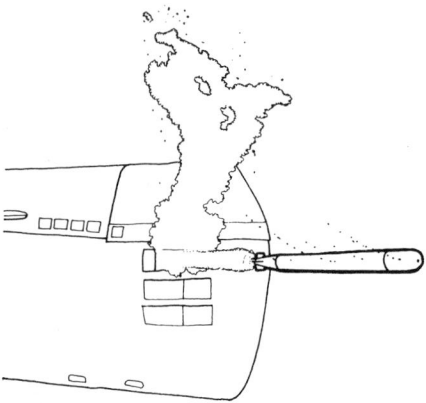

last century he was working in a shipyard in Fiume, then an important Adriatic port of the Austro-Hungarian Empire. Improving on ideas originating with an Austrian captain named Luppis, Whitehead in 1867 produced a torpedo propelled by a compressed air engine and fitted with devices to control depth and balance in the water. In 1870 the British Admiralty bought the manufacturing rights from Whitehead and soon the British and many other navies adopted the torpedo as an important weapon (*see SHAH*). Very quickly improvements in the torpedo's performance were introduced. TORPEDO BOATS were built to exploit the new weapon's potential, but it was the submarine which was to produce the most devastating effects with the torpedo, as a study of the losses of British and Allied shipping during the two World Wars will show. In the later years of the Second World War the German U-boats were fitted with electrically driven torpedoes which homed acoustically on to the sound of the propellers of the target ship. This and other improvements, the use of heated gases to provide propulsive power, sophisticated guidance systems, very powerful warheads and great speed, make the torpedo a formidable modern weapon.

The launching of torpedoes from aircraft continues to receive much attention. Of the many torpedo attacks by aircraft during the Second World War mention may be made of the successful attack by naval Swordfish aircraft on the Italian battle fleet anchored in Taranto harbour (November 1940; *see ILLUS-TRIOUS*), and it was the damage to the rudders of the *Bismarck* by torpedoes from *Ark Royal*'s aircraft that began her destruction in May 1941; her sinking was finally settled by torpedoes from the cruiser *Dorsetshire*.

A torpedo boat.

Torpedo boat: swift, light craft carrying torpedoes to attack larger ships. Torpedo boats first appeared in the 1870s with the development of the TORPEDO. 'Torpedo boat No. 1' was the name given to H.M.S. *LIGHTNING* when in 1879 (three years after her launching) she was fitted with two torpedo tubes. She was a small vessel, only 84 ft in length and 11 ft wide, but with the high speed of 18½ knots. Such was her success and potential that the Admiralty built many more torpedo boats, and foreign navies followed suit. It then became necessary to build a vessel which would counter the threat of the torpedo boat, and larger, faster and more heavily armed vessels were built in the 1890s as torpedo boat destroyers. These ships were again so superior to the earlier torpedo boat that they became a permanent class of warship which developed into the powerful DE-STROYER of modern times.

'Torpedo boat' is also commonly applied to a fast, engine-driven, small craft carrying torpedoes, and better-known as the M.T.B. or motor torpedo boat: *see also* MOTOR GUN BOAT.

Torres Strait: *see* TERRA AUSTRALIS INCOGNITA.

'Torrey Canyon': not a British ship, but notorious as the largest vessel to be wrecked off our coasts and responsible for oil pollution on the greatest scale then known. 975 feet long, and of 61,263 tons gross, she struck on the Seven Stones Reef, between Land's End and the Scilly Isles, on 18 March 1967 and shed some 30,000 tons of crude Kuwait oil. She was virtually destroyed by bombing in the hope of firing the remaining cargo.

The *Torrey Canyon* broken up on the Seven Stones Reef, 1967.

Torrington, Arthur Herbert, **Earl of** (1647–1716): admiral. His naval active service of some 27 years included actions against the Dutch and the Algerine pirates; he lost an eye during the capture of one corsair ship. He rose to become First Lord of the Admiralty and commander of the Channel fleet in 1689, having brought over William III the previous year as the result of the Bloodless Revolution. His naval career ended after he was defeated at the Battle of BEACHY HEAD (1690). *See also* FLEET IN BEING.

Torrington, George Byng, **Viscount** (1663–1733): admiral who combined a career in the Army and the Navy. He served in the Navy from 1678 to 1681, was in the Tangier garrison (1681–3) and then became an army lieutenant. His memoirs tell us that he was 'industrious to possess the Fleet in favour of the Prince of Orange', and, as a result of his support of William III, received his first naval command in 1688, rising thereafter to flag rank and to the First Lordship of the Admiralty (1727–33); he was raised to the peerage in 1721. His most famous naval action was the destruction of a large Spanish fleet off CAPE PASSARO (1718). He was the father of the unfortunate Admiral John BYNG.

Total war: war involving the whole population of a country, civil as well as military and naval (as distinct from engagements between the professionals), and into which the entire resources and capacity of a nation are thrown.

'Touch and take': the motto or watchword, perhaps never convincingly explained, adopted by Nelson before Trafalgar.

. . . the first Northerly wind will carry me to Cape St Vincent, where nothing shall be wanting on my part to realise the expectation of my friends. I will try to have a Motto, – at least it shall be my watch-word, *'Touch and Take.'* I will do my best.

> Nelson to the Rt Hon. George Rose,
> joint Paymaster-General
> (17 September 1805)

Touching the wind: sailing so close to the wind (*see* CLOSE-HAULED) that the weather edge of a sail shakes.

Toulon: great naval port and arsenal on the south coast of France and chief base for the French Mediterranean fleet. During the long struggle with France in the 18th century Toulon constantly featured in British calculations. In 1707, in the War of the Spanish Succession, Marlborough hoped that Prince Eugene would capture Toulon from the land whilst being supported from the sea by Admiral Sir Cloudisley Shovell. The fire of Admiral Shovell's fleet was effective in support of Prince Eugene's attack, and thousands of men and hundreds of cannon were landed from the ships. Nevertheless the siege failed, but not before great damage had been done to the harbour and to the French fleet. (It was on the homeward passage from this campaign that Shovell lost his life when the *ASSOCIATION* was wrecked off the Scilly Isles.) On 11 February 1744, during the War of the Austrian Succession, a British fleet fought a Franco-Spanish fleet off Toulon in an indecisive battle (*see* LESTOCK, RICHARD).

During the French Revolutionary and Napoleonic Wars Toulon continued its important role as a naval base. In 1793 Toulon was opened by French Royalists to forces under Admiral Viscount Samuel Hood in command of the British Mediterranean fleet, but after six months they were driven out by the young Napoleon, and

Toulon was re-established as a chief base for a French fleet. The port was thereafter blockaded for long stretches by the British, especially by Jervis, Nelson and Collingwood, though Nelson was more anxious to give the French fleet a chance to put to sea so that he could bring them to battle.

Tow: (1) coarse hemp fibre, of which ropes are made; (2) the operation of one vessel pulling another through the water by a hawser attached to the stern of the towing vessel and to the bows of the towed vessel.

Tower: *see . . . OF THE TOWER.*

Townshend, Jane: one of the authentic cases – dates uncertain – of a woman serving on one of H.M. ships. Details are always difficult, because females were never officially 'rated' and therefore do not appear on the muster-books. But Jane was on the *Defence* at Trafalgar and, more than 40 years later, proved her legitimate claim to the General Service Medal – with the support of no less a person than Queen Victoria. The Admiralty, however, resisted on the grounds that it would create too dangerous a precedent. Two other women, Ann Hopping and Mary Ann Riley, were rejected on similar grounds, though they could prove they fought at the Battle of the Nile.

Track: the line travelled by a ship through the water or by a torpedo after firing; or the onward movement of a storm, especially a tropical revolving storm such as a typhoon or hurricane.

Trade, protection of: along with command, and defence, of certain areas and routes (now much reduced), the chief function of the Royal Navy. In medieval times, since the king had no Navy of his own in the modern sense, merchantmen did their best to protect themselves. Not till the time of the Commonwealth in the 17th century did the Royal Navy assume, and thereafter maintain, its vital function of protecting merchant ships and engaging in convoy battles, e.g. against the Dutch. This was no accident. By this time the nation, i.e. the taxpayer, was maintaining the Navy and could virtually demand the protection of its sea-borne supplies of food and materials.

Trade winds: steady, regular winds which blow from the high-pressure belts or horse latitudes, lying approximately 30° N. and

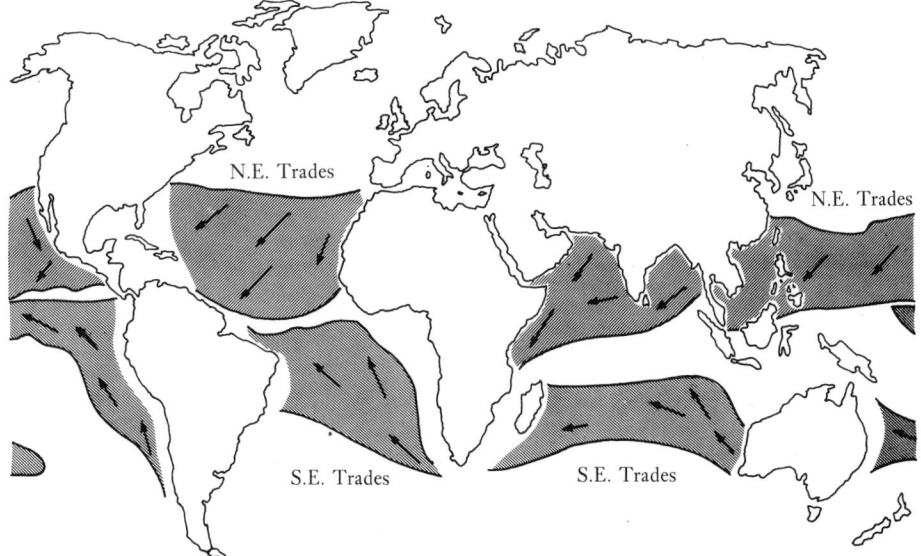

30° S., towards the low-pressure area around the Equator. Because of the spinning of the Earth, the Trade Winds both north and south of the Equator are deflected to the west, and therefore become the N.E. Trades in the northern hemisphere and the S.E. Trades in the southern. These wind belts shift slightly north and south with the passage of the seasons, but because they blow steadily and regularly with fair weather they were happy winds for trading ships in the days of sail; hence their name.

Trafalgar, Battle of (21 October 1805): 'At 11.30, the enemy commenced firing on the *Royal Sovereign*' (H.M.S. *Victory*'s log). 'Observed the *Victory*'s mizen mast go overboard, about which time [about 5.25] the firing ceased, leaving the English fleet conquerors' (H.M.S. *Euryalus*'s log).

Between these two laconic entries lies the story of one of the two greatest seafights in English history (the other being that of the Armada). What began with a fairly orderly approach to the combined French and Spanish fleets by the British ships in two lines (the lee and weather lines) developed into a furious mêlée, with every captain using his own initiative and doing the nearest job at hand or, at times, all that the battered state of his partly disabled ship permitted him to do. The first British ship to break the French line was the *Royal Sovereign*, flag-ship of the second-in-command, Admiral Cuthbert Collingwood, who led the lee line. (It is not always realized how protracted, because of the light and fitful winds, the first stages of the battle were. More than five hours elapsed between Nelson's last manoeuvring signal to his fleet and the guns of the *Royal Sovereign* opening fire on the French *Fougueux*.)

Nelson, heading the weather line, held on for about another twenty-five minutes before he, too, broke the line between the French Admiral Villeneuve's *Bucentaure* and the 74-gun *Redoutable*, one of the best led and trained ships in the enemy fleet; and, at last, the whole of *Victory*'s double-shotted broadside was loosed at *Bucentaure* from a distance of yards. Little more than an hour later, Nelson was dead.

At the end of the day, of the 33 enemy ships (including those captured later, on 4 November, and one that reached Cadiz in sinking condition), 23 were lost, their fates including capture, foundering, blowing up, running ashore and being taken to Gibraltar. The battle finally established British naval supremacy and destroyed all Napoleon's hopes for an invasion of England. For a time, despite the magnitude of the victory, the loss of Nelson seemed to outweigh every other consideration. One ordinary seaman wrote: 'I never set eyes on him, for which I am both glad and sorry, for . . . all the men in our ship who have seen him are such soft toads, they have done nothing but blast their eyes and cry ever since he was killed . . . Chaps that fought like the Devil sit down and cry like a wench.'

No battle in history has been more closely analysed, discussed and written about. Even so, a number of questions remain unanswered, especially regarding the famous pre-battle memorandum (*see* NELSON TOUCH). Captain Robert Moorsom of the *Revenge* (74) told his father in a letter that 'a regular plan was laid down by Lord Nelson some time before the action, but was not acted upon.' There are many discrepancies of time etc. in the entries in the various ships' logs, in the accounts of ships' movements, and even in such matters as the particulars of signal flags. But, in the end, as Dudley Pole rightly reminds us (*England Expects*, 1959),

Trafalgar was 'the final and calculated act in a campaign, and not an isolated action fought by chance off a Spanish cape.'

See colour section.

See also ACHILLES; AFRICA; AGAMEMNON; AJAX; BEATTY, SIR WILLIAM; BELLEROPHON; BLACKWOOD, SIR HENRY; COLLINGWOOD, CUTHBERT; COLOSSUS; CONQUEROR; DUFF, GEORGE; EURYALUS; HARDY, SIR THOMAS MASTERMAN; HARVEY, SIR ELIAB; KERR, LORD MARK ROBERT; LEVIATHAN; MEDALS; NELSON, HORATIO; NEPTUNE; PASCO, JOHN; PICKLE; QUILLIAM, JOHN; ROTHERHAM, EDWARD; ROYAL SOVEREIGN; TEMERAIRE; THUNDERER; 'TOUCH AND TAKE'; VICTORY.

The Sail Training Association's schooner *Malcolm Miller.*

Train ferry: type of ferry vessel used on short sea routes, an unmistakable feature being the long clear decks with two or more rail tracks. The deck rails line up exactly with those on a pivoted shore ramp which rises and falls with the tide. Though they are severely practical, the train ferries are not without amenities, including dining and sleeping accommodation. On some, passengers can remain in the train sleeping berths. Examples are the services carrying the London–Paris trains from Dover to Dunkirk; those in Denmark serving the numerous islands; and the many ferries over the North American lakes, maintaining a twelve months' service and therefore fitted as ice-breakers. The larger train ferries can carry a hundred or more loaded waggons.

Training ship: vessel used for training young sailors. The history of training ships includes such vessels as *Conway* and *Worcester*, permanently moored and used as long-stay school-ships for boys who mostly afterwards joined the merchant service. But these have given way to other methods of training either by direct entry as an apprentice with a shipping line or by long courses of professional training in sailing school-ships, the latter being specially favoured by the Scandinavian nations, Germany, Russia, Poland, Japan and other maritime nations, which train cadets in a number of fine sea-going full-rigged ships, barks, barquentines, brigs and topsail schooners. There is a strong belief among many sailors that training in sail is the best way to make a good seaman, and that, apart from any intended career, it can contribute as part of a general education to the formation of character.

Though not so well supplied with sailing training ships as some other nations, Britain has four topsail sailing schooners in which short training courses for boys and girls are regularly given. The ships are run by the Outward Bound Moray Sea School, the Sail Training Association, and the Dulverton Trust, for whom the latest British school-ship, the *Captain Scott*, was built in 1971. The *Sir Winston Churchill*, built in 1965 for the Sail Training

529

Association, is another training ship, well-known for her graceful lines.

Tramp: a cargo ship which operates on charter, taking up and discharging her cargo wherever and whenever her owners can get the trade. A cargo liner, in contrast, sails between ports on a fixed schedule.

Transom: a cross-timber or beam running from side to side in a vessel, particularly when fixed across the stern-post, as in old sailing warships, where transoms supported the square, overhanging stern quarters, giving what was known as a transom stern. *See also* SQUARE STERN.

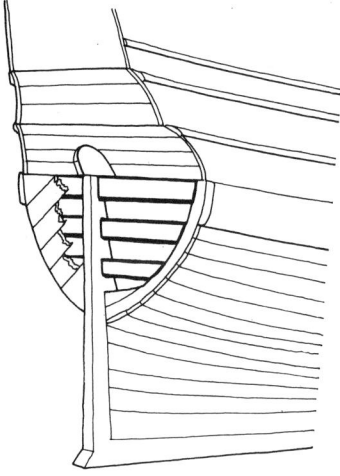

Transport: general name for any ship used for carrying military forces and material. In the 19th and early 20th centuries, when Britain maintained many garrisons overseas, the Royal Navy had a number of its own special transports; in the two World Wars many passenger and cargo liners were so employed (*see* TROOP-SHIP). In one sense the various kinds of LANDING CRAFT can also be described as transports.

Transportation: *see* PRISON HULKS.

Traveller: a general name for various

530

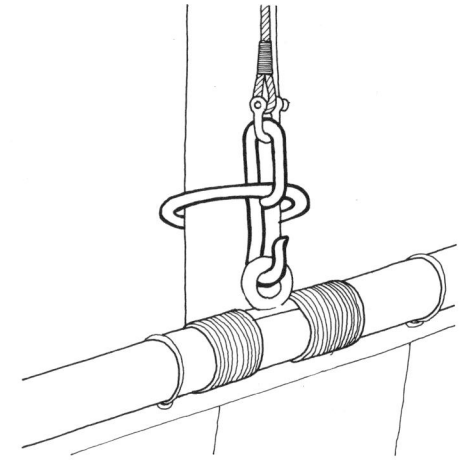

devices used in handling sails or rigging. The principle of a traveller is that a ring, thimble, sleeve or collar is allowed to move, slide or travel freely within a prescribed space and yet remain secure.

Traverse board: an early navigational device. It consisted of a board patterned with the compass-rose, from the centre of which radiated lines of eight holes to each point of the compass. Small pegs were placed in these holes according to the ship's estimated course and distance steered during each half-hour of the four-hour

A traverse board by a Scandinavian maker, *c.* 1800.

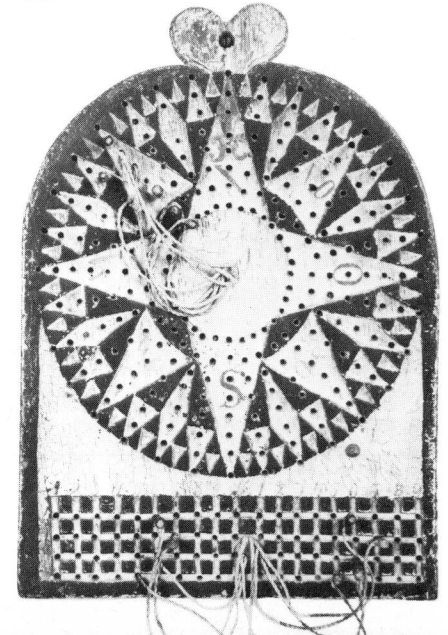

watch. Then from the position of the pegs the ship's progress during the watch was calculated to give an approximated dead reckoning position. *See also* INSTRUMENTS.

Traverse table: a printed mathematical table used by the navigator for calculating dead reckoning position and for plotting a course.

Trawl: a large, bag-like net, towed by a fishing vessel (*see* TRAWLER) to catch fish living on the bottom or in the lower layers of the sea. There are two main kinds of trawl, the beam trawl and the otter trawl. The beam trawl was formerly in common use, especially in the days of sailing trawlers. Its mouth is kept open by a stout beam at the upper edge of the net; at the ends of the beam D-shaped iron shoes or runners hold the sides and lower edge of the net and allow it to run along the sea-bed. The size of beam trawls varied according to the size of ship using them; the largest were up to 50 ft across their mouth. The otter trawl, which is now in general use, has its mouth kept open by OTTER BOARDS, and the net tapers away behind to what is known as the cod-end, in which the fish collect and are prevented from swimming forward again by devices known as flappers and pockets. There are various modern adaptations of the otter trawl, and the methods of use vary according to the type of fish being caught and the depth at which it is worked.

Trawler: a fishing vessel designed for catching fish on the bottom and in the lower layers of the sea by means of TRAWL nets. Trawlers are of several different kinds and sizes; some are designed to operate their trawls on the starboard side only, some on both sides, and others are equipped with modern machinery to land their catch over the stern. Inshore or near-water trawlers, working not far from their home ports, are relatively small compared with the larger vessels, known as middle-water and distant-water trawlers, which can travel to the far fishing grounds off Newfoundland and Iceland and within the Arctic Circle to the north of Europe. These trawlers have to be strongly built to endure the often stormy and icy conditions of northern seas. They also have to be capable of staying at sea for periods which have been extended from 10–14 days to the four or five weeks now spent at sea by the modern freezer trawlers and factory ships. These vessels, which range in size from over 1000 to 3000 tons, are equipped with electronic devices to identify shoals and aid navigation, and with machinery to clean, treat and freeze their catch on board; factory ships can also process the fish, e.g. into oil or fish-meal. *See also* FISHERIES.

The *Defiance*, a modern deep-sea stern trawler.

Treasurer of the Navy: chief officer responsible for the financial side of the Navy, a post created by Henry VIII. Holders of the office included the usual range from the efficient and incorruptible to the ineffective and avaricious (with occasional combinations of virtue and vice). One of the best was Elizabeth I's Sir John HAWKINS; for a less admirable example *see* CHIPS.

Trebuchet: a medieval device for hurling stones. Trebuchets were quite often carried in medieval ships, but were probably put on board for use against land-fortifications rather than against other ships.

Treenails (pronounced 'trennels'): pieces of well-seasoned oak, sometimes circular, sometimes many-sided in section, used in the old wooden ships to fasten the planks to the ribs etc.

Trelawney: a sea porridge concocted of barley, salt and water.

'Tremendous': 74-gun ship commanded by Captain James Pigott in Lord Howe's actions before and on the FIRST OF JUNE (1794). A gloomy note is struck by the Master in his log: 'Found stove [i.e. broken in] after the action one pipe of wine and two puncheons nearly full of rum.' *See also* MACKENZIE, DANIEL TREMENDOUS.

Trestle-trees: short timbers lying fore-and-aft at the head of the lower mast and supporting the top mast, its rigging, and the TOP.

Trice up: haul up and make fast.

Trim, to: to adjust the balance of a vessel or distribute the weight in her so that she floats level in the water. To achieve this many ships have trimming tanks or, in a submarine, ballast tanks, used to take in or expel water to give the vessel a good trim. If she is down in the water forward, she is 'trimmed by the head'; if she is down aft, she is 'trimmed by the stern'. To trim the sails or the yards is, however, to adjust them so as to get the best effect from the wind.

Trimaran: a small, light type of sailing yacht with a central hull and outrigger floats on either side. The design gives extra stability and allows a larger area of sail to be carried.

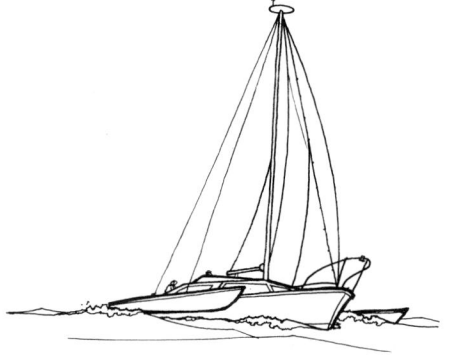

Trincomalee: seaport with a fine natural harbour in eastern Sri Lanka (formerly known as Ceylon). Trincomalee was taken by the Portuguese (1622) and then by the Dutch (1639). In the 18th century the rivalry between the British and French in India led to attacks on the harbour because of its strategic value. For a short while in 1782 it was taken and held by Admiral Sir Edward Hughes, but it was retaken by the French under the great Admiral Suffren later that year. It was finally captured by the British in 1795 and thereafter, when Ceylon became a Crown colony, Trinco-malee was an important fleet anchorage. In the Second World War after the loss of Singapore (1942), Trincomalee became the chief base for the Royal Navy in the Far

East; it was handed over to an independent Ceylon in 1948.

Trinidad and Tobago: two West Indian islands lying off the coast of Venezuela and to the south of the Windward Islands. In 1962 they became an independent republic within the Commonwealth. They were discovered by Columbus on his third voyage (1498). Both islands had different and varied histories until they were joined as a united colony in 1889. Trinidad was originally part of the Spanish Empire in the New World, but like so many islands in the West Indies it was at one time and another raided and fought over by English, Dutch and French. In 1797, during the Revolutionary War, a British expedition, sailing from Martinique, captured Trinidad, which at the Treaty of Amiens (1802) was ceded to Britain. In 1941 defence bases in Trinidad were leased to the United States, but except for a small tracking station they have since been given up. *See also* PORT OF SPAIN.

Tobago was unoccupied until 1632, when Dutch settlers arrived, soon to be followed by British. The island was claimed as a French possession in 1677, but in the following century, at the Treaty of Aix-la-Chapelle (1748), it was declared neutral and open to all nations. However, at the end of the Seven Years' War (1763) it was claimed by the British. Retaken by the French in 1783, and again by the British in 1793, it was restored to the French in 1802, only to be retaken in 1803. Finally it was ceded to the British Crown in 1814.

Trinity House: the authority responsible for the erection and maintenance of all lighthouses and seamarks around the coasts of England and Wales, and also the authority for the licensing of pilots in the ports of London, Southampton, Harwich,

Dover and about 40 others. The Corporation of Trinity House, to give it its full name, appears to have had its origins in a medieval guild of seamen based on Deptford, but its official recognition began with the granting of a charter by Henry VIII (1514) in response to a petition from shipmasters on the Thames. The powers of Trinity House were enlarged during the reign of Elizabeth I, when it became entitled to levy shipping dues and to issue certificates of competency to masters and pilots, for both home and overseas waters. Today Trinity House carries out a wide range of responsibilities under the direction of the Elder Brethren, consisting of the Master and ten others with long maritime experience. Elder Brethren may be called upon to sit as assessors with judges of the Admiralty Division when hearing marine causes. The sovereign and other distinguished people are elected as Honorary Elder Brethren; and Younger Brethren with seafaring experience are also elected, with voting but no executive powers.

In recent years the role of Trinity House has been under discussion. In July 1977 a Report of the Advisory Committee on Pilotage made a number of recommendations which will require legislation before they can come into force. Trinity House will continue as the main pilotage authority, but amongst proposed changes are a new executive board with representatives from shipowners, port authorities and pilots, able to take and vote on decisions concerning pilotage and the licensing and pay of pilots etc.

Trip, to: to release. To trip an anchor is to break it out of its hold on the sea-bed by hoisting on the cable; to trip any gear or tackle is to loosen it.

Tristan da Cunha: one of the small group

533

of volcanic islands in the South Atlantic, halfway between the Cape and South America. The island is named after the Portuguese discoverer who sighted it in 1506, but for long it was known as Lonely Island on account of its remoteness. For 300 years Tristan da Cunha was uninhabited, but a lone settler was found there when the British sent a party of soldiers to the island in 1816 in case it should be used as a base for the rescue of Napoleon, exiled on St Helena. The soldiers were withdrawn but some remained, headed by William Glass and his family. A few other settlers came as wives, and the little colony and their descendants remained on this distant island until 1961, when the volcano of Tristan, believed to be extinct, erupted and the whole population was evacuated to Britain. They returned two years later, and now number about 300 people, who rely on fishing for their livelihood.

In 1815 the seas off Tristan da Cunha were the scene of the last naval engagement in the war with America, when the British 19-gun sloop *Penguin* surrendered to the American 20-gun sloop *Hornet*. In 1942, during the Second World War, Tristan da Cunha was commissioned as H.M.S. *Atlantic Isle*, and became an important radio and meteorological station.

Tromp, Marten Harpertszoon (1597–1653): Dutch admiral who temporarily wrested control of the English Channel in the First Anglo-Dutch War but was subsequently heavily defeated on two occasions and in the second battle, against the English forces under MONCK, was killed by a musket bullet through the heart.

He is not to be confused with his second son, *Cornelius Van Tromp* (1629–91), buried, like his father, at Delft and also an admiral of great distinction. Although suffering reverses of fortune and at one time being deprived of command, he came back with honour and, though he had spent much of his sea service against Britain, he was received with every mark of respect by Charles II when he visited England in 1675.

Troop-ship: a ship carrying troops. Many liners were used as troop-ships during the two World Wars; the largest of these in the Second World War were the *Queen Elizabeth* and the *Queen Mary*, which were continually at work during the war years, each carrying thousands of troops at a time. In the later years of the war the *Queen Mary* was carrying as many as 15,000 men on a single trip from America to the British Isles. Because of their speed, both ships were able to sail independently in safety on their many voyages, but scores of other troop-ships sailed in convoy. *See also* TRANSPORT.

Tropics: the region of the Earth which lies between the two parallels of latitude marking the most northerly and most southerly points between which the sun appears directly overhead at noon during its apparent annual migration. The two parallels of latitude are each just under $23\frac{1}{2}°$ north and south of the Equator and are known respectively as the Tropic of Cancer and the Tropic of Capricorn.

Trot: 'a line some twenty yards long with eight or ten hooks upon it, having half a brick at one end, and a few bits of cork with a skewer stuck through them at the other.' (The description is from *A Sea-Painter's Log* (1886) by the Victorian painter Robert Charles Leslie, which contains a wealth of information about inshore fishing and small coastal craft.) 'Trotting' for flounders was a 'mode of fishing' with 'special charms for the poorer men among riverside people, the capital invested being small, and the tackle requiring little thought or after-care.'

Trotter, Thomas (1760–1832): physician to the Channel Fleet. He went to sea as a surgeon's mate, was at the Battle of the Dogger Bank (1781) and later served on a slaver. He was also present at the 'Glorious FIRST OF JUNE' (1794). He qualified as M.D. at Edinburgh in 1788, and became physician to the Channel fleet in 1794. He encouraged a number of reforms including the issue of regular uniform and a prescribed ration of lime-juice as a scurvy preventative (*see also* HASLAR). Among his suggested comforts was cocoa for the Channel fleet:

In a cold country it could be singularly beneficial. What a comfortable meal would a cup of warm cocoa or chocolate be to a sailor in a winter cruise in the Channel or North Sea on coming from a wet deck in a rainy morning watch!

Troubridge, Sir Thomas (?1758–1807): admiral. His distinguished career and the actions in which he was involved included Cape St Vincent and the Nile. His last years were embittered by a serious quarrel with Sir Edward Pellew whose Mediterranean command was, as a result of political pique at home, split into two, the more important part going to Troubridge, Pellew's junior in rank. In the end, Troubridge lost the inevitable heated arguments and, as some sort of compensation, was given the command of the Cape of Good Hope station. To support this command, Pellew sailed to Madras to meet Troubridge and hand over several ships of the line. But the disillusioned Troubridge, described by Lord St Vincent as the ablest adviser and best executive officer in the British Navy, refused to wait for any favours from his rival. In an old and leaking ship, the *Blenheim*, accompanied by only two small vessels, he left Madras for the Cape (12 January 1807) and went down in a gale off Madagascar.

Trough: the depression between two waves.

Trucial Coast: the name formerly given to the territories of seven sheikhdoms in the southern Persian Gulf and the Gulf of Oman. In the early 19th century this coastal area was a haunt of Arab pirates, and after acts of hostility had been committed against the East India Company the British government brought pressure to bear on the ruling sheikhs, who in 1820 signed the first of several treaties by which they agreed not to enter into relationships with other powers and to allow Britain to be responsible for their defence. This special relationship lasted until 1971, when British forces withdrew from the Gulf and a new treaty of friendship was made. In some parts of what was the Trucial Coast the development of the oil resources has now brought great wealth and rapid economic growth.

Truck: a small wooden disc at the top of a mast. 'From keel to truck' is a common measurement for the maximum perpendicular dimension of a ship.

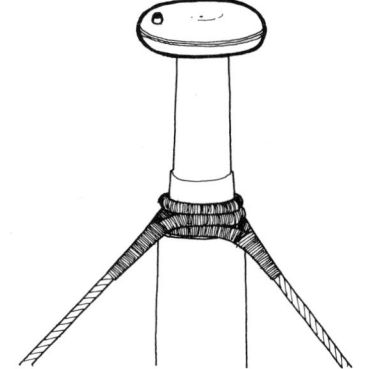

True North: the direction of the northernmost point of the world, that is the North Pole. All lines of longitude converge at the North Pole, and the direction towards this from any point on the surface of the globe is true north. This differs from magnetic north, the direction to which the compass needle points; *see also* MAGNETIC POLES.

Trunnions: a pair of short horizontal projections on either side of a cannon, acting as pivots on which it rests on the gun carriage and providing a balancing point for elevation.

Truss (or **parrel**): the bands of rope by which the yards were fastened to the masts, so as to slide up and down and to swivel when braced as required. Chain or a metal attachment replaced the rope truss or parrel.

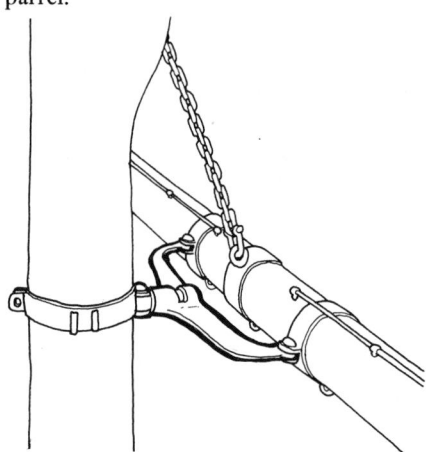

'Trusty': Royal Navy vessel of 1855 which led one despairing writer to say 'The Admiralty is decidedly masting mad!' She was a floating battery, pierced for 16 guns, with vast portholes measuring 3 ft 4 in. by 4 ft 10 in., and rigged as a three-masted schooner. According to those who sailed her and similar vessels, they would 'neither sail, steam, stay, nor steer'.

Trysail: a fore-and-aft sail set on a gaff.

Tsushima, Battle of: *see* CROSSING THE T; RANGE.

Tucker, Joseph (*fl.*1800–1831): Master-Shipwright of Plymouth Dockyard and (1813–31) one of the Surveyors of the Navy.

See also HUNDRED-AND-SEVENTY-GUN SHIP.

Tudor Navy: *see* ELIZABETH I; HENRY VII; HENRY VIII.

Tug: a vessel specially designed and built for towing and for assisting the berthing of larger ships either by towing or by nosing them into the required position. There are many different kinds of tugs, from quite small river tugs to large ocean-going salvage tugs, but all must have great power and manoeuvrability. These qualities were once achieved by steam paddle tugs, but these have been replaced by the modern motor tugs with propeller units of advanced design to give very powerful thrust, a small turning circle, and rapid response to control even at low speeds. Tugs generally have a short superstructure set well forward near high bows and an after-part designed for towing gear. Steel hoops (strongbacks) running athwart the stern are often fitted to keep the tow-lines clear of the deck. Some tugs are equipped for fire-fighting in addition to towing and berthing duties. Most river and harbour tugs are of relatively small size, under 300 tons, but ocean-going salvage tugs are much larger, the British *Lloydsman*, for example, being over 2000 tons. These ocean-going tugs are capable of being at sea for long periods, and can be used for a long tow such as moving a floating dock, or an oil-rig, over considerable distances. Some

The ocean-going tug *Lloydsman* employed in fishery protection off Iceland, 1976.

of them stand by at sea waiting for a distress call in the hope that they will be first on the scene and so gain the rewards of salvage work.

Tumble-home: the upward and inward curve of a vessel's sides to give on the upper deck a beam narrower than that nearer the water-line. Tumble-home is most clearly seen in the design of the old wooden warships, but it is also apparent in certain types of modern vessels.

Tunis: ancient city and capital of Tunisia, lying (with its outport, La Goulette) at the head of the Gulf of Tunis. Tunisia was for long nominally subject to the Ottoman Empire, and during the 17th and 18th centuries Tunis was one of the many bases of the Barbary corsairs, whose activities lasted into the first half of the 19th century. In 1881 Tunisia became a French protectorate. During the Second World War the country was the scene of the fighting retreat of the German forces in North Africa, and was captured by the Allies in May 1943. Tunisia achieved independence in 1956.

Turbine: an engine providing power by the action of high-pressure steam or gas on a series of blades set to revolve within a casing. Just as a water-wheel is turned by the force of the water on the blades of the wheel, so is a steam or gas turbine of more complex design forced to revolve, but at very high speeds. The steam turbine was invented by Charles Parsons, and he demonstrated its use in ships with the *TURBINIA* (1897). Its impressive performance and potential led to its rapid development and use in ships of all kinds by shipbuilding nations. The high speed of revolution within the turbine is reduced in reduction gearing before it is passed to the propeller shaft, but the efficiency of the turbine is much greater than that of the earlier steam reciprocating engines. The gas turbine is a more recent development over the last 30 years. The principle is the same, with hot gas providing the motive power to the blades of the turbine. A number of warships are now propelled by this method, amongst them some of the Royal Navy's fast patrol boats, which can reach a speed of 52 knots. Some vessels use turbines combining steam and gas to rotate their blades.

'Turbinia': innovatory vessel, the first to

At speed off Spithead, 1897.

be driven by a TURBINE; she received the official cold shoulder but chose her moment to display her efficiency in no mean fashion. She was a small steamer, only 100 ft long, of 44½ tons displacement, fitted experimentally with a new type of Parsons's turbines. At the great Naval Review of 1897, marking Queen Victoria's Diamond Jubilee, and with the eyes of the world on the massed shipping, the *Turbinia* appeared and steamed from one end of the fleet to the other at a rate no other destroyer or torpedo boat could match. Her makers proved their point and the success of the turbine engine was assured.

Turk's head: *see* KNOTS.

Turn turtle: a phrase generally used of a ship, meaning to capsize, turn over, but not necessarily sink.

Turret: *see* GUN TURRET.

'Turtle': *see* EAGLE; SUBMARINE.

Twain, Mark: *see* LEAD.

Twine: thin, but strong, twisted thread, generally of hemp, used for whipping a rope or for sewing canvas.

Two blocks: *see* CHOCK-A-BLOCK.

Tyneside: the chief seaport region of the N.E. coast of England, with a cluster of important industrial towns, of which Newcastle is the chief. From early times the export of the local coal became an important trade, and Tyne colliers were familiar ships in many ports. With coal and local iron ore available, Tyneside developed into a great industrial area in which shipbuilding was originally of first importance, being second only to the Clyde in the number and value of ships built. Mining machinery, marine engines, ships' fittings, locomotives and railway equipment are also produced on Tyneside, but today the electrical and chemical industries have replaced some of the older heavier iron and steel trades, though these are still important. Many fine warships have been built for the Royal Navy in the Tyne shipyards.

Typhoon: the name given to tropical revolving storms in the western North Pacific Ocean, particularly the China Seas. A typhoon consists of a deep low-pressure area outside and around which winds of hurricane force blow spirally towards the centre. In addition to this fierce circular motion typhoons have an onward progression known as the track, which tends to run west or north-west and to curve north or north-east. In the China Seas typhoons are most frequent from July to October, the latter month having the highest average number; but they may occur at any time of the year.

Tyrrhenian Sea: part of the Mediterranean Sea between Sicily, Sardinia, Corsica and the Italian coast.

U

U-boat: abbreviation of *Unterseeboot* (undersea-boat): a German submarine.

Ullage: the amount by which a cask or bottle of liquor is short of being full because of leakage or evaporation. The word is, however, commonly applied to what remains after leakage or evaporation, and as this is often no good, so a useless fellow may be referred to as mere ullage.

Umiak (or **oomiak**): *see* KAYAK.

'Uncle John': interesting experimental craft built in 1976–7 as a private venture by a group of London and Norwegian shipping companies. Costing around £17,000,000 and looking more like an oil-rig than any conventional vessel, it is designed for oil-rig work, such as pipe-connection, and floats on two enormous pontoons. Its construction will enable it to hold position and continue work even in hurricane conditions.

Under bare poles (or **sticks**): riding without sails on the masts (generally because of bad weather).

Under the weather: a phrase of nautical origin meaning indisposed, depressed or off-colour. A ship 'under stress of weather' is one affected by bad weather.

Undertow: a backward current, opposite to the one on the surface; particularly the backward thrust under waves breaking on the shore.

Underwater exploration: *see* DIVING; SALVAGE.

U-boat *U35* torpedoing a merchant ship from the surface, 1917.

Under way: a vessel is under way when she is moving purposefully, under command.

Under weigh: an incorrect spelling of UNDER WAY, resulting from confusion with 'weighing' (lifting) an anchor.

Underwriter: one who writes his name under an INSURANCE policy, as does an underwriter at Lloyd's. To underwrite a ship is therefore to take the risk of insuring her or her cargo.

Uniform, naval: for centuries, neither seamen nor officers wore any standardized official uniform. Blue was associated with the seaman from the Middle Ages (*see* NAVY BLUE), but at Court functions in the reigns of Elizabeth I and James I, masters of royal ships often wore scarlet suits, decorated with ships, roses and crowns. Green was often worn by seamen and, in the 17th century, red was as much associated with sailors as with soldiers. Early 18th-century Navy contracts mention 'red kersey breeches lin'd with Linnen' and there were some especially splendid red-flowered breeches decorated with gold thread. As late as the Nelson period, seamen gloried in highly-coloured waistcoasts, spotted shirts, and jackets edged with ribbon. Headgear included painted straws, rakish 'beavers' and felts, turbans, fur caps and woollen tam-o'-shanters.

Probably the first attempts at uniformity came from individual captains wishing their crews to present a less nondescript appearance. One lieutenant recorded that in 1815 the men '. . . were issued with twelve yards of duck [a cotton or linen fabric, whiter and finer than canvas], thread and needles and a black silk handkerchief.' By the next muster every seaman was expected to appear in a neat loose blouse (a 'frock') and trousers. 'You would see the fellows run to the galley fire, burn a stick, down on deck, dot off the shape and commence work at once. Others, unable to do this, would give their grog to those more expert.' Captains also liked their boat-crews to create a good impression and sometimes equipped them with highly individual uniforms at their own expense. But gradually more-or-less standard items began to appear. The petticoat-like garment of tarred sailcloth (*see* TARPAULINS) and short jacket and waistcoat gave way to the blue jacket and white, ankle-length trousers. The deep blue collar with the rows of white tape round the edge became common in the 1830s. Finally, though effects were slow at first, an official Admiralty order was issued in January 1857, standardizing dress for petty officers, seamen and boys.

Regulations for the uniform of officers appeared more than a century before those for the lower deck. Perhaps as a matter of professional pride, so that their calling and rank should be immediately apparent, the pressure was applied by the officers themselves and in consequence an order was issued by the Admiralty in 1748, outlining official requirements and stating that patterns were being lodged at various places where officers could examine them. The change was not immediate and dramatic, and there was still opportunity for the more showy (and the more wealthy) to indulge their fancies; but, in general, from that date began to appear the uniforms of the 18th and 19th centuries, so familiar from prints and portraits, before Victorian dowdiness stripped the quarter-deck of much of its sartorial glory.

Union: the Union flag, commonly known as the Union Jack, and officially as the Great Union. It is the national flag of Great

Britain, signifying the Union of England, Scotland and Ireland, with a combination of the crosses of St George, St Andrew and St Patrick. The Union flag is worn at the stern of warships when not under way between colours and sunset, and it is worn at sea when the ship is dressed with mast-head flags or escorting royalty. During the sitting of a court-martial in a ship the Union flag is flown from the yardarm.

Unship, to: to remove any piece of equipment, e.g. tiller or rudder, from its normal position; and occasionally used in the sense of discharging a cargo.

Up and down: said of the anchor cable when it is taut and running straight up and down from the ship to the anchor. This occurs when weighing, just before the anchor breaks out of the ground.

Up Channel: the eastern part of the English Channel, towards the Straits of Dover.

Up funnel, down screw: *see* SCREW.

Up helm: an order, when under sail, to move the tiller to windward.

Upper deck: (1) the deck above the main deck, stretching from stem to stern; **(2)** collectively, the officers, as distinct from the ordinary seamen or LOWER DECK.

Up spirits: the traditional pipe or order for bringing the day's ration of RUM.

Ushant: an island off the N.W. coast of Brittany; the most westerly point of France. Ushant has particular associations for many generations of British seamen, for it is a key point in navigation. To the north lies the entrance to the English Channel, to

the west lies the open Atlantic, and to the south lies the Bay of Biscay. The rocky island was a pivotal point in the struggle against France in the 18th and early 19th centuries, for it is only some 40 miles from the great French naval base of Brest, which was for such long periods watched and blockaded by the 'wooden walls' of England.

It was off Ushant that on 27 July 1778 Admiral Augustus KEPPEL, commanding 30 ships of the line, fought a muddled and indecisive action with the French, during which no ships were sunk or taken. Vice-Admiral Sir Hugh PALLISER, Keppel's third-in-command, later made charges of misconduct against Keppel; when these had been dismissed at Keppel's court-martial Palliser in turn was the subject of an inquiry.

In 1794, some 400 miles west of Ushant, the British and the French clashed again in the battle known as the 'Glorious FIRST OF JUNE'.

The name 'Battle of Ushant' is sometimes given to the engagement of 14 October 1747 also known as one of the Battles of FINISTERRE.

Ushant-eyed: applied to a man having one fixed eye. At one time the island of Ushant had one fixed signal light and one revolving.

Utrecht, Treaty of: treaty, or series of treaties, which concluded the War of the Spanish Succession (1702–13). By the Treaty of 11 April 1713, France ceded Newfoundland, Nova Scotia, and the Hudson's Bay territory to Britain. On 13 July of the same year, Spain ceded to Britain Gibraltar and Minorca and handed over the inglorious monopoly of the slave trade with Spanish America (*see* ASIENTO).

V

Vancouver, George (1758–98): naval captain and explorer. He sailed with Cook as seaman and midshipman, and later made an important voyage on his own account (1791–5), surveying S.W. Australia, New Zealand and the Pacific coast of North America (including Vancouver Island, which is named after him). His record of this voyage was published after his death (1798).

Van Diemen's Land: *see* TASMANIA.

Vang: one of a pair of guy-ropes steadying a gaff by running from its peak to the deck.

'Vanguard': a name well worthy of a whole book. In 1588 Sir William Wynter, standing out to sea in *Vanguard* to meet the Spanish Armada, wrote to the Officers of the Queen's Majesty's Admiralty:

> Our ships doth show themselves like gallants here. I assure you it will do a man's heart good to behold them; and would to God the Prince of Parma were upon the seas with all his forces and we in view of them; then I doubt not but that you should hear that we would make his enterprise very unpleasant to him.

H.M.S. *Vanguard* in 1947.

This *Vanguard* was launched in 1586 and rebuilt in 1612, with a keel of 102 ft and a beam of 35 ft – very close to the ideal dimensions for a large ship as given by Sir Walter Ralegh: 100 ft in the keel, 35 ft beam.

Another *Vanguard* (1787), dismasted in a gale and nearly driven ashore, almost missed the Battle of the Nile (1798), but was repaired in time to give a good account of herself against the *Spartiate*, which eventually struck to her and was boarded.

Drake and Nelson might have looked wide-eyed at the King George V class *Vanguard*, with her full-load displacement of over 50,000 tons, over-all length of 814 ft, sea speed of $29\frac{1}{2}$ knots and tremendous armament of eight 15-in. and fifteen 5·25 guns. She was the largest battleship built by Britain, laid down at Clydebank in October 1941, launched three years later and completed in April 1946 at a cost of £9,000,000. She was scrapped in August 1960.

See also RAM.

'Vasa' (or **'Wasa'**): *see* SALVAGE; SHIP-BUILDING.

Veer: (1) to change course away from the direction of the wind; (2) (of the wind) *see* SHIFT.

Velde, Willem (or **William**) **van de:** name of two painters, the Elder (1610–93) and the Younger (1633–1707), who came

A self-portrait by Willem van de Velde the Elder.

to England from Holland *c.*1672 and did much to record the history of English shipping. The father was originally employed by the Dutch government to paint sea-fights and in that capacity had sailed with the Dutch fleet during the Anglo-Dutch Wars. Both were appointed, first by Charles II, then by James II, at a yearly salary of £100 'for taking and making draughts of sea-fights', the son's chief function apparently being to reproduce in colour his father's drawings. This royal patronage of skilled draughtsmen and artists specifically as marine painters meant that, probably for the first time, English shipping was depicted in detail and with absolute fidelity. The National Maritime Museum at Greenwich possesses the finest collection of Van de Velde drawings in the world – some 1400 in all.

'Vengeance': *see* LORD'S OWN.

Venice: *see* ADRIATIC, MARRIAGE OF THE.

Venturer: *see* *ADVENTURER.*

Vernon, Edward (1684–1757): admiral whose chief claim to naval fame is that he introduced GROG. He had been nicknamed 'Old Grog' because he often wore a coat of grogram (a coarse material of silk with wool or mohair). The exploit that brought him his greatest popular acclaim was the capture (1739) of Porto Bello, its town, castle and harbour on the Isthmus of Panama, with a small squadron of six ships of the line and without any marines to back up the seamen. He also made a career as a politician, representing a number of boroughs over the years and being responsible for a number of speeches and pamphlets attacking, on occasion, the government and the Admiralty in language not conspicuous for its temperate nature. In 1746, apparently at the royal command, he was struck off the list of admirals and lived in retirement, retaining his seat as member for Ipswich.

Admiral Vernon was rather low in stature, of a brown complexion, a piercing eye, and his look and gesture commanding: he was remarkably strict, or, rather, perhaps severe in his discipline; naturally haughty, and impetuous, and sanguine in his expectations: his courage was unquestionable, and his abilities, as a seaman though not as a naval commander, were considerable.

Dr John Campbell, *Lives of the British Admirals* (1814 edition)

From a portrait by Charles Phillips, 1757.

A mighty bowl on deck he drew
    And filled it to the brink;
Such drank the *Barford*'s gallant crew,
    And such the Gods shall drink;
The sacred robe which Vernon wore
    Was drenchèd with the same;
And hence its virtues guard our shore,
    And Grog derives its name.

                    Old ballad

Versailles, Peace of (3 September 1783): treaty which closed the maritime war of Great Britain against France, Spain, the United States and the United Provinces (the War of AMERICAN INDEPENDENCE). Among its complicated provisions, France gave back to Britain Grenada, St Vincent, Dominica, St Kitts, Nevis and Montserrat. In return, France received Goree, St Louis and the French stations in India. The independence of the United States was recognized, and its boundaries defined so as to take in Louisiana. Other details concerned important fishing rights, the cutting of logwood, river navigation rights etc.

Versailles, Treaty of (28 June 1919): treaty closing the First World War (1914–18). The 15 parts included important military, naval and air-force clauses which imposed heavy restrictions; e.g. the German fleet was limited to six battleships, six cruisers and a few destroyers. It was unfortunate that the signatories to the treaty lacked the will or the means to maintain the effectiveness of these restrictions.

Vice-Admiral: rank between Rear-Admiral and full ADMIRAL.

'Victoria': the last wooden battleship built for the British Navy, launched at Portsmouth in 1859 and commissioned in 1864. She served as flag-ship in the Mediterranean but was removed from active service three years later.

Her successor (1887), a steel-armoured first-class single-turreted battleship, built at Newcastle upon Tyne, was sunk (1893) in collision with the *Camperdown* during naval manoeuvres in the Mediterranean, with the loss of Admiral Sir George Tryon (Commander-in-Chief, Mediterranean) and all the crew. The circumstances were bizarre and remain to some extent inexplicable, since Tryon, a distinguished and very experienced sailor of 45 years' service, put the ships on an inevitable collision course and, despite warnings from his navigating officer, declined to alter it.

'Victory': the most famous ship name in British naval history, imperishably associated with Nelson's flag-ship at Trafalgar (though there had been four earlier H.M.S. *Victories*). The ship herself can still be seen at Portsmouth, restored and preserved by every device that nautical knowledge and science can muster. It is a wonder that she survives, now almost in her old guise, since she was already over forty years old at the Battle of Trafalgar and, had Nelson been able to see her at the beginning of this century, he might not have recognized her, since she had been allowed to deteriorate at moorings at Portsmouth since 1835, and almost everything about her had been altered – masts, rigging, bow, stern, deck and cabin plans, guns, even the famous 'Nelson colours' of her outside paint.

Fortunately the appeals of enthusiasts succeeded in arousing both public and official support. In June 1921 the Society for Nautical Research (entrusted with the ship's rehabilitation) launched a determined crusade to save her and preserve her for posterity in dry dock. The Admiralty co-operated and only seven months later, on 12 January 1922, *Victory* was moved into No. 2 Dock at Portsmouth. By that time nearly a half of her fabric was so fragile and perished that the manoeuvre was delicate and hazardous. But it was safely accomplished and, fittingly enough, the oldest ship on the British Naval List was ready to be permanently safeguarded in the oldest dry dock in the world.

Tradition – glorious at times, incredibly stuffy at others – apparently dictated that no part of the official naval grant could be devoted to a ship no longer on the active fighting list; but a public appeal was launched by the Society on Trafalgar Day 1922. Response was slow at first, but in 1923 came a splendid gift from Sir James Caird, the Scottish shipowner, and soon the restoration fund stood at over £100,000 and the work could safely proceed. The result can best be expressed in the words of Sir Geoffrey Callender – himself one of the doughtiest of *Victory*'s champions – written in 1929:

A great change has come over the ship, a strangely mysterious metamorphosis, like that which converted the old hag of the nursery-tale into a fairy of radiant loveliness. All the imperfections and disfigurements and anachronisms have vanished and the *Victory* has recaptured the beauty that was hers when she flew Nelson's flag at her mast-head. The graceful bow, with its rails and brackets and spandrels, has been constructed afresh; the stern has been refashioned; and the backbone of the vessel, twisted and racked though it is with extreme old age, now snuggles cosily into a magic wall of concrete, which, moulding itself to the drag and droop of the keel, obliterates them, and (at the same time) lifts the ship so high above the dock floor that, with correct trim, the *Victory* seems to float, if not in water, then in air . . . This cunning arrangement makes it possible also for the . . . spectator to leave the imaginary water-level and descend by a solid staircase to the real bottom of the dock, and from that point of vantage to obtain a view of the

ship which Nelson never had – the entire underwater body poised above him, its mighty mass curved like the vaulting of a cathedral roof . . . But better pleased will be the spectator who lifts his eyes aloft to where the masts and spars raise themselves skywards in an interlacing maze of unforgettable beauty. With the magic of distance throwing its enchantments upon him, the spectator will do well to inform himself as to the dimensions of some of the ropes . . . If he knew, for example, that the shrouds, supporting the fore and main masts, are eleven inches in circumference, and the forestay eighteen inches, and the mainstay nineteen, he could amuse himself by computing the height of the fore topmast or the girth of the main topsail yard.

Similar work had proceeded internally, as the result of painstaking research among early plans and records, and in the summer of 1928 King George V unveiled a tablet which reads:

H.M.S. *VICTORY* LAID DOWN 1759 LAUNCHED 1765 WAS AFTER 157 YEARS OF SERVICE PLACED 1922 IN HER PRESENT BERTH THE OLDEST DOCK IN THE WORLD AND RESTORED TO HER CONDITION AS AT TRAFALGAR UNDER THE SUPERINTENDENCE OF THE SOCIETY FOR NAUTICAL RESEARCH. TO COMMEMORATE THE COMPLETION OF THIS WORK THIS TABLET WAS UNVEILED ON 17TH JULY 1928 BY H.M. KING GEORGE V

Victory became Nelson's flag-ship in 1803, having previously carried the flags of Admirals Augustus Keppel, Kempenfelt and Howe. After 1835 she was used as the stationary flag-ship of the Commander-in-Chief at Portsmouth. Her full history has been written in a number of books, e.g. Sir Geoffrey Callender's *The Story of H.M.S. 'Victory'* (1914).

When Nelson hoisted his flag in her, her main dimensions were: burden, 2162 tons; length of gun-deck, 186 ft; length of keel for tonnage, 153·1 ft; breadth, 51·5 ft;

depth in hold, 21·5 ft. Complement, 850 men. Guns carried at Trafalgar: gun-deck, thirty 32-pounders; middle deck, twenty-eight 24-pounders; upper deck, thirty 12-pounders; quarter-deck, ten 12-pounders; forecastle, two 12-pounders and two 68-pounder carronades. *See also* SAIL; WIDOWS' MEN.

See colour section.

Victualling: conveying or providing food etc. to a ship or fleet. In 1654 the government instituted Commissioners of Victualling as a department of the Navy. They, with an array of lesser officials, were responsible for the various Victualling Yards established through the country, usually associated with the dockyards. There had, of course, been earlier attempts to put the victualling of the fleet on some sort of systematic basis. In Elizabeth I's reign, for example, Edward Baeshe was appointed Surveyor of Victuals and was paid 4½d. a day for each man in harbour and 5d. a day when at sea. For this sum he was expected to provide a gallon of beer and a pound of meat per day for four days a week, the subsistence for the remaining days being largely made up of cheese and dried fish. In the 1590s the allowance was 7½d. a man per day on active service. On long voyages, in order to ensure that rations held out, the men were sometimes put on reduced rations of beer and meat.

The victualling scale of the Navy altered as slowly as the wage scale. For two hundred years the basic ship's provisions per man were 1 lb salt pork or 2 lb of beef on alternate days. There was a daily ration of 1 lb biscuit and 1 gallon of beer, and a weekly issue of 2 pints of pease, 3 of oatmeal, 8 oz butter and 1 lb of cheese. On southern voyages a pint of wine or half a pint of brandy was substituted for the beer which never remained fresh for long at sea. Rice was issued instead of oatmeal, olive oil for butter. When in port fresh meat was usually obtainable, but fresh vegetables did not become the rule until the end of the [18th] century. The full measure of all articles was reduced by an eighth to compensate the purser for wastage or seepage.

> Christopher Lloyd, *The British Seaman* (1968)

The invention or discovery which radically changed ships' victualling was the introduction of canned meat and vegetables, first experimented with in the Channel fleet in 1813. In 1866 the Victualling Office began to make its own version of the so-called 'bully-beef' (from the French *boeuf bouilli*).

Vigo, Battle of: *see* FERROL, BATTLE OF.

Vikings: Scandinavian seamen and warriors who, from the 8th to the 10th century, raided the coasts of Europe, including the British Isles, Iceland and Greenland. Some ranged further, reaching Russia and Constantinople and, according to some historians, North America. They are invariably associated with the famous LONG SHIPS. *See also* DANES.

Virginia: state on the southern Atlantic coast of the U.S.A., named (1584) in honour of Elizabeth I by Sir Walter Ralegh, who later made unsuccessful attempts to colonize Virginia. Climatic conditions, unreasonable demands from financiers back at home, and Spanish hostility combined to give the first settlers a rough time; but, after what is vividly called 'the Starving Time', a fresh arrival of immigrants brought new hope and determination, and such successes as the tobacco crop brought eventual prosperity.

'Virginia': *see* MERRIMAC.

Virgin Islands: group of many islands and

islets lying east of Puerto Rico and between the Greater and Lesser Antilles. They were discovered by Columbus (1493). The westernmost islands, of which the principal are St Thomas, St Croix and St John, are American territory; they were bought from Denmark by the United States in 1917 because of their strategic position, commanding a passage from the Atlantic to the Caribbean and one of the approaches to the Panama Canal. The British Virgin Islands, lying east of the American group, were claimed in 1666, but during the 18th century appear to have been a haunt of buccaneers and pirates. In 1812 the islands became part of the colony of the Leeward Islands, but today they are a separate colony within the Commonwealth.

Volunteers: apart from its usual general meanings, the word has several special applications in the Navy. In the ordinary sense, the king's ships, because of poor pay and conditions, never had enough volunteers – hence devices such as the press-gang.

On the other hand, the officers were always volunteers. In the old days, young men of good social standing were often taken to sea by some friendly captain as CAPTAIN'S SERVANT at the outset of their careers. Samuel Pepys added an Admiralty selection popularly known as KING'S LETTER BOYS, but officially 'Volunteers-per-Order'. In 1796, the old 'Captain's Servant' entry had their title established as 'First Class Volunteers'; *see also* BOY.

Wads: (1) compact masses of material rammed in to hold gun charges in place. They were normally of rope yarn, not too tight, so that they could be driven home quickly; but when the shot was used red-hot, as it often was in action, the wad was frequently a disc of green wood, wrapped in yarn. (2) Slang name for a naval gunner.

Waft: (1) (also **weft** or **wheft**) old name for a flag hoisted with its centre or fly stopped against the mast, staff or stay. Thus flown it would have different meanings according to the position in which it was displayed.

(2) To 'waft' is to convoy or sail smoothly along. The former use of the word 'wafter' to mean a convoying ship may possibly have been derived from the Dutch *wachter* meaning 'guard'.

Wager, Sir Charles (1666–1743): admiral whose long career embraced much service in the Mediterranean and the defeat of a Spanish treasure-fleet in Cartagena (1708). As an old man (for those days) and somewhat rusty, he presided over the Admiralty as First Lord (1733–42).

Waist: part of the ship between the quarter-deck and the forecastle, the equivalent of the more modern term 'well'. In time of action it was the most unenviable position in the ship.

It was the custom . . . to converge a broadside fire upon some central point in the opposing ship's side. The men stationed in the waist or main battery always suffered more in proportion than the men at the after or forward guns.

John Masefield, *Sea Life in Nelson's Time* (1905)

Waisters: the largest part of the old sailing Navy's ship's company; the least seaman-like and capable members, generally landsmen, employed on the ship's most menial work and likely to be stationed in the waist. To be 'good enough for a waister' was to be good for little else.

An early-19th-century table showing the organization of ships of the line includes the following numbers of 'waisters' for the various rates:

First-rates	171
Second-rates	151
Third-rates	115–125
Fourth-rates	39
Fifth-rates	15–32

Since they were not fit to go aloft, their chief duty (apart from swabbing, scavenging, livestock tending etc.) was heaving on the halyards. Though some of them doubtless developed into good seamen, the raw recruits came from such a diversity of previous occupations that it is hardly surprising that many of them remained 'waisters'. The *Elizabeth*, for example, a 74-gun ship with a company of 395, had only 117 proper seamen or men from callings associated with the sea. The rest included former tailors, stocking-makers, waiters, hatters, gardeners, labourers, painters, and a miner, chimneysweep, umbrella-maker and stay-maker.

Wake: (1) the track of smooth water left by a ship passing through water. Compare WASH. (2) Earlier, 'wake' was used for a space of water surrounded by ice, then for a passage cut through the ice for or by a vessel.

Walcheren Expedition (1809): an unfortunate enterprise conceived by the British government, on the renewal of the war between France and Austria, as a means of diverting French troops from the Danube valley. An enormous force of 35 ships of the line and frigates was dispatched, along with transports and over 40,000 troops and cavalry. Some modest initial success was achieved, including the capture of the Dutch island of Walcheren, but the failure of the Austrian armies knocked the bottom out of the enterprise. In the end, after a sad waste of life and effort, all forces and ships were withdrawn. It is said that 7000 men died from malaria alone. The failure had important (and unusual) political repercussions in that Canning and Castlereagh, the foreign and war ministers involved, had a violent quarrel, fought a duel (21 September 1809) and eventually resigned.

Wale: extra strengthening timbers secured in a projecting band round the hull of a ship to prevent damage. On sailing men-o'-war wales projected above and below the gunports, the lids of which were thus saved from damage when the ship came alongside another or a jetty.

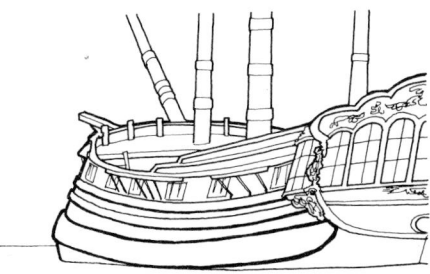

Wallis, Sir Provo William Parry (1791–1892): perhaps the longest-lived of British admirals, topping the century. Born in Nova Scotia (and, therefore, a 'bluenose' by origin), he served 53 years at sea. He was subsequently knighted and appointed Admiral of the Fleet (1877) at the age of 86.

Wallis, Samuel (1728–95): naval captain. His 37-year service at sea included a great voyage round Cape Horn, through the Polynesian group of islands and back by way of the Cape of Good Hope (1766–8). He later served two terms as a Commissioner of the Navy.

Wall knot: *see* KNOTS.

Walter, Rev. Richard (?1716–1785): naval chaplain who accompanied Anson on the first part of his voyage (1740–42) and later published a narrative of Anson's expedition, *A Voyage Round the World* (1748). After his sea-going experiences, Walter was chaplain at Portsmouth Dockyard for forty years. *See also* MANILA GALLEONS.

Warden of the Cinque Ports: *see* CINQUE PORTS.

Wardroom: the officers' mess in a warship or in a naval shore establishment. In a typical first-rate in the days of the sailing Navy the wardroom was usually found aft on the middle deck. Here lived the lieutenants and other officers – such as the master, the surgeon, the purser and the chaplain, all of whom were then classed as warrant officers of wardroom rank, but later became commissioned officers. There followed a period when the wardroom included only commissioned officers (excluding sub-lieutenants, who messed with the midshipmen in the gunroom). Today in the British Navy all officers mess in the wardroom, but commanding officers generally continue the tradition of messing apart in their own quarters, though practice depends on the size and class of ship.

Warhead: the head or component part of a torpedo or of a modern missile containing the explosive, which in the most powerful missiles may be nuclear.

Warm the bell: an old slang phrase in the British Navy, meaning to end a duty before the proper time.

Warp: (1) to 'warp a vessel' is to move her into a new position by hauling on a rope or ropes secured to a fixed position, e.g. a buoy or anchor (*see* KEDGE) etc.; **(2)** the name of the rope or hawser used in so moving a vessel; **(3)** the rope or wire by which a fishing trawl is lowered and hauled in; **(4)** the lengthwise threads of canvas, which are crossed by the weft or woof.

Warrant officer: a naval ranking of ancient origin but now obsolete. Warrant officers were those who were promoted from being a rating in the same branch; thus there were warrant gunners, warrant boatswains etc. They were not commissioned officers, though latterly before the grade was abolished they could become commissioned warrant officers and could rise to commander's rank. The origin of the warrant officer goes back to the time when the king needed permanent or standing officers to look after his ships and make them sail. Such important men as the gunner, the boatswain and the carpenter in the old sailing Navy carried heavy responsibilities and were appointed by warrant to a particular ship, in which they were relied upon to train the raw hands who formed the crew. Later such warrant officers were transferred from ship to ship as need arose within the fleet. Some who were at one time warrant officers of wardroom rank, such as the purser, the surgeon and the schoolmaster, became commissioned officers during the 19th century. Before the rank of warrant officer was abolished those who held it represented the best of skill, experience and leadership from the lower deck; today such men are promoted to commissioned rank and are not in a separate category. *See also* OFFICER.

Warren, Sir John Borlase (1753–1822): admiral. His career was unusual even for his period, when entry and methods of promotion were erratic and not reliably fair. Though his name was carried in ships' books from 1771 to 1774, he did not begin serving till 1777, having in the meantime taken an M.A. at Cambridge, become an M.P. and been created a baronet. In 1778 he was commissioned lieutenant, a year later commander and after another 18 months captain. This is not to say he was without merit. He defeated French squadrons in April and August 1794 and made many other captures. In 1798 he intercepted and defeated a French fleet on its way to Ireland.

Warren, Sir Peter (1703–52): admiral. He entered the Navy at the age of 14 and received his Vice-Admiral's flag 30 years later. He made a fortune from prize money in the West Indies, commanded a ship at the taking of Louisburg (1745) and represented Westminster in Parliament for the last five years of his life. This earned him a monument in Westminster Abbey.

'Warrior': British ship of revolutionary design, launched in 1860 as a counterblast to the French *La Gloire* of the year before. By the old standards she was a huge ship, of 9000 tons, and she was the first capital ship constructed of iron throughout. She was armoured with $4\frac{1}{2}$-in. iron plates and screw-propelled. She marked the beginning of a long and hard-fought transition

period in modern ship design; and, epoch-making though she was, she carried two legacies from the old days: she was also a fully rigged sailing ship, and she was still a 'broadside' fighting ship so far as her guns were concerned. These consisted of 28 7-in. smooth-bore muzzle-loaders, two smaller guns of the same type and two 20-pounder breech-loaders. Her 1250 h.p. engines gave her a maximum speed of nearly 15 knots. Despite her fighting power, in appearance she remained – apart from her length of 380 ft – an elegant, almost clipper-like vessel (*see above*).

'Warspite': a famous name for which it would be possible to select a dozen good representatives, beginning with the *Warspight* of Tudor times. The *Warspite* whose keel was laid 1912–13 belonged to what was probably the foremost British series of battleships ever built, the Queen Elizabeth class, which also included the *Barham*, *Malaya*, *Queen Elizabeth* and *Valiant*. With midships armour 13 in. thick, tapering to 6 in., the ships combined the great fire-power of the battleship with the speed of the cruiser. Their major armament consisted of 15-in. guns, which experiments had shown could pierce the thickest armour plating then in use, with an explosive force half as great again as that of the previous largest ships' guns. The cost

of each ship was about £2,400,000. Modified in the 1930s, they fought their way through both World Wars and, with the exception of the *Barham* (sunk in 1941), survived them. *See also* CAPE MATAPAN, BATTLE OF.

Warwick, second Earl of: *see* RICH, SIR ROBERT.

'Wasa' (or **'Vasa'**): *see* SALVAGE; SHIP-BUILDING.

Wash: the foaming and swirling of water caused by the passage of a vessel, considerable if the ship is a large one travelling at speed and a source of peril to small craft caught in it. Compare WAKE.

Wash, the: shallow bay of the North Sea in the Lincolnshire and Norfolk coast. Originally part of a much larger bay, it is now about 350 sq. miles in area.

Washington Conference: conference held in Washington in 1922 which sought to share control of the seas, thus ending the old conception of the PAX BRITANNICA. The three participants, America, Britain and (the most recent challenger) Japan, agreed that they should possess battleships on the basis of a ratio of five, five and three. An equal ceiling for submarine power was agreed for all three, and – an indication of how little appreciation there was of the future role of air power – a low limit was fixed of 35,000 tons in aircraft-carriers. By agreeing to such limitations Britain virtually relinquished her ancient claim to rule the waves of the world, since she retained control only of the Mediterranean, the Eastern Atlantic and the Indian Ocean.

Watch: a division of the day into periods of duty of four hours each, except for the first and last dog watches, which are each of two hours and run between 1600 and 1800 hours and 1800 and 2000 hours. The reason for this sub-division is that if there were six four-hour watches the same watch would be kept every day by the same men whether the ship's company were divided into two or three groups for watch-keeping. The names and times of the watches at sea are:

Middle:	midnight–0400 hours
Morning:	0400–0800 hours
Forenoon:	0800–1200 hours
Afternoon:	1200–1600 hours
First dog:	1600–1800 hours
Last dog:	1800–2000 hours
First:	2000–midnight

The ship's company is normally divided into either two or three groups for duty; these are generally known as the port and starboard watches, or the red, white and blue watches. 'The watch below' refers to those men on watch but not on deck, and 'the engine-room watch' etc. refers to those on watch in the part of the ship stated.

Watch-and-watch: ship organization which, usually because of undermanning, meant the company being split into only two watches, each on duty twelve hours a day in alternating four-hour spells.

Watch-bill: detailed list of the ship's company assigning to each man his watch and duty station for all occasions and emergencies.

Watch buoy: a buoy fixed near a light-ship from which the light-ship checks her own position and ensures that it has not shifted.

Watchkeeper: one who keeps watch and has some special responsibility.

Watch-keeping certificate: a written statement given by a commanding officer to a junior officer testifying to the kind of watch-keeping he is competent by experience and performance to carry out alone.

Water-blink: a cloud-like reflection in the sky in regions of Arctic ice, indicating the presence of open water.

Waterford schooners: type of sailing vessels used by the Waterford Line between Bristol and Waterford (in the south of Ireland) before steamers took over. They were rigged as two-masted schooners with square top and top-gallants on the fore mast. Well-known representatives of the line were the *Alexandra,* *Martha* and *Rapid*, plying in the 1830s.

Water-line: the line of the surface of the water around a ship's sides. The water-line will vary, of course, between the load water-line, when the vessel is fully laden, and the light or unladen water-line. It also varies with salt and fresh water (*see* LOADLINES).

Water-logged: saturated or filled with water so that very little buoyancy remains.

Water-sail: an additional fair-weather sail spread below the lower studding sail.

Waterside jockeys: landsmen with more money than sense, ready to buy unseaworthy craft without taking sound advice.

Waterside people are always in favour of the seller until after the purchase, when they become unpleasantly candid about his craft to the buyer.

R. C. Leslie, *A Sea-Painter's Log* (1886)

Waterspout: a pillar of water drawn up from the sea by a narrow, funnel-shaped mass of whirling cloud caused by intense low pressure such as occurs in tropical revolving storms. Waterspouts are generally quite narrow in diameter, but they can draw up a considerable volume of water, which when it descends is capable of swamping open boats and small craft.

'Waterwitch': well-known barquentine built (1871) at Poole, Dorset. She was 122 ft long, 207 tons gross. After her trading days were done, she finished up in an unusual role – as a training ship for Thames pilots, who, at a time when such ships had almost passed from human ken, still had to put in some time on a square-rig ship to complete their qualifications.

Water-sail.

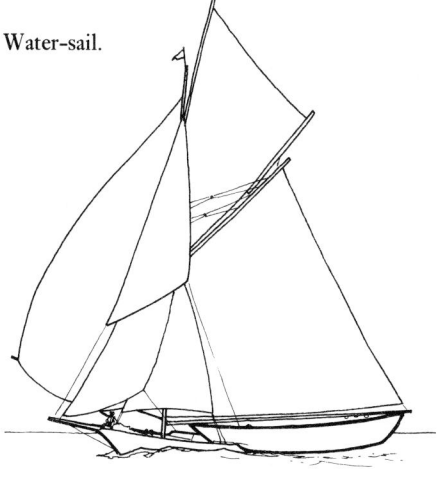

Watson, Charles (1714–57): admiral who, though he was accorded a monument in Westminster Abbey, has rarely had his services fully recognized. Yet without Watson Clive's great victories in India in the Seven Years' War would have been impossible.

When the news of the Black Hole reached Madras the British fleet on that station was under peremptory orders to return to England. Admiral Watson, however, declined to obey the Admiralty decree, and decided to stay and save the situation in India. Without his assistance, it is not too much to say, Clive would have been powerless. It was Watson who conveyed the punitive expedition to Bengal; Watson who steered the battleships into the Hooghly when the pilots declared the enterprise too hazardous; Watson who turned the Nawab's position from the river, and so effected the relief of Fort William; and Watson whose naval power made possible the conquest of Chandernagore.

Geoffrey Callender, *The Naval Side of British History* (1924)

Watson, George (*b*.1792): a refreshing lower-deck character who, despite harsh treatment and misfortune, displays an engagingly cheerful view of life at sea in his *Narrative of the Adventures of a Greenwich Pensioner* (1827). Even though he was personally thrashed with a stick by his captain (Sir Charles Collier) and subsequently given a dozen of the best with the cat-o'-nine-tails when he didn't deserve it, Collier still retained his respect and admiration. By the age of 20 Watson had been so badly wounded in action as to be virtually crippled for life. He received a Greenwich pension and lived on comfortably there to write his memoirs.

Wave: undulation of water caused when the surface of the sea is made to rise up in a ridge by the wind above. In deep sea there is no motion forward of the wave's water, but only its rise and fall. On reaching shallow water, however, the troughs are retarded, with the result that the waves rush forward and break.

Waves are measured by their height from trough to crest; by their length horizontally between crest and crest, or trough and trough; by their period or time taken for successive troughs or crests to pass a given point; and by their velocity, which is reckoned by dividing their length by their period. Such detailed measurement is not normally necessary, and a simple sea scale, based on the height of the waves (*see* SEA), may be used for recording the state of the sea in the log. The code runs from 0 to 9, that is, from calm to precipitous waves over 45 ft in height, which, though exceptional, have occasionally been reported.

Wavy Navy: colloquial name formerly given to the Royal Naval Volunteer Reserve because the gold braid worn on sleeves or shoulder straps by its officers followed a wavy pattern contrasting with the straight gold braid of the Royal Navy and the intertwined gold braid of the Royal Naval Reserve. *See also* RESERVES.

Way: *see* STEERAGE WAY; UNDER WAY.

Ways: frameworks down which ships are launched; *see also* SLIPWAY.

Wear: (1) to 'wear ship' is to put a sailing vessel on an opposite tack by bringing her stern to the wind. When this is done the ship is 'wore'.

(2) A ship is said to 'wear' a flag, especially when that flag denotes the presence on board of a particular person: e.g. when Her Majesty is on board *Britannia* the royal yacht will wear the Royal Standard at the main, the Lord High Admiral's flag at the fore and the Union flag at the mizen, while the White Ensign flies at the stern.

Weather: the combined result of all atmospheric conditions at a particular time and place. The weather has ever been of vital importance to sailors, especially during the centuries when man relied upon the sailing ship. But even in modern times the safety and efficient handling of power-driven vessels are dependent on the weather, and it remains of great importance too for yachts and other small craft which are more quickly subject to its effects. It is not surprising, therefore, that one of the first duties of a sailor in a sailing ship was to learn to read the weather, to note the wind's changes and what they foretell, to interpret the appearance of the sky and clouds, and to understand the rise and fall of the atmospheric pressure shown on his barometer. Observations of the weather were regularly recorded every watch in the ship's log, as they still are, and for this purpose a code of abbreviations known as the Beaufort Weather Notation is used. For example, 'r' stands for rain, 's' for snow, 'rs' for sleet, etc. A capital letter denotes 'intense' or 'heavy', and the repetition of the letter denotes 'continuous'; thus 'RR' means continuous heavy rain.

Sailors are no longer solely dependent on their own observations of the weather; forecasts are regularly transmitted by radio from stations ashore. Such weather forecasts are based on synoptic charts which are built up from a mass of reports received from specially stationed weather ships, H.M. and other ships, and aircraft. Photographs of cloud formations over vast areas are received from satellites circling above the earth's surface, and these too help in interpreting the likely course of the future weather. Forecasts are broadcast to shipping at regular intervals, but gale warnings are broadcast as soon as possible and repeated on the hour. For these forecasts the seas around the British Isles are divided into named areas, thus Dogger and Fisher are in the central part of the North Sea, whilst other names such as Hebrides, Faeroes, Thames and Wight cover the areas of sea which their names suggest. Forecasts for inshore waters, that is, up to twelve miles from the coast, are also broadcast every evening, and information on local weather and sea conditions is given by local radio stations. However, forecasts cannot always foresee the speed with which the weather may change, nor can they predict the local squall which may be dangerous to small craft, so all sailors should learn to read the sky and the coming weather.

The all-important place that weather has played in the story of ships and seamen is reflected in the many nautical uses of the word. Often it is synonymous with 'windward'. To 'weather a headland' is to pass it to windward, and to 'weather a storm' is to come safely through it. 'Under stress of weather' means affected by bad or heavy weather, likely when the weather-glass or barometer is low. Figuratively, however, to 'make heavy weather' of anything means to exaggerate difficulties. The 'weather line' of ships, as opposed to the 'lee line', is those in line of battle on the windward side, a position sought by British sailors when attacking the enemy, for it was thought to give the advantage by allowing the attacker to dictate time and place, to mass on a particular part of the enemy's line and to give better visibility as the smoke from the guns drifted away and down on to the leeward fleet; similarly, to have the 'weather gage' is to be to windward of another ship, and so have the advantage. A 'weather shore' is one that lies

to windward, and to 'keep a weather eye open' is to be on the alert, watching for any signs of change or possible danger, just like a sailor when watching the weather. A sailing boat is said to 'carry weather helm' if she tends to come up into the wind when the helm is amidships, and a boat is described as 'weatherly' when capable of sailing close to the wind. A ship's 'weather decks' are those exposed to the weather, though some part of them may be protected by a canvas screen known as a 'weather-cloth'.

Weather ropes: old term for tarred ropes. Compare WHITE ROPE.

Weather ship: a ship moving slowly about in a particular and limited area of the ocean for the purpose of recording and transmitting meteorological observations. In the North Atlantic the U.S.A., Britain, France, the Netherlands, Norway and Sweden maintain weather ships in nine different areas, of which the U.S.A. is responsible for four. Converted frigates, such as the British S.S. *Weather Monitor*, have been equipped for this task; others are specially designed. It may take three to five days for a weather ship to reach her appointed station. There she will remain for about three weeks before being relieved. Using an internationally understood code weather ships send hourly radio reports of their observations which are then plotted on a synoptic chart at weather-forecasting stations ashore. From this a forecast can be made and broadcast for the benefit of all.

Weddell Sea: sea lying within the Antarctic Circle between 20° and 50° W., named after a notable seaman, James Weddell (1787–1834). He had been sent into the Royal Navy because of insubordination on a merchant ship, but his qualities enabled him to rise to Master by 1812. Between 1819 and 1824 he made three voyages to the Antarctic during which he named the South Orkney Islands, charted the South Shetland Islands and part of the sea named after him, into which he sailed as far south as 74° 15′ S., 34° 16′ W., breaking Captain Cook's record of the most southerly exploration at that time.

Weft: (1) *see* WAFT (*1*); (2) *see* WARP.

Weigh (anchor): to raise the anchor or to start on a sea voyage. *See also* UNDER WEIGH.

Well: (1) *see* PUMPS; (2) *see* WAIST.

'West Country Waggon': *see ROYAL SOVEREIGN.*

Westerlies: winds that prevail in both the northern and southern hemispheres between latitudes 40° and 60°. In the northern hemisphere the westerlies blow mainly from the south-west; they often bring fierce gales and heavy seas but at other times they can be gentle and steady. Joseph Conrad in *The Mirror of the Sea* (1906) describes the westerlies in their fiercer mood as a

war-lord who sends his battalions of Atlantic rollers to the assault of our seaboard . . . The sky of the westerly weather is full of flying clouds, of great big white clouds coming thicker and thicker till they seem to stand welded into a solid canopy, upon whose grey face the lower wrack of the gale, thin, black and angry-looking, flies past with vertiginous speed. Denser and denser grows this dome of vapours, descending lower and lower upon the sea, narrowing the horizon of the ship.

In the southern hemisphere the strong prevailing north-westerlies often gave very fast passages to sailing ships bound for Australia, and between latitudes 40° and 50° S., were known as the ROARING FORTIES.

Western Approaches: the area of sea commanding the approaches to the western ports of the British Isles. During the Second World War, 'Western Approaches' was also the name of the naval command covering this area; at the start of the war the command was centred on Plymouth, but from early in 1941 the Commander-in-Chief of the Western Approaches was based at Liverpool.

Western Ocean: traditional name among British seamen for the North Atlantic.

West Indiaman: square-rigged merchantman engaged in the West Indies trade in sugar, fruit etc. The West Indiamen were normally much smaller than the East Indiamen, in the later part of the 18th century averaging 300–500 tons against the latter's 800.

West Indies: a long chain of islands spreading in an arc from south of Florida to the northern coast of South America and dividing the Caribbean Sea from the Atlantic. The larger, more northerly, group of islands, consisting of Cuba, Jamaica, Haiti, San Domingo and Puerto Rico, are called the Greater Antilles, while the many smaller islands of the Leeward and Windward groups are known as the Lesser Antilles, the whole arc being the peaks of a submerged range of mountains. The name West Indies is due to the belief by Columbus that he had discovered India by a western route. The islands and seas became the scene of two centuries of rivalry and war between Spain, England, France and Holland, and incidents of maritime adventure and naval endeavour are almost countless. After Columbus's voyages, the West Indies became the Vice-Royalty of New Spain. Here, in the Spanish Main, Hawkins and Drake won their early fame; here the buccaneers sailed and looted; here were the harbours receiving the huge numbers of negro slaves shipped from West Africa; here a succession of British admirals flew their flags and deployed their ships in protection of the West Indian trade, which in the 18th century was the richest part of Britain's commerce. In April 1782 a decisive victory over the French under de Grasse was gained by Rodney, with Hood as his second in command, at the Battle of the Saints, fought off the islands of Dominica and Guadeloupe. Here, on the West India station, Nelson saw much of his early service, and it was to the West Indies that he pursued Villeneuve in 1805 before finally gaining his victory over the French and Spanish fleets at Trafalgar.

Westing: the distance made good in a direction due west.

Westminster Palace of Varieties: one term – of many – for the Admiralty.

Weston, Agnes Elizabeth: *see* MOTHER OF THE NAVY.

Whack: old nautical term for proper share or due portion. 'A fair whack' referred to the provision of the correct ration of daily victuals aboard ship.

Whaleboat (or **whaler**): a double-ended clinker-built open boat used by British warships for pulling (five oars), sailing and general sea duties. They were modelled on the boats carried by the early whaling ships.

Whale Island: a small island in Portsmouth Harbour; home since 1891 of the Royal Navy's gunnery training school. Whale Island is 'commissioned' as H.M.S. *EXCELLENT*, and is colloquially known as 'The Island' or 'Whaley'.

Whaling: the commercial hunting and killing of whales for the products they yield, particularly oil. There are many different kinds of whales distributed throughout the oceans of the world; they vary in length from a few feet to a hundred, and in weight from 100 pounds to as many tons. Whales are warm-blooded, lung-breathing mammals, and must come to the surface of the sea to take in fresh supplies of air. When they do so they spout or blow a column of warm air which is visible from a distance as it looks like steam or spray. Thus the early whale hunters would cry 'There she blows' when a whale was spotted by the look-out at the mast-head. Then boats would be launched and the whale was attacked with a harpoon attached to a long rope. If the whale was struck it would sometimes tow the boat for miles, but once it was exhausted it was killed with long spears. The ship would then come up to the dead whale, which would be lashed alongside, and the process of 'flensing' (stripping off the blubber) would begin. Following that the blubber would be boiled down in great vats either on boats or at a whaling station ashore to extract the oil, which may be either edible or inedible according to the kind of whale. As well as the oil there are other valuable products, e.g. whalebone, much in favour in the 19th century for stiffening corsets; ambergris, useful in the manufacture of perfume; and spermaceti, a fatty substance put to a variety of uses, e.g. candle-making.

The classic story of the traditional whaler is told by Herman MELVILLE in

557

Casting the harpoon from the whaleboat.

Moby Dick, published in 1851, a time when the great whaling industry of New England was at its height. But before this, and indeed from earliest times, man had hunted the whale. In the Middle Ages the Basques were hunting the whale in the Biscay area, and the search was extended to the Newfoundland Banks during the 16th century. Soon other nations joined in and whaling was established at Spitsbergen in the Arctic, with the English, Dutch, Germans and Danes all involved. The hunt moved to other oceans and seas; the Americans, working out of NANTUCKET and other New England ports, now sought the whale in the Atlantic and southwards round Cape Horn into the Pacific and Indian Oceans.

The invention of the harpoon gun by a Norwegian in the 1860s and the coming of steam-powered whaling ships turned the scales so heavily against the whale that its numbers began seriously to decline. Enormous catches were made during the first half of the 20th century, and so serious was the depletion of the whale population that in 1947 an International Whaling Commission was set up to try to limit the numbers killed annually. But the agreement did not have the force of law and

success was less than that hoped for. The Commission still meets and in 1977 announced a 36 per cent reduction in the quotas of different kinds of whale to be killed in the following year, but even such a limit comes to as many as 17,839 whales to be killed in the North Atlantic, North Pacific and southern hemisphere. The Commission was concerned with the diminishing numbers of the sperm whale in particular, but the proposed limitation of kill was resisted by Japan and the Soviet Union, who have the largest whaling fleets. Of the Commission's 16 member nations only Japan, the Soviet Union, Australia, Denmark, Brazil, Iceland and Norway operate whaling ships. The other nine members are Argentina, Britain, Canada, France, Mexico, New Zealand, Panama, South Africa and the United States.

Modern whaling fleets consist of a whale factory ship attended by smaller ships which are whale catchers. The latter scout for and kill the whales with their harpoon gun in the bows. The whale is then inflated and marked with a flag or radio buoys so that it can easily be found again and towed to the factory ship for treatment. The whale factory ship is a specially designed vessel of between 16,000 and 30,000 tons displacement; indeed one Russian factory ship is of 36,000 tons. In the stern there is a slipway through which the whale is drawn, and it is flensed and treated in various processing plants to produce oil, meat and meat-meal for pet-food, and other by-products. Whale factory ships may carry helicopters to find the whales and direct the whale catchers to them; they also use electronic aids such as the echo whale-finder.

Wharf: a platform or place for loading or landing cargoes, more often associated with rivers, harbours and canals than with major ports, and ranging from proper stone-and-timber constructions to simple level spaces of rubble. The word derives from the Anglo-Saxon for 'bank' or 'dam'.

Wharfinger: the owner or manager of a wharf.

Wheel: a vessel's steering wheel, which moves the RUDDER and is controlled by the helmsman. It was introduced into ships towards the end of the 17th century and was generally sited on the quarter-deck; in a modern ship it may be housed on the bridge or in a separate wheelhouse. 'Wheel' is used as a general term and in phrases, e.g. 'Wheel's amidships, sir', 'Wheel's hard a-port, sir', or 'Five of starboard wheel on, sir', said by the helmsman when, having previously acknowledged an order, he has completed it. (In the last of these examples the helmsman is reporting that he has turned the wheel to alter the angle of the rudder by five degrees; the ship will continue to turn to starboard until the wheel is again brought amidships.)

Wheft: *see* WAFT (*1*).

Whelps: longitudinal raised ridges on the drum of a capstan or winch to provide an improved grip for a rope.

Where away?: the old call for 'In what direction?', 'Whereabouts?'.

Wherry: (**1**; see below) a kind of sailing barge with wide beam and shallow draught, used on the Norfolk Broads for transporting bulky freight. The wherry has a large mainsail on a single mast which can be lowered for passing under bridges.

(**2**) The name was also given to light, shallow rowing craft used on rivers or lakes for transporting passengers. R. C. Leslie, the painter, gives a wonderful description of the wherries he observed 'among the sheltered mud-lined estuaries that wander in behind such places as Portsmouth, Southampton, or Poole':

They remain masses of oak, copper and iron, held together more by paint, tar, or force of habit than by any strength of sail; their very timbers almost lost to sight, buried under many coats of paint and Stockholm . . . [The owner] will admit 'she veeps a trifle in her garboards, and hup and down her stem and starn-posts, and by rights she'd ought to have new topsides; but there, that would be making a new boat of her; she will last my time, and them as comes arter me may do that.' So with much putty,

brown paper, tar, and bits of old sheet lead, and with a few nails poked in here and there, the old boat with a great coat of bright green paint is once more ready, as summer comes round, to ply for hire, licensed to carry twelve persons.

A Sea-Painter's Log (1886)

Whip: (1) a simple form of hoisting tackle consisting of a single rope and block. When used from a derrick it is called a whip-and-derry. **(2)** To whip a rope: *see* WHIPPING.

Whipping: the operation of binding a rope's end to prevent it from fraying or unlaying; or the material, such as twine or yarn, used for so doing. Whipping may be done in several different ways, e.g. common whipping, West Country, American and sailmaker's whipping.

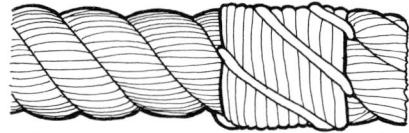

Sailmaker's whipping.

Whistle: (1) another name for the BOATSWAIN'S CALL or pipe; **(2)** a sound-making device, operated by steam or air, which must be carried by vessels over 40 ft in length to give signals of an intended manoeuvre or in fog.

Whistling down the wind: it was an old belief that certain people who were in touch with good or evil spirits could summon up a wind. Eric, King of Sweden, had the reputation of bringing the wind by simply turning his cap in the required direction and received the nickname of 'Windy Cap'. As late as 1814 Bessie Miller, of the Orkney Islands, eked out her living by selling favourable winds for 6d. a time.

An allied superstition was that the whistler forfeited a year of his life.

'Well, do you feel like whistling for it?' asked Simon. 'You know that it means a year off your latter end.' 'That'll be three of mine gone,' said Ralph with a laugh that sounded a little uneasy. 'I've paid once off the Bermudas, and once off Guinea' . . . And, then, clear and shrill as a nest of throstles they began to whistle. There was no tune, just the long pealing calls which men used when a dog has strayed . . . and for just that moment I could imagine, in some far corner of the sky, the recalcitrant wind lifting its head, listening, remembering, and obeying.

Norah Lofts, *Blossom Like the Rose* (1939)

White, Admiral of the: *see* ADMIRAL.

'White Bear' (or **'Bear'**): Armada ship of some 1000 tons, at one time flying the Lord Admiral's pennant, afterwards transferred to the *Ark Royal*. The *Bear* was commanded during the fight by Lord Sheffield, who was knighted for his services.

White Ensign: the official flag of the Royal Navy and the Royal Yacht Squadron: an ENSIGN with a white 'field' and the Union Flag in the upper corner next the staff.

Whitehead, Robert: *see* TORPEDO.

White rope: rope that has not been tarred, or does not need it. Compare WEATHER ROPES.

White Sea: a land-locked extension of the Barents Sea on the coast of N.W. Russia. The relative shallowness of the White Sea, combined with the mixing of North Atlantic Drift and Arctic waters, has produced a sea rich in fish and much favoured by trawlers in spite of the fearful weather often experienced there. Between November and May the White Sea is usually frozen over, though modern ice-breakers can maintain access to the chief port of Archangel.

'White Ship': ship in which Prince William (*b.*1103), only son of Henry I of England, was drowned off Barfleur in 1120 – after which, one chronicler affirms, the King was never seen to smile again.

When, therefore, it was now dark night, these imprudent youths, overwhelmed with liquor, launched the vessel from the shore. She flies swifter than the winged arrow, sweeping the rippling surface of the deep: but the carelessness of the intoxicated crew drove her on a rock, which rose above the waves not far from the shore. In the greatest consternation, they immediately ran on deck, and with loud outcry got ready their boathooks, endeavouring, for a considerable time, to force the vessel off: but fortune resisted and frustrated every exertion. The oars, too, dashing, horribly crashed against the rock, and her battered prow hung immovably fixed . . .; when the boat having been launched, the young prince was received into it, and might certainly have been saved by reaching the shore, had not his illegitimate sister, the Countess of Perche, now struggling with death in the larger vessel, implored her brother's assistance; shrieking out that he should not abandon her so barbarously. Touched with pity, he ordered the boat to return to the ship, that he might rescue his sister; and thus the unhappy youth met his death through excess of affection: for the skiff, overcharged by the multitudes who leaped into her, sank and buried all indiscriminately in the deep. One rustic alone escaped; who, floating all night upon the mast, related in the morning the dismal catastrophe of the tragedy. No ship was ever productive of so much misery to England . . .

William of Malmesbury, *Chronicle of the Kings of the English* (*c.*1125, trans. J. A. Giles, 1845)

Widows' men: one of the Admiralty's curious methods of providing a fund for the widows and dependants of seamen killed in action. The system was in force between 1733 and 1829. 'Widows' men' were imaginary seamen officially carried on the ships' books, and their wages were paid into the widows' fund. An early 19th-century document includes the following numbers:

Rate of ship	Full complement	Number of 'widows' men'
1st	837	8
2nd	738	7
3rd	491–700	5–7
4th	340	3
5th	252–294	2–3

It should be noted that the above figures for a full ship's complement are not absolute, and indeed they vary from document to document and book to book. It was, in any case, rare for a ship of the period to carry a full crew. At the last muster before Trafalgar, the first-rate *Victory* was some 200 men short of the figure shown above.

Wight, Isle of: island off the S. coast of England and commanding the approaches to Southampton and Portsmouth. It is separated from the mainland on the N.W. by the Solent and on the N.E. by Spithead. The latter has long provided a fine shelter and anchorage for the fleet, and has been the scene for naval reviews and the assembly of great convoys (*see* MUTINY). The Isle of Wight's strategic position has often invited invasion in the past, and from time to time it has been garrisoned and fortified. A Spanish landing was feared in 1588 before the Armada passed on up Channel; and a French invasion was feared at various times during the 18th century.

William IV (1765–1837): King of Great Britain (1830–37), often called 'the Sailor King' from his naval service, which was genuine and extensive. He entered at the age of 13, passed for Lieutenant in June 1785, and commanded a frigate (1786) and several other ships. Except for always having his own cabin, he lived the ordinary life of the gunroom and wardroom, acquiring in the process a considerable knowledge of seamanship. He became friendly with Nelson, and when the latter married Mrs Nisbet at Nevis (1787) he gave away the bride at the ceremony. Though he was promoted to higher rank, his active service, to his great disappointment, finished when he became a Rear-Admiral in 1790. When Canning in 1827 unwisely created him Lord High Admiral, a supposedly inactive office, he alarmed all and sundry by insisting on taking personal command of the Channel Fleet and promoting a variety of his own friends. He was almost at once persuaded, much against his will, to resign his office. Though a diarist (Greville) noted on his accession to the throne that he was a 'kind-hearted, well-meaning, not stupid, burlesque, bustling old fellow', he was in fact a fussy, quarrelsome type during his naval career and thoroughly irritated most of those under his command. In the words of the historian C. R. L. Fletcher:

> If he was a failure in the profession it was not from idleness, or from want of keenness, or want of readiness to go anywhere and do anything, but from want of balance, from fussiness, and, in spite of Greville's dictum, from stupidity.

Historical Portraits, Volume IV (1919)

'William Mitchell': one of the last two deep-water sailing vessels in service in the British merchant fleet, the other being her sister ship the *Garthpool*. The *William Mitchell* was built (1892) at Londonderry, a steel ship of gross register 2035 tons, length 272·7 ft, breadth 41 ft, depth 23·7 ft. She continued in service, apparently not very profitably, till 1927, when she was sold abroad and broken up.

Willis, John: *see* OLD WHITE HAT.

Willoughby, Sir Hugh (*fl.*1544–54): one of the heroes of early English navigation. He first saw military service and was knighted at Leith in 1544. He turned to the sea and in May 1553 sailed as captain-general of an expedition to discover the NORTH-EAST PASSAGE. Three ships set out, the *Bona Esperanza* (in which Willoughby sailed), the *Edward Bonaventure* (with Richard CHANCELLOR and Stephen Borough) and the *Bona Confidentia*. In August the *Edward Bonaventure* became separated from the other two ships in a gale. After a wandering and hazardous journey Willoughby reached the bay of Arzina on the coast of Lapland, where, although inadequately provisioned for the Arctic winter, he and his men apparently survived until at least the following January. Russian fishermen later discovered the two ships and the bodies of Willoughby and his company. His will and journal, which were found with him, were brought home and were published, though the originals have long since disappeared.

Willoughby, Sir Nesbit Josiah (1777–1849): admiral, undeservedly little-known but one of the true heroes of British naval history. In the words of William O'Byrne:

> The consummate gallantry indeed, the utter disregard of self, and the exalted devotion to his country's interests, which have emblazoned the acts of his hero's career, in every rank and under every circumstance . . . we confess to have never seen surpassed in any of the myriad soul-stirring deeds which have necessarily passed in review before us.

Naval Biographical Dictionary (1849)

High praise indeed; but not too high perhaps for a sailor who, in many adventurous exploits in the course of duty, lost one eye, seriously injured the other, had a cheek sliced in two and a pistol-ball lodged permanently near his brain, had his jaw shattered and could scarcely open his mouth to talk; and, again in O'Byrne's words, was put off 'with a simple C.B., an honour . . . he had earned on 10 different occasions'.

He added to his distinctions by being court-martialled several times. Serving with the Russian army in 1812 and escaping from a French prison appear comparatively trivial in the list of his exploits; and it comes as something of a surprise to find that he wrote *Extracts from Holy Writ and Various Authors, intended as Helps to Meditation and Prayer, principally for Soldiers and Seamen.*

A pleasant incident is recorded of Willoughby's days of retirement, when William IV, taking exercise with his court along the sea front at Brighton, met the battered old sailor and hailed him as a hero before all the company.

Willy-willy: name, borrowed from the aborigines, for the tropical revolving storms occurring off the north and north-west coasts of Australia.

Winch: revolving drum, generally on a horizontal shaft, moved by a crank or by steam or electric power, and used for hauling and hoisting.

Winchelsea: village near RYE, Sussex, a member of the confederation of the Cinque Ports and, until its harbour silted up in Elizabethan times, a famous seaport.

Winchester, Captain (*fl.c.*1890): one of the skippers of the famous clipper *Thermopylae.* He is recorded as being a 'bluenose', i.e. a Novascotiaman, therefore belonging to one of the finest breeds of seamen in the world. But, splendid sailor though he was, he got into trouble with the crew over his whiskers – a set of 'Dundrearies' of which he was inordinately proud. Apparently, after a long series of gales, the crew decided that the captain's whiskers were causing all the bad weather and, after a serious conference and in some trepidation, they approached him with the request to cut then off. Despite his tough qualities, he obliged and returned home clean-shaven. Cecily Fox Smith comments: 'I don't know if the desired improvement in weather conditions followed.'

Wind: the movement of air from areas of high atmospheric pressure to areas of low pressure. Winds are named from the compass direction from which they blow, though local winds with particular characteristics have individual names, e.g. the SIROCCO.

From man's first venture on the sea, and certainly from the first use of sail, it was vital for the sailor to know the winds and understand their likely behaviour, helpful or hurtful. In the ancient world the winds were given particular names, and the early mariners of the Mediterranean marked the direction from which they blew on a wind-board, wind-star or rose, having eight points corresponding to N., N.E., E., S.E., S., S.W., W. and N.W. This was indeed an early form of compass before the arrival of the magnetic needle, though a wind-rose could give only very approximate guidance.

Today the velocity of the wind is measured by an anemometer, an instrument consisting of wind-driven cups revolving a spindle which operates a pointer to show the speed. The BEAUFORT

WIND SCALE is used to record the force of the wind from calm to hurricane by the figures 0 to 12.

The wind was for so long of vital importance to sailors that many nautical phrases have taken on a figurative meaning in our everyday language. Thus to 'sail close to the wind' can also mean to go close to the edge of what is proper or legal, whilst to 'sail before the wind' means to prosper and proceed smoothly as a ship does when so sailing. To 'take the wind out of someone's sails', meaning to forestall him or put him at a disadvantage, reflects the situation when a ship sails to windward of another and takes the wind out of her sails. *See also* BETWEEN WIND AND WATER.

Windjammer: general term for a large, fully rigged merchant sailing vessel.

Windlass: a cylinder on an axle, turned by a crank or brace, useful for hoisting and hauling. Such a device was much used by merchant ships and was often placed athwartships at the break of the forecastle. In the Royal Navy it was normally fitted only in schooners and cutters, never in three-masters. One of its uses was to heave the anchor.

Wind-rose (or **wind-star**): *see* WIND.

Wind-sail: wide tube or funnel of canvas rigged up to direct a stream of fresh air to a particular part of a ship, often downwards into the lower regions, in oppressively hot conditions.

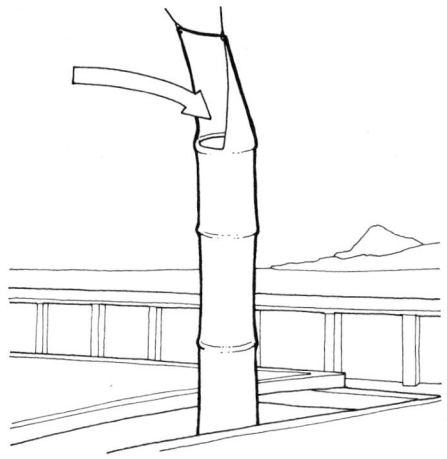

Windward: the side from which the wind blows; the opposite of 'leeward'. To be 'to windward' is to be in an advantageous position; the phrase dates from the days of sail, when British warships engaging the enemy would generally seek to have the windward position (the 'WEATHER gage').

Windward Islands: (1) group of islands in the West Indies at the southern end of the Lesser Antilles (*see also* LEEWARD ISLANDS). They comprise the French island of Martinique and the former British colonies of St Lucia, St Vincent, Grenada and the numerous islets of the Grenadines. During the long struggle with Spain and then with France in the 17th and 18th centuries, the British Navy was much occupied in Caribbean waters, and the West Indian station was of paramount importance for protecting the rich trade in sugar, rum and spices. The numerous attacks on the islands and the many naval engagements testify to the British concern with the West Indies, which in the 18th century received more naval attention and support than the Indian Ocean.

(2) *See* SOCIETY ISLANDS.

Wireless: a shortening of the term 'wireless telegraphy', the original name for RADIO.

Wire ropes: introduced in the mid 19th century in place of hemp. Among their advantages were the fact that a steel wire rope needed to be only about half the size of its hemp equivalent and its length of service was much greater. They were particularly useful for standing rigging and gave much more rigidity to the whole rigging system, small rigging screws being sufficient to take up any slack. Wire standing rigging, first used in the 1850s, rapidly became almost standard in the larger merchantmen. The Royal Navy was slower on the uptake; indeed, before wire rigging became common there, the sailing warship was out of date. *See also* ROPE.

Wolf-pack: name applied during the Second World War to groups of about ten German U-boats employing the tactic of converging for combined attacks on Allied convoys. The plan was for a pack of U-boats to patrol over a wide stretch of ocean, and when an Allied convoy was spotted by one of them it would be reported by radio to the German headquarters ashore. Messages would then be sent from this base to the other U-boats telling them the course to steer to converge for a combined attack on the convoy, which when conditions were suitable was carried out at night on the surface. The advantage lay with the U-boats because on the surface they were faster than the escorts, and the escorts were unable to use their Asdic for underwater detection.

Wolf Rock: the Rock lies at the entrance to the English Channel 10 miles S.W. of Land's End in Cornwall. On it stands a granite tower lighthouse, 135 ft in height, exhibiting an alternately flashing white and red light visible for 16 miles. The present lighthouse was established in 1870, replacing earlier structures. Over the light there was erected in 1973 an experimental helicopter platform, and in November of that year the first relief of Wolf Rock by helicopter was carried out, but without the aircraft landing.

Women at sea: a popular song used to celebrate a certain Captain Macpherson of the Merchant Navy, who was such a favourite with the ladies that they chased him from "Frisco to Perim'. He eventually put an effective stop to the pursuit by marrying. The song finished:

> East and West, North and South,
>   'Frisco to Perim,
> Didn't matter where he went,
>   The girls were after him.
> They chased him, pursued him,
>   They would not let him be,
> But they did when Mrs Captain Mack
>   Was Mistress of the Sea!

This reflects to some extent the attitude of the merchant marine who, not subject to governmental control, have usually been fairly amenable in the matter of women at sea, either working alongside the crew (and sometimes skippering a craft) or travelling with their menfolk.

The Royal Navy, on the other hand, have taken a more rigid attitude through the centuries, at the same time maintaining a remarkable degree of hypocrisy. In port, women on board were for long the accepted order of things, and were often allowed on voyages between home port and home port. Only very occasionally did a particularly strong- (or narrow-)minded captain, such as James Gambier in 1793, insist that all women coming aboard should be able to show their marriage lines. It is clear that the women were often a serious menace, not only to morals but to discipline, one of their chief offences being the amount of illegal liquor they smuggled on board.

At sea, when the ship was on active service, it was supposed to be a very different matter and the presence of women was completely contrary to regulations. But, even here, it is quite evident that women were smuggled aboard and hidden; sometimes, in an emergency, they would come out of hiding and help to handle the ship and even fight a gun. John Nicol records of the Battle of the Nile (1798), where he was stationed at the powder magazine in the *Goliath*:

> Any information we got was from the boys and women who carried the powder . . . I was much indebted to the Gunner's wife who gave her husband and me a drink of wine every now and then . . . Some of the women were wounded . . . One woman bore a son in the heat of action.

See also DARLING, GRACE; FREMANTLE, SIR THOMAS FRANCIS; MACKENZIE, DANIEL TREMENDOUS; PIRATES; SNELL, HANNAH; TALBOT, MARY ANNE; TOWNSHEND, JANE; W.R.N.S.

Women's Royal Naval Service: *see* W.R.N.S.

Wonderful Year, the: the year 1759, also known as 'The Year of Victories' and ANNUS MIRABILIS. Among the victories were the capture of QUEBEC and the Battle of QUIBERON BAY. David Garrick celebrated the year in the song HEART OF OAK.

Come, cheer up, my lads! 'tis to glory we
    steer,

To add something more to this wonderful
    year;
To honour we call you, not press you like
    slaves,
For who are so free as the sons of the waves?

Wood: *see* TIMBER.

Wooden walls: the old fanciful name for the sailing Navy as the best defence in the country. The conception is very old. Thomas, Baron Coventry, one of the judges of Star Chamber who assented to the levying of ship-money, said in a speech on 17 June 1635: 'The wooden walls are the best walls of this kingdom'.

Further back in history, when the Greeks sent to the oracle at Delphi to inquire how best to defend themselves against the invasion by Xerxes (480 B.C.), they received the answer:

Pallas hath urged, and Zeus, the sire of all,
Hath safety promised in a wooden wall.

The oracle did pretty well on this occasion, since the Persian fleet suffered a heavy defeat at the hands of the Greeks at the Battle of Salamis.

Woodget, Captain Richard: captain of the famous clipper *Cutty Sark* (1885–95), under whom she made her last and greatest voyages as a wool clipper. The son of a Norfolk farmer, he learnt his trade the hard way among the East Coast traders and

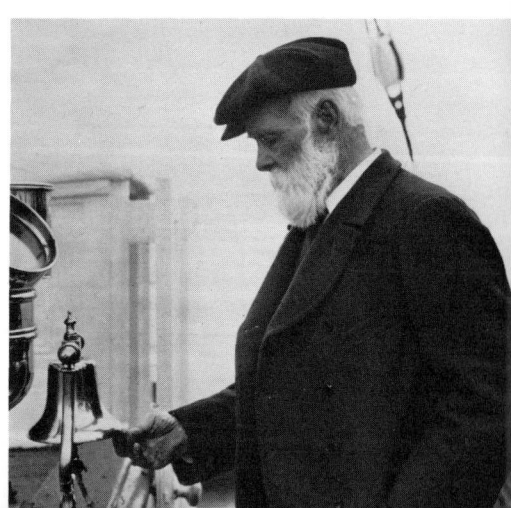

became a magnificent seaman whose success lay partly in the fact that, hard driver though he was, he never called on his men to do anything he was not prepared to tackle himself. It was a pleasant tribute to him that, nearly thirty years after he had last seen the *Cutty Sark*, the old man was invited aboard and took the wheel when, in 1924, she made a coastal trip to Fowey.

Wool clipper: clipper engaged in the Australian wool trade in the 19th century. Many former TEA CLIPPERS turned over to the wool run; some, indeed, including the famous *CUTTY SARK* and *THERMO-PYLAE*, made their great reputations in wool.

There was a great difference, not always realized, between the tea and wool trades. With tea, the anxiety was to be first home with the new season's crop for the London merchants. It was the reverse with wool, since it was the last clip that was wanted in London for the New Year sales; so, whereas with tea the fastest ships loaded first, with wool they were held back till last.

Wool Derby: the annual race home of the wool clippers from Australia.

Woolding: repairing a sprung yard or mast by binding it with rope.

'**Worcester**': one of the most famous of the training ships. On 7 October 1861, the Admiralty agreed to transfer the 50-gun frigate *Worcester* to the newly-formed 'Thames Marine Officers' Training Ship', instituted to provide officers for the merchant service and sponsored by some of the most notable shipowners and skippers of the day. *Worcester* was moored in Blackwall Reach and officially handed over on 29 May 1862. The first (temporary) commander was Captain J. F. Trivett, and Mr W. T. Read was appointed headmaster to organize the study courses, which included knotting, splicing, reefing, etc., navigation, nautical astronomy, various branches of mathematics, marine survey-ing, chart work and general subjects.

The difficulty which is experienced in providing proper qualified officers for merchant vessels has induced several gentlemen inter-ested in shipping and our increasing foreign commerce to form an association for the purpose of remedying in some degree this acknowledged deficiency; and it is hoped that the valuable results, which, from a national point of view, may be expected to flow from this undertaking, will secure for it general support.

From the first prospectus

In September 1863 the ship was moved to healthier surroundings at Erith and, four years later, gained much in reputation from the personal interest of Queen Victoria, who awarded the prize of a gold medal to the cadet who 'displayed the qualities likely to make the finest sailor'. Other moves followed, first to Southend, then to Greenhithe, an occasion celebrated by a salute of the ship's guns which is said to have shattered all the windows in Greenhithe.

The first *Worcester* training ship was superseded in 1875 by the screw line-of-battle ship *Frederick William*, which changed her name appropriately and was refitted to take in the greater number of cadets demanded.

There have, of course, been other *Worcesters*; for two notable examples, *see* NAMES, SHIPS'.

Wore: *see* WEAR.

Work, to: to labour with effort in a particular direction at sea, e.g. 'work to windward'. The word occurs in many other nautical expressions. To 'work double tides' was to do three days' duties in two; to 'work over' or 'work up' involved making over old materials such as worn rigging into something else; to 'work one's passage' was to pay for a passage by labouring with the crew and has passed into common parlance for anyone providing temporary work service in lieu of cash.

World War, First (1914–18): many references to actions, ships and personalities of the war will be found throughout this book (e.g. *see* DOGGER BANK, BATTLES OF THE; FALKLAND ISLANDS, BATTLE OF THE; GALLIPOLI). In historical perspective, the main features will be the introduction of unrestricted submarine warfare by the Germans (which eventually brought the U.S.A. into the arena) and the development, if belated, of efficient convoy work by the Allies. The main sea battle was that of JUTLAND (31 May 1916), which, though conflicting claims are made by both sides as to victory or defeat, at least sent the German surface fleet into harbour for the rest of the war.

World War, Second (1939–45): as with the First World War, it would be difficult, in a work of this nature, to give a comprehensive account of the role played in the war by the Royal and Merchant navies, in their convoy work, heroic encounters with surface raiders and capital ships, coastal raids and bombardments, minesweeping and other protective work, and the moving epic of the 'Little Ships' at DUNKIRK. To illustrate but one aspect of the struggle, Britain, her allies (and some neutrals) lost more than 5000 merchantmen, totalling over 21,500,000 gross tons. The Germans and their allies lost nearly 1000 submarines, nearly 800 of them German. The strange, and perhaps unique, fact remains that the British Navy did not fight a single gun-to-gun battle as a concentrated fleet. The day of the vast capital ship was virtually over; ship could destroy ship without ever coming in sight of it. The war was fought more under and over the sea than on its surface. *See also* ATLANTIC, BATTLE OF THE.

Worm, to: to fill in the depressions between the spiralling strands of a rope by winding into them smaller rope or line.

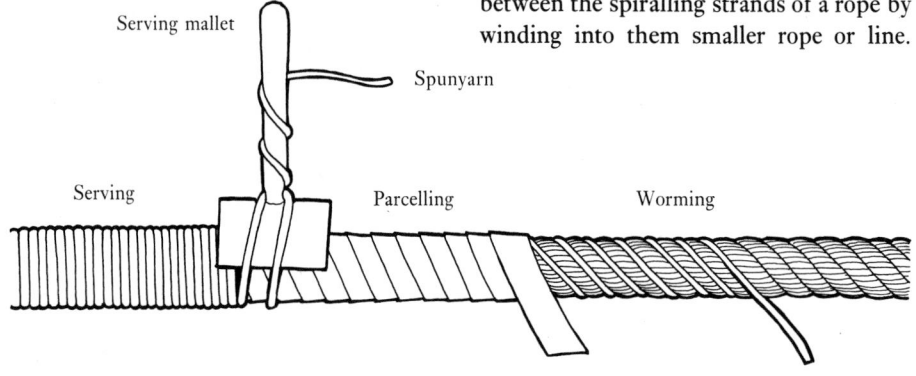

Serving mallet

Spunyarn

Serving   Parcelling   Worming

This is the first stage of the process known as 'worming, parcelling and serving', used to preserve a rope by protecting it from wet. The second stage (parcelling) consists of binding the wormed rope with strips of tarred canvas. In the third stage (serving) the wormed and parcelled rope is bound with taut and close turns of spunyarn; a wooden tool known as a serving mallet is used in the process to obtain maximum tautness of the spunyarn as it is passed round the rope.

Wrack (or **wreck**): shattered cloud; or the tangle of sea-weed thrown up on the shore.

Wreath-ports: an innovation in the reign of Charles II; gunports on and above the upper gun-deck were encircled with elaborate carved and gilded wreaths. They disappeared with later orders forbidding the expense of costly carved work, but reappeared occasionally in the 18th century.

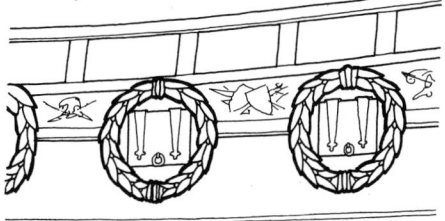

Wreck: *see* WRACK; SALVAGE; SHIP-WRECKS.

Wright, Mrs (*fl.c.*1720): women do not figure greatly in the annals of shipbuilding, except as providers of provender; so it is worth recording that in 1720 a Mrs Wright had a shipyard in St Clement's parish, Ipswich – and, judging from the rating assessment, the largest one in the town.

Writer: a rating in the Supply and Secretariat Branch of the Royal Navy concerned with correspondence, accounts, records of stores, pay, victualling, etc.

W.R.N.S.: abbreviation for Women's Royal Naval Service, originally formed in 1917 and disbanded in 1919. It was speedily re-established when the Second World War became imminent and has now been placed on a permanent footing. The creation of a suitable uniform has been described by one writer as 'a unique sartorial event' and it is not surprising that the combination of appropriate femininity and utility in service has been at times a major preoccupation in an effort to keep in touch with the civilian fashions. Few would deny that these efforts have been very successful since the days of ankle-length skirts, gaberdine hats and voluminous coat-frocks.

The Royal Naval College, Greenwich, includes, under its own director, the W.R.N.S. Officers' Course for Cadets qualifying for the rank of Third Officer.

Wrens: familiar name for members of the W.R.N.S.

Wynter (or **Winter**), **Sir William** (*fl.*1540–89): admiral and Surveyor of the Navy 1549–89. He was also Master of Ordnance for 30 years. *See also* *VANGUARD*.

X-craft: name for British MIDGET SUB-MARINES.

Xebec (or **xebeque, chebeck** etc., pronounced 'zebec'): spelt variously but appearing as 'xebec' in most ships' logs of the 18th and 19th centuries. Often used by the Barbary pirates, it was a type of three-masted fast-sailing vessel (sometimes supplemented by oars) much favoured by the French and Spanish and always featuring strongly in the British captures made in the Mediterranean. The xebec was a shallow-draught ship, often with the fore mast raking well forward over the bow, set with a large lateen sail. The other masts might be square- or lateen-rigged and, in fact, the name seems sometimes to have been loosely applied to ships with various rigs but the same general lines.

Off Malta we fell in with a xebeque, bound to Civita Vecchia, and the captain of the transport, anxious to proceed, advised our going on board of her, as the wind was light and contrary, and these Mediterranean vessels sailed better on a wind than the transport.

Captain Marryat, *Peter Simple* (1834)

Y

Yacht: a vessel, propelled either by sails or by engine power, and generally used for pleasure, for racing and cruising, but sometimes adapted for a particular task, especially in time of war. 'Yacht' comes from a Dutch verb meaning to hunt, and apparently has reference to the speed of such a vessel, suggesting a chase. The design of yachts, their different rigs, their classification, management and maintenance, are complex matters which require long study, as does the development of the powered yacht from the first early steam yachts with paddle-wheels to the modern very powerful engined boats of today.

Yard: a spar fastened to a mast to carry sails. A square yard is a spar, tapered at each end, held at its mid-point at right angles to a mast; a lateen yard is held, not necessarily at its mid-point, diagonally across a mast. The purpose of yards is to support sails, the angle of which in a square-rigged ship can be altered to catch the wind by hauling on the braces secured near to the yardarm or outer end of the yard. This allows the yard to swivel horizontally at the point where it crosses the mast and at which parrels, trusses or goose-necks hold the yard but allow it free movement. Vertical movement of the yard is controlled by lifts running from the mast-head to the yardarms and similarly by slings to the middle of the yard. The yards on a square-rigged ship are named according to the mast or the sail to which they are attached, thus 'lower main yard', 'topsail yard' etc.

In modern power-driven ships yards

The Earl of Dunraven's challenger for the America's Cup, *Valkyrie III*, on sailing trials in the Clyde, 1896.

may survive to carry signal halyards or radio aerials, but are generally lighter and made of metal compared with the sail-bearing wooden yards in square-rigged ships.

Manning the yards was once, in the days of sail, a ceremony to honour someone or to mark an important occasion. The yards were lined by members of the ship's company, with a single sailor standing on the extreme top or truck of each mast. The practice may still sometimes be seen in sailing training ships.

Yardarm: the outermost part of a YARD. In the days of the sailing Navy, signals were flown from the yardarm; it was also the point from which men sentenced to death by court-martial were hanged. *See also* PUNISHMENTS.

Yarmouth: Norfolk watering-place and seaport, which enters history as long ago as the 5th century, when the invader Cerdic the Saxon is believed to have landed there. King John gave it a charter in 1208 and Elizabeth I granted it another in 1552, giving it Admiralty jurisdiction. Its main industries have traditionally been herring and mackerel fishing and curing. The Yarmouth Roads, except in easterly or north-easterly winds, have for centuries provided an excellent anchorage. The entrance channel to the quays was cut by a Dutch engineer, Joost Jansen, as early as 1567.

Yarn: twisted fibres prepared for rope-making. *See also* SPUNYARN.

Yaw: fall away from the course being steered, either because of poor helmsmanship or (more often) from the effect of a strong following wind and sea.

Yawl: a small two-masted fore-and-

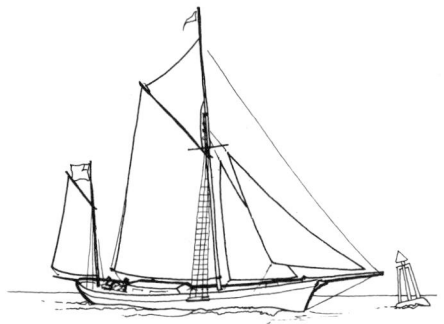

aft rigged sailing vessel, similar to a ketch.

The yawl rig one comes in time to love. It is, I should think, the easiest of all to manage.

Joseph Conrad, *The Mirror of the Sea* (1906)

Year of Victories: *see* WONDERFUL YEAR.

Yellow admiral: 19th-century term for a naval officer so long ashore that all hopes of re-employment and promotion are virtually gone. Presumably he was 'yellow' because he could no longer be of the Red, White or Blue (*see* ADMIRAL).

Yellow Jack: formerly, a colloquial term for yellow fever (*see* HEALTH AND HYGIENE) and also used with a special meaning at Greenwich Hospital, where drunkenness among the pensioners was punished by making the offenders wear a yellow jacket. *See also* QUARANTINE.

Yellow Regiment: the first regiment of sea-soldiers or MARINES, formed by James Duke of York, later James II. In 1664, the Admiralty obtained an Order in Council authorizing the establishment of 'The Duke of York and Albany's Maritime Regiment of Foot', consisting of a regiment of 1200 'Land souldgers prepared for sea service'. It did good service in the Dutch Wars and was disbanded in 1689. The regiment was recruited largely from London, and the marines have inherited the privilege of marching through the City with fixed bayonets, drums beating and colours flying.

Yellow Sea: the northern extension of the East China Sea enclosed by Korea and the coast of north-eastern China. It is so named because of its yellow colour, caused by the vast quantities of fine silt or loess brought into it by the Yellow River (Hwang Ho).

Yeoman: title given until recently to a petty officer or chief petty officer in the Signal branch, the full title being Yeoman or Chief Yeoman of Signals. Yeoman is also the name for a rating assisting an officer by undertaking certain clerical duties. In the old sailing Navy certain ships bore men rated as boatswain's, gunner's and carpenter's yeomen; there were also yeomen of the sheets, yeomen of the signals and yeomen of the powder room. All these had petty officer status.

Yoke: a cross-bar on a rudder to which steering lines are fitted; often found instead of a tiller on the rudder of small rowing or sailing craft.

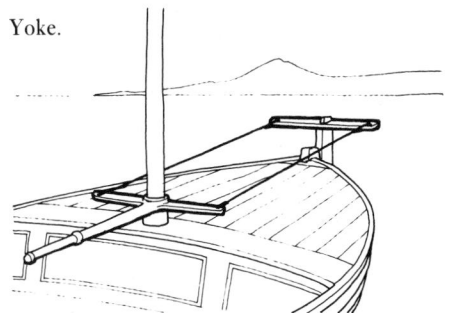

Yoke.

York, James Duke of: *see* JAMES II.

Yorktown: town with a fine harbour on Chesapeake Bay, Virginia, famous for the surrender of the British forces under Cornwallis (October 1781), which virtually ended the War of American Independence on land.

Young gentlemen: historical name for MIDSHIPMEN.

Young Nick's Head: Nicholas Young, surgeon's boy on Captain Cook's *Endeavour*, was the first to sight New Zealand (7 October 1769). In recognition, this promontory at the southern end of Poverty Bay was named after him.

Z

Zeebrugge: a small port on the coast of Belgium, linked by a canal to Bruges; celebrated in British naval history for the brave but not wholly successful attack made on it during the First World War. The purpose of the attack, which was carried out on the night of 22–3 April 1918, was to prevent German U-boats, destroyers and coastal craft from using the canal and the harbour at Bruges. Directed by Vice-Admiral Sir Roger Keyes, the plan was to sink three old cruisers across the mouth of the canal. At the same time a naval force of seamen and marines from the cruiser H.M.S. *Vindictive* was to attack the harbour mole, and the bridge linking it to the shore was to be destroyed by two submarines blowing themselves up beneath it. The cruisers were not able to position themselves properly and only partly blocked the fairway, but the bridge was destroyed. Although casualties among the landing force were heavy, and although the raid only temporarily incommoded the Germans, it did much for morale which at that stage of the war was at a low ebb.

Zenith: that point in the heavens which lies immediately above the observer; a term used in astronomical navigation, especially in 'zenith distance', which is the angle between the zenith and any celestial body being observed.

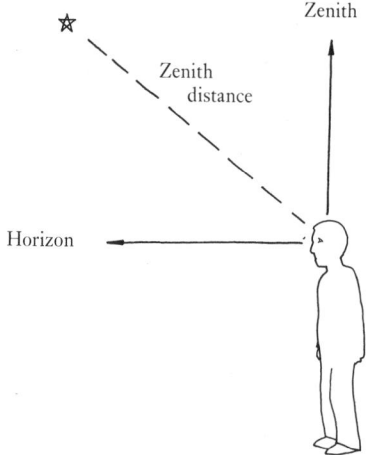

Zone: (1) in a general sense, any tract or belt of land or sea.

(2) One of the regions into which the earth is divided by parallels of latitude, i.e.: the frigid zones within the Arctic and Antarctic Circles, the torrid zones between the Tropics of Cancer and Capricorn, and the temperate zones between the torrid and frigid zones.

(3) A division of the world by lines of longitude into sectors or time zones within which an agreed uniform time is kept, differing from Greenwich Mean Time by an exact number of hours, fast or slow, according to longitudinal distance east or west of Greenwich.

Zopissa: mysterious term for the pitch or tar scraped off old ships, which formerly enjoyed a reputation as a cure for certain skin eruptions.

Appendixes

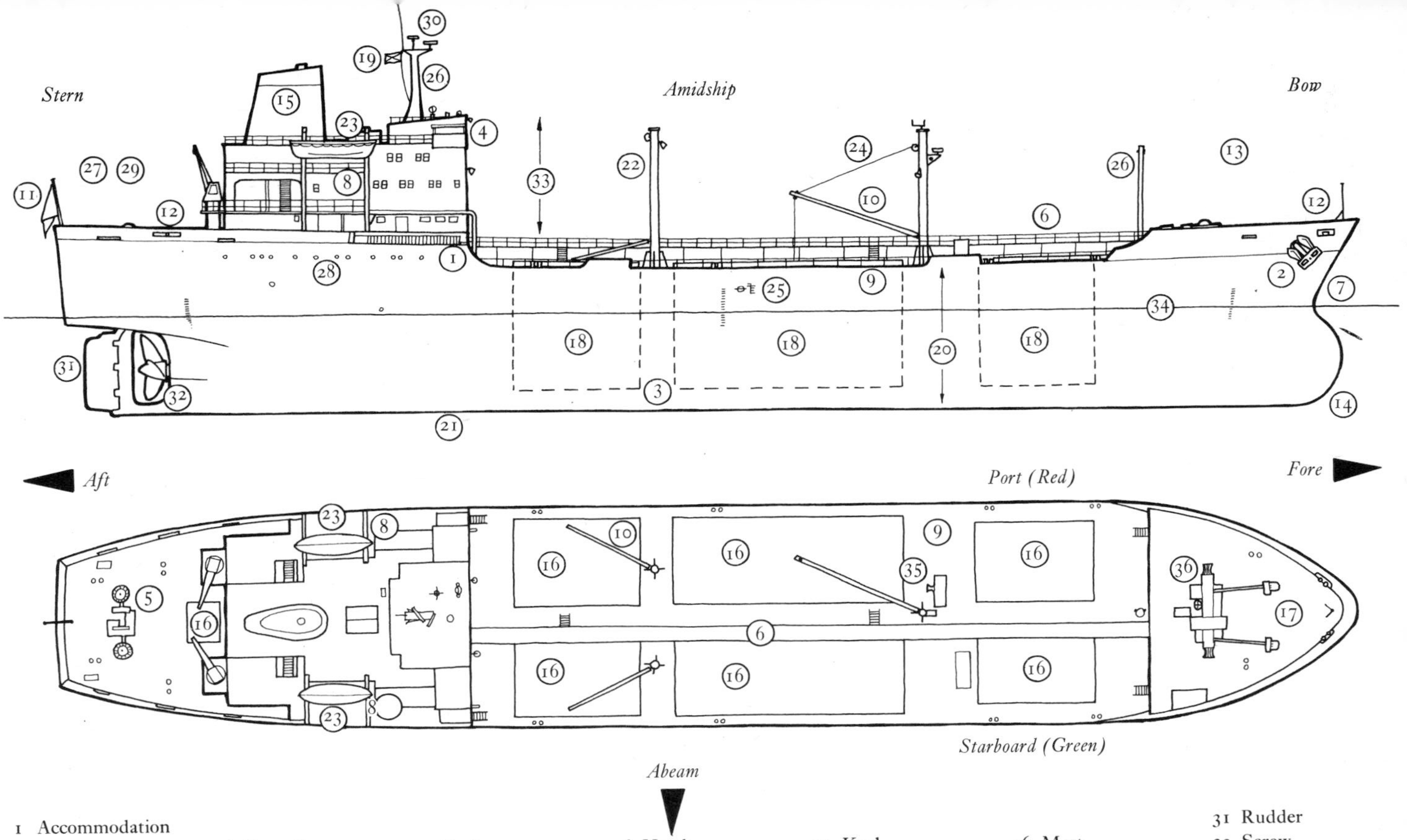

Bow

Fore

Port (Red)

Starboard (Green)

Abeam

Aft

Amidship

Stern

1 Accommodation
 ladder
2 Anchor
3 Bilge
4 Bridge
5 Capstan

6 Catwalk
7 Cutwater
8 Davit
9 Deck
10 Derrick

11 Ensign
12 Fairlead
13 Forecastle
14 Forefoot
15 Funnel

16 Hatch
17 Hawse pipe
18 Hold
19 House flag
20 Hull

21 Keel
22 Kingpost
23 Lifeboat
24 Lift, Topping
25 Loadline

26 Mast
27 Poop
28 Porthole
29 Quarterdeck
30 Radar

31 Rudder
32 Screw
33 Superstructure
34 Waterline
35 Winch
36 Windlass

1. Parts of the ship (shown here is a small general cargo carrier)

577

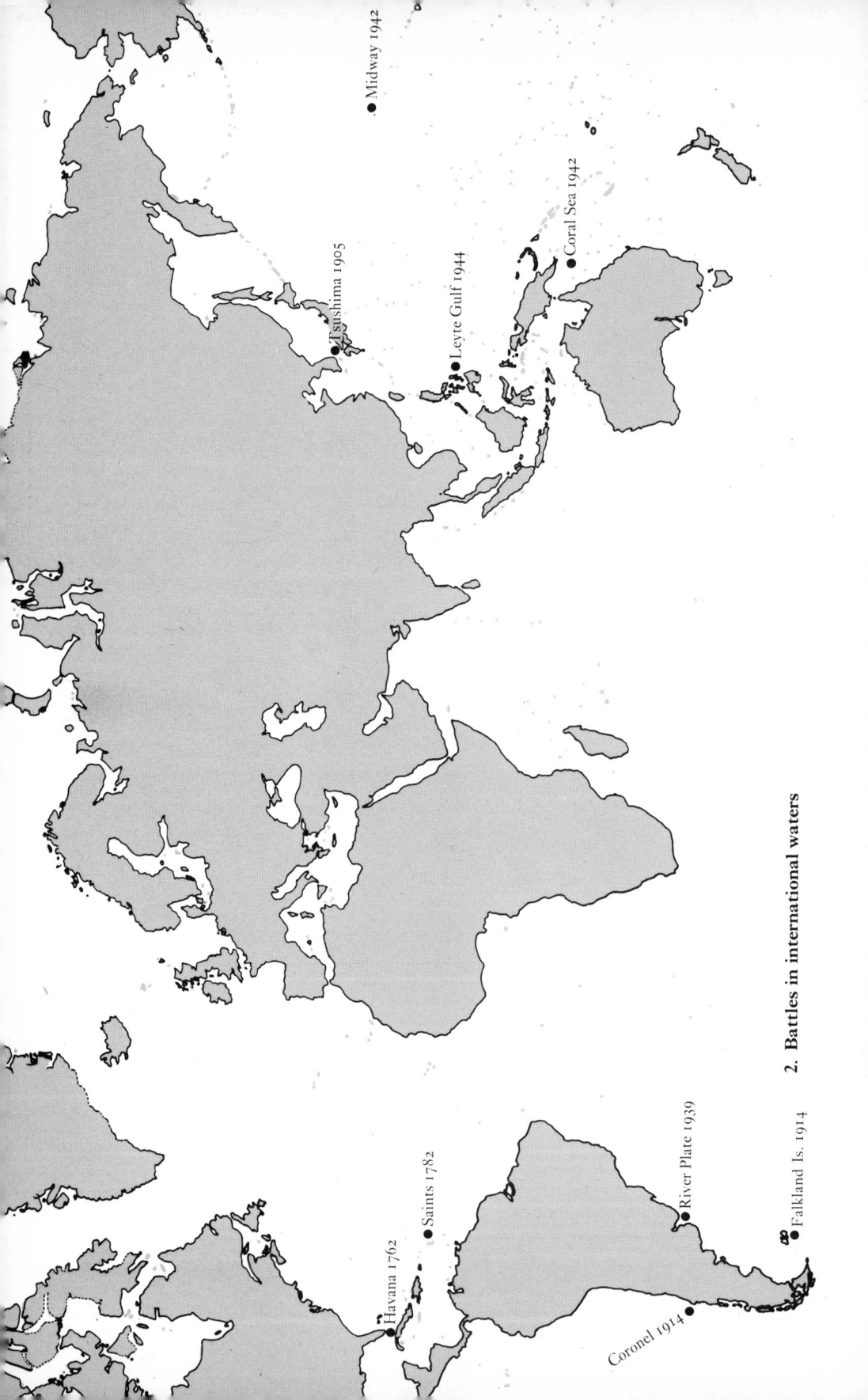

Midway 1942

Coral Sea 1942

Tsushima 1905

Leyte Gulf 1944

Havana 1762

Saints 1782

River Plate 1939

Falkland Is. 1914

Coronel 1914

2. **Battles in international waters**

Flamborough Head 1779

Lowestoft 1665
Solebay 1672
Gabbard 1653

Four Days Battle 1666
Gravelines 1588
Dunes 1657
Downs 1639
Dungeness 1652

Kentish Knock 1652

Beachy Head 1690

Portland Bill 1588

3. Battles in home waters

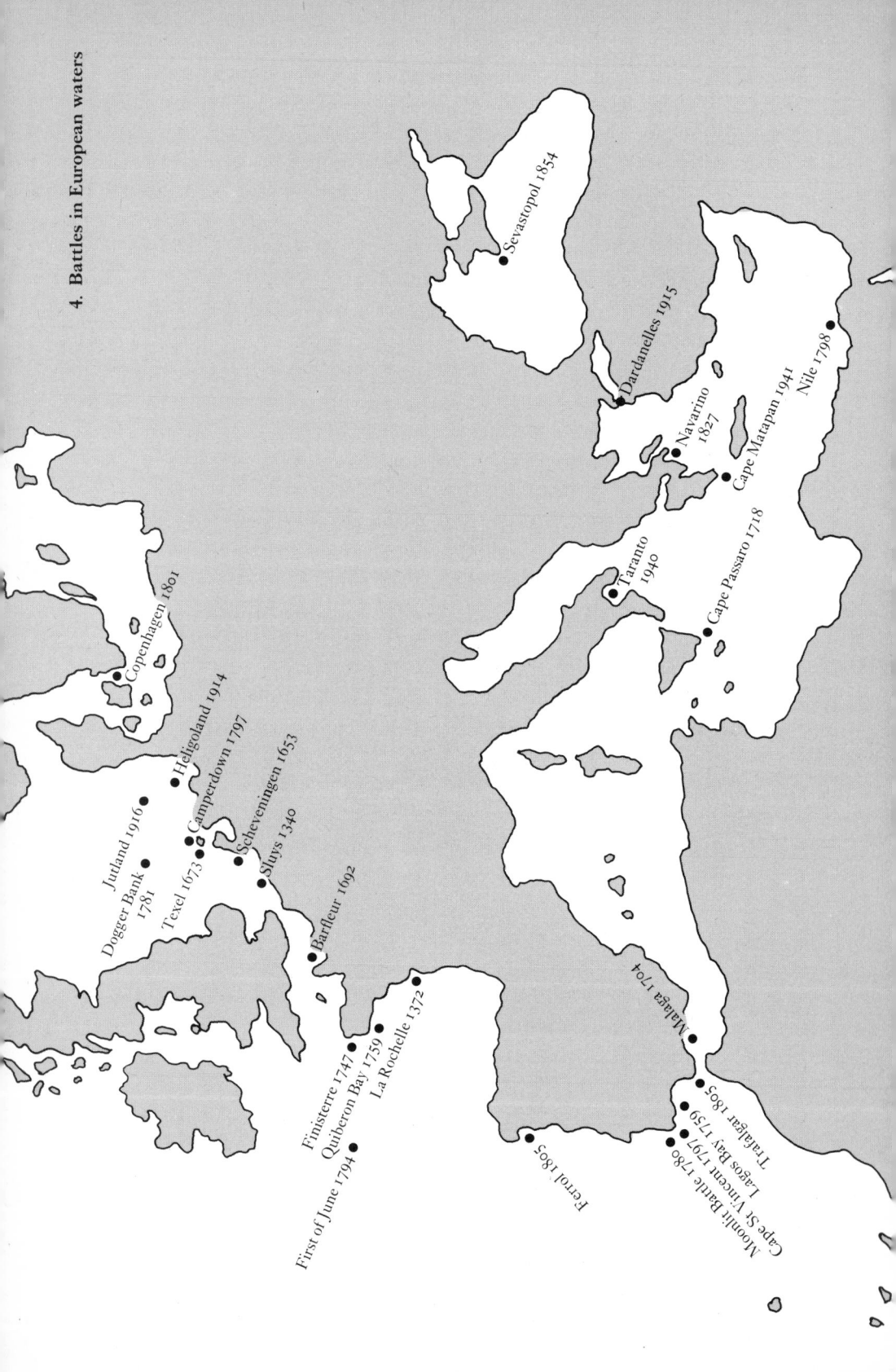

4. Battles in European waters

Sevastopol 1854

Dardanelles 1915

Navarino 1827

Cape Matapan 1941

Nile 1798

Taranto 1940

Cape Passaro 1718

Copenhagen 1801

Heligoland 1914

Camperdown 1797

Jutland 1916

Texel 1673

Scheveningen 1653

Dogger Bank 1781

Sluys 1340

Barfleur 1692

La Rochelle 1372

Finisterre 1747

Quiberon Bay 1759

First of June 1794

Malaga 1704

Trafalgar 1805

Cape St Vincent 1797

Lagos Bay 1759

Moonlit Battle 1780

Ferrol 1805

5. Place names in Europe

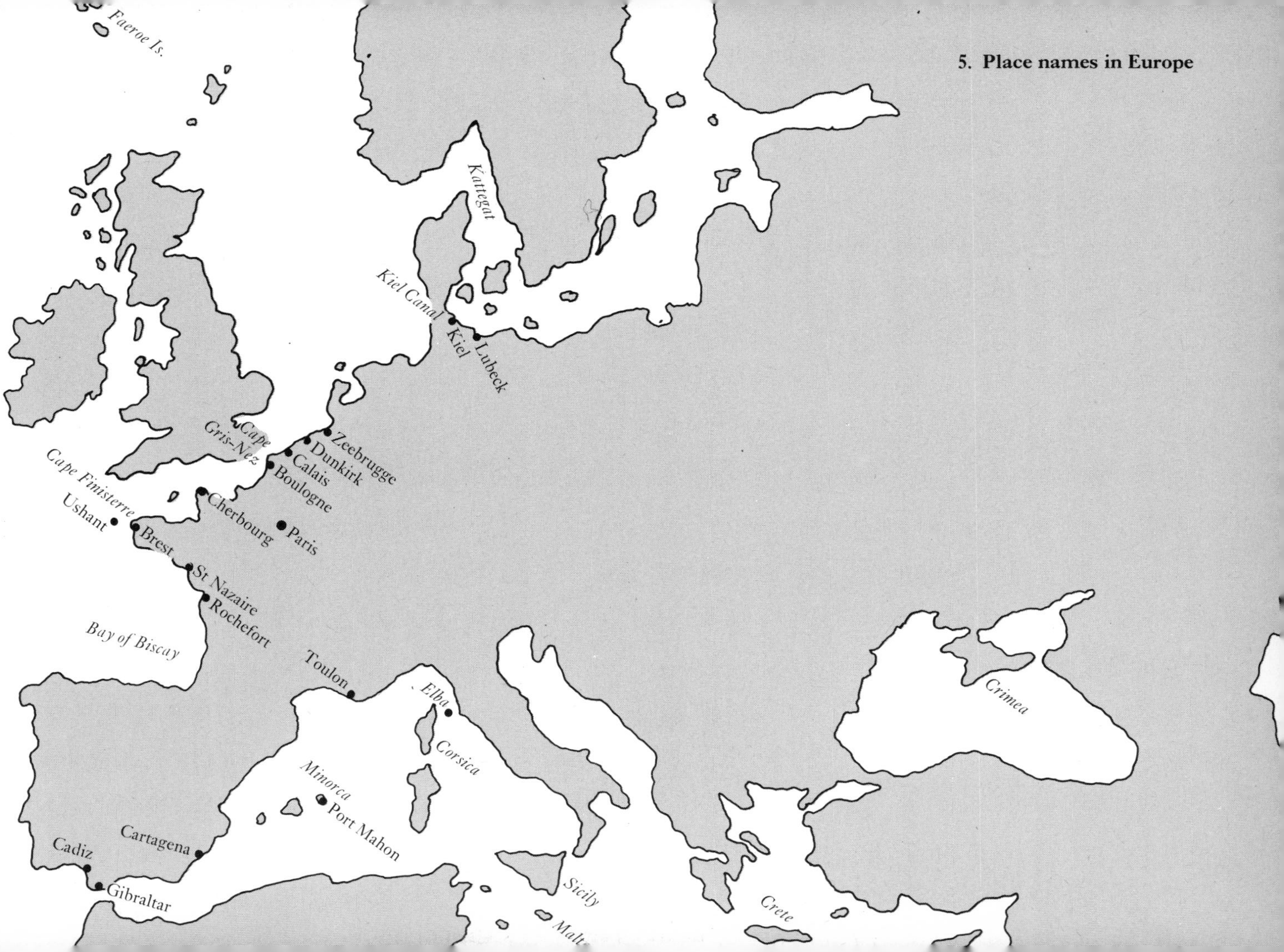
Faeroe Is.
Kattegat
Kiel Canal
Kiel
Lubeck
Cape Gris-Nez
Zeebrugge
Dunkirk
Calais
Boulogne
Cape Finisterre
Ushant
Cherbourg
Paris
Brest
St Nazaire
Rochefort
Bay of Biscay
Toulon
Elba
Corsica
Minorca
Port Mahon
Cartagena
Cadiz
Gibraltar
Sicily
Malt
Crete
Crimea

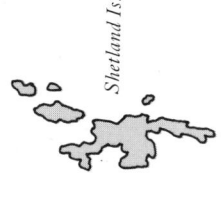

6. Place names in the British Isles

Shetland Is.

Orkney Is.

● Inchcape Rock

Rosyth ●

● Glasgow

● Greenock

Tobermory ●

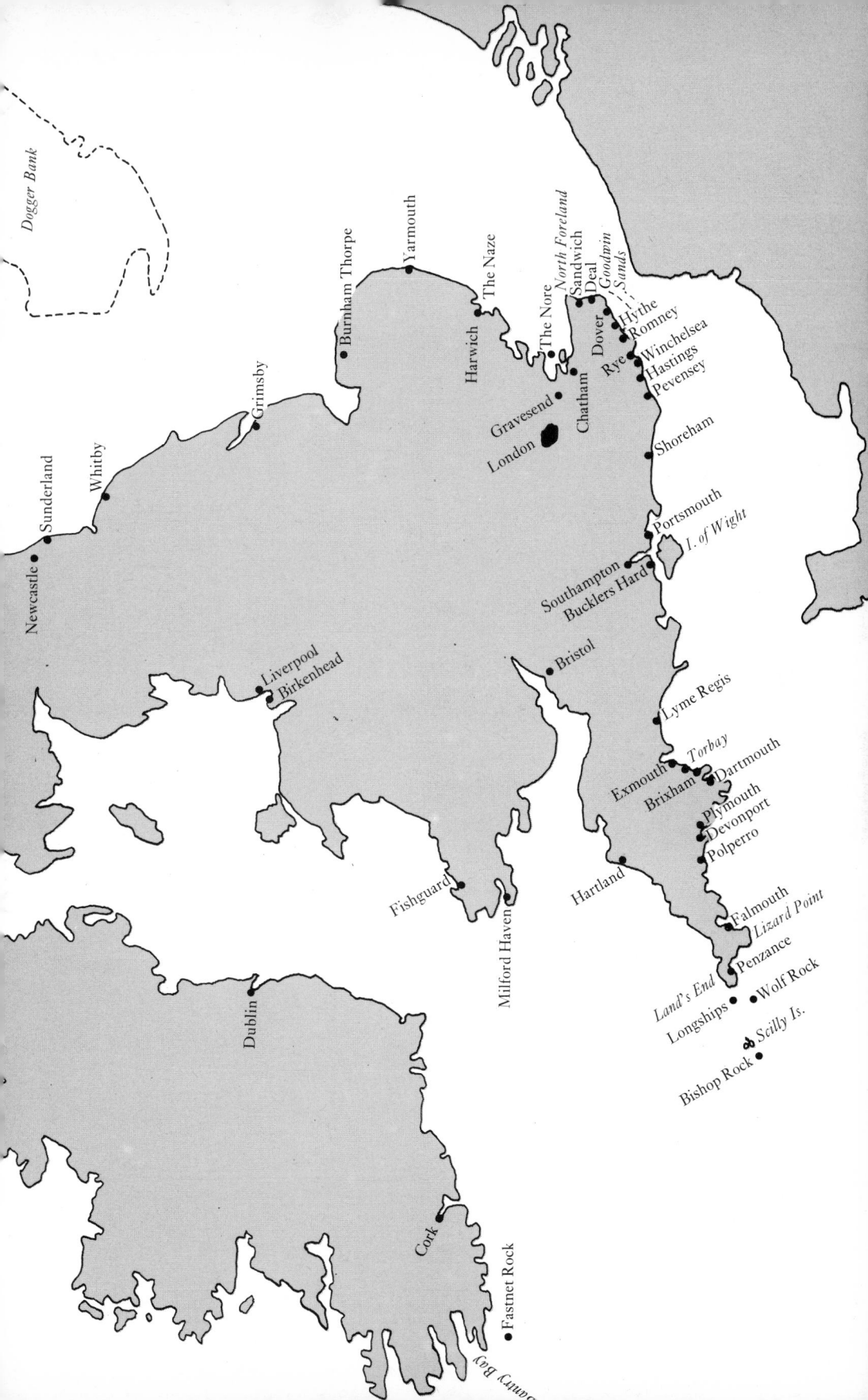

Dogger Bank

Newcastle
Sunderland
Whitby

Grimsby

Burnham Thorpe
Yarmouth

The Naze
Harwich

The Nore
North Foreland
Sandwich
Deal
Goodwin Sands
Dover
Hythe
Romney
Winchelsea
Rye
Hastings
Pevensey

Gravesend
Chatham
London

Shoreham

Portsmouth
I. of Wight

Southampton
Bucklers Hard

Bristol

Liverpool
Birkenhead

Lyme Regis

Torbay
Exmouth
Brixham
Dartmouth
Plymouth
Devonport
Polperro

Fishguard

Hartland

Falmouth
Lizard Point
Penzance
Land's End
Longships
Wolf Rock
Scilly Is.
Bishop Rock

Milford Haven

Dublin

Cork

Fastnet Rock

Bantry Bay

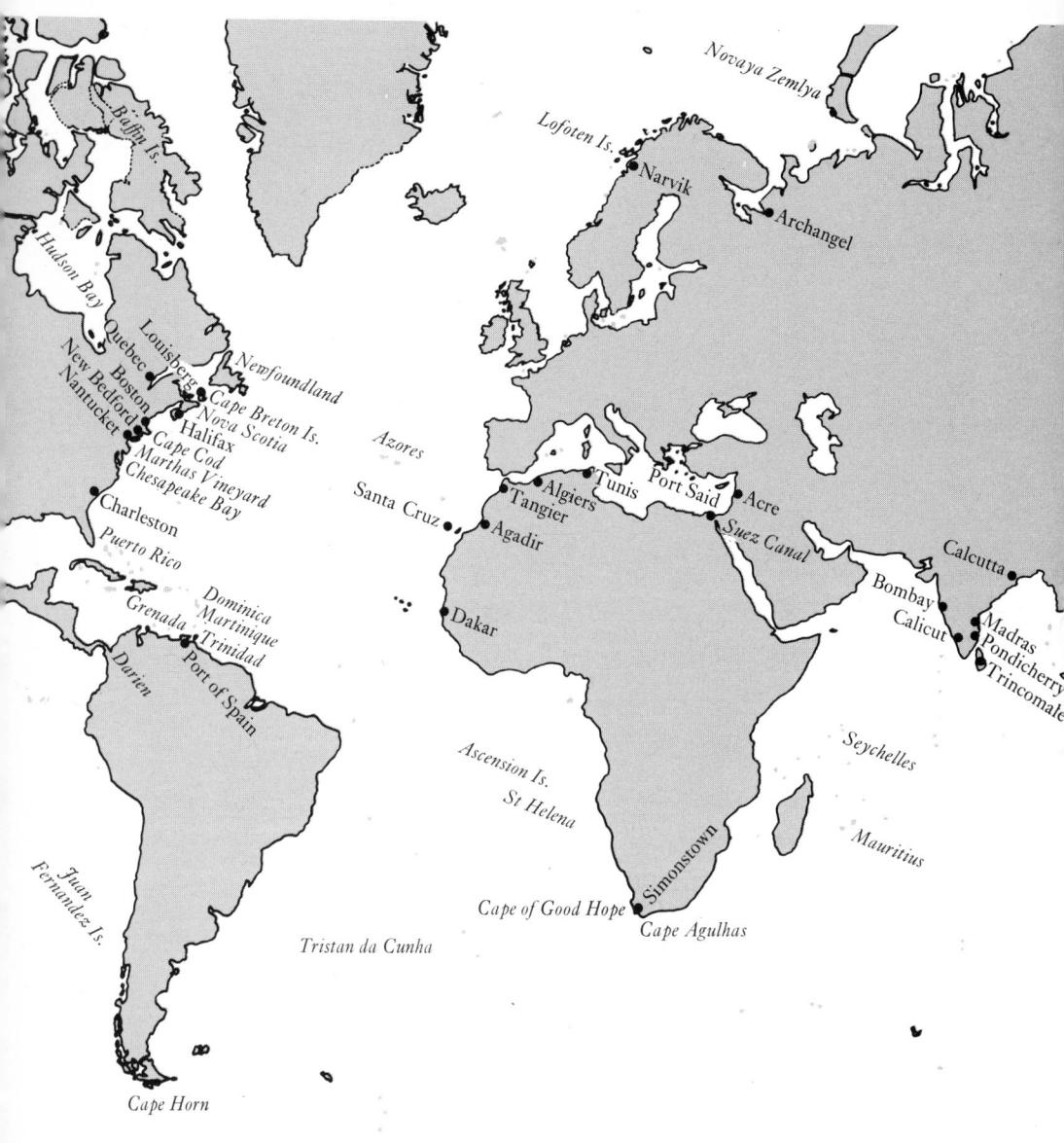

7. **International place names**

Massachusetts Bay
New York
Yorktown
Rhode Is.
Long Is.

St. Kitts

Sandwich Is.

Porto Bello

ng
g
Canton
Manila
Philippine Is.

Admiralty Is.

gapore
Amboyna

Tahiti
Society Is.

Pitcairn Is.

Sydney
Botany Bay
Melbourne
Tasmania

Prime Meridian | O° Longitude

Barents
Sea

Labrador Current

North
Sea

Baltic

Greenwich

English Channel

Ligurian
Sea

Adriatic Sea

Sea of Azov

Black Sea

Sea of Marmara

Sargasso Sea

Mediterranean

Tyrrhenian Sea

Ionian Sea

Aegean

Persian Gulf

Latitude

Caribbean

Atlantic
Ocean

Indian Ocean

Aghulas Current

8. Seas and currents

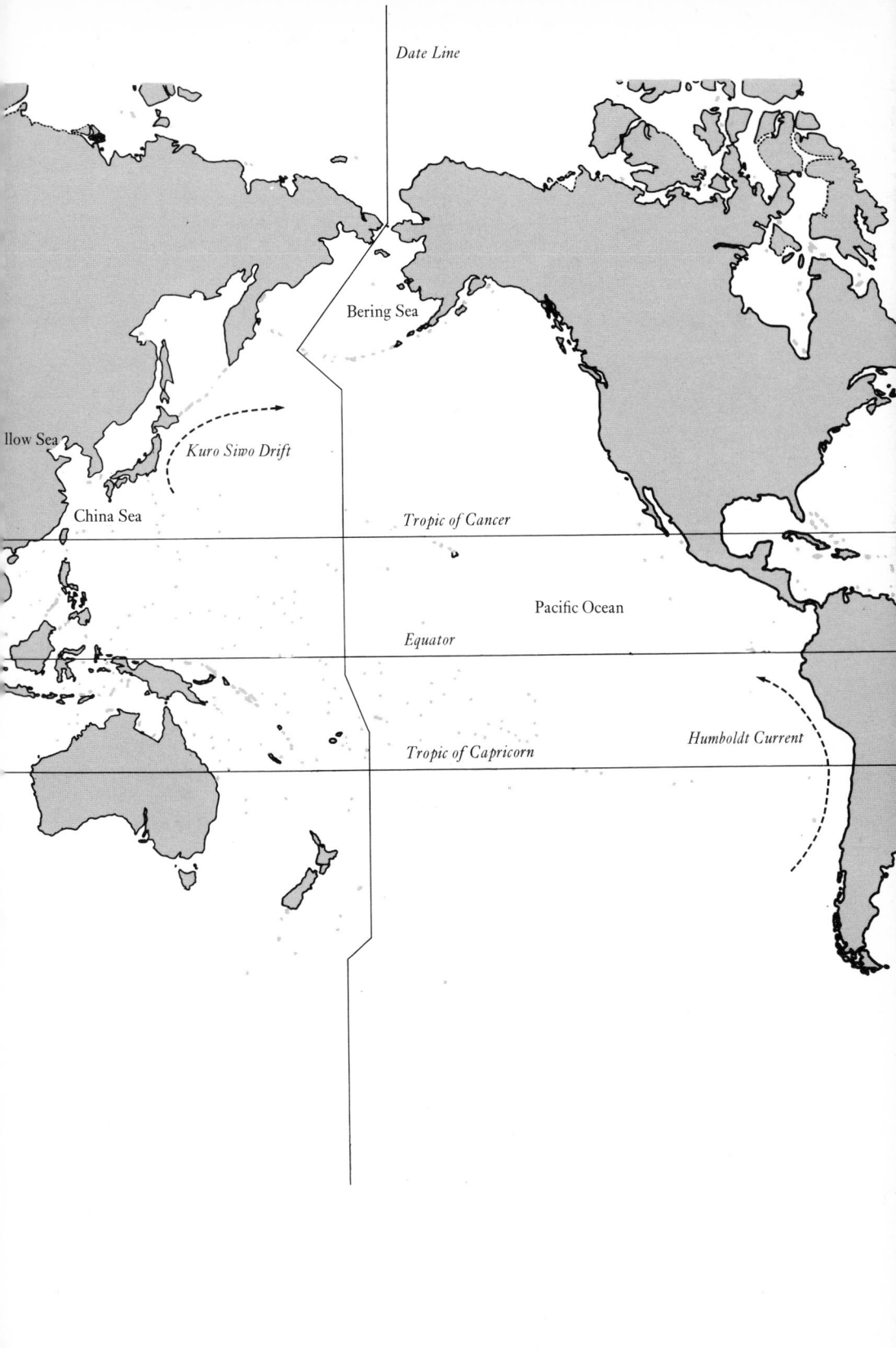

Date Line

Bering Sea

llow Sea

China Sea

Kuro Siwo Drift

Tropic of Cancer

Pacific Ocean

Equator

Tropic of Capricorn

Humboldt Current

Illustration acknowledgements

The author and publishers would like to thank the following for their kind permission to reproduce illustrative material:

Antikvarisk-topografiska arkivet, Stockholm for p.275; Beken of Cowes for pp.403, 571; British Antarctic Survey for p.418; British United Trawlers for p.531; British Waterways Board for pp.254, 323; A. Bromley-Martin for p.529; Canada House for p.448; Photothèque Cie Gle Maritime for p.270; David and Charles for p.450; Grace Darling Museum, Bamburgh for p.113; p.231 reproduced by Gracious Permission of Her Majesty the Queen; H.M.S. Osprey for p.264; Kelvin Hughes for p.466; Illustrated London News Picture Library for pp.31, 142; Imperial War Museum for pp.40, 94, 118, 126, 129, 176, 180, 183, 241, 242, 247, 256, 316, 382, 429, 430, 456, 525 *above*, 539, 542; Keystone Press Agency Ltd for pp.293, 525; pp.23 *below*, 35, by permission of the Master and Fellows, Magdalene College, Cambridge; Manchester Ship Canal Company for p.224; Mary Evans Picture Library for p.318; Crown Copyright with permission of the Ministry of Defence for p.537; National Maritime Museum for pp.9, 12, 13, 14, 16, 17, 23 *above*, 24, 26, 29 *above*, 29 *below*, 38, 47, 51, 52, 67 *above*, 67 *below*, 69, 78 *below*, 81, 92, 100, 106, 108, 109, 115, 119, 122, 123, 127, 135, 137, 143, 155, 156, 160, 161, 163, 165, 166, 167, 168, 175, 177, 179, 185, 186, 189, 199, 207, 211, 213, 218, 235, 239, 268, 277, 281, 286, 299, 300, 303, 308, 312, 313, 325, 331, 349, 358, 363, 366, 368, 369, 370, 377, 391, 394, 400, 414, 419, 420, 421, 433, 438, 452, 455, 458, 459, 463, 474, 479, 503, 509, 510, 511, 521, 530, 538, 543 *above*, 543 *below*, 551, 558, 559, 566; National Portrait Gallery for pp.52, 110, 141; Overseas Containers Ltd for p.97; *Come Hell or High Water* by Clare Francis published by Pelham Books 1977 for p.427; Plymouth City Museum and Art Gallery, on display at Buckland Abbey, for p.203; Press Association Photos for pp.232, 266, 345; Radio Times Hulton Picture Library for p.64; Royal College of Physicians and Surgeons of Glasgow for p.43; Royal Geographical Museum for p.467; Royal Naval Museum, Portsmouth (photo by J. A. Hewes) for p.395; Royal Naval Public Relations Office, Portsmouth for pp.153, 191; San Francisco Maritime Museum for p.78 *above*; Science Museum (Crown Copyright) for pp.82, 96, 159, 209 *above*; Skyfotos Ltd for p.416; Society for the Preservation of New England Antiquities for p.516; Sutcliffe Gallery, Whitby for p.436; p.209 *below* by permission of Teredo Books Ltd; University Museum of National Antiquities, Oslo, Norway for p.355.

City of Glasgow Museum and Galleries for PC8 *centre*; PC2 *centre* reproduced by Gracious Permission of Her Majesty the Queen; PC5 *above left* and PC7 *above left* reproduced with the permission of the Controller of Her Majesty's Stationery Office; National Gallery for PC6 *below*; National Library of Australia for PC3 *above*; National Maritime Museum for PC2 *above*, PC2 *below left*, PC2 *below right*, PC3 *centre*, PC3 *below*, PC4 *above*, PC4 *below*, PC6 *above*, PC8 *above*; National Portrait Gallery for PC7 *above right*; Novosti Press Agency for PC4 *centre right*; Peabody Museum of Salem for PC1 *above*; Royal Navy Submarine Museum, Gosport for PC8 *below left*, Timothy Severin for PC1 *centre right*; Universitets Oldsaksamling, Oslo for PC4 *centre left*; Vosper Thornycroft for PC7 *below left*; Lionel Willis for PC1 *below*, PC5 *below*, PC6 *centre*.

All maps and figures are by Lionel Willis.